MORE PRAISE FOR
ON EVERY TIDE

"What a fine book! It has all the virtues one wants in a work of synthesis. Sean Connolly has read almost everything in print on the Irish diaspora, and he distills the material in a gentle, generous, and highly readable fashion—and yet with an engaged and edgy quality. Thus, several of the myths about the Irish worldwide—such as that they had an instinctive sympathy with indigenous and racialized groups—are called into question. *On Every Tide* is the ideal place for anyone interested in the Irish diaspora to begin, and, for those with some previous knowledge, to recalibrate their compass."

—Donald H. Akenson, Queen's University

"A nuanced overview of Irish migrations, focusing on the experiences of both Catholic and Protestant Irish in United States, Great Britain, Canada, Australia, New Zealand, and, to a lesser extent, Argentina. Connolly offers a subtle analysis of the meaning of 'diaspora' in the context of the varied patterns of Irish demographics and integration across several societies. *On Every Tide* likewise presents shrewd observations on Ireland's interactions with its far-flung progeny as well as on the changing nature of what it means to be Irish, whether one lives on the island or elsewhere. All readers interested in the topics of international migration, ethnicity, assimilations, and globalization should put this book on their reading list."

—Thomas J. Archdeacon, University of Wisconsin-Madison

"*On Every Tide* is a richly detailed, deeply insightful, and beautifully written panorama of Ireland's history of migration. Connolly excels in explaining the causes of Irish emigration and the impact of that mobility on Ireland, the people who left home, and the societies they helped create. This impressive book constitutes a major contribution to the new, globally oriented scholarship on the Irish diaspora."

—Malcolm Campbell, University of Auckland

"*On Every Tide* is an expert survey of the Irish diaspora from the seventeenth century to the present day. Elegantly written, highly accessible, yet carefully researched and wonderfully comprehensive, the book displays the impressive skills of one of Ireland's foremost historians. Connolly's masterful contribution to our understanding of Irish emigration will not only be essential reading for students of Irish and American history, it will appeal to anyone interested in how Irish migration impacted the history of the modern world."

—Robert Savage, Boston College

"*On Every Tide* is the first comprehensive history of the Irish diaspora from pre-famine times to the present. This remarkable book, which is both readable and scholarly, ranging from North America and Britain to South America, Australia, New Zealand and South Africa, highlights the diversity of the Irish diaspora: Protestant and Catholic, unionist and nationalist, and their different experiences in the places where they settled."

—Mary E. Daly, University College Dublin

ON
EVERY
TIDE

ON
EVERY
TIDE

THE MAKING AND REMAKING
OF THE IRISH WORLD

SEAN CONNOLLY

BASIC BOOKS

New York

Basic Books
Hachette Book Group
1290 Avenue of the Americas, New York, NY 10104
www.basicbooks.com

Printed in the United States of America

First Edition: October 2022

Published by Basic Books, an imprint of Perseus Books, LLC, a subsidiary of Hachette Book Group, Inc. The Basic Books name and logo is a trademark of the Hachette Book Group.

The Hachette Speakers Bureau provides a wide range of authors for speaking events. To find out more, go to www.hachettespeakersbureau.com or call (866) 376-6591.

The publisher is not responsible for websites (or their content) that are not owned by the publisher.

Print book interior design by Amy Quinn.

Library of Congress Cataloging-in-Publication Data

Names: Connolly, S. J. (Sean J.), author.
Title: On every tide: the making and remaking of the Irish world / Sean Connolly.
Other titles: Making and remaking of the Irish world
Description: First edition. | New York: Basic Books, 2022. | Includes
   bibliographical references and index. |
Identifiers: LCCN 2022019418 | ISBN 9780465093953 (hardcover) | ISBN
   9780465093960 (ebook)
Subjects: LCSH: Irish diaspora. | Irish—Foreign countries—History. | Ireland—
   Emigration and immigration—History. | National characteristics, Irish.
Classification: LCC DA928 .C66 2022 | DDC 909/.049162—dc23/eng/20220616
LC record available at https://lccn.loc.gov/2022019418

ISBNs: 9780465093953 (hardcover), 9780465093960 (ebook)

LSC-C

Printing 1, 2022

For Iona and Paige

CONTENTS

1. Diaspora: Ireland and the World   1
2. The Beginning of Mass Migration   17
3. Flight from Famine   45
4. Castle Garden and Beyond: Emigration to the United States in the Post-Famine Years   77
5. Soldiers and Citizens: Nativism, Civil War and the Quest for Acceptance   119
6. Beneath the Southern Cross: Australia and New Zealand   143
7. The Making of Irish America   189
8. The Politics of Irish America   219
9. The Other America   257
10. An Irish World   285
11. War and Revolution   305
12. In the Melting Pot   327
13. From Tammany to Camelot   359
14. 'We've married Italian girls and moved to the suburbs': Irish Identities in a Changing World   385
15. A Last Hurrah? The United States and the Northern Ireland Conflict   411
16. Global Ireland Reimagined   443

Acknowledgements   455
Appendix: A (Short) Note on Statistics   457
Further Reading   465
Notes   471
Index   509

1

DIASPORA

Ireland and the World

Gerald O'Hara arrived in Savannah, Georgia, in 1822, at the age of · 21, with nothing but the clothes on his back, 'two shillings above his passage money and a price on his head'. He had fled his native County Meath after killing 'an English absentee landlord's rent agent' who had insulted him by whistling the opening bars of an Orange ballad. In Savannah he joined two older brothers, long ago exiled for their own activities involving preparations for rebellion and a cache of hidden weapons. Beginning life in America as humble waggoners, they had established themselves as wealthy merchants. Their younger brother, however, did better still. In a late night, whiskey-fuelled poker game, he won the deeds to a failing cotton plantation 250 miles inland, located dangerously close to territory still inhabited by potentially menacing Cherokees. Over the next ten years Gerald succeeded in building this unpromising prize into a profitable venture, and in establishing himself as a respected, if rough-tongued, member of landed society. His social ascent was confirmed when, at the age of 43, he married Ellen Robillard, twenty-eight years his junior and the daughter of an old French family in Savannah.

Thirty years after Gerald O'Hara, in 1853, the 19-year-old Patrick Durack, born in County Clare, arrived with his family in Britain's oldest Australian colony, New South Wales. After working for ten years on a smallholding bought with money earned during a foray into the goldfields of neighbouring Victoria, he relocated to the southwest of the new colony of Queensland. A prolonged drought that killed off the livestock they had brought with them took him and his associates close to disaster. Within a few years, however, they had built up a fortune by staking their claim to land that they could then sell on to later, less enterprising settlers, and by cannily investing in the first towns to take root in the region. Yet in 1883 Durack made the astounding decision to hazard everything he had gained by moving again, setting out with his relatives on a twenty-eight-month trek across 3,000 miles to Kimberley in northwest Australia, bringing with them more than 7,000 cattle to form the basis of a new ranching empire. By the 1920s the family controlled over seven million acres of land, and Patrick Durack's son was one of the region's representatives in the Australian parliament.

Only one of these two men actually existed. Mary Durack's *Kings in Grass Castles*, first published in 1959, is a lightly fictionalised account of the life of her grandfather Patrick Durack. Margaret Mitchell, author of *Gone with the Wind*, born in Atlanta in 1900, also had an Irish-born grandfather on one side, and an Irish great-grandfather on the other. But the Gerald O'Hara of her celebrated novel, with his violent past and his estate founded on a late-night poker game, was a product of her imagination.

Why then should Gerald O'Hara and Patrick Durack be mentioned together? What links the two men, one lightly fictionalised, the other wholly invented, is the prominent place that each holds in a national epic of his adopted country. *Gone with the Wind*, first published in 1936, remains America's most celebrated work of historical fiction. Mary Durack's family saga is widely regarded as a classic celebration of Australia's pioneering origins. Each tells the story of a society created, by force of will, out of a wilderness. And in each case the central figure in this act of creation is an Irish immigrant. In each case, moreover, it is the character's Irishness that provides the driving force behind his relentless urge to build and to acquire. Mary Durack, writing for an audience that was still firmly part of the British Commonwealth, does not go so far as to have her grandfather leave behind him in Ireland a dead representative of English tyranny. But *Kings in Grass Castles* begins by outlining the memories of 'ancient wrongs and of glories still more remote' that the Duracks brought with them from their homeland. Later chapters several times return—particularly at those awkward moments when some acknowledgement is required of the way in which the family's Australian triumphs were founded on the clearance of the Aboriginal population—to the status of their Irish protagonists as underdogs and victims of colonial oppression. In *Gone with the Wind*, Irish history becomes, much more directly, the force that drives Gerald O'Hara. The only literature with which he is familiar is the patriotic verse of Thomas Moore, and the only history 'the manifold wrongs of Ireland'. In Georgia, his only local enemies are the MacIntoshes, 'Scotch-Irish and Orangemen', who own an adjacent plantation. O'Hara calls the mansion he establishes on his property Tara, after the reputed seat of the ancient kings of Ireland, and he tries to explain to his sceptical daughter the importance of what he had built there. 'Land is the only thing in the world that amounts to anything, for 'tis the only thing in this world that lasts . . . to anyone with a drop of Irish blood in them the land they live on is like their mother.'[1]

Not all of the details from these two best-sellers need to be taken at face value. Some of those who emigrated to the United States, Australia and elsewhere did so, like Gerald O'Hara, as political exiles. But far more were driven, or attracted, by a flight from poverty, or the hope of economic betterment. Many Irish Australians prospered, but few achieved the fabulous wealth of a Patrick Durack. Few Irish Americans, equally, made their home in the American South, and fewer still became plantation owners. Any proper account of the Irish diaspora, equally, must look beyond the examples of both Patrick Durack and Gerald O'Hara to recognise that the global Ireland that emerged during the nineteenth century was Protestant as well as Catholic. But taken together *Gone with the Wind* and *Kings in Grass Castles*, tales from separate hemispheres, are powerful testimony to the worldwide impact, across the nineteenth century and beyond, of emigrants from a small island on the periphery of western Europe. And the true story of that impact is in many respects as remarkable as anything invented by either Mary Durack or Margaret Mitchell.

The appearance of stereotypical Irishmen as key figures in two national epics from opposite hemispheres is a testament to the massive scale of emigration from Ireland during the nineteenth and twentieth centuries, and to the way these migrants helped to shape the societies in which they settled. Between 1821 and 1901 around six million men and women moved permanently to another country. By 1961 another two million had followed. The population fell from a peak of just over eight million in 1841 to not much more than four million in 1926. By the end of the nineteenth century, two out of every five people born on the island were living beyond its shores. The largest number were in the United States, where they were by this time only one of a multiplicity of ethnic groups. But the Irish and their descendants also made up a quarter or more of the population of Australia. In Canada and New Zealand they constituted almost one-fifth, and there were smaller Irish settlements in Argentina, South Africa and elsewhere.[2]

The background to this outward movement, without parallel elsewhere in the Western world, lay partly in Ireland itself. It contained one spectacularly successful industrial region, centred on the northeastern city of Belfast, home at the end of the nineteenth century to two of Europe's largest shipyards. But it was otherwise a poor and underdeveloped country, lacking the industrial and urban growth that elsewhere in the United Kingdom provided a living for a steadily expanding population. In addition Ireland suffered, between 1845 and 1851, a devastating famine that drastically reshaped its economy and its population history. But the scale of Irish emigration was also a response to developments beyond its shores. The international economy of the nineteenth century was being transformed by three developments: industrialisation, the filling up of sparsely inhabited parts of the globe by settlers of European origin, and the knitting together of diverse parts of the world into a single complex system of international trade. It was this new world to which the Irish emigrated and which, equally important, opened up to receive them.

The extent to which Irish emigration was inextricably linked to the birth of a new economic order became evident at a very early stage. In 1834 a rising young barrister, George Cornewall Lewis, received a commission to investigate the Irish migrant population, numbering between three and four hundred thousand, that over the previous few decades had settled in various cities of England and Scotland. His report was a classic depiction, from above, of an urban underclass. The Irish, in his account, occupied the very lowest level of the economic system. Their employment was mainly in unskilled labour, or in work 'of a coarse, repulsive and often unwholesome character' that the established population were unwilling to undertake. Yet their degraded condition, Lewis insisted, was not due to any discrimination. If they lived in poverty it was because they chose to work no more than was required for a bare subsistence, spent any spare money on drink, and lacked the steadiness of character required to graduate to skilled employment. They were also a threat to the wider society: their tolerance for squalor and their willingness to crowd into substandard housing made them a menace to public health, while their drunkenness and brawling threatened to overwhelm a police establishment designed to preserve order among a more tractable native population.

To the modern reader all this has a depressingly familiar ring. Exactly the same depiction of immigrants as a threat to the morals and stability of the host society, and as the authors of their own misfortunes, can be encountered, in different parts of the world, at any time across the past two centuries. In two respects, however, Lewis showed himself to be a shrewd, rather than a merely prejudiced, observer. The first is his conviction that what he described was something entirely new. In earlier eras, he pointed out, people from advanced societies had colonised less developed parts of the world, as the Spaniards had done in South America. Here, however, was something different: 'a less civilized population spreading themselves, as a kind of substratum, beneath a more civilized community; and, without excelling in any branch of industry, obtaining possession of all the lowest departments of manual labour.' The second is his equally clear recognition that this 'less civilized population', whatever problems it had created, had been essential to the massive commercial and industrial growth that in recent decades had transformed British society. Their irregular habits were to be regretted. 'But it is to be remembered . . . that they came in the hour of need, and that they afforded the chief part of the animal strength by which the great works of our manufacturing districts have been executed.'[3]

Lewis was discussing the recent short-distance movement of Irish people to Great Britain. What gives his report a significance beyond the immediate circumstances of early nineteenth-century Glasgow or Manchester is that he was writing on the eve of a great age of migration, in which the pattern of mobile labour he described was to be replicated across the greater part of the world. In the century after 1840, nearly sixty million Europeans were to cross the Atlantic. More than two-thirds went to the United States or Canada. But millions of Italians and Spaniards also became tenants on the large estates created by the opening up of the Argentinian pampas, and replaced liberated slaves on the coffee plantations of Brazil. During the same period around twenty-nine million Indian and nineteen million Chinese immigrants found their way to all corners of the Pacific Rim and beyond, labouring on the tea, sugar, rubber and tobacco plantations of Cuba, the West Indies, Malaya, and East Africa; in the gold and mineral mines of southern Africa; and in the mines and on the railways of America's West Coast. Later, after the Second World War, it was the turn of the richer countries of western Europe to turn to emigrants from their former colonies, or from their poorer neighbours in or close to Europe, first to rebuild their economies, then to take advantage of the long economic boom that followed the return of peace. In 1975 one in seven manual workers in Germany and Great Britain was a migrant. And in all these cases the typical destiny of the migrant has been the same—to become part of a 'substratum', a despised and ill-treated underclass set apart from a society that resents their presence yet is unable to do without their labour.[4]

An emphasis on manual labour as the driving force for the creation of a new world economy might at first seem odd. The nineteenth century, after all, was the great era of technological innovation, especially in the use of steam power. But technology had its limitations. Steam engines could drive the machinery required for simple, repetitive tasks such as spinning or weaving, and could propel railway engines across land and ships across oceans. But the railway lines along which those engines ran still had to be constructed by traditional methods, with shovel, pick and sledge-hammer. The same was true of the roads and canals that provided alternative forms of inland transport, and of the ports and dock-sides where ships berthed, while the goods they transported still had to be loaded and unloaded at warehouses, piers and railheads. The cities that were the centres of the new civilization, whether built from the ground in a former wilderness or expanded to engulf long-established but often modest townships, had likewise to be constructed street by street, house by house, brick by brick. And where Europeans settled new lands there were forests to be cleared, prairies to be broken up, wells dug and fence posts sunk.

In previous centuries there would have been an obvious solution to this need for labour. In the period between Columbus's first westward voyage and 1820, Europeans established control of a large part of the Americas without the need for mass migration. But that was because the two and a half million or so white settlers who crossed the Atlantic in those three hundred years were accompanied by around ten million enslaved Africans. It was these captives and their descendants who cleared ground for the coffee plantations of Brazil and the cotton plantations of what became the southern United States. Even in the northern states, unfree Black workers played a large part in the task of converting a natural landscape into an environment fit for European habitation. In New York City, in the mid-eighteenth century, Black slaves performed at least one-third of the physical labour that kept the city going. All this makes it easy to understand why the Western world was so reluctant to abandon coercion. Slavery continued in the United States up to 1865, in Brazil and Cuba to the 1880s. And even where slavery had been abolished, other forms of bound labour continued, like the indentures imposed on Chinese and Indian migrants, or the use of transported convicts to complete the first stage of the colonisation of Australia, and of Indian prisoners, both criminals and political troublemakers, to clear land and erect buildings across Britain's Asian possessions. Over time, however, the political pressures to abolish slavery became impossible to ignore, and none of the other forms of bound labour available came near to meeting the demand. Instead what emerged was an international trade in people, providing the free but cheap labour essential to the continued growth of the emerging world economy.[5]

This is the background against which the experiences of the eight million men and women who left Ireland between the early nineteenth and the mid-twentieth century must be understood. They were migrants in an age of mass migration. If very many among them became part of the bottom tier of the labouring population of more affluent societies, this should not be seen as licensing some exclusively Irish narrative of victimhood. It was a logical outcome of the economic forces that redistributed them around large parts of the globe. It was also a destiny that they shared with tens of millions of others, many even more disadvantaged. If the Irish were distinctive it was for two things: their status, noted by George Cornewall Lewis, as the pioneers of a wholly new type of mass migration, and the impact, out of all proportion to their numbers, that they made in their new homelands.

From one point of view, then, the story of the migrant Irish is of disadvantage and exploitation. Their condition can be summed up in the language that Karl Marx used to characterise the navvies (many themselves Irish immigrants), unskilled workers who constructed the roads and railways of Victorian Britain: they became 'the light infantry of capital, thrown by it, according to its needs, now to this point, now to that'. But there is another side to the picture. The nineteenth century was also the era in which Europeans, of all nationalities and social classes, asserted their superiority over other races. As settlers on newly opened lands, in Australia,

New Zealand and British North America, the Irish became accessories in the great nineteenth-century land grab whereby European societies extended their possessions at the expense of indigenous peoples. The same was true, on a smaller scale, in Argentina. The *Southern Cross*, a newspaper of the Irish community there, carried articles denouncing the seventeenth-century colonisation of Ireland by British settlers. But the paper also, with no sense of contradiction, offered enthusiastic accounts of the success achieved by Irish immigrants on fertile lands 'so lately won from barbarism to civilisation'—in other words by the clearance of the indigenous population. In the United States, by the second half of the nineteenth century, the Irish, like most other new immigrants, were concentrated well away from the frontier. But there too, whether in the cities of the East Coast and Midwest or in the generally more open society of the West Coast, they emerged as prominent defenders of white supremacy. In a world of racial hierarchies and ruthless territorial expansion, the migrant Irish must be recognised as both victims and, inescapably, oppressors.[6]

———

George Cornewall Lewis's remark about 'animal strength' put the focus on heavy manual labour. But the trade in people that developed during the nineteenth century was never solely about men. Women, in fact, became even more clearly a commodity to be shipped across long distances in the service of economic development. In both agriculture and manufacturing they were a cheaper and, generally, more biddable workforce than men. They were cheaper still when they worked from home. The clothing trade, for example, was a major part of the new manufacturing economy, and everywhere it depended on legions of women tending factory machinery, or labouring hour after hour on monotonous, repetitive and poorly paid work, stitching and sewing. Immigrant women also provided the greater part of the cheap domestic labour that sustained more affluent households across Canada, the United

States, Australia and New Zealand, providing the essential foundations for a culture of leisure, genteel sociability, philanthropy and social activism.

In colonies of settlement, where migrants were sought not just as workers but to populate new lands, the recruitment of women alongside men became even more important, as a means of avoiding a dangerous gender imbalance. A pamphlet in 1849 spelt out the reasoning behind plans to ship hundreds of young women from Irish workhouses to New South Wales. The absence of female society 'has made the settlers wild, reckless men; it should be the province of the young women who now emigrate to win them back to home ties and duties, and to revive in their hearts many pure and hallowed feelings, which have long lain dormant.' An even cruder attempt at demographic engineering took place nearly ten years later in British southern Africa, where the colonial government was seeking to secure newly annexed lands on the eastern frontier of the Cape Colony. The first step was to settle more than 2,000 German mercenaries recruited to serve in the Crimean War (1853–6) but who were now no longer needed. The second was to begin providing these men with wives by importing 153 young single women, again recruited from Irish workhouses. In the event, most of the young women concerned showed little enthusiasm either for the inhospitable countryside of 'British Kaffraria' or for a population of foreign ex-soldiers who were already proving to be ill-suited to farming. Instead they moved to Grahamstown and other urban areas, where they quickly found employment in domestic service.[7]

The willingness of these former workhouse inmates to reject the destiny mapped out for them as instruments of colonial social engineering should not surprise. One of the most striking features of nineteenth-century Irish emigration, distinguishing it from the wider global migrations of which it was a part, was the appearance of women as independent actors. European migration was predominantly male. Seven out of every ten emigrants entering the United States between 1900 and 1909 were men. The female minority, moreover, came mainly as members of family groups. Emigration from Ireland initially followed much the same pattern. After 1850, however, Ireland became the only European country to send almost as many women as men across the Atlantic, the great majority as single women rather than as wives or daughters. This pattern of independent female migration was of central importance, giving Irish diasporic communities a stability they would not otherwise have had. In particular it helps to explain why Irish rates of return migration were so low: there was no need to return home to find a bride from one's own ethnic background. In the case of the United States there is also the suggestion that the typical life cycle of a female Irish emigrant—a period of domestic service followed by marriage—gave the families thus created a familiarity with American domestic culture that would never have been achieved by husbands employed in manual and semi-skilled work.

The idea of an Irish diaspora was popularised in the 1990s by the Irish president, Mary Robinson, who in 1995 addressed a joint session of the two houses of the country's legislature on the theme 'Cherishing the Irish Diaspora'. Among academic historians the term has caused some unease. *Diaspora* came into common use through the Greek version of the Hebrew scriptures, where it was employed to describe the repeated episodes in which Jews believed that an angry God had allowed their ancestors to be violently uprooted from their homeland. Applied to the two million or more people who fled Ireland during and immediately after the Great Famine of 1845–51, the suggestion of a catastrophic visitation has an obvious relevance. Applied to the much longer history of Irish emigration, from the early nineteenth century to the 1950s, the term is more problematic. By casting Irish migration in terms of diaspora, there is an obvious danger of succumbing to what one writer has memorably described as MOPE: a reading of history in which the Irish appear as 'the Most Oppressed People Ever'. But some notion of a forcible dispersal is necessary to capture the exceptional, even pathological, character of the outflow that continued long after an apparent economic normality had been restored.[8]

Diaspora, moreover, has a second implication. Dispersed around first the Mediterranean and then the wider world, Jews retained a strong sense of their condition as exiles, and of a shared connection with a lost homeland. Here again the Irish case offers obvious parallels. In North America, Australasia, Argentina and elsewhere Irish immigrant communities shared a transnational culture. Whatever the location, the pages of their newspapers were filled with the same material: news reports from Irish papers, poems, stories, slices of popular history. Successive nationalist movements sought to create support organisations in the main centres of Irish settlement, and from the late nineteenth century regular overseas tours, raising funds and promoting the cause of Irish self-government, were central to the success first of the Home Rule movement and then of the more radical republicanism that replaced it. More powerful still, as a force reaching into the heart of every overseas Irish community, was the Catholic Church, dominated throughout the English-speaking world by bishops and priests of Irish birth or descent, and offering these expatriates a potent blend of ethnic and religious identity. Once again, however, as with the Most Oppressed People Ever, some caution is needed. The image of a people defined by Catholicism, nationalism and a deep sense of historical grievance applies to only one part of the Irish immigrant population. Protestant Irish emigrants, too, had their international network, in the Orange Order and the worldwide circulation of the *Belfast Weekly News*, providing a militantly Protestant perspective on the affairs of the homeland. Yet Orangeism outside Ireland tended to shed its ethnic character, becoming a more broadly based

Protestant fraternal association. And Irish Protestant immigrants in general were far more likely than their Catholic counterparts to be quietly absorbed into the mainstream culture of the societies in which they settled. Irish Catholic emigrants, meanwhile, may have brought with them memories and attachments that formed the basis of stronger transnational networks. But continued attachment to the cause of Irish self-government took very different forms in the United States, in Canada and in Australia or New Zealand. There was no single Irish exile mentality.

These are some of the complexities that the chapters that follow will explore. Accounts of the main centres of Irish settlement—the United States, Canada, Australia and New Zealand, with a briefer discussion of Argentina and Great Britain—examine the shared allegiances and cultural traits that constituted a transnational emigrant culture. But they also draw attention to the different experiences of these separate Irish populations. In addition they give a place to those who were not part of the Catholic nationalist culture that most Irish emigrants carried with them overseas. In seeking to explain the extraordinarily high level of emigration from Ireland, the discussion will have to distinguish a series of phases: the years after 1815, when the number of people seeking a new life outside Ireland climbed to new levels, and a disposition to emigrate spread from its traditional base in the province of Ulster to most parts of the island; the Great Famine of 1845–51, when emigration became for many a flight from disaster rather than a search for opportunity; and the century that followed, when those emigrating were no longer driven by fear of starvation, but made choices determined by a rigid social system. It ends in the present century, when many of the traditional landmarks of the Irish diaspora have disappeared, and when a widening gulf has come to separate the people of an affluent and secular Ireland, now a receiver rather than an exporter of emigrants, from those they were once taught to see as their exiled kin. Yet as recently as the 1990s the legacy of the Irish diaspora was sufficiently strong to make the affairs of Northern Ireland a central concern of American foreign policy. And today a global image of Irish identity persists, even if it is one that Gerald O'Hara or Patrick Durack would only partly recognise.

2

THE BEGINNING OF MASS MIGRATION

Emigration from Ireland was not a new development of the nine-teenth century. Living on an island on the western periphery of Europe, with regular commercial traffic to both continental Europe and North America, its people were never imprisoned by geography in the way that the peasantry of southern and eastern Europe long continued to be. From the Reformation onwards, close ties of religious affinity linked the Catholic Irish to their coreligionists in continental Europe, creating a steady stream of migrants—merchants, students for the priesthood, and recruits for the armies of the Catholic powers. So it was an Irish-born priest, Henry Edgeworth of County Longford, who as Abbé de Firmont attended Louis XVI on his way to the guillotine, while at almost the same time, on the other side of the world, Sligo-born Ambrose O'Higgins was viceroy of Peru, where he had gone as a servant of the Spanish king. Other Irish emigrants made a more direct journey west: between 1718 and 1776 an estimated 150,000 crossed the Atlantic to Britain's North American colonies. The majority of these migrants were Presbyterians from the northern province of Ulster. These were already a mobile group, mostly from families who had settled in Ireland during the second half of the seventeenth century or even later. As a Bible-reading people who prized education and literacy, as commercial farmers and artisans rather than as peasantry, and as inhabitants of the Irish province with the closest trading links with the American colonies, they possessed the information, the resources and the confidence to respond to superior opportunities opening up on the other side of the Atlantic. In America they established a particular place for themselves as active, land-hungry pioneers, initially in western Pennsylvania, then in western Virginia and the Carolinas, and in what was to become Kentucky. An analysis of the census of population taken in 1790, based on the frequency of certain surnames, suggests that between one in seven and one in six of the white population of the newly independent United States were of Irish origin, and that more than two-thirds of these were of an Ulster Presbyterian background. In the thirty years following the end of the American War of Independence in 1783, these settlers of the colonial era were to be followed by another 150,000 emigrants from Ireland, with seven out of ten once again coming from Ulster.[1]

This well-established but geographically and culturally limited pattern of transatlantic migration continued after 1815. But it was now supplemented, and eventually overtaken, by a more broadly based outward movement. The first signs of what was to come were in 1816. The previous year an eruption at the Tambora volcano in Indonesia had propelled a thick blanket of ash into the upper atmosphere, creating a worldwide ecological crisis.

To contemporaries 1816 was 'the year without a summer', when crops struggled to grow in wet, sunless fields. Emigration from Europe to North America rose threefold; a Belfast newspaper saw the flight that took place as 'a spectacle without a parallel since the time of the Crusades'. In Ireland dysentery and typhus, running through a starving population, prolonged the crisis. Around 14,000 emigrants left Ireland for North America during 1816–7 and an unprecedented 20,000 in 1818. Numbers fell back from 1819, as news arrived of bank failures and industrial recession in the United States, but not to the same extent as in other parts of Europe. And from the mid-1820s they began a sustained climb. Some 115,000 emigrants left for North America between 1826 and 1830, and 244,000 during 1831–5. There was a further pause, in response to another American recession, during 1838–9. But overall, between 1815 and 1845, close to a million emigrants left for North America, three times the number that had done so in the preceding hundred years.[2]

At the same time that numbers multiplied, the culture of emigration expanded far beyond its traditional centre in Presbyterian Ulster. The surge in numbers during 1816–8 followed a long-standing pattern. Two-thirds of all emigrants in these years sailed from the Ulster ports of Belfast, Derry and Newry, and contemporaries believed that most of those leaving were Protestants. Twenty years later, on the other hand, Ulster was providing half or fewer of Ireland's emigrants. By this time, too, it was generally accepted that the majority of Irish immigrants were now Catholics. Over the next decade the geographical range became wider still. Of those arriving in New York, by this time the most important American point of entry, between 1835 and 1846 more than two-thirds still came from the commercialised and relatively prosperous provinces of Ulster and Leinster. One in eight, however, came from the much poorer western province of Connacht, previously insignificant as a source of emigrants.[3]

The massive increase in emigrant numbers, and the extension of emigration from its traditional base in Protestant Ulster to the greater part of the island, reflected tightening economic circumstances. From the 1730s to the mid-1810s Ireland had enjoyed a long wave of rising prosperity. Economic expansion was initially based on exports of beef, pork and butter to the British and French colonies of the Caribbean. Then, just as the agriculture of the newly independent United States had begun to displace expensive transatlantic imports in the Caribbean, an expanding market opened up closer to home, as the agriculture of industrialising Britain failed to keep up with the needs of a rising population no longer working on the land. The good times reached a peak between 1793 and 1815. As the long war with Revolutionary and Napoleonic France closed off other trade routes, Irish farmers had this expanding British market, further swollen by increased demand from the army and navy, largely to themselves. With the coming of peace, however, prices fell to around two-thirds of their wartime peak. Meanwhile what had looked like a healthy manufacturing sector began to weaken. Irish firms producing cotton, wool and other products, catering mainly to a local market and without local supplies of coal, failed to compete with the much larger enterprises emerging in Scotland and England. The exception was the manufacture of linen, where the development of machine spinning ensured the survival of Ireland's most important manufactured product. Dependence on coal, however, meant that the new factory-centered industry was based mainly in Belfast, the most convenient port for imports, and its immediate hinterland. Elsewhere the availability of cheap mill-spun yarn wiped out the earnings of wives and daughters in poorer households, who for decades had supplemented precarious family incomes by spinning flax into thread in their own homes.

The Ireland of the 1820s and 1830s was not a society in economic collapse: that was to come after 1845. Studies of the physical height of convicts and military recruits suggest that the Irish poor, three-fifths or more of the population, were in fact more physically robust than their counterparts in urban, industrial England. Among the better off—middling and large farmers, merchants and shopkeepers, artisans in trades not yet being undermined by cheap imports—rising imports of tea, sugar and tobacco indicate a gradual rise in living standards. But there was nevertheless a pervasive sense of opportunities contracting. In County Antrim, a government inquiry was told in 1835, the people emigrating were still 'in tolerable circumstances'. However they had become afraid that if they remained in Ireland 'the badness of the times might render them unable to go'. The shutting down of options affected in particular the younger generation aspiring to set up their own households. The Andersons, for example, were five sons born in the early 1800s to John Anderson, a farmer at Lisnamuck near the town of Maghera in County Londonderry. A generation earlier the family might well have provided one or two emigrants to North America, while the rest found a livelihood at home, on the land, in linen weaving, or in some other trade. Now, in the changed circumstances of the 1830s, this Ulster Presbyterian family adopted what was, by the second half of the nineteenth century, to become the survival strategy of farming households across Ireland as a whole. One son, William, remained in County Londonderry, working the family farm, while the other four made their way to the United States. John sailed to Quebec with his wife in 1832, and five years later he and his brother David were in Ohio. Robert, born in 1807, had already set up a household of some type in Ireland, but in 1840, three years after the death of his wife, he and his brother Joseph likewise set out for America, leaving Robert's two sons in the care, first of his parents, then of their Uncle William.[4]

Rising emigration was a response to diminishing prospects. But it was also a product of a widening awareness of opportunity beyond Ireland. By the early nineteenth century several decades of dramatic economic growth, combined with the country's political integration into the British state, had created a well-organised commercial society, crisscrossed with roads, canals and, from the 1840s, railways, and with a dense network of towns and villages. The late eighteenth and early nineteenth centuries also saw important changes in Irish popular culture. There had been a dramatic growth in the demand for education. More than three out of five men born between 1811 and 1820—the most likely potential emigrants of the 1830s and 1840s—and more than two out of five women in the same age group, could read. With literacy came a switch from Irish to English language: already by the 1830s only just over a quarter of all children grew up in a household where enough Irish was spoken for them to acquire the language.[5]

Literacy and the adoption of English do much to explain how, within just a couple of decades, familiarity with emigration and the opportunities it offered spread from a cluster of northern counties to the greater part of the island. But the drive for schooling, and for mastery of the language of power and status, were also evidence of a wider shift in mentality: a growing determination on the part of ordinary men and women to adapt to the demands of a rapidly changing world. It is a shift powerfully illustrated by developments in popular politics. The 1820s were the decade of the great campaign for the removal of the remaining restrictions on Catholic political activity—mainly the right to sit in parliament. Under the dynamic leadership of the lawyer Daniel O'Connell, hundreds of thousands of small farmers and artisans mounted a successful agitation that astounded observers in supposedly more advanced political societies such as England and France, staging giant public meetings and mass petitions, and eventually casting off deference to reject the control that landlords had long exercised over the votes of their tenants. Around the same time observers began to comment on the retreat of magic from the Irish countryside. Belief in fairies and in charms and spells, attendance at holy wells, and the observance of great seasonal festivals like St John's Eve (midsummer) and Lughnasa (harvest) were all in decline. A whole culture of beliefs and practices that had promised some sense of control over an imagined network of unseen forces was falling into disuse. Instead, as the lengthening passenger lists of the emigrant vessels made clear, growing numbers of men and women were finding alternative ways of coping with the unsatisfactory realities that surrounded them.[6]

Tightening economic circumstances and a growing awareness of the opportunities that existed elsewhere drove up emigrant numbers. But it is also important to recognise the extent to which emigration, once it got under way in new areas, developed its own momentum. The first emigrants to leave an area faced a largely unknown future. But their letters home provided advice, encouragement and promises of assistance to those who were to follow. A parish priest in County Cork, regularly called on to read letters received by illiterate parishioners, was struck by their positive tone. 'The general observation they make', he reported in 1845, 'is that there is no tyranny, no oppression from landlords, and no taxes.' With increased passenger traffic the facilities available to intending migrants also improved. Traditionally travellers had bought their passage from an individual ship's captain or a merchant who had chartered a particular vessel. By the 1820s, however, specialist passenger brokers regularly advertised places on a range of projected sailings. The main firms were based in Liverpool, Belfast and Dublin, but they employed networks of local agents, mainly shopkeepers or other dealers, in towns across the countryside. Shipping companies and brokers also began to offer facilities that enabled those who had already emigrated to assist relatives or others still in Ireland in following in their footsteps. By the mid-1830s the Liverpool firm of Fitzhugh and Grimshaw was receiving £6,500 annually in bank drafts and other remittances from their agents in America; of that annual amount, £2,500 was to be forwarded as cash remittances in sums of £1 to £10, while the rest was to pay for tickets to allow friends and relatives to join the sender in the United States.[7]

Rising emigration on the scale seen in Ireland from the 1820s was potentially a matter of interest to the government. The country's population had grown by more than half in thirty years, from 4.4 million in 1791 to 6.8 million by 1821. A few decades earlier, in 1798, the pioneering demographer Robert Malthus had argued that human populations had an inbuilt tendency to grow faster than the resources needed to sustain them, until at length they were brutally cut back by plague, war or famine. Ireland, as hopes of an industrial revolution faded while numbers continued inexorably to rise, seemed poised to bear out every part of his grim prediction. In the early 1820s the idea of emigration as a possible escape from the Malthusian trap briefly gained the attention of two key figures, Henry Goulburn, the Irish chief secretary, and Robert Wilmot Horton, under-secretary of state for war and the colonies. With their support, Peter Robinson, a successful Canadian-born businessman and brother to the attorney general of Ontario (at this stage known as Upper Canada), brought more than 2,500 settlers from County Cork and adjoining areas to the Canadian province between 1823 and 1825. The scheme, given that Robinson recruited mainly among paupers and recently evicted tenants, was surprisingly successful: a study of one of the places of settlement found that 45 per cent of the farms created in the 1820s were occupied by the same families forty years later. But success was achieved by generous financial support, at what subsequent governments regarded as prohibitive expense. There was also the argument that anything that reduced the pressure on resources within Ireland would simply encourage more improvident ventures into marriage and parenthood, so that the space created would quickly fill up again. Two later commissions of enquiry, into poverty in 1833–6 and into the occupation of land in 1843–5, nevertheless included state-assisted emigration in the bundle of reforms they recommended. But with so many continuing to leave the country each year without the need to lay out public money, their recommendations were quietly ignored.[8]

Landlords too had, in principle, an interest in emigration. During the long period of prosperity up to 1815 lax management and the pressure of population had encouraged the creation, through subletting and subdivision, of multiple small plots yielding little more than enough potatoes to feed a family. Subsidised emigration offered the possibility of consolidating largely worthless holdings into rent-paying farms. In 1831, for example, the agent of the Caulfield property in County Roscommon spent £723 to facilitate the emigration of thirty-six heads of families who between them had occupied fifty acres of land, for which they had paid an insignificant £46 a year in rent. But emigration on a scale large enough to make a real difference was expensive. The Wyndham estate in County Clare spent £7,634 between 1839 and 1847 to facilitate the departure of 1,582 individuals. For most landlords, burdened by mortgages and other encumbrances built up during the years of agricultural prosperity, spending of this kind was out of the question. There was also the very real risk that any attempt to move the rural poor off the patches of land they clung to, even with the offer of assistance to emigrate, would meet with violent resistance. Instead, the most that could normally be expected was that a landlord would not place obstacles in the way of a tenant anxious to leave the country. In County Cork, for example, a magistrate reported in 1836 that landlords who evicted a tenant generally forgave the arrears of rent, allowing him to sell livestock, furniture and other goods in order to pay the passage of himself and his family.[9]

The great majority of the rising number of emigrants leaving Ireland in the thirty years after 1815 thus paid their own way. In 1827 a passage to Canada cost between £2 and £3, while the minimum fare to New York was £5 from an Ulster port and £4 from

Liverpool. By the 1830s the fare to the United States from Liverpool had fallen to between £2 10s and £3, but Quebec could be reached for only £1 10s. Up to 1842, passengers also had to find a further thirty or forty shillings for provisions. In Ulster, and to a lesser extent in some other districts, a tenant was recognised as having a right of occupancy which he could sell to whoever succeeded him. This 'tenant right' was another reason why Ulster remained for so long the main source of emigrants. Elsewhere substantial tenants could still realise the necessary funds by the sale of livestock, standing crops, agricultural implements and furniture. Tradesmen and shopkeepers could likewise sell off premises, stock, tools and household goods. The many occupiers depending for a bare subsistence on small plots of land, on the other hand, faced difficulty in scraping together even the much-reduced fares of the late 1830s. A report from County Leitrim in 1836 described how the 'sons of small farmers of four or five acres . . . embarrass their parents very much' by pressing them to sell livestock in order to fund their passage. Where labourers were concerned, wages could be as low as six pence per day in winter and were rarely more than one shilling. Even the very cheapest passage thus represented the earnings from fourteen weeks or more of full-time work at average wages; the £10 to £12 for a family was wholly unattainable. For them the most likely escape from the bleak prospects they faced at home was the short sea crossing to Liverpool or Glasgow, with perhaps the hope of accumulating enough money there to make the onward journey across the Atlantic.[10]

This complex pattern of costs and resources meant that the Irish travellers crossing the Atlantic were a disparate group. Around one in five of the passengers arriving at New York during 1820–48 and Boston during 1822–39 were aged 14 or less. However, emigration by whole families—not surprisingly, considering the cost—was rare. Instead a little under half of passengers (45 per cent) travelled alone. Some of these would have been single migrants. But contemporary accounts make clear that others would have been married men leaving behind wives and children whom they hoped to send for once they had established themselves and begun earning money. Most of the remainder travelled in groups of two or three, suggesting that these were siblings or other relatives travelling together, married couples, either childless or with a single child, or single parents with one or two children.[11]

Another striking feature of the profile of these early emigrants is the role of women. Among immigrants from Ireland arriving in United States ports in 1831, there were only 559 women for every 1,000 men. Among those travelling in family groups the numbers were roughly equal. Among single migrants, however, men outnumbered women by about two to one. Men, in other words, still predominated, and those Irish women who did emigrate most commonly travelled as wives, sisters or daughters. But attitudes were beginning to change. Ten years later the ratio of women to men had risen to 788, significantly higher than the figure for England (538) or Scotland (575). There were good economic reasons why Irish women were more ready than others to take to the emigrant ship. The replacement of the cottage spinning wheel by the giant water-and-steam–driven machinery of Belfast and the surrounding area, and the failure of factory-based manufacturing to thrive in other parts of the country, sharply reduced the opportunity for women to find employment, and with it their prospect of marriage. But contemporaries also reported what they saw as a dramatic change in outlook. 'It is really amazing', a County Cavan land agent commented in 1845, 'to see the number that are going, when six or eight years ago there was scarcely a female emigrating.' As with other emigrants the reports sent home by predecessors seem to have been a major influence. A County Westmeath farmer who frequently acted as recipient of letters to local families was struck by the many letters reporting the opportunities that local women had found on the other side of the Atlantic. The willingness and ability of these and other Irish females to join their male counterparts in responding to diminishing possibilities at home by turning to the greater opportunities available in a wider world points forward to the second half of the nineteenth century, when Ireland stood out among the nations of Europe for the number and independence of its female emigrants. And it is further confirmation that the sudden rise in emigration from Ireland from the 1820s was the result, not just of poverty and despair, but of widening horizons and a weakening of restrictive traditions.[12]

The drivers of rising emigration were economic and cultural change within Ireland. But the mass movement of people was possible only because of the inexhaustible demand for settlers and workers in the expanding economy of the United States. The journeys that Irish migrants took were likewise shaped by the requirements of the Atlantic economy. The goods carried east from America to Europe—principally cotton, tobacco and timber—took up substantially more space than the textiles and other manufactured goods that Britain and Europe exported in return. A human cargo provided both income and the ballast needed to keep a vessel stable. In the early years of mass departure, Irish emigration was closely tied to the Canadian timber trade, in which during the Napoleonic Wars the forests of British North America had taken over from those of the Baltic as the main source of British imports, so that the capacious holds of returning vessels offered plentiful cheap accommodation. British ships were also allowed to carry more passengers than their American counterparts, reinforcing the price differential between the Canadian and American routes. Better-off passengers preferred to travel on the less crowded American vessels. But between 1826 and 1835 more than two-thirds of Irish emigrants, even the majority planning to move on to the United States, sailed to a Canadian port. By the early 1840s, however, a rising proportion of transatlantic traffic, including such former staples of the direct trade between Ireland and America as cotton, flaxseed and timber, was funnelled through two emerging megaports, New York on one side and Liverpool on the other. The concentration of commercial traffic on this single route meant both cheaper fares and more regular sailings, so that there was no longer an incentive to use British North America as a stepping stone. In 1844, on the eve of the Famine, some 38,000 Irish arrived in the United States, compared to only 18,000 in British North America.

Changing patterns of transatlantic trade also determined the places from which Irish emigrants departed. As emigration spread to other parts of Ireland, the Ulster ports lost their dominance: by the late 1830s Cork had displaced Belfast as the main port of embarkation, while Sligo and Limerick had also begun to send out significant numbers. It had also become more common for ships leaving major British or Irish ports to call in at smaller harbours, such as Westport in County Mayo, to pick up additional passengers. By the 1840s, however, the dominance of the New York–Liverpool route meant that Irish ports no longer attracted the same number of large ocean-going vessels seeking a returning cargo. More affluent travellers might still choose to sail from Belfast or Dublin, willingly paying an extra ten shillings or so for the convenience of a direct passage. Those forced to count every penny, on the other hand, could pay as little as a shilling for a passage to Liverpool, where they could be sure of finding regular and affordable sailings across the Atlantic. By the early 1840s this was the route taken by well over half of all Irish transatlantic emigrants, and four-fifths or more of those heading for the United States.[13]

Paying only the cheapest fare, and admitted on board primarily as ballast, the Irish emigrant could expect only the most basic accommodation. The ships that carried growing numbers to Liverpool were the steamers that from the 1820s had revolutionised the Irish trade in live animals, so that passengers stood on the open deck sharing space with cattle and pigs. To prepare ocean-going cargo ships for passengers, sailors constructed a lower deck in the middle of the hold, creating a compartment between the storage area for provisions and any cargo and the upper deck of the vessel. In this area, known as steerage, they would then knock together wooden berths, generally measuring 6 feet by 6, each to provide sleeping space for four persons. The only other furniture was long tables running between the berths, at which the passengers ate. Sanitation was provided by communal buckets, emptied overboard as they filled. Travellers brought their own straw mattresses. They were also responsible, up to 1842, for bringing their own food. After that date ship owners were required to provide each passenger with a weekly ration of seven pounds of bread, biscuit, flour, oatmeal or rice. Alternatively, in recognition of the preponderance by this time of the poor Irish, they could provide the equivalent in potatoes.[14]

The ships that thus transported the first great wave of European immigrants to America during the 1830s and 1840s have acquired a lurid reputation. And there is little doubt that conditions were often grim. A typical ship of 400 tons would have had a lower deck of around 95 by 25 feet. Into this space the first British Passenger Act, in 1803, allowed a captain to cram 200 passengers, rising to 300 from 1828, then falling back to 240 from 1835. In practice, ship's manifests often understated the true number sailing, and enforcement was rudimentary. In this crowded, hastily constructed accommodation, steerage passengers endured a voyage that typically lasted six or seven weeks. Their choice was to remain in the gloomy, cramped and airless space between decks, or to crowd onto whatever portion of the top deck was open to them, exposed to all the weather offered. During a storm they were forced to remain below, with closed hatches, enduring the tossing and pitching in the overcrowded darkness. At the same time, references to 'coffin ships' and comparisons with conditions on the vessels that carried slaves from Africa are wide of the mark. Of just under five million Europeans who set out for United States ports between 1820 and 1860, around 45,000 died at sea, about 3,000 were lost in shipwrecks, and an unknown number, somewhere between 16,000 and 39,000, died soon after arrival from diseases contracted aboard ship. In other words 98 per cent of those who set out reached their destination alive.[15]

––––––––––

Potential Irish emigrants, looking across the Atlantic, had the choice of two very different destinations. In British North America a long-established French population had created solid urban centres in Quebec and Montreal, along with mature agricultural settlements on the banks of the St Lawrence River. Large parts of the British provinces, however, remained thinly populated and underdeveloped. The earl of Durham, reporting in 1837 on recent political unrest in British North America, saw the Canadian–United States border as separating two different worlds. On the American side 'good houses, warehouses, mills, inns, villages, towns and even great cities are almost seen to spring up out of the desert'. On the British side, in contrast, was found 'a widely scattered population . . . separated from each other by tracts of intervening forest, without towns and markets, almost without roads'. Even on opposite shores of the Great Lakes, the difference was apparent in the number of ships on the water and the provision of harbours and landing places. So stark a contrast helps to explain why a large majority, around two-thirds, of those who chose the cheaper sailing to a Canadian port went on to cross the border into the United States. Some, however, stayed. By 1842 British North America had around 160,000 Irish-born inhabitants.[16]

For those who came to stay, a major attraction was the huge areas of virgin land being opened up for settlement, particularly in Ontario, along a corridor bordered by the Great Lakes to the south and the great mass of partially exposed rock known as the Canadian Shield to the north and west. Those who had come with some capital could buy immediately; others initially worked as labourers, either on other men's land or in non-agricultural occupations, while they built up the means to buy a holding, generally on reasonably easy terms of payment by instalments. In doing so they committed themselves to years of gruelling labour. Trees had to be cut down, one at a time, with axes, the brush between them cleared, and the ground broken up in preparation for a first crop. Meanwhile settlers endured freezing winters, the menace of wolves and bears, and the absence of even the most basic social amenities. The government of Ontario's chief agent for emigration admitted in 1837 that a settler on wild land 'can hardly expect in his life-time to see his neighbourhood contain a population sufficiently dense to support mills, schools, post-offices, places of worship, markets or shops'. But the long-term investment did in the end pay off. By the time of the Canadian census of 1871 the Irish stood out as both the largest and the most successful of all the ethnic groups engaged in farming in Ontario.[17]

The harsh life of a farmer on virgin land was not for all. Already by 1824 around one-sixth of the population of Quebec City was Irish-born. By 1842 perhaps a quarter were of Irish birth or descent. In Montreal the Irish population rose from around 1,000 in 1821 to three times that level just four years later, and to 12,000 by 1851. These urban Irish Canadians, particularly the Catholics among them, tended to be concentrated in specific, generally poorer, districts of their town or city—Griffintown in Montreal, the waterfront district of Quebec, Corktown in Hamilton, Ontario—and to be employed mainly in unskilled or at best semi-skilled manual work. On the other hand the large numbers moving on to the United States, and the attraction for so many others of new lands in Ontario and elsewhere, meant that those who remained in the towns had the benefit of reasonably good wages. In Quebec a government emigration agent, reporting in 1831, pointed to the receipts of the city's savings bank as evidence of the prosperous condition of immigrant workers. 'I have experienced very great satisfaction in witnessing the decent deportment and well-dressed appearance of the vast body of Irish servants and labouring classes that attend the Rev. Mr M'Mahon's church on Sunday, some of whom, perhaps only a few months previous, landed with scarcely a shoe to their foot.'[18]

Irish immigrant life in Canada also had its rougher side. Protestants and Catholics brought with them the sectarian animosities of their homeland, leading to occasional violent clashes. Itinerant Irish labourers employed in canal building or in the lumber trade shocked observers by their willingness to engage in pitched battles among themselves or against outsiders. In the neighbourhood of Bytown (later Ottawa), during 1835–7, the Shiners, former canal workers turned lumbermen, fought vicious battles against their French rivals for control of the district's waterways, then allowed themselves to be enlisted by a local merchant as strong-arm men supporting his attempt to gain control of Bytown politics. Nevertheless, the overall verdict of contemporary observers on the contribution of Irish immigrants to the development of the colony was favourable. 'The Irish', the deputy postmaster general for British North America reported in 1837, 'above any people, most readily conform to the new habits of life and labour which obtain in the Provinces; and it is found, also, that instead of the recklessness which is generally considered as belonging to the Irish character in their own country they become careful of their earnings, and go on progressively improving their circumstances.'[19]

The larger body of emigrants who went on from Canada to the United States, or sailed there directly, also had the option of seeking to acquire land. The frontier continued to move westwards, but the opportunities were there for those with the energy and commitment to seize them. This was the case, for example, with the brothers John and David Anderson. In 1837 they had well-paid work on farms in Ohio, earning $144 and $126 a year, along with their keep. By 1841 they had saved enough to buy uncleared land and to begin the grinding task of turning forest into farmland. 'We are quite well here', they reported to their brother in Ireland, 'but we earn our bread by the sweat of our brow.' The timber 'stands pretty thick on our land' and in the previous summer they had sold 1,200 bushels (more than 9,000 gallons) of ash produced by their clearing and burning. By the 1850s, however, John was living comfortably enough, on a farm of just over a hundred acres, to contemplate semi-retirement, while David had a well-established business producing cheese. A third brother, Robert, who had arrived in 1840, had also done well, building up 240 acres in Indiana. Only the fourth brother, Joseph, had failed to prosper, for which his brother David blamed his wife, who was 'too full of notions'.[20]

The Andersons were Ulster Protestants. They were thus part of a tradition that by this time extended over more than a hundred years. But emigrants of other backgrounds also made their way onto the land. David Curtin, from Bruree in County Limerick, had arrived in Quebec at about the age of 20. Because he spoke both Irish and English fluently, he was able to establish himself as a ganger, hiring other immigrants to work at quarrying stone. He moved to Detroit, where he married, and then, around 1837, to Greenfield, near Milwaukee, where he bought a farm. This was, much more than the Ohio of the Andersons, very much a frontier settlement. Curtin's son Jeremiah recalled being snapped at by a wolf when he stood, aged 3, in the doorway of their cabin, and his mother almost picking up a rattlesnake sitting on her windowsill, which she mistook for an iron ring. But two of Curtin's brothers-in-law bought land nearby, establishing the nucleus of an Irish colony, and he himself was to become a justice of the peace and superintendent of the local school.[21]

The contribution of Irish immigrants to the settlement of the westward-moving frontier is not at first sight impressive. In 1850 the Irish-born in Wisconsin accounted for just 7 per cent of the population, in Minnesota 4.5 per cent, and in Illinois 3 per cent. But it is important to remember that, contrary to legend, first-generation Americans of any kind made up a small proportion of the frontier population; the great majority of settlers were American-born. A better measure is the Irish share of the foreign-born population. In Wisconsin the Irish provided one in five of those born outside the United States. In Illinois the figure was two out of five, and in Minnesota almost half.[22]

Alongside the continuing movement of Irish settlers to the frontier, however, observers in the 1830s and early 1840s—before the disaster of the Famine—had begun to draw attention to the growing number who instead opted for a life of labour off the land. Some chose to settle in or close to their point of arrival. In New York, increasingly the main port of entry for immigrants, the Irish share of the city's population rose from well under 10 per cent in 1830 to just over a quarter by 1845. Others became part of a mobile labour force, in lumbering, road building, and above all in the massive canal building projects that by 1860 gave the country 4,254 miles of waterway. As the projects reached completion the large bodies of labourers they had brought together often became the nucleus of an Irish working class in the towns and cities growing up along the route. The Irish presence in Chicago began when navvies who had been employed in digging the Illinois and Michigan Canal settled there after work finished in 1842. In Massachusetts, similarly, labourers brought in to create the improved and extended network of canals and mill races that for a time helped Lowell to become the premier textile centre of the Northeast stayed on to become part of the labouring population of the growing town. In Buffalo, at one end of the great Erie Canal linking Upstate New York to the Great Lakes, a whole district to the south of what was now a rapidly expanding inland port city was to remain up to the 1950s a distinctively Irish quarter, again founded by former canal workers. In these towns, and elsewhere, the Irish continued to be associated with the toughest and most demanding manual work. In Buffalo, for example, the first businessman to experiment with a steam-powered elevator to be used for unloading grain from ships was told by competitors that 'Irishmen's backs were the cheapest elevators'.[23]

Irish women, meanwhile, were also finding their place in the American economy. One early opening, at a time when free Black women were not yet present in sufficient numbers to be serious competitors, was domestic service. By 1846 between 7,000 and 8,000 of the 10,000 to 12,000 servants in New York City were Irish. Since most servants lived in, this was an occupation primarily for young, single women. Others, in New York and elsewhere, found employment in the garment industry, labouring as needlewomen, paid by piecework, in workshops or in their own homes. Married women contributed to the family income by taking in washing, by catering to boarders, or by peddling fruit and groceries on street corners. Over time, as factory production spread, Irish women began to be recruited by textile mills and similar large-scale, mechanised enterprises. In Lowell, for example, from the 1840s, Irish women began to find work in the town's cotton mills. Their employment, however, coincided with a sharp fall in the status of Lowell's factory workers. Employers turned to the Irish in response partly to growing competition from other centres, and partly to increased industrial militancy amongst the existing workforce, the American daughters of farming households in Lowell's rural hinterland. Abandoning earlier ideals of a paternalistic and humane factory system compatible with republican notions of equality, they turned instead to the exploitation of the cheap and, for the moment, biddable labour of immigrant Irish women.[24]

The growing numbers of Irish emigrants who set out for British North America in the years after 1815 owed their freedom to seek new lives on the other side of the Atlantic to specific circumstances: the development of a huge west-to-east trade in timber, and a concern to strengthen Britain's hold on its possessions north of the Great Lakes. No other part of the empire, at the beginning of the nineteenth century, offered similar opportunities. The plantations of the West Indies had long settled on enslaved Africans, rather than poor white immigrants, as the manpower best suited to crushing labour in tropical conditions. India, with a dense population and its own already well-developed commercial economy, required military, political and fiscal control, not people. A minor exception was the Cape of Good Hope, seized from the Netherlands during the war against Napoleon. This was important primarily as a staging post on the sea route to India, as well as a trading hub for products from other Indian Ocean territories. Some settlement was nevertheless desirable, as a counterweight to the Dutch who made up most of the existing European population, and also to secure the colony's eastern frontier, where the cattle-herding Xhosa people had been driven beyond the Great Fish River. In 1820 the government provided free passage and grants of land to promote the settlement of some 4,000 emigrants. These included a small contingent, 325 divided into four parties, from Ireland. The colony was not a success. Early wheat crops were destroyed by the fungal infection known as rust, while in autumn 1823 a prolonged drought gave way to devastating floods. A visitor in 1825 found the settlers living in dire poverty. Three shoemakers from Longford reported that they were unable to pursue their trade because the majority of their neighbours went barefoot for lack of money. From the mid-1820s a switch from tillage to more environmentally appropriate cattle farming, along with the writing off of money owed to the government for seed, tools and rations during the early years, allowed those who remained to progress towards reasonable prosperity. But by that time close to half of the 1820 settlers had abandoned the land for work in Cape Town and other urban centres.[25]

Eastern Australia, claimed for Britain by James Cook in 1770, played a different, and much more important, part in the history of the Irish diaspora. The 12,000 mile voyage discouraged conventional settlement by voluntary migrants. When it came to finding a replacement for the lost American colonies as a penal settlement, however, distance became a positive advantage. The foundations of Irish Australia were thus laid almost exclusively by convicted criminals. The first fleet of six transports, carrying 543 male prisoners and 189 women, arrived at Botany Bay in January 1788. The first vessel to sail directly from an Irish prison, the *Queen* with 133 men and 22 women, left Cork in mid-April 1791 and arrived in Sydney on 26 September. By 1828 New South Wales, with a total population of less than 40,000, had around 8,000 Irish-born inhabitants, of whom no more than 500 had come to the colony as free immigrants. In all 30,000 or so men and 9,000 women were dispatched from Ireland between 1788 and 1853, to New South Wales up to 1840 and thereafter to Van Diemen's Land (later Tasmania). There were also an estimated 8,000 Irish-born prisoners convicted in the courts of the British mainland. A minority, by one count between 6 and 8 per cent, had been transported for political offences, or for crimes of protest such as cattle maiming or writing threatening letters. The majority, however, had been convicted of minor offences such as theft; for seven out of ten it was their first recorded offence.[26]

Transported offenders arrived in New South Wales as prisoners bound to forced labour. For many, this was the rough beginning to a new life. Convict discipline could be brutal. Francis McNamara, transported for a robbery in Kilkenny in 1832, was flogged a total of fourteen times during his fifteen-year sentence, endured three and a half years at hard labour in irons, and spent seven more in a facility for particularly recalcitrant convicts on Van Diemen's Land. A well-behaved male convict, on the other hand, could expect to be given, halfway through his sentence, a ticket of leave that allowed him to take paid work. He could thus hope to begin his life as a free man with some savings, and experience of local farming methods or of other types of work. Up to the mid-1820s, male ex-convicts could apply for a grant of thirty acres of land, increased to fifty acres in the case of a married man. By the 1830s the authorities had become alarmed at the number of letters from former convicts regaling friends and relatives in Ireland with accounts of the prosperity they enjoyed. In 1838 the Irish chief secretary went so far as to ask the senior Catholic clergyman in New South Wales to restore some of the dread the penalty had been intended to inspire by publishing a pamphlet on *The Horrors of Transportation*. Female convicts did not have the same opportunity to acquire land or set up in business, and they remained highly vulnerable to sexual exploitation by employers. But once they gained their freedom, the uneven gender balance in the convict population improved their chances both of finding well-paid domestic work and of contracting advantageous marriages. Some women transported for arson in the 1840s and early 1850s freely admitted that they had deliberately sought transportation to improve their circumstances.[27]

As its role as a dumping ground for convicts approached an end a more settled and self-regarding New South Wales, along with the new, non-convict provinces of South Australia and Victoria, turned instead to subsidised immigration by free settlers. The first schemes addressed the multiple social evils thought to arise from the acute shortage of women in the Australian population. In March 1831 fifty girls and young women from the Foundling Hospital in Cork, established to provide for abandoned children, were added to a convict transport bound for Sydney. The following year the *Red Rover* carried 202 women between 14 and 27 years old, the majority coming from the Foundling Hospitals in Cork and Dublin and the Houses of Industry, institutes for the relief of the destitute, in the same cities. After 1836 the focus changed again, to subsidising the passage of family groups. South Australia, proud of never having been a convict colony, and aggressively Protestant, made little effort to recruit in Ireland. In New South Wales, on the other hand, the convict past deterred potential British settlers. Instead it was the Irish who came forward willingly: between 1839 and 1851 there were over 37,000 assisted passages from Ireland, almost half the total. By 1846 one-quarter of the population of New South Wales was Irish-born. The numbers were modest in terms of over-all emigration from Ireland. But already before the gold rush of the 1850s convict transportation and assisted emigration had be-tween them laid the foundations for another Ireland in the south-ern hemisphere.[28]

Beyond the boundaries of the British Empire, men with an eye for profit were similarly quick to take advantage of the opportunities created by the emerging trade in immigrants. After the United States purchased Louisiana from France in 1803, the sparsely populated and hitherto neglected territory of Texas became the new frontier zone between Anglo and Latin America. After 1823 the govern-ment of newly independent Mexico, anxiously eying its aggressively expansionist neighbour, began to offer generous grants to entre-preneurs who would contract to settle immigrants on Texan land. Among those who came forward were two pairs of Irishmen. One partnership, comprising John McMullen and his son-in-law James McGloin, had been born in the northwest of Ireland, in Donegal and Sligo, while the other two speculators, James Power and James Hewetson, were from the southeast, Kilkenny and Wexford. All four were merchants who had come to Mexico for business reasons and integrated themselves into Mexican society. McMullen and McGloin recruited their immigrants among Irish families who had already crossed the Atlantic, mainly to New York. Power, on the other hand, returned to his native Wexford and used local contacts to recruit a party of between 250 and 350 to accompany him from Liverpool to the Gulf Coast. Around one-third never made it to Texas. Some deserted along the way; others died, many in a disastrous outbreak of cholera. In the end the 210 individuals who in 1834 received grants of land in the colony Power established around the former mission station Nuestra Señora del Refugio, located a few miles inland from the port of Copano, included not just Irish but American, Canadian, British and European settlers. Meanwhile McMullen and McGloin created their settlement on a new site, San Patricio de Hibernia, where sixty Irish-born and twenty-three Mexicans received grants of land. Neither of these ventures inspired the continuing stream of incomers they might have hoped for. But the Refugio Irish, in particular, recruited from among the farmers, merchants and tradesmen of the relatively prosperous Irish southeast, flourished in their new environment, particularly after Texas in 1846 became part of the United States. By the 1860s, as Texas cattle ranching entered into its golden age, at least a third of the large-scale stock raisers in Refugio county were of Irish background. One of them, Thomas O'Connor, a nephew of James Power who had come to Texas as a teenager in 1833, became the owner of half a million acres, making him one of the richest men in the state.[29]

Further south, in Argentina, the collapse of Spain's colonial empire created similar opportunities. For the Irish this was not wholly unknown territory. Already before independence, Irish and British merchants had engaged in an illegal but lucrative trade across the River Plate from two Portuguese-ruled towns in present-day Uruguay. Irish soldiers took part in British military expeditions in the region in 1806 and 1807, and some remained when the army withdrew. A few years later the South American wars of independence attracted further fighters from Ireland, some inspired by ideals of international liberation, others by the prospect of adventure and profit. In 1822 an Irish veteran of these wars, John Thomond O'Brien, originally from County Wicklow, signed a contract with the Argentine government to recruit Irish emigrants to be employed on public works and rewarded at the end of their service with plots of land. The British government, reluctant to antagonise Spain, had still not recognised the new Argentine state and intervened to block

O'Brien's mission. Over the next few years, however, Irish entre-preneurs active in Argentina turned to their homeland to recruit workers for their businesses and landed estates. Two of the most prominent were the banker and merchant Thomas Armstrong, and Patrick Browne, owner of a meat packing business.[30]

In Argentina, in contrast to Texas, Irish migration, once be-gun, became self-sustaining. By 1864 Fr Anthony Fahy, the priest responsible for the Catholic Irish of Argentina, claimed that his flock, comprising the Irish-born and their descendants, numbered 30,000. Conditions in Argentina were favourable to Irish migrants. An export-based trade, first in sheep, then in cattle, was expanding rapidly, and land was easily available as the new government ruth-lessly dispossessed the Indigenous population in the hinterland of Buenos Aires. But there was also a strong element of chain migra-tion, as letters from early migrants, offering advice and assistance, encouraged others from the same district to follow. Irish Argen-tina thus had a strong regional character. Armstrong was from a prominent landed family with lands on the border between the midland counties of Westmeath and Longford, and he recruited his migrants from that area; Browne sought his workforce in his native district of County Wexford. A twentieth-century genealogi-cal study found that just under three-quarters of the 3,667 original migrants identified had come to Argentina from the counties of Longford, Westmeath and Wexford. In the 1850s William Mulvi-hill, a grocer in the town of Ballymahon, County Longford, acted as agent for the River Plate Steamship Company, supplying pro-spective immigrants with tickets that would take them to Liver-pool and on to Buenos Aires. This distinctive movement of small and medium farmers, mainly Catholic, from the Irish midlands continued up to the 1870s. Thereafter emigration to Argentina continued on a smaller scale, but the immigrants were now mainly businessmen and white collar workers, with roughly even propor-tions of Catholic and Protestant.[31]

———

By the 1840s a new Ireland beyond the seas was beginning to take shape. Given that between four and five times as many immigrants went to the United States, either directly or through Canadian ports, as stayed in British North America, the 160,000 Irish-born recorded in the different Canadian provinces in 1842 suggests an Irish-born population in the United States of somewhere over 700,000. In Australia, New South Wales alone had 48,000 Irish-born inhabitants in 1846. Adding the 400,000 Irish-born living in Great Britain, it seems safe to say that one in seven of the 9.5 million Irish-born no longer lived on the island of Ireland. By comparison the few thousand Irish in Argentina were numerically insignificant. But the establishment of a sustained chain migration from a group of mainly rural counties in the Irish Midlands to such a distant and, initially, unfamiliar destination is further evidence of the openness to new opportunities created by a changing culture.

All this raises the question of what would have happened if there had been no Irish Famine. Between 1831 and 1841 the population of Ireland rose by only 400,000, from 7.8 to 8.2 million. The 426,000 emigrants departing for British North America and the United States, in other words, had cancelled out the greater part of the natural increase in population, through an excess of births over deaths, that would otherwise have taken place. If these trends had continued, the population of Ireland in 1851 would once again have shown only a moderate increase—perhaps, if emigrant numbers continued to rise, no increase at all. Emigration, in other words, was not just creating an Ireland overseas, it was well on the way to bringing population growth under control and averting the sort of disaster foretold by Robert Malthus. Before this could happen, however, the appearance in Europe of *Phytophthora infestans* was to give the history of the Irish both at home and abroad a decisive new direction.

3

FLIGHT FROM FAMINE

Phytophthora infestans is a fungus that attacks the growing potato plant, causing the tuber to degenerate into a blackened, slimy pulp. It was first reported on the Eastern Seaboard of the United States in 1843. Its appearance in Europe in the summer of 1845, probably carried across the Atlantic in a cargo of seed potatoes, caused widespread hardship. In Ireland, however, the consequences were disastrous. No other food of the same nutritional value could be grown in such quantities on small patches even of marginal ground, such as reclaimed bog or the upper slope of mountains. As the population of Ireland almost doubled, from 4.4 million in 1791 to more than eight million in 1841, the potato had become the staple food of the poor. According to one estimate, around one-third of the population depended on this single crop for 90 per cent of their food requirements. The potato fungus arrived late in the season in 1845, allowing roughly two-thirds of the crop to survive intact. In 1846, however, the fungus took hold and blighted the potato crop, creating a second successive year of crop failure. Harvest that year was only one-fifth of normal. The first deaths from starvation came in October, and the winter that followed saw horrific scenes: emaciated men, women and children begging for scraps of food, or foraging desperately for anything that could be eaten, while dead bodies lay unburied in obscure corners, or inside cabins that had been stripped of every last item that could be sold or bartered for food. The crisis continued for another five years. The last death from starvation was recorded at the end of April 1851, and it was not until after the healthy potato harvest of that autumn that something like normality returned. The census of 1851 recorded a population of 6.6 million, around two million fewer than might have been expected. There had been roughly one million deaths, over and above what would have been expected across the same period in normal years. Perhaps 10 per cent of these deaths had been caused from starvation, the rest from the spread of disease in a population weakened by malnutrition and forced into crowded and unsanitary workhouses. The remainder of the fall in population, another million or so, was a result of emigration.[1]

The initial impact of the potato blight on numbers leaving was modest. An estimated 109,000 people sailed for North America in 1846. This was well above the average of 66,000 emigrants a year between 1842 and 1845, though not dramatically higher than the pre-Famine peak of 93,000 departures in 1842. In the last months of 1846, however, the first signs appeared of an alarming new development. Sailings normally took place during the spring and summer. But after the second successive failure of the potato crop, in the autumn of 1846, unprecedented numbers were willing to accept the additional risk and hardship of an out-of-season crossing. Throughout the winter of 1846–7 reports continued of roads and canals unable to cope with the numbers making for the port towns, and of ports themselves crowded with people desperate for a place on any vessel willing to sail. Total departures during 1847 were 224,000, a level never seen before. By the end of the year, this panicked exodus seemed to be coming to an end. Mass starvation continued, because so few potatoes, about one-eighth of the normal acreage, had been sown. But what had been harvested was free of blight, a hopeful portend for the future. Departures picked up again in early 1848, but that was because of a rush to beat the expected rise in fares that would follow the tighter regulations imposed by a new Passenger Act. Instead it was the harvest of 1848, when spores that had lain dormant in the dry summer of 1847 revived to once again blacken field after field of potatoes, that shattered any remaining resistance to emigration. Large numbers of people, one newspaper reported in September, had up to this held back from leaving, simultaneously horrified by tales of the sufferings that had accompanied the mass exodus of 1847 and encouraged by that year's healthy crop. Now, however, 'the gambling root has cheated them anew' and huge numbers were preparing to flee the country. In every year between 1849 and 1852 the number emigrating was to remain above 200,000; in 1851 it was just short of a quarter of a million.[2]

The mass emigration that rescued hundreds of thousands from fever and starvation owed almost nothing to the assistance of government. British administrations, first Tory then Liberal, responded to the crisis unfolding on the other side of the Irish Sea with a succession of temporary expedients—a system of public works, soup kitchens distributing basic rations, and eventually a much-expanded workhouse system offering the desperate a bare subsistence. But their commitment to saving lives was diluted by a determination not to impede what policy makers saw as a painful but necessary restructuring of the Irish economy. That restructuring, it was clear from the start, would have to include emigration. The projected reorganisation of agriculture envisaged a class of labourers earning steady wages from enlarged farms created by the consolidation of small holdings. But the number so employed would be limited. Manufacturing industry, in an Ireland relieved of the burden of an impoverished agricultural sector and made more attractive to British capital, might expand to absorb some of those moved off the land. But there would also be a substantial surplus population whose only future lay outside Ireland. The British prime minister, Lord John Russell, the Irish lord lieutenant and others tried to make the case for state-subsidised emigration. However the British treasury was unwilling to meet the costs. There were ideological objections to what would be in effect a subsidy to Irish landlords, who were widely seen as having created the crisis by their lax management of their estates. And there was also the argument that large-scale emigration was taking place anyway, without state assistance. In this, as in other respects, government policy was that Ireland's future was to be decided by the workings of the free market.[3]

Local government played only a slightly bigger part in promoting emigration. From 1838, boards of Poor Law Guardians had the power to raise funds by a local rate to subsidise the emigration of poorhouse inmates. In practice, however, the cost of day-to-day relief ate up all available funds, so that these powers were little used. In the twelve months from September 1848, Boards of Guardians supported the emigration of just 201 men, 400 women and 270 children. It was only as the immediate crisis eased after 1850 that unions became able to think about subsidised emigration as a long-term investment that would reduce the cost of poor relief. New legislation, in August 1849, allowed unions to borrow rather than having to support emigration wholly out of current resources. Even then, however, the numbers involved remained insignificant. In a twelve-month period across 1851–2, unions sponsored 3,092 emigrants to British North America, nearly two-thirds of them women, mostly aged between 14 and 25. But total emigration across the same two years averaged 235,000 each year.[4]

At the same time that the government allowed the consequences of ecological catastrophe broadly to take their course, Irish landlords made their own contribution to the catastrophe by initiating large-scale clearances, evicting smaller tenants and their families and levelling their cabins to prevent them returning. Landlords were encouraged to do so by legislation making them, rather than the occupier, responsible for the rates payable on holdings of less than four acres. Statistics, available only from 1849, show that in that and the next four years nearly 50,000 evictions took place, representing perhaps a quarter of a million displaced persons. This figure does not include an additional number of tenants, unknown but probably substantial, who left under the threat of eviction, making a nominally voluntary surrender of their holdings in exchange for a small sum of money or the right to hold on to possessions that might otherwise have been seized to pay off their arrears of rent. A few landlords sought to ease the process by assisting the displaced to emigrate. The Palmerston estate in County Sligo, property of the British foreign secretary, spent over £8,000 assisting 2,000 tenants to emigrate during 1847. The Fitzwilliam estate in County Wicklow spent £25,000 to send out nearly 6,000 people, representing a third of the tenants. But these were prohibitive sums. Most Irish landlords, faced with collapsing rents and spiralling taxes, had no such resources. Removals, even if financed, were also unpopular. Major Denis Mahon, who arranged the departure of 833 tenants from his estate in Roscommon, was shot dead in November 1847, apparently following reports of the large number of deaths on a ship he had organised. For his part, Palmerston was vilified when he advertised for new tenants to take farms of 500 and 1,000 acres on the lands he had cleared by eviction. The best estimates suggest that between 1846 and 1855 landlords gave significant assistance to between 50,000 and 80,000 emigrants. This would amount to between 4 and 5 per cent of the total number leaving Ireland during that period.[5]

Without significant support from government or landowners, emigration did, as policy makers envisaged, play an important part in resolving the desperate crisis created by the destruction of the potato crop. But those it took away were not necessarily the destitute, or people in imminent danger of starvation. As in the period up to 1845 those who now crowded onto emigrant ships were drawn disproportionately from two areas: counties like Cavan and Longford, where emigration was already common, or prosperous, commercialised counties like Meath and Louth, where those affected by the crisis were most likely to have access to the necessary information, about tickets, routes and destinations, as well as resources that could be converted into the cost of a passage. There was a definite increase in the number of poorer emigrants. The proportion of Irish passengers arriving at New York who were classified in ships' manifests as labourers and servants rose from 60 per cent in 1836 to 75 per cent in 1846. Among those arriving in the same port during 1847–8, the western province of Connacht provided almost one in four, compared to only one in eight across the previous ten years. But some of the counties worst hit by the failure of the potato crop, such as Kerry, Clare and Mayo, sent out relatively few emigrants in relation to their population. A part of the rural poor, in these districts and elsewhere, were able to make the cheaper journey to Great Britain. Many others, however, had no choice but to stay where they were, and died in their hundreds of thousands.[6]

––––––––

The desperation of so many to escape from a collapsing economy and the risk of death by fever and starvation brought a revival in traffic from the Irish ports that over the preceding decade had lost business to Liverpool. In particular there was an increase in direct sailings from the southwestern ports of Cork and Limerick, and from Sligo on the west coast. There was also a rise in sailings from smaller Irish ports, especially in the panic year of 1849. Opportunistic attempts to capitalise on the sudden demand led to some dangerously under-resourced ventures. In July 1846, just as news of the second successive failure of the potato crop was spreading panic through the countryside, local speculators in Killala, County Mayo, chartered the 83-year-old *Elizabeth and Sarah* to carry 276 passengers, 121 more than the legal limit, to Quebec, with no provisions other than what the passengers brought with them. Seventeen passengers died on the voyage, and seventy-six were admitted to hospital on arrival, of whom seven died over the next two weeks. The *St John* from Galway was wrecked as it approached the port of Boston in October 1849, with the loss of all but fifteen out of around one hundred passengers. It had timbers so rotten that the writer Henry David Thoreau, viewing the wreckage on a Massachusetts beach, could almost push the point of his umbrella through them. But these seem to have been the exception. Figures collected at Quebec in 1847, a year of particularly heavy mortality, show that the number of deaths on sailings from Ireland was lower than on ships leaving Liverpool. Cork, on the other hand, had more deaths than either Liverpool or the smaller Irish ports. This would suggest that the quality of ships was less important than the conditions in which emigrants lodged while waiting to sail: it was the crowded and unsanitary conditions that prevailed in the larger ports, whether in Ireland or in Great Britain, that gave killer diseases their opportunity to gain an initial foothold.[7]

For the much larger body of emigrants who continued to sail from Liverpool, the huge increase in numbers, and the wretched state of so many seeking to travel, brought a sharp deterioration in conditions. A report in 1849 described the horrific character of the sea crossing from Ireland. With no system of booking tickets, passengers who had paid the basic fare were allowed to crowd onto each departing vessel, once the livestock had finished loading, until no more could be crammed in. One inspection of arriving steamers in 1849 found that there was one square yard of space for every two passengers. Travellers stood 'so jammed together in the erect posture that motion was impossible. . . . The common offices of nature, including vomiting from seasickness, were consequently done on the spot.' With emigration no longer confined to the summer months, travel on the open deck presented other dangers: Liverpool constables reported having found dead bodies frozen to the deck. In one notorious case in December 1848 the steamer *Londonderry*, attempting to make its way from Sligo to Liverpool with 203 deck passengers, encountered a heavy storm. The captain, apparently concerned that passengers might be washed away by the large waves crashing onto the deck, had 170 of them confined in a small below-decks compartment, where 72 died of suffocation.[8]

The main voyage, from Liverpool to the United States, was in theory more closely regulated. By 1845 emigration officers at Liverpool, Glasgow and the main Irish ports were charged with ensuring that ships carried only the permitted number of passengers and had adequate supplies of food and water. In practice, rigorous inspection was impossible. An outcry in 1851 over deaths on a grossly overloaded sailing to New Orleans led to the dismissal of the chief emigration officer in Liverpool, who was accused of accepting the paperwork presented to him while making no checks of his own. But the truth was that, with up to thirty sailings a day, leaving from separate docks as much as 4 miles apart, the three officers available in the port could not possibly have been expected to carry out the detailed inspection required by the law. There were frequent complaints of overcrowding masked by falsified passenger lists, and of provisions that were stale or adulterated or dispensed using false measures. The rations supplied, mainly oatmeal, rice and potatoes, had to be cooked over communal fires, but these were often inadequate, leading to brawls where 'sticks are used and hats knocked off', while those unable to assert themselves, or to slip a bribe to the cook in charge of the fire, went hungry.[9]

Although the Passenger Acts made no provision for sanitation, emigration officers had begun on their own authority to demand that ships clearing port install water closets, located on deck and emptied by chutes running into the ocean. The provision was not generous: commonly there was one or at most two closets for every hundred passengers. Some observers claimed that Irish emigrants ignored these facilities, instead defecating indiscriminately in spaces between the decks. But it was also the case that the flimsy huts that had been erected were sometimes carried away by the waves. In addition, women passengers were often unwilling to be seen entering and leaving the very visible on-deck water closets. Some used chamber pots or whatever utensil they could find, 'which they bring up under their aprons and empty overboard'. But others continued to seek out whatever dark, unoccupied corners of the ship they could find. A passenger on one voyage in 1850 noted without undue surprise that 'one of the female passengers played the dirty trick this evening of committing a nuisance on the deck at the top of the steps; being caught in the act, she was (very properly) made to take it up with both her hands and throw it overboard.' Matters became worse when bad weather forced passengers to remain below with hatches closed, and the pitching of the ship caused any receptacles used to spill their contents. One witness boarding a ship driven back to Liverpool by a violent storm compared the passengers' quarters to 'a regular dungeon. When we opened some of the hatchways under which the people were, the steam came up; the smell was like the smell of pigs.'[10]

Stench, cramped quarters and poor food were all familiar complaints, though probably made worse as the massive increase in numbers made effective regulation impossible and encouraged operators to cut corners. An apparently new element was the accounts that began to appear of physical violence inflicted on migrants by those who had charge of them. Passengers arriving in Liverpool on the ferries from Ireland, a parliamentary enquiry was told in 1851, were commonly driven off with sticks. The philanthropist Vere Foster, who in October 1850 travelled in steerage on an American vessel to inform himself of conditions on emigrant voyages, found much to criticise. Provisions were dispensed irregularly, and not in the proper quantities. The ship's doctor refused to attend passengers who would not offer him money. But his strongest complaint was of casual brutality. The sailor overseeing the distribution of provisions routinely laid about him with a rope's end, 'with or without the slightest provocation'. The first mate, walking past an elderly passenger, kicked him so violently that he passed blood. On another occasion the same officer 'took it into his head to play the hose upon the passengers in occupation of the water closets, drenching them from head to foot'. Foster himself was twice knocked down when he took it upon himself to act as spokesman for passengers complaining about a failure to issue the promised rations.[11]

The most likely explanation for this routine and gratuitous violence, apparently a new development of the Famine period, is the bewildered and demoralised condition of the emigrants themselves. An increased number of those who crowded into steerage in Liverpool and elsewhere during the second half of the 1840s were from the poorer classes within Irish society. Some would have been unable even to speak up for themselves in English. What possessions they once owned had generally been sold to raise the money for their passage. There was also the hunger and deprivation they had already endured. The County Limerick landlord Stephen de Vere, who like Foster had himself made a journey in steerage to investigate conditions, commented on the 'utter demoralisation' of the men and women coming ashore at Quebec. 'The emigrant, enfeebled in body, and degraded in mind, even though he should have the physical power, has not the *heart*, has not the *will* to exert himself. He has lost his self-respect, his elasticity of spirit—he no longer stands erect.' Alexander Carlisle Buchanan, the chief emigration agent in the port, went further, questioning 'whether the frightful extent of the mortality among the Irish emigrants at sea has not been in great part chargeable to their own want of moral energy, and their untractableness'. In a familiar process, refugees from economic disaster came to be seen as to blame for their own debased condition. And it is easy to see how, in such a context, the ordinary seaman, already accustomed to the rough ways of a sailing ship, found it tempting to respond to any irritation with the fist, the boot or the knotted rope.[12]

In the years before the failure of the potato crop, the attractions of the Liverpool-to-New York route had drawn an increasing share of emigrant traffic away from British North America. But in 1847, just as the crisis in Ireland neared its peak, the trend was temporarily reversed. A new American Passenger Act required that ships sailing to ports in the United States should have 14 square feet of deck space per passenger. One estimate was that the new requirement cut the carrying capacity of the standard emigrant ship by a fifth. Meanwhile individual American states, responding to the first reports of dangerous levels of disease in Ireland, introduced their own restrictions. Massachusetts in particular virtually closed Boston to emigrant traffic by requiring that masters of vessels post a bond for $1,000 to indemnify the state against any charge their passengers subsequently made on public funds. In response ships diverted to Canadian ports, and the fares on those still sailing to the United States rose sharply. In 1846, 69,000 Irish emigrants had sailed directly to the United States, compared to 41,000 to British North America. In 1847, as the Famine crisis deepened, Irish emigration to the United States rose by three-quarters, to 119,000; but sailings to British North America more than doubled, to 104,000.

What this meant in practice was that one of the most horrific episodes of the whole Famine era was played out largely in Canada. More particularly it was played out on Grosse Île, a wooded island in the Gulf of St Lawrence, 30 miles downriver from Quebec, where a quarantine station had been established during the European cholera epidemic of 1832. The chief medical officer, aware of conditions in Ireland, and also of the tightening of restrictions in the United States, had prepared for the 1847 emigration season by increasing capacity to 200 beds. But the facility was quickly overrun, as ship after ship appeared, bringing multiple cases of typhus and dysentery. By 28 May, eleven days after the first arrival, there were 856 patients on the island, and another 470 still on board ship, while 13,000 passengers waited to be inspected. Three days later there were forty ships at anchor, in a line stretching nearly 2 miles downstream. The provincial council drafted in extra medical staff and erected several hundred tents to provide emergency accommodation. But conditions quickly deteriorated. A priest working on the island described the scenes he had witnessed:

> Beside each tent lies fermenting waste which nobody has time to carry away, and inside, in two and sometimes three rows, lie living skeletons; with hardly enough straw on which to stretch out their limbs, men, women and children pell-mell; and so close together that one could hardly take a step without treading on some part of the breathing mass. Nearly all are suffering from dysentery as well as from fever, and are too weak to drag themselves outdoors, and hence must wallow in their own filth.

When the tents were eventually replaced, in August, by more permanent sheds, they were found to be too dirty for conventional washing. Instead soldiers had to drag the tents to the river, so that the current could carry away the worst of the filth that encrusted them.[13]

By the end of 1847 the doctors at Grosse Île had treated 8,691 patients, mostly for typhus or dysentery. Of these patients, 3,238, almost two out of every five, had not survived. The other main station for the reception of emigrants, Partridge Island in New Brunswick, had not been overwhelmed by the same number of arrivals, and so had fared somewhat better. At the end of the year the emigration agent reported 17,074 passengers, virtually all Irish. Of these an estimated 2,400 had died: 823 at sea, 1,196 at the quarantine station or the emigrant hospital near St John, and the rest at other locations. The staff manning the station at Grosse Île had also paid a heavy price. Almost all of the doctors had at some stage fallen ill, and four of them had died, along with four Catholic priests, two clergymen of the Church of England, and thirty-four ancillary staff.[14]

Yet, despite these sacrifices, the quarantine stations at Grosse Île and at Partridge Island in New Brunswick failed to achieve their primary purpose. The strategy was twofold. The sick were to be detained and if possible cured. The healthy, once clean, were not to be permitted to congregate in Quebec. Instead they were to be herded onto steamboats that would carry them up the St Lawrence to Montreal and then along Lake Ontario to Toronto. The results were predictably disastrous. Typhus was not the result, as most contemporaries believed, of the vapours given off by dirty bodies and decaying matter. It spreads through the bites or faeces of lice and other parasites, and has an incubation period of ten to fourteen days. Cases of typhus appeared in Quebec City itself within a few weeks, carried by immigrants passed as healthy at Grosse Île. Thereafter a succession of further reports confirmed the potential for lethal infection to radiate outwards from the quarantine stations. Some 1,200 died of typhus in Kingston, 1,100 in Toronto. Montreal, at a point where the waterway narrows, requiring travellers to transfer from the large sea-going steamers to smaller boats, became a particularly lethal bottleneck. A collation of the weekly totals published in local newspapers between June and November 1847 suggests that 2,499 immigrants died in the sheds set aside for the infected, while another 750 died in other parts of the city. Meanwhile the death rate among residents of the city rose by four-fifths, bringing an extra 400 deaths across the same period. In New Brunswick, equally, the emigration officer at Partridge Island admitted frankly that most of the emigrants being permitted to pass through quarantine were too feeble to work. Those who were able to do so frequently spread fever through the farmhouses in which they were employed, so that 'their course through the country was almost invariably marked by disease and death'.[15]

The lethal combination of mass emigration and epidemic disease that brought disaster to British North America also affected the United States, but not to the same degree. Boston, despite the extraordinary efforts of the state authorities to deter poorer migrants, had to send 4,816 new arrivals to its quarantine station on Deer Island, at that time still a separate island in Boston Harbor. The presence on the island of 852 graves suggests a death rate of a little below one in five, half that recorded on Grosse Île, although it is possible that some bodies were taken away by friends or family for burial elsewhere. In New York the Staten Island quarantine centre treated 3,259 cases of typhus during ten months of 1848, of whom just 433 died. In their primary purpose of protecting the resident population, moreover, the New York facilities were largely successful: the records of one city hospital show that, even at a distance from the port district, eight out of every ten typhus sufferers treated were newly arrived immigrants. One reason for the lower mortality and the greater success in containing the disease was that American facilities for the reception and treatment of diseased immigrants were superior to those found north of the border. The Marine Hospital in New York had 600 beds, and as numbers rose extra accommodations were quickly found at other sites. But the United States was also protected by its tougher regulations, which diverted the worst-maintained and most-overcrowded ships, and the poorest immigrants, to Canadian ports.[16]

The grim scenes enacted at sea and at quarantine stations and elsewhere during 1847 became part of the enduring memory of the Irish Famine. As early as 1848 Thomas D'Arcy McGee of the militantly nationalist Young Ireland movement announced in a speech that the ships carrying refugees from the crisis had become 'sailing coffins' that transported their passengers not to America but to eternity. McGee almost, but not quite, coined a phrase. The term 'coffin ship' came into widespread use from around 1870, in connection with the English reformer Samuel Plimsoll's campaign against the dangerous overloading of commercial vessels. During the 1880s, at a time of renewed agrarian conflict in Ireland, it was taken up by Irish nationalist commentators, who employed colourful accounts of the clearances that had accompanied the failure of the potato crop some forty years earlier to back up their attacks on what they presented as a ruthlessly exploitative landlord class. In that contentious context the image was quickly extended to suggest that across the whole period of the Famine, emigration was close to a sentence of death. The claim of catastrophic losses was not wholly political rhetoric. The most recent calculation suggests that the death rate among Irish passengers to British North America in 1847 was a little over 10 per cent. This, however, covers only those dying on board ship or in the quarantine stations at Grosse Île and Partridge Island. Other calculations, taking account of those who passed beyond the ports but died elsewhere soon after landing, point to a higher figure. The figures provided by the emigration agent for New Brunswick suggested an overall death rate among passengers from Liverpool and Irish ports of one in seven. The medical officer at Quebec suggested a death rate of one in six among those from all parts of the United Kingdom entering the provinces of Ontario and Quebec. All of these estimates, however, relate to a year in which passengers came on board ships carrying a deadly infection. In 1848 the death rate on ships to Canada was to fall to 1.5 per cent. There were lesser peaks of mortality in 1849 and 1853, when outbreaks of cholera pushed the death rate on ships from Irish ports to New York to between 3 and 4 per cent. Otherwise, however, the death rates for Irish passengers crossing the Atlantic between 1845 and 1855 remained at the normal level for voyages from Europe during the nineteenth-century age of sail, ranging from around 1 to 2.5 per cent. The transatlantic voyage, as the evidence of Vere Foster and others made clear, remained a debilitating, and sometimes brutal, ordeal. But, with the major exception of 1847, the great majority of those who undertook it survived.[17]

As well as searing itself into Irish memories, the crisis of 1847 reshaped the future pattern of Irish emigration. Provincial authorities in the different parts of British North America were horrified by the arrival of so many ragged, starving and disease-ridden Irish. Their response was to slap heavy additional taxes on arriving emigrant vessels: in the case of Quebec the levy rose in stages from the existing five shillings per passenger to thirty shillings by October 1848, and there were further taxes where ships were held in quarantine. Prohibitive charges of this kind eliminated the price difference that had previously made Canadian ports an attractive option for poorer emigrants. Across the next five years, 1848–52, 140,000 Irish emigrants sailed to British North America, compared to more than six times that number to the United States. The Famine did boost the Irish population of Canada: by 1861 there were 286,000 Irish-born, compared to 160,000 two decades earlier. The United States, however, now had 1.6 million Irish-born inhabitants. And it was that much larger community, enough to ensure that few young Irish men or women considering their future would be unable to identify a relative, friend or former neighbour, that was to become the magnet for future generations of emigrants.

The flight of refugees from the Irish Famine to other destinations was on a much smaller scale, but it was still significant for the societies concerned. Emigration to Great Britain went uncounted in official records since this was technically movement within the same state. The best estimate is that between 200,000 and 300,000

Irish arrived between 1845 and 1855, helping to increase the number of Irish-born living in England, Wales and Scotland from just over 400,000 in 1841 to 727,000 in 1851, and to 805,000 ten years later. In part this was a continuation of a movement that had been going on for some decades, and had already created the community described by George Cornewall Lewis. But Great Britain now became the destination of additional numbers desperate to escape Ireland, but who were without the resources to attempt an Atlantic crossing. There were also frequent allegations that landlords and estate managers, anxious to clear their properties on the cheap while at the same time avoiding resistance, solved the problem by providing displaced tenants with just enough money to take them to a British port.[18]

In 1847, the year of the typhus epidemic, this influx of poor, famine-stricken Irish produced a crisis similar in character if not in scale to that which affected North America. In Liverpool, during that year, the police recorded the arrival of 296,000 passengers from Ireland, 116,000 of whom they classified as paupers, 'half naked and starving'. Glasgow recorded around 50,000 arrivals of the same kind. Poorly clad, lice infested, and already worn down by malnutrition, many congregated in the ports of arrival, notably Liverpool and Glasgow, finding lodgings in crowded and unsanitary cellars. In March 1847 a Poor Law inspector in Glasgow reported finding four Irish families, twenty-three people in total, all of whom had arrived within the past few months, living in a cellar measuring 16 feet by 10 feet, eight of them suffering from typhus. But others fanned out from their ports of arrival in search of work, or in an attempt to make their way to friends or relatives. At Cheltenham in April an inquest jury met to consider the case of a 3-month-old boy pronounced dead of starvation. The family had been evicted from their holding in County Clare earlier in the year. They had paid for their passage from Cork to Newport in Wales with the eight shillings remaining from the sale of a horse and a cow, and had set out on foot for London, where an aunt of the father kept a shop. At Cheltenham a constable had found them sheltering in a ditch, attempting to keep the child warm, although he was in fact already dead. The local Poor Law Union found space for the rest of the family in a lodging house. But eight days later a second inquest investigated the death of two more of the couple's four children, carefully protecting the town's reputation by their conclusion that the deaths had been 'from the effects of starvation brought on from privation previous to their arrival in Cheltenham'.

The provisions of the English Poor Law allowed parishes to return paupers to their place of origin. On this basis Liverpool, during 1847, returned some 15,000 recent arrivals to Irish ports, most commonly Dublin, while Glasgow and other Scottish ports deported another 10,000 or so. But the numbers that remained were far beyond anything existing mechanisms of public health and poor relief could deal with. Liverpool created its own miniature Grosse Île: a ship serving as a quarantine station for new arrivals from Ireland, two more ships used as hospitals, and fever wards in disused dockland buildings. Other centres adopted similar emergency measures, with contemporary estimates suggesting that four out of five patients treated for typhus or similar diseases were Irish. As in North America those who came forward to provide medical aid and spiritual comfort to the victims of infectious diseases sometimes paid a heavy price. In Liverpool at least ten doctors and ten Catholic priests died of typhus, along with a Unitarian missionary, and an unknown number of nurses, Poor Law officials and others in the front line of relief work. In Glasgow the dead included four priests, two Irish and two Scots, four doctors, three nurses, three Poor Law inspectors, two clerks, and a van driver. Despite such sacrifices, disease and malnutrition combined to cut like a scythe through the immigrant population. One estimate is that Irish deaths from typhus and other famine-related diseases might have been as many as ten to fifteen thousand. If total Irish immigration to Great Britain during that terrible year was around 40,000, this made the emigrant's chances of survival even poorer than for those who risked the Atlantic crossing. But then these very poorest Irish, whose means took them no further than England, Scotland or Wales, are perhaps better seen, not as emigrants, but as refugees in panicked flight from an all-embracing economic catastrophe.[19]

The other secondary destination for those seeking to escape the Famine was Australia. Considered purely as a refuge from catastrophe in Ireland, this destination made little sense given the high costs to travel there. Instead the impetus came from the colonies themselves. The transportation of convicts to New South Wales had come to an end in 1840, and the supply of free settlers fell far short of what was needed. Conditions were so desperate, according to some accounts, that farmers were being forced to kill off their herds of livestock for want of stockmen to manage them. There was also the perennial problem of a skewed gender balance. In parts of the interior there were reportedly more than four men for every woman. In the more prosperous districts of Melbourne, meanwhile, there were horror stories of a shortage of domestic help so acute that 'the natural order of society is reversed', as servants confident of their scarcity value lorded it over their mistresses.[20]

Against this background the government launched two initiatives. The first was a resumption of the earlier system of subsidised emigration, which had been in abeyance since 1844. Unlike other schemes, this did not attract opposition from the British treasury, since the costs were met by the sale of Crown lands in the colony to settlers. Ireland was initially not well represented in the scheme, providing only 3,500 of the 18,000 emigrants who sailed during 1847–8. Over time, however, as poorer English and Scots continued to show their reluctance to accept even assisted passage to what they saw as a distant dumping ground for criminals, it was Irish settlers who came to predominate. Most came from Cork and

Tipperary, the two counties that already had a history of settlement in Australia, or from northeast Ulster. By 1856 a total of about 14,000 had been assisted to make their way to the colony.[21]

The second assisted emigration scheme was specifically directed at the shortage of women. Young female inmates of Irish work-houses were to be carried free to Australia, with the Poor Law Unions concerned covering the cost of outfitting them for the journey and delivering them to Plymouth in southwest England. The cost of their onward passage to Australia was once again covered from the proceeds of Australian land sales. As implemented it was probably the best-organised scheme of assisted emigration provided by any nineteenth-century agency. Between 1848 and 1850 a total of 4,175 girls and young women, mostly aged between 14 and 18, made the journey to Australia. Poor Law Guardians were required to supply each girl with a full set of clothing, possibly a better se-lection of apparel than anyone in their family had ever possessed. Each shipload was accompanied by a matron and a surgeon, and was well provided with food. On arrival those under 17 were ap-prenticed as domestic servants, while the rest were found ordinary positions in the same capacity, in both cases to approved employers. An orphan committee in each colony continued to monitor their progress, in some cases intervening to protect them from abuse or exploitation. The death rate across all the voyages concerned was less than 1 per cent.

Despite these careful preparations, what came to be known as the workhouse-orphans scheme aroused massive hostility. Irish newspapers denounced it in the same terms they had used towards Palmerston and other landlords subsidising emigration. One Tip-perary newspaper labelled the scheme a part of the white slave traf-fic. The *Nation*, an organ of Young Ireland, the militant nationalist movement that had initially supported Daniel O'Connell's consti-tutional campaign for Irish self-government but had subsequently adopted a more militant stance, compared it to Cromwell's attempt to banish the native population west of the River Shannon. Australians were no more enthusiastic. Instead of 'the rosy-cheeked girls of England', or 'the braw lassies of bonnie Scotland', a Melbourne newspaper complained, they were being sent 'coarse useless creatures . . . whose chief employment hitherto has consisted of some intellectual occupation as occasionally trotting across a bog to fetch back a runaway pig'. Another paper alleged that the barracks housing newly arrived orphans in Adelaide was, in effect, a government brothel. The Scots Presbyterian minister John Dunmore Lang of Sydney, a long-standing campaigner against Irish immigration, claimed that the orphans scheme, opening the way to several thousand religiously mixed marriages, was part of a plan to 'Romanise the Australian colonies'.[22]

Diatribes of this kind are a reminder of the deep ethnic and religious prejudices that existed, to be awakened wherever poor Irish emigrants, in particular poor Irish Catholic emigrants, appeared in any numbers. What is equally striking, however, is the extent to which this hostility was balanced by the social needs—for labour and a better gender balance—that had inspired the emigration scheme. A small number of the 'orphans' lived down to predictions, turning up in subsequent police records as prostitutes, drunkards or criminals. There were individual tragedies, like 16-year-old Alice Ball from Enniskillen, who drowned herself in the Yarra River after being made pregnant by her employer. Most, however, were quickly found places in households desperate for maids, cooks and childminders. From there the majority proceeded quickly to a household of their own. Two out of every three married within three years of arrival, at an average age of just over 19. The men they married were on average ten or eleven years older. This raises the possibility that there might have been a price to pay, in emotional terms, for being part of the solution to a demographic crisis as acute as that of colonial Australia. Early marriage certainly meant large families: the average number of children born to these couples was nine. Almost a third of these young women married men who had, like them, been born in Ireland. More than half, however, married men born in England, a further indication that the orphans, whatever prejudice they had to put up with, became integrated into colonial society.[23]

The two million emigrants who left Ireland in the ten years after 1845, and the smaller but still significant number who left in the years that followed, carried with them memories of a withering human tragedy. But the ways in which that memory was interpreted could be very different. In the United States the predominant view was that the Famine was a man-made tragedy, caused by the negligence and indifference of an alien government. In *The Last Conquest of Ireland (Perhaps)*, published in 1861, the former Young Irelander John Mitchel went further, arguing that British ministers had deliberately promoted mass starvation as a means of completing the political subjugation of the country. More than a century later, in the 1980s, Irish-American organisations revived Mitchel's ideas when they campaigned to have the Irish Famine included in mandatory school curricula as an example of genocide. Irish immigrants to Australia, in contrast, showed no interest in a narrative of victimhood. During the crisis the 70,000 or so Irish-born settled there responded generously to news of suffering in Ireland, contributing a total of around £10,000 for famine relief. But once the crisis was over they saw little reason to perpetuate its memory. Australia did eventually get a Famine memorial, in 1999, in response to an Irish campaign, headed by the country's president, Mary Robinson, to raise awareness of the event throughout the main areas of Irish overseas settlement. But the focus of the memorial at Hyde Park Barracks, Sydney, was very specific. It commemorated the 'workhouse orphans'. These were representative neither of the hundreds of thousands who died in Ireland from starvation and disease, or of the great mass of emigrants who had fled the disaster.

But, as a category of transportee, they were a group that Australians could identify with.[24]

The response of the Canadian Irish was more complex. In 1909 the Quebec branch of the Ancient Order of Hibernians, the most numerous Irish nationalist organisation in North America, sponsored the erection of a granite Celtic cross, 46 feet high, on Grosse Île. The man behind the project was Jeremiah Gallagher, who had arrived in Canada from County Cork around 1859 and had pursued an eminently respectable career as waterworks engineer and surveyor for the city. But he was also the Canadian organiser of the revolutionary Clan na Gael movement. The ceremonial surrounding the opening of the monument reflected his success at maintaining this double life. Among those present were cabinet ministers from federal and provincial governments, the Chief Justice of the Supreme Court, the Catholic archbishop of Quebec and the Papal Legate to Canada. The inscriptions on two sides of the monument, in English and French, contained nothing to disturb this assemblage of the great and the good. They spoke of 'Irish emigrants who, to preserve the faith, suffered hunger and exile in 1847–8 and, stricken with fever, ended here their sorrowful pilgrimage'. A third inscription, in Irish, read rather differently. 'Children of the Gael died in their thousands on this island, fleeing from the laws of foreign tyrants and an artificial famine.' The speeches on the occasion followed the same pattern. The head of the Canadian Ancient Order of Hibernians referred vaguely to 'our respect to the dead, who died for Ireland'. A visiting speaker from the United States branch of the Order spoke more provocatively of 'those poor Irish immigrants who were hunted like wild beasts from their native land'. But it was left to the third orator to echo the sentiments of the Irish inscription. Major Edward McCrystal, a veteran of the United States army, had advised Gallagher on the wording of the Irish text and now he repeated the same message: the emigrants 'were destroyed by England. . . . Our native country is in bondage still and our people are ruined.' His remarks, however, were once again delivered in Irish. The same message of victimhood and historical grievance that was openly proclaimed in the United States clearly had its Irish Canadian adherents. But it was equally clearly not a view to be too widely shared.[25]

The Famine brought major changes to the pattern of Irish emigration and to the character of the Irish population overseas. Yet its impact on the outlook of those emigrants and their descendants was by no means uniform. The sense of a major crime committed against the people of Ireland by an oppressive British government, not just indifferent to their sufferings but positively malevolent in its intentions, so widely accepted in Ireland, was replicated mainly in the United States. In Canada such attitudes were muted; in Australia they seem to have been largely non-existent. The reasons for these divergences will become clear as we come to look more closely at the different settings within which the Famine and post-Famine immigrants sought to create their new lives, and at the different versions of Irish identity that emerged as they did so.

———

The heavy emigration that had begun once the consequences of the potato failure became unmistakable declined only gradually as the crisis came to an end. From a peak of 250,000 emigrants to North America in 1851 departures fell to 134,000 in 1854. There was then a sharp fall to 63,000 the following year, and to only 34,000 in 1858. Some would-be emigrants might have been deterred by news of the rise in the United States of a militant anti-immigrant movement, the Know-Nothings. But with a parallel and equally steep tailing off in both the United States and Canada it seems clear that the main reason was economic. By this time the brutal readjustment of the country's population to changed market conditions was largely complete, and living standards for those who remained had begun to improve. News in 1857 of another economic downturn in the United States added further to the reasons for staying at home.[26]

Over the next six decades the level of emigration was to fluctuate in response to conditions both in Ireland and abroad. Numbers fell further in the late 1850s and early 1860s, years of high agricultural prices and general prosperity, reaching lows of just over 64,000 in 1858 and again in 1861. But they rose again, to more than 100,000 a year, during 1863–5, when a combination of drought, heavy rain and animal sickness brought renewed crisis of rural Ireland. In 1876–7, with the United States again in recession, emigration from Ireland to all destinations reached a new low of fewer than 40,000 a year. But numbers rose again with the catastrophic fall in farming incomes early in the next decade, reaching a peak of over 108,000 in 1883, before falling back to under 40,000 for almost all of the twenty years before the First World War. Even in the good years, however, emigration was a significant part of Irish social life. Overall a further three million emigrants were recorded as leaving Ireland between 1860 and 1910.

Continued emigration reflected the restructuring that the Famine had imposed on Irish society. The key fact was that *Phytophthora infestans*, though it had become less virulent, had not disappeared. It was not until around 1900, when spraying with copper sulphate or bluestone became available as a protection, that the potato could once again become the reliable resource it had been before 1845. And without this staple crop, there could be no return to the pre-Famine economy. No other type of cultivation could feed so many people on so little ground. And no other crop would allow cash-poor small farmers to employ the workers they needed to engage in labour-intensive tillage by way of allowing them a piece of fallow land as potato ground. Between 1845 and 1851 the number of holdings of less than one acre had been reduced by nearly three-quarters, the number between one and five acres by more than half. Farms remained small: in 1910 almost half of all holdings were between five and twenty-nine acres. But most now concentrated on livestock—cattle and dairying, sheep, pigs, fowl and eggs—all of which could be managed, on most holdings, by the work of family members. By the early twentieth century fewer than one person in three employed in Irish agriculture was a paid labourer; the rest were relatives contributing to the family farm. The new rural Ireland that thus emerged after 1850 was more prosperous, peaceful and stable than the one it replaced. But it was a society in which the army of smallholders and labourers that had provided the base of the pre-Famine tillage economy no longer had a place.[27]

Emigration also became an established part of the life cycle of the farming family. Already before 1845 the occupiers of medium and large farms had often sought to pass this asset undivided to a single son, rather than distributing the available land between heirs, as was common among labourers and small holders. Marriage in these circumstances was an economic arrangement, frequently negotiated through intermediaries, in which the bride of the inheriting son was expected to bring with her a dowry appropriate to the value of the farm she was marrying into. After 1845, these more substantial matchmaking farmers, formerly a minority in rural society, were now the largest social group. Meanwhile, the alternatives open to the less fortunate siblings of a farming family—the sons who would not inherit, the daughters for whom there was no dowry—had contracted sharply. Holdings were now being consolidated rather than subdivided. Employment opportunities for labourers were diminishing. The supply of waste land was contracting, as bog and mountainside no longer capable of yielding even a bare subsistence was abandoned. A well-off farmer might be able to set up a son as a publican or grocer, to finance a more bookish boy for a training as a priest, to assist a daughter in becoming a schoolteacher or nurse. In most farming families, however, emigration represented the only real option for a non-inheriting son or daughter unwilling to spend a lifetime as an unmarried helper on the family farm. The influence of this new pattern of inheritance was evident in the changing profile of those who now emigrated. Family groups of emigrants, still important in the 1830s and early 1840s, were now relatively rare. Instead emigrants were overwhelmingly young and single. In addition, and in sharp contrast to the general pattern of nineteenth-century European emigration, Irish women were now as likely to emigrate as men. Across the whole period of 1851 to 1910, 48 per cent of emigrants were women. In the 1890s and 1900s females actually outnumbered males.[28]

At the same time that it reshaped Irish rural society, the Famine transformed emigration itself. Before 1845 the geographical area from which emigrants were drawn had been slowly broadening. But those departing still came disproportionately from the more prosperous counties of the north and east. The experience of the Famine years, however, decisively broke down the remaining barriers, cultural, psychological and practical, to a general emigration. From the 1850s to the First World War, it was in fact the poorer counties of Connacht and, commencing a little later, the southwest counties, that consistently sent the largest proportion of each new generation overseas. There was now no part of Ireland in which emigration was not a familiar concept, or where those hoping to leave would not find relatives, friends or former neighbours waiting to smooth their entry into a new society. Heavy post-Famine emigration is generally seen as the result of a restrictive regime of marriage and inheritance. But the argument can be stood on its head. The Famine turned Ireland into a society of heavy emigration, and the availability of this easy escape route made it possible to adopt the rigid system of farm succession that prevailed across the century that followed.[29]

The continued decline in population in the decades following the Famine brought major benefits to those who remained. Real agricultural wages, for example, more than doubled between 1854 and 1913. Agriculture remained inefficient by western European standards. Manufacturing outside the northeast contracted further as improved shipping and the completion of the railway network opened up local markets to cheaper British products. But falling population numbers meant that, even with sluggish economic growth, a society previously swamped by an impoverished peasantry was now able to enjoy the benefits of an expanding consumer society. These gains, however, were achieved at the expense of the departure, year after year, of a substantial part of each new generation of men and women. A few observers, working from a starting point in contemporary economic theory, were prepared to acknowledge this uncomfortable truth, and to argue that continued emigration was of benefit to the nation. In 1848 Denis Heron, professor of Political Economy at Queen's College, Galway, argued that the outflow should continue until wages in the west of Ireland had risen to the same level as wages in Chicago. Most Irish commentators, however, chose to ignore the extent to which continued heavy emigration was an essential part of the new arrangements that had given the country its current modest prosperity. Instead they preferred to present the continuing procession of emigrants as the victims of a society oppressed by British misgovernment and an exploitative landlord class.[30]

Contradictory sentiments, if not downright doublethink, were also evident in the attitude of the Catholic Church. Some priests and bishops, in the first half of the nineteenth century, had been willing to see emigration as one way of reducing the problem of poverty. Faced with the massive outflow of the Famine years, and the continued high levels of the following decades, however, the majority became decidedly hostile. Bishops and priests denounced the loss of population, depriving the country of its youngest and most energetic inhabitants, and joined in the condemnation of landlords and the British government. They also warned of the danger to the moral and spiritual health of the emigrants, in the godless and materialistic societies to which they went. And yet, at the same time that they deplored the outcome, priests played an active part in facilitating continued departures, assisting in correspondence with those already overseas, acting as the recipients of remittances of passage money, and providing letters of recommendation for those about to sail. Schools run by nuns also played their part, providing the training in cooking, sewing and ironing that their pupils would need as domestic servants on the other side of the Atlantic. Some sought to reconcile formal opposition and pragmatic acceptance by declaring that what looked like a social evil was in fact the hidden hand of divine providence. The dispersal of the Irish throughout the English-speaking world was part of God's plan for the spread of the true, Catholic religion to all parts of the globe.[31]

What of the outlook of the emigrants themselves? It would be easy to see those leaving as the less fortunate in each generation, forced from their homes by the drying up of opportunities and the harsh family dynamics that came with the system of arranged marriage. Yet close studies of farm inheritance suggest something rather more equitable: a division of the family's resources between the holding inherited by one son, and the dowry provided for one daughter, and the financial assistance that allowed other siblings to emigrate. The heir to the tenancy was not necessarily the eldest son, making it possible for the more compliant to remain at home awaiting the farm (or the dowry) while the more adventurous sought a future elsewhere. Nor was eventual entry into control of a small farm in rural Ireland necessarily an unmixed blessing. The living standard of most Irish farmers, measured in terms of material consumption at least, was improving, but it remained well below that of industrial workers in Great Britain or the United States. And for women the prospects were even more unappealing. Lillian Doran, who had left County Westmeath in 1912 to become a domestic servant in New Haven, Connecticut, was in no doubt about her choice. In Ireland she would have been a farmer's wife, working 'outside, and every kind of hard work in the country, digging and everything. . . . I never could do that.'[32]

Against this background many emigrants, buoyed by letters from friends and relatives describing the opportunities that awaited them, may well have felt that they had the better part of the bargain. A newspaper reporter observing the crowd waiting to sail from Queenstown in 1866 concluded that it was composed entirely of people departing from choice rather than necessity, attracted by the prospect of employment at good wages or of acquiring land. 'All wear an appearance of pleasure, sometimes assuming the aspect of thoughtless gaiety and denote, by their dress, manner and deportment, the real satisfaction with which they exchange this for another country.' Representatives of two shipping lines, questioned in 1881, likewise rejected the suggestion that their passengers were 'dull, heavy, sorrowful'. 'From my experience', one insisted, 'they are generally rather jolly about it.' Much has been made of what came to be known as 'the American wake', when people gathered in the house of a person about to emigrate, in the same way that they did to mark the death of a friend, neighbour or relative. But it has also been suggested that the extravagant displays of grief common at such gatherings had a purpose. By presenting the emigrant's departure as a lamentable necessity the performance shifted attention away from the extent to which there was also an element of choice, thus reducing the risk of resentment and conflict within the family. As such it need not be taken wholly at face value. One observer, in 1909, noted the manner in which 'sometimes the lamenting girl seems to lose her grief as suddenly as she found it, and as she arrives at various railway stations, she leans out of the window to see if there are any friendly faces'.[33]

If some emigrants at least set off with a lighter heart than they could decently reveal, the grief of parents left behind is likely to have been more deeply felt. In December 1847 a Presbyterian minister in Portaferry, County Down, wrote to his son John Orr, who had recently settled in Chicago:

> No night passes in which, at the family altar, you are not remembered before the Throne of Grace. . . .
>
> Frequently, at dinner or tea, the question is put, what is poor John about now? We have come to the conclusion, by the study of Geography, that we are about 5¼ hours of time in advance of you, and that consequently when we are at tea you are going to dinner at one o'clock.

Similar calculations may well have continued between 3 November 1850 and 14 January 1851, the time it took for news to reach the manse at Portaferry that John Orr had died of cholera in Sacramento, where he had gone to seek his fortune in the goldfields.[34]

4

CASTLE GARDEN
AND BEYOND

Emigration to the United States in the Post-Famine Years

During the second half of the nineteenth century, emigrants left Ireland for a range of destinations. But the great majority, more than four out of every five, continued to look to the United States. The number of Irish arriving there between 1856 and 1880 was 1.1 million—about the same as the number recorded during the crisis years of 1846–52—amounting to an average of 44,000 emigrants a year.

For would-be Irish emigrants, this continued preference made sense, given the huge numbers already established in the US by the end of the Famine crisis. They were able to make this continuing choice, however, because of the astonishing development of the United States itself. In 1820 its economy had been, by one reckoning, the seventh largest in the world. By 1900 it was by far the largest, producing almost a quarter of all manufactured goods. In the intervening period white settlement had expanded to fill in the huge spaces between the Mississippi River and the Pacific Ocean. The transcontinental railroad, linking San Francisco to the eastern railway network, opened for traffic in 1869; the federal census of 1890 announced that the frontier no longer existed. The old cities of the East Coast, now massively expanded, were joined by new urban giants in the Midwest and West. As early as 1860, New York (with Brooklyn) became the first American city to reach a population of one million. The next to do so, by 1890, was Chicago, a city of stockyards and grain elevators, and the centre of a massive international trade. Growth on this scale was made possible by a huge and, initially, thinly populated land area, by abundant natural resources, and by ever-increasing technological sophistication. But it also required a constant supply of additional labour. And it was this that ensured that hundreds of thousands of Irish men and women to whom their birthplace offered no worthwhile future could find acceptance, if not necessarily a welcome, on the other side of the Atlantic.[1]

For those who sought to arrange a passage to America, whether in good years or bad, the process had never been easier. A dense network of railways, by the 1850s largely complete, ensured easy passage from all parts of Ireland to the main ports. Cost, too, was no longer a significant obstacle. Fares varied according to the time of year. But the rising volume of Atlantic shipping, and competition among shipping lines, ensured that across the 1850s and 1860s the average cost of a passage in steerage remained stable at between £3 and £3 10s. Irish incomes, on the other hand, were improving: the average weekly earnings of a labourer, for example, rose from four shillings and six pence in 1844 to seven shillings in 1860. There was also the continuing flow across the Atlantic of remittances and prepaid tickets. In the forty years between 1848 and 1887 Irish emigrants in the United States sent home an estimated forty million pounds, of which about two-fifths came in the form of prepaid passages. A newspaper report on emigrants leaving Queenstown in 1866 noted that about one-third had prepaid tickets, while another third had bought their tickets with money received from relatives or friends in the United States.[2]

For the best part of two decades after the end of the Famine, the great majority of emigrants continued to cross the Atlantic in sailing ships. New Passenger Acts introduced in the United Kingdom in 1852 and 1855, and in the United States in 1848 and 1855, had addressed some of the problems highlighted by Vere Foster and others, for example by requiring better ventilation between decks, and by further tightening up the arrangements for inspection. Meanwhile the shipping companies, adjusting to the increasing proportion of their business accounted for by fare-paying passengers, gradually improved the quality of accommodation. Yet complaints of brutal treatment, and flagrant neglect of legal requirements, continued. A doctor who had made six Atlantic voyages on emigrant ships reported in 1857 that passengers were not only intimidated by seeing the 'frightful bodily injuries' inflicted on one another by the crew, but were also convinced of their own helplessness by 'themselves getting a few drives and knocks and plenty of curses'. Officials dismissed his report. But a Donegal man who sailed to New York in the same year corroborated his claims. The passengers had received no more than one-third of the food they were entitled to, and when one protested at being denied water, the captain had him handcuffed then 'beat him in the face until it was all blackened and cut besides'.[3]

Even without such brutality, emigrants embarking on a sailing vessel committed themselves to spending an average of six weeks at sea, cooped up in cramped, poorly ventilated quarters, enduring the unavoidable build-up of smells and dirt, and vulnerable to any difficulties that might arise in the storage and preservation of adequate food and water. They did so for straightforward reasons of cost. The first regular service by steamship had begun in 1840, when Cunard Line introduced four paddle steamers carrying mail and cabin passengers between Liverpool and Boston. But the fares were typically between £20 and £40. Over time technological improvements—the adoption of iron hulls and the use of screw propellers rather than paddles—permitted more economical use of coal and the construction of larger vessels. By the late 1850s steamships had begun to offer cheaper fares to non-cabin passengers. There was still a substantial price difference: shipping advertisements in the early 1860s offered passages at six or eight guineas (£6 6s or £8 8s). But the attraction of a much shorter journey—initially two weeks, falling soon after to around ten days—was enough to persuade growing numbers of emigrants to make the extra investment. From that point on the main constraint on the transition from sail to steam was the ability of the industry to construct new steam-powered vessels fast enough. In 1855 fewer than three out of every hundred passengers landing in New York had arrived by steamer. By 1861 the figure was almost thirty-one in every hundred, by 1867 it was eighty-one, and by 1873 it was ninety-seven.[4]

The emigrants embarking on these new steam-powered ships travelled, like their predecessors, as steerage passengers, accommodated in the lower deck otherwise used to carry cargo. Typically up to a hundred passengers occupied the space between two iron bulkheads. By this time, however, the normal practice was to subdivide the area by constructing wooden or canvas rooms, generally holding twenty or twenty-four passengers in each. Passengers slept in berths arranged in two tiers, measuring 6 feet by 18 inches, separated from their neighbours by a strip of wood or canvas 10 inches high. They were required to bring on board their own mattresses, along with a metal plate and tins. At the end of the voyage the mattresses would be dumped into the sea before the ship docked to prevent any infestation of vermin being carried over to future voyages. Travel under these conditions was hardly comfortable. The big difference, however, was that such conditions were now to be endured for a much shorter time. One immediate benefit was that the danger to health from cramped and unsanitary conditions became much reduced. By 1869, according to the New York Commissioners of Emigration, a body established to administer the fees collected from arriving immigrant ships, the death rate on steam ships arriving in the port was 1 in 1,000, compared to 1 in 200 on sailing vessels.[5]

One area where contemporary sensibilities dictated a high level of regulation was in the accommodation of male and female passengers. In 1881 the nationalist writer Charlotte O'Brien published a lurid account of the supposed threat to the morals and sensibilities of women travellers, who were forced to sleep, dress and undress in crowded, mixed-sex accommodation. An official enquiry, however, heard from a succession of witnesses that emigrants were invariably quartered in three blocks, married couples, single men and single women, with the last two kept rigorously apart. There had been experiments with a complete separation of the sexes, but these had been abandoned due to opposition from the married emigrants, who refused to be parted from their spouses. Instead it became the custom for the men in married quarters to retire to the decks, to smoke their pipes, while the women and children readied themselves for bed. As the investigator's summary pithily put it: 'An obtrusive man soon finds his level.'[6]

For Irish emigrants the transition from sail to steam had another important consequence. Steamships, faster and more manoeuvrable, found it easier to call at an Irish port on their way west. In particular Queenstown, on the outward-facing side of the bay in front of Cork city, became a regular stop. Already by 1860 it had become necessary to lay on two steamboats to convey passengers, formerly accommodated on the tender that carried the mails, from the main railway station at Cork to the Queenstown docks. In 1865 an estimated 30,000 of the 82,000 Irish emigrants to the United States left from the port. For a time the Queenstown route had the disadvantage that passengers might find that the ship on which they were booked had already filled up at Liverpool. Hence many emigrants, whether seeking a steamship or a less expensive passage under sail, continued to prefer the short and cheap journey to that port. By 1881, however, nine of the ten shipping lines sailing from Liverpool made the stop at Queenstown, making the Liverpool route largely redundant. Meanwhile, serving the northern half of the country, a second Irish port of departure had emerged at Moville, located at the mouth of Lough Foyle, the large bay that separates the counties of Londonderry and Donegal. Moville owed its initial growth to its geographical position, allowing it to shave twenty-four hours or more off the journey time of a transatlantic mail packet. From the 1860s Moville, like Queensland, became a port of call for passenger liners sailing from Liverpool, with emigrants being ferried from nearby Derry by a regular tender service. During 1884, 154 steamers called there, taking away over 10,000 passengers to the United States and almost 5,000 to Canada.[7]

As in earlier decades the most important port of arrival, receiving three out of every four immigrants from Europe, was New York. (The two next most popular were New Orleans, with a little under 10 per cent of total arrivals, and Boston, with just over 6 per cent.) The presence there of so many inexperienced and disoriented travellers was a magnet for confidence tricksters, the notorious 'runners', who offered travellers worthless tickets for onward travel, or who steered them to lodging houses where they would be bullied and intimidated into paying huge sums for the release of themselves and their baggage. In 1855, however, the newly created New York Commissioners of Emigration opened a depot in a disused military base at Castle Garden, near the southern tip of

Manhattan Island. There, protected by high walls from the attentions of runners, the arriving immigrant was taken through a series of carefully organised steps. Baggage was labelled and stored, to be delivered free of charge to any dock or railway station. Agents of the railway companies offered tickets to all parts of the United States and Canada. An office exchanged gold and silver coins for dollars. Officials read out to the assembled immigrants the names of those who had friends or letters waiting for them, and they directed others to a letter-writing department staffed by clerks familiar with different European languages. The aim was to facilitate as many immigrants as possible in moving on to friends or employers beyond New York. But, for those who wished to remain in the city, boarding house proprietors licensed by the mayor were admitted to recruit customers, baggage could be delivered for a small fee, and a labour exchange in nearby Canal Street provided assistance in finding work.[8]

These were the new facilities as described in a celebratory account by one of the Commissioners of Emigration. A journalist visiting Castle Garden twelve years after it opened was less impressed. He found hundreds of newly arrived immigrants crammed into a large circular reception hall, 'a sink of filth, and unfit for human beings as a place of occupation', where 'large bluebottle flies haunt the seams of the planking on the floor . . . sucking and feasting upon the corruption'. The 'deadening, stifling smell' of which he complained was perhaps unavoidable, in a room crowded by men and women who had spent weeks in the cramped conditions of steerage. However the facilities provided for washing were grim— 'the huge blocks of soap and the damp, wet floor . . . present a very black and disconsolate aspect'—and there was no attempt to require immigrants to use them. The clerical staff manning the facility were also less than satisfactory: 'gruff when asked for information promptly, and rigidly impassive or deaf when questioned mildly'. However the report acknowledged the valuable facilities that the reception centre provided for immigrants: the careful storage of their luggage, the information office where women seeking positions as servants could meet potential employers, and most of all the exclusion from the premises of runners and rogue boarding house keepers.[9]

On balance, then, the opening of Castle Garden made arrival in the United States a safer and more orderly process, if quite possibly a harsh and disorienting one. But the moves towards a system of closer regulation also had a more negative side. The arrival in the Famine years of so many refugees from economic catastrophe, physically broken down and desperately poor, encouraged a movement towards closer scrutiny of the fitness of new immigrants. Already before the 1840s the state of Massachusetts, possibly reflecting the English Puritan origins of its ruling elite, had applied a system similar to England's Poor Laws: paupers were to be removed to the town or district to which they belonged, or else, if they had no legal settlement within the state, expelled beyond its boundaries. Between 1837 and 1845 Massachusetts sent 4,706 impoverished persons out of the state, including 715 who were deported to Ireland. In 1851 the state created a Board of Alien Commissioners, empowered to examine passengers arriving by sea or railway, and to carry out regular searches of alms houses and other public institutions. By 1863 they had removed from the state more than 15,000 individuals identified as an actual or potential burden on public resources. Most were returned to Canada or to other American states, but at least 1,841 were shipped back to Liverpool or other transatlantic ports. Over the next fifteen years a successor body, the Board of State Charities, deported a further 2,489 paupers, as well as an unknown proportion of the 2,891 persons removed from mental hospitals, either to Canada or back across the Atlantic. New York, where immigrants already made up an important part of the electorate, did not adopt compulsory deportation. But by 1863 the New York Commissioners of Emigration had sent at least 2,505 immigrants back across the Atlantic in what were purported to be voluntary repatriations. The Commissioners were also expected to provide a more effective protection against the entry of the old, the infirm and the incapable by carrying out a more rigorous inspection than previously performed on arriving immigrants, and requiring from captains a bond for every passenger who was at risk of becoming a public charge.[10]

The number affected by this new regime, when set against the hundreds of thousands arriving, was relatively small. But the consequences for individuals could be tragic. One case highlighted by the Irish Emigration Society concerned a man known only as O'Connor, who had landed in New York with his wife and three children. Suffering from fever, all five were placed in a poorhouse on arrival. O'Connor recovered first, travelled west to obtain money from his father in St Louis, then returned to collect his family. However his wife had died and the three children had been put on a ship to Liverpool. One had died on the voyage and the other two had disappeared into the teeming port city, lost forever. Another immigrant, Hugh Carr, was removed in 1854 from the insane asylum in East Cambridge, Massachusetts, and put on a ship to Liverpool, without the knowledge of the six sisters with whom he had been living during the thirteen years that he had worked and paid taxes in the state. He, too, disappeared from view. Five years later a group of sixteen Irish paupers deported from Boston to Liverpool was found to include five women with an average age of 71, who protested that they had been in the United States for forty years.[11]

For more than a century before 1850, immigrants from Ireland had been prominent in the westward expansion of white settlement in America, cutting down forest and breaking up new land. Settlement of this kind continued in the 1850s and beyond. The Famine, indeed, seems to have produced a temporary surge of new arrivals bent on acquiring land. In 1849, as faith in the future of the Irish agricultural system collapsed in the wake of yet another year of blight, there were reports of the holders of substantial farms harvesting their crops and departing for America with the proceeds, leaving their rent unpaid. On the other side of the Atlantic, meanwhile, an Irish-American newspaper claimed that over the preceding two years a new type of immigrant had appeared in the United States, 'the pith and marrow of Ireland', bringing with them between $100 and $5,000 per family, who 'go directly into the interior to seek out the best locations as farmers, traders and so forth'. And in fact the years 1848–50 saw an increase in the proportion of immigrants arriving in New York, including Irish, who immediately moved on to inland states. Over the next three decades, as the frontier of settlement moved steadily west, Irish immigrants continued to find opportunities to acquire land cheaply, or by free grant. When, for example, Andrew Greenlees of County Antrim made his first attempt at farming on his own account, in 1861, it was in Michigan. When he tried again, more successfully, in 1874, it was on a free land grant of 80 acres in Kansas awarded under the Homestead Act. In the same way Edward Hanlon, son of a farmer from County Down, found his foothold on the land in Nebraska, buying just over 215 acres in 1870. When his brother in Ireland contemplated giving up the family farm and joining him in the United States, Hanlon directed him to southern Nebraska, Kansas and Missouri, where they would each be entitled to a grant of 160 acres of newly released government land.[12]

The Famine, then, did not mark the end of the Irish contribution to western settlement. But it nevertheless marked a major discontinuity. Already in the 1820s and 1830s observers had drawn attention to the growing number of Irish immigrants, mainly poor and unskilled, who congregated in the cities of the Eastern Seaboard. After 1850 this became the norm, although the choice of urban centre had now widened to take in the rapidly growing new cities of the Midwest. By 1870 just over a quarter of all Irish-born inhabitants were concentrated in just five cities: New York, Philadelphia, Brooklyn (an independent city until 1896), Chicago and Boston. Where the Irish did not live in major cities, they were most likely to be found in smaller urban centres, in the mill villages that grew up where a river, a canal or a railway offered an advantageous site, or in mining districts. On this basis, just under three-quarters of the Irish-born living in the United States in 1870 can be classified as settled in an urban and industrial, rather than a rural, environment.[13]

Contemporary observers interested in the welfare of immigrants found this choice of destination baffling. A people drawn from an overwhelmingly rural and agricultural society turned their backs on the prospect of becoming masters of their own homesteads in the expanding west, in favour of the slum accommodation and the dependence on poorly paid manual labour, which was all that awaited them in the crowded cities. The Irish nationalist MP John Francis Maguire, touring North America in 1868, lamented that 'the hardy peasantry of Ireland madly surrender the roomy log-cabin of the clearing, and the frame house of a few years after, together with almost certain independence and prosperity', for the misery and degradation of the inner city. But attempts to redirect the pattern of settlement proved largely futile. One early scheme, in 1856–7, foundered largely due to the opposition of John Hughes, the Catholic archbishop of New York. His public argument was that Catholics transplanted to the far west, without ready access to priests and churches, would drift away from their faith. But Hughes also feared that colonisation would strip cities like New York of the more vigorous and enterprising Catholics, leaving behind the poor and weak. Later, in 1879, a meeting of Catholic clergy and influential laymen in Chicago established the Irish Catholic Colonization Association, with the object of financing schemes for land purchase and settlement through the sale of bonds. But the venture collapsed when not enough subscribers came forward to provide the necessary capital.[14]

More localised projects had greater success, but there too the overall impact was limited. The Minnesota Colonization Company, founded in 1877 by a successful businessman, William O'Mulcahy, settled at most forty-five families. In 1881 John Sweetman, a County Meath landlord and later Nationalist MP, sponsored the emigration to America of eighty-one families whom he settled on lands he had purchased in Minnesota, only to find that most quickly deserted their holdings to take employment in the city of St Paul. In 1875 John Ireland, Catholic coadjutor bishop of St Paul, launched an ingenious scheme that exploited the anxiety of railway companies to secure their profits by promoting settlement along their routes. Rather than trying to raise capital, his Catholic Colonization Bureau acted as broker in the distribution of some 379,000 acres of railway land available on easy terms, establishing 4,000 Catholic families in ten rural villages and farming communities in western Minnesota. Only six of the settlements, however, were predominantly Irish. Even there, moreover, the majority of the inhabitants were families already successfully settled on farms in other states, or craftsmen and shopkeepers seeking to reinvest their capital in cheap western land, rather than refugees from the inner city.[15]

It is sometimes suggested that this apparently anomalous preference of immigrants from rural Ireland for life in the crowded industrial cities, or in mine and factory towns, was due to the cultural baggage they carried with them. As tenants in an overcrowded and exploitative land system they had experienced poverty and insecurity, before being catastrophically let down by the staple crop on which they had staked their whole future. Was it any surprise that they were unwilling once again to wager all on the uncertain fortunes of agriculture? Another suggestion is that people raised within tight-knit communities of relatives, friends and neighbours were ill-equipped to cope with the open spaces and isolation of the rural frontier. Yet immigrants from the same Irish background, in Australia and British North America, showed no reluctance, when given the opportunity, to embark on the life of a pioneer farmer, accepting risk and loneliness as the price to be paid for the chance of becoming an independent proprietor.

A more convincing explanation is that commentators like Maguire underestimated the practical obstacles to taking up the life of an American farmer. Many of the Irish rural poor, accustomed to nothing more than the spadework required to plant and dig potatoes, had neither the commercial outlook nor the technical skills demanded by this new environment. The one major catastrophe of Bishop John Ireland's colonization project in Minnesota was when he was persuaded, in 1880, to suspend his usual strict requirements and accept a group of just over 300 desperately poor peasants recruited directly from Connemara in the Irish west. Some failed to settle to farming, preferring the short-term gains of labouring for wages. Others ignored advice to prepare for winter by insulating their houses with sod and digging pits to protect their potatoes from freezing, and Ireland had to rescue them from starvation by moving them to St Paul. He then distributed the land they abandoned among their neighbours. Men who had managed medium and large farms, by contrast, brought with them the experience of carrying out mixed farming in a commercial environment. But there was still much to learn. Andrew Greenlees, in his first year as an agricultural labourer, had to be taught how to milk a cow, which at home in Antrim had been women's work. Edward Hanlon estimated that a nephew joining him on his Nebraska farm would need a year to learn what he needed. Such examples help to explain why so few of the Irish who did take part in the settlement of the Midwest came there directly from the emigrant ship. Census records for Irish households in Wisconsin and Minnesota commonly include children born in several other American states, indicating that the parents had moved west in stages, probably building up resources and acquiring useful skills, and an equally valuable knowledge of American ways, as they came. In the case of Wisconsin the average time spent by Irish settlers in other states was seven years.[16]

Meanwhile the resources needed to gain a foothold on the land had risen substantially. For immigrants in the 1830s like the Anderson brothers, who took uncleared land in Ohio and neighbouring states, the main task for establishing a homestead was to remove stands of trees. This work required only simple tools and vigorous muscle. By the 1850s, however, the frontier had moved to the prairie. The lightweight steel plough, developed in 1837, made it possible to break up what had seemed impossibly tough topsoil, but a lengthy process of ploughing and cross-ploughing was needed before a crop could be sown. The large acreages involved also required other expensive equipment, such as mechanical reapers and drills for planting seed. Settlers in many districts had to depend on expensively imported timber, and to dig deep wells to obtain water. Distances were also greater: in the 1870s, even with a well-developed rail network, a family of four could expect to pay $100 to travel from New York or Philadelphia to Minnesota. Rail tickets were just one cost. Bishop John Ireland, for example, stipulated that anyone seeking to take up the lands he controlled had to have a minimum $400 capital to cover the cost of a house, furnishings, agricultural implements, and a first year's food and fuel. Later estimates put such costs higher, at $700 or even $1,000. This was at a time when average earnings in the state of Massachusetts ranged from $747 a year for the best-paid skilled workmen to $414 for an unskilled labourer.[17]

The simplest explanation for the tendency of the Irish to congregate in the cities of the East, therefore, is that many of them could not afford to go any further. Those arriving during the Famine, in particular, were economic refugees, bringing little more than the rags they stood up in. Later immigrants, in the 1850s, 1860s and 1870s, were better provided for. The huge volume of passage money and prepaid tickets now flowing back each year to relatives in Ireland could in theory have included the cost of travel beyond New York or Boston to the interior. But by then the pattern of Irish settlement was already established. The predecessors sending these remittances were concentrated in the major cities of the Northeast, and it was to there that those they financed came, in order to join their benefactors and begin their induction into American life. It was a choice, moreover, that reflected the needs of the American economy. Canada and Australia were mainly rural societies, with modest urban centres and limited manufacturing. The United States was on its way to becoming an industrial giant. Opportunities still existed on an ever more distant frontier. But the great demand, much closer to hand, was for workers to fill its factories and workshops, and to maintain the fabric of an ever more complex urban infrastructure.

In the eyes of many contemporaries, and in the imaginations of later generations, the typical Irish immigrant to the nineteenth-century United States was a wielder of pick and shovel, engaged in work whose only qualification was extreme physical endurance. The image is understandable. The Irish arrived in the United States at a comparative disadvantage. Two-thirds of those landing in the 1840s were classified as unskilled, compared to fewer than half the English and Scots and fewer than one in ten of the Germans. With the beginnings of mass emigration from southern and eastern Europe still thirty years in the future, and with only limited competition from free Black workers, they had the market for the lowest and cheapest forms of labour largely to themselves. But this did not mean that every Irish immigrant became, or remained, a ditch digger or a hod carrier. In New York, for example, the 17,000 Irish labourers recorded in 1855 accounted for more than four out of five of the city's workers in that category. But they nevertheless made up only just over one-fifth of the 88,000 Irish-born male workers in the city. In Philadelphia at the same time the equivalent figure was just over one-third, falling to a quarter two decades later. In Boston, with a much narrower industrial base, the Irish were more heavily dependent on unskilled manual work. But even there labourers accounted for a little under half the Irish-born workforce.[18]

What of the remainder? Some Irish immigrants practiced traditional crafts. In the New York construction industry in 1855 three out of five masons, bricklayers and plasterers were Irish. American apprenticeships, however, had never been as formal as in the Old World, and craft boundaries were less rigorously policed. By mid-century the line between craftsmen and others had become even more blurred. The development of the canals, and then of a railway network, enabled the creation of huge markets for cheap, mass-produced consumer goods such as clothing, footwear and furniture. But technology had not yet advanced to the point where goods could be assembled by machines. Instead manufacturers responded by breaking down the production process into a succession of individual tasks. By 1860, for example, the making of a single shoe had been broken down into forty separate operations. The more complex of these, such as cutting leather to shape or fashioning a complex joint, might still be done by skilled craftsmen. But elsewhere in the sequence ordinary workers could be fairly quickly trained to perform a single, repetitive task. This world of what have been described as 'mediocre skills' absorbed tens of thousands of Irish immigrants, some employed in workshops or factories, others labouring in their own homes, in some cases drawing in wives and children to assist in the work. Others found work in the rapidly expanding factory system. In eastern textile towns like Lowell, Massachusetts, it was Irish immigrants, later joined by French Canadians, who became the backbone of the factory workforce. Further west, and somewhat later, similar opportunities for assembly line employment opened up in the great centres of the food industry, in particular the stockyards and grain stores of Chicago and the pork processing enterprises of Cincinnati. Others again, assisted by their knowledge of English, were employed in the expanding service industries. In both Boston and New York the Irish-born in 1850–5 accounted for three out of five of all waiters. In New York they likewise supplied just under half of the city's carters, draymen, teamsters and porters, becoming an indispensable part of the huge transport infrastructure required to keep a nineteenth-century city moving.[19]

That the majority of Irish urban workers were not engaged in the most basic forms of manual labour does not mean that they were prosperous, or even comfortable. The work of a waiter or a carter was less arduous than that of a general labourer in construction or on the docks, and they could be more confident of continuous employment, rather than being hired by the day or for the duration of a specific project. But their wages were well below those of a skilled craftsman, and they remained vulnerable to economic fluctuations that could suddenly throw them out of work. Even in good years such employment was often highly seasonal. The freezing of the main rivers and canals during the winter months meant that in cities like New York and Philadelphia trade came to a near standstill. There were also periods in the hottest part of the summer when any sort of outdoor work became impossible. Many working-class families thus had to rely on what savings they could build up in spring and summer to see them through the leaner months that followed. The estimate of a New York newspaper in 1853 made clear just how tight was the typical family budget. The average workman, it estimated, spent $600 a year, of which $550 was required to meet the cost of food, clothing, rent and household expenses, with $15 for other essential items.[20]

In exchange for these wages workers had to adjust to the intense demands of an American workplace. Immigrants of all nationalities commented on the contrast between the pace of work in their new home and what they had been used to in Ireland, Britain or continental Europe. Frank Roney, arriving in New York in 1867, had worked in an iron foundry in Belfast, so he was no stranger to an industrial environment. But he had never seen men working 'in so exhausting a way' as those he encountered in his new workplace. 'The American moulders seemed desirous of doing all the work required as if it were the last day of their lives.' The 'railway pace' of the American workplace probably reflected the predominance in the labour force of young men, and the superior diet that America afforded even to the working classes. There may also have been a difference in mentality: a sense that opportunities to work and earn were abundant, not something to be rationed and shared out, as in the Old World. Immigrants could try to cling to their old habits. In 1826 the sole American-born man in a group of carters reported that his Irish workmates told him 'to work slower, like the rest', and beat him up when he refused. But in the long run those who wished to make their way in the new society had little choice but to conform to its ways.[21]

By opting to remain in the industrialising eastern states Irish immigrants exposed themselves to the worst aspects of nineteenth-century urban living, as runaway population growth outstripped the development of basic facilities such as water supply and drainage. The huge number of poor Irish immigrants crowding into the major cities between 1845 and 1855 found shelter where they could, as speculators threw up jerry-built tenements, or subdivided dilapidated former warehouses, or the former residences of affluent families, into multiple units. In Boston, where more prosperous immigrant groups, Germans, English and others, joined the native-born in moving to new residential districts on the periphery, the Irish remained heavily concentrated in the old commercial city centre, close to the harbour. Public health officials struggling to cope with the cholera epidemic of 1849 discovered 586 cellars occupied by between five and fifteen persons each. In New York the Five Points area, once the home of tradesmen and merchants, had by 1855 developed into a notorious slum district, where two out of three adult inhabitants were Irish-born. The lurid reputation of Five Points as a centre of vice and crime was such that tours of the area, under police protection, became a fashionable excursion. The same image was revived in Martin Scorsese's film *Gangs of New York*, depicting an exotic criminal underworld in which Irish gangs like the Dead Rabbits battled with one another and with hostile American-born nativists. Recent archaeological investigations reveal a somewhat different picture. Five Points was not just a neighbourhood of taverns, brothels and gambling dens. It was also home to hundreds of working-class families who have left behind traces of their work at tailoring, shoemaking or other trades, along with modest household implements.[22]

The makeshift accommodation that first greeted the immigrants of the 1840s and 1850s gave way over time to purpose-built working-class accommodation. In New York the most common provision was the tenement, by this time a brick structure, normally two or three storeys high. Amenities were basic. Water had to be carried from a pump or a communal tap located at ground level. Shared privies frequently overflowed. Gas lighting was rare, forcing residents to grope their way along gloomy hallways and staircases, and leaving the windowless rooms in the middle of the building in permanent darkness. New regulations after 1879 required buildings to have a central airshaft so that every room could have a window. But this proved to be a mixed blessing, as the bottoms of the shafts filled with refuse thrown out of upstairs windows by residents reluctant to descend several flights of dark stairs to make use of an overflowing privy or rubbish heap. Everywhere, meanwhile, space was limited. In 1868 the nationalist MP John Francis Maguire, touring the United States to report on the condition of the Irish immigrant, visited a typical New York tenement, the home of a couple from West Cork. The building, he emphasised, was by no means the worst he had seen. 'There was no squalor, no dilapidation; the place appeared to be in fair order.' The apartment, too, showed 'no actual want of essential articles of furniture, such as a table and chairs; and the walls were not without one or two pious and patriotic pictures, Catholic and Irish.' The entire space, however, consisted of a living room measuring 9 feet by 12, a large part of which was taken up by a stove, and beyond it a single bedroom, where the floor space was almost entirely occupied by a four-post bed. Yet this provided the entire living space for seven people: the parents, four children, and a female relative.[23]

In other urban centres the housing available to working-class Irish immigrants varied according to the layout of the town and the precise circumstances of the residents. In Philadelphia, thanks to firm urban planning and adequate building land, the dominant type of house was the terrace or row house, lining streets laid out on a regular grid pattern. The town also had its poorer districts, in some cases identified as specifically Irish quarters. But the average number of people per house in 1851 was between six and seven, only half the density recorded in New York. In the Massachusetts mill town of Newburyport, with a population of around 13,000, two-thirds to three-quarters of those working-class residents who remained for at least two decades were able, not just to occupy a house of their own but, through a mortgage, to become the owner. In Buffalo, New York, the people of the Irish-dominated First Ward likewise had individual dwellings: 'hundreds of wood frame houses, most of which had little picket fences, gates and tiny front yards set back from wooden sidewalks and dirt streets'. The ground, however, was low-lying and vulnerable to flooding, making the whole district unattractive to those with more choice. In Worcester, Massachusetts, another medium-sized town, the Irish quarter was the poorer East Side, where around one-third of families lived in small, plain houses, in this case set flush against the street, while most of the remainder lived instead in three-storey tenements. The whole district suffered from the existence of a stream, the Mill Brook, running through its centre, which received the contents of the town's sewer lines and was not culverted over until the very end of the century.[24]

For that great majority whose journey ended in a city in the northeastern states, then, emigration to the United States meant an intense regime of work in a degraded urban environment. In return they could hope to achieve, if all went well, a level of material consumption greater than anything they could have known at home. The New York tenement that John Francis Maguire visited may have been noisy, crowded and smelly, but the table, chairs and four poster bed would have represented a level of furnishing significantly more elaborate than would have been found in the cabin of a rural labourer, or even a small farmer. The occupants would also have been better dressed: immigrants commented frequently on the difficulty, outside the workplace, of telling the middle and working classes apart. Most of all, they enjoyed a hugely superior diet. Immigrants of all nationalities contrasted the abundant meals that were standard in America with the sparse routine that had prevailed at home. 'We can find better here', one County Londonderry man reported from Philadelphia in 1873, 'for our regular diet in this country is the same as a set day at home.' Three or four years later his death would leave the family in poorer circumstances. But his daughter could still boast to an Irish relative of how 'the people eats and drinks well here. For our part it takes eight dozen of eggs to do us in the week, and thirty pounds of beef and mutton, one pound of tea and one pound of coffee, fourteen pounds of sugar, four pounds or five pounds of cheese, besides a great deal of vegetables which is too numerous to mention.' A widely circulated joke concerned the Irishman who wrote home that he had meat twice a week. When his employer indignantly pointed out that in fact he was served meat three times a day he replied, 'Faith . . . my friends would disbelieve all I have said, if I told them that.'[25]

The very large minority of Irish immigrants who were women—more than two out of five in the 1860s, a clear majority by the end of the century—had their own place in the American labour market. Their most common occupation was domestic service. Irish dominance of this market, like other aspects of the Irish contribution to the mid-nineteenth-century American economy, depended on an effective combination of supply and demand. On one side there was a new ideal of female domesticity. The middle-class woman was to be a lady of leisure, devoting herself to cultural accomplishments, to a formal round of visits and social gatherings with her peers, and possibly to appropriate philanthropic activity, while managing her household according to the demanding standards of a new bourgeois gentility. It was a lifestyle that could be supported only by abundant cheap domestic labour. But native-born American girls, products of a self-consciously republican culture, had always been brought up to despise the prospect of waiting on others, and they became even more reluctant to enter service as the social distance between mistress and servant grew. African-American women dominated domestic service in the South, but until the Great Migration northwards commenced at the beginning of the twentieth century the free Black population of northern cities was not nearly sufficient to meet demand. Germans and Scandinavian women dominated domestic service in the Midwest, but they too were less numerous in the eastern cities. Italians and other new immigrants from southern and eastern Europe became numerous only towards the end of the century. Even then women made up only a quarter to a third of their number, and there was strong cultural resistance to suggestions that they should leave the protection and supervision of their family for any reason other than marriage. That left the Irish. They were the largest body of foreign-born in the United States, until overtaken by the Germans after 1880. They represented an immigrant population that, uniquely, contained almost as many women as men. They also had the advantage, compared to Germans, Swedes and others, of being mainly native English speakers. In 1890 four out of every ten white women employed as domestic or personal servants across the United States were Irish, and domestic service accounted for three out of every five employed women of Irish birth.[26]

The prominence that immigrant Irish women thus enjoyed within the market for domestic servants was not accepted with good grace. Employers who could afford to do so advertised their preferences explicitly, with advertisements carrying the notorious rubric 'No Irish need apply', or specifying that the position was for a German, Swedish or 'colored' maid—or, equally effective, a Protestant. Those who had no choice made their dissatisfaction plain. Contemptuous depictions of 'Bridget', the dim-witted and incompetent Irish maid, became a staple of middle-class American culture. Much of the criticism focussed on the inability of servants brought up in an Irish cabin to meet the standard of gentility required. According to one commentator, himself Irish-born, hostility to the Irish had been shaped by 'the memory of burnt steaks, of hard boiled potatoes, of smoked milk. . . . It is in the kitchen that the Irish iron has entered into the American soul.' Religion was another line of division. Parents worried that conspicuously pious Irish servants would fail to provide the right religious instruction to their children, would even, perhaps, seek to draw them into the errors of Rome. Employers fumed at demands for time off to attend mass, not only on Sundays but on holidays and festivals, and to take part in other devotions. Servants, for their part, resisted attempts to make them attend Protestant family prayers.[27]

For Irish immigrant women domestic service nevertheless had definite advantages. They came from a culture where the role of servant carried no particular social stigma. Arriving as individuals rather than as part of a family, they had less reason to resist living in an employer's household; indeed such accommodations may well have seemed a safer and more secure option than the lodgings that would otherwise have been available to a single female. The often spartan living conditions—cramped sleeping quarters and food that comprised either their employers' leavings or inferior rations bought specifically for their consumption—were less burdensome to women brought up on small farms or in labourers' cabins than they would have been to many others. A servant's employment was more stable than other unskilled jobs. It was also better paid. In Philadelphia in 1883 a maid could expect to earn $2 or $3 a week, compared to the $7 to $12 that a family of male emigrants to the same city were earning a few years earlier in various factory jobs. But with food and lodging provided, the money was hers to save and spend. Domestic servants were prominent among depositors in the Emigrant Savings Bank in New York and similar institutions. They were also widely praised for their generosity in sending regular remittances to support family members back in Ireland, or to pay for the passage of sisters or other relatives to join them in the United States. At the same time it is clear that they also knew how to enjoy themselves. Observers frequently commented on the fashionable clothes that servants wore on their days off. And those, the majority, who worked in the major cities used their free time to take full advantage of the dance halls, amusement parks and other amenities that an urban environment offered.[28]

This money, however, was hard earned. Wealthy families might retain a household staff. But most middle-class families kept only one servant, a maid of all work. Outside of limited free time—generally Sunday afternoons and a single evening, usually Thursday—a servant of this kind was expected to be permanently available for whatever instructions their employers cared to give them. Meanwhile household manuals set out a formidable round of tasks to be completed, with different days of the week designated for major chores. There were parlours and reception rooms to be maintained in perfect order, with rugs swept and glass and wood repeatedly dusted and polished, elaborate tea and dinner parties, with showpiece crockery to be produced, cleaned and stored, wardrobes full of clothing to be cleaned, pressed and stitched. The words of one letter from New York State in 1899 are simple but eloquent. 'I do hate to get up every morning, I am so tired.'[29]

Despite this crushing routine, it would be wrong to see these women as passive victims. On the contrary what emerges from the endless complaints about the inadequacy of Irish servants is a strong sense, not just of religious and ethnic prejudice, but of the impotent anger that went with enforced dependence. Employers might find Irish women uncouth and slapdash. But they were what was available, at an affordable price, and both they and their employers knew it. Bridget, in contemporary accounts, was not just incompetent, but belligerent. A Philadelphia magazine, in 1872, appealed to what it called 'sufferers who are wearied out with the ignorance and arrogance of Celtic rule, . . . familiar with the scowl or the growl with which each fresh order is greeted by the Irish cook-maid'. (Its proposed solution, moving from a hostile ethnic stereotype to a condescending paternalistic racism, was to turn instead to the city's substantial African-American population, a 'simple and kindly people' who adapted more easily to 'a higher civilization'.) A newspaper in 1890 recounted the magnificent response of an Irish servant eventually dismissed following repeated episodes of drunkenness. 'And then, in a loud voice and with a martyr-like air, the girl exclaimed: "What do I care? They did the same to our Saviour."'[30]

The experience of domestic service in middle-class native houses, however fraught, had important implications for the future. On one side, close contact must have made the Irish working class a more familiar, if not necessarily a more warmly regarded, presence. On the other, service in middle-class homes made immigrant women from poor rural backgrounds in Ireland familiar with American modes of speaking and behaving. For most, moreover, service was not a lifetime career. They would go on, assisted by their savings, to marry and set up households of their own. There, in their new role as wives and mothers, they were able to pass on some of the standards of decorum, cleanliness and order they had learned as domestics, thus contributing further to the eventual emergence of an Irish-American culture that was reasonably integrated into the wider society.[31]

For Irish women who did not enter domestic service, the alternative was to join immigrant men in becoming part of the army of cheap labour that sustained the transformation of the United States into an advanced industrial economy. From the 1840s onwards manufacturers in towns like Lowell recruited Irish immigrant women to replace native-born Americans in the textile mills and other factories. The work was poorly paid: one estimate is that the wages of three or more mill workers were required to support a household. Employment of this kind was attractive primarily to married women or to daughters still living with their family, particularly in mill towns where the small middle class meant that there was a limited demand for servants. The other main form of employment outside domestic service was in the needle trades, the repetitive, labour-intensive stitching of seams, buttonholes and pockets that constituted the last stage in what was by now a highly organised garment industry. An important development here was the coming of the sewing machine, with which a newcomer could become sufficiently adept within a week to start earning money. But the same ease of entry meant a downgrading of handicraft skills, opening the way to the reduction of wages to a pittance. Workers in the needle trades were frequently brought together in workshops. Others were outworkers in their own homes, paid by the piece, and pushed by the miserable returns into constant self-exploitation, labouring for interminable hours to make enough for a bare subsistence. In New York in 1855 two-thirds of those in the sewing trade were foreign-born, and seven out of ten of these were

Irish. In the country as a whole one-third of those working in 1900 as seamstresses and dressmakers had been born in Ireland.[32]

Irish immigrant women did not generally take employment outside the home after marriage—or at least not as long as their husbands remained alive. Many, however, contributed to the family income by doing paid work in the home. Home work in the clothing industry in particular often involved whole families, with husbands, wives and children each labouring at a particular part of the cutting, assembly and finishing of garments. Married women also earned money by taking in laundry, or by accommodating lodgers and catering to their needs. Another common resource was selling fruit, vegetables or other goods, either door-to-door or from carts or stands. The journalist who visited Castle Garden in 1867 was clearly drawing on a familiar ethnic stereotype when he offered his readers a description of the stalls set up on the site selling bread, sausage, peanuts and lemonade to the immigrants within, run by 'aged but vituperative Irish women of masculine frame, with bleary eyes, tawdry garments and faces lined with the wrinkles of hardship'.[33]

For Irish women emigration to the United States was no easy option. Most immigrants embarked on a life of arduous labour, either as domestic servants or as unskilled and poorly paid workers. As with men, many found the struggle more than they could cope with. Women, in fact, were doubly vulnerable, since their lives—particularly once they had children—could be derailed, not just by their own misfortune, but also by a husband who fell ill, took to drink, or simply deserted his family. Across the country Irish women were overrepresented in America's prisons, alms houses and mental hospitals. The wrinkles of hardship were no journalistic invention. At the same time the American world of work, with all its hardships, had to be contrasted with the limited prospects and meagre rewards that faced poorer women in Ireland. There was also the question of marriage. Irish women in the United States married on average a couple of years later than native-born Americans in the same region and social class. But that was understandable, given the extra time needed to settle down in a new country, and perhaps accumulate some savings with which to set up a household. In the early twentieth century, for reasons that remain unclear, the proportion of bachelors and spinsters was to rise, making the American Irish somewhat unusual. For those who emigrated in the thirty or forty years after the Famine, on the other hand, the chances of their marrying or not marrying in their new homeland were about the same as for other sections of the population. In this respect too, life in America opened up possibilities that in Ireland would almost certainly have been denied them.[34]

Few Irish by this time headed purposefully to the frontier. But the same ever-increasing demand for labour that kept most immigrants in the cities of the East carried others much further. During periods of depression and high unemployment workers from the eastern cities sometimes took to the road, seeking work or better wages. Others were recruited for specific projects, to build a canal or a railroad, or became part of mobile labour gangs moving from one large construction project to the next. Much of this movement was temporary and circular: a long-term study of immigrants of all nationalities arriving during the 1840s found that nearly one in five of those located in the West in 1850 had returned to the East a decade later. But parts of this floating population eventually came to rest, creating small islands of Irishness far from the main centres of immigrant settlement. In Erin Prairie, Wisconsin, for example, Irish labourers left stranded by the suspension of work on the Superior and Bayfield railroad during the economic panic of 1857 became the nucleus of an enduring community. In this case the immigrants turned to farming. Ten years later a local newspaper reported that 'the Irish have not alone possessed themselves of every acre of this fine prairie for six miles square', but were buying up improved land in surrounding townships to be able to farm on a grander scale. But many others, as in the East, preferred to find work in the towns. In 1890, for example, more than one-third of the Irish-born inhabitants of Minnesota lived in the twin cities of Minnesota and St Paul.[35]

Alongside this more or less random drift to the farms and towns of the interior, there was also a more concerted westward movement. Following the discovery of gold in California in 1849 Irish immigrants from all over the United States joined the tens of thousands rushing to seek a fortune on the Pacific Coast. Some made the three- to six-month voyage by sea round Cape Horn, or took the shorter but more expensive route that used the Isthmus of Panama as a land bridge between oceans. Most joined wagon trains setting out from Iowa or Missouri across the Great Plains and through the Rocky Mountains. At Fort Laramie, Wyoming, John Orr, the clergyman's son from Portaferry in County Down, who had abandoned a profitable business in Chicago, described the scene: 'At night you could see campfires as far as the eye could reach, and during the day wagon following wagon for miles without a break in the line'. There was also some migration across the Pacific: of the 4,223 Irish-born who had settled in San Francisco by 1852, 589 had come from Sydney. By 1870 California had an Irish-born population of over 54,000, accounting for just under one-tenth of the population.

The overland journey to California was an arduous one, at times recalling the terrible Atlantic crossings of 1847. John Orr's wagon train suffered outbreaks of cholera, then fever and dysentery; in the final stages 'hundreds died of scurvy'. Bill Williamson of County Armagh described 'truly awful suffering' on the route beyond the Sierra Nevada mountains. 'I have seen 5 dollars offered for a small loaf of bread and men going along crying for something to eat.' The hoped-for reward for these hardships was sudden riches. In practice, the life-transforming lucky strike was rare. Instead most miners reckoned their gains in terms of a monthly income. Bill

Williamson's brother James, for example, estimated his profit from various claims at between $3 and $8 a day, and eventually concluded that he would do better at other work, where he might expect to make $100 to $125 a month and 'not be so apt to be sick as when you are at work in the water all the time'. Later in life he appears to have become an extra hand, generally known as 'Uncle Jim', on the ranch of his cannier brother, who had made his money running a store and boarding house, then invested in land.[36]

Bill Williamson was not alone. California created few gold millionaires, but it was nevertheless a place of opportunity. As its population rose from less than 10,000 before 1849 to over 90,000 by the middle of 1850, there were multiple opportunities for those able to respond to the explosion in demand for food, housing, and all the other necessities of life. Dennis J. Oliver, born in Galway in 1823, established himself as San Francisco's leading importer of paint, oil and glass. John Sullivan, born in County Limerick in 1824 into a family that emigrated to Canada six years later, was one of several who built up fortunes in real estate. John Downey, born in County Roscommon in 1827, had arrived in the United States at the age of 15, and had trained as a pharmacist in Washington, DC, before moving west. There he invested the profits from a partnership in San Francisco's first drugstore in what became an extensive ranch. He went on to win election to the state legislature, and in 1860 became California's first Irish-born governor. Success stories like this reflected not just the opportunities created by a population explosion, but the absence of an established elite that might have closed ranks against newcomers. By 1870 the Irish population of San Francisco was one-third that of Philadelphia, and half that of Boston. But San Francisco had twenty-seven Irish-born bankers and brokers, compared to eighteen in Philadelphia and just four in Boston.[37]

For ordinary Irish immigrants, too, the move to California was an advantageous one. Some turned to agriculture. By 1870 around one-third of the Irish living south of Monterey were successful farmers, and Irish farmers had also established themselves in other parts of the state. Once again, as in parts of the Midwest, it is clear that the Irish were more than ready, when the opportunity was there, to take to the land. The majority, however, like their counterparts in the East, preferred the town to the countryside. In 1870 almost two-thirds of Irish-born Californians lived in San Francisco, or in the five neighbouring counties, while one in every six residents of the city proper had been born in Ireland. Arriving without capital or skills, most took their place on the lower levels of the occupational ladder. In 1852 just under half of all Irish-born men in San Francisco were unskilled labourers, making them significantly poorer, not just in relation to the native-born, but also in comparison to the city's German immigrants. Thirty years later, however, the proportion of Irish-born men in unskilled work had fallen to less than three out of ten. The change was not due to any great turnover of population. Instead what counted was the environment. As San Francisco developed from a hastily thrown-together boom town to a major regional centre with a complex economy, its Irish inhabitants were well-placed to move on from manual labour to work involving a degree of skill or responsibility.[38]

The progress that the Irish were able to make in San Francisco was part of a wider pattern. The minority of Irish who travelled to other locations in the urban west started off at a social disadvantage. In Detroit in 1850, for example, half of all Irish-born heads of families were in low-status, poorly paid occupations, compared to just over one-third of German-born. In St Paul in 1880 almost two out of five Irish-born workers were classified as labourers, twice the average of the workforce as a whole. In St Louis a large part of the Irish population lived in an Irish ghetto known as the Kerry Patch where, according to one visitor in 1878, 'the shanties are not always kept in the best of repair . . . the hinges of the windows are often broken, the doors have fallen down and a bundle of rags often do service to keep the wind from circulating too freely'. Yet the concentration of the Irish-born in the poorest and least desirable work, measured statistically, was from the beginning less in these centres than in the major cities of the East. There was also, as in San Francisco, more scope for improvement over time. In St Louis, for example, the number of Irish households in the Kerry Patch fell by two-thirds between 1880 and 1900, as its inhabitants moved out to the more salubrious (though still ethnic) neighbourhood of Dogtown, leaving the Kerry Patch to more recently arrived Poles and Russians. Irish urban dwellers in the West were in part better off because they were less likely to have been drawn from the very poorest immigrants. In Detroit, for example, four-fifths of those arriving even at the height of the Famine crisis, during 1845–50, were able to read and write. But they also had the advantage, as in San Francisco, of arriving in towns and cities still in the early stages of development, with room for newcomers to take a place and a widening circle of opportunities as the local economy matured. Edward Hanlon, at a low point in his fortunes, berated himself for not having stayed in Milwaukee 'when the place was then young, and worked for myself'.[39]

The Irish were drawn to California by gold. In two other western states a different type of mining underpinned the emergence of distinctive Irish communities. In the first half of the nineteenth century, copper mines providing skilled though dangerous work operated in parts of the Irish counties of Cork, Waterford and Wicklow. When the removal of protective duties caused the collapse of these ventures after 1842, groups of skilled workers, mainly from Cork and Waterford, emigrated to the United States. Some found employment in the copper mines that were then just beginning to open up where Michigan's Keweenaw Peninsula projected into Lake Superior. Around 1870 Irish and Cornish men dominated the skilled positions in Michigan's mines, while German, Canadian and even native-born workers were predominantly labourers.

The great magnet for Irish miners, however, was Butte, Montana, where the Irish-born Marcus Daly had made the crucial decision to switch his mining operations from silver to copper just as Thomas Edison's experiments were making clear that copper wiring was about to become an essential commodity in advanced societies. By 1900 the Irish-born, along with their immediate offspring, made up just over one-quarter of the population of Butte. Nine out of ten were employed in mining, and a high proportion had brought their skills with them from the former mining district of County Cork. Their experience reflected in extreme form the combination of risk and reward that characterised so much of the immigrant experience. Hard-rock mining was both gruelling and dangerous. The physical wear and tear, along with a high accident rate, meant that the working life of a miner was, on average, no more than fifteen years. Such grim conditions help to explain why so many of Butte's Irish miners moved on after short periods. Only 15 per cent of the Irish miners recorded in the town in 1900 were still there ten years later. But this was enough to create a stable community of around 2,000 settled Irishmen, with their families, enjoying steady employment in relatively well-paid work. In the early twentieth century more than half of those who had been in the town for between four and seven years, and almost two-thirds of those who had been there for longer, either owned their own houses or were paying a mortgage.[40]

Of all the regions of the United States, the South was the least attractive to Irish immigrants. The dominance of plantation agriculture, where cotton, tobacco and rice were farmed by armies of slaves, meant that opportunities either for the wage earner or for the settler hoping to become owner of his own modest farm were far fewer than in other parts of the country. A few individuals of Irish birth managed, by skill or good luck, to insert themselves into the slave-owning planter elite, often on the basis of fortunes made in the cotton trade. But the numbers were small. Gerald O'Hara had few real-life counterparts. Migrant Irish workers, on the other hand, were employed throughout the South, on heavy work such as digging canals and laying railroad tracks. There were even suggestions that they were favoured, as an expendable labour force, in hot, swampy and often disease-ridden locations. One observer, noting the number of Irish labouring on canal construction, commented that their employment made sense, since a good slave would cost the equivalent of £200 sterling. There was also a more settled Irish population, but the numbers remained low. In 1860, across the whole eleven states that were soon to make up the Confederacy, there were just 85,000 Irish-born, amounting to 1.6 per cent of the white population. These were heavily concentrated in the major urban centres, where the majority were unskilled labourers. In Louisiana, the southern state with by far the highest number of Irish, more than four out of five, a total in 1860 of 24,000, lived in New Orleans; in North Carolina, likewise, two-thirds of the Irish-born were found in the city of Charleston.[41]

One consequence of moving beyond the cities of the Northeast, whether west or south, was that Irish immigrants were brought more squarely face-to-face with the brutal realities of America's racial hierarchy. Those settling land on or near the frontier were aware of, but largely indifferent to, the Indigenous populations they dispossessed. In 1857 a cousin of the Andersons of Ohio noted dispassionately that they had settled in a district that local Indians, having sold their other lands to the government, had tried to retain for themselves, 'but the whites drove them off'. In 1868 an Irish railway superintendent in Nebraska sent home an enthusiastic account of a skirmish with a party of Sioux, 'damned skunks', who had attacked one of his trains, and of the punitive expedition that followed. The cavalry had returned with nine scalps, one of which he had acquired, 'to take home to show the folks'. Even if relatively few Irish became proprietors on the huge territories seized from Native Americans, a good number of them had a hand in the process of seizure. The Irish, like other immigrant groups, were heavily overrepresented in the armed forces of the United States. In 1870 just under a quarter of the soldiers stationed in western forts and barracks, patrolling the frontier of white settlement, had been born in Ireland.[42]

Settlement on the Pacific Coast could also involve encounters with Native Americans. In 1850 John Orr reported cheerfully that there had been 'some little disturbance' with the Indians on the Yuba and Feather Rivers north of Sacramento. 'Some companies of US troops and some miners went out and chastised them pretty severely, killing 300 to 400 while they only lost three men killed.' But the main targets for the hostility of the California Irish were the Chinese, who had begun to appear in numbers from the time of the California gold rush, competing with the Irish for work in the mines, on the railroad and elsewhere, and on occasion acting as strike-breakers. During 1877–8 the Workingmen's Party, founded by a County Cork–born small businessman, Denis Kearney, briefly challenged the established Democrat and Republican Parties, with strong Irish support, under the slogan 'The Chinese Must Go'. In 1885–6 the Knights of Labor, another movement in which the Irish were prominent, was a major force behind a campaign of boycotts and evictions directed against Chinese communities in Washington Territory and other parts of the Pacific West.[43]

For the minority of Irish immigrants involved, settlement in the southern states meant coming to terms with the South's 'peculiar institution'. On his journey to join his uncle in Augusta, Georgia, J. B. Hamilton, a pious young man from County Antrim, was happy to recount the derogatory account he was given of free African Americans, 'a pest on society'. But on his uncle's farm, the home of fifty-six slaves, he was nevertheless shocked to hear the sounds of one of their number being flogged. 'I can scarcely write down what were my feelings. Certain that I felt my own flesh creep.' Whatever the initial scruples, however, the great majority of those who chose to remain in the South came to accept slavery as necessary and beneficial. 'If you only want to see a happy and contented lot of creatures', one County Antrim man wrote home in 1852, 'you should see a number of slaves meet together after their day's work is done and hear them play the banjo and see them dance.' His brother, settled in the same neighbourhood, painted a similar picture: slaves attended Sunday church with the women dressed in silks and the men sporting gold watches, and had liberty to earn money on their own account. Another Antrim man, William Hill, in America from the early 1820s, had brought with him many of the radical instincts that had made Ulster Presbyterians such enthusiastic participants in the Irish republican insurrection of 1798. Yet none of this stood in the way of his becoming a slave owner in South Carolina, and he objected strongly to an Irish acquaintance who questioned the religious commitment of the clergy of the Southern states, 'as if slavery and Christianity were inconsistent'. At the end of the Civil War he remained totally unreconciled. Freed slaves, formerly 'happy and contented', were now (he claimed) reduced to starvation because they were too lazy to work without compulsion. In the legislature 'an irresponsible body of negroes' imposed crippling taxation on the impoverished whites. 'A war of extermination either of the white or the black race is, in my opinion inevitable, and the conflict will not be long postponed.'[44]

One part of the Irish story in the United States, then, is of concentrated settlement in a few locations: New York, Boston and Chicago. It is a story that, especially when taken in conjunction with the chorus of criticism of the Irish for not being pioneers, encourages an image of immobility founded on caution and conservatism. But there is also a parallel narrative of constant mobility. Even the majority who placed themselves in the major cities of the East could, where necessary, set off for distant parts in search of work.

In logging, canal digging or the construction of roads and railways teams of workers formed and dispersed as they moved from project to project. There was also movement back and forth across frontiers, between Canada and the United States, or, in the case of the gold rushes of the early 1850s, between Australia and California. In 1914 one Butte miner, William O'Brien from County Cork, told a visiting committee of enquiry that he had worked in mines 'all over the world. Africa, Australia, New Zealand, Tasmania, Canada, Alaska, Mexico, this country, and South America'.[45]

What did this mean for the individuals concerned? The career of John Doherty of Belfast provides a glimpse of the energy and optimism that could inspire the continued wandering of someone who had already crossed 3,000 miles of ocean, as well as, it seems likely, a reminder of the potential cost. In 1848 Doherty was working as a railway superintendent in Pennsylvania. However he gave up that position after being threatened by 'some of my countrymen from the South'. (Doherty, despite his name, seems from some religious expressions in his letter to have been a Protestant.) Having looked fruitlessly for work in Philadelphia he accepted a nine-month engagement on a whaling ship sailing from New London, Connecticut. After fifteen months of hunting, in the waters off New Zealand and then in the Arctic, they had collected '2,500 Barrels of oil, from 18 whales, 9 of which I helped to take, that is, our boat took them'. But the ship had still not filled its quota of 3,500 barrels, and Doherty and others had to go to law to force the captain to release them. Discharged in Hawaii without his promised pay, he found work and scraped together the fare to California, where 'the gold mines were in every body's mouth'. Arriving in San Francisco in April 1850 he found 'it was too soon for the mines, so I looked about me what I could do'. He 'went to work at the first thing that offered' and built up a nest egg of $300 on a wage of $5 a day. His next thought was a speculation of the kind that allowed some others in the booming town to make their fortune. With coffee in San Francisco in short supply and expensive, he reckoned he could make a 400 per cent profit by bringing in supplies from Hawaii. Now an experienced seaman, he was able to contract to assist in bringing a vessel to the Islands for a fee of $200—enough to fund his coffee venture. Just as the voyage began, however, 'all my airy castles were pulled down. . . . I had my leg below the knee, broken to pieces, and myself almost killed'. In Hawaii he spent four months recovering. When he wrote home in November 1850 he was working as a caretaker in the missionary station at Honolulu and living frugally. 'I owe nothing, I am as it were beginning afresh, for it took all my money I saved to pay my doctors' bills, and attendance. There is, however, good prospects in view, I will make another trial, and on the event, please God, go home.' Where he went next is not clear. We know only that in 1860 his wife, whom he had left with their children in Baltimore when he set off whaling, reported that she had been shown a newspaper report of his death. His last letters to her had been 'full of confusion. There are many little incidents that lead me to think he fell by his own hands.'[46]

Moving on from this striking individual case, is it possible to draw up an overall balance sheet for the gains and losses of the Irish immigrants who during and after the Famine made the journey to the United States? The most ambitious attempt to do so is a major statistical study that tracked the experience of a large sample of immigrants—6,776 Irish, 9,022 British and 6,871 Germans— who landed in New York, by this time by far the most common port of arrival, between 1840 and 1850, following those who could be located through the American censuses of 1850 and 1860. The results suggest that, in terms of social mobility, the rewards for a journey across 3,000 miles of ocean were meagre. Among white-collar and skilled workers from Germany and the United Kingdom, whatever work they may have taken on first landing, seven out of ten had regained their previous status within four years of their arrival. Among the Irish, on the other hand, two out of every five of those classified on arrival as skilled workers, and more than half of those classified as white collar, were still in unskilled occupations even in 1860. Movement upwards, meanwhile, was negligible. By 1860 around one-fifth of German unskilled workers, and almost the same proportion of British, had risen to skilled or white-collar occupations. But the Irish making the same upward progress were too few to quantify from the imprecise statistics available.[47]

This poor performance can be explained in more than one way. The relegation of so many former skilled and white-collar workers to the ranks of the unskilled would suggest that what counted as a skill or a qualification in Ireland did not have the same status in the more developed economy of the United States. Even among the unskilled, equally, a young man brought up among subsistence farmers in the western counties of Ireland probably had less to offer in that new environment than someone who had spent time in an English or Scottish town, or in one of the more prosperous German states. The decision of so many Irish to remain in the overcrowded cities of the Eastern Seaboard also helped to ensure that they remained trapped in low-status, low-wage work. But it is also necessary to allow for significant discrimination. The notorious rubric 'No Irish need apply' was most common in advertisements for domestic servants. But formal and informal mechanisms of ethnic exclusion operated throughout all sections of the economy. Leading employers in Worcester, Massachusetts, for example, favoured Swedish workers as superior to other immigrant groups. In Newburyport, in the same state, factory managers kept immigrant workers of all kinds in a minority, as the only way, in their view, of bringing them up to standard. (On the other hand there were claims that some employers of large workforces deliberately fostered an ethnic mix as a means of undermining worker solidarity and reducing industrial disputes.) An existing workforce in a strong bargaining position could likewise refuse to work alongside these unwelcome newcomers, effectively excluding them from skilled employment. Banks, too, were frequently singled out for their unwillingness to lend to Irish Catholic businesses, or to employ members of the small but slowly expanding body of white-collar workers from an Irish Catholic background.[48]

Other evidence, too, suggests that the Irish coped less well than other groups with the challenges they encountered in their new environment. In New York the Irish-born accounted for two-thirds of the paupers admitted to the city's alms house. In Philadelphia in 1855 they made up more than half of the inmates in the House of Industry, a charitable institution which catered for the city's destitute inhabitants. They also made up two-thirds of the inmates admitted to Philadelphia's state hospital as suffering from a mental disorder, and just under half of all admissions to New York's lunatic asylum during 1849–58. The figures cannot be taken at face value. Native-born individuals fallen on hard times, or afflicted with mental illness, were more likely to have family willing to provide for them; non-Irish immigrants, too, were more likely to have arrived as part of a family group. But the figures are nevertheless a sharp reminder that the lives of many Irish men and women who took their chances in this difficult new environment ended badly. At its worst the American city could also drastically shorten lives. An Irish immigrant arriving in Boston, it was claimed in 1849, had a life expectancy of not more than fifteen years after their arrival, and figures from the following decade confirmed that the Irish death rate was in fact almost one and a half times that of the native-born. The situation in other cities was less stark. But across the second half of the nineteenth century, and indeed into the twentieth, life expectancy for Irish-born Americans, and for their children, remained lower than for non-immigrant Americans, and also lower than for the Irish still living in Ireland itself.[49]

Emigration to the United States, then, rarely brought advancement to a higher social class; for many, as seems to have been the case with John Doherty, life did not end well. But another set of results from the same long-term study of Irish, British and German immigrants present a more optimistic picture. In 1850 the Irish-born in the sample had on average only just over one-third of the wealth, in real estate, of the average German or British immigrant, a further indication of their poorer circumstances at the time of their arrival. By 1860 the Irish still owned less, per head of population, than the other two main immigrant groups, but the gap had narrowed. It was now no greater than could be accounted for by the fact that a much higher proportion of the Irish were unskilled or semi-skilled workers. Irish immigrants, in other words, were no longer significantly poorer than other immigrants in the same social class.[50]

Behind these abstract statistics lies a history of prolonged sacrifice, collective effort and formidable determination. Living in grim tenements, labouring at onerous, poorly paid and often insecure jobs, Irish immigrants in the 1850s and after single-mindedly acquired assets. Where circumstances permitted, as in Newburyport, they took on mortgages to become the owners of their houses. Elsewhere they concentrated instead on building up savings. A study of account holders at the Emigrant Savings Bank of New York, looking solely at Irish immigrants who had arrived during the Great Famine period, 1845–51, found that the median maximum balance they achieved was $163; for those in unskilled occupations the figure was, remarkably, slightly higher, at $165. This was at a time when the wage for labourers in construction and on the docks was between $1 and $1.25 a day. Among the savers were former tenants of the Lansdowne estate. They had been removed from their smallholdings in County Kerry during 1850–1, in one of the most notorious land clearances of the Famine era, causing outraged comment at their destitute condition on arrival in

America. Around a thousand found their way to the notorious Five Points district of New York. From there 153 individuals, representing probably half of the families concerned, opened accounts over the next five years with the Emigrant Savings Bank, with a median opening deposit of $100.[51]

These details are important for the light they cast, not just on the economic position that these migrants had achieved within a few years of arrival, but also on their aspirations. What they suggest is a strong preference for security over adventure. Idealists like Thomas D'Arcy Magee and John Francis Maguire lamented the opportunities that were lost by the refusal of Irish immigrants to embrace the risks and opportunities of settlement on the ever-receding frontier of white civilization. But the great majority of the Irish who emigrated to the United States during the Famine, and of those who followed them in the decades afterwards, were not eager pioneers. They left Ireland as refugees from the collapse of an entire economic system, or from a post-Famine economic order in which they had no place. In America they found themselves in cities where opportunities for work were infinitely varied and, in normal times, abundant, and where the frugal lifestyle they had brought with them from Ireland made it possible for even a poor family to build up a financial hedge against the uncertainties of urban life. It is hardly surprising, given their background, that this seemed to them a future that was not only more readily achievable than that of a pioneer settler, but also more attractive.

5

SOLDIERS AND CITIZENS

Nativism, Civil War and the Quest for Acceptance

In March 1863, just under two years after Confederate forces attacked the federal garrison at Fort Sumter, Matthew Brooks, a County Tyrone man who had been a resident of Philadelphia since the late 1820s, wrote to his sister with a mixture of political and personal news:

> There have been a great many of my acquaintances killed and wounded in this war. It is grievous to see what men are going up and down the street on crutches and their legs shot off. I met one James the other day, that lived with the Reverend Clark when a boy, going on crutches

with one of his legs off. David White of Cavendarragh went to the army and before he was 15 minutes in the first battle he got the half of his head blown off by the bursting of a shell.

What Brooks described was the local manifestations of a conflict marking a new and terrible episode in the history of Western warfare. The Civil War of 1861–5 was to cause 618,000 deaths. In relation to population this was six times the loss that the United States was to experience in the Second World War. Many others had been maimed for life by the loss of sight or limbs or by other injuries. The main reason for this harvest of death and mutilation was improved military technology. From the seventeenth century, when firearms had first become the standard battlefield weapon, soldiers had sought to kill each other with smooth-bore muskets that sent a ball wobbling unsteadily across a relatively short distance. Rifled guns existed, but the time spent forcing a ball between the grooves that would give it force and direction made them unsuitable for most military purposes. By the 1860s, however, Captain Claude-Étienne Minié's invention, a ball that slid easily down between the grooves, but expanded in the hot gases of the exploding gunpowder to provide a tight fit on exit, gave battlefield soldiers the rifled musket, with an effective range of a thousand metres or more, three times that of its smooth-bore predecessor. The new weapon had its limitations. It was still a single shot firearm, and the 'minié ball', gunpowder and percussion cap had each to be loaded separately. But the rifled musket, in a society where far more people were familiar with firearms than was the case among the workers and peasants of Europe, made battle enormously more costly, in terms of numbers killed and wounded, than in earlier conflicts. It also changed the likely outcome of a large-scale military engagement. Frontal assault on an enemy position was not yet, or at least not always, the suicidal option it was to become in the era of barbed wire and machine guns. But increased firepower meant that victory was less likely to be achieved by a charge or a succession of charges leading to a breakthrough. Instead war came to follow the grim logic of attrition. Union General Ulysses S. Grant's bloody Overland Campaign of 1864 was a limited strategic success, forcing his adversary, Confederate General Robert E. Lee, back into a defensive position at Richmond and Petersburg in Virginia. But the real point was that the Federal side could accept the 55,000 killed, wounded and missing more easily than the South could cope with its smaller total of 33,000 casualties.[1]

Into this brutal conflict, in which manpower was increasingly recognised as the key to victory or defeat, the Irish in the United States, and some of those still in Ireland, were drawn in large numbers. Many hoped that their participation would counter the disdain with which they continued to be viewed by much of American society, and establish their claim to be equal citizens of the republic. But these hopes were to be at best partly realised.

Hostility to the presence of Irish immigrants had a long history. In the colonial period Ulster Presbyterians, an often disruptive presence on the fringes of white settlement, found themselves categorised, to their indignation, as 'wild Irish'. Tensions of a different kind emerged after 1798, when a radical movement, the United Irishmen, in alliance with revolutionary France, organised an armed insurrection to liberate Ireland from British rule and create an independent, democratic republic. When fugitives from the failed rising made their way to America, Thomas Jefferson's Democratic-Republicans welcomed them as fellow victims of British tyranny. Their Federalist opponents, on the other hand, introduced legislation to curb the political activity of what they saw as dangerous aliens. As total emigrant numbers rose after 1815, from 60,000 during 1820–6 to 777,000 in 1836–45, concern grew about the implications for the well-being of the young republic. Not all of the hostility was directed at the Irish. There was a fear that

European immigrants in general, steeped in an Old World culture of divine-right monarchy, aristocracy and the suppression of ideas, could not be trusted to uphold democratic values—a mindset typified by the inventor Samuel Morse's bizarre vision in 1835 of 'some scion of the House of Hapsburg' being installed as emperor of an America purged of democratic institutions. But the Irish, accounting for two-fifths of all arrivals in the ten years up to 1845, were too numerous not to attract special attention. In 1834, in America's first major outbreak of anti-Catholic violence, a mob destroyed the Ursuline convent in the Boston suburb of Charlestown. In Philadelphia in 1844 two rounds of fighting in and around the predominantly Irish district of Kensington brought twenty deaths, as well as the burning of two Catholic churches, a convent, and the houses of prominent Irish figures. In the county elections that followed three months later an American Republican Party was able to exploit its role as defender of native values to win control of local government, remove Irish members of the police force and replace them with reliable supporters of its programme.[2]

Against this background it is no surprise that a huge increase in immigrant numbers in the late 1840s and after should have provoked a strong reaction. Between 1846 and 1854 American ports received 2.8 million immigrants, almost four times as many as had come in the preceding ten years. Of these almost one-third were German, fleeing economic recession at home as well as the repression that followed the failed revolutions of 1848. But the largest single group, 1.3 million, were Irish, most of them impoverished refugees from the disasters that had followed repeated failures of the potato crop. What made the early 1850s the high point of American nativism, however, was that this unprecedented increase in arrivals should have coincided with an upheaval in the political party system. In 1854 the Whig Party, hopelessly divided on the issue of slavery, fell apart. The movement that stepped into the resulting vacuum had begun as an obscure society, the Order of the Star-Spangled Banner, established in New York about 1850 as a militantly nativist and anti-Catholic association open only to Protestants of American birth. By 1854 it had become the American Party, but was also known colloquially as the Know-Nothings, based on the answer ('I know nothing') that members were supposedly told to give if asked about party business. Between June and October membership rose from around 50,000 to one million, and during 1854–5 the party achieved a series of spectacular electoral successes. The most striking was in Massachusetts, where in November 1854 it gained every seat in the senate, and all but three out of 378 in the lower house, as well as electing the governor. Know-Nothings also gained control of state governments in Connecticut, Rhode Island and New Hampshire, and became the mayors of Philadelphia, Boston and Chicago. At the national level, the new Congress that met at the end of 1855 contained 234 members, of whom 123 are estimated to have at some stage attached themselves to the Know-Nothing movement.[3]

The American Party saw itself as a movement of national regeneration. At the heart of its programme was a belief that the republic created by the American Revolution, with its core values of civic virtue and political freedom, was being undermined by corrupt politicians, immigrant voters ignorant of democratic values, and the decline of public morals. Members were also alarmed by American Catholicism, its numbers swelled by Irish and German newcomers, and its repressive, authoritarian character confirmed by recent moves on the part of American bishops to end the involvement of the laity in the management of parishes and to renew the demand for separate denominational schools. The American Party's remedy for these multiple ills was that immigrants should be required to complete twenty-one years of residence before they could become naturalised citizens and acquire the right to vote, and that election to public office should be reserved to native-born Americans. In addition most northern Know-Nothings were opponents of slavery, and the party also campaigned for restrictions, or an outright ban, on the sale of alcohol. None of this applied to the Irish alone. But in all the most important respects—their Catholicism, their aptitude for urban machine politics, and their taste for drink—they stood out as the most prominent targets.

The triumph of the American Party in 1854–5 had serious consequences. In different cities and states Know-Nothing mayors and legislators disbanded Irish militia companies, dismissed foreign-born policemen, introduced new regulations requiring Bible reading in schools, imposed literacy tests on voters, and tightened the procedures governing the admission of immigrants as citizens. In Maryland and Massachusetts committees were set up to carry out compulsory inspections of convents, awakening memories of the assault on the Ursuline convent in Charlestown. Pennsylvania, New York, Connecticut and Michigan all introduced legislation requiring that church property be vested in the laity rather than in bishops or other ecclesiastics. Outbreaks of lethal violence also occurred. In St Louis, fighting between Irish and Know-Nothings during the municipal election of 1854 led to six deaths. In Louisville, Kentucky, the following year, American Party supporters forcibly took over the polling booths and later invaded the German and Irish quarters of the town, destroying houses and a brewery. In all between nineteen and twenty-two people, two-thirds of them immigrants, died in Louisville's 'Bloody Monday'. Even in the far west, generally more politically open, the appearance in California of a branch of the Know-Nothings inspired the formation of a Committee of Vigilance that during 1856 lynched, imprisoned or exiled twenty-nine Democrat Party activists, most of them Irish.[4]

The reign of politically organised nativism was short-lived. As the presidential election of 1856 approached, the American Party, like the Whigs before it, became divided between a pro-slavery Southern wing and an abolitionist Northern wing. Its candidate, running on a compromise platform of abiding by existing laws, carried only one state, and over the next three years the party faded away. Most of its supporters transferred their votes to the emerging Republican Party, comprising former anti-slavery Whigs and other abolitionists. The new party was able to win their support without having to make more than a few token gestures towards a nativist agenda. But memories of the excesses of the Know-Nothings, and a perception of the Republicans as their successors, nevertheless form part of the background to the ambivalent response of the Irish in the Northern states to the Civil War that erupted less than a decade later.

———————

As the issue of slavery moved to the centre of political life during the 1850s, the Irish were noted for their lack of sympathy with the abolitionist cause. At a personal level relations between Irish and African Americans were not always hostile. Even in a notoriously unruly district like Five Points, there are indications that Irish and Black residents could coexist and interact in reasonable peace; there are even instances of intermarriage. But the Irish response to the anti-slavery movement, what the Boston-based Catholic newspaper the *Pilot* denounced as 'nigger lovers', was openly hostile. In a notorious incident in 1854 Boston's Columbian Artillery, an Irish Catholic militia unit, turned out as part of the armed guard holding back a furious crowd as Anthony Burns, arrested under the controversial Fugitive Slave Act, was loaded onto a ship that would take him back to servitude in Virginia. Opposition to emancipation was based in part on economic rivalry. The Irish, as the poorest section of the white working class, were the group most likely to compete with African Americans for unskilled manual work, and to fear that emancipation would liberate more Black workers to undercut their wages and conditions. But in other respects too the abolitionist cause had, for the Irish, very negative associations. Many of its strongest supporters were evangelical Protestants, whose opposition to slavery was matched by their enthusiasm for the compulsory reform of the manners of the poor, particularly through an aggressive campaign against alcohol, and by their hostility to Catholicism. Harriet Beecher Stowe was not just the author of *Uncle Tom's Cabin*, supposedly hailed by Lincoln as the little book that started a great war. She was also the daughter of the Reverend Lyman Beecher, whose fierce anti-Catholic preaching was blamed by many for preparing the way for the destruction of Charlestown's Ursuline convent in 1834. To the working-class Irish of the northern states, extravagant concern for the welfare of enslaved Africans in the distant South was at best an irrelevance, at worst the battle cry of an establishment that despised and exploited them.[5]

When Irishmen enrolled in the Northern Army, then, it was rarely out of any commitment to the anti-slavery cause. 'The feeling against niggers', wrote Peter Welsh in 1862, while serving as a soldier in the 28th Massachusetts Infantry, 'is intensely strong in this army. . . . They are looked upon as the principal cause of this war and this feeling is especially strong in the Irish regiments.' Instead, like the majority of those they fought alongside, the commitment of Irish soldiers was to the defence of the political institutions of the republic. Welsh himself had entered the Union Army in inglorious circumstances. Born to Irish parents in British North America in 1830 but long settled in New York, he had lost all his money in a drinking bout during a visit to Boston and enlisted rather than face his family's disapproval. But he was nevertheless able to write to his wife rationalising his decision in terms strikingly similar to those that Lincoln was to use, a full nine months later, at the opening of the Soldiers' National Cemetery at Gettysburg. The war, he told her, was 'the first test of a modern free government in the act of sustaining itself against internal enemies and matured rebellion'. If it could not do so, 'then the hopes of millions fall, and the designs and wishes of all tyrants will succeed'. A further powerful influence was the close connection, in contemporary minds, between masculinity, citizenship, and the bearing of arms.

The Irish had participated enthusiastically in the pre-war fashion for service in local militia companies, where training and parading offered a badge of communal identity, and perhaps a warning to others that these were not people to be interfered with. The coming of war was a challenge to match this rhetoric with action, and the opportunity to progress from ethnic self-assertion to a display of patriotism. Loyal service to the nation in its hour of need would be the ultimate answer to nativist slurs on the Irish population.[6]

What of the Irish who fought for the South? Some of them were outspoken advocates of slavery. The Irish-born T. W. McMahon, in 1862, published a full-blooded defence of the Confederacy as a struggle to protect white racial superiority. His pamphlet enumerated forty-six anatomical differences between the African and the Caucasian, including the claim that a crucial part of 'the skull of the negro approximated to its situation in that of the chimpanzee and Ourang-Outang'. John Mitchel, the former Young Irelander and prisoner in Tasmania who sent two sons to fight in the Confederate Army, had in 1854 published a notorious editorial insisting that it was no crime to own slaves, or to keep them to their work 'by flogging or other needful coercion'. The great majority of Southern Irish, however, were poor whites with no personal stake in the institution of African-American bondage. In the series of political crises that preceded the coming of war they showed no inclination to support secession, instead giving their support to pro-Union, southern Democrats. Once the war began, however, they responded to the demands of local or regional patriotism. As in the North, the flow of willing recruits to what became a long ordeal by battlefield slaughter testifies to the desperate longing of a marginalised immigrant population to be accepted by the society in which it lived.[7]

The Civil War was not the first appearance of the Irish on American battlefields. For immigrants struggling to gain a foothold in American society the regular pay, with board and accommodation, provided by military service had always been attractive. Irishmen had made up around a quarter of the force that invaded Mexico in 1846. The exploits of a small group, nicknamed the San Patricios, that defected to the enemy during the conflict have detracted from the memory of the much larger number who helped bring about further large territorial gains for the United States. In the 1850s two-thirds of soldiers in the American army were foreign-born, with the Irish making up more than half of that number. In the Civil War, with both sides desperate for manpower, the incentives became greater. By 1864 men entering the Federal Army could expect a bounty of $700 or more, and there was also the possibility of being paid to enlist as a substitute for men selected for the draft. The great majority on both sides, however, enlisted as volunteers. In all nearly 150,000 Irish-born soldiers are recorded as serving in the armed forces of the federal government, as well as an unknown number of American-born men of Irish descent. This compares with a total of almost 600,000 Irish-born men of military age living in the Northern states. It was not the exceptional level of participation sometimes claimed: compared to Germans and other immigrant groups, the Irish were in fact somewhat underrepresented. However this might have been due, not just to a lack of enthusiasm for the crusade against slavery, but to the modest social profile of the Irish-American population: unskilled workers of all nationalities seem to have been less ready than other groups to volunteer for service. For the Confederate forces we have only an estimate based on an analysis of surnames, thus covering both the Irish-born and those of Irish parentage. But compared to a population in the South of only around 39,000 Irish-born men aged 15 and over, the total of around 20,000 suggests a high level of participation, possibly twice that seen in the North.[8]

Not all the Irish who bore arms in the Civil War were enlisted men. Irish-born commanders also appeared on both sides, their profiles a reminder of the diverse range of positions that Irish immigrants had established for themselves in the forty years since the beginning of large-scale immigration. The Union Army included twelve generals born in Ireland. James Shields, born into a middle-class Catholic family in County Tyrone around 1806, had qualified as a lawyer in Illinois, rose to prominence in state politics and then, after service in the Mexican-American War, became the first Irish-born member of the United States Senate. Thomas William Sweeny, born in County Cork, began life in America more humbly, as a printer's apprentice, but became a career soldier after serving, and losing an arm, in Mexico. He was active in campaigns against Native Americans in the 1850s, and by the time the Civil War began had risen to the rank of captain. Among senior officers on the Confederate side Patrick Cleburne, from a modest Protestant background in County Cork, had served in the British army before emigrating to the United States, where he set up a successful legal practice in Arkansas. His exploits in Kentucky and Tennessee led Jefferson Davis to hail him as 'the Stonewall [Jackson] of the west'. Richard Dowling, the son of a County Galway farmer, had prospered as a bar owner and real estate speculator in Houston, Texas. He was celebrated for his defence of a fort on the Sabine River, where in September 1863 his artillery company of just 40 men blocked a projected invasion of his state by driving off some 5,000 Union attackers. A plaque commemorating the 'American Civil War hero and Texas businessman' unveiled in the town hall at Tuam, County Galway, in 1998 was hailed at the time as a tribute to a local man made good. More recently there have been calls for its removal.[9]

Governments on both sides acknowledged the Irish contribution to their war effort by sanctioning the creation of ethnic units. New York already had a largely Irish-born militia unit, the 69th New York Infantry Regiment. When the war began its commander, Donegal-born Michael Corcoran, was in custody awaiting court martial for having refused to parade the regiment as part of the official welcome during a visit to the city by the Prince of Wales in 1860. Released to lead his men into battle, he was taken prisoner at the First Battle of Bull Run. His successor, Thomas Francis Meagher, was something of a political adventurer: a veteran of the Young Ireland rebellion of 1848 who had escaped from the penal colony of Tasmania, he had been angling for some time for a government position, and now he became concerned primarily to use his credit with the Irish immigrant population to win for himself a position in American public life. A month after Bull Run, in late August 1861, he was authorised to create a brigade comprising the 69th New York, two other New York regiments, and regiments from Massachusetts and Pennsylvania. One of the initial Massachusetts regiments, later redeployed, was made up of native-born Americans, and one Pennsylvania regiment was partly German. For the most part, however, Meagher's force was Irish-born or second-generation Irish American. Regiments were in part based on pre-war Irish militia units, and the Brigade fought beneath a green flag carried alongside the Union colours. Later Corcoran, released from a Confederate prison, raised an Irish Legion comprising a further four regiments. Irish units were also established in other states: one Illinois infantry regiment called itself 'the Irish Brigade', while another was known as 'the Irish legion'. The Confederacy had no equivalent to Meagher's or Corcoran's brigades. But there, too, units composed wholly or largely of Irishmen proclaimed their nationality with names such as Irish Volunteers, Emerald Guards, Hibernians, Shamrock Guards and even, in Louisiana, Southern Celts.

The creation of ethnic units helped promote Irish support for the war effort on both sides. Their formation also contributed to the development of an Irish-American identity. Among other arguments, Peter Welsh and others presented their service in the army as the payment of a debt of gratitude that the Irish in particular owed to the United States for having provided a home for so many refugees from famine and oppression. The widespread perception that Britain supported the Confederate cause further helped to stiffen Irish support for the Northern war effort. Most important of all there was the belief that military experience won on American battlefields would someday be of service nearer to home. The idea of the Civil War as a training ground for a future struggle to liberate Ireland was a standard part of the recruiting speeches of both Meagher and Corcoran. Meagher himself, with his eyes on an American career, was never more than a cautious fellow traveller to the militant republican movement in the United States. Corcoran's Irish Legion, on the other hand, was dominated by committed members of the revolutionary Irish nationalist movement, the Fenian Brotherhood.[10]

For the Irish, as for native-born Americans, the Civil War was a war of brothers. Meagher admitted as much in an oration in September 1861, when he called on an audience that had just cheered the 69th Regiment to do the same for the two sons of his fellow Young Irelander John Mitchel, 'who are fighting as bravely on the other side'. On occasion, unavoidably, Irishmen on opposite sides met one another in combat. In the very first major engagement of the war, at the First Battle of Bull Run on 21 July 1861, Corcoran's 69th New York came up against the Louisiana Zouaves, whose ranks included Irish dock workers from New Orleans. Later, in October 1862, the Southern Celts saw action against Federal forces that included a mainly Irish regiment from Kentucky. But with only 20,000 Irish soldiers in Confederate service, distributed across all the theatres of war, such encounters cannot have been common. The most widely cited episode, at Fredericksburg, where the Irish Brigade were cut to pieces as they charged at Marye's Heights, has been heavily mythologised. Their opponents included what has been presented as an Irish regiment from Georgia. But this contingent in fact contained only four or five Irishmen, apart from its Ulster-born commander. Another Confederate unit stationed nearby was indeed Irish, but it contained only forty-seven men. Claims that a defender sighting the Brigade was heard to exclaim, 'Oh, God, what a pity! Here comes Meagher's fellows', may have originated with a poem later published by the Irish nationalist John Boyle O'Reilly.[11]

The same strong regional loyalties that put Irish immigrants on opposite sides of the battlefield also divided what was by this time the predominantly Irish leadership of the American Catholic Church. Catholic teaching contained no prohibition of slavery. The papal encyclical *In Supremo Apostolatus*, published in 1839, had condemned the international trade in human beings. But on the institution itself, it said only that Christians should regard their slaves as brothers, and be 'more inclined' to set free those who deserved it. In the Southern states, bishops, priests and religious orders commonly owned, bought and sold slaves. Their counterparts in the North, like their congregations, generally had little time for the abolitionist movement. Archbishop John Hughes of New York, for example, saw slavery as an evil, but argued that it should be allowed to die out naturally. Once the Southern states seceded, however, he gave full support to the war to preserve the union, flying the Stars and Stripes from the roof of St Patrick's Cathedral and formally blessing the 69th Regiment as it marched out of the city towards its first engagement at Bull Run. Other northern bishops, in Philadelphia, Milwaukee, Pittsburgh and Cincinnati, also displayed the Federal flag from their churches. In Boston, Harvard University took the unprecedented step of conferring an honorary degree on Archbishop John Fitzpatrick, who had enthusiastically supported the formation of an Irish regiment. Southern bishops were equally vocal on the other side. In Charleston, South Carolina, Bishop Patrick Lynch presented a regiment of Irish Volunteers with their flag, combining the shamrock and harp with the stars of the confederacy. Bishop John Quinlan of Mobile, Alabama, blessed the Emerald Guards, and announced his belief that the South had been 'too long on "leading strings"' and 'must cut adrift from the North'.

As the war continued both sides took their case to Europe. In late 1861, at the direct request of Lincoln's Secretary of State William Seward, an old political ally, Archbishop Hughes travelled to Paris and Rome as one of three envoys sent to counter Confederate appeals for international recognition. For the Confederacy, Martin Spalding, bishop of Louisville, prepared a dissertation in 1863 for submission to Rome, blaming the war on abolitionists who 'hate the Catholic religion with an almost Satanic hate', and insisting that emancipation would be the ruin of the Black population. The following year Bishop Lynch followed in Hughes's footsteps, appealing first to the Emperor Napoleon III in France, and then to Pope Pius IX. The response of the Vatican was cautious. The pope appeared to give Hughes a sympathetic hearing. But a subsequent letter addressed jointly to Hughes and a Southern bishop, instructing them to work for peace, was widely interpreted as a rebuke to the archbishop for his partisanship, and he was never to receive the cardinal's hat that a clergyman of his standing might have expected. By contrast the promotion of Spalding to the premier see of Baltimore seemed to indicate that his defence of the Confederacy had done him no harm, and the pope admitted to Lynch his private view that the South was a separate nation. However there was no formal recognition of the Confederacy, and the pope also made clear his view that something must be done to bring about an eventual end to slavery.[12]

The American Civil War broke out at a time when immigration from Ireland had been in decline for several years, as living standards rose and the shock of the Famine receded. The early years of the war saw numbers fall further still, as letters from the United States brought dire warnings of the collapse of economic activity. 'The times is miserable in this country', one Ulster immigrant reported. 'This rebellion has stopped all public works and men is going about in thousands that can't get anything to do.' In 1861 only 28,000 emigrants from Ireland came to the United States, followed in 1862 by 34,000, numbers last seen in the late 1830s. There was also the fear of being drawn into what was developing as a bloody and prolonged military conflict. In Ireland, however, the years 1863–4 brought a succession of disasters—drought and excessive rain, diseases of cattle and sheep—that wiped out most of the gains in living standards achieved since the Famine, and left large numbers once again facing destitution. Prospects in the United States, on the other hand, were now much improved, as the recruitment of massive armies left the factories and farms of the North short of labour. During 1863–5 270,000 Irish immigrants arrived in the United States, more than four times the number seen in the first two years of the war. Apart from some middle-class radicals and some radically inclined workers in the industrial Northeast, there was little support in Ireland for the Federal cause. But an effective Union naval blockade that closed off the Southern ports ensured that almost all of this emigration was directed to the Northern states. As the economic crisis deepened, American consuls in Irish ports found themselves besieged by two types of enquirer. Potential emigrants in a position to fund their own passage sought assurances that they would not be liable for conscription. Poorer men, on the other hand, made desperate offers to enlist in the Federal Army, if the government would pay for their passage across the Atlantic.[13]

The federal government was acutely aware of the potential contribution of Irish immigrants either directly to the war effort, or to the Northern economy that supported it. 'To some extent', Secretary of State Seward told his consul general in Paris in September 1862, 'this civil war must be a trial between the two parties to exhaust each other. The immigration of a large mass from Europe would itself decide it.' Consuls across Europe, including those in Dublin,

Cork, Belfast and four other centres, received instruction to do all they could to boost emigration to the United States. But they were also warned that to become involved in any way in direct military recruitment might put them in legal peril. Confederate agents in both Ireland and Great Britain hunted vigorously for evidence that Federal representatives were enlisting soldiers, at one point even hiring private detectives. The British government, in response to their complaints, also kept a watch on the activities of the consuls. On one occasion, when the vice consul in Dublin found his office crowded with young men excited by word that a railway company in Ohio was looking for hands, he recognised two plainclothes policemen lurking in the throng. However the only clear-cut case of official Federal representatives taking up recruits concerned the USS *Kearsarge*, which arrived in Queenstown harbour in November 1863. Witnesses agreed that some 150 to 300 men surrounded the vessel in small boats, clamouring to be taken on board. When sixteen of their number were later found to have made their way onto the ship, the captain claimed they were stowaways. Six of the men stood trial at the next assizes, still wearing the American naval uniforms they had been issued (supposedly because they were 'otherwise utterly destitute'). However, they were acquitted, allowing both governments to bury an embarrassing episode.[14]

If official representatives of the federal government had to be circumspect, private contractors could operate more freely. In April 1863 police in Mullingar reported that a man ostensibly recruiting hands for public works in the United States had been observed recording the height and chest measurements of applicants, and rejecting any man less than 5 feet 6 inches tall. It is not clear whether, in this case, the recruits themselves were privy to the deception. But sharp practice was certainly involved in an episode the following March, when an entrepreneur, Jerome Kidder, brought 120 tradesmen from Dublin to Portland, Maine, and then to Boston. The men had been promised employment on railway construction or on the city's waterworks. But they arrived in an American winter, with rivers icebound and ground frozen hard, so that no work was available. Instead they were told they could enlist in the 28th Massachusetts Infantry, part of the Irish Brigade. They refused. But observers were clear that, if they had complied, Kidder and his associates would have found a way of appropriating the greater parts of the enlistment bounties to which they would have been entitled. Meanwhile seven of the party who had stayed behind in Portland were taken to a liquor store, made drunk, then arrested and kept without food and water until they agreed to sign up. One of the seven, a veteran of the British army in India, was found unfit for service and hospitalised. By the time, two months later, that the British minister in Washington had pushed a reluctant American government to enquire into the case, the other six had been sent into combat, where two had been killed and two wounded.[15]

———

Supporters of the Union cause had argued that loyal and courageous service in the Federal Army would counter the numerous slurs that nativists had over the years directed at Irish immigrants. Such hopes were at best partially realised. When Corcoran's 69th Regiment marched through New York to the steamer that would carry them towards the front line, they were cheered by enthusiastic crowds. Other responses, however, were grudging, or even hostile. An official in Wisconsin told an Irish militia company that there were enough young Americans available to suppress the Southern rebellion, so that 'red-faced foreigners' were not required. An officer in Massachusetts described the men of the Irish 13th Volunteer militia as 'the sweepings of our jails', who were now electing 'officers of their own stripe'. Elsewhere the authorities dealt with similar concerns by imposing native-born officers on Irish units. In Philadelphia hostile residents went further, pelting the largely Irish 69th Pennsylvania with stones and bricks as they marched out of the city in the autumn of 1861.[16]

From these mixed beginnings, the Irish contribution to the Union war effort became steadily more contentious. Almost from the start the Irish Brigade was pushed forward into a succession of bloody encounters. It suffered heavy losses during General George McClellan's attempt to force his way up the Virginia peninsula during March–July 1862. At Antietam on 17 September 1862, the 63rd and 69th New York lost 60 per cent of their numbers, killed or wounded, as they charged Confederate defenders firmly entrenched in a sunken roadway. Meagher's strategy, he later reported, was to rely 'on the impetuosity and recklessness of Irish soldiers in a charge'. But in the event Confederate fire 'literally cut lanes through our approaching line'. The battle of Fredericksburg, in December, brought another suicidal charge, uphill against enemies sheltered by a low stone wall. The Irish Brigade's losses were estimated at 45 per cent. By April 1863 the Brigade had been reduced to 520 men; losses at Chancellorsville in the first days of May reduced its strength further, to 418. Alongside these major bloodlettings, there were the numerous casualties being sustained by Irish soldiers in other units, all liable to be reported back, week after week, to close-knit communities in the major centres of Irish settlement. Some of the blame for the carnage was directed at Meagher, widely suspected of caring more for his own military glory than for the lives of his men. But there was also a sense that the sacrifices of Irish soldiers were not being properly acknowledged, and a resentful awareness of continued nativist prejudice. After Chancellorsville, Meagher resigned as commander, in protest at what he claimed was unfair treatment of the Brigade, in particular a refusal to allow its men a period of leave. The shrunken Brigade went on to fight at Gettysburg in July 1863, losing 202 out of its 530 men, though a reorganisation in 1864 brought its numbers back up to 856.[17]

Alongside the ever-growing casualty lists, and resentment at what was perceived as continuing nativist prejudice, Irish

Americans became increasingly unhappy with the conduct of the war. Two decisions in particular, taken after the bloodbath of Antietam, rankled. The first was the removal from command of the Union forces of George McClellan. Although he was hailed by at least one enthusiastic admirer as an Irishman, McClellan's family background was in fact Scottish. However he was popular with Irish Americans, as a personable commander in chief, as a fellow Democrat, and as a commander who did not waste lives unnecessarily. His removal, justified on the grounds that he had failed to prosecute the war with sufficient vigour, was further apparent confirmation that the Irish were giving their lives in a war run by their enemies. The second decision, even more unpopular, was Lincoln's Emancipation Proclamation of September 1862. The proclamation granted freedom only to those slaves held in the states in rebellion. But the discovery that a war to preserve the Union had become a war for abolition produced a furious reaction. Irish-American newspapers condemned 'Negrophilism' and 'the irredeemable malignity of the Abolition hatred of our race', and warned that Irish workers would be 'degraded to a level with negroes'.[18]

It was against this background of growing Irish alienation that the Lincoln administration embarked on its most divisive measure, the introduction of conscription. The first draft, in states held not to have produced their quota of volunteers, provoked riots by Germans in Wisconsin and Irish in the mining districts of Pennsylvania. The most bitter resistance, however, came when the draft was extended to New York in July 1863. Opposition initially focussed on a class issue: the provision that affluent conscripts could buy their way out for a fee of $300. The first day's protest, on Monday 13 July, was a broadly based workers' demonstration. Crowds forcibly closed places of work, cut down telegraph poles and tore up railway track, attacked draft offices and other federal buildings and beat up policemen and other agents of government. In the days that followed, however, skilled workers, and German

Americans, largely withdrew from the protests, leaving the streets in the hands of labourers and industrial workers, the majority of whom, reflecting the city's occupational structure, were Irish and Catholic. Over the next four days large crowds continued to fight with police and soldiers, and to threaten government buildings and the homes of prominent Republicans and abolitionists. But they also turned their aggression on the city's Black population. Already on that Monday evening a crowd had set fire to the Colored Orphan Asylum, though mercifully not before the children inside had escaped through a rear door. Others in the city were not so lucky. Of the 105 or so deaths that can be documented, at least 11 were of Black males lynched or otherwise killed by the rioters. The killings were accompanied by savage displays of racial hatred: one corpse had the fingers and toes chopped off; another was dragged round the streets by a rope attached to the genitals.[19]

The draft riots were suppressed by military force, using National Guard regiments drafted in from neighbouring states. In the longer term the local Democratic Party resolved the draft issue by promising that any poor man with a family selected for the draft would have his exemption fee, or the cost of a substitute, paid out of municipal funds. The scheme, financed by a bond issue, added greatly to the city's debt. But it allowed the draft to go ahead unchallenged the following month. It also powerfully reinforced the bond between Tammany Hall, the Democratic Party's New York headquarters, and the city's Irish-American population. Other reactions were less emollient. The rioters had been predominantly Irish Catholics. But so too had the police force against which they battled. The riot also claimed prominent Irish Catholic victims. Colonel Robert Nugent, former commander of the 69th New York but now in charge of implementing the draft, had his house wrecked. Colonel Henry O'Brien, from another New York regiment, who had ordered a cannon fired to disperse one crowd, was subsequently taken prisoner and battered to death across a period of six hours. The federal government, presumably mindful of the need for continued Irish support for the war effort, reacted to the disturbances with caution. It held back from imposing martial law on the city, instead allowing Tammany Hall to buy off popular discontent. Lincoln's only public comments were cautious, deploring the way worker had turned on worker, but saying nothing to single out the Irish. The conservative patrician George Templeton Strong, on the other hand, had no hesitation in identifying the rioters, from the very first day, as 'the lowest Irish day labourers. . . . Every brute in the drove was pure Celtic.' Their actions, in his view, confirmed long-standing fears of a republic swamped by uncivilised aliens. 'Long live the sovereigns of New York, Brian Boru *redivivus* and multiplied. Paddy has left his Egypt—Connaught—and reigns in this promised land of milk and honey and perfect freedom.' By the end of the week Strong noticed frequent placards saying 'Sam organise', a call for the revival of the Know-Nothing party. The intervention of Archbishop Hughes of New York, addressing a crowd of 3,000 on the Friday morning and seeming to excuse rather than condemn the events of the preceding days, only added to the belief of a collective Catholic complicity in treason and racist murder.[20]

Irish Americans had hoped that service in the Civil War would be a route to acceptance. Those hopes, as the choleric spluttering of George Templeton Strong make clear, were not realised. By this time, in fact, the character of anti-Irish hostility had taken a new, and at first sight menacing, turn. The ideas of the Know-Nothing movement had been conservative and backward-looking. Drawing on the same language of civic virtue that had inspired the Founding Fathers of the republic, they saw immigrants as dangerous because of the corrupting influences they had brought with them from the Old World. The solution was not to exclude them permanently from full citizenship, but to require them to serve a period of probation in which they could acquire the values of a democratic, egalitarian society. This set the movement firmly apart from a different set of ideas, originating in Europe, that by the mid-nineteenth century had begun to circulate in the United States. Going beyond broad distinctions based on skin colour, influential writers argued that humanity could be divided into a whole hierarchy of ethnic groups, destined by biology to a higher or a lower place on the ladder of civilization. The influence of the new pseudoscience quickly became apparent in images of the immigrant Irish. Alongside continued accusations of drunkenness, violence, ignorance and superstition, negative depictions came to include a new emphasis on physical marks of inferiority. Cartoonists in particular developed a whole visual shorthand to convey the idea of an inferior species, using facial hair, sloping foreheads and protruding jaws to give Irish figures an unmistakably simian appearance.[21]

To some later writers the spread and popularity of this new style of caricature, framed in the language of biological inferiority, is evidence that the Irish should be included among the victims of the pervasive racism of the nineteenth-century United States. But it is important to avoid misleading parallels. The Irish competed with Black and (on the West Coast) Chinese Americans for some of the most arduous and poorly rewarded forms of manual labour. They were also the victims of widespread but informal discrimination. But to compare their grievances to the legal inferiority, reinforced by ruthless repression, imposed on African Americans, and on Chinese and other Asian immigrants, is to trivialise the experience of the victims of real racism. There are echoes here of the shameless attempt, in the 1980s, to claim a place for the Irish experience in the emerging discipline of Holocaust studies.[22]

In terms of popular culture, equally, it is important to recognise the distinction between a visual shorthand and a fully developed ethnological theory. Cartoonists and sketch writers were happy to reach for ready-made signposts to identity. But, in the absence of the objective marker provided by skin colour, there was always a certain fuzziness to conceptions of the Irish as not just ridiculous or badly behaved, but as a separate species. The superficial character of what at first sight can look like a clear case of racist imagery can be seen in a cartoon strip of 1883. The topic is the perennial middle-class problem of how to deal with an unsatisfactory Irish maid. In early frames the gaunt, pipe-smoking harridan, with distinctly ape-like features, keeps open house in her employer's kitchen for her equally ill-favoured friends. But once the mistress (instructed by her husband) puts her foot down and imposes discipline, the maid not only mends her ways but is physically transformed into a fresh-faced Irish colleen, cheerfully going about her work.[23]

The final reason for not exaggerating the importance of the new fashion for anti-Irish caricature is a simple matter of chronology. The pseudoscience of innate ethnic characteristics began to gain ground in the 1840s and 1850s. But this was just at the time when the rise and fall of the Know-Nothings, whose anti-immigrant policies were based on very different ideas, marked the high point of direct action against the Irish. Nativist agitations would recur. But there was to be no instance of violence to match the Charlestown or Philadelphia riots, and no further attempt to tighten the rules on political participation in a way that would exclude the Irish. The immediate benefits of participation in the Civil War were disappointing, and they may have been partly cancelled out by the appalling events of the July 1863 draft riots in New York. But the second half of the nineteenth century, the heyday of ethnic 'science', was to be the period when the Irish moved towards a degree of acceptance as a part of American society.

6

BENEATH THE
SOUTHERN CROSS

Australia and New Zealand

In the Ireland of the 1850s emigration to Australia was by no means an unfamiliar prospect. Over the previous half century it had been the destination of a little under 40,000 Irish convicts. Most of these were freed within a few years of arrival and made their way as settlers; many wrote home to friends and family describing their new lives. From the end of the 1830s these involuntary migrants had been joined by almost the same number of government-assisted immigrants, as well as a smaller number paying their own way. But familiarity had to be set against cost and distance. The 12,000-mile voyage was a daunting prospect, and the

£10 to £15 fare was beyond the reach of even reasonably comfort-able farming or artisan families. The Famine years, 1845–51, were a turning point in the general history of Irish emigration. But the one small ripple to reach far-off Australia was the 4,000 female in-mates of Irish poorhouses, the so-called 'orphans', dispatched un-der a special scheme. There was no equivalent in Australia to the hundreds of thousands of refugees from a collapsing economy, rag-ged, starving and diseased, that were cast up on the shores of Great Britain and North America.

Instead the turning point in Irish emigration to Australia came in the 1850s, following the discovery of gold in New South Wales and Victoria during 1851–2. Left to themselves, few Irish would have been in a position to respond directly to the huge excitement the news aroused. At the height of the mining frenzy, in 1852–3, only 6 per cent of self-financing immigrants to Victoria came from Ireland. But subsidised passages continued, driven by the contin-ued demand for labour on farms and sheep runs, in the developing towns, and in the homes of the servant-keeping classes. Even Vic-toria, during the gold rush years, felt it necessary to spend money on immigration in order to compensate for the flight of workers from other sectors to the goldfields. As before, colonial govern-ments regularly expressed their preference for sturdy ploughmen and shepherds, or deft and neat housekeepers, from Scotland and rural England. But in practice it was the Irish, men and women, who came forward willingly to fill every place offered to them. Ire-land's share of the population of the United Kingdom fell from just over a quarter in 1851 to just over one-seventh in 1881. Yet a third of all assisted immigrants arriving in the Australian colonies were Irish. By this time, too, earlier Irish settlers were increasingly well-positioned to offer financial assistance to relatives and others, although remittances from previous emigrants never assumed the importance in Australia that they did in the United States. To-tal Irish emigration to Australia and New Zealand combined (in practice, overwhelmingly to Australia) rose from 23,000 in the decade 1841–50 to 102,000 during the next ten years, with a further 200,000 arriving over the period 1861–90. These were small totals compared to the annual outflow to North America. But then total emigration to Australia was also smaller. The 5 per cent or fewer of Irish emigrants who across the nineteenth century made it their destination was enough to ensure that the Irish-born and their descendants consistently accounted for one-quarter of the population.

The arrival of large numbers of free migrants to Australia tends to mask the continuation, for almost two more decades after 1850, of the practice of transporting criminals. New South Wales ceased to receive convicts from 1840. However just under 10,000 Irish prisoners were transported instead to Van Diemen's Land between 1840 and 1853, while there were also Irish among the 9,635 prisoners from all parts of the British Isles dispatched to Western Australia between 1850 and 1867. Once again, the Irish convicts included some whose offences were clearly political. Twelve men sentenced for their part in the Young Ireland movement, either before or during the ineffective rebellion its leaders had attempted in 1848, were sent to Van Diemen's Land during 1849–51, while among the last arrivals in Western Australia were sixty-two men convicted for their part in the more formidable Fenian movement of the 1860s. As in earlier decades, however, the majority had been tried for routine criminal offences. Like their predecessors, they endured a period of labour on public works before receiving tickets-of-leave entitling them to work for wages for the remainder of their sentence. For the most part, however, their future was not bright. Records from Tasmania (as Van Diemen's Land became in 1856) indicate that most Irish ex-convicts remained in unskilled, low-status work, with a significant minority falling into poverty or being convicted of further offences. A high proportion, in a society where the continuing gender imbalance gave women the power of choice, remained unmarried. There were few equivalents, after

1850, of the chains to riches stories encountered in the first half of
the century. Instead the future lay with the free immigrant.[1]

———

The transfer during the nineteenth century of around one and a half
million immigrants from Europe to the Australian colonies was
achieved almost entirely with the technology of the pre-industrial
world. A steam-powered vessel made its way from Southampton
to Sydney, taking just eighty days, as early as 1852. But the cost of
coal, and the lack of stations at which to refuel on the last long leg
of the voyage, meant that sailing ships remained common even in
the 1870s and 1880s. Reliance on sail in turn meant that travel to
Australia was largely unaffected by the opening in 1869 of the Suez
Canal, where wind-powered vessels had to be expensively towed the
length of the waterway. Ships' captains, in fact, continued to rely on
a trick devised by Portuguese navigators in the fifteenth century,
allowing their vessel to drift westward towards the coast of South
America in order to pick up the countervailing westerlies that
would carry them eastward back towards Africa and the Pacific
Ocean. In the 1830s this had meant a sailing time of about four
months. By the early 1880s piecemeal technological improvements,
in particular the increasing use from the 1850s of iron hulls, or of
wooden hulls sheathed in an alloy of zinc and copper, had made
ships more efficient, while the use of larger vessels eliminated the
need for a stop to take on provisions at the Cape of Good Hope.
But journeys of a hundred days or more remained common.

Accommodation on a typical emigrant ship was almost the same
as on the much shorter transatlantic crossing. Steerage passengers
were packed in beneath the main deck (on some ships on the two
lower decks), with headroom of just over 6 feet. They slept in two
tiers of bunks, measuring 6 feet by 3 for married couples, and 6 by
2 for those travelling alone. Adjoining bunks were divided by a partition, which for more fortunate travellers extended all the way to
the ceiling, but by law needed to be no more than 23 inches. Water

closets for female passengers were located below decks, but those for men were outside, on the main deck, so that in bad weather many chose to remain below, using whatever receptacle, including dishes and cooking pots, came to hand. As the ship passed through the stifling heat of the tropics male passengers frequently chose to sleep outside, on the open deck. Women, for reasons of decency, generally felt they had no such choice, so they remained in the cramped airless space below, already heavy with the stench of waste and bodies that had built up over weeks at sea.[2]

Steerage passengers thus faced an uncomfortable passage. Because the great majority were subsidised, however, and because both ends of their journey lay within the jurisdiction of the British government, the voyage was more closely regulated than the much larger number of sailings to North America. Effective monitoring slackened briefly in the early 1850s, as news of the gold discoveries created an unprecedented demand for passages. During 1852 one in sixty adult passengers on ships chartered by the British Colonial Land and Emigration Commissioners, and an appalling one in five children under four, died during the voyage. There was particular criticism of the decision, quickly reversed, to use American double-decked ships, more capacious but less well-ventilated than British vessels. Two additional Passenger Acts, in 1852 and 1855, further tightened the system of regulation, and as the gold fever passed its peak, conditions on the Australian run returned to normal. After 1854 the death rate for adult passengers was no higher than for the home population as a whole. For the very young, however, the emigrant vessel remained a death trap. Among infants of less than 1 year of age, around one in seven did not survive the voyage. The main reasons were the spread of measles and other infectious diseases, the risk of dehydration in the heat of the tropics, especially when combined with diarrhoea, and, in the case of infants being weaned, the absence of fresh milk. For children born while at sea, of whom again around one in seven would die before landing, the main problems seem to have been premature births induced by the multiple stresses of shipboard life, and the inability of women who were themselves weakened by prolonged seasickness to feed or care for the newborn.[3]

Not all Irish emigrants to Australia travelled steerage. Ireland, a poor society with a well-developed educational system, produced more than its share of disappointed aspirants to a middle-class career. William Foster Stawell, chief justice of Victoria and one of several Irishmen to prosper in the Australian legal system, made his decision to emigrate as a newly qualified barrister in 1842. 'When I saw forty hats on the Munster circuit, and not enough work for twenty, I felt it was time to go, and so I came to Australia.' Irish doctors likewise came in search of opportunities denied them at home, where a general lack of affluence limited the scope for private practice while public appointments combined drudgery with low pay. In particular, reflecting the high reputation of the Dublin Lying-in Hospital as a centre of teaching, a succession of Irish-trained practitioners dominated the obstetrics profession in Victoria for a period of half a century. The Church of Ireland, forced by Whig reformers to accept drastic cuts to its establishment, was another source of genteel immigrants. Around a quarter of the Anglican clergy who served in the Australian colonies in the period up to 1850 were Irish, with graduates of Trinity College, Dublin, as numerous as graduates of Oxford. Not all of those who looked to the colonies for the status denied them at home, however, could hope to be successful. When James Cumine Parkinson, son of an Ulster Protestant clergyman, set out for Victoria in the 1850s, neither his failure to gain admission as a medical student nor an abandoned apprenticeship as a ship's officer had done anything to damage his sense of entitlement. 'This country', he lamented in 1858, 'would be very pleasant if one had good society to mingle in, but the bulk of the population is of the lower caste, so one cannot expect to meet with much kind or refined feelings among them.'

But by 1874, after a failed attempt to run a grocery store, and more time at sea, he was glad to obtain a position as superintendent of a lighthouse just off the Tasmanian coast, with a salary that enabled him to support his wife and six children, but not to keep a servant. He had even acquired a little self-knowledge. 'People in the old country', he wrote to his mother in 1880, 'have queer notions about position. . . . I have long ere this dropped my Irish pride. It does not pay in a new country.'[4]

In Australia, to a much greater extent than in Canada or the United States, the Irish thus contributed, not just to the labour force, but to an emerging professional and social elite. But immigrants of this social class were nevertheless a small minority. Around four out of every five moving from Ireland to Australia received financial assistance from the Colonial Land and Emigration Commissioners or from state governments. Nine out of every ten reported their occupation as labourer or agricultural labourer for men, or domestic servant for women. Just under half of those arriving in the 1850s were able to read and write; by the late 1860s, reflecting a rapid growth in literacy in the Irish population as a whole, the proportion rose to around two-thirds. About seven in ten immigrants, and four out of five of those assisted, were Catholics. As in the case of Argentina, another distant and unfamiliar location, emigrants frequently followed a route established by predecessors, while assisted passages often involved nomination by friends or relatives already in Australia. Both circumstances help to explain why migrants came disproportionately from two regions: a band of counties in the south midlands, extending from Clare and Limerick in the west through Tipperary to Kilkenny and King's County, and the south Ulster counties of Fermanagh, Cavan and Armagh. As in the case of emigration to North America, the Irish differed from other ethnic groups in that the number of men and women was roughly equal. But the future Irish Australians differed from those going to America in the higher proportion, around two out of every five, who travelled as part of a family group. This was because Australian immigration policy, reflecting concerns about the severe gender imbalance in the settler population, was slanted in favour of married couples and single women.[5]

The high proportion of assisted passages claimed by unskilled Irish Catholics outraged many. Employers complained of women ignorant of even the basics of middle-class housekeeping and men whose skills extended no further than digging with a spade and reaping with a hook. Some of the complaints had a basis in fact. 'It's not the same as home', Michael Normile, brought up on a thirty-acre farm in County Clare, explained to his father in 1855. A labouring man had to be 'handy for many different works', such as stock driving on horseback, fence building with axe, saw and adze, or handling a plough, and a newcomer, especially an Irishman, 'is nothing but a real fool for the first year'. Women raised in a typical labourer's or small farmer's cabin were equally unprepared for the duties expected of them as domestic servants. But the criticism also had an edge of ethnic and religious prejudice. As elsewhere in the English-speaking world, cartoons in Australian newspapers and periodicals made frequent use of a standardised visual shorthand, giving Irish characters low foreheads and protruding jaws. Meanwhile, comically loquacious, drunken and belligerent Irishmen passed back and forth across the stages of theatres and music halls. Advertisements for workers, particularly for domestic servants, sometimes carried the notorious rubric 'No Irish need apply'. From the 1880s, as the proportion of potential candidates actually born in Ireland declined, alternatives like 'Protestant preferred' or 'English and Scotch only' became more common.[6]

Explicit antagonism of this kind recalls the experience of Irish immigrants in America. But the two situations were different. Unlike the long-established society of the United States, Australia was a new and therefore a more open society. Just as talented Irish professionals could make their way in medicine, in politics and at the bar, so working-class Irish men and women could take their place in a fluid population largely composed of former convicts or of assisted immigrants drawn from the poorest classes of England and Scotland. There were few Irish among the large-scale industrialists, and the first statistics linking birthplace and occupation, collected for New South Wales in 1901, shows that they were somewhat overrepresented among the unskilled and semi-skilled. But there was no sign of the concentration in particular occupations, characterised by heavy manual work, that was so obvious in both Great Britain and the United States. Men born in Ireland made up 7 per cent of the male workforce, 8 per cent of those employed in construction, and 9 per cent of those involved in transport. Women were most commonly employed in domestic service or in shopkeeping. For most, however, their working career was relatively short. The continuing surplus of men within the population allowed women their choice of marriage partners, and the generally high living standards of late nineteenth-century Australia made it possible for most working-class women to give up paid employment and devote themselves instead to the care of household and children.[7]

Just as Irish Australians were not conspicuously concentrated in particular areas of work, they showed little tendency to crowd into specifically Irish districts. Instead the majority were fairly evenly dispersed both across the different states and within their boundaries. There were a few places where the effects of chain migration, or the natural tendency of immigrants to settle close to those with whom they felt an affinity, produced what was seen as an unusual concentration of Irish. Westbury, in northern Tasmania, was already noted in the nineteenth century for the regular celebrations of St Patrick's Day that have continued to the present day. But even in cases such as this it was unusual for the Irish to be an actual majority. Kiama, south of Sydney, for example, had a reputation as a centre of Ulster Protestant sentiment, with a strong Orange character. Yet in 1861 just 21 per cent of the inhabitants had been born in Ireland, and these would have included a substantial proportion of the 9.5 per cent of residents who were Catholic. In the cities the Irish naturally tended to be more numerous in working-class districts than in the more affluent sections of town. But there was nothing resembling the ethnically defined neighbourhoods of a Chicago or a New York.[8]

None of this means that the new life they found in the different Australian colonies was anything other than arduous and demanding. The reason immigrants could obtain the financial assistance needed to make the long journey south, and could find employment when they arrived, was that the great need of these new societies, as with frontiers of settlement elsewhere, was for the endless supply of workers required to convert a trackless wilderness into what Europeans considered a habitable landscape. 'This country is curious, dear Father', Michael Normile wrote in 1856. 'It is only in its infancy as yet. There is no roads. No bridges cross the rivers.' The labour that was required to gradually subdue this wildness took its toll. 'There is no great deal of comfort in this country', the 32-year-old Edward O'Sullivan, from County Kerry, reported in 1857, after three years in Victoria. 'Every man must work for his livelihood, even men better than 60 years of age.' James Hamilton Twigg, a solicitor's son from County Tyrone, arrived in Western Australia as a young man of 17 in 1891. Having worked on a sheep station, on railway construction and tree felling, he took a grant of land in 1898 but had to go on taking labouring jobs to make ends meet. By 1900, at the age of 26, he was complaining that 'the constant hard living and hard work is making me stiff already. A man here of 30 is to all appearance as old as a man of 45 in the old country.'[9]

The reward for this punishing regime of physical labour, for those able to sustain it, was a standard of living significantly higher than anything those who came from a labouring or small farm background could have hoped to achieve at home. Irish Australians, like their counterparts in the United States, wrote regularly of the profusion and variety of the diet that ordinary wages permitted them to enjoy. A survey in 1891, in fact, suggested that the people of New South Wales had the highest level of food consumption per head of population in the world. The 1850s, when immigration fuelled by gold fever caused the population to more than double, produced a temporary housing crisis: by 1861 almost a third of all houses were classified as temporary dwellings. Thirty years later, on the other hand, the average house had increased in size from three to five rooms, with one room for every resident, compared to two for every three in 1861. The major towns had their separate working-class and middle-class districts. But Australian cities were noted for not having crowded and dangerously insanitary slum districts of the kind that continued to be found in the larger urban centres of the United States, Great Britain and elsewhere. In Victorian Britain urban death rates were around one and a half times what they were in the countryside. Yet Sydney in the 1880s had a death rate no higher than in Great Britain as a whole.[10]

Alongside the availability of work at good wages, and the comfort this brought, immigrants, again like their American counterparts, celebrated their release from the deference and subordination that governed life in their homeland. 'This is the place where a man makes all for himself, independent of any master', a former convict from Tipperary assured his brother in 1856, 'for once you purchase land here you have it for ever without taxes or any other cess.' A farmer's son from County Cork, thirty years later, wrote in a similar vein of friends 'all happy out here away from perhaps tyrannical landlords and Irish bailiffs'. Nor was it only landownership that conferred a release from deference. Before taking up land, John Maxwell of County Down worked as an assistant gardener at a gentleman's house outside Melbourne, and hoped to take over as the coachman. 'The sound of coachman', he told relatives at home, 'will jar in your ears I suppose, but servants in this country are never so much looked down on about gentlemen's places as they are at home, and you are not obliged to do flunkey so much or touch your hat and say yes mam and yes sir, simply yes or no, I will or I haven't time.'[11]

Chronology was also an important influence on the Irish-Australian experience. Immigrants arriving in the 1850s, like Michael Normile, might well encounter a country 'in its infancy', especially if they moved far from the major cities. Over the next few decades, however, they were firsthand witnesses of its transformation into a prosperous, technologically sophisticated society. The McCance family arrived in Victoria in 1853 and settled near Castlemaine, one of the boom towns created by the discovery of gold, where the first stone buildings were just being erected alongside a sea of tents put up by hopeful miners. Five years later John McCance, now working for a mining company, wrote home to County Antrim to describe how the town, and his own township of Chewton, were growing 'as if it were by magic'. By the following year, 1859, work had started on the railway that was to link Chewton to Melbourne and Bendigo. But McCance was more impressed by the four stage coaches a day, with two more at night, that ran between Castlemaine and Melbourne, 'so you may think we are not living in a wilderness or desert. . . . We have also about twenty of all sorts of cabs or busses running to and from Chewton and Castlemaine.' A few months later he was able to send a newspaper with reports of the public gardens at Chewton as well as of 'our great procession which we had in Castlemaine at the laying of the foundation stone of our Benevolent Asylum'. It was at this point that the Irish-Australian and the Irish-American experiences diverged. Whereas the Irish in the United States became the first mass movement of poor immigrants into an already well-developed society, the Irish in Australia had every reason to see themselves as among the builders of a new country, and to demand a share in the credit for what had been achieved.[12]

———

One of the several ways in which Irish immigrants in Australia stood apart from their counterparts in the United States was in the number that chose a rural way of life. In New South Wales in 1901 one-third of men born in Ireland were engaged in agriculture. This was just below the figure for the population as a whole, but significantly higher than the one in four of those born in England and Wales who had followed the same path. The Irish were not well represented among the major stockholders. A study of the 360 most substantial pastoralists in Victoria in 1879 found that 45 per cent were of Scottish origin, holding between them over three million acres, while the Irish made up only 11 per cent, with total land holdings of 640,000 acres. But the opportunities were there for smaller men to become farmers, as well as sheep shearers, herdsmen and general labourers. The free grants of thirty-acre holdings that had allowed emancipated convicts to gain a foothold on the land ended in 1825. But from the 1860s, as the colonies moved towards representative government on a broad male franchise, a new set of land laws allowed would-be farmers to 'select' or apply for plots of Crown land, to be paid for in instalments. The main concentration of Irish landholding, reflecting early grants to convicts and subsequent chain migration, was in the southern part of New South Wales. Selectors also fared relatively well in South Australia, or at least in the region south of the 10-inch annual rainfall line mapped out by the surveyor-general, George Goyder, which emerged as Australia's prime wheat-growing region.

Queensland, as a newer colony, made it relatively easy for newcomers to acquire land. In addition the state government required immigrant vessels to begin disembarking passengers at stops along the coastline before reaching the capital Brisbane, an effective way of placing newcomers on the frontier rather than having them congregate in the towns. The Irish, in consequence, became well represented among graziers and also, in the warmer and moister north, among sugar planters.[13]

To become a selector was a precarious undertaking. Political pressures had forced the different states to declare their commitment to the small farmer. Across much of Australia, however, a dry climate and a grassland of inferior quality created an environment in which large-scale cattle or sheep herding, with stock free to range across wide areas of grazing land, was often the only enterprise capable of sustaining itself. A great deal thus depended on the precise quality and location of the land selected. The inexperienced or poorly informed could make disastrous choices, especially when trees and scrub made land quality difficult to ascertain. Selectors also faced obstruction from the well-established stockholding elite, who were determined to preserve the extensive tracts of Crown land they rented. A favourite technique was 'peacocking': stockholders created a landownership map spotted like a peacock's tail by making claims as selectors, either directly or through intermediaries, for strategically located plots containing water holes or river frontage. This technique ensured that the rest of the district was impossible for anyone else to work profitably. In Victoria, a Royal Commission in 1879 found that one-third of selectors who had acquired land under the most recent land act, ten years earlier, had since lost their holding, one-fifth of the remainder were heavily mortgaged and arrears payments amounted to one-quarter of the state's annual income from land. The selector also committed himself and his family to years of manual labour and frugal living. The early houses of Patrick Durack and his neighbours, according to family lore collected by his granddaughter, were 'of slab timber and stringybark, with thatched roof and shutters swung on greenhide hinges'. There were two rooms, one providing sleeping space for the women and children, the other a living room where the men slept on the floor in their bedrolls or 'swags'. 'The kitchen was an open lean-to. Floors were of hard beaten mud and strewn with hides.'[14]

Yet the rewards, if things went well, were considerable. 'A man who selects in this country', John Maxwell insisted in 1884, 'would have more he could call his own in 10 years than he would have in 20 at home.' One important advantage, once the purchase price was paid, was that with 'no rent to pay and no landlord to fear', a selector could hope to survive a bad year by taking paid work elsewhere until things improved. Maxwell himself did not live to enjoy this security. In 1888 he took 350 acres in Gippsland, New South Wales, but he died three years later, two weeks before the date set for his wedding, of the tuberculosis he had brought with him from Ireland. However two of his brothers, both of whom had up to this point worked as shop assistants or storekeepers, took over his land, and by 1911 one of them was the owner of 1,100 acres freehold and 200 sheep.[15]

For Irish immigrants moving onto the land, particularly in the early years of colonial settlement, drought and crop failure were not the only hazards they had to face. In Tasmania in 1851 the Young Ireland leader John Mitchel, describing his visit to a family named Connell who had emigrated from County Cork thirty-two years earlier, recalled the trials of their early years—'a wild forest to tame and convert into green fields—wilder black natives to watch and keep guard against—and wildest convict bushmen to fight sometimes in their own house'. By the time of Mitchel's visit, however, bushrangers had become less common, while 'the black Tasmanians have all disappeared before convict civilization'. Here Mitchel's bland phrasing concealed an uncomfortable truth: that the Irish, just as much as other immigrants, were inescapably complicit in the often brutal process by which the Aboriginal inhabitants were killed, exiled or beaten into submission in order to make way for the steady expansion of European settlement.[16]

The relationship between Irish Australians and Aboriginal people is today an emotive topic. The well-established image of the Irish as defiant rebels against oppression has encouraged the assumption that those who found themselves in Australia would have been more disposed than other settlers to deal fairly with Indigenous people, their fellow victims of colonialism. In recent decades this image of the Irish as virtuous settlers has encouraged people of mixed Aboriginal and European descent to select an Irish heritage as the ancestry with which to identify. A rugby team in Moree, New South Wales, for example, calls itself the Shamrock Aboriginal Warriors. Yet there is little evidence that Irish settlers were more likely than others to treat Indigenous people as equals, or to see them as anything other than an obstacle to their aspirations for land and profit. In the early days of the colony there were reports of runaway Irish convicts, operating as outlaws in the bush, who had formed expedient alliances with Aboriginal peoples. But there is also a report from a missionary lamenting the violence towards these Indigenous inhabitants of what he called escaped 'croppies' (a nickname for the Irish insurgents of 1798). The appearance of Irish surnames among Aboriginal peoples has been taken as evidence of a willingness on the part of Irish Australians to go beyond casual sex and instead form stable and equal relationships with Indigenous women. But in reality Aboriginal peoples required by officialdom to provide a surname often gave the name of an employer; in other cases, reportedly, the police, among whom the Irish were well represented, assigned whatever surnames came to mind. And other evidence suggests that, as with settlers in general, sexual relationships between Aboriginal women and Irish settlers were most commonly transitory and exploitative, with any children abandoned and disowned.[17]

Attitudes did of course vary among individuals and with circumstances. High-ranking officials, removed from the realities of frontier life, could more easily adopt a moral tone. When settlers massacred around thirty Aboriginal men, women and children at

Myall Creek, New South Wales, in 1838, it was the attorney general, John Hubert Plunkett of County Roscommon, who took the lead in securing the execution of six white men and an Afro Caribbean. But the comments of ordinary emigrants make clear that casual racism was common. To Michael Normile, the farmer's son from County Clare, 'the native blacks' were 'an ugly race of people' who 'go about cadging for the price of drink or tobacco; they don't work'. Nearly thirty years later Alexander Crawford, born into a middle-class, Methodist family in Belfast, wrote casually to his fiancée of the 'nigger hunts' in which he dealt out summary punishment to 'blacks' who had stolen his sheep. In the case of the Duracks, attitudes are filtered through the narrative constructed by Patrick's granddaughter. But the comments, and the silences, are revealing. In relation to the family's selection in New South Wales the tone is condescending: 'The new settlers found their dark-skinned visitors good-humoured and amusing, even helpful in a desultory fashion, until a whim seized them and they were on their way.' A comment attributed to a great-aunt—'there was no fight in the poor things by that time'—follows Mitchel in quietly evading the question of how that submissiveness had been achieved. Later, in the unexplored reaches of Queensland, the attitude shifted to a degree of pragmatic respect. Patrick kept his firearms under lock and key 'for he had strong views on riding armed into the blackman's country'. In the Durack family's final destination, in the Kimberley region of Western Australia, the tone shifts again. The explicit mentions are now of faithful Aboriginal servants. But there are also references to the spearing of cattle and other depredations, and to the sometimes lethal reprisals that regularly followed, accepted if not participated in by the Duracks, whose interests such summary justice helped to protect.[18]

On Thursday 30 November 1854 a large crowd of gold miners assembled on Bakery Hill, a low rise just outside the town of Ballarat in the colony of Victoria. Earlier that day armed police looking for men prospecting without a licence had staged a raid on the pits, in one case firing on a fleeing digger. A 27-year-old Irishman, Peter Lalor, prospecting on the Eureka diggings further from town, called on the miners to organise themselves into a force capable of resisting any repeated aggression from the police or military. Around 1,000 men formed into companies, some with firearms, others with hastily made pikes or even picks and shovels. They withdrew to a hill at Eureka, where they erected a defensive perimeter from the wooden slabs used in the diggings, and began to drill in military style. After Friday and Saturday had passed without incident the number of men on the hill fell to around 150. But on the morning of Sunday 3 December a force of 276 police, cavalry and infantry mounted a surprise attack and overran the miners' camp. Lalor subsequently listed twenty-two miners known to have died, and it is possible that others escaped with wounds that later proved fatal. Five soldiers were also killed and a dozen seriously wounded, while more than a hundred miners were taken prisoner.[19]

The background to this brutal encounter was the gold rush that had followed the discovery of substantial deposits in Victoria in 1851. The number of settlers arriving from overseas—mostly British and Irish, but including some from continental Europe and the United States—rose from around 15,000 in 1851 to more than 90,000 in each of the next two years. There were also migrants from other parts of Australia. Across what had been a sparsely inhabited interior, at Ballarat, Mount Alexander, Bendigo and other sites, disorderly settlements developed, with thousands of tents spread across a blighted landscape that lay stripped of all timber and dotted with roughly excavated pits interspersed with heaps of waste. The licencing system was the colonial government's attempt to maintain some control over these undisciplined conglomerations of transient fortune hunters. The fee of thirty shillings a month was contentious because it had to be paid whether or not a miner found any gold. This was particularly an issue in Ballarat, where the gold lay in long-buried riverbeds at a depth of well over one hundred feet. In effect, the licence fee was a tax on months of what might prove to be wholly profitless digging and bailing. But the miners also resented the thuggish behaviour of the goldfield police as they carried out their regular sweeps in pursuit of unlicensed diggers. An incident in October 1854, when the proprietor of a local hotel had faced no charges after violently ejecting two drunk but apparently inoffensive miners, beating one so badly that he died, added further to the sense of injustice.[20]

Irishmen played a prominent part in the miners' revolt at Bakery Hill. They made up about one in six of those working in the Victoria goldfields. But at the Eureka diggings, chosen by the protesters as their rallying point, they were the largest ethnic group. Of the seventeen miners who were killed in the assault on the stockade and whose nationality is known, ten were Irish, as were ten out of twelve who were wounded. The man who emerged as their leader, Peter Lalor, was a member of an important Irish political family. His father, a prosperous landholder in Queen's County, was an active supporter of Daniel O'Connell's Repeal Party, and from 1833–5 served as Liberal MP for the county. Peter's recently deceased brother, James Fintan Lalor, had been a prominent member of the Young Ireland movement. Peter Lalor's instruction to his followers to equip themselves with pikes has been seen as a conscious echo of the armed rising, inspired by the French Revolution and organised by the United Irishmen, that had convulsed Ireland in 1798. In reality the miners' 'pikes', used only when guns were not available, were put together by a local German blacksmith who was accustomed to turning out similar implements for use against wild dogs and kangaroos. What is true, however, is that one of the passwords used to control entry into the stockade was 'Vinegar Hill', the scene of a celebrated last stand by those engaged in the longest and bloodiest part of the United Irishmen's revolt.[21]

The prominence of Irish-born miners in the revolt at the Eureka Stockade must have confirmed the worst fears of those who regarded immigration from Ireland as a threat to good order. In reality, however, what is striking about the whole episode is the rich mix of influences that were on display. Raffaello Carboni, who became one of Lalor's lieutenants and later stood trial as a ringleader, had fought alongside Garibaldi in defence of the short-lived Roman Republic of 1849. When miners from the Creswick diggings, 12 miles away, arrived to join the Ballarat protest, they marched behind a German band playing the French radical anthem *La Marseillaise*. More prominent still was the influence of the British radical tradition. Several leading figures in the agitation were veterans of the Chartist movement, which between 1837 and 1848 had mobilised large numbers of industrial workers in a campaign for a radical reform of the British political system. When a Reform League was formed on 11 November to accompany the miners' agitation, its objectives—more frequent elections, manhood suffrage, the removal of property qualifications for members of the Legislative Council, and salaries for members of parliament—closely followed the British movement's foundation document, the People's Charter. A poem circulating on the gold field hailed 'brave Lalor' in typical Irish ballad style, but ended with the call 'United Britons, you are omnipotent'. It also referred to the flag raised by the protesters, which incorporated the five stars of the Southern Cross constellation, an emblem already used by bodies campaigning for the different colonies to be united in a self-governing confederation. Here the Ballarat protesters aligned themselves with an emerging Australian national identity, and it is in this light that their brief stand at the Eureka Stockade entered collective memory and continues to be celebrated in Australia to the present day.

Seen in context, then, the Eureka Stockade episode stands out, not as an example of distinctive Irish rebelliousness, but as a landmark in the integration of the Irish into Australian society. These immigrants had clearly not forgotten their country's history of revolt, and they were ready to stand up, in their new homeland, for what they considered their rights. In doing so, however, they merged their grievances with those of fellow immigrants, English, Scots, Germans and others, to create a shared and specifically Australian working-class radicalism. Their stand, moreover, was largely vindicated by subsequent developments. In the aftermath of the attack on the stockade, thirteen leaders of the diggers' protest were put on trial for high treason. However all were acquitted by a jury verdict. Soon afterwards the government of Victoria abolished the system of monthly permits, substituting the much less contentious £1 annual licence and a duty on all gold actually found. There were also important political concessions. Westminster had just granted the colony of Victoria its own parliament, and the new licence conferred on holders the right to vote; when the first parliament met it went on to grant the franchise, by secret ballot, to all adult males. The other Australian colonies acquired parliaments, and adopted adult male suffrage, at about the same time.

Two years after the affray at the Eureka Stockade a new spokesman arrived to articulate precisely this sense of an assertively Irish yet firmly Australian identity. Charles Gavan Duffy's links to Irish revolution were more direct than Peter Lalor's: he had been a leading figure in the Young Ireland movement, escaping prison or transportation only when a jury failed to agree a verdict. He then became a member of the British House of Commons, establishing himself as a friend and associate of leading reformers. Arriving in Melbourne in 1856 he made no secret of his revolutionary past. He was still, he insisted at a dinner in his honour, 'an Irish rebel to the backbone and to the spinal marrow', justifiably so since 'tyranny has supplanted law in my native country'. But he was now in a different world. 'I recognised', he later recalled, 'that this was not Ireland but Australia—Australia, where no nationality need stand on the defensive, for there was fair play for all.' His words were borne out by his own subsequent career. Despite sectarian hostility and gibes about his Irish rebel past, he went on to serve as minister for lands in the government of Victoria, as prime minister of the state during 1871–2, and as Speaker of its Legislative Assembly from 1877 until he left politics in 1880. After his retirement he returned to Europe, but two of his Irish-born sons remained in Australia and enjoyed prominent political careers, one as a government minister and attorney general in Victoria, the other, after federation, as a judge and eventually chief justice of Australia.[22]

'Fair play for all' did not mean equal representation. In the first elections to the parliament of Victoria in 1856, sixteen of the sixty members returned were Irish-born, but only six of these were Catholics. Catholics were also poorly represented in state service, making up only 4 per cent of magistrates and only three out of fifty electoral returning officers. In New South Wales, similarly, only ten Catholics were returned in the elections of 1859, although the Catholic *Freeman's Journal* had estimated that their share of the vote entitled them to twenty-seven seats. Underrepresentation of this kind, however, reflected not just sectarian prejudice, but the small proportion of the Catholic population with the qualifications required for public employment, and the financial means to take up a political career. And in some respects the limitations of Irish political power were an advantage. Because they made up only a quarter of the population, and because, unlike their counterparts in the United States, they did not huddle together in specific Irish neighbourhoods, there was much less temptation to build political platforms around a narrow ethnic vote. Instead the way to political success was through alliances with other groups behind shared political objectives, such as land redistribution or reform of the electoral system. On this basis those Irish Catholics with the means and status to compete for political office achieved some notable successes. Duffy's ally, then rival, in Victoria politics was John O'Shanassy, born in Tipperary in 1818, who had come to Australia in 1839 and built up an impressive fortune, first as a draper then in land and banking. In the unstable factional politics of the late 1850s and early 1860s he served three times as prime minister, and both he and Duffy received knighthoods for their political services. A third Irish Catholic, Sir Bryan O'Loghlen, was prime minister during 1881–3. New South Wales got its first Irish Catholic prime minister, Sir Patrick Jennings, born in County Down, in 1886–7. In Queensland two Irish-born Catholics, John Murtagh Macrossan and Andrew Thynne, held ministerial office during the 1880s and 1890s, and Thomas Joseph Byrnes, son of Irish Catholic immigrants, became prime minister in 1898, only to die five months later.[23]

One other political career confirms the accuracy of Duffy's assessment. When Victoria had its first parliamentary elections in 1856, one of those who came forward was Peter Lalor, for a time in hiding with a price of £200 on his head, but now returned unopposed for a district including Ballarat. In a political career spanning three decades, he was twice to hold government office and spent the last eight years as Speaker of the Legislative Assembly. As a member of parliament he was something of a disappointment to the diggers who had originally supported him. He voted in favour of measures to slightly dilute the new franchise by imposing a minimum period of residence before men became qualified to vote, and by giving extra votes to property holders. In addition, true to his background in the middle ranks of Irish rural society, he opposed demands to 'unlock the lands' by allowing successful miners to invest their profits in small plots of ground, insisting that the multiplication of small-holdings was incompatible with profitable farming. Yet this shift to the conservative centre did not wholly wipe out the memory of his earlier exploits. In 1893, four years after his death, he was commemorated in a granite statue in Ballarat, his Speaker's robes draped so as to conceal the missing left arm, amputated after he was wounded in the assault on the Eureka Stockade. By this time the Australian colonies had come a long way from their origins as a dumping ground for convicted criminals. The career of Peter Lalor, one-time insurgent turned senior parliamentarian, was evidence of how fully their Irish inhabitants, whether free immigrants or former convicts, had shared in that progress.

When Charles Gavan Duffy praised the openness of Australian society, he specified nationality. But he may also have been thinking of religion. The colony had begun as an outgrowth of the confessional state that was the mother country. Convicts were required to attend services of the Protestant episcopal Church of England, and land was set aside for the support of its clergy. But a new Church Act in 1836 took a major step towards denominational equality. For the future, any Anglican, Catholic or Presbyterian congregation that raised £300 towards the cost of erecting a church and a minister's dwelling would receive matching funding from the state, as well as a small continuing stipend for the minister. Meanwhile the successful campaign back in Ireland for Catholic Emancipation had permitted the appointment to public office of two Irish Catholics. In 1829 Roger Therry, a Cork-born barrister, arrived in Sydney to take up an appointment as commissioner of the Court of Requests. When his wife accompanied him to their first mass in the colony, she entered local folklore as supposedly the first woman to appear in that congregation wearing a bonnet, rather than a shawl or mob cap. A second, more prestigious, appointment followed three years later when John Hubert Plunkett, credited with having delivered the Catholic vote in his native Connacht to O'Connell's Repeal Party, became the solicitor general of New South Wales, at a salary of £800. Both men were to have long Australian careers. Plunkett remained in office, first as solicitor general then as attorney general, until 1856, earning fame and notoriety for his prosecution of the Myall Creek killers, and later won election to New South Wales's Legislative Assembly. Therry went on to sit as a judge in the colony's supreme court.[24]

The shift towards pragmatic acceptance of a variety of religious denominations encouraged the development of a more formally organised Australian Catholic Church. William Ullathorne became vicar general in 1833, followed two years later by a bishop, John Polding. In 1842 Polding was promoted to archbishop of Sydney, presiding over suffragan bishops in Hobart and Adelaide, joined by Western Australia in 1845 and Melbourne in 1847. To cater to the rising flow of emigrants from Ireland, the bishops set about an ambitious building programme, erecting parish churches and cathedrals in the fashionable Gothic revival style. William Broughton, the Anglican bishop of Sydney, complained in 1842 of being forced to walk past 'the walls of a vast edifice to be called the Church of "St Patrick"', and worried about the 'sophistries which at no very distant date [are] to be addressed . . . from the gorgeous altars of which I can already trace the foundations'. He was to be further outraged five years later when the government, in a further gesture of religious neutrality, ruled that Polding's status as archbishop meant that he took precedence at official functions over Broughton, a mere bishop.[25]

Protestant disquiet was reinforced by developments in the personnel and management of the expanding Catholic Church. Ullathorne and Polding were both Englishmen and both were Benedictines, members of a religious order that in Britain catered primarily to the education of the small Catholic upper class. Polding's dream was to make this genteel monastic foundation the basis of the Australian mission. However the superiors of the English order were unwilling to release scarce personnel. Instead Polding was forced to turn to Ireland: by the 1850s three-quarters of the clergy serving in Australia were Irish-born. The majority had been trained at All Hallows College, Dublin, established in 1842 to prepare priests for overseas service. Academic standards were less rigorous than at Maynooth, where priests were trained for service in Ireland itself, and the students were drawn from a lower social background. An ethnic division between the leaders of Australian Catholicism and the clergy they ruled over was thus reinforced by a social and cultural gulf. Before long, disgruntled Irish clergy began to complain to Rome about the shortcomings of Polding's leadership and the imperative necessity of appointing bishops of the right nationality to minister to an overwhelmingly Irish Catholic population.

In the contest for control that followed, the Irish party had the advantage of a powerful ally at the heart of Vatican decision-making. Paul Cullen, born in County Kildare in 1803, had been a star student, and then a professor, at the Roman College maintained by Propaganda, the papal department responsible for the Irish mission. From there he went on to become rector of the Irish College in Rome, before being sent back to Ireland as archbishop, first, in 1849, of Armagh and then, in 1852, of Dublin. His fluent Italian, his high reputation in Roman circles, and his knack for maintaining key personal contacts allowed him to become the papacy's main adviser on episcopal appointments across the English-speaking world. One of his protégés, James Quinn, became bishop of Brisbane in 1859. Later, in 1865, Cullen himself promoted the appointment of Quinn's brother Matthew to Bathurst, and of his own secretary, and a distant cousin, James Murray, to Maitland. In addition he and his Australian followers mounted a shameless campaign of slander to block the appointment of Polding's choice of auxiliary and potential successor, whom they improbably accused of frequenting the bedroom of a nun. By the late 1860s the Irish were dominant everywhere except in Polding's Sydney and in Western Australia, which was controlled by Spanish Benedictines. In 1873 Polding was able to take advantage of the waning of Cullen's power at Rome, following a change of papal secretary of state, to secure the appointment of a different candidate, the English Benedictine Roger Vaughan, as his coadjutor and successor. But when Vaughan died in 1883 his successor was Patrick Francis

Moran, bishop of Ossory and a son of Cullen's half-sister. The Irish takeover of Australian Catholicism was complete.[26]

These developments had consequences, not just for the management of the Australian church, but for its public face. By the middle of the nineteenth century the Catholic Church in Ireland had become a self-confident and authoritarian institution, inflexibly committed to upholding its version of theological orthodoxy and the complete separation of Catholics from members of other faiths, in particular through an exclusive control of education. The priests and bishops recruited to staff the expanding Australian mission were the products of this narrow environment, and their outlook had been further shaped by the closed world of All Hallows College and other seminaries. In 1869 the Irish bishops, against the wishes of Archbishop Polding, pushed through a ban on 'mixed' marriages between Catholics and persons of other denominations. Ten years later they turned their attention to education. Following the failure in the 1830s of plans for a single school system acceptable to all denominations, state governments had run a dual system, combining wholly secular state schools with financial support for schools run by the different churches. By the 1860s, however, attitudes had hardened on both sides. State governments scaled down their support for denominational schools. The Irish bishops, meanwhile, denounced the state schools as a dangerous threat to Catholic faith and morals, and in 1879 a joint pastoral letter ordered Catholics throughout the country to withdraw their children. In doing so they initiated a conflict that was to poison for almost a century the relationship between their church and the wider Australian society.

The spectacle of an increasingly combative Catholicism, linked to a steady flow of Irish emigrants, produced a predictable reaction in sections of Australian Protestantism. Already in 1841 the Presbyterian clergyman John Dunmore Lang had published *The Question of Questions: or is the Colony to be Transformed into a Province of Popedom?.* In the first elections to the Legislative Council of New South Wales, in 1843, Lang stood against a wealthy stockholder, Edward Carr, on the explicit grounds that Carr, as a Catholic, was not a fit public representative. In 1849 he came forward again, to lead the campaign of vituperation directed at the 'workhouse orphans'. In the decades that followed politicians like Duffy, O'Shanassy and later O'Loghlen were regularly attacked on the grounds that their religion meant that they could not be trusted to uphold political freedom and that their election would introduce an unhealthy papal influence into government. The Catholic campaign for separate schools launched in 1879 provoked a particularly strong reaction, contributing to the disastrous Victoria election of 1883 in which O'Loghlen and at least half of the Catholic members of the Legislative Assembly lost their seats.[27]

Not all Irish emigrants to Australia were Catholic. The Protestants among them, amounting to about three out of every ten arrivals, also brought with them elements of their distinctive culture. The first lodges of the Protestant supremacist Orange Order appeared in the 1840s. In 1846 the movement achieved brief prominence, when members meeting in a Melbourne hotel to celebrate the Twelfth of July, the anniversary of a victory by Protestant forces in 1690 and the most important event in the movement's public ritual, came under attack from a Catholic crowd. The Orangemen retaliated by firing on the attackers, wounding several. This incident apart, Orangeism remained for the next two decades a relatively obscure transplant from its Irish home. Its status changed in 1868 when Henry James O'Farrell shot and wounded Alfred, Duke of Edinburgh, the second son of Queen Victoria, who was undertaking the first-ever royal tour of Australia. O'Farrell, born in Dublin, had come to Victoria with his family in 1841, at the age of 7 or 8. A failed candidate for the priesthood, an unsuccessful businessman and an alcoholic, he seems to have been mentally disturbed, and to have acted alone. But his actions, coming just a

year after the unsuccessful Fenian rising in Ireland and a number of well-publicised acts of violence on the British mainland,
produced panic and a wave of anti-Irish sentiment. Against this
background the Orange Institution enjoyed an immediate surge
of recruits. By the end of 1868 its membership in New South
Wales had doubled, to 2,000. By 1876 membership had risen to
19,000, and by 1882 to 25,000.

The O'Farrell affair seemed for a time to usher in a new period of religious conflict. In the long run, however, the effect of
the dramatic growth in Orange numbers was to demonstrate the
limited potential of Australian sectarianism. With numerical expansion came a change in ethnic composition: by the last quarter
of the nineteenth century Irish-born members were outnumbered
by English and Scots. Orangeism in this new phase became less the
transfer to Australia of an Irish factional feud than a general Protestant protection association, concerned primarily with favouring
their coreligionists in commercial dealings and employment. The
Twelfth of July continued to be celebrated in Australian towns, but
in many cases noisy processions gave way to picnics and tea parties, still sectional but much less divisive. And where Orange events
did continue to provoke disorder, the attitude of wider Australian
society was one of disapproval, reflecting a widely held view that
insistence on ethnic or sectarian divisions was contrary to the fun-
damental values of this new society. In 1895 a County Tyrone man
who had emigrated in middle age to join a daughter in New South
Wales commented tellingly on the contrast he perceived between
his old and new environments: 'You won't be asked what you are.
At least I haven't yet.'[28]

Irish Catholics, then, did not have a smooth introduction to
Australian society. But the hostility they encountered was not sufficient to produce the defensive tribalism shown by their counterparts in the United States. Australian Catholics were willing
to support their clergy in an ambitious programme of church

building, and also to bear the costs of a separate school system. On the other hand they did not respond to periodic calls, from the church authorities and from Catholic newspapers like the *Freeman's Journal*, to use their electoral muscle in support of Catholic claims in education or other areas. There was no cohesive Catholic vote. Instead Australian Catholics for the most part chose to vote for the candidates that best reflected their social and economic interests. In religious behaviour, too, they were closer to Australian norms than to what was taking shape in the society they had left behind. In Ireland the second half of the nineteenth century saw what has been described as a devotional revolution, producing a near universal compliance with the regime of weekly mass attendance and regular participation in the sacraments that had no parallel in western Europe. In Australia, by contrast, only about one in five Catholics in the mid-nineteenth century were regular church attenders, possibly rising to around twice that level as a result of intense efforts by an expanding parish clergy, but falling back to below one in three by the end of the century. The prohibition of mixed marriages pronounced by the bishops in 1869 had little immediate impact: both before and after around one-third of Catholics married partners of another denomination. By 1911 the proportion of religiously mixed marriages had fallen, but still remained significant, at between one-fifth and one-quarter.[29]

Where the politics of the homeland were concerned, the contrast with Irish America was even more marked. Immigrants in Australia contributed generously to collections for the relief of distress at times of crisis in Ireland, for example following the sudden collapse of agricultural prices in 1879–80. They were less interested in the politics of Irish nationalism, and positively hostile to its more militant varieties. Despite the wild stories that circulated in the press and in establishment circles following O'Farrell's attempt to assassinate the Duke of Edinburgh, there was minimal Australian support for the Fenian movement. Even the centenary of the birth of the much more moderate Daniel O'Connell, in 1875, attracted only lukewarm support. By the 1890s there was more consistent, though still not particularly demonstrative, backing for home rule. But that was only after its endorsement by the British Liberal Party had made this a respectable cause, and only on the basis that what was being demanded for Ireland was the self-government within the empire that Australia already enjoyed. Irish Australians continued to honour their ethnic origins in public celebrations of St Patrick's Day. But the dominant tone was a careful blend, in which national pride and support for moderate nationalism sat beside professions of Australian patriotism and loyalty to queen and empire. In 1900, for example, the organising committee of the Melbourne celebrations took the opportunity to send a telegram in the name of 'the Irish people of Victoria, enjoying the blessings of self government', thanking the queen 'for the kind friendliness displayed by her proposed visit to Ireland', which they hoped might be a prelude to home rule.[30]

At this point a problem looms. How is an account that emphasises largely successful assimilation to be reconciled with the life of nineteenth-century Australia's most famous Irishman? Edward 'Ned' Kelly was born in Victoria in 1854, the son of a Tipperary man transported in 1841 for the theft of two pigs. He had his first brush with the law when he was arrested, aged 16, as a suspected associate of the bushranger Harry Power. In 1878, following further arrests and periods of imprisonment, he and others killed three police who were tracking them in the bush. Now irredeemably committed to a life as outlaws, Kelly and his gang robbed the bank at the small town of Euroa in December 1878. In February 1879 they crossed the border into New South Wales to take over the small but thriving town of Jerilderie. They remained there for two days, during which they took £2,000 from the local bank and burned documents from its safe, wiping out the evidence of mortgages and other debts owed by the local farming population. After a lengthy manhunt, during which his men killed an associate who had been assisting the police, Kelly was taken prisoner in June 1880. He was hanged four months later.

Perceptions of Ned Kelly's criminal career as an Irish revolt are not entirely unfounded. Of 124 individuals identified by the police as supporters of the gang, just over three-quarters were either Irish-born or of Irish parentage. Kelly's own testament, the 8,000-word manifesto that he left behind at Jerilderie, is a personal apologia, detailing with evident passion the victimisation at the hands of the Victoria police that had pushed him into a full-blown criminal career as a horse thief and bank robber. But the text is shot through with Irish references: Irish members of the police force are a disgrace to their ancestors and country, having 'deserted the shamrock, the emblem of true wit and beauty to serve under a flag and nation that has destroyed massacred and murdered their forefathers'. There are references to the penal colony at Tasmania, where 'many a blooming Irish-man rather than subdue to the Saxon yoke, were flogged to death and bravely died in servile chains but true to the shamrock and a credit to Paddy's land'. There is speculation about a possible war between Britain and the United States, where the numerous Irishmen in the British army might take up 'the colour they dare not wear for years, and to reinstate it and rise old Erin's isle once more, from the pressure and tyrannism of the English yoke, and which has kept in poverty and starvation'. The idiom too has striking Irish features. The denunciation of the police, with its piling up of adjectives ('a parcel of big ugly fat-necked wombat headed big bellied magpie legged narrow hipped splaw-footed sons of Irish Bailiffs or English landlords') is a clear echo of the Gaelic Irish literary tradition. And the final admonition, following the warning against helping the police, has an incantatory formality characteristic of the threatening letters that commonly accompanied agrarian protest in faraway Tipperary: 'I am a widow's son out-lawed and my orders <u>must</u> be <u>obeyed</u>'.[31]

Ned Kelly thus stands as a reminder that the Irish story in Aus-tralia had its darker side. The selector system allowed many Irish immigrants to achieve a prosperity and independence that would never have been possible in their homeland. But there were oth-ers, like the Kellys, who had merely exchanged one state of rural poverty for another, while enduring the contempt and hostility of wealthy stockholders and harassment at the hands of police and magistrates. It is no surprise that some among them responded will-ingly to Kelly's flamboyant defiance, and to gestures like his public destruction of the record of poor men's debt. Yet his short and vio-lent life, for all its drama, must be seen in context. He was not the only Irish outlaw to trouble Australian society. Of one hundred of the most prominent bushrangers active between 1789 and 1901, twenty-two were Irish-born. Fifteen of the thirty Australian-born were Catholics, and therefore probably also of Irish descent. But then the Irish, as Kelly's own invective indicated, were also prom-inent in the police. Two-thirds of the New South Wales police in 1865, and no less than four-fifths of the Victoria police in 1874, were Irish-born, roughly evenly divided between Protestant and Catholic. The judicial statistics also rule out any suggestion either of concerted opposition to the law or of systematic victimisation. Irishmen were overrepresented in the overall statistics for those arrested and convicted by the courts. But the offences concerned were for the most part minor misdemeanours such as drunkenness and brawling. That is a pattern that might be explained, at least in part, by the preponderance in the Irish immigrant population of young, single, working-class males. Where more serious offences are concerned, about one-quarter of the men hanged in the state of Victoria between 1842 and 1891 were Irish Catholics. That is roughly their share of the total population. The hanged made up only a minority of those actually sentenced to death. But here again a study of the commutation of death sentences reveals no evidence of an anti-Irish bias in the choice of who was and was not to die. In political terms, too, Kelly's armed rebellion against an oppressive social order must be set against the preference of the great majority of his countrymen for assimilation rather than confrontation. Conflict, ethnic and sectarian, certainly existed. But Peter Lalor's progress from the Eureka Stockade to the parliament of Victoria is a better symbol of the trajectory of Irish Australia than Ned Kelly's short career as a widow's son outlawed.[32]

What, then, should we make of the Jerilderie letter? Images of Ned Kelly as the heir to some proud tradition of nationalist-inspired rebellion are not borne out by the record. His father had been transported for the theft of two pigs from a neighbour, a landless labourer as poor as himself, and there are indications that he earned a lighter sentence by giving evidence against some confederates. His reputation in Australia was of 'a timid man, averse to quarrelling'. But that makes it all the more striking that his son, growing up under his roof, should nevertheless have absorbed so much of the language of Irish nationalist grievance. Some of the more baroque details in Kelly's manifesto ('by the greatest of torture as rolling them down hill in spiked barrels pulling their toe and finger nails and on the wheel, and every torture imaginable') seem to relate to an early Christian, or possibly English, martyrology, rather than anything identifiably Irish, pointing perhaps to memories of sermons or of some particularly lively piece of religious instruction. Tales of the sufferings of transportees may well have been based on things heard from former convicts. But if so, both elements were folded into a wider narrative of an oppressed nation struggling to free itself from 'the Saxon yoke'.[33]

To read the Jerilderie letter is thus to trace the route of a road not travelled. What it offers is a glimpse of the political culture that poorer Catholic immigrants brought with them from Ireland: a strong sense of past wrongs, blending memories of political oppression and religious persecution. In the United States these traditions provided the basis for a continuing culture of grievance, in which Irish immigrants saw their exile from the homeland as part of the broader story of an oppressed nation, and gave their support to a militant Irish nationalism. The same folk history may well have led many Irish Australians to experience a vicarious thrill as they observed Ned Kelly blaze his defiant path across Victoria, or as they sang the ballad of 'Bold Jack Donahoe', who 'scorned to live in slavery, or humble to the Crown'. In their real lives, however, the great majority preferred to buy into the dominant narrative of their new home, the notion of Australia as a land where the conflicts and inequalities of the Old World were left behind. Faced with a new, growing and still fluid society, in which they were not denied the right to claim their place among its founders, they followed Charles Gavan Duffy in proclaiming that this was not Ireland but Australia.[34]

More than 2,500 miles to the east, on the other side of the Tasman Sea, another 'new Ireland' was taking shape. For several decades English and other settlers had been present in New Zealand, trading with the Indigenous population, the Maori, for whalebone and whale oil, flax, sealskin and timber. Eventually the British government, anxious to impose order on an unregulated frontier, and uneasily aware of French interest in the territory, declared the islands a Crown colony. Under a charter issued on 16 November 1840, what had been known as the North Island was now to be New Ulster. The South Island became New Munster, and a minor offshore island New Leinster. The names were probably the choice of William Hobson, born in Waterford in 1793 and one of several Irishmen to play an important part in the history of New Zealand. Having served with distinction against pirates and slave traders in the Mediterranean and West Indies, he had been appointed lieutenant governor of the territory in 1839 and had negotiated the agreement with

the Maori, the Treaty of Waitangi, that became the colony's founding document. In naming the two large islands and their minor
appendage he may conceivably have looked back to the two large-
scale plantations that had been the main building blocks of British settlement in sixteenth- and early seventeenth-century Ireland.
More probably he simply reached for familiar place names. But in
either case the Irish themed—colony in the southern hemisphere did
not last long. In 1846 New Ulster and New Munster became provinces, giving the names an administrative as well as a geographical
significance. But in 1853 London reorganised the growing colony
into six provinces, and the two main land masses once again became North and South Island.

Nomenclature aside, the Irish presence in the early years of
New Zealand was marginal. The voyage was even longer than the
journey to Australia, taking anything from three to six months,
and the fare—£18 to £24 in the mid-1850s—was much higher
than the cost of crossing the Atlantic. There was also no penal
transportation to provide the involuntary immigrants who might
become the nucleus of an Irish population. Even in 1858, when
the Pakeha, or non-Maori, population stood at just under 60,000,
only 4,554, fewer than one in ten, had been born in Ireland. Many
of these had probably come from Australia, in search of work or a
less extreme climate. Following the discovery of gold in two parts
of the South Island, Otago in the southeast in 1861, and the West
Coast in 1865, the Irish-born population rose sharply, to just under
30,000 by 1871. But this was still just under one in eight of what
was by now a much-expanded white New Zealand population.
Many of these new immigrants had, once again, come to New
Zealand via Australia, or in some cases via California.

Direct immigration from Ireland to New Zealand became significant only after the gold rush had ended. As the number of new
settlers fell, threatening the colony's future, Julius Vogel, treasurer
and later prime minister, launched an ambitious programme of

assisted immigration. One part of the scheme involved the appointment in 1871 of an agent in London, who would direct a network of subagents charged with recruiting suitable candidates for free or subsidised transport to New Zealand. It quickly became clear, however, that the agent, with what looks like the tacit support of Vogel, was largely ignoring Ireland. By 1873 a campaign of protest, headed by the *New Zealand Tablet*, the campaigning Catholic newspaper recently established by the Irish-born bishop of Dunedin, Patrick Moran, forced the government to provide direct sailings from Ireland. However only ten vessels sailed during the 1870s, seven of which left from Ulster ports. Of much more importance in the rest of Ireland was a second scheme that permitted those already in the colony, on payment of a fee, to nominate relatives or others for free or assisted passage. Again there were complaints that the London agent and his assistants put unreasonable obstacles in the way of Irish Catholic nominees. The Irish, however, already familiar with the procedures of British bureaucracy, proved to be tenacious applicants. In addition, as in Australia, they had on their side the colony's pressing need for labourers, servants and female marriage partners. Of the 100,000 assisted emigrants who arrived in New Zealand during the 1870s a quarter or more were Irish. By 1886 almost one in five (18.8 per cent) of the non-Maori population was of Irish birth or descent.[35]

A destination as distant and unfamiliar as New Zealand made it even more desirable than usual that emigrants should have the example and assistance of predecessors. Heavy reliance on the nomination system had the same effect. So it is no surprise that settlement from Ireland had a strong regional character. Three-quarters or more of the New Zealand Irish in the second half of the nineteenth century came from two of Ireland's four provinces, Munster and Ulster, with the counties of Antrim, Down, Cork, Limerick and Clare standing out as the most prominent. The prominence of Ulster is understandable, given that it was the main focus of the limited attention that the New Zealand government's agents devoted to Ireland. The three shiploads that, under pressure, they had eventually organised from other parts of Ireland, equally, had all sailed from Cork. Beyond this Clare and Limerick were two of the three counties topping the list of those sending the largest number of emigrants to Australia, and were thus presumably well represented among the significant number of Irish who made their way from there to New Zealand. Of the assisted emigrants, three out of five were single adults. Where Australia had succeeded in attracting roughly equal numbers of male and female emigrants, however, Irish women seem to have found New Zealand a less attractive, or a more daunting, prospect. Single men outnumbered single women two to one, so that the gender balance within the Irish population improved, but remained skewed. The number of Irish women for every 1,000 Irish men rose from 679 in 1874 to 784 by 1881. Protestants were also overrepresented, making up around a quarter of the population of Ireland, but two-fifths or more of those coming to New Zealand.[36]

A few Irish settlers brought resources with them. The parents of William Massey, the future prime minister, disposed of small amounts of freehold and leasehold land near Limavady, County Londonderry. This allowed them to travel to New Zealand in 1862 as fare-paying passengers, which in turn entitled them, as a couple with two children, to a grant of eighty acres near Auckland. The great majority, however, were assisted emigrants, and of these most men were categorised as agricultural labourers, and most women as domestic servants. But in a setting where a landscape featuring cleared fields, roads and bridges was still taking shape, and rough settlements were only gradually maturing into towns and cities, this was not necessarily a disadvantage. 'There is nowhere else on earth', a new resident of Auckland informed a friend back in Ulster in 1864, 'that the willing working man or woman can be so well rewarded for their labour. . . . Many lay by the surplus of their earnings, purchase building ground and soon knock up a weather-board house, which will last some 20 years. They are then on the way to independence.' An Antrim man, eighteen years later, was surprised to find that 'there is no such thing as poor people. I have been in Port Chalmers, Lyttleton, Wellington and Waganui, and I have not seen a beggar or a house that you would say was a poor man's.' In this favourable environment Irish immigrants, like their Australian counterparts, were quickly integrated into economic life. Their distribution across the different provinces, and between cities and rural areas (roughly 45 per cent rural), closely matched that of the population as a whole; there were no notable Irish ghettos. Nor was there any marked religious distinction. Statistics collected in 1921 showed that the occupations of Catholics, the great majority of whom were of Irish descent, closely matched those of other New Zealanders. Fourteen per cent of Catholic men, for example, were farmers, compared to 16 per cent of the whole male population.[37]

New Zealand was closely tied to the United Kingdom by its exports of meat, cheese and butter. It also depended on the Royal Navy for protection against the predatory great powers—first France, later Germany and Japan—that were active in the Pacific. This made it the most British of what became the white dominions. Irish Protestants thus had little difficulty finding a place in its public life. Ethnic stereotypes could not be escaped entirely. Opponents of Edward Stafford, three times prime minister and a dominant figure in the first two decades of responsible government, were quick to dismiss his sometimes bumptious manner as the behaviour of 'a bragging Irishman'. His much less eminent rival, James Edward Fitzgerald, like Stafford the son of a landed family, could be praised as a 'thorough Irish gentleman—quick, impulsive, witty and winning in manner and conversation'. Both Stafford and Fitzgerald, however, were southern Irish, the first from County Louth, the second from Queen's County. In contrast, two Protestant Ulstermen seem to have become the key figures in the shift towards a more clearly defined party politics in the 1890s without their origins becoming the subject of significant comment. John Ballance, born in County Antrim in 1839, and living in New Zealand from 1866, marshalled a loose coalition of parliamentarians into an effective party, and became prime minister at the head of the first Liberal government in 1891. In the following decade William Massey, whose parents had left Limavady in 1862, organised the opponents of the Liberals into a Reform Party, and went on to head a series of administrations between 1912 and 1925.[38]

No Irish Catholic achieved the same prominence, in this period, as Ballance and Massey. A number, however, rose high enough to make clear that their background did not exclude them from a successful public career. Patrick Dignan from County Galway became a successful hotelier and businessman in Auckland, which he represented in the House of Representatives from 1867 until 1879. His son became the city's first New Zealand–born mayor in 1897. Patrick Buckley, born in County Cork in 1840 or 1841 and a veteran of the Irish force raised to defend the Papal States against Italian nationalists in 1859–60, was a member of the appointed upper house and held portfolios in three governments between 1884 and 1895. John Tole, born in Yorkshire to Irish Catholic parents, was minister of justice during 1884–7. At a higher level of achievement Joseph Ward, born in Melbourne in 1856 to Irish immigrant parents, became postmaster general in Ballance's Liberal government, and received a knighthood in 1901. His religion did cause problems. In particular he was dogged by complaints that under his control the rapidly expanding postal system came to employ disproportionate numbers of Catholics. But when Ballance's successor Richard Seddon died in office in 1906, Ward succeeded him as prime minister and went on to lead the Liberals to victory in the election of 1908. He later served as deputy prime minister, under Massey, in a wartime coalition between 1915 and 1919, and had a last, sad spell as prime minister during 1928–30, when, old and ailing, he presided over a chaotic mixed ministry as New Zealand was drawn into the world economic crisis of the Great Depression.

Outside the sphere of party politics, there were occasional episodes of friction between Catholic and Protestant settlers. The most serious were in 1868, at the high point of excitement about the activities in Ireland and abroad of the revolutionary Fenian movement. In February and March, Catholics in several centres organised events to honour the Manchester Martyrs, three men executed for the death of an English policeman who had been killed by a stray bullet during the attempted rescue of a prisoner. The demonstrations passed off peacefully. Soon after, however, the news from Sydney of O'Farrell's attack on the Duke of Edinburgh pushed the authorities into arresting seven organisers of the most elaborate Fenian procession in New Zealand, at Hokitika on the West Coast. Two of them, a journalist who had earlier been acquitted of treason following his part in the Eureka Stockade revolt, and a Catholic priest who had delivered the oration at Hokitika, received short jail sentences. An episode in nearby Addison's Flat, where Irish Catholics attacked Protestants assembled to celebrate the duke's escape from death, added to the excitement. A local official, however, dismissed the affair as 'a miserable little street row', easily mended with 12 inches of sticking plaster and a ten shilling note. Equally important, there was no surge of local Irish support for the imprisoned priest and journalist. A second open display of sectarian animosity occurred just over a decade later in 1879, when groups of Catholics mobilised to oppose attempts by Orange lodges to stage Boxing Day processions in the two main centres of the east-central region of Canterbury on the South Island. At Timaru between two and three hundred opponents surrounded the forty loyalists and forced them to remove their Orange regalia. Events at Christchurch to the north took a nastier turn, as around thirty men armed with pickaxe handles charged the Orange marchers. But the excitement was short lived. Orange lodges had spread through New Zealand only in the preceding fifteen years, and the 1879 Boxing Day displays were a first attempt by Canterbury's Orangemen to claim public space for processions in full regalia. In the aftermath they made their point by staging large-scale processions on 12 July 1880. Having done so, however, they then reverted to their less provocative previous routine of balls and dinners.[39]

Events on the West Coast in 1868, and in Canterbury eleven years later, make clear that both Catholics and Protestants brought with them allegiances and animosities that could provide the basis for violent sectarian conflict. In New Zealand, however, they found a society with no entrenched system of denominational privilege or sectarian exclusiveness, but instead a rough equality of opportunity. In this new climate, inherited animosities failed to thrive. The town of Katikati on the Bay of Plenty, established by the entrepreneur George Vesey Stewart, who recruited his settlers through Orange lodges, became the centre of a community of just over 500 Ulster Protestants. But their Twelfth of July marches were low-key affairs, reportedly supported even by the district's Catholic residents. By the late 1880s the marches had been abandoned in favour of a ball, and in 1892 the Twelfth of July went wholly unobserved. Letters home from Irish migrants, whether Catholic or Protestant, included few references to sectarian discord. The Anglican bishop of Auckland, travelling in 1906, noted wryly in his diary that a hotel kept by 'church people' had 'as usual, charged the bishop double'. The following night, on the other hand, 'Stayed in hotel kept by R.C.'s, who, as usual, charged nothing'.[40]

As elsewhere the arrival of large numbers of Irish immigrants forced major changes on the New Zealand Catholic Church. Since 1838 responsibility for ministering both to the Maori and to the Pakeha population had lain with the French Marist order. In 1870, however, Cardinal Cullen used his influence at Rome to secure the appointment of County Wicklow–born Patrick Moran to the new diocese of Dunedin. This was followed a year later by the succession to Auckland of Cullen's former student at the Irish College in Rome, Thomas Croke. For a time it looked as if the Marists were to follow the Australian Benedictines in being shouldered aside by aggressive Irish empire building. Croke, however, sabotaged his patron's plans by engineering his own transfer back to the more congenial environment of Ireland. When he left in 1874 to become archbishop of Cashel, his successor was a Dutch Jesuit. Meanwhile the Marists proved more adept than the Australian Benedictines at fighting their corner in Rome. To meet the argument that the English language was now central to the New Zealand mission they successfully put forward English-born members of their order for Wellington in 1872 and for the new diocese of Christchurch in 1887. They also imported Irish priests from the order's seminaries at Dublin and Dundalk. The Marists thus retained a place within the New Zealand Catholic Church, but only at the price of themselves becoming more Irish. Even then, once the need for an English-speaking clergy had been accepted, they could do no more than postpone the inevitable. Of the eighteen New Zealand bishops appointed between 1869 and 1950, fifteen were of Irish birth or descent, including all of those appointed after 1890. Among the lower clergy, meanwhile, the Irish, many recruited from All Hallows College, steadily eclipsed the French. As late as 1976, in all but one of New Zealand's dioceses, more than a quarter of the priests employed had been born in Ireland.[41]

New Zealand's Irish Catholics, like their counterparts in Australia and the United States, were thus offered an appealing blend of religious and ethnic allegiance. Yet the Catholic Church was never able to achieve the level of control that by this time had become the norm in Ireland. It is true that Catholics did not contribute to the general decline in religious practice that affected late nineteenth- and early twentieth-century New Zealand. Between 1886 and 1926, when overall church attendance fell from 48 per cent to 27 per cent of the population aged 15 and above, Catholic attendance varied between 47 and 58 per cent, with no clear trend over time. But this was well below the near-total conformity that by this time prevailed in Ireland. In education the Irish bishops, backed by Rome, condemned the free, non-denominational provision offered in the state system, instead demanding that Catholic parents support an independent network of Catholic denominational schools. Yet in 1926 just under three out of five primary school pupils were in Catholic schools. Irish voters also largely ignored calls from their bishops and clergy to give their votes only to candidates willing to support state funding for separate Catholic provision. Instead they preferred to support candidates whose other policies they found attractive. This was especially true, as in the case of many in the Liberal Party, when a candidate's strong commitment to secular education was compensated for by their support for the granting to Ireland of some form of self-government. Where marriage was concerned, the bonds of community were stronger. A study of Christchurch between 1860 and 1889 found that all but 3 per cent of Irish Catholic bridegrooms chose partners of the same background. Among women, however, the proportion opting for Irish partners was not quite three-quarters, and of those choosing otherwise, three out of four married a non-Catholic. The most likely explanation, as in the cases of Australia and California, is that their scarcity value as marriage partners gave women more opportunity to trade up in social and economic terms. Taken together, the statistics on church attendance, schooling and marriage suggest the same broad picture. There was clearly a New Zealand Catholic identity but it was not all-encompassing. What we see is a subculture rather than a ghetto.[42]

One reason for this relatively smooth integration into the wider society may have been the extra pressure for white solidarity in the face of the Indigenous population. Between 1860 and 1872 the Maori engaged in a series of wars; at their peak 18,000 British troops were deployed to contain around 5,000 fighters. Nationalist journalists in Ireland and America depicted the Maori as counterparts of the Irish, defending their homeland against Anglo-Saxon invaders. In New Zealand itself there were claims that Irishmen with Fenian sympathies had supplied the Maori with arms, or even fought alongside them. But any such renegades were hugely outnumbered by the number of Irishmen, Catholic as well as Protestant, who took part in the violent re-assertion of imperial control, either as part of the regular British army or in the colonial militia. The sophisticated structure of Maori society, and the effective military resistance it made possible, led some observers to accord it a respect denied to Aboriginal people in Australia, or to Native Americans. But a County Antrim immigrant, writing in 1884, was dismissive. Indigenous people adopted Western dress outside their villages, but did not know how to wear it: 'You would think they had been thrown on with a pitchfork. . . . There is some of them intelligent enough looking, but to me they are nearly all repulsive looking.' Other Irish letter writers resorted to casually racist language, referring to the Maori as 'niggers'.[43]

7

THE MAKING OF
IRISH AMERICA

The participation of Irish Americans in the Civil War failed to
secure them the acceptance many had hoped for. That much was
evident in the conflict's long ceremonial aftermath. In the South,
where the Irish had never been numerous enough to be resented,
and where they could be seen as fellow victims of Reconstruction,
the service of Irish units, and the exploits of noted Irish commanders, readily found a place in the monuments, statues and
ceremonies with which the defeated supporters of the Confederacy demonstrated their continued devotion to the Lost Cause. In
the North, however, the main vehicle for commemoration was the
Grand Army of the Republic, a fraternal organisation for Union
veterans. Dominated by former Yankee officers, and with a strong

Protestant and Republican Party flavour, it attracted few Irish former combatants.[1]

In the immediate postwar period two further sets of incidents seemed to confirm that the Irish still lay beyond the boundaries of respectable American society. In 1871 troops once again battled Irish rioters on the streets of New York. This time the occasion was a planned Twelfth of July parade by members of the Orange Institution. The previous year Irish labourers employed on major public works, including the laying out of Central Park and of what was to become the upper part of Broadway, had attacked an Orange gathering in Elm Park, allegedly in response to the playing of sectarian tunes. The Orangemen fought back with knives and pistols. As the fighting spread through the surrounding district, eight men were killed and, according to one estimate, around a hundred injured. Now, in 1871, the lodges attempted a formal parade from their headquarters on the corner of Eighth Avenue and Twenty-third Street. Around a hundred marchers set out, accompanied by a strong escort of police and National Guard, but immediately came under attack. In the fighting that followed, sixty-two civilians were killed, as well as three members of the National Guard and two policemen.

Responsibility for this bloodshed lay partly with the city and state government. The mayor, A. Oakey Hall, was a Democrat elected with the help of Irish votes. He initially prohibited the planned Orange parade, but sought to ward off criticism by having the superintendent of police, James Kelso, a Protestant, sign the order. The state governor, John T. Hoffman, had also come to office with Irish backing. However he was now in search of the broader support base that might allow him to seek nomination as a Democratic candidate for president. As protest mounted against what was seen as a surrender to the threat of Irish Catholic violence, he intervened, on 11 July, to countermand Kelso's proclamation and insist that the parade go ahead. (His claim that he had not been consulted about the ban in advance was disputed by others.) The uncertainty that these self-interested manoeuvrings created undoubtedly contributed to the build-up of tension. More serious blame was attached to the National Guard. Some of their number openly displayed their loyalties by cheering the Orangemen when they appeared. And at a certain point they responded to attack by firing volleys directly into the crowds that surrounded them. Of the fifty-six civilian deaths whose cause can be identified, all but one was due to military gunfire. To many observers, however, the blame for the violence lay, once again, with the Catholic Irish. Kelso's ban, one newspaper complained, was a surrender to 'this same Irish Catholic mob, which hung negros and killed babies and burned orphan asylums'.[2]

The other set of events that kept alive the image of the Irish as an alien and threatening presence in American society took place over a number of years, in the coalfields of eastern Pennsylvania. Here what was involved was not the depredations of the urban crowd but a transfer to North America of the well-developed Irish tradition of the secret society. During 1862–3 Schuylkill County, home to around 13,000 Irish immigrants in a total foreign-born population of 31,000, was the scene of violent demonstrations against the draft. The same years saw the first of a series of killings and assaults that continued into 1868. The victims were all mine owners or officials, and the motives, as far as they can be ascertained, combined labour grievances, punishment for cooperating in the implementation of the draft, the settling of private scores, and in two cases highway robbery. The violence was reported to be the work of a society, the Molly Maguires. This was a name frequently used in parts of the north and west of Ireland from the 1840s onwards. It described a variety of secret organisations that sought to protect the interests of the rural poor by threatening and where necessary attacking landlords and their agents, large farmers or shopkeepers. After a period of relative quiet the Pennsylvania Molly Maguires became active again during 1874–5. Two of the eight further kill-ings attributed to the society arose out of a succession of violent clashes between Irish and Welsh miners; another was of a Welsh mine official alleged to discriminate in favour of his own country-men. There was also a policeman, shot at the instigation of a miner he had beaten up. By this time, however, the leading employer in the area had hired the Pinkerton National Detective Agency, which had dispatched an agent, Armagh-born James McParland, to infil-trate the Irish community. During 1876–8 the authorities staged a series of trials of alleged Molly Maguires, for offences going back to 1862. Ten of those convicted were hanged on the same day in June 1877, an act of concentrated retribution clearly intended to intimi-date the unruly coalfields. Ten more alleged culprits were executed over the next two years, following further trials and the rejection of appeals.[3]

At first sight the murderous activities of the Molly Maguires, and the ruthless repression that followed, was further evidence that the immigrant Irish had no hope of finding acceptance in Ameri-can society. But appearances were deceptive. The eastern Pennsyl-vania coalfields were an exceptionally harsh environment, where men laboured underground in narrow, poorly ventilated shafts, and were in constant danger from cave ins and flooding. There were bitter divisions, not just between management and workers, but between miners and unskilled labourers and between ethnic groups, in particular between Irish and Welsh. The Irish who re-sponded to these conditions by turning to the brand of crude pro-test, shading into gangsterism, represented by the Molly Maguires, were not typical. They were disproportionately drawn from the northwestern corner of Ireland, in particular from Donegal. This was a region where the name of Molly Maguire was well known. But it was also one of the poorest parts of Ireland, largely Irish speaking and dominated by subsistence agriculture. The violence in Schuylkill County, in other words, was the response of a section of the immigrant population particularly poorly equipped to adjust to the new world they encountered. Other Irish immigrants were more likely to turn to trade unionism. The Workingmen's Benevolent Association, despite the innocuous name, was a campaigning trade union that spread through the mining district from 1868. Roughly half of the executive board of the union had Irish names. The leading organiser, John Siney, was a very different type of Irish immigrant to the Irish-speaking Donegal men of the Molly Maguires. Born in Queen's County in 1831, he was the son of a small farmer whose family had moved to Lancashire, England, when he was five. He worked in a cotton mill and on building sites, and was actively involved in British trade unionism, and in the radical Chartist movement, before making the move to the United States in 1863. Under his leadership the Workingmen's Benevolent Association forcefully rejected violence, emphasising instead the common interests of labour and capital and the potential of peaceful collective bargaining. One of its major achievements was local legislation dramatically improving safety standards in the mines of Schuylkill County.[4]

What was true of the Irish in Pennsylvania was also true elsewhere. Provoked or threatened, some among them were still capable of violence. But violence was no longer their only resource. In the case of the New York anti-Orange riot of 1871, the issue was not just the potential for Irish mobs to take to the streets as they had done the previous year. Instead, as the political manoeuvrings of the mayor and governor made clear, the real problem for those in charge of the city was that the Irish had become a cohesive political body, allied to, but never to be taken for granted by, the Democratic political machine run from Tammany Hall. If the Irish stood aloof from—or were frozen out of—mainstream commemorations of the Civil War, equally, they responded by creating their own alternative organisations to make sure that their contribution to the Union cause could not be ignored. In 1888, for example, they erected a monument at Gettysburg to the New York regiments of the Irish Brigade. There was also a celebratory history of the Brigade, published in 1867 by David Power Conyngham, a journalist and staff officer for Thomas Francis Meagher, the Young Ireland leader and commander of the Irish Brigade. In all three cases the message was the same. The Irish were still not fully accepted. But they had begun to develop resources that would ensure that their interests were defended and that their place in American society would be acknowledged if not admired.[5]

One of the most important of those resources was the Catholic Church. This was not an outcome that should be taken for granted. Immigrants arriving in the United States in the second half of the nineteenth century, shaped by the dramatic remaking of religious culture known as the devotional revolution, were increasingly likely to be regular church attenders. But many of their predecessors, including those who had arrived in such huge numbers during and just after the Famine, brought with them a Catholicism that rested on a much looser body of belief and practice. Their religious identity was then subjected to further trials as the majority entered mushrooming urban centres where the familiar social landmarks that had kept them in some sort of contact with organised religion no longer existed, and where the clergy struggled to maintain even sporadic contact with ever-increasing flocks. In Ireland the ratio of one priest for every 3,000 Catholics that existed on the eve of the Famine was regarded as much too high; by the 1870s it was to fall to one to every 1,560. In New York in the mid-nineteenth century that ratio was one to 4,500, and in western states one to 7,000. John Hughes, the future archbishop of New York, who took his first position as a priest in Philadelphia in 1826, estimated that only one out of every fifteen of that city's Catholics was a regular communicant. Yet from these unpromising beginnings there developed a strong religious culture. In the second half of the nineteenth century there was general agreement that church attendance among Irish Americans was significantly higher than among other Catholic ethnic groups, suggesting a level somewhere above the overall American average of around 50 per cent. This was not as high as the 90 per cent or more attendance rate that came to prevail back home in Ireland. But by the standards of most predominantly urban, industrial populations it was an impressive pastoral achievement.[6]

From another point of view the importance that the Catholic Church came to assume in the lives of the American Irish is understandable. For immigrants of all kinds, transported to a new and difficult environment, the familiar language and rituals of the religion into which they had been born were a link with home. Religious faith could also be a powerful source of strength in an often hostile new country and could likewise underpin the habits of industry and self-discipline required to prosper and achieve respectability. But, for the Irish, Catholicism was also much more. In Ireland itself an overlap between religion and national identity had been apparent almost since the sixteenth-century Reformation left the majority of the inhabitants of the island on the other side of the religious divide from the people of England, Wales and Scotland. In popular tradition, and in a developing body of nationalist historical writing, memories of the proscription of Catholicism and the suppression of political revolt came together in a single mythology of martyrdom. The conflation of religious and political loyalties continued in the campaigns of the charismatic popular champion Daniel O'Connell for Catholic Emancipation and for repeal of the Act of Union that in 1800 had incorporated Ireland, previously ruled by laws made in its own parliament, into a unitary British state. And when Irish immigrants arrived in the United States, they encountered a situation that seemed directly to mirror what they had left behind in Ireland—a disadvantaged Catholic population and a Protestant establishment that was at best condescending, and at worst openly hostile.

If the immigrant Irish found in the Catholic Church a familiar and valued institution, they also encountered, in the United States, a church that was itself increasingly Irish-dominated. From an early stage, clergy of Irish birth or descent had alarmed other sections of the American Catholic establishment by their ambition and cohesion. The English-born archbishop of Baltimore complained to Rome in 1833 of 'warm-headed' priests 'with strong Irish predilections in favour of Irish bishops'. As was later to be the case in Australia, those predilections were seconded by the influence of Paul Cullen, the Irish powerbroker who was just beginning his ascent to influence in Rome. Already by 1850 bishops of Irish birth or descent controlled all of the main centres of population. Along with their clannishness, the Irish had strong pragmatic arguments on their side. Up to the 1880s they were by far the largest body of immigrant Catholics. The appointment of church leaders who were native English speakers also made sense, both to those who wanted to see Catholicism brought into the mainstream of American life and to those who hoped that continued immigration would eventually conquer the whole of North America for Rome. This did not mean that the Irish always had things their own way. In the diocese of Fort Wayne, Indiana, created in 1857, the first four bishops, serving up to 1924, were German-born or of German descent. Here it was Irish priests and congregations who complained that their interests were neglected. In 1890 a ferocious lobbying campaign led by John Ireland, the archbishop of St Paul, failed to block the appointment of the Austrian-born Frederick Katzer to Milwaukee, the third of four German-, Austrian- or Swiss-born clerics who governed the diocese from its foundation in 1844 up to 1930. But by the end of the nineteenth century almost two-thirds (62 per cent) of bishops in the United States were of Irish descent, and more than half were Irish-born.[7]

Irish dominance was equally evident at parish level. As immigrant numbers rose in the first half of the century, the church had begun to permit the formation of national parishes, where German, French or other immigrants could confess their sins and listen to sermons from a priest who spoke their language. In some cases these included specifically Irish parishes. Most Holy Trinity Parish in Detroit, for example, was created in 1833 to cater for Irish Catholics previously forced to accept services in French and German. In the major cities of the Northeast, however, the more common pattern was for the ordinary Catholic parishes, English speaking and organised on the basis of territory rather than ethnic affiliation, to become in practice Irish dominated, with separate provision for others. In Chicago, for example, across the period 1844–1900, there were sixty-one English-speaking parishes, in practice overwhelmingly Irish, and sixty-seven others, including twenty-seven German parishes, sixteen Polish, eight Czech, five French, four Italian, three Lithuanian and one each for African Americans, Slovaks, Slovenes and Dutch.[8]

Many of the priests serving in these de facto Irish parishes were American-born but of Irish descent, trained in the seminaries that by this time existed to provide pastors for most American dioceses. But there was also a continued reliance on priests imported from Ireland. Between 1842 and 1891 All Hallows College in Dublin, the main training centre for overseas service, sent 652 priests to dioceses in the United States. Another 466, in the period up to 1922, came from the seminary at Carlow, and there were also recruits from other Irish institutions. Nor was it only in the major centres of Irish settlement, like New York or Chicago, that Irish priests were numerous. In the southern states, where the Irish immigrant population was much smaller, bishops were if anything more reliant on Irish recruits than their colleagues in the Northeast. In Charleston, for example, 71 of the 101 priests who served between 1820 and 1880 were Irish-born or of Irish descent. For American bishops struggling to provide for an ever-increasing population, priests recruited from Ireland had two great advantages. First, they spoke English, allowing them to fit easily into American civic life. Secondly, as members of a society where emigration was a familiar option, and where a newly ordained priest could look forward to many years as a lowly curate before acquiring his own parish, they were willing to come.[9]

At least as important as this continued reliance on priests from Ireland, from the point of view of the development of a strong Irish Catholic identity in the United States, was the importation from the same source of large numbers of religious women. Priests were essential to the central liturgical functions of Catholicism. But it was female religious orders that did the often gruelling day-to-day work of assisting working-class Irish immigrants to survive in their new environment. It was they who ran and staffed schools, hospitals, orphanages, homes for the aged, reformatories, asylums for the rescue of 'fallen women' and a range of other charitable and reforming institutions. Some of the religious orders involved were distinctively Irish. The Sisters of Mercy, founded in Dublin in 1831, sent their first nuns to Pittsburgh in 1843 and went on to spread across the United States, relying almost entirely on sisters imported from Ireland. But other orders too, like the French Sisters of the Good Shepherd, recruited heavily both in Ireland and among Irish-American women. When an emissary of the Indiana-based Sisters of the Holy Cross arrived in Ireland on a recruitment mission in 1870, she found that 'the Dominican Sisters first, then the Sisters of Mercy and their Bishop . . . have thoroughly gleaned the country'. Even so she returned to the United States with nineteen Irish women ready to enter the order.[10]

In the middle decades of the nineteenth century, then, American Catholicism had its own version of Ireland's devotional revolution, as a vigorous and expanding church offered immigrants both the consolations of religion and a vehicle for ethnic solidarity. In cities and towns across the country, and in rural areas where numbers permitted, the parish became their central social institution. While attending Sunday mass and other services they sat surrounded by familiar faces and accents, were addressed from the altar by a fellow countryman, and exchanged news and gossip with friends and acquaintances. Initially the functions of the typical parish were confined to religious practice. Any organization established within it would have been of a purely religious nature, such as a men's confraternity or a women's sodality. From the 1880s, however, Catholic parishes everywhere became the basis of a lively culture of clubs and societies, devoted to charity, recreation and self-improvement. By 1896 the Chicago parish of Holy Family, containing 25,000 Catholics, had a total of twenty-five societies, with a combined membership of around 10,000. As well as relief for different categories of the needy, night classes, and meetings for prayer and devotion, parishes now offered bands, baseball clubs, dramatic societies, picnics, bazaars and parades marking local religious festivals. Meanwhile national organisations aimed at Irish Americans—the Ancient Order of Hibernians, the temperance movement, the charitable Saint Vincent de Paul Society—all took the parish as their local unit of organisation.[11]

Central though the parish thus became to the lives of Irish immigrants, there was one revealing exception to their commitment. In the 1840s Hughes and others had fought bitter battles against city and state authorities as they campaigned for schools that would protect the faith of Catholic children. In the decades that followed, the demand for denominational education remained the official policy of the church, reiterated in plenary councils of the American bishops in 1852, 1866 and 1884. Yet in Chicago the proportion of Catholic children attending parochial schools in the second half of the nineteenth century was about half; in San Francisco in the 1870s it was 55 per cent. Elsewhere the proportions seem to have been about the same. A survey in 1908 confirmed that 60,000 Catholic children across twenty-four cities were attending parochial schools, compared to 67,000 in public schools. Part of the reason for this limited participation was that not all Catholic bishops and priests, despite the resolutions of successive plenary councils, were convinced that parochial schools were a priority, at a time when budgets were stretched by the demands of a constantly growing and generally poor immigrant population. There was also the question of language. German parents were more committed to parochial schools than Irish, because at them their children received an instruction that was not just Catholic but was delivered in their mother tongue. The choice of the Irish, by contrast, was between two English-language schools, parochial or public. At the same time there were also consistent reports that Irish parents preferred the public schools simply because the quality of teaching there was higher. Catholicism had become central to their identity. But when its dictates conflicted with their ambition to achieve for their children success and respectability, their obedience had clear limits. Their decision to entrust their sons and daughters to the public school system was made easier because so many young women of the first American-born generation, the daughters of domestic servants, chose teaching as their route to a better life than their mothers had known.[12]

Despite their shared ethnic origins, the Irish bishops now firmly in charge of the management of American Catholicism were by no means united in their vision of the future. In the 1880s a party emerged, under the informal leadership of John Ireland, archbishop of St Paul, and John Spalding, bishop of Peoria, Illinois, advocating what came to be known as Americanism: the view that Catholics should embrace the republican and democratic values of the United States and make themselves part of the wider society. Ireland and Spalding were also the leading advocates of assisting Irish Catholics to abandon the slums and factories of the East Coast cities in favour of the opportunities available on the plains and prairies. Their thinking in both cases can be seen as reflecting the optimism of the more prosperous and assimilated Catholics of the

West and Midwest. On the other hand, their main opponents—
Archbishop Michael Corrigan of New York and Bishop Bernard
McQuaid of Rochester—spoke for what still saw themselves as the
embattled Catholic communities of the East Coast inner cities.
The United States, in their view, was a hostile environment, dominated by secular and materialist values and by a militant, intolerant
Protestantism, and Catholics could preserve their faith and morals
only by holding themselves rigorously apart. In 1899 the conservatives scored a major victory. A papal encyclical rejected 'those views
which, in their collective sense, are called by some "Americanism"',
and in particular the idea that 'the church should shape her teachings more in accord with the spirit of the age'. The liberals protested
that they had never held the views specified in the condemnation.
But they had suffered a serious public defeat.[13]

On another issue, however, and one probably of greater significance, it was the liberals who won the argument. In 1884 the
French-Canadian archbishop of Quebec obtained a decree from
Rome condemning the most important workers' organisation of
the day, the Knights of Labor. The decree, however, applied only
in Quebec. Archbishop James Gibbons of Baltimore, a supporter
of Ireland and Spalding, used a visit to Rome, where he was to receive his cardinal's hat, to present detailed arguments against making the condemnation general. The Knights, he insisted, were not
a secret society, their aims were legitimate, and since a majority of
their members were Catholic there was no danger that their faith
would be undermined by contact with heretics. He also warned
pragmatically that condemnation would destroy the church's influence among the working class. Gibbons's arguments prevailed
and there was no wider condemnation. The Knights were soon
to fade away. But by ensuring that their followers were not forced
to choose between their church and their class, Gibbons and his
liberal allies avoided the large-scale alienation from organised religion that was to take place in France, Italy and other European

countries. Instead the Irish were able to make both the union local and the parish central pillars of their Irish-American identity.[14]

In the second half of the nineteenth century the American Catholic Church became distinctively Irish, and the Catholic parish became the social institution at the heart of most Irish-American communities. But Irish America had never been wholly Catholic. For over a century, up to the 1830s, the majority of emigrants to what became the United States had been Protestant, and after that date Protestant immigration, though less visible beside the hugely increased movement of Irish Catholics, nevertheless continued. In the eighteenth and early nineteenth centuries Protestants of Irish birth had had no difficulty in calling themselves Irish. Many had joined with Catholics in establishing fraternal and philanthropic societies like Philadelphia's Friendly Sons of St Patrick, New York's Irish Emigrant Society, and the Hibernian Societies of Charleston, Savannah and other southern towns. Many had also supported liberal and patriotic causes, such as Catholic Emancipation and repeal of the Act of Union. In the second half of the nineteenth century, however, Protestants of Irish origin found themselves in a society where Irishness was associated with a large body of generally poor, often unruly and stridently Catholic immigrants.

To some it seemed to make no difference. David Bell, a Presbyterian minister, left his County Monaghan congregation in 1853, partly at least because of hostility to his radical views on land reform. In 1864, under threat of arrest for his involvement in a militant nationalist conspiracy, he emigrated to the United States, where he joined the executive council of the Fenian movement. Thomas Addis Emmet, grandson of a United Irish exile, served between 1892 and 1901 as president of the Irish National Federation of America, supporting the Irish Parliamentary Party's campaign for home rule. Other Irish-American Protestants continued to participate in the work of non-political bodies like the Friendly Sons of Saint Patrick in New York. But even those still anxious to give expression to their Irishness could not ignore the widening gap between their ethnic and religious identities. William McCarter, who had been born in County Londonderry in 1840 or 1841, was by 1862 working as a tanner in Philadelphia. He was proud to enlist in the new 116th Pennsylvania Infantry, making him part of the Irish Brigade. He wrote enthusiastically of his admiration for Thomas Francis Meagher, whose orderly he became. As a Protestant, however, he clearly felt some unease about the implications of his choice. Meagher and other senior officers, he insisted, were Catholics, but 'only by profession, certainly not in practice'. He also claimed, contrary to all the evidence, that the Brigade as a whole contained fewer Catholics than any other unit of the army, and that 'twenty attended the Protestant services for every two who went to Mass'.[15]

Others chose the more straightforward path of denying any kinship with Catholic Irish America. 'I never saw genuine Irish until I came to this country', County Antrim–born Andrew Greenlees wrote from Illinois to his brother in 1859, 'and I assure you I don't think it strange that they are everywhere spoken against and looked upon with a certain degree of suspicion.' 'The low Catholic Irish' and the 'Dutch' (by which he possibly meant Germans), 'addicted to drinking and loafing around shops', were 'abhorred here as in every other civilized community'. Another Antrim man, William Hill, had been in the United States since the 1820s. He had brought with him the same political radicalism that had led an earlier generation of Ulster Presbyterians to take the field in the Irish rebellion of 1798: he had named his son after the martyred patriot Robert Emmet, expressed his distaste for the Orange Order, and rejoiced at the prospect of a British defeat in the Crimean War. By 1859, however, he regarded the emigrants now arriving from Ireland as 'of the lowest rank . . . and reflect discredit on the better class of their countrymen'. His hometown, Abbeville, South Carolina, contained 'a good many of the rowdy class of Irish . . . mostly of the real Irish or Papist stock, and their looks and uncouth appearance often bring to my mind the pigmen that I had seen when a boy in Ballymena fairs'.[16]

One obvious vehicle for a Protestant sense of separate Irish identity was the Orange Order. New lodges appeared after the Civil War, and in 1870 the Grand Orange Lodge of Ireland authorised the creation of an American grand lodge. But the emphasis on loyalty to Crown and empire that allowed Orangeism to flourish in British North America did not sit so easily with American anti-Catholicism, whose exponents saw themselves as defending the founding values of the republic. The numbers involved, in consequence, remained small. On 12 July 1872, for example, 172 Orangemen paraded in New York, protected by 750 police; in 1873 there were 337 marchers and over 1,000 police. Even the celebration of the bicentenary of the Battle of the Boyne in 1890 was to bring out fewer than 1,000. Across the United States as a whole, the Order in 1900 claimed 120 lodges with 10,000 members. Canada, by contrast, had 1,450 active lodges. For those of Irish Protestant descent who did feel the urgent need to combine against the threat to society of the pope and his followers, a safer avenue was to join any one of the numerous nativist societies, anti-Catholic but impeccably American. And for those whose main interest was in sociability and ritual, rather than political and religious controversy, Freemasonry was an attractive alternative. Of 135 high-ranking masons active in New York in the second half of the nineteenth century more than one-third were Protestants of Irish background.[17]

Another option, for Protestants wishing to set themselves apart from a stridently Catholic Irish America, was to create a new ethnic identity. The foundations had been laid during the bitter factional conflicts of America's first age of party, between 1790 and about 1820, when the Federalists accused their Jeffersonian and later Jacksonian rivals of relying on the support of the 'wild Irish'. Affluent conservatives of Ulster Presbyterian background sought to exempt themselves from their own party's rhetoric by insisting that they themselves were 'Scotch Irish'. The term reappeared a generation later with the massive immigration during the Famine and immediate post-Famine years, and the rise of nativism that followed. When the Irish nationalist politician John Francis Maguire, in 1868, published an account of his travels among his countrymen in America, he devoted several pages to an attack on those 'unnatural Irish . . . sleek and well fed' who rejected any connection with the mass of poorer immigrants by claiming to be 'Scotch Irish'. In 1889 this sense of a separate Irish Protestant identity found an institutional base with the creation of the Scotch-Irish Society of the United States of America, whose annual congresses commemorated the contribution of the 'Ulster Scot' to the making of the United States. An American Irish Historical Society, established eight years later in 1897, vigorously asserted the rival claims of Catholics of Gaelic ancestry. In America as in Ireland itself, the notion of 'the common name of Irishman', the slogan with which the United Irishmen of the 1790s had proclaimed the unity of Catholic and Protestant, had given way to a revived set of confessionally based distinctions.[18]

———————

Alongside the Irish parish was the Irish neighbourhood. The Irish, like other immigrants, liked to live close to others of the same ethnic background. There they could have the support and companionship of relatives, friends and former neighbours, and become part of wider social networks. They could hope to meet with a welcome, or at least civility, from saloon keepers, grocers and landlords of their own nationality. In the event of conflict with other ethnic groups, they had the protection of numbers. The frequency of chain migration, in which immigrants crossed the Atlantic to join relatives or friends who would then assist them in establishing themselves in their new homeland, further reinforced their tendency to cluster in specific areas. Where numbers permitted, in fact, immigrants showed a preference for living, not just among other Irish, but among their own sort of Irish. In Detroit the area round Most Holy Trinity Parish church, known locally as the Irish section, had distinct pockets occupied by natives of Kerry, Cork, Limerick and Tipperary. In New York the residents of the cele-brated Five Points were drawn disproportionately from Kerry and Sligo, while immigrants from Limerick were concentrated further east, in the Fourth Ward.[19]

How far this natural tendency to congregate led to the creation of entire Irish neighbourhoods, however, depended on circum-stances. In the cities of the West and Midwest, where economic opportunities were wider and Irish immigrants found it easier to move up the social scale, the level of segregation was modest. In San Francisco there were wards with an above-average or below-average proportion of Irish, but no exclusively Irish districts. In Detroit in 1853 the Eighth Ward, containing the 'Irish section', housed only 1,864 of the town's 5,123 Irish Catholics, along with 2,324 resi-dents of other backgrounds. In Chicago only 11 out of 303 census districts returned a clear majority of Irish residents in 1884. In the industrial centres of the East, where Irish immigrants were most likely to be poor, were grouped in the same narrow range of occu-pations, and were on the defensive in a hostile environment, their urge to cluster together was stronger. In Worcester, Massachusetts, in 1880, the four districts regarded as Irish neighbourhoods were home to two-thirds of the town's Irish immigrant adults. But that was within a total population of 58,000. In the larger cities that attracted the greatest number of immigrants, a more complex ur-ban geography, the need to live close to places of work and the sheer numbers involved all combined to make any neat distribution into homogenous ethnic neighbourhoods impossible. In New York in 1855 the greatest concentrations of Irish were in the First and Fourth Wards, where they made up 46 per cent of the population. Even in the Five Points, so often cited as the archetypal Irish slum, only just over two-thirds of the adult population had been born in Ireland. For really clear-cut divisions of space along ethnic lines it was necessary to look at a much lower level, the individual street, or even part of a street, or a particular tenement block.[20]

Even in the great urban centres of the East, then, the level of residential segregation should not be exaggerated. A study of Boston, often taken as the home of a particularly cohesive Irish population, shows that in 1880 the Irish were in fact the immigrant group least prone to separate themselves from other nationalities, with a 'segregation index' less than half that of Germans and just over one-fifth that of Italians. It would also be wrong to imagine that urban neighbourhoods somehow recreated on the other side of the Atlantic the rural communities that most immigrants had left behind, where one could be born, live and die surrounded by the same circle of faces and family names. All the evidence is that the first generation of immigrants, Irish and otherwise, were highly mobile. In Detroit, for example, fewer than half of the Irish-born residents listed in the census of 1850 were still living in the city ten years later. An Irish or a German neighbourhood may have retained its ethnic complexion over time, but this was because the large numbers leaving every year were replaced by newcomers of the same nationality. Residence there may well have fostered a strong sense of communal identity, as when New York Irish tenement dwellers in 1863 battled fiercely to keep Federal troops out of what they saw as their territory. But personal bonds between neighbours, at this early stage at least, must often have been transitory.[21]

This is not to suggest that residential segregation did not have a part to play in the establishment and maintenance of an Irish-American identity. Living in the Five Points or St Louis's Kerry Patch, or even in the Seventh Ward, San Francisco's most Irish district, where more than a quarter of the inhabitants were Irish-born, the immigrant would have found it natural to turn to Irish neighbours for companionship and support. Particular saloons and grocery stores, owned and patronised by the local Irish, provided a meeting place to supplement the parish church. Meanwhile the American-born children of these immigrants would have grown up surrounded by the accents, songs and memories of an Ireland they had never seen. The bonds of community were strengthened by living arrangements. Very few Irish Americans lived alone. If they were not part of a household, they generally boarded, almost always with an Irish family. But it is nevertheless important to recognise that, contrary to what is sometimes claimed, the American Irish did not generally live in ghettos, surrounded exclusively by their fellow countrymen and cut off from the wider society. Instead the neighbourhood should be seen, not as the retreat of an alienated minority, but as a stage in the process of assimilation: a safe base from which the immigrant could begin the process of learning how to behave in a complex new environment.[22]

Another part of the glue that held together Irish immigrant communities was the ties of kinship. Most Irish immigrants, by the second half of the nineteenth century, came to the United States with the assistance of relatives who had preceded them, and once arrived continued to look to family members for assistance and support. They also, overwhelmingly, looked to fellow Irish immigrants for partners in marriage. Even in San Francisco, with its relatively low level of residential segregation, more than 85 per cent of Irish-born men chose Irish-born wives, with no significant change in this preference between 1852 and 1880. In Detroit the pattern was roughly the same, while in Worcester, Massachusetts, on the other side of the continent, the figure was more than 90 per cent. In the first American-born generation the desire to marry one's own kind remained strong. In Worcester more than seven out of ten American-born sons and daughters of Irish parents chose partners of Irish birth or descent. In San Francisco the proportions were even higher—more than three-quarters for women and seven out of eight for men. In Detroit, on the other hand, slightly over half of American-born sons of Irish immigrants chose wives with no Irish ancestry.[23]

Like other immigrants the American Irish showed a strong preference for associating with their fellow countrymen and women. At work they were often found in occupations like construction, road and rail making, or dockside loading and unloading, all jobs that involved working in teams, generally put together on an ethnic basis. In religion they sought Irish congregations with an Irish priest. In marriage their choice was overwhelmingly a partner of the same nationality as themselves. They also liked to live close alongside other Irish families. Yet here they were significantly less inclined than other groups to form exclusive ethnic enclaves, cutting themselves off from the wider society. One obvious reason for this was language. For Germans, and later for Poles, Italians and others, life in an ethnic neighbourhood was attractive because it offered the convenience, for many the absolute necessity, of conducting the business of life through their native language. For the Irish this did not arise. The first half of the nineteenth century had seen a distinctive shift to English as the language of power and opportunity. About a quarter of Irish immigrants arriving in the United States in the 1850s and later would still have been Irish speakers. But even among these it is likely that many knew some English. For the majority of first-generation Irish Americans, meanwhile, one major obstacle to moving outside the boundaries of their ethnic community did not apply.[24]

What the majority of Irish immigrants brought with them to the United States was thus something distinctive. They had a clear sense of national identity, giving birth to a strong, and where necessary aggressive, instinct for solidarity and collective self-defence. But it was an identity whose components were historical tradition and recent experience of grievance, as well as an increasingly close identification with Catholicism, rather than a unique language or culture. This distinctiveness was reflected in the institutions they created for themselves in the United States. Germans, the other sizeable immigrant group at mid-century, were noted for the number and variety of the associations, or *Vereine,* that they created, dedicated to fostering German language, literature, music, drama and sports. In Irish America, as in Ireland itself, on the other hand, movements seeking to revive or defend a distinctive national culture became significant only from the beginning of the twentieth century. Before that the Irish were noted instead for their distinctive contribution to the mainstream popular culture of the United States.

In the case of sport, for example, the Irish early on made their mark in boxing. John L. Sullivan, born in Boston to Irish immigrant parents, became heavyweight champion in 1882 by defeating Tipperary-born Paddy Ryan. He lost the title ten years later to Jim Corbett, born to Irish parents in San Francisco, though reportedly never forgiven by the more numerous Irish of the East for overthrowing their hero, Sullivan. Boxing was perhaps a natural route to success for a mainly poor ethnic group with a strong culture of hard manual labour (although Corbett, dubbed 'Gentleman Jim', had in fact been a bank clerk). But the Irish also made a major impact on the republic's national sport, baseball. Amateur teams proliferated in Irish communities across the country, rivalling militia companies in their choice of patriotic names—Shamrock, Hibernian Green, Celtic, Emmet and Fenian. Irish professional players also prospered. In 1872 it was claimed that one-third of players in the major league were of Irish birth or descent. There were even reports of players of other backgrounds adopting Irish names in order to help their careers in the sport. Irish professionals were also prominent in the short-lived sport of pedestrianism (walking races), as well as in rowing.[25]

Success on the sports field, or in the boxing ring, lent itself to a straightforward celebration of Irish strength, courage and skill. The

Irish contribution to popular theatre involved a more ambiguous presentation of national character. Early depictions of the Irish on the American stage drew on existing English stereotypes. Just as African-American performers rolled their eyes and distorted their voices so as to conform to the image of a dim-witted, credulous and by nature dependant people, so Irish-American performers adopted the outlandish brogue, the comically dishevelled appearance and the drunken and pugnacious mannerisms of the stage Irishman. By mid-century the image had begun to soften. Paddy was still poor, feckless and rumbustious, but he was also good-natured and on occasion witty. The arrival in the 1850s and 1860s of the plays of Dion Boucicault, notably *The Colleen Bawn* (1860), helped to establish a new fashion, in which the Irish appeared as colourful rather than ridiculous. Boucicault's plays were set in Ireland, but from about the same time contemporary urban America found its interpreters in the vaudeville sketches of Edward Harrigan, New York–born grandson of Irish immigrants, and Tony Hart, born in Worcester, Massachusetts, to parents from County Mayo. Boucicault himself was to comment that they had done for the Irish of America what he had done for the Irish in Ireland. Yet even at this point, the traditional-stage Irishman had been modified rather than rejected. A New Yorker recalled in his memoirs the plays he had seen in the Bowery Theatre of the 1870s, including the 'stock Irish play' involving 'a virtuous peasant girl and a high-minded patriot with knee-breeches, a brogue and an illicit whiskey-still', who 'utterly expose and confound a number of designing dukes, lords etc'. One of Harrigan and Hart's greatest successes, equally, was a series of sketches depicting the adventures of a militia company, the Mulligan Guard, presented in a modified brogue. 'When we get home at night boys', one chorus ran, 'the divil a bit we'd ate / We'd all sit up and drink a sup / of whiskey strong and nate.' By the early 1900s a new generation were angrily rejecting this type of ethnic stereotyping. But the Irish of the post–Civil War era, it appears, preferred to adapt the prevailing American perception of their national character into something they could accept, and even enjoy.[26]

Just as the Irish of mid-century and after did not feel the urge to create distinctive cultural institutions, so when it came to creating associations offering companionship, self-improvement and protection, their response was to create their own versions of American models. This was particularly the case with the two most prominent forms of association at mid-century. One was the volunteer fire company. In the period before cities established professional municipal fire brigades, these were the property owner's only protection. But they were also boisterous male fraternities, often with a strong ethnic identity, Irish, German or American, whose sometimes violent rivalries led some contemporaries to see them as more akin to street gangs than to a public service. One reflection of their importance was the frequency with which the leadership of a fire company could be a stepping stone to a career in local politics. The other key institution was the militia company. Irish companies advertised their origins by displaying green flags or other insignia, and by taking the name of an Irish or Irish-American hero. New York's Napper Tandy Light Artillery Company, for example, was named after a leading United Irishman, while both Richmond and Boston had Montgomery Guards, named after an Irish-born commander killed in an attack on Quebec during the American War of Independence. Their marching and display, including their prominent part in celebrations of St Patrick's Day, allowed them to serve at the same time as an assertion of communal pride, a claim to status, and a social outlet for young energetic males.

Over time, as part of a broader process of settling down, the rough male camaraderie of the fire company and the volunteer militia gave way to associations more focussed on self-improvement. These included the temperance societies, religious confraternities, sporting clubs and educational societies sponsored by Catholic parishes. Savings banks and friendly societies also became more common. Already in the late eighteenth and early nineteenth centuries middle-class Irish Americans had formed a range of associations that provided charitable relief to the Irish poor and at the same time functioned as a social club for their better-off compatriots. Philadelphia, for example, had the Friendly Sons of St Patrick, established in 1771. In New York a society of the same name appeared in 1784, followed around 1816 by a Shamrock Friendly Association. From the 1850s or 1860s, however, these elite philanthropic bodies were joined by others that sought to introduce the working class themselves to a culture of thrift and mutual insurance. In San Francisco, for example, the Hibernian Society and the Sons of the Emerald Isle, both established in 1852 in what was still very much a new settlement, seem to have been attempts at middle-class philanthropy of the traditional sort. However the Irish American Benevolent Society and the St Joseph's Benevolent Society, both of which followed in 1860, were more focused on working-class self-help. The Irish American Benevolent Society had a social aspect, organising parades and picnics. But the main function of both was to collect regular subscriptions, out of which they made payments for the support of sick members, to meet the funeral expenses of those who died, and to assist their dependants.[27]

A survey of voluntary associations in Lowell, Massachusetts, in the period 1859–85 gives an indication of the range of options it offered to its Irish inhabitants. The Knights of St Patrick and the St Patrick's Catholic Union were primarily religious societies. There was also a St Patrick's Temperance Association. The Lowell Irish Benevolent Society and the American Society of Hibernians identified themselves as charitable bodies. The Young Men's Catholic Lyceum and the Young Men's Catholic Literary Association were dedicated to self-improvement through literature. There were two marching bands, the Erina Coronet Band and the Manchester Coronet Band, and two military companies, the Sargeant Light

Guards and the Sheridan Guards. There were also four branches of the Ancient Order of Foresters, a friendly society that combined fraternal gatherings with mutual insurance, and five branches of the Catholic, nationalist Ancient Order of Hibernians. In some of the larger cities, where numbers made it feasible, there were also associations bringing together immigrants from a particular county. New York, in particular, had no fewer than twenty-one county societies in 1883. Some were purely social organisations, like the Kerry Men's Association. Others, like the Meath Football Club, were sporting clubs, others again, like the Limerick Guards, military societies. As well as providing dinners, dances and excursions, county associations might provide sick pay or death benefits out of the dues collected from members. They differed from other Irish clubs and societies, like the range of bodies listed for Lowell, in providing for women as well as men. Female county clubs, however, were generally separate from the men's, and they catered mainly for young, single women, so much so that their usual night for meetings was Thursday, widely recognised as the 'maid's night out'. On marriage, the assumption was family life would take the place of organised sociability.[28]

The rising importance of these Irish associations, and their growing self-confidence, can be seen in the development, from mid-century onwards, of the St Patrick's Day parade. In the early nineteenth century observances of Ireland's national festival had been for the few not the many. The members of elite Irish societies—merchants, professional men and similar individuals of substance—met to dine together and drink patriotic toasts. By the 1840s, however, these socially exclusive gatherings were being overshadowed, as a growing population of working-class Irish immigrants sought a form of celebration more in keeping with their tastes and resources. Boston had its first parade in 1841. In New York, parades on 17 March became common during the 1840s, and in 1851 supporters established a Convention of Irish Societies to coordinate arrangements. By 1874 the newspaper *Irish World* could count over 120 parades in the United States, as well as 9 in Canadian cities. Typically the procession brought together Irish militia companies, along with in many cases a detachment from the police, followed by a variety of religious, charitable and self-help societies, as well as political clubs. A report from New York in 1868 conveyed something of the flavour of what remained the country's largest parade. As the day began, 'Second Avenue was alive with swords and sashes, jingling spurs and sabers, glittering badges and gold fringed collars, green shirts and red caps, while above all floated in the sunlight the banner of the harp.' The selection of music was eclectic. Irish tunes like 'The Wearing of the Green' and, inevitably, 'St Patrick's Day in the Morning' alternated with American standards like 'The Star-Spangled Banner'. Marchers and spectators alike dressed themselves in green or decorated their clothes and hats with green ribbons. From the 1880s new techniques of refrigeration made it possible to supply American processionists with fresh shamrock imported from Ireland.[29]

The rise of the St Patrick's Day parade was a further indication of the place that the Irish had established for themselves, from mid-century on, in the United States. The event was not popular with all. Nativists and patrician conservatives complained of the freedom claimed by the Irish to take over town centres, on what was normally an ordinary working day, disrupting business and the routines of daily life. Political reality, however, required that the Irish, a sophisticated, cohesive and numerous body of voters, should not only be allowed to have their day, but should have their procession treated with respect. In New York, Tammany Hall, not surprisingly, was particularly quick to respond: as early as 1857 the mayor and other office-holders reviewed the military and civic companies as they marched past. In Boston in 1868 the mayor, along with the chief of police and members of the Board of Aldermen, likewise took up their station along the processional route, and acknowledged the salute of the parade marshals as they passed the spot. In Philadelphia the mayor reviewed the parade in 1872, while two years later President Grant and his cabinet reviewed the Washington parade as it passed the White House. For the Irish the celebration of 17 March thus had two functions. It was an opportunity to reaffirm their Irish identity through music, slogans, banners and emblems. And it was also a defiant assertion of their status in American society, and of their entitlement to make themselves a part, however unwelcome to some, of its civic rituals. William Russell, the celebrated correspondent for the London *Times*, observing the New York parade in 1861, believed that the participants were 'proud of the privilege of interrupting all the trade of the principal streets, in which the Yankees most do congregate'.[30]

Alongside this growth in clubs and societies, there was also the growth of specifically Irish newspapers. The first titles aimed at an immigrant readership had been Catholic rather than Irish in their focus. In 1822, for example, Bishop John England of Charleston, South Carolina, published a *United States Catholic Miscellany* that was to continue in circulation for almost forty years. Boston too had a Catholic paper, called first the *Jesuit* and then the *Catholic Intelligencer*. But in 1836 the bishop of Boston sold the paper to one of its journalists, County Cavan–born Patrick Donahoe, who renamed it the *Pilot*, in imitation of the Dublin paper that had become the main organ of Daniel O'Connell's political campaigns. Under his editorship the paper became 'the Irishman's bible', carrying information on naturalisation procedures and missing relatives, as well as political news from both Ireland and the United States. The new focus raised the paper's circulation from 680 in 1838 to 7,000 by 1844. In 1849 Patrick Lynch, a former editor of the *Pilot*, joined with others to launch the *Irish-American*, which by the time of his death in 1857 was the best-selling Irish-American paper in the country. The success of this and other titles was made possible by the huge surge in emigration during and immediately after the

Famine. Not all sections of this much-expanded Irish population were equally interested in Irish-focussed materials. In San Francisco, for example, a succession of attempts between 1850 and 1880 to launch an Irish newspaper failed to attract readers in an Irish population more interested in the relatively open, dynamic society being constructed around them than in events, past or present, in the cities and counties of Ireland. But elsewhere Irish newspapers proliferated as editors and entrepreneurs responded to a rising market, and the most successful titles expanded beyond their city of origin to reach a national readership. The circulation of the *Irish-American* rose to a peak of 35,000 in 1882. By the 1890s the *Pilot* in Boston had reached 75,000 and the *Irish World*, launched in 1870 by Patrick Ford, stood at 125,000. All of these titles followed the pattern successfully developed by Donahoe's *Pilot*, combining news and information from the Irish-American world with reports from Ireland itself, all reviewed from the perspective, according to editorial policy, of the more or less radical varieties of Irish nationalism.[31]

The development of a thriving newspaper industry was another sign of the emergence of a strong Irish ethnic culture. But the place of these different papers in the lives of their Irish readers was also significant. All of the leading Irish newspapers were weeklies. This was because the Irish, and in particular those of them who were literate, were mainly English speaking. They could therefore read the same local or national papers as the non-immigrant population. This in turn had implications for their relationship to the wider society of the United States. Other immigrants might be forced to rely entirely for news on publications written in their own languages—German or, later, Italian, Polish or Yiddish—and which had a sectional ethnic perspective. The Irish, on the other hand, took their ordinary, day-to-day news from American sources, then turned to their own weekly papers to supplement and interpret what they had read. The Irish-American press, in other words, was the voice of an increasingly confident and assertive interest within American society, not of an ethnic ghetto.[32]

In the second half of the nineteenth century, then, Irish Americans created their own network of institutions and associations. With the powerful assistance of a Catholic Church whose management they largely controlled, they established their own hospitals, orphanages, asylums and poorhouses and, where they wished to have them, their own schools. They formed clubs and associations to supplement the bonds of family and neighbourhood with a mixture of sociability and mutual support. In none of this, however, did they seek to erect barriers that would separate them from the mainstream of American life. On the contrary, as with the fire company and the volunteer militia unit, what they did was to create their own versions of American institutions. Their aim, as they demonstrated in their tens of thousands during the four bloody years of the Civil War, was to establish a place for themselves while still retaining their Irish identity. By the end of the nineteenth century there were even complaints that the American Irish were no longer naming their children after the patron saints of their homeland. Patrick and Bridget, distinctively Irish and so easily vulgarised as Paddy and Biddy, were giving way to the no less Catholic, but nevertheless in American eyes unexceptional, John and Mary.[33]

8

THE POLITICS OF
IRISH AMERICA

At the same time that they developed a community life based on church, neighourhood and a rich array of associations, the Irish in the United States began to create a place for themselves in politics. From small beginnings as foot soldiers of the Democratic Party they established themselves as masters of a particular style of urban politics. They also took an increasingly prominent position in the turbulent world of labour organization. At the same time, to a degree not seen in any other part of the Irish diaspora, they became supporters of Irish nationalism, particularly in its more militant varieties.

At two o'clock one morning, sometime around the year 1900, a bartender rang the doorbell of George Washington Plunkitt, a

Democratic member of the New York Senate. Roused from sleep, Plunkitt made his way to the police station to bail out the bartender's employer, who had been arrested for some violation of the licensing laws. Back in bed, he was awakened at six by the sound of fire engines. He hurried to the scene to supervise his lieutenants in collecting the tenants removed from a burnt-out building, taking them to a hotel, feeding them, providing them with clothes, and moving them on to temporary quarters. At 8.30 a.m. he was at the police court, where he secured the discharge of four constituents by a quiet word with the judge, and paid the fines levied on two others. Later, at the civil court, he paid the rent of one family facing eviction and arranged legal representation for another. In the late morning and early afternoon he spent three hours finding jobs for three men who had come to him for help, and saving another from threatened dismissal by the railway company. Later in the day he attended two weddings, one Italian the other Jewish, and a church fair, where he bought a ticket for every attraction. At his district headquarters he presided over a meeting of his electoral district captains, responded positively to requests to buy tickets for a forthcoming church excursion and for a baseball game, subscribed to a church fund for the purchase of a new bell, and promised some street peddlers that he would deal with their complaint of police harassment.

Plunkitt had been born in New York in 1842, the son of Irish-born parents, both illiterate. After a few years in public school he had begun work at the age of 11, first driving carts, then apprenticed to a butcher. By 1865 he had his own butcher's shop but he gave it up around 1876 to go into business as a contractor and dealer in real estate, and to develop his political career. He duly won election to the State Assembly and then the Senate, and held office as a police magistrate and as deputy commissioner for street cleaning, both positions that provided wide opportunities for patronage. William Riordan's *Plunkitt of Tammany Hall*, published in 1905, was ostensibly a series of monologues delivered by the great man as he held court from his favourite spot, the shoeshine stand at the county courthouse. The format can hardly be taken at face value. Riordan had all too clearly recast his original material as a series of mini-essays, arranged under thematic headings. But he was a star political reporter, and his book built on interviews with his subject that he had conducted and published between 1897 and 1905. The result is a literary artifice, but it is also an insider's account of a real political world.[1]

The world in question was that of Tammany Hall. The Society of St Tammany, or the Columbian Order, had been founded in 1788 as a fraternal club, then developed as a political organization for supporters of Jefferson's democratic republicanism. It took its double name from two venerated figures from the founding of white America: *Tammany* from the Native American chief Tamanend, who had welcomed the first European settlers in what became Pennsylvania, and *Columbian* from Christopher Columbus. From 1805 the party organization separated itself from the club, but continued to operate out of Tammany Hall. In the first half of the nineteenth century the city's Democratic Party remained a collection of squabbling local fiefdoms. By the 1860s, however, William Tweed had established sufficient control over the party's local organisers to be recognised as the city's first 'boss'. Boss Tweed himself was New York–born and of Scottish descent. But several of his key lieutenants were of Irish birth or parentage, including County Cork–born Richard 'Slippery Dick' Connolly, the city's chief financial officer, and Peter 'Brains' Sweeny, son of Irish immigrants, who served as city chamberlain and park commissioner. Tweed also devoted much of the patronage at his disposal to cultivating the Irish vote. The *New York Times* claimed in 1869 that his administration had given 46 city jobs to Germans and 754 to Irishmen. Indeed when Tweed fell from grace in 1871, after his corruption had become too blatant to be overlooked, his arrest was carried out by another son of Irish immigrants, Matthew Brennan, whose election as sheriff Tweed himself had organised. As Tammany Hall rebuilt itself following the scandal it was men of Irish birth or parentage who one after another took charge of the machine. 'Honest John' Kelly, the son of immigrants, replaced an unstructured organization, in which local party functionaries handed out favours on a freelance basis, with a tightly controlled, top-down hierarchy. Admirers said that he inherited a mob and transformed it into an army. Richard Croker, born in Cork and brought to the United States at the age of 3, helped Tammany adjust to changing times by creating a network of clubhouses to replace saloons as the party's local places of business, and by having them cater, not just for the Irish, but for immigrants from eastern and southern Europe. In 1903, when his massive profiteering threatened to catch up with him, Croker retired to Ireland, where he used his considerable fortune to buy an estate at Malahide, north of Dublin, and settle down to breed racehorses. His successor, 'Silent Charley' Murphy, another American-born son of Irish parents, was, as the name suggests, a less flamboyant figure, avoiding flagrant corruption. He also began the process of nudging Tammany away from a narrow preoccupation with the procedures and rewards of machine politics to support for moderate social reform in areas such as factory regulation and the introduction of a minimum wage.[2]

The Tammany in which Plunkitt made his career was the one created by 'Honest John' Kelly. As leader of one of the city's twelve assembly districts, a working-class area on the Middle West Side popularly known as Hell's Kitchen, Plunkitt sat on Tammany's executive committee and answered directly, first to Kelly, later to Croker, and then to Murphy. Reporting to Plunkitt were the captains responsible for the wards and electoral districts of his assembly district. The rewards for this army of local workers were the favours that came with electoral success: licences to traders and peddlers, for example, or jobs with employers who looked to Tammany for contracts, or a place on the city payroll. It was a system that had come into existence, in New York and elsewhere, to fill a vacuum of leadership. Up to the 1840s politically ambitious men of property had been willing to take part personally in the business of building up an electoral following, for example by dispensing charity, acting as foremen of volunteer fire companies, and presiding over convivial gatherings. By mid-century, as urban society divided more clearly into employers and wage earners, this sort of face-to-face management was no longer congenial or effective. Instead a new type of operative appeared on the lower slopes of the political system: the saloon keeper, captain of a fire company or leader of a local gang who delivered the votes of his local district in exchange for jobs, trading permits and other favours for himself and his followers, and who over time developed into the more or less full-time political organiser represented by Plunkitt.[3]

The Irish did not invent what came to be known as the political machine. But they came to its practice with considerable advantages. Unlike the other main immigrant group, the Germans, they were mainly English speaking. They were easily organised through ready-made networks based on neighbourhood, family connections and counties of origin. In addition, those who had been adults in Ireland from the 1820s onwards had direct experience of political participation of a type denied to those coming from the restored old regimes of post-1815 continental Europe. They brought with them to the United States a familiarity with the ways and means of electoral competition, a pragmatic acceptance of politics as a series of transactions rather than a cause, and a keen appreciation of the value of sticking together. Their understanding of the potential value of politics as a means to desirable ends was evident in the eagerness with which they completed the formalities necessary to become part of the electorate. In Boston in 1885, 60 per cent of Irish-born men were registered to vote, compared to only 37 per cent of other immigrants. In San Francisco in 1900 it was 70 per cent of the Irish-born compared to, again, 37 per cent of other foreign-born. In New York in 1890 the Irish-born and the sons of Irish parents together made up one-quarter of the population, but one-third of registered voters.[4]

The benefits available to lubricate the working parts of this emerging political machine were initially modest. But in the second half of the nineteenth century the gains to be made from the business of urban government expanded out of all recognition. Between 1850 and 1900 the population of New York rose from just over half a million to 3.4 million, of Philadelphia from 121,000 to 1.3 million. These accumulations of people required a massive new infrastructure—trams and railways, water and sewage, gas, electricity, telegraph and telephone—all major sources of profit and employment, and all either provided by government or open to municipal regulation. Changes in finance also widened the opportunities open to urban political operators, as cities discovered they could imitate railways and other private enterprises by paying for long-term projects through the issue of bonds secured against future taxes. It was against this background that the late nineteenth and early twentieth centuries became the golden age of American urban machine politics, with Irish bosses and their lieutenants occupying a prominent role. Yet colourful accounts of wholesale plunder are misleading. The wider political system, as Boss Tweed discovered in 1871, imposed its own restraints. The main period of high borrowing and dramatic expansion of city budgets was between the 1850s and the 1870s, as city machines sought to consolidate their authority. Thereafter party bosses, now firmly in control of their mainly immigrant, working-class electorates, became more concerned with establishing a working relationship with business, and minimising the threat of attack from reform movements by placating middle-class taxpayers. From the 1880s, spending in the cities controlled by machines actually lagged behind the growth of population. Tammany and its counterparts, in other words, did not represent a license to squeeze unlimited profits from the public purse. Instead the political machine is better seen as an intermediary between the political establishment and a poor, largely immigrant electorate, securing for its followers the largest share of public resources that could be achieved without risking a wholesale breakdown of the system from which both boss and immigrant stood to benefit.[5]

To secure their grip on municipal government, political machines turned to a variety of well-publicised forms of electoral malpractice. Ballot boxes could be stuffed or mislaid, as occasion required, and 'repeaters' slipped from one polling station to another to cast multiple votes in the names of deceased or otherwise absent voters. But the real basis of a machine's power, as the more perceptive of their critics recognised, lay not in these black arts but rather in the protection that it could offer to an otherwise powerless urban poor. When the Chicago-based activist Jane Addams, in 1898, wrote an article entitled 'Why the Ward Boss Rules', her starting point was 'kindness': the constant regard, largely invisible to those higher up the social scale, that the poorer classes displayed for one another, by sharing their meagre resources with those in distress. This was the same quality that the local alderman displayed when he paid the rent of a poor family, found a job for an unemployed father and husband, financed the funeral of a pauper, or, at a lower level, handed out turkeys at Christmastime or buckets of coal during the winter freeze. It was a display of kindness, moreover, that did not make moral distinctions. 'A man stands by his friend', as Addams put it, 'when he is too drunk to take care of himself, when he loses his wife and child, when he is evicted for non-payment of rent, when he is arrested for a petty crime.' The ward boss was expected to do the same. The reformers who denounced Tammany's corruption may well have been active also in philanthropy. But their charity would have been of the bourgeois, often evangelical Protestant, type that sought to separate the deserving from the undeserving poor. For Tammany and its counterparts elsewhere, in contrast, the only criterion was need. The rising Boston politician Martin Lomasney made the point explicitly when he spoke of rescuing his people from 'the inquisitorial terrors of organised charity'.[6]

Tammany Hall was not unique. In Albany and Jersey City the same pattern of a dominant machine, with a single boss exercising control across the whole city, emerged in the 1870s and 1880s. In San Francisco, a new city, where the Irish were present at every level almost from the beginning, there was less pressure to maintain ethnic solidarity. Instead Irish voters could be found supporting the Democrats, the Republicans, the racist and populist Workingmen's Party, and even the political wing of the Committee of Vigilance whose purge in 1856 had included so many Irish among its victims. By 1882, however, the temporary disarray of the Democrats, as voters defected to the Workingmen's Party, provided the opportunity for the rise of a truly formidable city boss. Christopher Augustine Buckley had been born in Ireland in 1845 and came to California at the age of 17. He initially attached himself to a rising Republican activist, who described him, revealingly, as 'a handy man behind the ballot box'. After a spell in nearby Vallejo, where he dealt in lucrative contracts at the naval yard, Buckley returned to San Francisco and opened a bar. The loss of his eyesight, apparently through heavy drinking, did nothing to stop his rise. In place of a loose federation of squabbling local bosses, he created a network of forty-seven districts, each with a clubhouse managed by a leader answerable to Buckley himself, and all held together by the lavish distribution of favours great and small. On the foundation of this efficient electoral machine Buckley then created an edifice of graft that would have made George Washington Plunkitt blush. Control of the city's board of supervisors, which fixed the price of gas and water, allowed him to collect regular bribes from the companies concerned. Contracts for public works invariably included a percentage payment to the Buckley machine. The price of a teaching post was around $200. One outraged reformer wrote of young women being forced to make their way through the gamblers and other undesirables gathered in Buckley's saloon, popularly known as 'Buckley's City Hall', to plead for a lower price.[7]

If the tactics of Tammany were widespread, however, its centralized structure was less common. A systematic survey of thirty cities between 1870 and 1945 suggests that at any one time around six out of ten had some type of organised machine. Fewer than one-third, however, would have been centralized operations under the control of a single boss. More commonly, machines operated at the level of the individual ward, each providing the base from which its boss engaged others in factional competition for power and profit. This was the case, for example, in Chicago, partly because the municipal constitution gave aldermen almost complete autonomy within their district, and also because a Republican state government consistently limited the freedom of action of the Democrat-controlled city, and with it the patronage available to any potential citywide boss. The dominant figure was Roger Sullivan, born in rural Illinois to poor Irish parents, who from the 1880s slowly worked his way up the party hierarchy. Along the way he laid the foundations for a substantial personal fortune when he joined with the mayor and other office-holders in securing a franchise for a gas company that they were then able to sell to the municipality at a large profit. However he was opposed by Carter H. Harrison I and II, father and son, wealthy Democrats who between them held the office of mayor for twenty-one years between 1879 and 1915. They owed their success to a careful compromise, whereby they opposed blatant corruption while quietly allowing a group of Irish ward bosses, rivals of Sullivan, to enjoy the spoils of office.[8]

Boston, where an unsympathetic state government once again imposed limits on municipal largesse, was initially another centre of competing fiefdoms. The elite of long-established, wealthy,

Protestant families, the so-called Brahmins, were content to accept Irish domination of the city's Common Council, while choosing one of their own as mayor. The first important leaders to emerge from the city's Irish population, Patrick Collins and Patrick Maguire, promoted this alliance by downplaying religious and ethnic divisions. 'There are no Irish voters among us', Collins proclaimed in 1876. 'There are Irish-born citizens . . . but the moment the seal of the court was impressed on our papers we ceased to be foreigners and became Americans.' In 1905, however, John 'Honey Fitz' Fitzgerald, boss of the North End, won election as mayor, having defeated the candidate of his rival Martin Lomasney, who controlled the eighth ward, in the Democratic primary. He brought to city hall a full-blooded imitation of the politics of Tammany. Non-jobs created for clients and followers—like the eight 'bicycle tallymen' paid to follow street sprinklers round the town and ensure that they did their job—inflated the municipal payroll, while the budgets of city projects expanded to accommodate the sums extorted from contractors. Fitzgerald's outrageous behaviour inspired the creation of a progressive reform movement, and he lost the office in 1908, only to win re-election in 1910. In doing so he jettisoned the conciliatory language of Maguire and Collins, instead rallying his supporters through an appeal to ethnic and religious pride and an open contempt for Protestant and patrician Boston. Running against the banker and former Harvard champion oarsman James Jackson Storrow, Fitzgerald had himself photographed with his six children. The accompanying caption 'Manhood against Money' was not just an appeal to class resentment, but a blatant swipe at the Protestant practice of birth control.[9]

In party political terms Irish politicians and their voters were generally aligned with the Democrats. Their support was not unanimous. Following the Civil War the Republicans saw the need to reward those who had supported the Federal cause. The Lincoln administration, in 1865, appointed Thomas Francis Meagher governor of Montana, where he drowned two years later, falling overboard from a riverboat during what seems to have been a drunken search for a privy. During his first administration, between 1869 and 1873, President Grant appointed Irishmen to all of the main New York offices that were in the gift of the federal government. In 1872 one of his nominees, Tom Murphy, collector of the Port of New York, persuaded Jeremiah O'Donovan Rossa, a militant Irish nationalist who had come to New York on his release from prison in England, to challenge the Democratic machine by running against Tweed for his seat in the state senate. Rossa lost, but only after a contest marked by blatant ballot stuffing. One precinct with a total male population of 1,407, not all of them citizens entitled to vote, cast 1,813 votes. Other leading figures, like the newspaper editor Patrick Ford, likewise turned their backs on what they saw as the grubby politics of the Democratic Party, where Irish support was taken for granted, and instead supported the Republicans. But Republican efforts to build on support of this kind were regularly undermined by reminders of the party's nativist heritage. A programme of 'reconstruction at home' sought to undermine the Democrats in their areas of strength by placing new restrictions on the naturalisation and enfranchisement of immigrants, and by removing the licensing of saloons, and the appointment of police and firemen, from municipal political control. Initiatives of this kind, with their clear echo of the Know-Nothing movement, helped to ensure that the Democrats became overwhelmingly the party of the Irish. And the Irish, as their grip on urban politics tightened, became increasingly influential within the party. In the early 1890s, 69 per cent of members of Chicago's Democratic Committee, and 61 per cent of the officers of the Tammany society, were of Irish birth or parentage. In San Francisco in 1886 the figure was only slightly lower, at 58 per cent.[10]

The development of highly organised machine politics meant that Irish immigrants and their offspring became a prominent part of the public workforce in cities across the country. In the fourteen largest cities of the United States, by one calculation, the proportion of public employees of Irish parentage rose from 11 per cent in 1870 to 30 per cent by 1900. Policing, in any case a natural choice for immigrants brought up in a culture of hard, unskilled manual labour, was one particularly fertile source of patronage. In New York, as early as 1855, more than a quarter of policemen had been born in Ireland. By 1869 there were thirty-two Irish police captains, but no Germans. In Chicago by 1860, where the Irish were roughly one-fifth of the population, they supplied 49 out of 107 members of the city's police force. (In Philadelphia, where the Irish had less political clout, they made up only 7 per cent.) Many Irish beneficiaries of machine patronage were employed in unskilled manual labour, as street sweepers, doormen in public buildings, or labourers on construction sites or other public works. But public employment could also be important as a means of upward social mobility. In Worcester in 1880, 30 per cent of Irish immigrants who had found their way into clerical positions had done so on the public payroll. Teaching positions in the public schools were of particular importance in allowing women of Irish descent to achieve a better position in life than their Irish-born mothers. By 1908 more than one-fifth of teachers in the public schools of Boston and New York were the offspring of Irish parents. In Chicago the figure was more than one-third, and in San Francisco about half.[11]

Access to more prestigious positions in public life came more slowly. As in other areas of life, opportunities were greater in the new states of the West. St Louis elected the first of four Irish-born mayors, George Maguire, a former superintendent of Indian Affairs, as early as 1842. San Francisco's first Irish-born mayor, Frank McCoppin, who had come to the United States in 1853 after a period of service in the Irish Constabulary, took office in 1867. New York, on the other hand, elected its first Irish-born mayor only in 1880. To secure his election Tammany had to look beyond its own

ranks to a more respectable figure, William Grace, son of a well-
to-do farmer in Queen's County, who had made a fortune in South
America through shipping before settling in New York. Even then
Grace was only narrowly elected against a background of vehement
anti-Catholic agitation. In Boston, similarly, Patrick Collins put
forward a successful businessman, Hugh O'Brien, to secure the
election of the city's first Irish Catholic mayor in 1884. In Chicago, Roger Sullivan was bolder in his choice of candidate. In 1893
he put forward John Patrick Hopkins, born in New York State to
Irish immigrant parents, and Sullivan's partner in the infamous gas
works deal, to become the city's first Irish Catholic mayor.

In national politics, too, advancement came more easily to those
who moved west. Of the seven men of Irish birth who sat in the
United States Senate between 1850 and 1890, two were elected
by California and one by Nevada. A fourth, James Shields, a Civil
War general and later an active sponsor of Irish settlement in Minnesota, sat at different times for that state, Illinois and Missouri.
But overall progress was once again slow. In 1871 the *Irish World*
complained that there were only two Irish-American representatives in Congress, and only one in the Senate. By the 1890s, however, the formidable presence that the Irish had established within
the Democratic Party organisation had begun to pay off. In 1890
and 1892, both good electoral years for the Democrats, nine Irish-
born candidates were returned to Congress, along with eleven more
of Irish parentage.[12]

———

In one other important area the Irish were equally successful in
creating their own distinctive place within the structures of American society. This was the labour movement. Trade unionism in the
first half of the nineteenth century had been largely confined to
the skilled trades and had easily shaded into aggressive nativism,
as craftworkers sought to resist the intrusion of cheap immigrant
labour. In the decades after the Civil War, however, the completion

of a nationwide railway network, and the introduction of a new generation of machines, finalised the triumph of mass production. Outside of a few highly specialised crafts, the artisan gave way to the factory operative. It was this new type of industrial wage earner who now became the backbone of the trade union movement. And in that movement Irish immigrants played a prominent part. Their initial role was modest. Irish-born William McLaughlin became president of the shoemakers' union in 1869; his near namesake Hugh McLaughlin became president of the iron puddlers' national union two years later. However a survey of seventy-seven individuals prominent in the labour movement in the years 1860–75 includes only eleven born in Ireland. By the 1880s, on the other hand, a clear majority of American unions would be led by men of Irish descent.[13]

In establishing themselves as leaders of the new mass trade unionism of the post–Civil War years, the Irish had the same advantages that allowed them to carve out a place for themselves in the world of urban machine politics. Their knowledge of English made them natural and confident spokesmen in dealings with employers and other figures of authority. They also brought with them from Ireland experience in political organisation. Some, like the miners' leader John Siney, could draw on experience gained in the British labour movement. Yet more was involved than a capacity for organisation. The Irish were also tough. This was important, because labour disputes in the post–Civil War United States were, by European standards, extremely violent. Employers and government routinely unleashed state and Federal troops, police, and armed Pinkerton detectives against strikers and their supporters, while union leaders faced arrest on charges of conspiracy and treason. But the American Irish had repeatedly demonstrated their ability to hold their own on the streets, whether against nativists, other ethnic groups or, quite commonly, rival groups of Irishmen. They may have been more at home than many other immigrants in the union committee room or at a public meeting. But they were also not easily cowed by official or private thuggery.

Alongside their involvement in trade unions, the Irish also took a leading part in a broader federation, the Knights of Labor, established in 1869 and growing rapidly from about 1880 to reach a peak of 750,000 members by 1886. Terence Powderly, the leader who presided over this expansion, was the son of poor Irish immigrants who had come to America in 1826. Most other significant positions of leadership in the Knights were also in Irish hands. In 1884 Powderly estimated that about half of the membership were Catholic, most of whom would have been Irish. The ideology of the Knights was in many respects backward-looking. They idealised the active producer, whether a wage earner or a small employer, while blaming the evils of industrial society on banks and giant corporations. But on these conservative foundations they formulated a far-reaching political programme, calling for the nationalisation of the banks and the railway companies, as well as workers' cooperatives, government intervention to regulate conditions in the workplace, and a system of arbitration in industrial disputes. They also broke new ground in opening membership to Black as well as white workers. Performance did not always live up to rhetoric. In practice the number of Black members remained below 10 per cent, largely due to rank and file resistance. The limits of racial tolerance were even more crudely revealed in western states, where local branches were heavily involved in the vicious campaign of boycott and violence directed at Chinese immigrants. But the Knights, under strongly Irish leadership, nevertheless represented a huge step forward for the progressive wing of American labour.[14]

A second way in which the Knights moved beyond traditional practice was in their provision for women workers. The movement recognised housework as labour, and it admitted housewives, domestic servants and boarding house keepers as members, and demanded equal pay for male and female wage earners. It also advocated universal female as well as male suffrage. In practice total female membership never rose above 10 per cent, two-thirds of it grouped in special 'ladies' locals'. But at the leadership level the commitment was real enough to allow two Irish women to rise to important positions. Leonora Barry, the first director of the Department of Women's Work, was a widowed factory worker who had emigrated from County Cork with her family as a child. The annual reports she produced in the late 1880s established her as a pioneer of occupational statistics. Elizabeth Rodgers, another child immigrant, brought up in Ontario, appeared before the 1886 convention of the Knights with her tenth child, a 2-week-old daughter. In 1882 she became 'master workman' of a Chicago local assembly, and in 1886 'district master workman' of Assembly No. 24, in charge of a membership of 50,000. The Knights also provided a first step in the career of Mary Jones, born Mary Harris in Cork in 1837, who went on to become a fiercely combative organiser for a mineworkers' union. Widely known by the nickname Mother Jones, she was one of the founding members of the Industrial Workers of the World.[15]

In nineteenth- and twentieth-century Ireland the politics of the nation and the politics of class appear as competing commitments: the call for unity in the cause of independence repeatedly relegated the labour movement to the sidelines, ensuring conservative hegemony. In the United States, on the other hand, the 1880s saw Irish nationalism and working-class radicalism brought together in a single movement. In 1879 Charles Stewart Parnell, a rising member of the Irish Home Rule Party with ambiguous links to the revolutionary Fenian movement, had launched a campaign of militant resistance to the attempts of Irish landlords, at a time of tumbling agricultural prices, to extort the usual rents from their tenants. In March 1880, at the end of a three-month tour of North America, Parnell secured the establishment of an American Land League, to raise funds in support of the farmers' struggle. Its leadership was dominated by middle-class, often socially conservative, Irish Americans. At the local level, however, the Land League organisation sometimes overlapped with that of the Knights of Labor, and members looked instead to the more radical leadership offered by Patrick Ford of the *Irish World*, which set up its own fund to support the Irish struggle. By autumn 1881 the American Land League had sent to Ireland a respectable $180,000. Ford, however, had sent $350,000, collected mainly in donations of less than a dollar, with particular support coming from the mining districts of Pennsylvania and the West, and from industrial towns throughout the northeastern states.

Many of those immigrants who contributed to Ford's fund would have had their own experiences of landlordism before leaving Ireland; even if not, tales of rapacious rent collectors and ruthless evictions were by this time part of nationalist folklore. Yet there was more to the American Land League than a transfer of Irish grievances across the Atlantic. Up to the middle of the nineteenth century Irish immigrants had revelled in the rough egalitarianism of the United States, and the opportunities it offered of achieving independence. There was no need, as the County Down man William Porter, by this time an Illinois farmer, observed in 1869, to take off one's hat to any man. By this time, however, the much larger number of Irish who were now industrial workers were coming to terms with a different America. They might not have to take off their hats to the steel baron Andrew Carnegie or to the railway magnate Jay Gould, but it was nevertheless clear that men like these wielded a degree of power more despotic than anything that might be encountered on an Irish landed estate. The defence of the tenant farmer in Ireland fused, in the minds of embattled Irish-American workers, with their own struggle against a predatory capitalism. In the celebrated phrase of the *Irish World*, 'The cause of the poor in Donegal is the cause of the factory slave in Fall River'.[16]

The recognition that the battle against monopoly and the exploitation it permitted was the same on both sides of the Atlantic found an echo several years later in the work of American economic writer Henry George. His book *Progress and Poverty* (1879) argued that the root cause of poverty and exploitation in all societies was the private ownership of land, which created an unproductive elite that appropriated the profits of capital and labour alike. George was a close associate of Patrick Ford, who sent him to Ireland as a reporter for the *Irish World*. In 1886, George ran for mayor of New York, challenging both Republicans and Democrats under the banner of the United Labor Party. His platform included his central proposal of a single tax that would confiscate the profits of unproductive landowners. But there was also an ambitious programme of labour reforms, including shorter hours, control over working conditions, and the right to peaceful assembly. Tammany Hall sought to undermine George's campaign, and shore up the Democratic vote, by mobilising the Catholic clergy to denounce his dangerous ideas. Despite this George polled 68,110 votes, not all that short of the victorious Democrat's 90,552, and a little ahead of the Republican candidate, a young Theodore Roosevelt, who polled 60,435. In particular the results from working-class Irish districts showed that he had made substantial inroads into the Democratic vote.

A similar capacity to link specifically Irish grievances to wider concerns was evident twelve years later, when the United States went to war against Spain in Cuba and the Philippines. The war was a fresh opportunity to provide the ultimate proof of Irish loyalty to the United States. The 69th New York Infantry Regiment, with 400 Irish-born members, was in action again, and Irish regiments came forward from Massachusetts, Illinois, California and elsewhere. But when the United States went on to annex the Philippines, and embarked on a brutal counterinsurgency to subdue its newly acquired possession, Irish-American spokesmen, and the majority of Irish and Catholic newspapers, were overwhelmingly hostile. Part of the concern was the safety in American hands of the Filipino Catholic Church, part the prospect of an influx of cheap—and non-white—labour from the newly acquired territory. But opponents also pointed to the dangerous consequences for America itself of abandoning the principles of republican freedom and joining the imperialist powers of the Old World. The *Irish World*, meanwhile, drew a more direct connection with the Irish past. Like the Irish at the time of the 1798 rebellion, the Filipinos 'see their religion insulted and their most sacred rights infringed on by insolent foreigners who are trying to steal their country from them'. When the patrician Henry Cabot Lodge defended the military commander in the Philippines, Ford claimed to hear in his words 'an echo of the nasal cant of his Puritan forebears who in Cromwell's time defended the atrocities perpetrated upon the Irish'.[17]

By this time, however, Irish participation in the mainstream labour movement had taken on a more pragmatic character. The Knights of Labor reached the peak of their influence in the mid-1880s, then lost ground rapidly when Terence Powderly failed to provide sufficiently militant leadership during the major industrial conflicts of 1884–6. Instead the dominant force in the trade union movement became the American Federation of Labor (AFL). Its leader, Samuel Gompers, was London-born and of Dutch ancestry. But Irish Americans were also prominent in the organisation, and in the individual unions affiliated to it. The Federation's watchword was 'pure and simple unionism'. This meant turning away from wider issues of social reform, and proposals to create a political movement, in favour of a concentration on wages and conditions of work. The new pragmatism also meant a focus on conflicts that could be won. The AFL was not exclusive in the sense of the old craft unions; it admitted unskilled and semi-skilled workers as well as artisans. But it backed away from confrontation with giant corporations of the kind ruled by Gould or Carnegie, instead drawing its members from areas such as construction, printing and transportation, where smaller firms predominated. There was also an ethnic dimension. Gompers, like Powderly before him, favoured the inclusion of women and African Americans, although strong rank and file resistance meant that few of either were in fact recruited. But he was firmly opposed to opening membership to the growing number of eastern and southern Europeans now entering the labour force. These, in his view, were precisely the sort of unskilled, politically inexperienced workers, recruited in huge numbers by the large corporations, that could assert themselves only by mass revolt. And experience had shown that action of the kind would inevitably be suppressed by well-resourced employers backed by a state willing to employ ruthless coercion. Instead the American Federation of Labour was for the most part a movement of Germans, of those who considered themselves simply American—and of the Irish. The former outcasts, thanks partly to their own efforts and partly to the changing composition of the American workforce, were now a prominent part of the old working class, organised in its own defence.[18]

A further prominent feature of Irish-American political life, as revealed in the story of the American Land League, was passionate support for nationalist movements in Ireland. A continuing engagement with the affairs of the homeland was not unusual in immigrant communities. But what is striking in the case of Irish America is the vehemence of this commitment, transmitted to second and third generations that had never seen Ireland, and broadening into a reflexive but savage Anglophobia. Peter Welsh of the 28th Massachusetts Infantry had been born in 1830 at Charlottetown on Prince Edward Island, Canada. But writing to his father-in-law in County Kildare he was nevertheless able to reel off a catalogue of atrocities from Ireland's past: 'seven centuries of persecution, churches, convents and monasteries plundered and destroyed, confiscated property, murdered patriots and innocent women and children slaughtered in cold blood'. Like many others in the Federal Army he believed that Irish participation in the Civil War would prepare the way for the raising of an army 'that will strike terror to the Saxon's heart'. The socialist campaigner Elizabeth Gurley Flynn, born in New Hampshire in 1890, was even further removed from direct experience of Ireland. But she had been raised on stories of great-grandfathers who had taken part in the Irish insurrection against British rule in 1798, and a grandfather who had emigrated sometime before 1840 and took part in the Fenian invasion of Canada in 1866. 'As children we drew in a burning hatred of British rule with our mother's milk. Until my father died, at over eighty, he never said "England" without adding "God damn her!".[19]

Flynn's image of Ireland came primarily from her family. But there were other ways in which a folk memory of historical wrongs, heroism and suffering could be transmitted. The Irish neighbourhoods that took shape in most American towns and cities were not ghettos. But they provided multiple opportunities, in saloons, at church gates, on doorsteps and street corners, for the passing on of shared narratives. There was also the increasingly rich network of voluntary associations and sporting clubs, many with titles (Sarsfield, Emmet, later Meagher and Mitchel) that recalled key figures in the same patriot mythology. Ballads, whether newly composed or carried over from Ireland, were a further repository of names and images to be passed on to new listeners. Then there was the extensive Irish-American press. Some newspapers had an explicitly political agenda, such as Thomas Francis Meagher's *Irish News* (1856), one of the most important organs of Irish opinion in the years before the Civil War, with a circulation of 50,000; the Boston-based *Pilot,* edited from 1876 by the former Fenian activist John Boyle O'Reilly; and Patrick Ford's *Irish World.* But even less ideologically driven, more commercial Irish newspapers found it necessary to give full coverage of Irish events, past and present. Readers were thus kept informed of the ups and downs of current political controversies and of successive nationalist movements. They were also offered regular refresher courses on the catalogue of historic wrongs that underpinned the sense of national grievance, with features on topics such as the penal laws that had circumscribed the lives of Irish Catholics during the eighteenth century, or the brutal violence that agents of the state indulged in during and after the Irish Rebellion of 1798.[20]

Another institution was important in sustaining the tradition of Irish-American nationalism: the Ancient Order of Hibernians, established in 1836 in New York and in Schuyler County, Pennsylvania, was an offshoot of the Ribbon Society, a Catholic nationalist society that in the years after 1798 sought to keep alive something of the revolutionary ideology of the United Irishmen. Official histories speak of a formal warrant, never seen by outsiders, in which the Irish organisation authorised the creation of an American branch, to be open to all Catholics of Irish birth or descent. More probably some immigrant Ribbonmen decided on their own initiative to replicate an institution familiar from home. The new organisation initially called itself the Friendly (or Ancient Friendly) Sons of Erin, but the name Ancient Order of Hibernians also appeared in the early years, and from the 1850s became common. By the 1870s branches of the Order existed across the United States, recruited mainly from semi-skilled or unskilled workers, the great majority of Irish birth. Membership rose from 53,000 in 1886 to 132,000 by 1908, by which time there were also 55,000 members of a Ladies' Auxiliary created in 1894.[21]

The Hibernians, like the Ribbon movement they grew out of, defined themselves as part of a long tradition of Irish Catholic resistance to domination by a British Protestant state. In the 1860s the Order gave encouragement and financial assistance to the Fenians. In subsequent decades it offered similar backing to both parliamentary nationalists and supporters of physical force. On occasion members took direct action, most notably in New York in 1871, when it was Hibernians who led the violent counter demonstration against the Orange Order's Twelfth of July parade. For the most part, however, the Order operated like any other nineteenth-century working men's fraternity. It collected regular dues from which it provided sickness and death benefits to members and their families. At the same time it offered members regular opportunities to socialise in congenial company. It also organised larger social events, such as picnics and other family outings. The central event of its year was the St Patrick's Day procession on 17 March, but lodges also marched with their banners on other occasions, such as the Fourth of July.

Despite the Order's self-proclaimed role as defender of Catholic interests, the Church initially regarded it with suspicion, as part of its general opposition to oath-bound secret societies. The crisis came during the violence in the Pennsylvania coalfields, when hostile contemporaries sought to present the Molly Maguires as the Hibernians under another name. At its convention in Boston in 1878 the Order adopted a new constitution which it submitted to the church authorities for approval. When delegates next met, in Cincinnati the following year, the archbishop of the diocese gave them a high mass in the cathedral. Having shed the trappings of secrecy it had inherited from its Ribbon antecedents, the Order was now able to become a formidable lobbying body, campaigning on issues like the teaching of Irish history in schools and the provision of Irish texts in public libraries. It was also the Hibernians whose noisy demonstrations, in the last years of the nineteenth century and the first years of the twentieth, drove from the stage the comic Irishman, whose brogue, blunders and enthusiasm for whiskey and fighting had entertained American theatre goers, including the Irish among them, for half a century or more.[22]

The survival in America of a tradition of Irish nationalism is easy to understand. Immigrants brought with them a strong sense of historical grievance that they passed on to their children and built into the fabric of the social institutions they created in their new homeland. To understand the political expression of that nationalism, however, we need something more. Peter Welsh's letter from wartime Virginia immediately recalls the manifesto left behind in Jerilderie, Australia, nearly twenty years later, by the outlaw Ned Kelly. Welsh wrote more coherently, and with a sounder grasp of detail, but where the Irish past was concerned the two men clearly inhabited the same mental universe. Yet neither in Canada, where Welsh's immigrant parents initially settled, nor in Australia, where the young Ned Kelly grew up, did support for militant Irish nationalism become the major force that it was in the United States. To understand the unique ferocity of Irish-American nationalism we need to look beyond the ideological baggage that successive cohorts of Irish emigrants brought with them to different types of immigrant experience. In British North America, and even more so in Australia, the Irish were able to participate from almost the beginning in the construction of new societies. In the United States, or at least in those parts in which they settled in largest numbers, they were forced to take their place at the bottom of an already well-established social order. Despised and exploited, they were more prone to perceive themselves as victims, and to allow historical memory to harden into active grievance and resentment. American society also exerted its own pressures on the immigrant population. In a political culture built around the idea of an aggressively egalitarian liberty, the Irish could be all too easily written off as an inferior people, refugees from political defeat and passive victims of poverty and starvation. A militant spirit of national self-assertion, directed towards the goal of winning a free and independent homeland, was thus a means of establishing the Irish as worthy participants in the life of the American republic. The Irish Land League leader Michael Davitt, speaking in 1880, made the point explicit. 'You want to be honoured among the elements that constitute this nation . . . aid us in Ireland to remove the stain of degradation from your birth . . . and [you] will get the respect you deserve.'[23]

Irish-American support for nationalist agitation in the homeland first became significant in the 1840s, when an American-based Repeal Association movement offered financial and rhetorical support to Daniel O'Connell's campaign for the restoration of the Irish parliament that had been dissolved in 1800–1 by the Act of Union between Ireland and Great Britain. The campaign attracted support from both Catholic and Protestant Irish Americans, as well as from such prominent figures as the former Democratic president Martin Van Buren; Robert Tyler, a son of the sitting president; and a future president, James Buchanan. Support faltered when O'Connell refused to moderate his condemnations of slavery. But the real crisis came in 1845 when O'Connell, ever the pragmatist, announced that in return for self-government Irish nationalists would be willing to support Great Britain in its dispute with the United States over ownership of the Oregon Territory. Not for the last time Irish Americans were forced to choose between their allegiance to Ireland and to the United States. In the southern states the Repeal movement, already exposed to local hostility through the slavery issue, collapsed. In the north it struggled on, as supporters tried to differentiate between O'Connell's personal views and the issue of Repeal. But the cause had been irreparably damaged.[24]

In 1848, as popular revolts erupted across continental Europe, and the Young Ireland movement, having broken with O'Connell, seemed poised for militant action, Irish Americans once again mobilised in support. The Irish Republican Union, launched in New York on 21 March, announced plans to recruit an Irish Brigade of 1,000 men, including veterans of the Mexican-American War, to be shipped to Ireland. The British authorities kept an anxious eye on men arriving in Ireland from the United States, and Crown forces in Canada were put on alert. In the event, the rising staged by the Young Irelanders in July was an embarrassing anticlimax. Some of those involved took refuge in the United States. In 1854 John Mitchel, who sought sanctuary there after escaping from penal confinement in Australia, created an Irishmen's Civil and Military Republican Union, and tried to take advantage of the Crimean War by appealing unsuccessfully for the support of Britain's opponent, Russia. The following year two less prominent veterans of 1848, John O'Mahony and Michael Doheny, formed the Emmet Monument Association—an apparently innocuous title that drew its force from the celebrated speech from the dock in which Robert Emmet, about to be sentenced to death in 1803, had insisted that his epitaph should not be written until Ireland had taken its place among the nations of the earth. Members did military drill once a week, with talk of a full-scale invasion of Ireland to take place in September. That summer, however, one of the members, a 22-year-old tailor called Joseph Denieffe, was summoned home to see his dangerously ill father. When he asked Doheny to whom he should report when he reached Ireland, he was taken aback when he was told that 'we have no one there as yet' and was invited to see if he could put anything together.[25]

What provided the stimulus to more purposeful organization was the appearance in 1857–8 of two serious threats to the British Empire: the prospect of war between Britain and France, and a major revolt against British rule in India. In March 1858 Denieffe, still in Ireland, joined James Stephens, another 1848 veteran recently returned from Paris, and three others to create the Irish Republican Brotherhood, swearing allegiance to 'the Irish Republic, now virtually established'. In New York O'Mahony and Doheny renamed their organisation the Fenian Brotherhood, a term chosen by O'Mahony, a Gaelic scholar, which related to a mythical band of warriors in the distant Irish past. Though formally adopted only by the American movement, the name *Fenian* came over time to be widely used for the movement on both sides of the Atlantic. In 1861 the two organisations achieved a propaganda triumph when they arranged for the body of Terence Bellew McManus, a not particularly distinguished Young Irelander who had died in California, to be exhumed and transported to New York, where Archbishop Hughes arranged a requiem mass in St Patrick's Cathedral. A month later the coffin passed on to Dublin, where a massive crowd, defying the vehement opposition of the city's archbishop, Paul Cullen, escorted it to a new resting place in the city's main Catholic cemetery at Glasnevin.

The outbreak of the Civil War saw members and potential recruits to the American organisation drawn off into the ranks of the Union Army. But the Lincoln administration, frustrated by what it saw as British support for the Confederacy, made no attempt to curb Fenian recruitment and organisation within its armed forces or elsewhere. The Catholic Church, too, was less open in its opposition than in Ireland. In 1865 Bishop Spalding of Baltimore obtained a ruling from Rome that membership of the Brotherhood was incompatible with Catholic teaching. However this was kept secret. The bishops were wary of taking a stand that might encourage the sort of anticlericalism that strident episcopal condemnations had provoked in Ireland. They were also aware that wider American public opinion would see any attempt by the church to dictate the politics of its members as a violation of the republican ethos. In November 1863 the Brotherhood held its first convention in Chicago, attended by eighty-two delegates representing twelve states, the District of Columbia, and several units of the Federal Army. In 1865 the movement took a further significant step by creating a women's auxiliary body, the Fenian Sisterhood, run by a formidable Chicago schoolteacher, Ellen O'Mahoney, which organised balls, fairs and other events to raise money for the movement. (The Irish movement, in the same year, created a rather less prominent Ladies Committee, dedicated to the same sort of fund-raising.) At

Easter 1864 Chicago Fenians organised a hugely successful Great National Irish Fair. The artefacts on display, including a coin 'from the time of Saint Patrick', and two dozen arrows once used by the legendary Gaelic hero Finn McCool, were at times dubious. But the event was a triumphant success, raising an estimated $54,000. The lieutenant governor of Illinois attended the opening, along with a municipal delegation headed by the mayor, while national politicians and three Union generals sent contributions and messages of support.[26]

These were public triumphs. But without progress in Ireland towards an effective insurrection they remained a façade. By the mid-1860s Stephens had recruited around 50,000 followers, supposedly organised in a tight conspiratorial system of self-contained 'circles'. Modern research, however, suggests that for many the Brotherhood was more a social club than a serious commitment to armed action. Stephens himself clearly had limited confidence in the military potential of his organisation, repeatedly postponing the planned rising. The first signs of impatience among his American backers came as early as 1863, when a militant group calling themselves the 'men of action' challenged the leadership at the convention in Chicago. At the third Fenian convention, in 1865, the militants forced through a new constitution, transferring power to an elected senate. When they went on to impeach O'Mahony for alleged financial irregularities, the American movement split into rival factions. The leader of what now became known as the Senate Wing was William Randall Roberts, an immigrant from County Cork and, unusually for a Fenian, a Protestant. Although his roots were in New York, where he had made his fortune as proprietor of a Manhattan department store, his support came mainly from the Midwest, while O'Mahony's supporters were concentrated in the East.[27]

By this time the police had arrested most of the leaders of the Irish movement, and Stephens had fled the country. The government went on to suspend habeas corpus, permitting the arrest and detention without trial of hundreds of Fenian activists. As the prospect of an Irish insurrection faded, the Senate Wing turned instead to the idea of an attack on British North America. Supporters offered a range of arguments. An offensive across the Canadian border would tie up British troops that might otherwise be deployed in Ireland. The use of an American base might draw the United States into a war against Great Britain. More fancifully there was the idea of seizing territory that could be traded for a British withdrawal from Ireland, or possession of which would give those engaged in future Fenian operations the legal status of belligerents, protecting them from charges of piracy or banditry. For many, it seems likely, the real appeal was the prospect of striking at the British enemy where it could be reached.

In the event it was O'Mahony, desperate to restore his credibility, who organised the first attack. In April 1866 around 1,000 Fenians gathered on the coast of Maine, under the command of a former Union infantry officer, Bernard Doan Killian, and supported by a decommissioned naval vessel loaded with rifles. But Killian's force was outnumbered five to one by the soldiers that the British government, well informed through its agents, had stationed along the Maine–New Brunswick frontier. British warships were patrolling the Bay of Fundy, and the United States army was also standing by. Killian's men made two raids on an uninhabited island, seizing a flag and burning a couple of buildings, before withdrawing. In the aftermath O'Mahony tried to save face by denouncing Killian as a British spy who had sabotaged the operation. The Senate Wing's more ambitious plan, the following month, was initially more impressive. From Buffalo, John O'Neill, born in County Monaghan and a battle-hardened veteran of the Civil War, led a party of around 800 men across the Niagara River to Ridgeway, Ontario, where he defeated a party of local militia. The Battle of Ridgeway was a small-scale affair, with ten dead on each side. But it was to be remembered for years as a morale-boosting victory, vigorously re-enacted at Fenian picnics. Soon after, however, the American military was deployed to prevent any further incursions across the Niagara. With larger British forces closing in, O'Neill had no choice but to retreat to his crossing point at Fort Erie, where he defeated another small Canadian force before taking his men back over the river to the American side. On 7 June, in what was meant to be the main Fenian offensive, a force of around 1,000 men crossed the frontier. However they carried only 250 muskets for which they had ammunition. Those who did not flee when British troops appeared sustained no casualties, because the cavalry that dispersed them had been ordered to use only the flats of their swords.

Two further efforts at a Canadian offensive were on a smaller scale. In May 1870 O'Neill, still basking in his status as the victor of Ridgeway and now heading his own faction within the movement, led a force of 400 men across the frontier from Franklin, Vermont. The ostensible target was Quebec, though it is not clear whether there was any real strategic goal beyond a show of armed aggression for its own sake. The invaders skirmished with local Canadians who had formed an unofficial home guard, then retreated when the reinforced defenders charged, leaving three dead. Two days later a second party of around 480 crossed the frontier from New York State, erected a defensive breastwork, but then retreated in the face of a smaller Canadian force, having spent a total of ninety minutes on British soil. In October 1871 O'Neill made one last attempt, this time in the new province of Manitoba, where the mixed-race Métis were seeking to defend their rights against the encroaching government of the new Canadian Confederation. Without the backing of the wider movement, O'Neill pinned his hopes on picking up recruits from the many Irish labourers employed on the Northern Pacific Railway, as work wound down for the winter. But when his party of seventy or so entered Canada and seized a post belonging to the Hudson's Bay Company, United

States soldiers crossed the frontier, with Canadian permission, and arrested them.[28]

The Fenian threat to Canada was at first sight formidable. At the time of O'Neill's raids across the Niagara there were as many as 10,000 men massed along the frontier, many with recent military experience. Yet the movement was never able to translate numbers into effective force. The Fenians could assemble recruits and stockpile weapons. But they did not have the organization or the funds to supply large bodies of men, for any length of time, with the necessities of life. Instead there was a constant turnover of personnel, as would-be Fenian fighters came forward but then melted away when they could no longer pay for their board and lodgings. The number available at any one time was counted in the hundreds, not the thousands. There were also serious political miscalculations. The Fenians placed too much faith in the supposed disaffection of French and Irish Canadians, and of provincial opponents of Confederation. In addition they wholly misread the attitude of the United States government. President Andrew Johnson and Secretary of State William Seward were happy to see Great Britain put under pressure as they negotiated for compensation for wartime losses chargeable to its collaboration with the South. Awareness of the strength of the Irish vote also meant that neither this administration nor the later one headed by Ulysses S. Grant would bring charges against those involved in any of the Canadian offensives. But no American government could contemplate being dragged into a war with Great Britain by Irish military adventurers, and where necessary the United States military intervened to head off any such risk. Tolerance for Fenian antics became more limited still after 1871, when Britain ended the long-running dispute by agreeing to pay reparations for the depredations of Confederate warships built in its shipyards.

By this time the long-awaited Irish insurrection had come and gone. At the end of 1866 a group of American Fenians headed by

Thomas Kelly, a Galway-born veteran of the Civil War, forced Stephens to stand aside and constituted themselves as the provisional government of a free Ireland. But the rising they staged on 5–6 March 1867 petered out after a few small-scale clashes, mainly in County Dublin and in parts of Munster. Reports that Ireland was up in arms inspired O'Mahony's faction to send a supply ship, the *Erin's Hope*, carrying a formidable array of weapons—three artillery pieces, 5,000 rifles, crates of revolvers, sabers and 1.5 million rounds of ammunition. However the rival Senate Wing bribed the courier sent to alert Fenian leaders in Ireland to arrive deliberately late, so that when the ship arrived off the Irish coast on 10 May there was no eager throng of volunteers waiting to unload its lethal cargo. Twenty-four passengers, the majority of those on board, went ashore near Dungarvan, County Waterford, and were fairly quickly arrested. The remainder lingered for a few days off the coast then set off, already dangerously short of food and water, on a gruelling voyage back to the United States.

Following these repeated failures, a much-diminished Fenian movement continued for a few years, led by O'Mahony and then by Jeremiah O'Donovan Rossa, the former prisoner who had failed in his 1872 attempt to capture Boss Tweed's New York State Senate seat. But leadership of militant Irish nationalism had now passed to a new organisation. Clan na Gael, founded in 1867, began as an obscure secret society with masonic rituals. But it found a new leader in John Devoy, who like O'Donovan Rossa had come to the United States after serving a prison sentence for Irish Republican Brotherhood activities. In 1876 Devoy established the movement's credentials, and revived the sinking morale of Irish-American nationalists, with a spectacular success. The whaling ship *Catalpa* sailed from New Bedford, Massachusetts, to the coast of Western Australia, where it picked up six prisoners transported for their part in the 1867 rising and carried them to freedom in America. By 1877 the Clan had 10,000 members and had re-established links with the Brotherhood on the other side of the Atlantic. In a second ambitious, though this time secret, project the Clan, between 1876 and 1883, spent almost $35,000 subsidising the attempts of the County Clare–born engineer John Philip Holland to construct a submarine. Two decades later Holland's designs were to become the basis of the United States Navy's first commissioned fleet of 'Holland-class' submersibles. His designs were also to be taken up by the Imperial Japanese Navy and even—to his annoyance—by the British Admiralty. But none of the three prototypes he built for the Irish republican movement proved satisfactory.[29]

The ostensible aim of the revived transatlantic nationalist movement was the traditional one: an armed insurrection to liberate Ireland from British rule. But in 1873 the supreme council of the Brotherhood had already turned its back on the idea that a revolutionary vanguard could force events forward by armed action. A revised constitution made clear that any future 'war against England' would have to wait until it was clear that it had popular support. Devoy, too, seems to have been looking beyond a simple repeat of the tactics of 1867. In 1878–9, at the same time that he was organizing a scheme to provide Irish supporters with up-to-date American rifles, he was in discussions with Michael Davitt, a former Fenian now committed to the emerging campaign of resistance to the demands of Irish landlords. What emerged was the New Departure, a tripartite agreement whereby American nationalists would support Charles Stewart Parnell, from the militant wing of the parliamentary Nationalist party, on the understanding that Parnell would commit himself to a vigorous campaign for Irish self-government and reform of the land system. Devoy did not abandon the idea of revolution. Part of his thinking seems to have been that the refusal of the British government to respond to peaceful protest would produce mass support for more extreme methods, and he continued to organise arms shipments to Ireland. But his deviation into politics left the way clear for a militant faction headed by Alexander Sullivan and two associates, collectively known as the Triangle, to take control of Clan na Gael. The headquarters of the new leadership was Chicago. There they could draw on the support of the new, assertive, often more prosperous Irish population that had been attracted to the rapidly growing capital of the Midwest. They also had the advantage of a Catholic archbishop, Patrick Feehan, who was more tolerant of militant nationalism than many of his colleagues.

The move away from armed insurrection was part of an international trend. European revolutions in the first half of the nineteenth century had begun with barricades in the streets of major towns, or bands of peasant insurgents. But in the world of railways, the electric telegraph and soldiers equipped with fast-loading firearms, those tactics had little future. By the 1870s and 1880s anarchists and other revolutionary groups across the Western world were turning to new tactics. Pitched battles in the streets or fields gave way to terror and assassination, pikes and rifles to revolvers or, more particularly, to explosives, as in the bomb that killed the Russian Tsar Alexander II in 1881. In 1875 O'Donovan Rossa, in cooperation with Patrick Ford, launched a 'Skirmishing Fund' to finance operations with dynamite, the more stable solid form of nitroglycerin that had been invented eight years earlier. Two years later Devoy, far more skilled in political in-fighting, seized control of the fund, large parts of which went to support Holland's experiments. But O'Donovan Rossa, now at the head of a new organisation, the United Irishmen of America, went ahead with a bombing campaign in Great Britain, beginning in January 1881 with an explosion at a military barracks in Salford. Further attacks targeted the Mansion House, the official residence of the Lord Mayor of London, an army barracks in Chester, and Liverpool Town Hall. In January 1883 the Triangle group, now in control of Clan na Gael, launched its own campaign with bombs at three locations in Glasgow, a railway station, the gasworks and a bridge. Other attacks followed, at government offices, the headquarters of the *Times* newspaper, and elsewhere. The campaign reached its climax on 24 January 1885, when more or less simultaneous explosions took place at the House of Commons, Westminster Hall and the Tower of London. The Salford bomb had brought down a wall that killed a 7-year-old boy. Later, in October 1883, glass and debris from a bomb on the London Underground caused injuries to seventy-two passengers, thirty of whom required hospital treatment. But these were the only serious injuries. The main victims of the bombing campaign in fact were three of the dynamiters themselves, killed in December 1884 when the bomb they attempted to position under London Bridge detonated prematurely.[30]

The bombing campaign came abruptly to a halt after January 1885. One reason was a desire to allow the Home Rule Party, now led by Parnell, to take full advantage of the opportunity created by the Representation of the People Act of the previous year, which had extended the right to vote to almost all male heads of household. And indeed the Irish party achieved a sweeping victory in the general election of November 1885, leaving Parnell holding the balance of power in the United Kingdom parliament. But the dynamite campaign had in any case proved disappointing. Explosions in major British cities caused alarm and outrage, but not the chaos or collapse of morale that had been predicted. With failure, meanwhile, came internal divisions. Sullivan had from the start a dubious reputation. In the past he had been acquitted of arson following a fire in the shoe shop he had run in Detroit and had fled New Mexico leaving a deficit of $10,000 in his accounts as Collector of Internal Revenue. In Chicago he had been controversially acquitted after shooting dead a school principal who had accused his wife of corrupt dealings. But he nevertheless became a figure of influence, cultivating both Democrat and Republican politicians, and with their assistance turning the local Clan into an effective machine for the dispensing of municipal patronage. Now, however, opponents attacked the disasters of the bombing campaign, as well as Sullivan's failure to provide for the families of men killed or imprisoned. There were also questions about money not properly accounted for. In May 1888 one of Sullivan's main critics, Doctor Patrick Cronin, well-regarded in the city both for his medical work among the poor and for his performances as a singer at public events, disappeared from his lodgings. His body was found eighteen days later in a sewer, with head wounds indicating he had been beaten to death. A detective in the Chicago Police Department, Sullivan's main hunting ground in matters of patronage, was one of three men convicted of the murder, although he was acquitted on appeal. Eight other police officers were dismissed for their handling of the case. Sullivan himself was never charged. But the scandal put an end to his political career. It also left Clan na Gael divided and largely ineffective.[31]

For two decades, from the end of the Civil War to the suspension of the bombing campaign, the United States had provided the base for a series of armed offensives against British rule in Ireland. In retrospect, this can be recognised as a period of transition. The most impressive appearance of Irish nationalists in arms had come in the immediate aftermath of war, when the United States was awash with guns and large numbers of ex-soldiers had yet to reintegrate themselves into civilian life. Over the next few years, as veterans found work, established a settled residence, perhaps married and began a family, the pool of potential recruits for serious military action became more limited. Support for militant nationalism was also the response of what was still, in the immediate postwar years, a marginalised and often vilified underclass. Two decades after the end of the Civil War, on the other hand, the Irish, through their powerful position in the labour movement, in urban government and in municipal employment, as well as in the Catholic Church, had become a strong and firmly established interest. The economic status of many was also beginning to improve.

With these changes came a softening of attitudes. Statistics from Pittsburgh in the 1880s reveal differences in both class and generation. Irish-American residents of the city had a choice of two political causes: the Skirmishing Fund, linked to the dynamite campaign, and the American Land League, implying a commitment to vigorous resistance to the claims of landlords, and to the pursuit of home rule, but stopping short of revolutionary violence. Working-class residents contributed to both, but an emerging middle class of professionals, businessmen and shopkeepers only to the second. Equally important the great majority of subscribers to the Skirmishing Fund—more than nine out of ten—were Irish-born. Immigrants might pass on a broad sympathy for the cause of Ireland, and an associated Anglophobia, to sons like Peter Welsh or even granddaughters like Elizabeth Gurley Flynn. But few beyond the first generation were active supporters of physical force nationalism.[32]

None of this meant that the Irish in America abandoned the cause of the homeland. The Ancient Order of Hibernians and other Irish societies organised lectures, concerts and excursions, all with a patriotic theme. They turned out, with their green flags and other Irish regalia, for Fourth of July parades and similar civic occasions. It was also during the 1890s that a more self-conscious revival or invention of traditional Irish culture took place, with the spread of Gaelic football and hurling, and festivals dedicated to Irish music and dancing. In all of this, the rhetoric of an oppressed nation denied the freedom that should belong to it remained prominent. But the emphasis had switched from political action to commemoration and celebration, and much of the appeal to those taking part lay in the opportunities for recreation and sociability. In Chicago, on every 15 August, the United Irish Societies organised a picnic to celebrate the anniversary of one of the great battles of late Elizabethan Ireland, the defeat of Crown forces at the Yellow Ford, in County Armagh, in 1598. In 1894 the sardonic saloon keeper–philosopher Mr Dooley, created by Finley Peter Dunne in the pages of the *Chicago Evening Post*, gave his commentary on the proceedings:

> In th' ol' days they wint over with dinnymite bombs in their pockets, an' ayether got their rowlers on thim [got drunk] in Cork an' blew themselves up or was arristed in Queestown f'r disorderly conduct. 'Twas a divvle iv a risky job to be a pathrite in thim days.

Today, however, 'they give picnics that does bate all. By hivins, if Ireland cud be freed be a picnic, it'd not on'y be free to-day, but an impire, begorra'.[33]

9

THE OTHER AMERICA

At two o'clock on the morning of 7 April 1868 Thomas D'Arcy McGee left the imposing Gothic revival–style federal parliament buildings in Ottawa, where he sat as a member for Montreal West, at the end of the evening's business. An ulcerated leg required him to walk with a cane, but he was in good spirits, exchanging greetings with some of the House of Commons staff. As he neared his lodgings, however, he seems to have become aware that he was being stalked. He quickened his pace and knocked urgently on the door of his lodgings. As his landlady opened the door, she was knocked back by a flash and the sound of an explosion. As she recovered she became aware that her nightgown was splattered with blood. It had gushed from McGee's mouth as he slumped in the threshold, shot in the back of the neck.

McGee's assassination came at the end of a life marked by dramatic personal changes of direction. Born in 1825, the son of an Irish revenue official, and brought up mainly in the town of Wexford, he had begun his career as a journalist, first in Boston and then back in Ireland. Having initially supported Daniel O'Connell's campaign for repeal of the Act of Union, he abandoned constitutional nationalism for the more militant Young Ireland movement. He fled Ireland after the failed rising of 1848, and then, back in the United States, renounced revolutionary politics in favour of the peaceful pursuit of Irish self-government under the British Crown. As a revolutionary he had denounced the Irish Catholic clergy for interfering in secular matters by their opposition to armed rebellion. But by 1852 the Know-Nothing movement had turned him into an ultra-Catholic conservative, arguing that an unquestioning submission to the authority of the church, and a militant defence of its rights, were the only defence against religious indifference, Protestant heresy and the collapse of social order. Appalled by the concentration of the American Irish in squalid industrial cities, he for a time supported proposals to establish Irish colonies on the western frontier. In the end, however, his eyes turned north. Visiting Montreal in 1854, he wrote enthusiastically of 'the glitter of a hundred crosses crowning the tin-covered domes and spires, which glisten like silver in the sun . . . the high-walled and deep-gated nunneries, the clergy, secular and regular, walking abroad in their proper habits'. In 1857 he moved to Canada and by the end of the year had been elected to the Legislative Assembly of the Province of Canada as an independent MP for Montreal.

McGee's Canadian career brought further dramatic shifts in his allegiances. Catholics in British North America had two less than ideal political options. The Liberal-Conservative Party had ties to the Orange Order, while the rival Reform Party shared with radicals elsewhere a distaste for denominational education, at times shading into positive anticlericalism. The Liberal-Conservative leader, John A. Macdonald, was himself an Orangeman, but he was also a supreme political pragmatist, whose power rested in part on an alliance with Catholic French Canadians. The leaders of the Canadian church generally looked to his party as most likely to favour their interests. McGee, on the other hand, opted initially for the Reform Party, and was president of the executive council in the Reform administration of 1862–3. Disillusioned by the experience, he joined the Liberal-Conservatives, and was back in government between 1864 and 1867. During these years he played an important part, as orator and as behind-the-scenes facilitator, in the negotiations that brought about the union of Ontario, Quebec, Nova Scotia and New Brunswick as the Dominion of Canada.

McGee's support for Canadian Confederation was inspired by a highly personal vision of 'a new northern nationality'. The British colonies in North America, he argued, should become a self-governing federation, but should be kept within the British Empire by the creation of a Canadian monarchy, held by a junior branch of the royal family. The federal parliament, in line with McGee's continuing concern to balance democracy with social order, should include a hereditary upper house. Within this framework the inhabitants of British North America would grow into a Canadian nation, assisted by an ambitious programme of railway building and economic development. Their unity would be founded, not on the surrender of existing identities, but on compromise and respect for difference. McGee remained a strong champion of publicly funded Catholic schools, and a vocal critic of the Orange Order. But he insisted that it was also up to the Catholic Irish to move away from anything that might be a cause for conflict. On this basis he called for an end to St Patrick's Day processions. He also became a fierce critic of militant Irish nationalism, denouncing as murderers the three executed Fenians that most of his countrymen regarded as the 'Manchester Martyrs'. Exactly how these provocations led to his murder remains unclear. The Fenian leadership in the United States reportedly deplored the assassination. The man convicted of firing the shot, Patrick James Whelan, was an unstable character, who apparently developed a fixation on McGee. But Whelan also had Fenian connections, and his comments before he faced the hangman suggest that he did not act alone, but was part of a squad of like-minded Irish Canadian militants.[1]

Thomas D'Arcy McGee was not a typical Irish immigrant to Canada. His middle-class background, his high political office, and his literary distinction, as well as his ideological and political somersaults, all mark him out as an exceptional case. By the time of his death, in fact, there were signs that his uncompromising hostility towards the Fenians, even when they were dead or in prison, had become too much for some of his Irish Canadian supporters. He had been expelled from the Montreal branch of the St Patrick's Society, an organisation that had once been part of his power base, and he had only narrowly retained his seat in the election to the new federal parliament. But in his death all was forgiven. Across the four days that his body lay in his Montreal home, between forty and fifty thousand people came to pay their respects. Some 80,000 turned out to watch the funeral procession, itself 15,000 strong. Canada's political elite joined in the tributes. As McGee's body left Ottawa, Macdonald, now federal prime minister, and other leading figures acted as pallbearers for a man hailed as one of 'the Fathers of Canadian Confederation'.

It is this acknowledged status as a national political figure that makes McGee's career significant. It is impossible to imagine an Irish Catholic newcomer to the United States of the same period achieving a comparable distinction. The nearest parallel is the Australian career of McGee's friend and mentor Charles Gavan Duffy. British North America in the nineteenth century was no showpiece of communal harmony. There were deep divisions along the lines of language, nationality and religion. But Canada's circumstances— the haphazard accumulation of distinct colonies, each with its own character and interests, and the presence of a French-speaking and Catholic population too large to be marginalised or suppressed— encouraged the development of a political culture based on compromise and expedient alliances. European settlement in this part of North America had a much longer history than in Australia. But the Canada that took shape in the course of the nineteenth century was a new society, one which its Irish residents, like their counterparts in the southern hemisphere, could feel that they had had a part in building.

———

The creation of Irish Canada was concentrated into a period of just over forty years. In the seventeenth and eighteenth centuries there were Irish communities in Newfoundland and Nova Scotia. But settlement in mainland Canada did not get under way until after 1815, when economic conditions in Ireland deteriorated while, at the same time, the British government began to promote settlement as a way of securing the southern frontier of its North American possessions. By the early 1840s there were roughly 160,000 Irish-born in British North America, three-quarters of them in Ontario and Quebec. The punitive levy imposed on arrivals following the disastrous year of 1847 succeeded in its aim of directing refugees from the Famine elsewhere. But it did not mean the end of significant migration. Between 1848 and 1854 British North America received a further 179,000 Irish immigrants, roughly the pre-Famine level of 25,000 a year. Where the Famine did make a difference was in making Irish America, with its hugely expanded population, the natural magnet for future emigrants. The young man or woman concluding there was no place for them at home was now far more likely to have relatives or friends in Chicago or New York than in Toronto or Montreal. After 1855, as the total number leaving Ireland suddenly fell away, the contrast became apparent. Between 1861 and 1910, 2.6 million Irish emigrants made their way to the United States. Canada received just 160,000, accounting for fewer than one in twenty of those choosing to emigrate to destinations outside the United Kingdom.[2]

In economic terms, too, Canada had less to offer. Its economy expanded modestly in the second half of the nineteenth century, assisted by rising world demand for food and lumber, a surge in railway building, and the development of mining and manufacturing. But none of this development could compare with what was taking place in the emerging industrial giant to the south, with its insatiable demand for labour. When, after Confederation in 1867, the Canadian government sent agents to Ireland to recruit emigrants who would help to populate the vast empty territories in the west, they reported that one of the greatest obstacles that they faced was the superior attractions of the United States. The only part of Ireland where the agents achieved a degree of success was Ulster, where earlier emigration patterns meant that potential migrants were more likely to have contacts in Canada, and where there was a large Protestant population likely to welcome the opportunity to emigrate while remaining within the dominions of the British Crown.[3]

The main attraction of Canada, apart from cheaper passages, had been the easy availability of land. But those who took advantage had to cope with the challenge of the Canadian climate. In 1866 an Irish immigrant settled in Indiana contrasted his new home, where cattle in need of winter feed found the stalks of last year's corn protruding above the level of any normal fall of snow, with the conditions he had known in British North America, where 'they have to hand feed for 6 months and the life is almost froze out of them into the bargain'. By the 1860s, moreover, most of the best agricultural land in the eastern half of Canada had been settled. The Ontario government attempted to relieve pressure by opening up lands bordering the southeastern corner of Lake Huron, but the thin soil and exposed granite of what this far north became the Canadian Shield proved unrewarding. Better lands lay further west, but progress was slow. There was some settlement in British Columbia, assisted by gold strikes in 1858 and 1862, and by the 1880s in Manitoba. But it was not until the early 1900s, fifteen years after the completion of the Canadian Pacific Railway in 1885, that a determined government campaign succeeded in promoting settlement on the landlocked prairie provinces of Alberta and Saskatchewan. At this point there was, significantly, a small increase in the number of migrants arriving from Ireland.[4]

The period of large-scale emigration was short. But the 160,000 or so Irish who settled before 1845, reinforced by whatever proportion remained in Canada from the 300,000 or so who arrived in the following ten years, became the foundations of a significant component of what was still a fairly small population. The first census of the new Dominion of Canada, in 1871, broke new ground in recording not only the nationality of the immigrant population, but the ethnic origin of the Canadian-born. The results revealed that persons of Irish birth or descent made up just under a quarter of the inhabitants of the new dominion, coming second only to the French. In Ontario and New Brunswick the figure was more than one in three. Over the next few decades, as fresh arrivals from Ireland remained insignificant, while emigration from other sources continued, their prominence gradually diminished. Even so, in 1901 the proportion classified as of Irish descent was still more than one in six, and in Ontario well over one in four.[5]

In contrast to the United States, whose Irish immigrant population was by now predominantly Catholic, the Irish of British North America were, in religious terms, more evenly divided. In 1871 just over half (54 per cent) of the Irish in modern Canada (the Dominion plus Newfoundland and Prince Edward Island) were Protestant. Catholicism was strong in the eastern provinces, which had long had links to southern Ireland. Newfoundland's Irish population was almost entirely Catholic. In Nova Scotia, Catholics accounted for half of those of Irish ancestry, and two-thirds of the

Irish-born. In Quebec, unattractive to Protestant immigrants because of the dominance there of the French language and of French Catholicism, two-thirds of the Irish-born were Catholic. In New Brunswick, on the other hand, Protestants made up three-fifths of those of Irish descent and almost half of the Irish-born. And in Ontario, which by 1871 contained two-thirds of the entire population of Canadians who were Irish by birth or descent, roughly the same proportion, two out of three, were Protestant rather than Catholic.[6]

Even as Irish emigration to British North America collapsed, those immigrants who in the first half of the century had taken on the laborious task of settling new lands were beginning to enjoy the reward for their efforts. Nathaniel Carrothers from County Fermanagh had emigrated in 1835 and taken a first plot of 100 acres in Westminster Township, Ontario. By 1853 he was the owner of 187 acres, of which 96 were cleared and fenced, and could boast of a mature farmstead: 'a good, decent frame house decently finished', with a large barn and stabling for livestock, a vegetable and flower garden, and an orchard of fruit trees, 'such as apples, pears, plums, peaches, cherries'. The isolation of early pioneer days had given way to life in a settled neighbourhood. London, the nearest town, 'has become a large and fine place since we came to this country. There is a great many fine churches, and merchant shops and wholesale warehouses, all of brick.' The Great Western Railway, linking Niagara and Windsor and passing through London, was under construction. All in all, it was 'a fine country for a man to live in. . . . I never was sorry for coming, but ever shall be that I spent so many of my days in Ireland.'[7]

Nathaniel Carrothers was not alone in savouring the results of labour and enterprise. In the census of 1871 just over half of all men of Irish birth or descent listed their occupation as farming. In Ontario, the most common destination for Irish newcomers from the 1820s onwards, the Irish were not only the largest ethnic group within the farming population, they were also the most successful. They were slightly more likely than others to be the owners rather than tenants on the land they occupied, and their farms were also significantly larger. At a time when fifty to sixty acres was reckoned to be sufficient to provide a family with subsistence but little more, the average Irish farm was eighty-five acres, compared to seventy-six acres for all Ontario farmers and only sixty-five acres for those of English and Welsh descent. In contrast to the social hierarchy they had left behind in Ireland, this rural prosperity was enjoyed by both Protestants and Catholics. The farms of men of Irish Catholic background were only slightly smaller than those of their Protestant counterparts (eighty acres as compared to eighty-five), putting them on a par with the Scots and better placed than any other ethnic group. They were also just as likely as Irish Protestants to be the owners of the land they farmed.[8]

What of other sections of the Irish population? Statistics on occupations in 1871 suggest that across Canada as a whole both Irish Protestants and Irish Catholics were as well represented as other ethnic and religious groups among merchants, manufacturers and professional men, and in white-collar occupations. At regional level Irish Protestants were less well off in Nova Scotia than elsewhere. Irish Catholics had a strong presence in commercial and professional occupations in Quebec. In New Brunswick and Nova Scotia, on the other hand, they were underrepresented in farming and overrepresented in labouring and semi-skilled work. A study focussing more directly on wealth reveals a sharper religious differential. Probate records for men dying in Ontario during 1891 show that Irish-born Protestants left on average $7,275, only a little less than the $7,763 left by those who were neither Irish nor Catholic; Irish Catholics, on the other hand, left an average of only $5,427. However this was true only for men aged over 50 at the time of their death. Later immigrants, Catholic men born in Ireland after 1840, died with significantly more assets than those of the same age born elsewhere, suggesting that they had either brought with them better skills and resources, or else found it easier than their predecessors to make their way in Canadian society.[9]

Irish Catholic disadvantage was most evident in the towns. In 1871 three out of ten urban Catholics of Irish birth or descent were unskilled labourers, twice the level in the overall population. Among Irish Protestants the figure was fewer than one in eight. In Hamilton, Ontario, a modern study concluded, just over one-third of the population in 1851 could be classified as living in poverty. Among Irish-born Catholics, however, the figure was more than half, rising to over two-thirds in 1861. There was also little social mobility. Three-quarters of the sons of Irish Catholic labourers in Hamilton were also unskilled manual workers, while more than one in five of the sons of the minority of Irish Catholic artisans failed to follow their fathers into skilled work. Hamilton was perhaps a special case, a town that grew very rapidly from small beginnings during the 1840s and 1850s, and possibly attracted more than its share of impoverished Irish immigrants during the Famine years. But even in Quebec City, where Catholics were the dominant religious group, the Irish-born heads of household among them were still twice as likely as their Protestant counterparts to be unskilled labourers. In places, indeed, the condition of the Irish Catholic urban working class may not have been very different from that of their counterparts in the United States. One French-language newspaper explicitly compared parts of Montreal's Griffintown, the city's Irish quarter, to the slums of Boston and New York. The difference was that in Canada these were the conditions of just one part of a diverse Irish population. Others within that population had found it possible, in a newer and more open society, to realise the promise of emigration in a way that remained beyond the reach of their American counterparts.[10]

Statistics on property ownership, given contemporary law and practice, apply overwhelmingly to men. Limited industrial growth, prior to the last years of the nineteenth century, meant that the main area of employment open to women was domestic service, and both the Irish-born and the Canadian daughters of Irish immigrant parents became a familiar fixture in middle-class parlours and kitchens. As in the United States there were frequent complaints that Canadian servants, aware that demand for their services exceeded supply, were lacking in due deference. Servants, a manual for prospective British emigrants warned in 1870, had to be treated well, 'for if one party is not inclined to do so, another will, and knowing this, the servant is more independent of the employer than *vice versa*'. Canadian humorists and newspaper writers were nevertheless quick to ridicule the naivety and lack of refinement of the docile but slow-witted Bridget. But the stereotype was misleading. In Hamilton, 60 per cent of servants were Irish-born (compared to only one-third of the overall population) but only 47 per cent were Catholic. In Toronto, Canada's Orange capital, where newspaper advertisements unashamedly advertised a preference for Protestant domestics, half the domestic servants in the town's elite residential areas were of Irish birth or descent, but fewer than one-third were Catholic. Bridget, it seems, was often joined in the kitchens and parlours of the affluent by Florence and Betsy.[11]

Domestic service was for most a stage in a life cycle. Working-class girls left the family home from the age of 13 on, to become live-in servants. From the age of 19, however, the proportion of women in paid employment fell sharply, as more and more married. Instead, married working-class women contributed to the family budget outside the world of wage labour. They raised pigs, chickens or a single cow, or grew vegetables on the small allotments that were common in urban areas, peddling anything they produced above the needs of the family from their houses or on the streets. Others sewed at piecework rates, took in laundry, or kept boarders. In rural areas the options were different. Once again many young women went into service as a combination of maid and farmhand. Wives and stay-at-home daughters, meanwhile, became part of the family enterprise, keeping house and assisting on the land, perhaps taking particular responsibility for an area such as poultry or dairying, as well as providing additional hands at peak times, such as harvest. Their working life was thus not all that different from what they would have known if they had remained in Ireland. The rewards, however, were for many significantly greater.[12]

The St Patrick's Society of Montreal came into being in 1834. It was a late addition to an array of such societies created by merchants and professional men of Irish birth or ancestry in the cities of British North America. Halifax, for example, had its Charitable Irish Society, created in 1786, while St John's, Newfoundland, had a Benevolent Irish Society, established in 1806. Like their counterparts in Philadelphia, Baltimore and other cities in the United States, these foundations in British North America combined the functions of social club and philanthropic agency. They offered assistance to widows, orphans and other distressed Irish immigrants, donated money to hospitals, schools and poorhouses, and combined these good works with a round of lively social gatherings. The Halifax society was noted for having as many as fifty toasts at its St Patrick's Day banquets; on one occasion the festivities did not end until sunrise on 18 March. The success of such proceedings, bringing together Catholic and Protestant members of a local urban elite, depended on steering clear of divisive sectarian and political issues. The Charitable Irish Society in Halifax, for example, became over time increasingly Catholic, but continued to elect some of its presidents from the Protestant minority. In 1838 it joined enthusiastically in the public celebrations for the coronation of Queen Victoria, setting up a hospitality tent and sponsoring a not very successful attempt to roast a whole ox.[13]

The St Patrick's Society of Montreal initially followed the same pattern of apolitical and cross-denominational patriotism. Its members included both Catholics and Protestants, and at dinners it exchanged toasts and fraternal greetings with its sister bodies, the St Andrew's and St George's Societies. By mid-century, however, this solidarity of the comfortable and benevolent had begun to break down. A report in 1853 that officers of the St Andrew's Society attending a 17 March dinner had been embarrassed to find themselves expected to drink to the health of the pope suggests that the nondenominational character of the society was already being eroded. Meanwhile a new parish priest had begun to establish alternative charitable ventures, such as an orphan asylum and a home for the aged, that were exclusively Catholic. In 1856, partly at the priest's instigation, the St Patrick's Society dissolved and reconstituted itself as an explicitly Catholic body. Protestant members responded by establishing their own Irish Protestant Benevolent Society. In 1864 this body joined with the St Andrew's and St George's Societies to create a United Protestant Immigrants' Home.[14]

The collapse of mutual accommodation within the Montreal society was part of a general hardening of religious divisions within British North America. Immigrants from Ireland had already introduced their tradition of Catholic-Protestant conflict during the first half of the nineteenth century. During the 1830s, for example, Protestant gangs in the hinterland of Peterborough, Ontario, used nighttime raids and other forms of intimidation to deter Catholics from settling in what they considered their territory. In Woodstock, New Brunswick, Catholics turned out to stop a newly formed Orange lodge marching on 12 July 1847, leading to fighting in which ten, all on the Catholic side, died. Two years later there was further serious violence, with twelve deaths, after Orange marchers insisted on forcing their way, with flags and drums, through the mainly Catholic residential area of York Point in Saint John. But new developments in the 1850s and 1860s deepened existing divisions, and extended them to a broader section of Canadian society. The Fenian movement reawakened the spectre of

Catholic conspiracy, this time extending to North America as well as Ireland. Meanwhile the Catholic Church was taking on a new voice, dogmatic and uncompromising, in particular in its assertion of papal authority. On the other side the rising influence of evangelicalism in all of the main Protestant denominations encouraged a similar, more confrontational approach. Against this background it is no surprise to find that the years after 1850 stand out as the period of most rapid expansion for the Orange Order, with almost one-third of the lodges established during the nineteenth century founded between 1854 and 1860.[15]

Throughout the second half of the nineteenth century Orangeism remained a central institution of Canadian Protestant society. By 1900 there were perhaps 60,000 active Orangemen. Branch records, however, indicate that turnover within the movement was very high, so that a much larger number, up to one-third of the Protestant male population, had been initiated at some point. By this time the Irish-born represented only a small minority, and Canadian-born Protestants of Irish descent were joined by large numbers whose ancestry was English, Scottish or other, but who were attracted by the Order's combination of imperial patriotism, sociability and a firm assertion of Protestant primacy. This was particularly the case as Orangeism spread to Nova Scotia and Prince Edward Island, where it appealed mainly to Scots, and to Newfoundland, where it was taken up by those of English descent. There were even lodges on several First Nation reserves, where, since white men were not allowed to join, there was no Irish element whatever. In the western provinces, Orangeism was carried to Manitoba by internal migrants from Ontario and from there to Alberta and Saskatchewan.[16]

The appeal of Orangeism did not depend solely on a spirit of sectarian aggression. In setting up Orange lodges Irish Protestant immigrants were recreating something of home, maintaining or establishing contact with others of the same background as themselves, and providing opportunities for companionship and conviviality. For those labouring to establish pioneering home-steads, in particular, the regular meetings of the local lodge must have stood out as brief but valued points of light and warmth in an otherwise lonely existence. The central role of sociability helps to explain why Canadian Orangeism had a more complicated and exotic body of ritual than its Irish counterpart, with five degrees of membership rather than two. Drinking, too, was initially a prom-inent part of the proceedings, although temperance was to gain ground within the movement as the century went on, and from 1859 lodges were forbidden to meet in hotels or saloons. There was also an element of social insurance: lodges commonly provided sickness benefits and contributed to the funeral cost of members, and from 1881 the Order ran a mutual benefit fund, although this never became big enough to rival friendly societies such as the Oddfellows and the Foresters.

Although Orangeism spread to all parts of Canada, its most im-portant stronghold remained Ontario, and in particular the city of Toronto. There Orangeism was central to what developed as the closest parallel within British North America to the machine pol-itics of the urban United States. The city elected its first Orange mayor in 1845; of the twenty-three men who followed him into that office during the rest of the nineteenth century, twenty were also members of the Order. In 1847 Irish Protestants, at least half of whom were Orangemen, held fifteen of the eighteen seats on the municipal council. Membership of the Order likewise became almost a requirement for employment in the police force, the fire service, or the municipal bureaucracy. The city's huge Twelfth of July parade became a central part of urban civic ritual, attended by local politicians and leading city officials, with public employees given a day off to enable them to attend. What was particularly striking was that this dominance was not just religious, but eth-nic. By the 1890s just under one-tenth of Toronto's population had been born in Ireland. Yet these Irish-born held a full quarter of jobs in the public payroll. Another quarter of all municipal employees had at least one Irish parent. The Protestant Irish, in other words, had acquired a stranglehold on municipal employment in Toronto reminiscent of the achievement of their Catholic counterparts in Tammany Hall. Critics drew a different but equally obvious parallel, labelling Toronto the Belfast of Canada.[17]

Religious divisions, in Toronto as elsewhere, also found expression in violence. In 1858, two weeks after D'Arcy McGee had used his maiden speech in the Ontario parliament to denounce Orangeism, angry Protestants attacked the hotel at which he and others were celebrating St Patrick's Day. In 1864 a crowd invaded the grounds of the Catholic cathedral to attack a Corpus Christi procession carrying the consecrated host. The potential for violence increased in the late 1860s with the introduction to Toronto of a youth auxiliary to the Orange Order, the Young Britons, which became a rallying point for young men in search of the rougher kinds of excitement. The 1870s saw sixteen significant clashes, most of them arising out of parades and demonstrations on 17 March or 12 July. There was also, in 1875, another attack on a Catholic religious procession, when protesters stoned and tried to attack a large body of pilgrims walking between two churches as part of the observances of a jubilee year.[18]

Despite incidents of this kind, the label 'Belfast of Canada' was something of an exaggeration. The Protestant near monopoly of municipal patronage, and the privileged access to public space granted to the Orange Order, offered undeniable parallels. There was also a degree of residential segregation in Toronto, with distinctively Catholic and Protestant districts. But here there was no comparison with Belfast, where three out of every five inhabitants in 1901 lived on a street where nine-tenths or more of their neighbours were of one religion. Belfast's sectarian violence was also on a wholly different scale. In Toronto, a Catholic man was fatally stabbed during the St Patrick's Day riot of 1858. But this appears to have been the only death of its kind. There were reports, both during the Corpus Christi riot of 1864 and the jubilee riot of 1875, of revolvers being brandished, and in some cases fired, but no one was killed on either occasion. In Belfast, by contrast, twelve people died during the riots of 1864, and at least thirty-two during the riots of 1886. Belfast's religious wars, moreover, were to continue, up to and including the murderous communal conflict of 1920–2, when 498 people died. In Toronto, sectarian clashes became less common from the 1880s, as the Young Britons lost the endorsement of the Orange Order and the police took a tougher line with on-street troublemakers.[19]

Sectarianism, then, was an inescapable part of the public life of British North America. But in general, as in the case of Toronto, animosities remained largely within bounds. One reason may have been the drying up of immigration from Ireland after 1855. The Irish Catholics and Protestants who clashed at Woodstock and Saint John had been born in Ireland, mainly in Ulster. Their counterparts thirty or forty years later were more likely to be the sons or grandsons of Irish immigrants; indeed many enrolled in the Orange Order by that time had no family connection with Ireland whatever. Their attachment to the political and religious values of one side or the other may have been as strong as ever, but it lacked the edge of personal animosity that came with an upbringing in the overcrowded, feud-ridden countryside of Armagh or Tyrone.

Political structures were also important in keeping sectarianism in check. For Great Britain the price of taking over the French colonies of North America in 1763 was the recognition of the civil and political rights of the Catholic population of Quebec province, and of the entitlements, including the legally enforceable right to collect tithes, of the Catholic Church. The law was different elsewhere, but the Quebec precedent made it difficult to present Catholics as political non-persons, especially after Ontario and Quebec were amalgamated in 1840 into a single province. Where circumstances were favourable, Canadian politicians were happy to appeal to sectarian solidarity. In 1872 George King, premier of New Brunswick, having forced through legislation to create a non-denominational school system, fought an election on the slogan 'Vote for the Queen against the Pope'. More commonly, however, the key to political success was to balance the claims of competing religious factions. As prime minister, John A. Macdonald, for example, normally took care to have one or two fellow members of the Orange Order in his cabinets. But he never forgot his party's dependence on the French Catholic vote in Quebec, and he was also aware of the need to compete for a share of the minority Catholic vote in other provinces. His response to the attack on Toronto's Corpus Christi procession in 1864 was to write a letter of apology, in his capacity as provincial premier, to the Catholic archbishop, whom he addressed by his formal ecclesiastical title as 'My dear lord'. (The city's mayor, in contrast, had written to 'Reverend Sir'.)[20]

What this meant in practice was that the Orange Order, though influential, never entirely got its own way. Attempts by D'Arcy McGee and others to have the Order legally categorised as a secret society, and its members excluded from the administration of justice, came to nothing. But in 1858 the parliament of the united provinces of Ontario and Quebec rejected a proposal to give the Order a charter of incorporation, intended to make it easier for lodges to hold property, but also important as conferring a degree of symbolic recognition. The charter did not in fact come until 1890, and then only as part of another typical Canadian compromise: it was a concession intended to soothe Protestant resentment of a bill to compensate the Catholic Church for property confiscated from the Jesuits at the time of the British conquest in 1759. Another consequence, equally important, was that Canadian Catholics were never pushed into the position of seeing the political establishment as indifferent or hostile to their interests. The Catholic clergy, for their part, avoided any potentially divisive linking of their church to one particular party. A Presbyterian newspaper compared the position of Thomas Connolly, archbishop of Halifax from 1859 until 1876, to that of a commercial company taking care to have partners associated with each side of party politics. 'It is very much better that denominations should be politically divided, and it was both wise and politic on Connolly's part to permit his flock freedom. In this he showed much shrewdness.'[21]

The political issue of greatest importance to the Catholic Church, in Canada as elsewhere, was schooling. Here again Quebec was crucial, as a precedent and in setting the ground rules. Its publicly funded school system was under the control of the Catholic Church, so that the protection offered to religious minorities was for the benefit of the province's Protestants. In Ontario, Michael Power, bishop of the new diocese of Toronto from 1842 until 1847, was prepared to accept a non-denominational public school system, with safeguards for Catholic children, as the best that could be achieved at a time when the Catholic population was too small, and too poor, to support its own institutions. His successors pressed more insistently for support for Catholic schools. An act of 1841, following the unification of Ontario and Quebec, had already permitted any group of inhabitants whose religion differed from that of the majority to request the establishment of a denominational school. In practice Catholic initiatives in Ontario remained vulnerable to obstruction from unsympathetic local authorities. But in 1863 new legislation established the right of Catholics to public funding for their own schools. The act was forced through the parliament of the united province only by the voting power of Quebec. However the measure also had the support of some Orange representatives. Their argument was in part that the principle of separate schools had already been conceded. Some were also interested in the right of minority Protestant groups, such as High Church Anglicans, to have their own schools. Others again calculated that the departure of Catholic pupils from the public schools would allow them to become de facto Protestant institutions. Once again sectarian animosities interacted with pragmatic calculation. When Nova Scotia introduced a system of free, non-denominational schools the following year, the government rejected Catholic demands for separate provision similar to that provided in Ontario and Quebec, but conceded that Catholic schools in the city of Halifax should be eligible for funding as public institutions.

During 1866–7, as the act to create the new Dominion of Canada was being finalised, Archbishop Connolly of Halifax travelled to London alongside the official Canadian delegation, and sought to use his influence as a leading supporter of Confederation to ensure that the settlement included guarantees for the religious rights of minorities. However the French Catholic delegates, more concerned with protecting Quebec's unique privileges than with the welfare of Catholics elsewhere in Canada, determinedly opposed anything that would increase the power of the federal government. The British North America Act, in consequence, stipulated only that provincial governments should not interfere with educational rights already existing by law. The stage was thus set for further conflicts, but also further compromises. Conflict over New Brunswick's Common Schools Act of 1871, which required Catholics to pay taxes for a new system of non-denominational public schools, escalated into violence in 1875 when two men died in a confused confrontation. The participants here were French rather than Irish Catholics, and a compromise quickly followed whereby Catholic children could be grouped in particular schools, members of religious orders would be facilitated in gaining recognition as teachers, and textbooks would be selected to exclude anything offensive to Catholics. In Manitoba the Catholic bishops, again French rather than Irish, responded to the introduction in 1890 of a mandatory non-denominational school system, with English the only medium of instruction, by forbidding their followers, on pain of sin, to vote for candidates from the governing Liberal Party. In response the Liberal leader, Wilfrid Laurier, negotiated a compromise along the same lines as in New Brunswick. In addition, in a remarkable reversal of the normal Liberal attitude to Roman intervention, he persuaded the Vatican to send an apostolic delegate to put a stop to episcopal attacks on his party.[22]

If a spirit of pragmatic compromise helped to keep the sectarian animosities of nineteenth-century Canada under control, one other circumstance was also important. This was the extent to which the country's Irish Catholic inhabitants steered clear of the bellicose nationalism so popular among their American counterparts. There had been a flurry of interest in Irish affairs in the last stages of the campaign for Catholic Emancipation. Friends of Ireland societies appeared in Quebec, Montreal, Halifax and elsewhere. But an attempt in 1831 to move on to the new cause of Repeal of the Act of Union failed to take off. After 1848 the issue of Irish nationalism assumed a new importance in Canada, as American-based activists turned to the idea of a direct attack on Britain's closest imperial possession. In 1858, in response to Orange attacks on the St Patrick's Day procession and dinner, Catholics in Toronto formed the Hibernian Benevolent Society. Its president was Michael Murphy, born in County Cork but brought as a child to Ontario, where he had begun as a cooper but was now proprietor of a tavern. Further branches of the Hibernian Benevolent Society followed, in Quebec, Montreal and other centres. Its ostensible purpose was to defend the Catholic community from Protestant aggressors, combined with the provision of benefits to sick or otherwise distressed members. But in reality it quickly became a front for the extension into Canada of the Fenian Brotherhood. On 5 November 1864, a night when Protestants would traditionally have assembled to celebrate the failed Catholic attempt to blow up the English parliament in 1605, the Toronto Hibernians showed something closer to their true character by a dramatic show of strength.

While the city's Orangemen prudently kept their commemoration of gunpowder, treason and plot indoors, around 500 Hibernians, armed with guns and swords, took control of the streets until two o'clock in the morning, when they dispersed after firing a volley.[23]

The Guy Fawkes Day demonstration of 1864 was a dramatic moment. But it marked the high point of Fenian credibility in Canada. When American Fenians staged their long-awaited incursion into British North America in 1866, Murphy received a telegram instructing him to bring a detachment to join Killian's force. The cipher was easily broken by the Canadian police, and Murphy and six companions were arrested on their way to Montreal. The government worried that the arrest had been premature, as there was not enough evidence to ensure a conviction, but Murphy resolved the issue by escaping from jail and fleeing to the United States, where he died in 1868. Later, after 1870, when the arrival of figures like Devoy and O'Donovan Rossa, newly released from British jails, injected new life into militant nationalism in the United States, some of the new activity spilled over into Canada. Both the United Brotherhood, the secret wing of Clan na Gael, and O'Donovan Rossa's United Irishmen had what they called circles in Montreal, Quebec and other centres. In 1882 O'Donovan Rossa's followers considered a proposal that would have attracted even more attention than the killing of D'Arcy McGee: to kidnap Princess Louise, a daughter of Queen Victoria, conveniently accessible because her husband, the Marquis of Lorne, had become governor general of Canada. However this came to nothing. And membership numbers remained insignificant. The United Brotherhood and O'Donovan Rossa's organisation had between them possibly as few as 300 members, with another 1,000 or so who bought their publications or contributed to their funds. The most that the small group of militant nationalists could hope to achieve was thus to act as a behind-the-scenes influence within larger, more moderate organisations—as when in 1909 Jeremiah Gallagher inserted a strong anti-British message into the Irish-language (though not the English or French) version of the inscription on the Famine memorial at Grosse Île.[24]

The Canadian Irish did not wholly lose interest in the politics of their homeland. Catholic newspapers continued to cover the progress of successive constitutional nationalist movements, from Isaac Butt's Home Government Association to the Irish Parliamentary Party of John Redmond in the years before the First World War, and Irish Canadians contributed some of the funding on which the continuing agitation depended. But support for moderate, constitutional agitation of this kind was well within the limits of the politically acceptable. What was being asked for, after all, was no more than what Canada itself already enjoyed. In 1882, in fact, John Costigan, the Canadian-born son of an Irish immigrant and a leading representative of the Catholics of New Brunswick, was able to get the federal parliament to approve a mild resolution in favour of home rule for Ireland. But such residual allegiances were now framed firmly in Canadian terms. Nationalist speakers on tours of North America were generally welcomed in the main centres of Irish Canadian settlement. But when the Nationalist Member of Parliament William O'Brien arrived in 1887 intending to denounce the governor general, Lord Lansdowne, for his exploitative management of his Irish estates, he found most Irish Canadians unwilling to be associated with this direct attack on the queen's representative. It was a mentality summed up by one of the great success stories of the Canadian part of the Irish diaspora. Frank Smith, born in County Armagh in 1822, had been left in poverty when his immigrant father had died before he was able to establish himself as a farmer in Ontario. However he had gone on to work his way up from grocer's assistant to become the millionaire owner of his own extensive retail business and a union-busting railway baron. He was also a senator, won over from the Reform Party in yet another of Macdonald's shrewd moves, and a cabinet minister.

'We love the old country', he observed in 1897, 'we love our own too; and we also see the beneficial results of home rule would apply to the whole empire.'[25]

The emergence of an Irish Catholic Canadian identity involved one further complication. What had to be established was not just a relationship with mainstream Canadian culture, English-speaking and Protestant, and with the British government and its local representatives. In Canada, Irish Catholic newcomers encountered another Catholic population, with its own unique political position, its own traditions, and its own strong sense of identity. For a time it seemed as if the two might forge a political alliance. In Montreal and Quebec roughly one in seven of subscribers to the Friends of Ireland were French Canadians. Irish activists reciprocated by emphasising the parallels between the positions of Catholics in Quebec and in Ireland, both majority populations denied representative government and instead subjected to the rule of a corrupt and despotic Protestant oligarchy. Edmund Bailey O'Callaghan, editor of the main English-language Catholic newspaper, the *Vindicator*, described Quebec as 'the Ireland of North America', and became a close associate of the *patriote* leader and speaker of the Legislative Assembly, Louis-Joseph Papineau. Others hailed Papineau as 'the O'Connell of Canada'.[26]

The sense of common enterprise, however, did not last. The sudden spike in Irish immigration during 1830–4, most of it focussed on Quebec and coinciding with the first outbreak of cholera, had seriously damaged the Irish in the eyes of French Canadians. On the Irish side, equally, the Shiners' War of the mid-1830s, when hard-bitten Irish gangs had used extreme violence to break the French-Canadian monopoly of employment in the timber trade of the Ottawa Valley, made clear that shared religion, or a shared antipathy to the established order, was no guarantee of amity. More important, most Canadian-based O'Connellites, unlike O'Callaghan, were no more ready to follow the *patriotes* into armed insurrection than their counterparts in Ireland were to follow Young Ireland in the same direction. Instead the Irish disassociated themselves from the *patriotes* as their language became more militant, and most played no part in the two rebellions mounted by discontented Francophone residents of Lower Canada during 1837–8. Later, in the 1860s and 1870s, American supporters of an invasion of Canada were to convince themselves that the people of Quebec would welcome the overthrow of the British oppressor, but made no attempt to establish links with those they proposed to liberate. By contrast, an Irish engineer resident in Ottawa warned in 1866 that 'no people are more disliked in Quebec than our countrymen'. It was also the French Canadians, he pointed out, whose votes were mainly responsible for keeping in power the 'Orange governments' of the Liberal-Conservative Party.[27]

The divergent interests of French and Irish Catholics were particularly evident in the management of church affairs. There was from the start a major cultural difference between the French system of ecclesiastical management, in which committees of laymen had a well-established role in the management of a parish, and the more top-down system of episcopal governance to which the Irish were accustomed. For most of the nineteenth century open conflict was kept in check by a quite clear-cut territorial division. The Maritime provinces were initially a missionary territory supervised by the archbishop of Quebec. But most of the clergy, reflecting their settlement history, were Irish or Scots, and it was from among them that, as independent dioceses were created, the region's bishops came. Atlantic Canada, despite the presence of a substantial French-speaking minority, did not get a French bishop until 1912. Quebec remained firmly in the hands of a French clergy and episcopate. But west of the Ottawa River, in English-speaking Canada, what emerged was a 'hibernarchy', a Catholic Church dominated, as in the United States, by bishops and priests of Irish birth or descent, and supported in schools, hospitals and orphanages by sisters of Irish religious orders. New questions of jurisdiction arose in the late nineteenth and early twentieth century, as immigrants began to pour into the prairie west. The French church, with a tradition of often heroic missionary service going back to the seventeenth century, believed that it had not just a historic destiny but a God-given mission to bring Christianity to this corner of North America. The Irish, however, had different ideas. The Catholic Church Extension Society, established in 1908, was intended to provide pastors for the Italian, Polish, Ukrainian and other settlers of Manitoba, Alberta, Saskatchewan and British Columbia, while at the same time facilitating their assimilation by having them taught English. The competing claims of French and English Catholicism were fought out in a series of contests over appointments to new or vacant bishoprics. The odds, however, were weighted heavily in favour of the Irish: as in the United States, where it promoted Irish over German claimants, the Vatican took the pragmatic view that an English-speaking clergy was the most effective instrument in the great drive to win North America for the one true church. So, with a few exceptions, Catholicism west of Ontario, like Catholicism in the older English-speaking parts of Canada, came to have an Irish face.[28]

A political alliance of Irish and French Catholics was the dog that did not bark in the night. There were, of course, practical reasons why Irish Catholic Canadians should have been wary of political extremes. A mainly rural population provided fewer opportunities for clandestine organisation than the great cities of the United States. For a fairly small minority living in a British dominion, equally, militant nationalism posed risks that did not exist in often Anglophobic America. Yet episodes like the Guy Fawkes Day demonstration in Toronto in 1864 make clear that Canadian Irish Catholics were not slow to assert themselves when they felt the need. For the most part, however, they were not driven to do so. Life in Canada was no idyll. Immigrants faced hardship, discrimination, and at times violence. But it also offered opportunities to achieve at least modest comfort and security, and a political system characterised by negotiation and compromise rather than unbending exclusion. In these circumstances the response of most Irish Catholics was not to join their French co-religionists in an ideological ghetto, but to seek to become part of an English-speaking, imperial, but reasonably open new society.

10

AN IRISH WORLD

In the years before the First World War emigration remained a central fact of Irish life. Between 1891 and 1910 there were a further 780,000 permanent departures. In relation to population, the emigration rate was now about two-thirds of what it had been in the 1860s and 1880s. To this extent Ireland had at last achieved a better balance between people and resources. But there were still those, year after year, to whom an economy dominated by the small family farm offered no place. A high birth rate among those who remained partly compensated for the loss caused by emigrant departures. But the population nevertheless continued to decline, from 4.7 million in 1891 to 4.4 million twenty years later.

By this time the Irish no longer stood out as one of Europe's main migrant peoples. The three-quarters of a million emigrants who left Ireland in the 1890s and 1900s were a small part of the twenty million who crossed the Atlantic in these years. Italy alone sent more than five million, Austria-Hungary more than three. The transport of passengers, once a minor supplement to the carriage of goods, was now a major industry in its own right. The new immigrants from southern and eastern Europe still for the most part made the journey in steerage of the traditional kind: each adult allocated a berth measuring 6 feet by 2, arranged in giant compartments holding up to 300 passengers or more, their only escape from the foul air and cramped conditions a small area of open deck. In northern Europe, on the other hand, competition between shipping firms for the custom of a somewhat better off population had encouraged the replacement of steerage by a new category, the third class passage. The best of the new accommodations put passengers in compartments holding from eight to as few as two berths, with hooks for clothes, a chair, a mirror, possibly even a separate washstand. Other versions still put each class of passenger—single men, single women and family groups—in a single large compartment. But where traditional steerage passengers had been required to eat in their berths, or at best on rough tables in the passageways in between, this version of third class offered a separate dining room, which outside mealtimes served as a general recreation area, giving passengers a space away from their berths without having to brave the crowding and variable weather of the open deck.[1]

A third class passage was not necessarily a comfortable experience. In October 1921 Genevieve Forbes, a 27-year-old feature writer for the *Chicago Tribune*, sailed from Queenstown to New York aboard the *Celtic*, disguised as an Irish immigrant. The third-class passengers, she reported, were treated 'as though they were doing us a favour to bring us over'. The *Celtic* had been refitted to accommodate more second-class passengers, so that the 580 travelling in third class were confined to the rear poop deck, with benches holding just 64 passengers and two small shelters, for use during rainfall, with room for just 30 to 40 people at a time. Forbes did not witness the sexual harassment of female passengers by crew that had been reported as common in the old steerage system, and that another investigator had found still existing on ships from continental European ports. 'I went over there', she admitted, 'because 9 or 10 people had definitely made charges of gross immorality. I found none. I found what I thought were distinctly indiscretions.' But the indiscretions were unpleasant enough. On arrival at New York female passengers had to strip to the waist to be examined for possible skin diseases. The examination was conducted by women, but the passengers were conducted there by male stewards, who gloatingly informed them that they would be present to see everything, while afterwards they were 'thrown out on an entirely open deck . . . where there were men around, with our clothes in our hands'.[2]

From the ship, immigrants passed into the hands of the American authorities. The opening of Castle Garden in 1855 had initially been welcomed as a means of protecting the newcomers from exploitation, while also screening out undesirable arrivals. By the 1880s, however, there were complaints that its officials, appointed through the patronage politics of New York State, were corrupt and incompetent. There were even claims that the notorious 'runners' had been able to resume their business within the centre's walls. In 1890 the federal government took direct charge, establishing a new reception centre on Ellis Island, in the city's harbour. Here Forbes's account of her experience was mixed. She witnessed some rough handling: a girl's cap roughly torn off when she was slow in removing it for an examination, and a Frenchman pushed down a flight of stairs when he made a fuss about being separated from his family. And, as on board the ship, some of the male attendants on the island enjoyed taunting the women with comments on the intimate examination they were about to undergo. The officials, too, were brusque, but in Forbes's view 'they were simply in a hurry or simply businesslike. . . . I distinguish very much between the ordinary incivility and the humiliation and indecency.' She also reported a rough paternalism. The inspector who processed her agreed to let her stay a few nights in New York rather than putting her on a train to Chicago, her official destination, but only after she had supplied the address of a well-regarded women's hotel. Even the officer who threatened her with detention when she intervened to help five young women in difficulties was, she conceded, carrying out his duty of protecting new arrivals from unauthorised persons who might seek to take advantage of them.

At the Ellis Island reception centre, the newly arrived passed before a line of doctors searching for signs of a physical or mental deficiency that might debar them from entry. Next, inspectors questioned them about their background, personal history and future plans. From 1917, males aged between 16 and 55 had to pass a literacy test in any language of their choosing. Those with medical problems might be forced to spend a period in quarantine. But the number refused admission was low, fewer than one in a hundred up to 1910, and fewer than two in a hundred thereafter. Here new Irish immigrants may well have coped better than most. They spoke English, they had enjoyed the benefit of one of the best systems of public health in western Europe, and most would have been briefed on what to expect by friends or relatives who had already made the journey. But the alien and impersonal setting, the heat and stench of the overcrowded reception rooms as numbers peaked in spring and summer, the gruffness of hard-pressed officials, and a knowledge of how much was at stake must nevertheless have made the whole process uncomfortable and anxious.[3]

The coming of the purpose-built passenger vessel had one other consequence. The bulk transatlantic trade, by its nature, was from east to west. To avoid having their vessels make the return journey empty, shipping lines began to offer heavily reduced fares on sailings to Europe. Irish emigrants who had achieved at least modest prosperity in the United States were quick to seize the opportunity. For every 100 Irish travellers who sailed to North America between

1895 and 1911, about 47 sailed in the opposite direction. A few among these travelled home for good. Contemporaries complained of well-heeled returnees bidding up the price of land. And indeed the census for County Leitrim in 1911 includes fifty-one men with American-born children, forty-five of whom were farmers. There were also stories of female 'Yanks' armed with the dowry that would allow them to purchase the husband of their choice. But the only available statistics suggest that the number of women seeking to exchange the amenities of Chicago or New York for the life of an Irish farmer's wife was smaller than folklore suggests. Permanent returnees of any kind, in fact, were not numerous. In the early twentieth century more than half of all Greek emigrants to the United States, just under half of Italians and one-third of Poles returned to their homeland. Among the Irish the figure was 10 per cent or less. Instead the great majority of those Irish who made the eastward journey were clearly happy to take the opportunity to visit family and friends, but were firmly committed to a new life on the other side of the Atlantic. A schoolteacher sailing from Moville to New York around 1901 wrote scathingly of these short-term returnees, who after a few years in the United States 'had picked up most of the American slang and catch phrases. I guess, yeh (for yes), the double negative and so on. "Stooard if I were in Noo York I guess I'd have a good square meal" was the remark of one of these Irish girls.'[4]

Between the 1840s and the 1880s the failing economy of the Famine years, and the more prosperous but rigid social order of post-Famine Ireland, had between them forced the departure of 4.5 million people to destinations round the world. In 1891 just over three out of every five of all those born in Ireland still lived there. The great majority of the remainder were unevenly distributed across four locations: 645 out of every 1,000 were in the United States, 225 were in Great Britain, 79 were in Australia and 51 were in Canada. Yet it was in the lesser among these destinations that the overall impact of Irish settlement was most significant. In Great Britain and the United States the Irish population in the late nineteenth century, even when expanded to take in the estimated number of children and grandchildren of the original immigrants, amounted to well under one-tenth of the total population. In Australia on the other hand, those of Irish birth or descent accounted for just over a quarter of the population in 1891; in New Zealand and in Canada the figure was a little under one in five. This, however, marked the high point of the Irish diaspora. Mass emigration to Canada had already come to an end in the mid-1850s. Emigration to Australia had reached a high point between the 1850s and the 1880s, but was to fall away sharply in the 1890s, as a severe depression brought a brutal end to several decades of prosperity. A deteriorating economy, along with the phasing out during the 1880s of the assisted passages that had made the 14,000-mile voyage possible, also reduced what had always been the much smaller Irish movement to New Zealand. Future emigration was to be largely to just two destinations, Great Britain and the United States.[5]

What position had Irish immigrants and their immediate descendants achieved in these different locations? In the United States at the end of the nineteenth century newly arrived Irish immigrants faced much the same prospects as their predecessors. They were more likely to be able to read and write, and to speak English confidently. But most were still from small farms or labourers' cottages, without the skills industrial and commercial America was likely to reward with any generosity. Instead their future lay in meeting the continued demand for hard manual labour and the most poorly rewarded personal services. In 1900 the most common occupations of Irish-born men were listed as 'servants and waiters, masons, saloon keepers and bartenders, labourers and iron and steel workers'. Irish-born women were most commonly domestic servants, janitors and laundresses. It was in the second generation that the changing position of the American Irish was evident.

The sons of Irish immigrants were still often found in the building trades and as barmen and saloon keepers. But they were now overrepresented, relative to the white male population as a whole, among bookkeepers and accountants, clerks and copyists, and had reached rough parity in terms of the number in the professions. The daughters of immigrants, meanwhile, had moved decisively away from domestic and personal service. An Irish-born woman was nearly two and a half times more likely than white working women in general to be a domestic servant; in the case of her daughter the likelihood dropped to two-thirds. Many second-generation Irish women were employed in factories, but they were also overrepresented in office work, as clerks, stenographers or telephone operators, as shop assistants and saleswomen, and also as teachers. The American Irish were no longer the poorest section of the American workforce. Instead, taking first and second generation together, their profile broadly resembled that of the native-born. They, or at least the Catholic part among them, remained poorly represented at the upper levels of commercial and industrial wealth. But they had a particularly strong base in skilled, unionized occupations and—a testament to the continued power of the urban political machine—on municipal payrolls. And with this improved economic position came the confident brashness that so irritated the censorious Ulster schoolteacher in 1901.[6]

The improved status of the Irish was reflected in their depiction in popular culture. Anti-Irish and anti-Catholic prejudice had not disappeared. In 1887 Harry F. Bowers of Clinton, Iowa, outraged that Irish mill hands organised by the Knights of Labor had secured the defeat of his favoured candidate for mayor of the town, formed the American Protective Association. Echoing the Know-Nothing movement of thirty years earlier, the Association warned of the threat that Catholics, constantly reinforced by new waves of immigrants, presented to the values of the American republic. Its membership peaked in 1894, at 2.5 million. In newspapers and magazines, on the other hand, the images of murderous, ape-like Hibernians that had proliferated in the years after the Civil War had now become uncommon. Stereotypes continued, as they did for other ethnic groups. Paddy was still a simple soul, and Bridget, in domestic matters, a dunce. But the edge of hostility was gone. Condescending amusement had replaced fear and dislike. Meanwhile a new subject for satire had emerged: the 'lace curtain' or 'steam heat' Irish, who had done well enough to leave the inner-city working class but struggled to adapt to the respectable society they aspired to join. The most enduring embodiment of this theme was Jiggs, the Irish bricklayer brought to life in 1913 by the cartoonist George McManus, himself the son of Irish immigrants, in the comic strip *Bringing Up Father*. When Jiggs wins a million dollars in a sweepstake, his wife, Maggie, is determined to install them in high society, while Jiggs wants nothing more than to sneak back to his old neighbourhood for a drink, a game of poker and a plate of corned beef and cabbage. Jiggs retains elements of the old physical stereotype: a forward jutting chin, a low, backward-sloping forehead, and a short stocky body. And at times he is the butt of the joke, as he fails dismally to adjust to his new surroundings. But he also serves, in his role as henpecked husband, and in his encounters with snooty servants and snobbish hosts, as a put-upon everyman. There is also an implied contrast between his down-to-earth authenticity and Maggie's inept social climbing. And on occasion, when one of Jiggs's strategies succeeds and he escapes back to his old haunts, he becomes the hero of the strip. These multiple layers of meaning help to explain why the series continued until 2000. For a time in the early 1960s it even appeared, alongside other American offerings, on the cartoon page of a Dublin Sunday newspaper, for an audience that appears to have been only vaguely aware, if at all, that it had a specifically Irish reference.[7]

It would be wrong to suggest that this relatively privileged position had been achieved at no cost. The novelist J. T. Farrell's trilogy on the early life of Bill 'Studs' Lonigan, son of Irish parents in pre–First World War Chicago, is rightly seen as a classic account of the new 'steam heat' Irish. Lonigan's father, Paddy, the son of 'a pauperized Greenhorn', began his career as an apprentice painter but built up his own business. Yet, as he sits on the veranda of his house in a pleasant middle-class street, his thoughts are of less fortunate friends—Spike Kennedy, 'bit by a mad dog and died', and 'poor Paddy McCoy . . . whose ashes rested in a drunkard's grave at Potter's Field'. Then there was his own family.

> Bill had run away to sea at seventeen and nobody had ever heard from him again. Jack, Lord have mercy on his soul, had always been a wild and foolish fellow, and man or devil couldn't persuade him not to join the colours for the war with Spain and he'd been killed in Cuba. . . . And Mike had run off and married a woman older than himself, and he was now in the east, and not doing so well, and his wife was an old crow, slobbering in a wheel chair. And Joe was a motorman. And Catherine, well, he hadn't even better think of her. Letting a travelling salesman get her like that, and expecting to come home with her fatherless baby; and then going out and becoming—a scarlet woman.

In the early twentieth century, pioneering ventures into social statistics confirmed Farrell's pessimistic vision. Ireland had one of the lowest death rates in Europe. But in the United States the offspring of Irish-born mothers, in other words both immigrants and the second generation, stood out as having the highest death rate of any ethnic group, only slightly better than that of the non-white population. The excess was particularly notable in the age range 45 to 64. The two main killers were tuberculosis and vascular diseases of the heart and brain. Deaths from tuberculosis could be linked to the high proportion of Irish immigrants living in crowded urban accommodation. Where other killer ailments were concerned, some observers suggested that the rural environment and temperate climate of Ireland left its emigrants particularly ill-equipped to cope with conditions in America. Alcohol could also have played a part. But it is hard not to wonder how far Irish immigrants were simply worn out by the heavy manual labour in which so many were employed. In addition, coronary and other vascular ailments, and for that matter heavy drinking, could be seen as symptoms of the stress so many experienced as they sought to make their way in a foreign, and often hostile, environment. Out of every 100,000 Irish-born inhabitants in New York State in 1911, 34 were patients in mental hospitals suffering from an alcohol-related disorder; 122 were confined on account of other mental conditions. The comparable figures for the American-born were 5 and 30, for the Italian-born 2 and 45, and for the German-born 11 and 87. Becoming a part of American society, in other words, came at a cost, for many a greater one than they were able to sustain. But for those who survived, and even more for their sons and daughters, the benefits were, by the beginning of the twentieth century, becoming clear to see.[8]

———

This modest improvement in the social status of the Irish took place at a time when the ethnic make-up of American society was being transformed. Between 1820 and 1860, 39 per cent of immigrants entering the United States, almost two out of five, had been Irish. The rest were mainly British or from northwestern Europe. Between 1899 and 1924, on the other hand, the four largest groups of immigrants, accounting between them for just under half of the total, were Italians, Jews (three-quarters of them from Russia), Germans and Poles.[9]

Relations between the Irish and these new arrivals were often hostile. American cities had always had their territorial divisions, with German, Irish, Black, and in some cases Chinese, districts. But what now took shape was a much more complex patchwork of neighbourhoods, whose boundaries constantly shifted as new arrivals staked their claims and upset existing territorial divisions. On building sites and dockyards, meanwhile, the poorer sections of the Irish population found the near monopoly they had established, partly by violently excluding African Americans, under threat from growing numbers of Italians, Poles and others. The response, once again, was violence and intimidation. In New York in 1906 the coroner investigating a series of suspicious deaths among Italians working on the building site for Grand Central Station heard evidence of a feud that had begun several years before when an Italian working with dynamite had accidentally caused the death of an Irish labourer. The frequent deployment of Italians and others as strikebreakers further contributed to resentment and distrust among the unionised Irish.[10]

There was more to the Irish relationship with the new immigrants, however, than brawls on building sites or scuffles on the edges of residential districts. Violence and intimidation were no more effective in fending off the threat of the newcomers than they had been, half a century earlier, when used by nativists against the Irish. And for the same reason: the newcomers were leaving their homeland because they had no other realistic choice, and the American economy needed their labour. The only sensible response to the appearance of these new immigrants in the workplace was to put class solidarity ahead of ethnic rivalry, which meant bringing them into the organised labour movement. For urban political machines, equally, the arrival of large numbers of poor voters in desperate need of intermediaries to assist them in dealing with an alien officialdom could be seen as an opportunity rather than a threat. In Chicago, for example, the Democrats opened a naturalization bureau in party headquarters and dispatched party workers to take charge of different ethnic groups. By such means the Irish were, in the short run, able to bring the newcomers under their control without surrendering the firm hold that they had acquired over these areas of American life. In the Chicago stockyards the Irish in 1904 made up only a quarter of the workforce, but they constituted 57 per cent of local union officials, representing a workforce that now included Germans, Czechs, Slovaks, Poles and Lithuanians. In New York and San Francisco, immigrant groups other than the Irish made up three-fifths of the workforce, but held just over one-third of all places on the public payroll.[11]

In their other great centre of institutional power, the Catholic Church, the Irish made even fewer concessions to the newcomers. They had already seen off a challenge from their longer-established rivals when in 1886 they defeated a call by the clergy in the so-called German Triangle of Milwaukee, St Louis and Cincinnati to be allowed their own separate ecclesiastical organisation. The Germans and the French Canadians did, however, have their ethnic parishes, and the Germans were allowed a minor share in church government, holding around 15 per cent of American bishoprics in 1900. The newcomers fared less well. Dioceses continued to create ethnic parishes and even imported priests from Italy and Poland. But in districts with the highest levels of immigration church building could not keep pace with the explosion of numbers, so that the new arrivals often had to be satisfied with masses squeezed into a schedule dominated by English-language services, or conducted in a basement or annexe. There were also cultural conflicts. In particular, bishops made clear their disapproval of Italian popular religion with its strong focus on the celebration of festivals and the cult of particular saints, combined in many cases with a truculent anticlericalism. The resulting clashes had a certain irony. One of the features of the 'devotional revolution' that had transformed Irish Catholicism in the middle decades of the nineteenth century had been a lengthy but ultimately successful campaign by bishops and priests to tame or eliminate practices such as ritual observances at holy wells or the lighting of bonfires on St John's Eve, replacing them with a strictly orthodox routine of mass, the sacraments and officially sanctioned devotions such as Benediction and the Stations of the Cross. Now, half a century later, an Irish clergy whose outlook had been shaped by that religious revolution were in turn seeking to impose their values on another peasant people deeply wedded to its own traditions.[12]

The great surge in emigration from southern and eastern Europe had two major implications for the place of the Irish in the wider society of the United States. In the first place, in a familiar process, the addition to the ethnic hierarchy of a new bottom tier brought promotion to those on the existing lower levels. In comparison to the other main immigrant groups of the early and mid-nineteenth century, English, Scottish and German, the Irish, and in particular the Catholic majority among them, had been easily categorised as inferior. Now, however, they were being compared with a very different type of newcomer, as poor and apparently uncouth as the Irish had ever been, and in addition suspected of bringing with them the dangerous political doctrines of socialism and anarchism. In relation to the new emigrants themselves, meanwhile, the Irish came to occupy a distinctive intermediate position. In the American city, as the economist and social reformer Emily Balch observed in 1910, the newly arrived Polish or Italian immigrant encountered at every turn a people who had established their own secure niche. Faced with 'Irish policemen, Irish politicians, Irish bureaucrats, Irish saloon keepers, Irish contractors and Irish teachers, [they] could be excused for thinking that "Irish" equalled "American"'. The Catholic Irish might still be excluded from the social and sporting clubs, the dinner tables and the schools and colleges of the elite. But for millions of newcomers they were in a very real way the gatekeepers to the New World.[13]

The second-largest group of Irish living outside their own country is easily overlooked. The 653,000 Irish-born residents of Great Britain in 1891 had travelled a short distance and remained within the boundaries of the same political unit. But the place they came to occupy in their new environment was that of an immigrant under-class. Early Irish settlement in Great Britain, in the late eighteenth century and up to the 1820s, was in many cases a movement of weavers and other skilled workers. By the 1830s, however, Britain was becoming the destination of those too poor to seek the broader opportunities offered by Canada or the United States. These were the Irish immigrants whom George Cornewall Lewis, in 1834, described as supplying the 'animal strength' that made British in-dustrial growth possible. The arrival from 1846 of huge numbers of starving and diseased refugees from the Famine confirmed the status of the Irish as the bottom layer of urban society; they were poor, largely unskilled and widely regarded as a threat to the soci-ety in which they had settled. Statistics collected from seven towns between 1851 and 1871 show that well over half of the Irish-born population were in unskilled or semi-skilled work. In Cardiff in 1851 the number was more than four out of five. In addition some of the minority in what were classed as skilled occupations, such as weavers, tailors and shoemakers, were in practice employed in repetitive, poorly paid piece work, as competition from machinery destroyed their bargaining power.[14]

From this low base the Irish, over the next few decades, only gradually improved their position. They did reasonably well in the iron-making areas of the north of England, where technological in-novation created new skills open to all comers: in parts of Cumber-land, up to nine out of ten Irish-born men were in skilled work by the late nineteenth century. In more traditional industries, however, strict apprenticeship regulations, enforced by strong trade unions, were a powerful instrument of exclusion. It was possibly easier for the diligent and able son of an Irish immigrant to rise to a white-collar position as clerk or bookkeeper than for either him or his father to become a skilled worker. Instead the Irish, into the early twentieth century, remained overrepresented among dockers, build-ers, labourers, carters and in other types of hard manual labour. Irish women worked in factories or, after marriage, as washerwomen, lodging-house keepers and street sellers. They did not, however, feature as prominently as their sisters overseas in domestic service. This was not just because of prejudice, which existed everywhere. Rather it was because English, Scottish and Welsh women were willing to take on the role, liberating middle-class householders from the necessity of admitting a 'Bridget' to their homes.[15]

In other respects, too, the immigrant Irish remained at a distance from the rest of British society. There were few areas, in the major cities, that did not have some Irish residents, and few that were inhabited exclusively by the Irish. In that sense there were no Irish ghettos. But the major centres of Irish settlement, such as London, Glasgow and Liverpool, had districts particularly associated with the Irish, like Manchester's 'Little Ireland', where immigrants and their descendants tended to congregate. As in other overseas destinations the Catholic Church provided a central focus that set the immigrant community apart from the host population. Throughout the second half of the nineteenth century, equally, the Irish were consistently overrepresented among those falling foul of the criminal justice system. Between 1861 and 1911 the Irish-born in England were five times more likely to go to prison than the population as a whole; in Scotland, the figure was almost ten times. Unlike the picture in American and Australian cities, moreover, the offences for which they were incarcerated included not just drunken or disorderly behaviour, or brawls in the street, but burglary, pickpocketing and other forms of professional crime.[16]

Militant nationalism, by comparison, was less of a threat to the position of the Irish in British society than might have been imagined. The United Irishmen in the 1790s, the Ribbonmen in the 1820s and after, and O'Connell's Repeal movement in the 1840s all extended their organisation to the industrial centres of England and Scotland. Matters took a more dangerous turn with the rise of Fenianism in the 1860s, with incidents such as the killing of a Manchester policeman during a failed attempt to rescue two activists in 1867, and the bomb outside Clerkenwell prison, two months later, that killed twenty people in nearby houses. Yet British politicians and the police responded with restraint, avoiding anything resembling a crackdown on the immigrant population as a whole. The absence of a reaction was partly due to a recognition that support for militant nationalism was never universal: after the Clerkenwell explosion representatives of the London Irish were able to procure a declaration of loyalty, containing 22,000 signatures, for presentation to Queen Victoria. But the political status of the Irish was also relevant. They were, in law, citizens not alien immigrants, and the presence of one hundred Irish members in the House of Commons made it impossible to brand the whole population as enemies. After 1886, when the Liberal Party committed itself to a policy of home rule for Ireland, their integration into the political system was complete. The main expression of Irish nationalism, for the next thirty years, was to be through the perfectly respectable form of electoral support for one of the two main British political parties.[17]

On the other side of the political divide, and equally revealing, Irish Protestant loyalism, though a noisy and often aggressive presence on the streets, failed to find a foothold in the political mainstream. The Orange Order, introduced to Great Britain by soldiers returning from Ireland in the 1790s, expanded rapidly from the 1860s, combining the functions of a social club and a benefit society with a frequently aggressive defence of Protestantism and British patriotism. In Liverpool, where a shortage of skilled work brought native and Irish immigrant workers into direct competition for unskilled, often casual, employment, adroit Tory politicians were able to use a militant anti-Catholic rhetoric to gain Protestant working-class support. But elsewhere Orangeism, despite its devotion to empire and to the reformed religion, was too Irish, and too openly sectarian, to become part of popular Conservatism.[18]

In their economic circumstances and social standing, Irish immigrants in Great Britain were in much the same position as their counterparts in the United States. In both cases a rural people became urban dwellers, largely employed in low-status and poorly paid labour, and, particularly in the early years, the target of a degree of nativist and sectarian hostility. The picture is a familiar one: it is what happens when immigrants arrive to fill a gap in the economy of a country with a firmly established social hierarchy and a substantial native working population. By contrast the other main Irish overseas communities at the end of the nineteenth century had developed in colonies that were still in the process of construction. The Irish in Canada, New Zealand and Australia had to contend with ethnic and sectarian hostility, and with colonial authorities who were less than enthusiastic about their presence. But in these more open societies it had not been possible to prevent them claiming a place. In all three cases the immigrant Irish spread out across the social and occupational hierarchy, including farmers and urban workers, labourers and skilled craftsmen, wage earners, businessmen and professionals. They also became a part of the political system in ways that reflected but were not defined by their ethnicity and religion. The same was true, to a lesser extent, of the minority among the Irish in the United States who moved beyond the major cities of the East to more fluid societies still in the process of creation further west.[19]

In one less important emigrant destination, Argentina, a different type of Irish community developed, fitting into neither of these larger patterns. The chain migration from a group of midland counties that continued from the 1820s to the 1870s created the fifth-largest Irish overseas population, and the only one to take shape in a Catholic and non-English-speaking country. It was an inward movement closely linked to the dramatic expansion of sheep ranching and wool production. Newcomers generally began as shepherds or farmhands, or took charge of a herd of sheep under a sharecropping arrangement that entitled them to a portion of the wool produced and of the natural increase in the size of the flock. A minority were able to build up the capital to acquire their own land. Most, however, remained tenants or employees. Only a quarter of Irish men identified in the census of 1895 described themselves as landowners, compared to two out of five who were farmhands, shepherds, servants or labourers. By this time a proportion of the Irish, like other sections of the population, had moved from the countryside to the cities. As English speakers, many found work with the growing number of British and later American firms operating in the country, laying the foundations for an urban middle class of Irish origin.[20]

What made the Argentine Irish community distinctive was the extent to which its members remained a self-contained group within Argentinian society. The pattern was established in the first decades of settlement, when the merchant Thomas Armstrong made himself virtual director of the colony he had played a large part in creating. His partner in this work was a Dominican priest, Fr Anthony Fahy, who in 1843 became chaplain to the Irish community. Together they presided over a remarkable closed environment. As new arrivals landed in Buenos Aires, Armstrong and Fahy's agents were waiting to take them to Irish boarding houses. From there the men were assigned to work for established Irish settlers, while single women were encouraged to find husbands among the Irish residents. Armstrong, by acting as banker to the migrants, retained control of the economic affairs of the expanding Irish community. Meanwhile Fahy built up a church within a church, recruiting twelve priests from All Hallows College, and a congregation of Sisters of Mercy nuns, all under his personal direction. These provided the Irish with religious services, schools and hospitals, all working in the English language. Indeed the libraries attached to the churches subscribed to local newspapers from Westmeath and Wexford. If any community of the Irish overseas can be described as living in a ghetto, this was it, though not with any of the negative associations normally attached to the term. The 'chaplaincies' catering exclusively for Irish congregations faded away after Fahy's death in 1871: the Passionist and Pallottine religious orders continued to supply Irish-trained priests, but their parishes were now part of the ordinary diocesan structure. By the mid-twentieth century many Argentines of Irish origin spoke only Spanish. But the *Southern Cross*, a newspaper of the Irish community, continued up to the 1960s to be published in English. As late as 2013 a visiting Irish journalist met Dickie Kelly, grandson of a Westmeath man who had emigrated in 1862, who spoke English with a distinctive Irish midlands accent that made clear he had learned it at home rather than in school. Marriages, up to at least the 1920s, generally involved a partner from the Irish community. There was particular hostility to unions with the Hispanic population, referred to as 'blacks'.[21]

Yet at the same time that they thus perpetuated their distinctive national identity, the Argentinian Irish also made themselves part of a wider subculture, that of the British. Argentina was not a colony. But its economy depended heavily on exports to Britain, and British capital and technical expertise were central to its banks, its railways and the rest of its infrastructure, to the point where it can be seen as part of a British informal empire. It thus made sense for the Irish to steer well clear of Fenianism and other forms of militant nationalism, and instead to seek the status and protection that came with proclaiming themselves British subjects. Celebrations of St Patrick's Day included toasts to the queen, and Irish families joined other expatriates in flying the British flag above their homes. At the same time their Catholicism gave them a special status, to Argentinian eyes, among the *Inglés*. Uniquely, in the history of the Irish diaspora, religion and politics combined to give a small Irish community the best of both worlds.[22]

11

WAR AND
REVOLUTION

Diaspora, to mean anything, must point to the existence, not just of large numbers of an ethnic group living outside their homeland, but of some continuing sense of shared identity and allegiance extending across national boundaries. The clearest sign of such a diasporic identity, in the case of the migrant Irish, is in the continued active support that they gave, within all of the major areas of settlement, to nationalist movements in the homeland. The foundations had been laid in the 1880s, when repeated fund-raising drives in North America, Australia and New Zealand had given Parnell's Home Rule Party the resources, not just to fight elections, but to look beyond the narrow circle of men of private means for candidates more representative of popular nationalism. But in

1890, following a sensational divorce case, the Home Rule Party split into supporters and opponents of Parnell's continued leadership. The vicious factional conflict that followed, continuing after Parnell's death in 1891, largely destroyed overseas enthusiasm for parliamentary nationalism. Indeed it was the poor returns from a fund-raising trip to the United States in 1899 that convinced John Redmond, leader of the Parnellites, of the need to negotiate a settlement with his rivals. When he returned to America in 1901 it was at the head of a reunited Home Rule Party. While there he established an American branch of the main support organisation of parliamentary nationalism, the United Irish League. By 1910 the United Irish League of America had contributed over £50,000 to Redmond's movement; his opponents labelled him 'the dollar dictator'. Other parts of the diaspora also made their contribution. A year-long tour of Australia and New Zealand by two Home Rule Party MPs in 1906 yielded £22,000, and there was a further fund-raising visit in 1911.[1]

It was not only Irish nationalists who by this time were part of a transnational network. Irish Protestant loyalists could point to the existence across all the main areas of Irish settlement of the Orange Order. An Imperial Grand Orange Council of the World came into existence in 1867, with meetings held every three years, the venue alternating among Ireland, Britain and Canada. Yet Orangeism, as an expression of ethnic identity spanning national frontiers, never achieved the same substance as successive Irish nationalist movements. Its numbers were very unevenly spread. A return in 1903 showed 53,000 members in Canada, 42,000 in Great Britain, but only 12,000 in the United States and 5,000 in Australia and New Zealand. Nor was Orangeism an ethnic organisation. In Canada and Australasia the Irish-born and those of Irish descent were, by the late nineteenth century, a minority in a membership attracted by the Order's combination of Protestantism, loyalty to empire, sociability and mutual assistance. It was this lack of ethnic exclusiveness that made it possible for the small South African branch of the Order to include some Dutch lodges, and for the appearance in Toronto of a Giuseppe Garibaldi lodge, catering for immigrants from Italy's small Protestant community who cherished the memory of the man who had unified their country.[2]

Diasporic nationalism was more firmly based on the shared culture of Irish Catholic communities overseas. Yet here too there were important differences. The Catholic Irish of Canada, Australia and New Zealand overwhelmingly supported the programme of the reunited Home Rule Party—an Ireland enjoying control of its domestic affairs while remaining a possession of the British Crown, all to be achieved by parliamentary means. This allegiance had the advantage of being wholly compatible with the values of the societies in which they lived. The Canadian federal parliament declared its support for Irish self-government in 1882, and did so again in 1903. The Australian parliament passed a similar resolution in 1905. The principle also had the support of leading New Zealand politicians, mainly, though not exclusively, in the Liberal Party. Dominion support for Irish claims reflected a commitment to the general principles of popular representation and responsible government. But the specific plan for Irish home rule, where the country would have its own parliament but retain a reduced representation at Westminster, was also attractive as a precedent; its achievement would add force to the argument that, for a true imperial federation, the dominions too should be represented at the centre of power. Touring Irish Nationalists, for their part, were happy to highlight the parallels between their proposals and dominion self-government, and to argue that home rule would strengthen rather than weaken the empire. One senior figure, John Dillon, went even further in catering to the prejudices of his audience, telling a gathering in New Zealand that the Irish deserved self-government because 'we are white men'.[3]

Irish nationalism in the United States wore a very different face. At the same time that Home Rulers in Ireland ended a decade of squabbling that had begun with the Parnell scandal, militant Irish-American nationalism had also begun to regroup. A convention at Atlantic City in July 1900 announced the reunification of Clan na Gael, ending divisions that went back to the machinations of the Chicago Triangle and the murder of their leading critic, Dr Cronin, in 1889. The president of the revived organisation was the veteran Fenian John Devoy. There were two other key figures. Joseph McGarrity, son of a County Tyrone farmer, had come to Philadelphia in 1892 and built up a chain of hotels and a wine and spirits business. He was to remain a central figure in American support for an uncompromising Irish republicanism up to his death in 1940. Daniel Cohalan, by contrast, was a first-generation Irish American. His father had come to America as a 12-year-old boy in 1848, and had risen through the construction industry to become owner of a successful glass company. A comfortable middle-class background allowed Daniel to be called to the New York State Bar in 1888. From there he went on to achieve wealth and professional success by becoming legal adviser to Tammany's 'Silent Charley' Murphy. During 1908–11 he was Grand Sachem of the Tammany Society, and in 1911, through Murphy's patronage, he became a judge in the state Supreme Court. But Cohalan's horizons were never limited to the narrow, intense world of New York machine politics. He had joined Clan na Gael in 1898 and played a central part, along with Devoy, in bringing about its reunification. Later he used part of what was now a significant fortune to buy a house in County Cork, where he regularly spent summer holidays. He was also active in Irish cultural affairs, serving on the executive of the Gaelic League of America and on the Council of the American Irish Historical Society. In all these respects he made clear that neither American birth nor an ascent to lace curtain status necessarily meant a loss of emotional and political commitment to the cause of the Irish homeland.[4]

Under the guidance of this formidable trio, the revived Clan na Gael set about making its mark. Its particular focus was a campaign against what it presented as the dangerous influence of Great Britain on American foreign policy. The first edition of the movement's newspaper, the *Gaelic American*, on 19 September 1903, warned of 'an organized movement to destroy the old American spirit and substitute for it a servile dependence on England'. The issue was well chosen. It tapped into a still lively Anglophobia, present in American culture since the Revolution and the War of 1812, and reinforced by Britain's devious behaviour during the American Civil War; it also appealed to a widely accepted doctrine, given almost scriptural status in George Washington's farewell address as president in 1796, that the United States should avoid becoming entangled in permanent diplomatic alliances. On this basis Clan na Gael joined in strident opposition to proposed treaties on issues such as the management of the Panama Canal and the creation of a system of arbitration in international disputes, on the grounds that they unduly favoured British interests. It also led agitations on questions not directly involving America, campaigning against British atrocities in the Boer War, and in 1904–5 supporting Russia in its war against Britain's recently acquired ally Japan. The Clan was joined in these campaigns by the Ancient Order of Hibernians. In 1907 the Hibernians announced an agreement with the National German-American Alliance. Their immediate aim was to campaign together against proposed new restrictions on immigration. But they also demanded a wholesale revision of history teaching, complaining that 'in all of our current school histories, and most others in fact, the Anglo-Saxon has been glorified and exalted to the exclusion of those others who did so much for this country, like the Irish and the Germans'.[5]

The more radical character of Irish-American nationalism was also evident in its response to the new forms of cultural nationalism that emerged in the late nineteenth century. A Gaelic League of America was established in 1898. However the labour of acquiring a language of which most even among the Irish-born had no prior knowledge was beyond all but a dedicated few. Fund-raising tours to support the movement in Ireland were reasonably successful. But otherwise the Gaelic League of America concentrated on social events, such as picnics and dances, or joined with the Ancient Order of Hibernians in campaigning for the teaching of Irish history and in opposing derogatory stereotypes of Irishness on stage or elsewhere. Sport was a different matter. In the second half of the nineteenth century Irish Americans had distinguished themselves mainly by their prominence in the American sporting mainstream. In 1886, however, the Irish Athletic Club of Boston, founded seven years earlier, played its first game of football according to the newly codified rules of the Gaelic Athletic Association. In 1898 clubs in New York opened a purpose-built stadium, later named Celtic Park, in the borough of Queens. The inclusion of Gaelic games at the 1904 World's Fair in St Louis was a major opportunity to raise their profile. In 1914, after various false starts due to local rivalries, a Gaelic Athletic Association of the United States came into being. Throughout there were close connections between the sporting movement, the Ancient Order of Hibernians, and the revived Clan na Gael. Daniel Cohalan, for example, among his many other roles, was on the board of the Irish American Athletic Club, the body responsible for the management of Celtic Park.[6]

Once again the support of the Irish Americans for cultural nationalism contrasted with the more muted response of their counterparts in the British dominions. In Toronto in the 1860s the Fenian-affiliated Hibernian Benevolent Society supported pre-codification versions of hurling and Gaelic football. Later in the century, however, Catholics of Irish descent continued to have their own sporting associations, but they now concentrated on Canadian games—lacrosse, rowing and tug-of-war—at which they could compete with other sporting clubs. In Australia, similarly, immigrants continued at local level to play the games they had brought with them. There is even the suggestion that the modern game of 'Australian rules' football was an adaptation of Gaelic football. However there was no attempt to create a nationwide Gaelic sporting culture. One major reason was the refusal of Catholic schools to abandon rugby, football and cricket. Religious principle may have prescribed separate, denominational schools. But in a society where sport was central to national life, those responsible for the education of the Catholic middle class had no interest in consigning their charges to a cultural ghetto.[7]

In the United States, then, emissaries from the Home Rule movement faced an audience very different to what they encountered in Canada or Australasia or indeed, at this time, in their own country. The main reason Redmond had insisted on creating his own fund-raising body, the American branch of the United Irish League, had been to keep control out of the hands of the militants of Clan na Gael. Even then, to achieve this end, he had had to resort to a rhetoric very different to his normal tone, assuring an audience in New York in December 1901 that he had no quarrel 'with any man or anybody who wants to strike a blow at the English government'. His reconstituted movement gained the support of the *Irish World*, still run, until his death in 1913, by the former enthusiast for dynamite warfare Patrick Ford. The Ancient Order of Hibernians also supported Redmond, while at the same time insisting that its goal was not merely home rule but full Irish independence. Devoy and Clan na Gael remained hostile. By 1910, however, the Irish Parliamentary Party held the balance of power in a British parliament where the Conservative and Unionist-dominated House of Lords had just been stripped of the power to block new legislation indefinitely. Home rule, it seemed, was imminent. Redmond's support in Irish America swelled, and Clan na Gael found itself pushed to the political margin.[8]

The outbreak of the First World War further widened the split between the United States and other centres of Irish settlement. With a home rule measure enacted, though postponed until after the war, Redmond declared that it was now the duty of nationalists to give full support to the British war effort. His followers in Ireland complied in large numbers. Irish Americans, on the other hand, were horrified. Support for the United Irish League of America collapsed. Clan na Gael, recently sidelined, moved in to fill the gap. In March 1916 it brought together some 2,300 representatives of different Irish-American bodies at an Irish Race Convention in New York, and used the occasion to launch a new front organisation, the Friends of Irish Freedom. By this time the Clan's leaders were also working in secret with the minority in nationalist Ireland that had opposed Redmond's support for the war. A key contact was Tom Clarke, who had come to America in 1898 after serving a fifteen-year sentence in England for his part in the dynamite campaign of the 1880s. He returned to Ireland in 1907 and set about reviving the dormant Irish Republican Brotherhood behind the cover of a newsagent's and tobacconist's shop in Dublin. Cohalan's summer visits to his house in County Cork allowed him to meet Clarke and other militants, including Patrick Pearse, who was to lead the long-awaited Irish rising. In July 1914 Roger Casement, a former British diplomat turned revolutionary nationalist, came to New York, where he met Devoy and Cohalan before going on to Germany to seek military assistance. Meanwhile McGarrity raised around $20,000 for the purchase of weapons in Ireland. Exactly how much these American supporters knew in advance of the insurrection that began in Dublin on 24 April 1916 is not clear. But six days earlier American Secret Service agents had raided the New York office of a German agent, Wolf von Igel, and uncovered a cable relaying a plea by Cohalan for the Germans to assist an

apparently imminent Irish rising by a diversionary air raid and naval attack directed at the English mainland.

The response of the Irish in the British dominions was very different. Political and church leaders gave unqualified support to the
war effort. William Cleary, the Wexford-born bishop of Auckland,
had earlier published a book denouncing the sectarian bigotry of
the Orange order, and had organised celebrations to mark the centenary of the insurrection of 1798. But he now not only proclaimed
the justice of the British cause but gave a practical demonstration of
his commitment by spending three months on the Western Front
as an army chaplain. In Australia Catholics, who at this point were
overwhelmingly of Irish birth or descent, made up 19 per cent of
those enlisting for military service. This was a little below the proportion of Catholics among males over 15 (22 per cent), but the
difference was at least in part a reflection of lower enlistment in
the working class, where Irish Catholics were overrepresented. In
Canada the only comprehensive statistics indicate that the Catholic presence among those coming forward to serve (14 per cent)
fell well short of their share of total population (39 per cent). But
scattered evidence from individual units makes clear that it was
French Canadians who declined to play their part; Scottish and
Irish Catholics came forward at least as readily as other groups.
In proclaiming their support for the war bishops, priests and the
Catholic press insisted on the patriotic duty owed, not just to Canada, but to the empire. Early in the conflict Canadian branches
of the Ancient Order of Hibernians came close to breaking away
from the parent organisation in the United States, because of its
pro-German views. At a Hibernian convention in Boston in July
1916 a New Brunswick priest, C. J. McLoughlin, delivered a combative speech insisting that 'the fires of patriotism burn not the
less bright within the bosoms of the Canadian Hibernians for the
British flag than it does within the breast of the American citizens
for the Star Spangled Banner. . . . Canadians of all classes, Irish

included, are prepared to stand by Britain in this crisis to the last man and the last dollar.'[9]

———————

McLoughlin's speech was all the more significant in that he gave it three months after the week-long Easter Rising (or, for its opponents, Easter Rebellion) that had taken place in Dublin in late April 1916. In all three of the main centres of Irish settlement within the British Empire, namely Canada, Australia and New Zealand, Irish Catholic bishops and Irish Catholic newspapers rushed to denounce the resort to armed insurrection as illegitimate and as a betrayal of home rule. But the severity of the British government's response—sixteen executions (including Casement) and mass arrests that went far beyond those involved in the conspiracy—caused uneasiness, especially when contrasted with the tolerance that had earlier been shown to unionists like Edward Carson, who had raised an armed force to defy parliament over home rule yet now held places in the wartime government. The surrender of Germany in November 1918 relieved the pressure for wartime solidarity. But with peace came even greater embarrassments for would-be Irish Catholic loyalists. The general election of December 1918 left Redmond's project of home rule in ruins. A new Sinn Féin party, claiming to be the heirs of 1916 and committed to the goal of complete independence for Ireland, took all but a handful of Irish seats and boycotted the Westminster parliament. Instead, its successful candidates met in their own assembly, Dáil Éireann, claiming to be the true representatives of the Irish people. Meanwhile advocates of armed action had begun to create their own organisation, what came to be known as the Irish Republican Army, or IRA. On 21 January 1919, the same day that the Dáil held its first meeting, republican activists in County Tipperary seized a consignment of gelignite, shooting dead both members of the police escort. This marked the beginning of a guerrilla campaign that was to continue, with rising levels of bloodshed, until July 1921, provoking an increasingly ruthless government response.

In the atmosphere of recrimination that developed, the Canadian Irish fared best. Bishops and other Catholic spokesmen condemned the indiscriminate violence with which Crown forces sought to crush the developing Irish insurrection, and the failure of the government to meet legitimate Irish demands for some form of self-government. But they stopped short of any general expression of hostility to Britain or to empire. That they provoked no hostile backlash may also have been due to the firm support Canada's Catholic Irish had given to the war effort, especially when contrasted with the disloyalty of their French coreligionists. In Toronto, the 'Belfast of Canada', the mayor, himself an Orangeman, attended the unveiling of a monument to the fallen in one of the city's Catholic parishes and praised the contribution to the war effort that it represented. In Australia, on the other hand, there had already been grumbles, however unjustified, about the alleged unwillingness of Irish Catholics to do their patriotic duty. When news arrived of the Dublin rising, Daniel Mannix, assistant archbishop and successor-in-waiting in the archdiocese of Melbourne, joined in the general condemnation. But he provoked outrage by adding that blame also lay with the British government, for its failure to deal with 'the treason of the Carsonites' and for its 'shifty policy on home rule'.[10]

Further conflict followed when the Australian government twice organised plebiscites, in October 1916 and December 1917, seeking support for conscription. Once again Mannix was the most outspoken figure. His stance, however, had nothing to do with Ireland. Instead his arguments echoed those of the labour movement: Australia had already contributed more than it should to what he called 'an ordinary trade war' (in some versions 'a sordid trade war'), the burden of conscription would fall mainly on a working class that had already suffered disproportionately from wage cuts and unemployment, and employers would seize the opportunity to replace conscripted workers with cheap female and 'coloured' labour. The other Catholic bishops, meanwhile, remained silent during the first plebiscite, arguing that conscription was a political not a religious matter; some privately supported the government's plans. But when the electorate voted to reject conscription, the government nevertheless blamed the outcome on the 'disloyal' Catholic vote. In the rancorous aftermath, ministers refused to exempt Catholic clergy from a new 'Bachelor Tax' designed to push single men into the armed forces, and then failed to provide adequate guarantees that either members of the Christian Brothers, a lay order essential to the running of Catholic schools, or those in training for eventual ordination would be exempted from a renewed conscription plan. What looked like displays of open hostility pushed other Catholic clergy into joining Mannix in calling openly for a 'no' vote. The government's second defeat, like its first, almost certainly owed more to the opposition of the trade unions and of socialist political groups than to anything said by Mannix or others. But the idea that an Irish Catholic enemy within had undermined the war effort was for decades to poison relationships in Australian politics.[11]

As the war ended, reports of violence in Ireland increased, producing new tensions. In June 1918, following a series of raids and the seizure of documents, the government interned seven leading members of the Irish National Association, a small Irish republican organisation that had been founded in Sydney three years earlier by Dr Albert Dryer, an Australian-born customs official of mixed German and Irish parentage. An enquiry into their detention suggested that some at least were part of a group with Irish Republican Brotherhood connections operating, unknown to the wider membership, inside the Association. In November 1920 the government had a Labour MP, Hugh Mahon, expelled from parliament. Mahon, born in King's County and a former Land League activist, had been in Australia since 1882, and had served as Minister for External Affairs in the Labour government of 1914–6. His offence was a speech at a public meeting in which he had denounced British rule in Ireland as a 'bloody and accursed despotism' sustained by 'spies, informers and bloody cutthroats'. He failed to regain his seat in the subsequent by-election and dropped out of political life. The most dramatic standoff arising from accusations of Irish disloyalty, however, took place thousands of miles from Australia. In May 1920 Mannix sailed for San Francisco, on the first leg of what was intended to be a journey to Ireland and then Rome. By this time his views were uncompromising. British rule in Ireland, he told American audiences, was dead, and the prime minister, Lloyd George, was to be compared to the wartime German governor of occupied Belgium. His planned visit, Mannix insisted, was not to British soil but to 'the ground of the Irish republic'. In the event the British government ordered his ship, the White Star Line's *Baltic*, to divert to Liverpool. Then, as Irish activists gathered to provide a triumphal reception, a destroyer intercepted the *Baltic* and carried the archbishop to the quiet Cornish port of Penzance. By the time Mannix left England, after a prolonged standoff lasting to March 1921, his status as the bogeyman of loyalist and Protestant Australia was even more firmly established.[12]

Meanwhile what was now an open confrontation between Irish nationalism and the Australian establishment had found further expression in a succession of disputes over the annual St Patrick's Day parade, once again centring on Mannix's city, Melbourne. The trouble began in 1918 when marchers carried banners relating to Sinn Féin and to the 1916 rising. There was no parade in 1919, ostensibly due to the influenza pandemic, although the organisers may have been avoiding a confrontation with the mayor, who had threatened to ban the event. In 1920 Mannix, working with John Wren, a millionaire son of Irish immigrants who had made his fortune in illegal gambling, used the occasion to convey a powerful assertion of Irish-Australian patriotism. The 20,000 marchers included 6,000 returned soldiers and sailors, in uniform. At the head walked two ex-servicemen carrying Australian flags. And the centrepiece of the display was a group of fourteen winners of the Victoria Cross, mounted on white horses and forming a guard of honour round Mannix's car. Not all of the fourteen, in fact, were Irish, and only eight were Catholics. But the point was made. On the other hand the Union Jack, on which the mayor had insisted, appeared only as small insets on two larger flags. The stipulations for the next year's parade were explicit: a British flag, measuring 6 by 3 feet, was to be carried at the head of the procession. The organisers retaliated by hiring what the police described as a vagrant, 'dirty in appearance and attire', to carry the banner while the crowd booed and jeered. Irish defiance went a stage further the following year, when the parade went ahead despite the refusal of the city council to grant permission. An attempt to prosecute the organisers collapsed when a court ruled that the bylaw they were accused of breaking was invalid.[13]

Sectarian rancour had been a feature of Australian politics since at least the days of Governor Richard Bourke. Relations in New Zealand had traditionally been more relaxed. But there too the war brought a deterioration. Already before 1914 the very success in public life of Catholics like Sir Joseph Ward had alarmed Protestants. News of the Easter Rising reawakened charges of Catholic disloyalty. In July 1917 members of the Orange Order created a Protestant Political Association to counter the 'growing aggressiveness and assertion of the political aims of the Roman hierarchy'. Meanwhile Catholics protested at the extension of conscription to the Christian Brothers and Marist Brothers, members of religious orders but not ordained clergymen, and to students in Catholic seminaries. As in Australia the bitterness continued into the postwar years. In 1922 the government prosecuted the assistant bishop of Auckland, James Liston, born in New Zealand to Irish parents, for a speech in which he had reportedly described the leaders of the 1916 rising as having been 'murdered by foreign troops'. Catholics blamed the influence of the prime minister, William Massey, an Ulster-born Orangeman who had briefly been the grand master for the North Island. Massey had in fact opposed the prosecution of Liston, who was in the end acquitted of sedition. However the Reform Party benefitted in elections from the support of the Protestant Political Association, and Massey's government reciprocated by introducing in 1920 a Marriage Amendment Bill, a wholly symbolic measure that was nevertheless appreciated as a repudiation of the notorious papal encyclical of 1908 on the subject of mixed marriage.[14]

In both Australia and New Zealand, then, the First World War and the rise of militant nationalism created serious divisions. But relations were damaged, not fractured. Irish Australians and Irish New Zealanders might express outrage at the double standards exhibited in the handling of nationalist and unionist treason, and at the increasingly brutal response to the challenge of Sinn Féin and the IRA. But many remained wary of radical nationalism. When the self-proclaimed government established by the Dáil organised support organisations in Canada, Australia and New Zealand during 1920–1, it avoided references to Sinn Féin and to the demand for an Irish Republic, wholly independent of Britain. Instead it created Self-Determination for Ireland Leagues, a less punchy title than Friends of Irish Freedom, but calculated to appeal to more moderate supporters as well as to the militant minority. Presented in these terms, moreover, the agitation did not, in any of the three dominions, set the Irish wholly apart from the rest of society. In March 1917 the Australian senate approved, by twenty-nine votes to two, an address to the king hoping that 'a just measure of home rule may be granted (immediately) to the people of Ireland'. In the labour movement, too, sympathy for the Irish case went well beyond those of Irish background. When the Victoria state railway sacked two employees in January 1921 for their part in a protest against the killing of three Irish railwaymen by Crown forces in County Cork, both men turned out to be Protestants of Scottish descent.[15]

Irish Americans, unlike their counterparts in Canada and Australasia, had long been free to indulge their Anglophobia without restraint. All this changed on 6 April 1917, when the United States declared war on Germany. Membership of the Friends of Irish Freedom slumped to no more than about a thousand, as its leaders scrambled to declare their wholehearted support for the American cause. Daniel Cohalan, now dangerously compromised by the papers seized from Wolf von Igel, withdrew from the political front line. Meanwhile the New York 69th Regiment, redesignated the 165th Infantry Regiment, went into action once again, drawing 95 per cent of its numbers from the Irish of the city. Their outstanding performance in the waterlogged trenches of northern France added further to the legend of the Fighting (and patriotic) Irish.[16]

For those militants forced reluctantly to swallow a war in alliance with the hated British, the main hope was now the postwar peace settlement. The American president, Woodrow Wilson, a Democrat, presented the war as a crusade to create a more just and stable international order by securing for the smaller nations of Europe the right to determine their own future. This opened the way for Irish-American nationalists to demand that their country should be one of the beneficiaries. A series of mass meetings in the early weeks of 1919 prepared the way for another Irish Race Convention, in Philadelphia in February. The gathering attracted over 5,000 delegates, including more than 30 Catholic bishops. A money-raising campaign, the Irish Victory Fund, brought in over a million dollars. Meanwhile Congress, in March 1919, passed a resolution expressing its earnest hope that the peace conference underway in Paris 'will favourably consider the claims of Ireland to self-determination'. A delegation from the Irish Race Convention had met Wilson in February to press him to take up the Irish cause, and in April 1919 three of their number arrived in France hoping to make the case directly to the Paris Peace Conference.[17]

Later, after the Paris Peace Conference had failed to deliver any of the gains expected from it, Irish nationalists blamed Wilson's Ulster Presbyterian ancestry. The allegation of religious bigotry is not particularly convincing. Wilson's private secretary during his presidency was Joseph Tumulty, a New Jersey lawyer of middle-class Irish Catholic background. The president had, however, clashed with the bosses of the great urban political machines, such as 'Silent Charlie' Murphy, by refusing their demands for patronage. Wilson also repeatedly expressed his disdain for those immigrants who, in his view, allowed their ethnic attachments to interfere with their allegiance to the United States. In May 1914 he chose the unveiling of a monument to an Irish-American hero, John Barry, a naval commander during the Revolutionary War, to set out his view in detail. Barry, he proclaimed, was an Irishman, but 'his heart crossed the Atlantic with him':

Some Americans need hyphens in their names, because only part of them has come over; but when the whole man has come over, heart and thought and all, the hyphen drops of its own weight out of his name. This man was not an Irish American; he was an Irishman who became an American. . . . That is my infallible test of a genuine American, that when he votes, or when he acts, or when he fights, his heart and his thoughts are centred nowhere but in the emotions and the purposes and the politics of the United States.

Wilson did not invent the term 'hyphenated Americans'. It had been used by Theodore Roosevelt, again as a term of reproach, as far back as 1895. But he gave it currency, and allowed his distaste to colour his attitude to men like Daniel Cohalan whom he saw as seeking to bend American foreign policy to Irish ends.[18]

Wilson's preferences, however, are at best only part of the story. The rhetoric of the Paris Peace Conference was the freedom of small nations. But the political reality, ignored by the Irish Americans, was that this applied only to the territorial possessions of the defeated powers; there was no prospect of the victors being required to give up anything. Alongside the territorial settlement, moreover, Wilson was desperate to implement the other part of his great project, the creation of a League of Nations that would uphold a rules-bound international order. And for this he needed the cooperation of Great Britain. Against this background Wilson, as he had promised, worked behind the scenes to push the British government towards an Irish settlement of some kind. The establishment in July 1917 of a constitutional convention charged with seeking an accommodation between nationalists and unionists, for example, was a response to American warnings that the unsettled state of Ireland was the main obstacle to more effective wartime cooperation. But this behind-the-scenes pressure was the most that Wilson, regardless of his private feelings, was in a position to deliver. When nothing concrete emerged, all he could offer was a vague suggestion that the Irish question might be something that a League of Nations could at some future point take up as an issue threatening world peace. Unimpressed, the Friends of Ireland joined with American isolationists in campaigning for the Senate to reject both the Treaty of Versailles produced by the Paris Peace Conference and the League of Nations.

In June 1919, as the debate over the League of Nations and the Treaty of Versailles continued, a new and disruptive figure appeared in America. Éamon de Valera, born in New York to an Irish mother and a Spanish Cuban father but brought up by his mother's family in rural County Limerick, was the senior surviving rebel commander from the Easter Rising. He was now president of Sinn Féin and, from 1 April, president of Dáil Éireann. Recently escaped from prison, and without a passport, the spindly, bespectacled former mathematics teacher had crossed the Atlantic unconvincingly disguised as a sailor. In New York, however, the Friends of Irish Freedom presented him to the press as president of the Irish Republic, calling on all of the resources of the world's most developed mass media. There were newspaper articles, magazine interviews, offers to produce recordings of his speeches, even a bid to purchase the film rights to his life story. But as de Valera's eighteen-month tour of the United States proceeded, relations with his Irish American hosts deteriorated. During 1919 the two sides managed to work together to promote a new fund-raising drive through the sale of bond certificates to be redeemed by a future Irish government. In February 1920, however, open hostilities erupted. De Valera suggested in a newspaper interview that an independent Ireland could meet British concerns over security by accepting something similar to the restrictions on external relations that the United States had imposed on Cuba. Irish Americans were outraged at this abandonment of Ireland's claims to full nationhood. By the summer of 1920 relations were so poor that de Valera and Cohalan sent rival delegations to the Republican Party convention, where their public squabbling allowed the party to avoid making any commitment on Irish issues. Following a final showdown at a meeting of the national council of the Friends of Irish Freedom in September, de Valera launched a rival body, the Association for the Recognition of the Irish Republic. Meanwhile his supporters had the Irish Republican Brotherhood announce that it no longer recognised Clan na Gael as an affiliate. By the end of 1921 the Association for the Recognition of the Irish Republic claimed a membership of up to 800,000. Membership of the Friends of Irish Freedom, meanwhile, had fallen from over 100,000 to just 20,000. Daniel Cohalan no longer spoke for Irish America.

The clash between the leaders of nationalist Ireland and of Irish America was in part a matter of personality. More than one contemporary found de Valera overbearing in manner and inflexibly wedded to the products of his own sometimes convoluted reasoning. A letter to Cohalan following the attack on his 'Cuba' interview provides a glimpse of the almost messianic conception of his own status that had come with his elevation to the presidency. 'I am answerable to the Irish people', he told the judge, 'for the proper execution of the trust with which I have been charged. I am definitely responsible to them, and I *alone* am responsible. It is my obvious duty to select such instruments as may be available for the task set me.' Cohalan, the veteran of Tammany Hall and of Democratic Party conventions, a man of sufficient standing to be a personal antagonist of Woodrow Wilson, could hardly be expected to take kindly to being addressed in such terms. But there was also a question of priorities. De Valera did not share Cohalan's antipathy to the League of Nations. More important, he objected to the use of money from the Irish Victory Fund to finance the campaign against it. Instead, he made clear, the Friends of Irish Freedom should devote themselves exclusively to supporting the struggle in Ireland.

To Cohalan and others, on the other hand, the battle against a malign British interest was an American as well as an Irish cause. There was some attempt to give opposition to the League of Nations an Irish slant, by suggesting that its provisions for mutual defence might require the United States to collaborate in putting down a future Irish insurrection. But the real objection was that the League of Nations would be bad for America. To join would be to abandon the long-standing principle of avoiding foreign entanglements. It would undermine the Monroe Doctrine established in 1823, whereby events in the Americas were the business of the United States alone. And it would tie the country to the British Empire, whose poisonous influence remained the greatest threat to American values and interests. Wilson had attacked 'hyphenated' Americans. But in reality Cohalan and his associates were clear that, however passionately they committed themselves to the cause of Ireland, they did so as citizens of the United States. Bishop Michael Gallagher of Detroit, president of the Friends of Irish Freedom, set out their position in a pamphlet published following the final break with de Valera. They were 'American citizens who never intend to live their lives in Ireland, who neither owe nor pay allegiance to the Irish Parliament or President thereof, but who, out of love for their race and loyalty to American principles of liberty, work for the recognition of the Irish Republic'.[19]

Support from the United States was crucial to the success of the Irish nationalist revolution. But the scale of that support must be seen in perspective. The 800,000 Irish Americans who reportedly came forward to enroll in the Association for the Recognition of the Irish Republic was an impressive total. But they represented only a fairly small minority among the more than four million first- and second-generation Irish in the United States. The presidential elections of the period confirmed that, for a much larger number, Irish issues were at best a small part of their concern. In 1916 Wilson publicly told an Irish-American activist who threatened him with electoral disaster if he did not change his position on Ireland that he would be 'mortified' to receive the votes of 'disloyal Americans' of his kind. But in the event, Irish-American districts responded instead to Wilson's labour-friendly social policies by voting solidly Democrat. In 1920, on the other hand, the Democratic candidate lost heavily. But detailed studies of the voting pattern have failed to find evidence that the Irish contributed more than other groups to this outcome. In any case the victorious Republican, Warren Harding, had not only offered no commitment regarding Ireland's future, but had reportedly said that he considered the matter one of 'the internal affairs of a foreign power'.[20]

Even as American dollars poured into the hands of Sinn Féin, then, the underlying picture is of an Ireland and an Irish America that had grown apart. Even those Americans with the strongest sense of their Irish background, as the spat between de Valera and Cohalan makes clear, were well on the way to developing an identity of their own. And among the wider population there were signs, even before the First World War, that the ethnic revival of the late 1890s and early 1900s was beginning to lose momentum. Newly arrived immigrants might still find in the Ancient Order of Hibernians, the Gaelic League or the Gaelic Athletic Association a familiar set of cultural markers and a chance to meet and mix with fellow countrymen. Among the American-born, however, the fastest growing organisation was now the Knights of Columbus, established in New Haven, Connecticut, in 1882. Between 1899 and 1922 membership rose from 42,000 to 782,000. The original purpose of the Knights was as a fraternal society, providing social insurance for the widows and children of deceased members. But in response to continued nativist and Protestant militance it developed into a campaigning organisation, playing a particularly important part in challenging the revived Ku Klux Klan of the 1920s. It was a movement largely led, and widely supported, by Irish American Catholics. But it was not a specifically Irish organisation. Instead their choice of patron, Christopher Columbus, neatly summed up the movement's twin values: militant Catholicism combined with a strident American patriotism. And it was here, once the troubles of their ancestral homeland no longer forced themselves on their consciousness, that the loyalties of the great majority of Irish Americans were to lie.[21]

12

IN THE MELTING POT

Between 1916 and 1922 Ireland was torn apart by a cycle of violence and repression that deepened antagonisms and created new borders. The crisis, occurring against the wider background of the First World War, affected the Irish diaspora in contradictory ways. At first sight its effect was to reduce the distance between different sites of settlement, and between diaspora and homeland. The Irish of Canada, Australia and New Zealand were enlisted in a common cause, bringing them closer to the Irish of the United States and of Ireland itself, and putting them at odds with large parts of the societies they lived in. From another perspective, however, what the crisis highlighted was the extent to which each part of the diaspora was well on the way to developing its own distinct identity. The Irish of Australia and New Zealand were more outspoken in their opposition to the policies of the British government, and their support for self-determination, than the Irish of Canada. But they were much less so than their counterparts in the United States. And even in America, where attitudes most closely mirrored those of the homeland, Daniel Cohalan and others made clear to de Valera that their support for the Irish cause took second place to their allegiance as citizens of the United States.

Over the next several decades this fragmentation of the Irish diaspora into a series of local identities with an Irish inflection became steadily more obvious. At the political level, involvement in the affairs of Ireland became less urgent following the Anglo-Irish Treaty, concluded between Sinn Féin and the British government in December 1921. Under its terms most of Ireland became a self-governing dominion within the British Empire. For many Australasian and Canadian Irish the settlement seemed wholly reasonable: Ireland now had the same status as their own countries. However there were those, in particular among Irish Americans, to whom the outcome remained unsatisfactory. Ireland was still tied to the British Crown, and the new state comprised only twenty-six counties; six others, two of them with Catholic majorities, became Northern Ireland, a devolved region within the United Kingdom. But with an Irish government in Dublin committed to upholding the settlement, the issue of national freedom was no longer so clear-cut. The short but vicious civil war that took place during 1922–3, between supporters and opponents of the Treaty, acted across the diaspora to diminish enthusiasm for further involvement in the affairs of the homeland. In New York attendance at the St Patrick's Day parade fell from 50,000 in 1922 to a mere 5,000 the following year.[1]

A second reason for the widening distance between the different Irish communities was that their links with Ireland were no longer being refreshed by the regular arrival of new immigrants. Already by 1921 the number of Irish-born people living in the main overseas immigrant destinations had fallen to around half of what it had been in 1891. Over the next thirty years the number of first-generation immigrants, men and women who had brought with them the speech, the culture and the outlook of the old country, continued to decline. In 1950 the Irish-born population of the United States was 520,000, compared to just over a million in 1920. In Australia the number had fallen from 106,000 in 1921 to 48,000 in 1954, in New Zealand from 34,000 to only 17,000 by 1951, in Canada from 93,000 in 1921 to 81,000 in 1950. Only Great Britain showed an increase, a substantial one, from 524,000 Irish-born residents in 1921 to 716,000 thirty years later.

––––––––––

In theory, following the long-awaited achievement of national independence, there should have been no emigrants of any kind. In a free Ireland, the Dáil had proclaimed in June 1920, 'no Irishman would ever leave his native land in order to live under decent conditions'. The reality was rather different. Between 1891 and 1911, the last two full decades of unchallenged British rule, emigration from the twenty-six counties that were to become the Irish Free State had averaged 31,000 persons a year. Between 1926 and 1961 the average was a lower but still substantial 25,000. As in earlier decades the emigrants were mainly the young. One in six of all male teenagers (aged 15 to 19) who were living in Ireland in 1926, and more than one in five of all females in the same age group, were to leave the country over the next ten years. This continued amputation of a large part of each rising generation was sufficient to ensure that by 1961 the population of what was by now the Irish Republic stood at 2.8 million, more than 150,000 lower than it had been in 1926.[2]

A part of this continued drain on population, especially in the first years of the new state, was driven by politics and ideology. Protestant numbers in the southern counties had already been in decline before the First World War, largely due to the difficulty of finding marriage partners in a thinly spread minority population, and to the insistence of the Catholic Church that the children of religiously mixed marriages be brought up Catholic. From 1919, during the IRA's campaign of violence, many became the target of murder and intimidation, whether as real or alleged collaborators with Crown forces, as reprisals for actions against the nationalist population, or (in the case of the houses of the landed gentry) as symbols of the political order that was in the process of being over-thrown. And even when the threat of violence faded, with the victory of Free State forces in the civil war of 1922–3, the ethos of the new state was hardly congenial. Its public rhetoric equated Irishness with Catholicism, and dismissed symbols of the Britishness with which most Protestants identified (such as the place names that disappeared from Irish maps) as an alien implant. Legislation on divorce, contraception and censorship explicitly deferred to the teachings of the Catholic Church. The Irish language became a compulsory school subject and proficiency in it a requirement for public employment. Between 1911 and 1926 the Protestant population fell from 327,000 in 1911 to 221,000, a decline of one-third. Part of the decline, around 30,000, reflected the departure of British soldiers and administrators brought home as the Free State came into being. Another 15,000 can be attributed to deaths and a depressed birth rate during the First World War. But the largest component remains the 60,000 or so southern Protestants who concluded that they had no future in the new Ireland. Records of school attendance, and of marriages in Protestant churches, suggest that the largest number of departures was during the years 1921–3. The fall in Protestant numbers over the next ten years was more modest, to 195,000 by 1936. But that still represented an emigration rate almost twice the level seen in the population as a whole (an annual average of 9 per thousand among Protestants compared to 5.4 overall). Many of these emigrants (or refugees)—around 24,000 in the period up to 1926—sought a safer or more congenial environment in Northern Ireland. Most of the rest moved to Great

Britain. But there was also an increase in emigration to Canada and South Africa.[3]

Otherwise continued heavy emigration from the Irish Free State reflected economic realities that independence had done nothing to change. On the contrary, the partition of the island had stripped the new state of Ireland's only region of concentrated manufacturing industry, leaving it dependent on the export of agricultural produce—live cattle, bacon, butter, eggs—to help feed the population of urban and heavily industrialised Britain. Fianna Fáil, the party of former opponents of the Treaty that displaced its more conservative pro-Treaty rival in 1932, attempted to realise the republican dream of economic regeneration. High protective tariffs brought a modest increase in manufacturing jobs, but the firms they shielded from foreign competition remained small. By the end of the decade, as the domestic market for what could be produced locally became saturated, growth levelled off. (A parallel policy of increasing agricultural employment by encouraging labour-intensive tillage at the expense of livestock ran contrary to the facts of climate and landscape, and it was wholly unsuccessful.) So Ireland remained a country of small family farms. Conservative commentators, unable any longer to see the continued loss of population as one of the many evils of British rule, lamented the corrupting influences that unsettled the young with false promises of glamour and material prosperity. The solution, one writer suggested, was to prohibit commercially sponsored programmes on the nation's only radio station. But the truth was that for large numbers of each new generation emigration held out the best chance of life as an independent adult.[4]

The 1930s, along with the period during and immediately after the Second World War, was of course a period of hardship everywhere. From the late 1940s, in contrast, the Western world entered on a quarter century of economic progress. But independent Ireland, isolated by a rigid protectionist economic policy, largely missed out on the first part of what in retrospect was to be seen as a golden age of rising prosperity. Emigration continued to carry off those for whom there was no place in a stagnant economy. But they were now joined by others who contrasted the meagre benefits of even a secure position in Ireland with the brighter prospects opening up elsewhere. Alarmist reports noted the departure of emigrants who were abandoning permanent, pensionable jobs in the police or public service. Farming families began to face the novel problem of a succession crisis. In the 1920s, one Irish sociologist observed, brothers had competed to be the one inheriting the family farm. Now, in the 1960s, 'they vied to escape it'. Women were even less willing to settle for the drudgery and tedium of farming life. In rural areas, by 1961, there were 244 single men aged between 45 and 54 for every 100 single women in the same age bracket. Emigration from the Irish Republic between 1951 and 1961 reached 405,000, the highest level since the 1880s. The title of a collection of essays published in 1953, *The Vanishing Irish*, was unduly melodramatic. But it accurately summed up the sense of malaise that hung over the Ireland of the 1950s, as around a third of young people chose or were forced to leave the country as they came of age.[5]

Partition may have dealt Northern Ireland a somewhat better hand. But it too faced grave difficulties in the decades that followed. Shipbuilding, one pillar of its economy, struggled to find customers in a world first glutted with new vessels constructed to meet the needs of the First World War and then, in the 1930s, paralysed by the Great Depression. Demand for the region's other main product, linen, also fell, as fashion and convenience favoured lighter, more easily cared-for fabrics. Northern Ireland farms, meanwhile, were, like those in the south, mainly small in acreage, and no better placed to provide a living for all the members of each new generation. So emigration continued, much of it, in contrast to independent Ireland, directed to Canada rather than the United States. But the level was lower than in the southern state.

Between 1926 and 1961 Northern Ireland, with less than one-third of the population of the island, contributed only around one-fifth of those emigrating, an average of about 6,000 a year. This meant that it achieved a modest increase in population, from 1.3 million in 1926 to 1.4 million thirty-five years later, although most of this came about after the Second World War had delivered a massive boost to the region's manufacturing industries.[6]

In the 1920s, continuing the pattern of earlier decades, more than four out of every five emigrants from the Irish Free State went to the United States. There the Johnson-Reed Immigration Act of 1924 for the first time imposed limits, in the form of country quotas, on inward movement. The purpose of the act, however, was to reduce immigration from southern and eastern Europe. The Irish Free State's quota, 28,567 a year, was comfortably above the actual average of around 20,000 Irish arrivals. A new calculation in 1927 brought the limit down to 17,853, possibly implying a small cut in numbers. Before any such effects could become clear, however, the United States had slid into the prolonged period of economic paralysis that became the Great Depression. By 1933, with one in four American workers unemployed, many of them wandering from place to place, or gathered in miserable shanty towns, desperate for even the poorest-paid work, the prospects for migrants were bleak. In any case, friends and relatives already in the United States could no longer send back the remittances that in the mid-1920s had covered the cost of an estimated 95 per cent of emigrant fares, or provide the required guarantees that a new arrival would not become a charge on public funds. In 1930, 14,072 immigrants from independent Ireland entered the United States; in 1931 the figure was 801.[7]

Those who continued to see no future for themselves in their own country instead turned to Great Britain. It too suffered from the worldwide drop in economic activity. Traditional areas of heavy industry, such as shipbuilding on the Clyde and in northeast

England, continued to languish throughout the 1930s. But by the middle of the decade new forms of manufacturing, such as motor car assembly and the production of radios and domestic appliances, had begun to flourish, and there was also work in areas like construction, transport and, for women, catering and domestic service. Between 1931 and 1937, when just 3,139 emigrants from the Irish Free State made the journey to the United States, 133,400, twice the number over the previous seven years, travelled to Great Britain.

The Second World War reinforced the change of destination, making the journey across the Atlantic perilous, while at the same time the demand for workers on the home front in Great Britain rose spectacularly. During the years 1939 and 1945, between 100,000 and 150,000 workers from independent Ireland travelled to England, Scotland and Wales. By 1950 the number of Irish-born people living in Great Britain—and hence the number able to provide advice and assistance to future migrants—was larger than the number in the United States. The demands of wartime had also brought Irish workers in Britain into a much wider range of occupations: many still found work on building sites and in the construction of roads and railways, but there were now others in factories, on trains and buses, in shops and warehouses. Fewer households could by now afford domestic servants, but Irish women found openings in hotels, boarding houses and restaurants. Others benefitted from the on-the-job training provided for nurses by the expanding National Health Service. In the postwar decades Great Britain continued to receive four-fifths or more of all emigrants from independent Ireland. It was the end of an era. Ireland remained as dependent as ever on emigration as a means of matching population to limited resources. But a diaspora based on mass movement across oceans had given way to a transfer of people across a narrow sea, within the boundaries of what had been up to a few decades before a single political unit.[8]

In 1948 Éamon de Valera, the one-time president of the revolutionary Dáil, set out on an ambitious foreign tour, ostensibly to raise international support for a campaign to end the continuing partition of Ireland. The timing was advantageous. His political party, Fianna Fáil, in office since 1932, had unexpectedly lost power to a coalition of its opponents. He himself was about to face the embarrassment of a court case to determine ownership of funds that had belonged to the Sinn Féin party in the period before the Irish Civil War, an inquisition likely to raise awkward questions about his behaviour in that contentious period. A world tour, under the anti-partition flag, was an opportunity to advertise his international standing, to touch up his image as the custodian of the true republican vision, and to make a strategic withdrawal from an unrewarding domestic scene. The first part of his progress was a four-week tour of the United States during March and April. The second part, beginning on 22 April, included brief visits to Singapore, Burma, India and Egypt, all former British colonies in which he was received as a hero of the struggle against imperialism. But the main focus was a five-and-a-half-week tour of Australia and New Zealand. In Canberra, de Valera and his foreign minister and travelling companion Frank Aiken had the rare honour of being allowed to sit in the chamber during a meeting of the Australian federal parliament. In New Zealand the Scottish-born prime minister, Peter Fraser, hailed him as 'a staunch champion of democracy', citing in particular his role as a supporter of the League of Nations.[9]

The enthusiastic welcome thus offered to the self-proclaimed Irish republican was not something that could necessarily have been predicted. In both Australia and New Zealand, the First World War had created tensions between the Irish Catholic population and the wider society. More recently there had been much resentment at de Valera's insistence that independent Ireland should remain neutral during the Second World War. And indeed there was some negative comment on the visit in sections of the Australian press. But the political establishment in both countries had clearly decided to put the past behind them. They showed no interest in being drawn into a campaign to push Northern Ireland into a united Irish state. But they happily indulged their visitor with symbolic invocations of Ireland's nationalist past. In Wellington, Fraser recalled his own period, nearly thirty years before, as an official in the Irish Self-Determination League. In Victoria, a government minister accompanied de Valera and Aiken to the Eureka monument at Ballarat. Later he was to visit the cottage where the Young Ireland leader William Smith O'Brien had lived during his period as a convict, and the monument to Michael O'Dwyer and other participants in the rebellion of 1798 in the Waverley Cemetery in Sydney. Another reminder of an earlier, contentious period, de Valera's much-publicised meeting with Daniel Mannix, still clinging flintily to power as archbishop of Melbourne, likewise passed without adverse comment.

One reason for the benign tolerance shown to the former enemy of all things British was that the Irish, in both Australia and New Zealand, were now so thoroughly embedded in the social structure of both countries. Free Irish settlers (as opposed to convicts in Australia) had never been an underclass in the way they became in Great Britain and the United States. And by the twentieth century the level of economic disadvantage had been greatly reduced. In Australia in 1933 Catholics (the great majority of whom would have been of Irish descent) made up 18 per cent of all heads of household, 22 per cent of the poorest, and 15 per cent of the richest. In New Zealand the distribution of Catholic men (again, at this period, almost all were Irish) across occupations, from professionals to farmers, was roughly equal to that of the population as a whole. There was thus no sense, except perhaps among diehard Orangemen, that Irish Catholics constituted a dangerous or disruptive presence. Memories of hard words exchanged during and after the First World War, equally, had by now been erased by the wholehearted support that Irish Australians and New Zealanders had given to the more recent conflict of 1939–45, support that also compensated for the refusal of de Valera's Ireland to play its part in the same struggle.[10]

The Irish in both Australia and New Zealand were still set apart from the wider population by their Catholicism. Religion and ethnicity, moreover, were closely linked. It was not until after the Second World War, and the arrival of immigrants from Italy and elsewhere, that *Catholic* and *Irish* ceased to mean virtually the same thing. The personnel of the church, too, had a firm Irish stamp. Fourteen of the eighteen Catholic bishops appointed to New Zealand dioceses across the whole period 1869–1950 were Irish or of Irish descent. In Australia the first four native-born bishops had all completed their ecclesiastical training in Ireland. The first truly Australian bishop took office only in 1930. Priests and nuns trained in local seminaries and convents, likewise, only slowly supplanted those imported from Ireland. As in Ireland itself, the church in both countries offered its followers a vast range of organisations, covering every aspect of social life: sodalities and other devotional societies, charitable and philanthropic bodies, sporting clubs and cultural associations. In addition the church authorities in both countries insisted on maintaining a separate system of denominational schools, despite the additional cost to the laity, whose taxes already supported the secular state system.

To some critics this comprehensive network of exclusive institutions amounted to the creation of a Catholic (and in practice Catholic Irish) ghetto. But this perception was misleading. Catholic associations in both Australia and New Zealand sought to preserve and strengthen a distinctive identity. But that was to be achieved, not by withdrawing from the wider society, but by equipping those involved to participate safely in national life. Catholic schools and clubs regularly took part, under their distinctive banner, in sporting competitions. Cultural societies and charitable bodies collaborated enthusiastically with kindred bodies. Attempts to promote a distinct Catholic identity, in any case, were influential only in so far as they succeeded. Separate education and specifically Catholic clubs and associations were intended to encourage commitment to the church's teachings and to promote regular religious practice. But the New Zealand census of 1921 put Catholic Church attendance at 56 per cent, an improvement on the 27 per cent recorded in 1874 but well short of the level of popular devotion that had by that time been achieved in Ireland. In Australia scattered statistics from the early twentieth century put the attendance rate at below 50 per cent. A further part of the rationale for the proliferation of clubs and societies was the hope that a social life conducted through exclusively Catholic associations would maximise the chances of an individual marrying within the faith. Yet around one-third of marriages involving Australian Catholics, and a third to a half in the case of New Zealand, were to non-Catholic partners. By no means all parents, equally, complied with the repeated insistence of priests and bishops that children must be educated in Catholic schools; in New Zealand in 1926 the number doing so was only 58 per cent. Even the Irish character of the church did not necessarily promote the group solidarity that might have been expected. The historian Patrick O'Farrell, born in New Zealand in 1933 to parents who had emigrated from County Tipperary, remembered the priests of his youth, mainly trained in All Hallows College, as boorish and authoritarian, characterised by a 'domineering clericalism' that might have been effective in the villages of the west of Ireland but that jarred with parishioners raised in the egalitarian ethos of New Zealand society.[11]

The integration of Australian and New Zealand Catholics into the wider population also had implications for de Valera's hopes of creating a new worldwide mobilisation of the expatriate Irish and their descendants behind the aims of Irish nationalism. O'Farrell recalled how little real interest in Irish affairs had persisted even among his Irish-born parents and their peers. Instead, he suggested, the culture he grew up in during the 1930s and 1940s was 'residually "Irish", but in a colonial way'. *Colonial* in this sense meant a culture derived from Ireland, but remoulded in unique ways by the new environment in which it had taken shape. During and just after the First World War the Self-Determination for Ireland Leagues had briefly united Irish Catholics of differing political outlooks. But with the creation of the Irish Free State this weak coalition collapsed. 'It is quite evident', the former president of the New Zealand Self-Determination League, Patrick O'Regan, wrote in his diary in 1926, 'that the Irish question is now dead as far as this country is concerned, and after all we have enough to do to mind our own affairs.' In Australia, similarly, de Valera attracted large crowds when he appeared alongside Mannix in Melbourne. But the turnout for other events—5,000 in Perth, for example, and too few to cover the administrative expenses in Hobart—was less impressive. Attempts to build a political movement on the basis of the visit, equally, failed dismally. Before leaving, de Valera commissioned Dr Albert Dryer, the leader of the seven members of the Irish National Association so contentiously interned thirty years earlier, to set up an Australian League for an Undivided Ireland. But the organisation never took off, and by 1953–4 it ceased to exist.[12]

Australia's welcome to de Valera may also have owed something to the presence there of a Labour government. One of the long-term consequences of the contentious plebiscites of 1916 and 1917 had been to solidify the link between the Catholic Irish and the Australian Labour Party, the two main groups that had opposed conscription. Just under half of the Labour Party members in the federal parliament at the time of de Valera's visit in 1948 were Catholic, the majority of Irish descent; the prime minister, Ben Chiffley, was himself the son of an Irish-born mother and an Australian-born father of Irish background. It was an electoral alliance initially endorsed by the Australian Catholic Church. The mildly progressive policies of the party were no threat, particularly in the light of the papal encyclical *Rerum Novarum* (1891), which had called for a more just distribution of the fruits of economic progress between capital and labour. There was also the hope that Irish votes would, over time, encourage the party to address Catholic grievances, especially in education. Already at the time of de Valera's visit, however, a hidden influence was working, behind the scenes, to undermine this consensus. Bartholomew Augustine ('Bob') Santamaria, son of Italian immigrants, had established himself as adviser to the Catholic bishops on social issues. In 1945, with their support, he created a secret organisation, the Catholic Social Studies Movement. The immediate purpose was to combat Communist influence in the Australian labour movement. But in the longer term the aim was to detach Australian Catholics from even the mild socialism of the Labour Party. In its place the Movement promoted the ideal, popular with Catholic intellectuals of the period, of escaping the conflict between capital and labour by returning to an economy based on small-scale independent producers. Santamaria's campaign was brought into the open in 1954, when Labour unexpectedly lost a federal election, due partly to the Red Scare tactics of its opponents. Its leader, H. V. Evatt, angrily denounced 'disloyal' elements within the party. His attack, and subsequent moves to curtail the influence of the Catholic Social Studies Movement and its affiliates, provoked a conflict within the party between left and right, with the conservative faction breaking away in 1957 to become the Democratic Labour Party.[13]

The schism within Labour split the Catholic vote, partly on class lines. Supporters of the Democratic Labour Party were about equally divided between white-collar and manual workers; among supporters of the Australian Labour Party, two-thirds were working class. For the party, the result was disastrous. Democratic Labour never achieved more than 10 per cent of the vote, but its challenge was enough to keep Labour out of power at the federal level until 1972. For the Catholic Irish, on the other hand, the split, and the subsequent realignment of their votes along a conventional left/right spectrum, can be seen as a further stage in their assimilation into the mainstream of Australian politics. There was also a collateral benefit. One of the most contentious outstanding issues between Australian Catholics and the wider society, from the late nineteenth century onwards, had been the refusal of governments to subsidise denominational schools out of public funds. Now, with the Irish vote no longer unshakeably committed to Labour, there were potential gains for others in taking up the question. Hence it was the Liberal Party leader Sir Robert Menzies who in 1963 introduced legislation extending federal funding to Catholic schools. In New Zealand change came a bit more slowly. But by the 1970s anti-Catholicism had ceased to be a political force, and there too the weakening of traditional loyalties meant that Labour and the National Party competed for Irish votes. A new education act in 1975 extended state funding to denominational schools, with the exception of some capital costs.[14]

Éamon de Valera was not the only Irish leader to visit the centres of Irish settlement overseas. Sir James Craig, prime minister of Northern Ireland from 1921 to 1940, travelled to Canada in 1926. In 1929–30, now Viscount Craigavon, he made an extended tour of Australia and New Zealand. Sir Basil Brooke, prime minister of Northern Ireland from 1943 to 1963, visited the United States and Canada in 1950, and Australia and New Zealand in 1955. Their visits brought to the fore a very different part of the Irish diaspora. 'It is wonderful', Craig wrote home from New Zealand, 'the number of men and women of Ulster blood out here, it is the backbone of the Dominion; they are a splendid lot.' His wife recorded in her diary how, travelling by train through Canada, they had repeatedly to stop to receive the greetings of 'people of Ulster and Irish extraction. . . . It was pathetic sometimes the eagerness they displayed in asking questions about the old country, and one of the features we enjoyed most on our trip were these little informal gatherings with natives of our homeland.' Brooke, visiting Cooke's Church in Toronto (named after the celebrated Ulster Presbyterian evangelist Henry Cooke), received presentations from, among others, the Sons and Daughters of Ireland Protestant Association. 'This was really very moving', he reported. 'Some had not seen Ulster for 30 or 40 years and tears were streaming down their cheeks. I shook hands with most of them. What fine people they are.'[15]

Brooke's visit to North America was primarily to promote trade, and the British government had made clear that it did not want him to stir up controversy on the issue of the partition of Ireland. In the United States he confined his speeches to topics such as the role of immigrants from Ulster in the American Revolution and the contribution of Northern Ireland to the Allied cause in the Second World War. In Canada, where a majority of the Irish population were Protestants, mainly of Ulster descent, he felt freer to speak his mind. 'Irishmen the world over', he announced in Toronto, 'can cancel any plans they may have for a wedding of the North and South'. The Irish Republic was 'a charming colleen', but one that Northern Ireland had no wish to marry. Earlier, in Ottawa, he had swapped mockery for menace, telling the Sons and Daughters of Northern Ireland that 'we will hurl back anybody who tries to introduce sedition into a country which is loyal to the King'.[16]

At first sight Sir Basil Brooke's progress through Canada was a political triumph. If the anti-partition movement could mobilise crowds in the United States, Northern Ireland also had its diaspora, who had not forgotten their Ulster Protestant heritage. In the wider society, however, there were signs that the old Orange warrior's rhetoric had struck a false note. An official Canadian government communique noted that 'there was too much insistence upon "British" and "Empire" to make his speeches completely compatible to Canadian audiences'. Canadians, like Australians and New

Zealanders, no longer thought of themselves primarily as inhabiting dominions of the British Empire or Commonwealth. Instead they had a growing sense of their own national identity. Even the Orange Order was not immune to the change. Toronto, at the time of Brooke's visit, still had an Orange mayor, as had been the case, with only occasional interruptions, since 1864. But only four years later a stridently Orange candidate was to be defeated. The last Orangeman to serve as mayor of Toronto left office in 1972. At the national level, membership of the Order had been in decline since the 1920s. By 1950 there were only 1,521 lodges, compared to 2,205 thirty years earlier. By 1970 the number would fall to 1,044. Ten years later there were to be fewer than 20,000 active members, with an average age of over 50. The Irish, in the late twentieth century, were still the fourth-largest ethnic group in Canada, after the English, the French and the Scots. But there as elsewhere, and in the Protestant as well as the Catholic diaspora, new identities had largely taken the place of older allegiances.[17]

––––––––

Sir Basil Brooke's easy passage through Canada stood in contrast to the rather different reception he had received on the first leg of his tour in the United States. Things got off to a bad start when he had to cancel plans to travel by sea, following a warning from the British embassy that Irish-American dock workers might refuse to unload the vessel. When he landed instead at Idlewild Airport in New York, a crowd of around 200 appeared to boo and jeer. The Irish-born mayor of Chicago, overriding the objections of supporters, agreed to meet him. However the mayor of New York, also Irish-born, had already publicly announced that Brooke would not be welcome in city hall, and throughout his visit groups up to a thousand strong paraded in protest outside his hotel. Brooke was able to use contacts established during the Second World War, when American forces had been stationed in Northern Ireland, to secure a visit to the Pentagon, an armed forces reception, and a military parade in his honour in Chicago. He was also granted a ten-minute courtesy call with the secretary of state. President Truman, however, had announced in January that he would not be available, a decision that Brooke admitted had been 'rather a jolt'.[18]

The prospect of dockworkers combining to frustrate the landing of the visiting champion of Protestant Ulster brought together all the stock elements in the conventional image of Irish America: manual labour, clannishness, and a continued commitment to the cause of Irish nationalism. It was an image that remained partly accurate. In 1950 just under three-quarters of Irish-born men worked in what would be classified as blue-collar jobs. But even here the nineteenth-century stereotype was misleading. Some immigrants continued to contribute what George Cornewall Lewis had described as 'animal strength'. But much larger numbers even of the first generation were now employed in work that was still often of low status, but was less physically arduous than that of a docker or builder's labourer. They were janitors and building superintendents, watchmen and porters, bus and taxi drivers, waiters and bartenders. The second generation, American-born sons of immigrants, were often found in the same service roles. But they also had a respectable presence across a wide range of skilled and semi-skilled jobs. Law enforcement was another constant across the generations: the share of policing jobs held by Irish-born men was three times their presence in the workforce as a whole; for the second generation it was four and a half times greater. Irish-born women were still more likely than other working women to be employed as servants. But their daughters, continuing a pattern already evident at the beginning of the century, tended to steer clear of domestic service, while holding more than their share of jobs as teachers, nurses and office workers.[19]

Alongside the improving position of the blue-collar Irish there was by this time a gradual but progressive movement into white-collar work. In Boston, by 1950, less than one in five Irish-born workers was in a white-collar occupation, and they had three times their share of unskilled labouring jobs. The second generation, on the other hand, were only slightly overrepresented among the unskilled, and just over two out of five were in white-collar positions. Across the country as a whole, accounting and law had now been added to what the census bureau called the occupational specializations of the second-generation Irish. The result was to introduce new divisions into the Irish American world. As early as the 1930s a team of social scientists engaged in an in-depth study of Newburyport, Massachusetts, noted

> the sharp antagonisms which exist between the Irish of the two lowest classes (lower-lower and upper-lower) and of the two higher classes (upper-middle and lower-upper). The former refer to the latter as 'lace curtain Irish', a term with reproachful connotations, and associate them with the Hill Street 'codfish aristocracy'. The higher-class Irish, when aroused, will apply to the Irish of the lower classes the familiar epithet, 'shanty Irish'. The lower-middle-class Irish seem to keep to the fence in this conflict between the two class factions in the group.

Resentment, in this case, was deep enough to fracture the legendary political solidarity of the American Irish. A recent mayoral election had divided along class rather than ethnic lines: a populist candidate of Irish background carried the whole working-class vote, both Irish and non-Irish, while his defeated rival, also Irish, had the support of the social elite but of only about one-fifth of the town's Catholics. Awareness of social divisions could also appear in more intimate settings. A biography of the Boston politician James Curley, himself the son of an immigrant labourer, recalls that the only occasion on which he struck his son was when the boy dared to greet him as 'Dad' rather than 'Father'. When the tearful boy protested that this was the word he had picked up at school, Curley was unrepentant. 'They're shanty Irish. If they wish to allow such things in their homes, that is their business.'[20]

With improving status came a change of neighbourhood. The New York Irish had long ago abandoned districts like the Five Points. After the First World War they spread from lower Manhattan, north to areas like Washington Heights, where the Irish population grew almost fourfold between 1920 and 1940, and outwards into the city's other boroughs. Here, thanks to new building techniques and tighter municipal regulation, they became tenants or owners in larger, brighter, airier and better-serviced apartments and houses. In Chicago families like the Lonigans, depicted in James T. Farrell's classic novels of Irish-American life, moved south from the old Irish stronghold of Bridgeport into new districts such as Washington Park. In Newburyport, Massachusetts, only a handful had by the 1930s penetrated the elite residential district of Hill Street, with its solid mansions set back from a 40-foot-wide boulevard shaded by an arch of ancient elms. But the majority, by this time primarily third or fourth generation, had moved away from the Merrimack River waterfront that had been their first home, and were making their way steadily along the residential streets that ran upwards from the river to connect with Hill Street.[21]

The new respectability of the Irish was also evident in patterns of marriage. The impulse to marry within the same ethnic group remained, but was gradually weakening. In New Haven, Connecticut, in 1930 three-quarters of men and women of Irish descent married others of the same background. Sixty years earlier it had been more than nine out of ten. By 1940, the proportion choosing an Irish partner had fallen to 45 per cent, rising slightly to 50 per cent ten years later. In the population as a whole the indications were that religion rather than ethnic background was becoming the main limitation on the choice of partner. Here, however, the Irish departed significantly from the general pattern. When they looked beyond their fellow Irish for a husband or wife they could choose in a population that included Italians, Poles and Germans, the last both Catholic and Protestant. In practice, however, the Irish more commonly opted for partners of English, Scottish or American descent. Their preference, in other words, was to intermarry with long-established ethnic groups like their own, even though these were overwhelmingly Protestant, rather than with more recent, imperfectly assimilated immigrants who shared their religion. This did not mean that religion had become irrelevant. On the contrary the other major finding to emerge from the New Haven records was that the majority of marriages involving an Irish and a British or American partner took place in a Catholic Church. Given the uncompromising policy towards 'mixed marriages' laid down in the papal decree *Ne Temere* (1907), that could only have meant that the Protestant partner had agreed that the children of the union would be brought up as Catholics. American and British spouses, it seems, were willing, not just to see Irish men and women as acceptable partners, but to submit to the demands of an inflexible and authoritarian church as the price of winning their hand.[22]

Change was also evident in the manner in which the Irish were depicted in popular culture. Hostile images of the violent, drunken, simian-featured Hibernian had long ago given way to the gentler satire typified by Jiggs and Maggie. By the 1930s and 1940s the prevailing tone in cinema, now the dominant popular medium, had moved on to positive approval. In 1938, just ten years after a presidential election had let loose a last great paroxysm of anti-Catholic protest, *Angels with Dirty Faces* presented Pat O'Brien as a charismatic priest who persuades gangster Jimmy Cagney to turn his young followers away from a life of crime, at the cost of seeming to lose all dignity on the way to the electric chair. Two years later O'Brien was back in clerical dress, portraying Francis Patrick Duffy, the real-life First World War chaplain of the celebrated New York Irish regiment in *The Fighting 69th*. In 1942 Cagney played George M. Cohan, grandson of an immigrant from County Cork and author of the First World War ballad 'Over There', as well as the doggerel but hugely popular celebration of Americanism 'The

Yankee Doodle Boy'. In *Going My Way* (1944) Bing Crosby was the affable but shrewd Father Chuck O'Malley, who rescues a New York parish from financial ruin by transforming a group of potential juvenile delinquents into a commercially successful choir. Irish women did not initially have the same distinctive screen image. Maureen O'Hara's first major success, in 1941, was as a Welsh heroine, while Maureen O'Sullivan's enduring image was as Tarzan's partner Jane in six films between 1932 and 1942. But by the 1950s, when the film studio MGM organised publicity for its star Grace Kelly, granddaughter of an immigrant and daughter of a wealthy Philadelphia building contractor, it deliberately promoted her as the epitome of a specifically Irish elegance and beauty.[23]

By the mid-twentieth century, then, the American Irish had clearly improved their position. Instead of a reservoir of cheap labour, they were a well-established part of the settled working population, with a small but expanding middle class. Yet there were those who argued that they should have done better still. In particular critics pointed to the absence of entrepreneurs. Irish Americans most commonly entered the middle class as lawyers, accountants, managers and administrators, only rarely as owners of their own businesses. (The exception was in construction, an area of traditional Irish strength, and also one where an ability to create and cultivate political relationships was a distinct advantage.) One common comparison, with Jewish immigrants, is perhaps misleading. Jews came to America with the advantage of being products of a commercial rather than a peasant society, and with an exceptionally strong communal solidarity forged by centuries of persecution, of a kind that made the failings of British government in Ireland trivial by comparison. A more telling comparison is with Italians. Here the Irish should have been at a definite advantage, in terms both of their mastery of English and their earlier arrival. Yet a celebrated study of ethnic mobility in Boston between 1880 and 1970 showed the two groups progressing at roughly the same level. The most common explanation points to what was in other respects the most striking achievement of the American Irish, their success in local politics. The main aim of the great urban political machines was to create a payroll vote. But here it made sense to maximise the number of modestly paid jobs that could be distributed to supporters. The result was to trap Irish Americans, the main beneficiaries of the system, in a blue-collar cul-de-sac.[24]

The idea that Irish America lacked dynamic entrepreneurs because it was too easy for talented young men to opt for the secure mediocrity of a lifetime as firemen, policemen or city clerks is plausible. But it also has a familiar ring. It echoes closely the complaints of nineteenth-century observers like J. F. Maguire that too many Irish immigrants chose to remain in the eastern cities, with their constant and varied opportunities of employment, ignoring the brighter prospects offered by life on the frontier. And, as with those earlier criticisms, some context is needed. By the time the great urban machines reached the height of their power, the trauma of the Famine was no longer part of living memory. But these were still people who had been forced by the dire lack of alternatives at home to trust themselves to an uncertain future, on the other side of a vast ocean. Against that background, a reliable income that would allow a working-class family to live in decent comfort was not something to be underestimated. When the historian Lawrence McCaffrey, born in Chicago in 1925, sought to explain his opposition to the gloomy view of immigrant life offered by younger colleagues, he pointed out that he had grown up in an America where 'a large number of streetcar motormen and conductors, subway drivers and maintenance personnel, railroad men, policemen, firemen, priests, nuns and brothers' all spoke with Irish accents and told their children that the United States 'was the greatest country in the world'.[25]

Even in purely economic terms the idea that, by opting for life on the public payroll, the individual Irish immigrant made a poor choice should not necessarily be accepted without question. In Boston in 1909, 45 per cent of Jews were engaged in business on their own account, compared to only 5 per cent of the Irish. But the average income of Jews was $396 a year, compared to $510 among the Irish. It is also worth noting that the era of contented streetcar conductors and beat cops described by McCaffrey was also the period of the Great Depression. The same study that criticised the Irish for not outstripping the Italians by economic risk-taking drew attention to the extent to which workers of all ethnicities who were pushed into poorer-paid and less skilled work during the Depression went on to suffer life-long economic disadvantage. For once, but in important ways, the Irish, concentrated in areas like municipal services and transportation that continued to function even as manufacturing withered, may well have been rewarded for their lack of ambition.[26]

Earnest sociological enquiries into immigrant life and behaviour, such as the Newburyport study and the analysis of New Haven marriage patterns, were shaped by an abiding concern among academics and policy makers with the issue of assimilation. The term 'melting pot' became popular through the play of that title by the British author Israel Zangwill, first staged in 1908. Zangwill's play was a melodrama in which emigration to the United States allows its Jewish hero to leave behind the destructive passions of the Old World, even to the point of falling in love with the daughter of the Tsarist officer responsible for the slaughter of his family. But its title became the shorthand for a much broader vision, going back to the eighteenth century, of America as a society uniquely capable of absorbing immigrants from different backgrounds and blending them into a single, cohesive whole. In time it became clear that this comfortable vision was not being realised. A turning point was the appearance in 1963 of *Beyond the Melting Pot*, a study of ethnic groups in New York by the sociologists Daniel Patrick Moynihan and Nathan Glazer. 'The point about the melting pot', they memorably announced in their preface, 'is that it did not happen.' Glazer and Moynihan did not wholly reject the idea of assimilation. The city's Germans, they noted, had been largely absorbed into what they called 'the Anglo-Saxon centre'. Among other groups the second and third generations had shed most of the outward signs of difference, such as language and dress. Intermarriage between ethnic groups, but within the same religion, was becoming more common, raising the possibility, as already suggested by the New Haven study, that what was emerging was a 'triple melting pot', with separate compartments for Protestants, Catholics and Jews. But for the moment, forty years after mass immigration had come to an end, the Italians, Irish, Jews, Puerto Ricans and African Americans of New York City still thought of themselves as members of particular ethnic groups. If each had become fully American, it had done so in its own distinctive way.[27]

What, then, was distinctive about the Irish way of being American? St Patrick's Day was now firmly established in the civic ritual of towns and cities. From 1933 the completion of a new radio transmitter at Athlone in the Irish midlands allowed Éamon de Valera, as head of the Irish government, to broadcast a St Patrick's Day address directly to the United States. Gaelic hurling and football, disrupted by the First World War, also flourished in the 1920s. After 1930, however, the games were no longer nourished by a continuing supply of newly arrived emigrants, while the Depression brought a collapse of gate revenue. In 1940 the New York Gaelic Athletic Association could no longer afford the lease on Innisfail Park in the Bronx, opened with much fanfare in 1925, and had to hand the grounds back to the city. The Ancient Order of Hibernians, once the premier organizational expression of Irish identity, also suffered badly from the dwindling supply of new arrivals. Membership fell from 132,000 in 1908 to around 20,000 in 1940. Fading interest in the ethnic past was also evident at local level. Catholic parochial schools in Newburyport had at one time taught

Irish history, and the Hibernians had offered an annual prize for the best essay on the subject. By the early 1930s, however, both the teaching and the prize had been abandoned. 'When I was a child', one woman told investigators, 'I and all my family knew all about the Irish heroes, but the children of today know nothing about them.'[28]

In place of culture or history, the Newburyport study concluded, the core basis of Irish identity was Catholicism. The 100 or so inhabitants of Ulster Protestant birth or descent, they found, were largely indistinguishable in culture and behaviour from those of southern Irish, Catholic background. Yet they had simply blended into (in the language of the report, 'are undifferentiated from') the non-immigrant population, whereas the Catholic Irish 'present themselves as a highly organised community system within the [Newburyport] social system'. The Catholic Church, of course, was not exclusively the property of the Irish. But they were without question the majority shareholders. In the 1920s more than half of the bishops in the United States, and more than one-third of the clergy, were of Irish birth or, by this stage more commonly, descent. Parochial schools introduced successive cohorts of children to a close-knit social world, in which Sunday mass served as a weekly gathering. Parishes also continued, as in the late nineteenth century, to offer a comprehensive array of community associations, including religious sodalities and fraternities, charitable and philanthropic organizations, sporting clubs, musical societies and study groups. Meanwhile the Knights of Columbus, a movement of Catholic rather than specifically Irish solidarity, took the place in communal life formerly occupied by the Hibernians.[29]

At the same time that Catholicism helped to sustain a distinct ethnic identity, it also further advanced the integration of the Irish into American life. The aggressive defence of Catholicism represented by the Knights of Columbus went along with an equally bold assertion of American patriotism. 'Proud in the olden days', the order's ceremonial proclaimed, 'was the boast "I am a Roman Catholic". Prouder yet today is the boast, "I am an American citizen". But the proudest boast of all times is ours to make: "I am an American Catholic citizen"'. Catholic schools, like their public equivalents, prominently displayed the flag of the United States, began the school day with the Pledge of Allegiance, and taught American history. Here Catholics were at a distinct advantage during the difficult interwar years. The Great Depression raised doubts about the future of the entire economic system; democracy, once apparently an unstoppable force, faltered and retreated in much of Europe; new work in science and psychology undermined what had seemed the certainties of space, time and human rationality; modernist artists abandoned the task of representation. The Catholic intellectual world, however, remained untouched by these disturbing trends. A well-established network of universities and colleges stuck to an alternative tradition, rooted in the teachings of St Thomas Aquinas. Liberal and left-wing intellectuals were appalled by what they saw as a retreat into the Middle Ages. But to many others the authority and confidence conferred by a philosophy of life that presented itself as rigorously deduced from first principles and the laws of nature was highly attractive. One conspicuous beneficiary was Francis Spellman, archbishop of New York from 1939, whose prominence as a national spokesman earned him the title 'the American Pope'. Alongside his firm defence of Catholic moral teaching on issues such as birth control, Spellman articulated a deeply conservative American patriotism. He was prominent in the anti-Communist crusade of the 1950s and after, served from 1939 as military vicar of the armed forces, and up to his death in 1967 gave outspoken support to the war in Vietnam.[30]

The other expression of an Irish ethnic identity, from the time of the Fenians onwards, had been organised support for Irish nationalist movements. Here the messy end of the final struggle for independence—a short but brutal civil war between supporters and opponents of the compromise settlement embodied in the Anglo-Irish Treaty of December 1921—left Irish America divided and confused. McGarrity, as head of a reorganised Clan na Gael, backed de Valera in rejecting the Treaty, and gave $17,000 to the anti-Treaty wing of the IRA. Devoy and Cohalan, who had earlier revolted against de Valera's high-handed manner, supported the pro-Treaty party that now became the government of the newly established Irish Free State. The recriminations were bitter. McGarrity's faction accused Devoy of being a British agent, and decried the 'silk-hatted' Irish Americans who turned out to greet W. T. Cosgrave, premier of the Irish Free State, when he visited New York in 1927. Devoy's *Gaelic American* accused Austin Ford, nephew of Patrick Ford and now editor of the anti-Treaty *Irish World*, of being an opium addict, and described de Valera as a 'half breed Jew'. McGarrity's movement, from 1929 renamed 'the Clan and IRA clubs', drew much of its support from the several thousand veterans of the defeated anti-Treaty IRA, denied employment and the target of aggressive police action, who in the years after 1922 joined the continuing flow of emigrants to the United States. A major part of the Clan's activities was to secure medical treatment for former fighters suffering from the after-effects of wounds, hunger strikes, or long periods on the run. The organization also appealed to other recently-arrived immigrants, to whom it offered a ready-made social life. Clan clubs played on local loyalties by adopting the name of county heroes of the independence struggle (Austin Stack for Kerry, Sean Tracy for Tipperary), and offered outings, dances and concerts, presided over by groups like Sean Hayes and his IRA Radio Orchestra. After 1930, however, the supply of newly arrived recruits dried up, and the clubs and dance halls closed for lack of paying customers. By 1942 the total membership of the anti-Treaty Clan in the United States was no more than 750.[31]

The bleak economic environment of the 1930s was not the only reason for the dwindling appeal of militant republicanism in America. The victory of the Irish Free State in the civil war, and electoral results during the 1920s, seemed clearly to indicate that the Treaty, however imperfect, was accepted by the majority within Ireland. There was also the powerful influence of de Valera. The American Association for the Recognition of the Irish Republic, following his lead, had joined the Clan in rejecting the Anglo-Irish Treaty. In 1926, however, de Valera led the more pragmatic opponents of the Treaty, now organised as Fianna Fáil, into parliamentary politics; from 1932 he headed the government of the Free State, and quickly began to treat his former IRA allies as an enemy within. In all this he succeeded in taking his large body of American supporters with him. Against this background supporters of a continued military campaign for a republic encompassing all Ireland, on both sides of the Atlantic, became a marginalised extreme. Their most creative minds were found in the small faction that envisaged a revitalised popular movement combining nationalism with socialism. But this was not a strategy likely to appeal to most Irish Americans. Mainstream republicanism, meanwhile, slipped into the politics of the gesture. Occasional resort to militant action, such as the planting of bombs in British cities in 1939, was intended more to assert that the physical force tradition was alive than to achieve any clear political objective. The bombing campaign had the support of McGarrity, militant to the end. But to most Irish Americans the idea of a struggle pursued with proud disregard for the chances of success or failure ran totally contrary to the pragmatic philosophy of politics that they had developed in their transatlantic exile.[32]

This did not mean that the cause of Ireland was wholly forgotten. De Valera's four weeks in the United States during his world tour in 1948 drew large and enthusiastic crowds. The parallel anti-partition campaign launched by the coalition government that had ousted him from power also made some impact. In 1950 John Fogarty, a congressman from Rhode Island, and three others, among them the future Senate majority leader Mike Mansfield, sponsored an amendment that would have denied Marshall Plan aid to the United Kingdom until the issue of partition was resolved. There was no realistic prospect of the Truman administration inflicting damage of this kind on its recent wartime partner, now a key ally in the Cold War. But midterm elections were approaching, and the amendment passed in a thin House, with explicit assurances that there would be an opportunity to reconsider. The anti-partition campaign, however, soon ran out of steam, in the face of general international indifference. And in the absence of any credible lead from within Ireland itself, Irish issues came to receive no more than token acknowledgement in American political life. In Edwin O'Connor's classic novel of machine politics, *The Last Hurrah*, published in 1956, the veteran boss Frank Skeffington, loosely based on Boston's Jim Curley, is careful to spice up a speech to local fishermen, most of them of Portuguese origin, with a reference to Prince Henry the Navigator. ('I've been trying to find a more contemporary figure . . . but with Portugal that's not so easy.') But the Portuguese were not numerous enough to be important:

> When you come right down to it, there are only two points that really count.
>
> . . . Skeffington held up to two fingers. 'One', he said, ticking the first, '*All Ireland must be free*'. Two, he said, ticking the second, '*Trieste belongs to Italy*'. They count. At the moment, the first counts more than the second, but that's only because the Italians were a little slow in getting to the boats. They're coming along fast now, though; in twenty years the Irish issue will be about as burning as that of

Unhappy Ethiopia. Fortunately, I don't expect to be among those present at the time.

At the time it seemed a credible prediction. But in practice the picture was to be transformed, well before that time limit, by developments that the wily old pragmatist had no means of imagining.[33]

13

FROM TAMMANY
TO CAMELOT

As the United States emerged from the First World War, Irish politicians retained a firm control on the political life of many of its major cities. The 1920s and early 1930s were in fact the heyday of the strongest form of machine, in which a single boss controlled an entire city. From then on Irish dominance was to be slowly eroded, as other ethnic groups began to assert themselves, as the New Deal transformed the provision of welfare services, and as suburbanisation began to break up the traditional inner-city neighbourhoods that had been the city boss's power base. But some political fiefdoms proved remarkably durable. Meanwhile the Irish, at the same time that their control of ward and city hall began to weaken, began to penetrate the centres of national power in a way that would earlier have been unimaginable.[1]

———————

The basis of the machine's power, as in earlier decades, lay in building up a body of compliant voters, then drawing on the resources of the municipality to reward and retain their support. The means of doing so varied. In Albany, New York, where voters often owned their homes, newcomers to a district might be served with an eye-watering assessment for property tax, which could then be reduced on application to a precinct captain. In Jersey City, patients treated at the New Jersey Medical Center might receive punishing bills that could similarly shrink or disappear following a suitably deferential interview with a party functionary. But the most common currency in the exchange between voters on the one hand, and the boss and his ward heelers on the other, was jobs. In New York City, Albany and Jersey City, between 1900 and 1930, the municipal workforce tripled in size. In addition, construction firms winning public contracts, and transport, electricity and other utilities subject to municipal regulation, were routinely required to make room on their payrolls for clients of the politicians they dealt with. In return, job holders were expected to remember their obligation. Public sector workers in some cities had to tithe a proportion of their earnings at election time to help cover the machine's expenses. And above all they had to turn out to vote. In Democratic-controlled Albany, it was claimed, the Republican lever on the city's voting machines was left unoiled, so that the audible squeak as the handle was pulled betrayed the elector who failed to keep his side of the bargain.[2]

Malpractice of this kind can encourage facile caricature. And it is important to remember that the terms 'machine' and 'boss' were developed by would-be reformers to stigmatise a system they sought to destroy. Urban political machines had always had a positive role, as a source of assistance to the inner-city poor, in particular the immigrants among them, in their dealings with an otherwise unfriendly world. By the early twentieth century the more far-sighted among those involved had also become supporters of more thorough-going measures of practical social reform. The outstanding example of the new type of urban politician was Al Smith, born in New York in 1873, the son of a German-Italian teamster and a second-generation Irish-American mother. Smith was a classic product of Tammany: leaving school at age 15 following the death of his father (his degree, he quipped, was from FFM, the Fulton Fish Market), he came to the notice of ward organisers as a bright and energetic activist, and progressed from an appointment as subpoena server to a seat in the state assembly, and then, in 1918, to election as Democratic governor of the state of New York. In the assembly he served as vice chairman of the commission set up to investigate conditions in factories, following the horrendous blaze that destroyed the Triangle Shirtwaist Factory, and killed 146 workers, in 1911. He then used the full Tammany repertoire of bargaining, bullying and cajoling to have the assembly pass the commission's reform proposals into law. As governor from 1919 to 1920 and again from 1923 to 1928 he promoted slum clearance, housing development and compensation for injured workers. He also gave women a forty-eight-hour working week and women teachers equal pay with men, and used bond issues to construct parks and bathing beaches on Long Island. By 1928 it seemed to be time to aim higher still. In June of that year the Democratic Party convention, meeting in Houston, Texas, voted overwhelmingly to make Smith its candidate for president.

The election of 1928 was a milestone in the political history of America's Catholics. To conservatives the years since the First World War, an era of industrial unrest, of brash new fashions in dress, dance and entertainment, and of suddenly independent women, had been deeply disturbing. In response the 1920s saw a revival of xenophobia and militant Protestantism on a scale not seen since the days of the Know-Nothing movement. One dramatic manifestation was the rebirth of the Ku Klux Klan, in the years after the Civil War a southern movement seeking to maintain white supremacy by terror, but now focussing its animosity primarily on Jews and Catholics. In this new guise the Klan spread rapidly in the North as well as the South. In Chicago it had, at its peak, 50,000 members, in Philadelphia, another Irish stronghold, 35,000. Meanwhile a number of states, notably Ohio, sought to close down Catholic denominational schools. Against this background, the emergence as presidential candidate of a Catholic of immigrant descent aroused predictable outrage. Protestant preachers across the country terrified their congregations with a lurid account of the impending popish tyranny, when the United States would become a vassal of the Vatican and it would become illegal to own or read a Bible. Handbills depicted Smith on his knees kissing the ring of a papal delegate. Smith polled well in the major cities. But across the South and Midwest, and even in the rural parts of his home state of New York, Democratic voters deserted him in droves. The Republican candidate, Herbert Hoover, carried forty states and dominated the electoral college with 444 votes to Smith's 87.[3]

Religious bigotry was not the only reason for this disastrous outcome. Prohibition was also a central issue in 1928, and in Smith the Democrats had a candidate not only not dry, but dripping wet. Even in the industrial North and Midwest a booming economy depressed the working-class Democratic vote. Smith had also done himself no favours with his party by his behaviour at the 1924 Democratic convention, when he had refused to abandon his own by now hopeless candidacy for fear of letting in William Gibbs McAdoo, a rival with links to the Ku Klux Klan. In addition his unmodified New York accent, his cigars and loud suits, even his chosen campaign song, 'The Sidewalks of New York', did little to appeal to rural and small-town voters. But the ferocity with which opponents attacked the very idea of a Catholic running for the presidency nevertheless left a deep impact. Smith himself was taken aback and frustrated by challenges based on a version of Catholicism he did not even recognise. 'Will someone please tell me', he reputedly demanded of his aides, 'what the hell a papal encyclical is?' And to his disappointed supporters the message was clear. Catholics, and in particular Irish Catholics, might rule the cities. But they were still not accepted as a wholly legitimate part of American political life.

Al Smith represented one face of Irish-American politics in the period after the First World War: a progression from the initial banding together for mutual protection of an inner-city immigrant group to a broader movement for social justice. But there was also another, darker face. By the 1920s and 1930s more people of Irish birth or descent had moved into relatively secure and well-paid employment. A minority had risen into the category of 'lace curtain' Irish (or, in one comedian's alternative formulation, families who had fruit in the house even when no one was sick). But there were many others who remained in low-status, poorly paid, physically demanding work. There was a resentful awareness, heightened by the brutal rejection of Smith's candidacy and the rebirth of the Ku Klux Klan, of the hostility and contempt with which large sections of American society continued to regard all things Irish and Catholic. Meanwhile the hard-won status of the Irish was also being threatened from another direction. By 1930 they made up less than 7 per cent of the foreign-born population, as compared to 20 per cent from Germany and Poland, 13 per cent from Italy, and 8 per cent from Russia. Many of these new immigrants were competitors only for the lower types of manual work. But central and eastern European Jews, from non-peasant backgrounds and with a strong tradition of education, had begun to claim their share of areas of white-collar work formerly dominated by the Irish.

Between 1900 and 1930, for example, the Jewish share of teaching jobs in New York rose from 11 to 44 per cent. There was also the growing number of African Americans migrating from the South to the industrialised cities of the North, less well-placed to compete with the Irish for jobs but even more unwelcome when they sought to expand their living space in ways that encroached on established Irish districts. Despised from above and threatened from below, Irish Americans of the interwar period, particularly the economically less fortunate among them, were easily drawn into a politics of rancour and insecurity, quite different to the progressive, aspirational outlook that Smith had represented.[4]

Among the practitioners of rancour few came close to James Curley, born a year after Smith and into a very similar background: his parents had both emigrated from County Galway, and his father, a hod-carrier, died when the boy was 10, leaving the family in poverty. Curley dominated Boston's political life for thirty years, serving four terms as mayor (1914–18, 1922–6, 1930–34, 1946–50), two as a member of Congress for the state (1911–14, 1943–7), and one as governor of Massachusetts (1935–7). Like John 'Honey Fitz' Fitzgerald, for a time his rival, he turned his back on the conciliatory tradition of Patrick Collins, instead casting Boston politics as a struggle between a privileged but decadent Yankee elite and an Irish Catholic people whose day had come. 'The Massachusetts of the Puritans', he proclaimed, 'is as dead as Caesar, but there is no need to mourn the fact. Their successors—the Irish—had letters and learning, culture and civilization, when the ancestors of the Puritans were savages running half-naked through the forests of Britain.' Like Fitzgerald, too, Curley used not very coded references to birth control to point up the contrast between Irish dynamism and 'Puritan' decadence. Later in his career, running for the Senate against Henry Cabot Lodge Junior, a representative of one of Boston's oldest families, Curley dismissed his opponent as 'Little Boy Blue', 'a young man who parts both his name and

his hair in the middle'. Curley's corruption was flagrant. He won
election to the Board of Aldermen in 1899 while serving a two-
month jail sentence for taking a written entrance examination for
a constituent who aspired to be a postman, campaigning on the
slogan 'He did it for a friend'. He was jailed again, for fraud in
connection with wartime contracts, in 1947, drawing his full salary
as mayor while incarcerated. At the time of his conviction he enjoyed a 62 per cent approval rating among voters who regarded his
flamboyant misdeeds less as offences than as acts of defiance. The
twenty-one room, neo-Georgian mansion he erected in 1915, with
its Italian marble fireplaces and shutters decorated with shamrocks,
cost incriminating multiples of a mayor's salary. But that was less
important than the triumphant message it sent to Boston's 'codfish
aristocracy' (a term, Curley quipped, that was an insult to the fish)
and to his own Irish working-class supporters.[5]

All this was in Boston, a city of finance capital with a particularly well-entrenched Brahmin elite. Elsewhere Irish social resentment was directed downwards and sideways, rather than up.
African Americans were one obvious target. In Chicago, where the
Black population had doubled between 1910 and 1920, a Black
youth, in July 1919, made the mistake of letting his raft cross the
imaginary line between white and Black space on the water off a
lakefront beach. There followed a vicious racist offensive, mainly
pursued by Irish gangs, which left thirty-eight people dead and
over a thousand homeless. But many Irish Americans were also
drawn to the great political poison of the interwar years: antisemitism. Here their spokesman was the hugely successful radio
priest, Father Charles Coughlin of Royal Oak, Michigan, whose
broadcasts brought him an audience of almost thirty million and
required him to engage a staff of fifty clerks to handle his daily
postbag. Addressing his audiences in what listeners took to be a
slight brogue, even though his family had been in North America
for four generations, Coughlan was initially a campaigner for social

justice, denouncing the devastation of ordinary lives by the misdeeds of bankers and financiers, and backing President Franklin D. Roosevelt's New Deal. By 1936, however, he was denouncing the massive expansion of federal activity as economically ruinous and a step towards communism. Two years later his attacks on high finance moved on from the occasional, partly coded reference to Jews to wild assertions of a worldwide Zionist conspiracy. Ominously, Coughlan also encouraged his followers to establish rifle clubs and paramilitary squads under the title of the Christian Front. Not all Irish Americans followed his lead. When a candidate for his hastily formed Union Party contested the presidential election of 1936, the great majority remained loyal to President Roosevelt and the Democrats. But in Boston's working-class Irish districts, his candidate took 11 per cent of the vote. And even in the 1940s, after Coughlin himself had been forced by his bishop to abandon the airwaves, Irish gangs in Boston and New York, inspired by the Christian Front organisation, continued to carry out vicious attacks on Jews, and to vandalise synagogues and graveyards.[6]

From 1933, the workings of the urban machines in the United States were transformed by the blizzard of federal government initiatives with which Franklin D. Roosevelt sought to reverse the collapse of the American economy. Across the country, the Public Works Administration built airports, highways, bridges, tunnels, hospitals and schools. The Works Progress Administration, during a period of eight years, put 8.5 million unemployed to work. All this involved federal spending on a scale multiple times greater than the state and municipal budgets within which bosses were accustomed to operating. Yet the New Deal did not, as the conventional wisdom once held, bring the end of machine politics. The tidal wave of new spending was financed by the federal government. But it had to be administered locally. And here Roosevelt proved to be ruthlessly pragmatic. As a young senator before the First World War, he had been a loud critic of Tammany. As a presidential candidate, and then a president with his eye on re-election, on the other hand, his dealings with the urban machines were governed strictly by his assessment of their political value to him.

Dealt with on this basis, some prominent figures fared badly. James Curley had been an enthusiastic supporter of Roosevelt from the start. But his base in Boston was too narrow to give him wider influence in the state, and at the Democratic convention he spectacularly failed to deliver the votes of the Massachusetts delegation, which instead supported Al Smith's campaign for a second nomination. So control of the massive patronage created by the New Deal went to the state governor, Joseph Ely, and to Democratic Senator David Walsh, both of whom had also backed Smith, but now reconciled themselves to Roosevelt's ascendancy. Curley, who had hoped for a Washington appointment, was fobbed off with what he regarded as the derisory offer of becoming ambassador to Poland. (When an aide queried the propriety of even this appointment, Roosevelt replied with a question: 'What is there in Poland that Curley could steal?') Thomas Pendergast, the political boss of Kansas City, had also been an early Roosevelt backer, yet ended up in prison after the president permitted the FBI and Treasury to investigate his administration's finances. But this happened, not just because his corruption was too flagrant for the government to turn a blind eye, but also after he had lost out in a power struggle with the governor of the state, leading Roosevelt to believe that Pendergast was no longer worth protecting. Frank Hague in Jersey City was even more corrupt than Pendergast, a man not above using his control of the police and courts to have political opponents jailed on trumped-up charges. Hague had also been an enthusiastic Smith partisan in 1932. But once he had demonstrated his ability to deliver both votes and delegates to future conventions he gained complete control of federal patronage in both state and city. Other bosses who proved their worth, like Edward Crump in

Memphis, were similarly rewarded. In Chicago, run by the equally reliable Edward Kelly, Roosevelt insisted on pouring money into huge projects like the subway, despite complaints from the director of the Public Works Administration that one-fifth of the federal dollars would disappear in corrupt payments.[7]

The real threat to the Irish-run urban machines came, not from the expanded role of the federal government, but from another feature of the New Deal era: the political awakening of the newer immigrant groups. Up to the 1930s the Irish had been remarkably successful in retaining their privileged position, even as their share of the urban population shrank. Immigrants from southern and eastern Europe, especially those intending to stay only a few years, were often slow to take out citizenship or register to vote. This meant that they could be relatively easily conciliated through minor favours—the distribution of food to the needy, loans, assistance in obtaining trader's licences or in getting round municipal regulations. There were also symbolic gestures. In Boston, Curley appropriated the worldwide hit 'Isle of Capri', published in 1934, as his campaign song. Earlier, in 1922, he had hailed Mussolini as the saviour of Christian civilization. More substantial benefits—jobs and election to local office—continued to be monopolised by the Irish. In New York and Jersey City in 1930 more than half of all local government employees were first-, second- or third-generation Irish Americans, representing more than one-fifth of the total Irish workforce. In New Haven in 1933 Irish Americans made up only 13 per cent of a sample of the population, yet again held nearly half of all public service jobs.[8]

By this time, however, the era of Irish domination by default was coming to an end. The non-Irish ethnic population now included not just immigrants but a second and third generation, American-born and English-speaking. A sense of ethnic identity remained strong, as Glazier and Moynihan were to discover even three decades later. But new forms of entertainment—the cinema, the radio, professional sport—provided the elements of a popular culture common to all ethnic groups, just as the spread of chain stores fostered a shared consumerism. These developments provided the basis for the mobilisation of a more homogeneous, less fragmented urban working class. The first signs of change came in 1928. Al Smith may have been overwhelmingly rejected at national level, but in the country's twelve largest cities he took a clear majority of the votes, attracting the support of Irish, Jews, Italians and Poles. Over the next decade, with the shock of the Great Depression and the charismatic leadership of Roosevelt, the transformation became complete. In the immigrant wards of the great industrial cities voter turnout rose by nearly one-third between 1932 and 1936. Membership of labour unions rose from three million in 1933 to eight million by 1940.[9]

Just how dangerous this political awakening could be for long-established Irish political machines was demonstrated in New York. In 1880 more than one-third of the city's residents had been of Irish descent. By 1945 it was fewer than one in ten. In 1932, a poorly led Tammany had been discredited by the removal of Jimmy Walker, the flamboyantly corrupt mayor supported by the machine, and had also backed Al Smith against Roosevelt. When the Depression forced massive cuts to municipal spending, the machine protected Irish-dominated sectors of the workforce, allowing the axe to fall instead on other ethnic groups, in particular the Italians. In 1933, Fiorello La Guardia, a gifted demagogue of mixed Italian and Jewish ancestry, brought together a coalition of non-Irish ethnic groups, reformers, and Republicans to defeat Tammany's candidate and become mayor of New York. La Guardia had run as a Republican, but Roosevelt, as always, chose to ally with the side that had proved itself a winner. Edward Flynn, boss of the Bronx, a long-term associate of Roosevelt, saw federal dollars pouring into his borough. But in the rest of the city Tammany watched helplessly as La Guardia used his complete control of New Deal funding to create a rival machine. The damage was lasting. Shrunken and demoralised, Tammany sought to shed its past by adopting a new name, the Democratic County Committee. When La Guardia eventually retired, after three terms in office, in 1945, the committee's nominee, Mayo-born William O'Dwyer, succeeded him as mayor. But the next mayor, in 1950, was an Italian Democrat, Vincent Impellitteri. A year earlier it had been another Italian, Carmine De Sapio, who emerged as head of the much-weakened New York Democratic machine. The Irish remained an important interest group. But they no longer owned the city's politics.[10]

Elsewhere, however, the impact on established Irish interests of the new ethnic politics varied both with local circumstances and with the political agility of the politicians involved. In Jersey City in 1949 Frank Hague's nephew and would-be successor lost to a dissident Democrat supported by Poles, Italians and younger Irish voters. In Chicago, on the other hand, Irish leaders, facing a strong Republican Party with its own machine, had already during the 1920s begun sharing power and patronage with southern and eastern Europeans. In the late 1920s Anton Cermak from Bohemia was able to organise Jews, Poles and his fellow Czechs to seize temporary control. But the Irish remained influential within the organisation, and when Cermak died in 1933, hit during a political rally by a bullet aimed at Roosevelt, it was two Irishmen, the former city engineer Edward Kelly and the businessman Patrick Nash, who took charge. In Pittsburgh another Irish boss, David Lawrence, was able to use New Deal patronage to organise southern and eastern European voters and create a machine that ran the city until 1969. In Boston, the city that consistently recorded the highest Irish population in the United States, the challenge from other European ethnic groups never materialised. The city got its first Italian mayor in 1994, by which time the Irish and the Italians were the two main components of a white working class feeling itself under siege from African Americans and Hispanics.[11]

In the twenty-five years or so that followed the end of the Second World War, Irish Americans completed the last stage of their long journey from an immigrant underclass to equal participants in prosperity and status. This was, for the United States, the golden age of economic growth. Between 1942 and 1950 national income had already risen by three-quarters; by 1970 it had increased to more than three times its 1950 level. The Irish, mainly employed in blue-collar jobs, but with a strong concentration in unionised and public service work, were well-placed to ensure that their boat was among those most effectively lifted by this rising tide. A survey of ethnic groups in 1969 adopted a broader definition of ethnicity. Instead of focussing on immigrants and their immediate descendants, it examined a sample of the whole population, asking those interviewed to say what ethnic group they believed themselves to belong to. Those who defined themselves as Irish, 6 per cent of the total, were distributed across the occupational hierarchy—professionals and managers, lower white-collar occupations, skilled workers, labourers—in almost exactly the same proportions as the United States population as a whole. The median income of an Irish family was $8,127, higher than the national median of $7,894, and not far short of what was recorded for families of English and German descent ($8,324 and $8,607 respectively). Among those aged over 35, one-third of the Irish had completed four years at high school, slightly higher than the national average (31 per cent); 9.3 per cent had completed four years in college, just under the national average (9.8 per cent).[12]

Another survey, in 1977–8, confirmed the picture of an ethnic group now firmly established in the middle levels of American society. This survey, however, included religious affiliation, and its findings were startling. It was Catholics of Irish background who

371

had enjoyed this rise in wealth and status. Protestant Americans of Irish background were significantly less well-placed in terms of high-status occupations, educational achievement, and family income. The explanation for this unexpected finding was historical and geographical. In the eighteenth century Protestant settlers from Ireland had played a major role in pushing back the frontier to and then across the Appalachians. But this left their descendants concentrated in the economically backward South. The predominantly Catholic immigrants of the nineteenth century, on the other hand, had settled overwhelmingly in precisely those areas, the cities of the East and Midwest, that were now the centres of America's dramatic economic growth. And by the late 1970s they had become, on the evidence of this survey at least, the most prosperous of all white, gentile ethnic groups, outstripping even the so-called WASPs, Protestants of English or German descent.[13]

One consequence of the economic boom of the postwar years was suburbanisation. Increased car ownership and huge highway construction schemes allowed populations to move from the inner city to a new landscape of houses, lawns and carports sprawling over what had been fields and woodland, while federal subsidies and guarantees to lenders, a legacy of the New Deal, made mortgages available to millions on ordinary incomes. Here the Irish were somewhat slower than other groups to abandon city living. But already by 1950 more than half of the Irish Americans in the New York metropolitan area lived outside the city. In the archdiocese of Chicago, by 1965, half of the Catholic population—heavily, though not exclusively, of Irish origin—lived in the 100 new parishes, 72 located in the suburbs and the rest on the city's outskirts, that had been created since 1940. Movement to the suburbs brought more living space, privacy, and new-built houses equipped for modern electrical amenities. But withdrawal from the inner city was also a response to the changing ethnic complexion of traditional Irish neighbourhoods. In New York, for example, Irish families had moved north from Lower Manhattan, following the extended subway, to take up residence in newly built tenements in the Washington Heights and Inwood neighbourhoods on the northern portion of Manhattan Island. By the 1950s, however, that area was being colonised by African Americans moving north from Harlem, by Puerto Ricans and, most of all, from the mid-1960s, by new immigrants from the Dominican Republic. History repeated itself as beleaguered Irish residents denounced the newcomers, using very much the same accusations that nativists had directed at the Irish a century before: the Dominicans, they claimed, were dirty, they were dangerously violent, and they showed no signs of assimilating in the way earlier immigrants had done. Already by 1960 the Irish population of these two neighbourhoods had fallen, in just ten years, by almost a third, from 27,000 to 19,000. And there, as elsewhere, white flight of this kind, once it had begun, became a self-sustaining process, as those who remained came to feel more threatened still.[14]

Membership of new suburban parishes like those created in Chicago would have helped to maintain a continuing sense of identity. In 1974, 58 per cent of Irish Catholics still attended mass every week, higher than the average (50 per cent) for Catholics as a whole. But life in the suburbs nevertheless brought more frequent and closer social contact with people of other ethnic backgrounds, and other religious denominations. The movement of population also had implications for the network of parochial schools, both in the inner-city areas that Catholics were abandoning and in the new, sprawling, ethnically and religiously mixed areas to which they moved. Of the eighteen Catholic elementary schools in Albany, New York, in 1954–5 only six remained by 1993–4, while only in four of the new suburbs was there a sufficient concentration of Catholic parents to support a parochial school.[15]

The flight of the white ethnic population to the suburbs had obvious implications for the legendary grip of the Irish on urban political life. Other changes in the postwar period further contributed to the decline of old-style machine politics. New laws requiring that posts be filled by competitive examination, affirmative action programmes aimed at directing a fair share of jobs to African Americans, and the emergence of strong public sector labour unions all imposed increasingly tight limits on the patronage available for political purposes. Yet the demise of the Irish city boss was a remarkably protracted process. By 1950, the Irish-controlled Tammany machine in New York and the Hague machine in Jersey City were no more. But in 1965, Boston, Philadelphia, Detroit, Chicago and San Francisco all had mayors of Irish ancestry. Most of these political leaders no longer commanded an organisation so powerful as to constitute a machine. But there were exceptions. In Chicago, Richard Daley took over from Edward Kelly in 1955 and remained undisputed master of the city's politics until his death in 1976. In his early years he ran an old-fashioned patronage-driven organisation, funded by a doubling of taxation. From 1963, threatened with a taxpayer revolt, he turned instead to an alliance with business, basing his appeal on the promise of efficient municipal services. Chicago, in the new slogan, was the city that worked. He also changed tack on race, abandoning the Black voters to whom he had earlier directed a share of patronage, and instead wooing the white electorate by enforcing rigid racial segregation in schools and housing. Throughout all this his administration continued disproportionately to be staffed by people of Irish background. Albany provides another example of Irish political longevity. Erastus Corning 2nd, who served as mayor from 1942 to 1983, with a short break for war service, was from an old Anglo-Dutch family. But he was closely connected, throughout his political career, to Daniel P. O'Connell, chairman of the local Democratic party and an old-style political boss. O'Connell's powerful machine continued to function in the classic style through the 1960s and 1970s, dispensing favours and patronage in exchange for votes. As late as 1991–3 investigators studying the Catholic population of Irish background in Albany discovered that almost one in three of those interviewed had at some stage approached their ward leader—an unelected party official—for assistance. These might, of course, have been memories stretching back over decades. But there was also a continuing perception that, as one informant put it, 'if you are smart you still register as a Democrat just for taxes and things like that'.[16]

At the same time that their control of city machines was slowly and unevenly eroding, Irish Americans were achieving a new prominence in the upper regions of the political system. Their ascent had begun in the era of the New Deal. Franklin Roosevelt's keen awareness of the importance to his regime of Irish support had ensured that city bosses who served him well could steer the parts of the federal gravy train that affected them. The same awareness was reflected in his higher-level appointments. James Farley, a New York–based Democrat and the grandson of Irish immigrants, became postmaster general for the new administration in 1933. As Roosevelt's campaign manager in 1932, and then chair of the Democratic National Committee, Farley was a key figure in the president's attempt to build up an alliance of labour, ethnic groups and progressives in the industrial North and so reduce his party's dependence on the voters of the racist and conservative South. He at one time hoped to make his own bid for the presidency, but was frustrated by Roosevelt's decision to run for unprecedented third and fourth terms in 1940 and 1944. Thomas Corcoran, a Harvard graduate from a middle-class Irish Catholic background, used a modest position within the Reconstruction Finance Corporation to coordinate activity across a range of projects central to the New Deal. Frank Murphy, formerly mayor of Detroit and governor of Michigan, where he had refused to authorise the customary use of troops to break a major strike by autoworkers, became attorney general in 1939, and was appointed a year later to the Supreme Court.

More controversially Roosevelt's choice as chairman of the Securities and Exchange Commission, established to curb the recklessness and dishonesty that had brought about the crash of 1929, was Boston-born Joseph Kennedy. The problem here was not Kennedy's family background, as the son of the long-serving political boss of East Boston and the son-in-law of John 'Honey Fitz' Fitzgerald. Instead it was his own career as a financier, where he had built up a fortune through precisely the practices of insider trading and short selling that he was now called on to curb. In the event he proved to be a vigorous and effective reformer. Later he went on to become head of the Maritime Commission, established to revive the struggling shipping industry. Roosevelt was unwilling to give Kennedy what he really wanted, a place in the cabinet. He considered him, as he explained to his son-in-law, 'a temperamental Irish boy', too opinionated, thin-skinned and power hungry to be a member of a governing team. But it is a measure of Kennedy's importance, as a fund-raiser, a man of influence, and a potentially dangerous enemy, that something had nevertheless to be done for 'Joe'. The consolation prize for his exclusion was the most prestigious diplomatic posting in the president's gift, ambassador to London. Roosevelt's patronage also extended lower down the administrative hierarchy. About one-quarter of all his judicial appointments were Catholics, many though by no means all Irish. And, in an important gesture, the clergyman he chose to pronounce a benediction at his inauguration for his second term, in January 1937, was Monsignor James Ryan, a professor at the Catholic University of America in Washington and a leading advocate of the gospel of social justice.[17]

The New Deal era was of course an exceptional time. But the rise to national prominence of men like Farley and Kennedy meant that a ceiling had been ruptured. Roosevelt's successor, Harry Truman, had been an associate of the Pendergast machine in Kansas City, and worked easily with senior Irish figures. Among his appointments was Maurice Tobin, who had defeated James Curley in

1937 to become mayor of Boston, and who in 1948 became Truman's secretary of labor. Robert Emmet Hannegan, another Missouri politician who had helped Truman disentangle himself from the scandal created by Pendergast's conviction, became postmaster general. Two successive attorneys general were likewise of Irish background. The passing of the presidency into Republican hands, with the election of Dwight Eisenhower in 1952, brought a leaner period for Irish aspirants to high office. By this time, however, it was becoming clear that not all Irish votes were unshakeably tied to the Democrats. So, a few judicious appointments made electoral sense. Eisenhower initially experimented with a cross-party appointment, making Martin Durkin of the Plumbers and Pipefitters Union secretary of labor. When, after a few months, Durkin found his position as a Democrat in a Republican cabinet untenable, Eisenhower replaced him with another Irish Catholic, this time a Republican of middle-class background, James Mitchell. As the Eisenhower administration neared its end, his vice president, Richard Nixon, who had worked closely with Mitchell on labour issues, for a time considered him as a possible running mate in his first bid for the presidency.[18]

International developments further contributed to the rising status of the Irish. For Ireland itself the Second World War brought a sharp deterioration in relations with the United States. The Roosevelt administration regarded Britain's survival as essential to the preservation of European civilization, and demanded that Ireland play its part. Specifically it called for Britain to have access to the country's ports, potentially crucial—particularly in the early stages of the war—to control of the North Atlantic. De Valera refused to budge from his policy of strict neutrality. But in 1941 he nevertheless appealed to America for food to relieve shortages created by a British naval blockade, and weapons for self-defence. The White House received his emissary, Foreign Minister Frank Aiken, with barely concealed contempt. But Ireland continued to have its champions, whether moved by electoral expediency or genuine sentiment, within the political system. During his American tour Aiken received official welcomes in Boston, Philadelphia and Los Angeles; when he sailed home from New York, Fiorello La Guardia turned up to see him off. So pragmatism prevailed. In response to Irish-American lobbying, Roosevelt agreed to send two shiploads of food to Ireland, and sanctioned a donation of half a million dollars from the American Red Cross. His administration also intervened on more than one occasion to restrain the British government, advising strongly against any attempt to take control of Irish ports by force, and later cautioning against proposals to extend conscription to Northern Ireland, where it would meet with resistance from a large nationalist minority.[19]

Where wider issues of foreign policy were concerned the two main Irish-American newspapers, the *Irish World* and the *Gaelic American*, campaigned strongly for the United States to avoid involving itself in another European conflict. Even after the attack on Pearl Harbor had left them with no choice but to support the war effort, they continued to pursue sectional grievances. They published complaints that British forces were not taking their proper share in the fighting, and drew invidious comparisons between the attention given to Nazi antisemitism and the supposedly greater problem of anti-Catholicism. In August 1945, four months after battle-hardened British and American soldiers had recoiled in horror at what they found on entering Bergen-Belsen and Dachau, the *Gaelic American* claimed that conditions in Northern Irish jails matched anything that had happened in the 'infamous Nazi concentration camps'. Among the wider population of Irish descent, however, attitudes were less clear-cut. A Gallup poll taken a few weeks after Pearl Harbor found that more than four out of five Irish Americans (82 per cent) believed that Ireland had in fact already entered the war. Follow-up questions revealed that more than half believed it should be part of the Allied war effort, and nearly three-quarters that it should at least permit access to its ports. An incident at the end of the European war, when de Valera visited the German legation to offer his formal condolences on the death of Adolf Hitler, their country's head of state, further highlighted divergent attitudes. Those in the United States who defended the visit as a legitimate assertion of Ireland's sovereign independence seem mainly to have been the Irish-born. De Valera's post bag, on the other hand, contained numerous letters from Irish Americans of the second, third and later generations expressing their outrage and dismay at what they saw as an inexplicable gesture.[20]

After 1945, with the coming of the Cold War, matters became more straightforward. In the new conflict between Western democracy and Eastern Communism there was no ambiguity about whose side the Catholic Church was on. Irish America's part in the ideological struggle had its darker side. Between 1950 and 1954 Senator Joseph McCarthy ruined lives and poisoned political debate by creating and sustaining a mood of hysteria regarding the supposed influence of covert Communists in politics, the civil service, the armed forces and academia. In giving enthusiastic support to McCarthy, Irish Americans were in part rallying to one of their own. McCarthy was a Republican, but he had been born and brought up in a small Irish Catholic enclave in rural Wisconsin. There was also a suggestion of scores being settled. The high-flying administrators and professors brought low by McCarthy's scattergun accusations were representatives of the Anglo-Saxon, Protestant establishment that had treated Irish Catholics, even a plutocrat like Joe Kennedy, with a mixture of condescension and contempt. (Kennedy's son, Robert, was a McCarthy aide.) There was also scope, in some of the targets chosen, for a degree of antisemitism. In this sense McCarthyism was a further exhibition of the same frustration and resentment that almost two decades earlier had driven the career of Father Coughlin. At the time, however, Irish commitment to the anti-Communist crusade was another step towards acceptance into the American mainstream. In 1952 Hollywood introduced a new variant on the Irishman as all-American hero when John Wayne appeared in the title role of *Big Jim McLain*, playing a two-fisted investigator for the House Un-American Activities Committee. A year later thousands of real-life Irish policemen were present to roar their approval as Cardinal Francis Spellman declared his support for McCarthy at a breakfast of the New York Police Department's Holy Name Society.

It was against this background that a new figure began his political career. John Fitzgerald Kennedy, second son of the buccaneering financier Joseph Kennedy, had come of age as part of his father's entourage in London. He then served in the Pacific during the Second World War, winning praise for his leadership after his patrol torpedo boat was sunk by a Japanese destroyer, before completing his degree at Harvard. But Kennedy also had roots in the intense world of Irish factional politics in Boston. As Joe's son he was the grandson of Patrick Joseph Kennedy, former boss of East Boston. Through his mother he was also the grandson of the two-time mayor John 'Honey Fitz' Fitzgerald. And it was to Boston that John Fitzgerald Kennedy returned to campaign successfully for election to Congress in November 1946. In 1952 he moved up to the Senate, defeating the incumbent Henry Cabot Lodge Junior. His victory continued a family rivalry within Massachusetts that had begun in 1916 when Lodge's grandfather defeated Honey Fitz in a Senate election. The rivalry was to continue when Kennedy's younger brother Ted defeated Lodge's son, in 1962, in another contest for the Senate seat.

By 1956, after only ten years in politics, John F. Kennedy was already looking beyond the Senate to the White House. His ambition clearly reflected the driving force of his father, who had long made clear his hope that one of his sons—initially his eldest son, Joe Jr.; then, after Joe's death in combat during the Second World War, his second son, 'Jack'—should become America's first

Catholic president. But when Jack began to be talked of as a possible running mate with Adlai Stevenson in 1956, his father was not in favour. The younger Kennedy had commissioned, then leaked, a report by his aide Ted Sorensen, which argued that a Catholic candidate would win back Catholic voters who had deserted the Democrats in 1952 because their candidate, Stevenson, was divorced and was perceived to be soft on Communism. Kennedy senior, however, warned that Stevenson was a weak candidate. For Jack to join him in defeat would simply reinforce the stigma of failure left by Al Smith's losing campaign of 1928. In the event Kennedy allowed his name to go forward at the convention then, when it became clear he could not win, withdrew with a graceful speech endorsing Stevenson. Over the next three years, however, he used his Senate seat to position himself for the 1960 contest, with strong speeches attacking the administration's foreign policy and some carefully calibrated stances, calculated to maximise his appeal within the party, on Black civil rights. In 1960, this time with his father's full support, and the massive financial resources that went with it, he launched his bid for the nomination. He contested primaries, bargained with or bullied local party bosses and, in one state at least, the notoriously corrupt West Virginia, paid handsomely to have the right names put forward during the selection process. Having won the nomination, despite challenges from Stevenson, the well-liked Minnesota senator Hubert Humphrey and Senate Majority Leader Lyndon Johnson, he went on to campaign for the presidency against the outgoing vice president, Richard Nixon.

Kennedy's Catholicism was a central issue throughout the contest. During the primaries Hubert Humphrey chose as his campaign song 'Give Me That Old Time Religion'. Following his nomination Protestant spokesmen came forward to repeat the central charge heard in 1928, that no Catholic could give his full allegiance to the United States because his religion commanded him to give priority to the dictates of the pope. In West Virginia, during the primaries, Kennedy answered critics with a powerful and emotional speech emphasising his wartime service and his brother's death in combat. But in September, as candidate, he had to appear before a group of Protestant ministers in Houston, Texas, to insist that his private religious beliefs would have no influence on his conduct as president. In the event he won fewer than half of the votes of Protestant electors, and beat Nixon by a margin of 118,574 out of a total of 69 million votes cast. This included at least one highly dubious majority, of just 8,800 votes, in Illinois, where the Daley machine had gone into overdrive on his behalf. The ghost of 1928 had been exorcised. But it had been a close-run thing.[21]

The significance of Kennedy's status as the first Irish president is less clear cut. His ethnicity, as opposed to his religion, was not an issue in the debate. On the contrary, some attacks were directed at his privileged background and the backing he received from his father's millions. In his first Congressional election a Boston newspaper labelled him 'Jawn Kennedy . . . ever so British', and parodied his campaign as 'Congress seat for sale. . . . Only millionaires need apply'. Nor were these gibes unfounded. Joe Kennedy had at best an ambivalent relationship to the country his grandfather had left in 1848. A visit to Dublin in 1938 to receive an honorary degree from the National University of Ireland appears to have been a genuinely emotional moment for him. 'My parents and grandparents', he told the gathering at a state banquet in Dublin Castle, 'talked ever of Ireland and from my youth I have been intent upon this pilgrimage.' Yet on another occasion, when a Boston newspaper described him as Irish, he exploded in rage. 'Goddam it. I was born in this country. My children were born in this country. What the hell does someone have to do to become an American?' His second son's interest in his heritage seems to have deepened over time. He spent the summer of 1937 travelling through France, Spain, Italy, and Germany. During 1939, based in London with his father, he devoted several more months to touring in continental Europe and the Middle East. Yet he made his first visit to Ireland only in the summer of 1945. He was writing newspaper articles at the time, and the visit seems to have been primarily a fact-finding trip. A second Irish stay, in 1947, was primarily to see his sister, Kathleen, who was staying in Lismore Castle, County Waterford, owned by the aristocratic family of her deceased British husband. But Kennedy also took the trouble to seek out relatives in County Wexford, and he subsequently took holidays in Ireland in 1949 and 1955. His decision in 1963 to end a European tour with a four-day state visit seems to have been for wholly sentimental reasons. There were no major diplomatic issues to address (certainly not in comparison to Berlin, where he had just made his celebrated speech designating the city the front line in the defence of democracy). In terms of domestic politics, as his irritated aide Kenny O'Donnell pointed out, 'you've got all the Irish votes in this country that you'll ever get'. Taken as a whole, the chronology supports the view of the Irish ambassador of the day. Kennedy's interest in Ireland, he believed, 'was something which grew, which wasn't there at the beginning, because he wanted above all things to be a good New Englander'.[22]

When Robert Frost visited Kennedy with a copy of the poem he had read at the inauguration ceremony, he told him that as president he should be 'more Irish than Harvard'. The injunction has been much misunderstood. Frost's point was that what he called an Augustan government must be prepared to work with power as well as poetry. The truth was that Kennedy was already Irish to just the right degree. To those so inclined, his name recalled the glory days of P. J. Kennedy and Honey Fitz. He had the support of key Irish politicians of his own day, like Daley. His inner circle of advisers was partly but never exclusively Irish. (When the *New York Times* referred carelessly to an 'Irish Mafia', its roll call included the names Kenny O'Donnell, David Powers and Lawrence O'Brien, but also the distinctly un-Hibernian Ted Sorensen and

Pierre Salinger.) Yet for others, including many Irish Americans, it was part of Kennedy's appeal that he did not fit the image of the traditional Irish politician. David Powers, himself the son of Irish immigrants, called him 'a completely new type of Irish politician':

> There was a basic dignity in Jack Kennedy, a pride in his bearing that appealed to every Irishman who was beginning to feel a little embarrassed about the sentimental, corny style of the typical Irish politician. As the Irish themselves were becoming more middle-class, they wanted a leader to reflect their upward mobility.

Kennedy never went to a wake, another aide noted tellingly, unless he had known the deceased personally. Even more revealing, perhaps, was his private comment that the overweight, heavy-drinking, rabble-rousing Joseph McCarthy, a favourite with the Massachusetts Catholic electorate whom Kennedy did not dare to criticise in public, was 'just another shanty Irish'. When John Fitzgerald Kennedy captured the White House, the American Irish celebrated the victory of one of their own. But what had taken place was not a straightforward ethnic triumph. Rather it was confirmation that a much-changed Irish America was at last receiving something close to the recognition it craved.[23]

14

'WE'VE MARRIED ITALIAN GIRLS AND MOVED TO THE SUBURBS'

Irish Identities in a Changing World

In 1965, at the high point of the drive to purge the United States of the most obnoxious abuses in its treatment of race, a series of amendments to existing legislation transformed the immigration system that had been created in the 1920s. The national quotas, with their overt bias towards northern European countries, disappeared. Instead would-be immigrants applied for entry visas whose main criteria were a relationship to an American citizen or legal

resident alien, and professional or other high-level skills and qualifications. The Irish-American speaker of the House of Representatives, Thomas 'Tip' O'Neill, later recalled his bewilderment at the
lack of response from the Irish government. 'I could have walked
out on the floor of the House, and got an exemption for Ireland
in five minutes flat. All I needed was a phone call from the Irish
embassy. But the call never came.' Irish diplomats may simply have
miscalculated. An official at the Washington embassy reported to
Dublin that 'the comparatively high level of education of our people and the fact of their being English-speaking', along with the
large numbers with relatives already in the United States, would
ensure that the new qualifications would pose no problems. In reality most of those seeking to emigrate had only a primary school
education, and the emphasis in the new system on the reunification
of close relatives also worked against Irish applicants. The number
of Irish immigrants admitted each year to the United States was
to fall from 5,000 or more in the early 1960s to less than 1,500
a decade later. In another interview, however, O'Neill went further, claiming that the Irish ambassador had in fact asked Irish-
American politicians to vote for the emigration bill, 'because there
was a tremendous brain drain out of Ireland and they wanted to
stop it'. And the recollections of a former Irish diplomat confirm
that at a later stage he and his colleagues were indeed discouraged by their superiors from associating themselves with protests
against its impact.[1]

The willingness of the Irish government to accept, or perhaps
even welcome, the loss of Ireland's guaranteed allotment of immigration permits is not wholly surprising. The United States had long
ceased to be the main destination of Irish emigrants; during the
1950s it took fewer than one in every seven. By the 1960s, moreover, emigration of all kinds was in sharp decline, as a new policy
that abandoned the quest for economic self-sufficiency in favour
of targeted state spending and foreign direct investment allowed

the country belatedly to claim a share in the postwar economic boom. Between 1961 and 1966, for only the second time since the Famine, an Irish census revealed an increase in population, from 2.8 to 2.9 million. Then, in the 1970s, a balance that had prevailed for more than a century was reversed. A rate of economic growth among the highest in Europe encouraged the return of large numbers of emigrants from earlier periods, so that the number of people entering the country between 1971 and 1979 exceeded the number leaving by over 100,000.[2]

The new prosperity did not last. Instead what took place, for the economy and emigration alike, was a four-decade switchback ride. The unaccustomed prosperity of the 1970s encouraged a political spending spree, as rival parties wooed the electorate with tax cuts and investment projects, paid for by borrowing. When, in 1979, the Iranian Revolution brought a second oil crisis, and a worldwide recession, the chickens came home to roost. Public finances lurched into crisis, while a contracting economy could no longer provide livelihoods for a population now one-fifth larger than it had been in 1961. Between 1983 and 1993 some 472,000 emigrants left Ireland; the census of 1991 once again recorded a fall in population, of just under 15,000, over the preceding five years. By the early 1990s a determined campaign to rebalance the public finances cleared the way for a new and even more dramatic period of prosperity. These were the years of the 'Celtic Tiger', a label borrowed from the high-growth economies of Southeast Asia. By 2006 the population of the Republic stood at 4.2 million, one-fifth higher than in 1991 and the highest level recorded since 1861. The increase was due, not just to natural increase and to falling levels of emigration, but also to an unprecedented level of inward migration. During 2002–6, when the population grew by an average of 81,000 each year, 48,000 of these new faces were the result of a surplus of immigrants over emigrants. Once again, however, runaway growth proved to be unsustainable. The early years of the 'Celtic Tiger' owed their dynamism to the growth of manufacturing, especially in pharmaceuticals and computer products, driven by mainly American investment. But from about 2002, growth became heavily dependent on the expansion of services, and on a boom in property prices. The worldwide economic crisis of 2008 brought a painful correction, and a new rise in emigration. Between 2009 and 2015, 265,000 Irish citizens left the country.[3]

These renewed surges in departures, seeming to threaten a return to the dark days of the 1950s or earlier, caused widespread dismay. In fact this was emigration of a wholly different kind. In an age of cheap and frequent global travel, movement abroad could be seen as a short-term solution to difficulties at home, rather than a permanent and irrevocable choice. Already in the 1980s people with professional qualifications or managerial experience were overrepresented among those leaving, and more than two out of five were giving up a job within Ireland, indicating a quest for better prospects rather than a flight from destitution. After 2008 the pattern was even clearer: two-thirds of the emigrating Irish citizens were university graduates, and nearly half had been in employment up to the point when they left the country. For poorer Irish citizens, on the other hand, emigration was no longer an attractive option, not just because they lacked marketable skills, but because wages for unskilled work, and unemployment benefits, were significantly higher in Ireland than what they could hope to find elsewhere. Emigrant destinations had also changed. During both periods of crisis the largest numbers went to Great Britain. During the 1980s many others turned to the United States. Legal immigration was still severely limited by the 1965 immigration act. But lax enforcement allowed a large number, perhaps as many as 50,000, to enter the country as visitors, or on student visas, and disappear into the informal economy. After 2008, in contrast, tighter regulation following the terrorist outrages of 11 September 2001 ruled out that easy option. Instead the most popular destination, outside the

British Isles, was Australia, enjoying an economic boom and offering two-year 'working holiday' visas to suitable applicants. Canada began offering similar temporary work visas from 2013. Other Irish emigrants, especially those with engineering skills, found work in the Gulf States, others again in the European Union. And growing numbers moved back and forth between these different destinations. Ireland, by the early twenty-first century, was no longer a reserve of mainly unskilled labour for the neighbouring United Kingdom. It was the source of a mobile, well-qualified workforce that responded flexibly to changing conditions at home and abroad.[4]

Meanwhile Ireland had become a major importer of people. Even during the depressed years between 2009 and 2015, the 265,000 Irish emigrants, along with the 295,000 residents of other nationalities who also left the country, were balanced by the arrival of 120,000 Irish and 285,000 non-Irish immigrants. Most of the arrivals during the 1970s had been the emigrants of earlier periods, and returning migrants remained important in the Celtic Tiger years; in 1998–9 they made up just over half of those entering the country. But they were now joined by others from much further afield. In 1991 Ireland had just 55,000 residents born outside Ireland and the United Kingdom. By 2011 the number had risen to 432,000, just under 10 per cent of the population. The census of that year identified more than twenty-five towns in which over a quarter of the population were non-Irish nationals, and a further thirty-five in which the proportion was between a fifth and a quarter. The newcomers included Indians and Filipinos attracted by openings for qualified workers in the Irish health service, Brazilians recruited through a process of chain migration as experienced workers in meat processing, and Chinese, officially reckoned to number 11,000 by 2006, although one report suggested that the true number, concealed in the black economy, was as much as six to ten times higher. The largest group, however, were from the ten new countries, mainly in eastern Europe, admitted to the European Union in 2004. Between 2004 and 2007 almost 400,000 of these new Europeans registered to work in Ireland. The biggest single group was Polish, with 63,276 citizens resident in Ireland by 2006, and an astonishing 122,585 (more than the 112,259 citizens of the United Kingdom) five years later.[5]

By the early twenty-first century, then, a nation of emigrants had to come to terms with being itself the host to a growing immigrant population. The precedents were not encouraging. In perhaps the most shameful episode in its diplomatic history, independent Ireland, both before and after the Second World War, had refused to accept Jewish refugees from Europe. The relevant government department cited the supposed unwillingness of Jews to become assimilated and 'the murmurs against Jewish wealth and influence'. Even in 1946, when the full horrors of the Nazi regime were public knowledge, it took a personal appeal from the former chief rabbi, Isaac Herzog, to Éamon de Valera to gain temporary admission for 137 orphaned children freed from the Bergen-Belsen concentration camp. Later, in 1964, a spate of attacks on the small number of Black students studying in Dublin caused concern, and subsequent research has documented the appalling ill treatment during this period of mixed-race children taken into care in orphanages and industrial schools. Against this background it was perhaps fortunate that the great majority of immigrants coming to Ireland in the 1990s and after were Europeans. This has helped ensure that Ireland has not produced an anti-immigrant party comparable to France's Rassemblement National or Germany's Alternative für Deutschland. But in the early 2000s, until a change in policy in 2011, the success rate among applicants for political asylum in Ireland, mainly African, was the lowest in Europe. When some women began to circumvent the system by contriving to give birth in the country, the government responded with a constitutional amendment, passed at referendum by a majority of four to one, that stripped children born in Ireland of their automatic right to citizenship. And a survey in 2009 placed Ireland among the five worst countries in Europe for violence against Africans.[6]

The boom years of the Celtic Tiger did not affect migration patterns alone. By the 1990s Irish people were more prosperous than ever before. Far more of them worked in manufacturing, and particularly in services; far fewer worked in agriculture. Many travelled abroad regularly and a rising proportion had spent some part of their lives outside the country. Against this background, long-accepted ideas and codes of behaviour began to crumble. The most dramatic changes were in the area of religion. The proportion of Irish Catholics attending church at least once a week declined from 91 per cent in 1973 to 30 per cent by 2011. Part of the change reflected widespread disillusionment, following revelations of the predatory activities, going back over decades, of paedophile priests, and of the extent to which religious superiors had allowed the preservation of the church's reputation to take priority over the protection of the children concerned. But the extent of the collapse suggests a deeper shift in attitudes and aspirations. Change was not uniform or linear. In 1983 supporters of traditional Catholic values won a referendum that reinforced the long-standing prohibition on abortion by inserting an assertion of the rights of the unborn child into the country's constitution. In another popular vote, three years later, the same lobby defeated an attempt to remove the prohibition on divorce. However the first steps towards a liberalisation of the previously rigid ban on contraception came in 1979, homosexuality was decriminalised in 1992, and divorce finally became available in 1995. Earlier, in 1990, the academic and lawyer Mary Robinson, a strong supporter of women's rights, unexpectedly won election as the country's president. The post was a largely ceremonial one, and Robinson's victory came about only when the establishment front-runner unexpectedly plunged into a political scandal. But her election was widely hailed as evidence of a society bounding free from a drearily repressive past.[7]

The emergence of a more affluent, outward-looking society, and the dispersion round the globe of a more confident and cosmopolitan expatriate population, coincided with a worldwide explosion of interest in Ireland and its culture. This was not entirely new. Already in the 1960s some notable performers had achieved success outside Ireland by adapting their repertoire to international trends, in particular to meet the rising demand for accessible folk music. The Clancy Brothers, Paddy, Tom, and Liam, were natives of County Tipperary. The fourth member of the group, Tommy Makem, was from County Armagh. But they had developed their musical style in the Greenwich Village of the 1950s, appearing on the same stages as Pete Seeger and the young Joan Baez. (The other Irish musical superstars of the 1960s, The Dubliners, stayed closer to home, but took their style, and some of their songs, from the pioneer of the British folk revival, Ewan McColl.) The immediate success of the white Aran sweaters that the Clancys wore for their breakthrough appearance on *The Ed Sullivan Show* in 1961 was an early example of successful ethnic branding. The 1990s, however, saw the fusion of cultural forms, and a level of international interest, rise to a wholly new level. From 1994 the Riverdance ensemble, based in the United States, enjoyed massive commercial success by adapting the country's distinctive and highly specialised style of traditional dancing to form the basis of a musical and visual extravaganza skilfully attuned to the demands of an international market. The Irish tourist board, responding with equal astuteness to new circumstances, abandoned the traditional iconography of thatched cottages and winding roads. Instead of an escape from the modern world, Ireland became an up-market but uniquely characterful holiday venue, where the tourist could discover all the familiar comforts while still encountering 'a sense of fun and spontaneity' and the possibility of unique, unpredictable experiences.

The most striking manifestation of this new fashion for all things Irish was the appearance, from Cape Town to Stockholm, from Madrid to Hanoi, of a distinctive new creation: the Irish pub. Assembled from ready-made kits, intensively promoted by the two main companies producing Irish beers (Guinness alone claimed to have opened 1,700 Irish pubs between 1992 and 1998), hostelries like the Loafing Leprechaun in Atlanta and Molly Malone's in Hiroshima were a carefully calculated synthesis of old and new. The décor—historical photographs, walls hung with agricultural implements, old bicycles and similar bric-a-brac, posters displaying fragments of supposed folk wisdom—attempted to create an impression of authenticity rooted in tradition. Yet the interiors, with their padded seating, tables and carpets, bore little resemblance to the local bars that at one time were characteristic of rural and small-town Ireland, where drinkers typically sat on round stools along a bare wood counter. Their model instead was the lounge bars that proliferated in towns and suburbs from the newly affluent 1960s onwards. And the music, though by recognisable Irish names, was that of mid-Atlantic performers like U2 or Van Morrison, rather than those working in more specifically Irish genres. Whatever the anomalies, however, the underlying implication of this hugely successful marketing operation was clear. The republican ideologues who had created the independent Irish state, and the policy makers who directed the first four decades of its development, were inspired by an austere vision of a pious, rural society whose distinctive values were to be protected against the corrupting influences of modern life. By the 1990s that vision was gone forever. In its place was a new concept of the Irish personality, at ease in its interactions with a wider world, and characterised, more than anything else, by a convivial secular hedonism.[8]

Changing economic fortunes also made possible a new attitude to the country's diaspora. Up to the 1970s the official stance of denial cast emigrants as having needlessly abandoned their country. Embassies, even in Great Britain and the United States, extended only a bare minimum of facilities to expatriates, and there was no attempt, as in other countries of high emigration like Italy, to enable non-resident citizens to vote. In an affluent, internationally respected Ireland, by contrast, it became possible to see the prominent Irish presence in so many parts of the world as a source of pride rather than evidence of national failure. An early sign of change was the public commitment of Mary Robinson, following her election to president of Ireland in 1990, to represent not just the inhabitants of Ireland, but the 'over seventy million people living on this globe who claim Irish descent'. Robinson's initial commitment, symbolised by the electronic candle placed in an upstairs window of her official residence, as a beacon to 'our exiles and emigrants', retained the concept of a national tragedy. By the time of her next address to the Irish parliament in February 1995, however, the tone had changed. The diaspora was 'not just a chronicle of sorrow and regret'. It was also 'a powerful story of contribution and adaptation', and an invitation to replace simplistic notions of Irish identity with a recognition of the complexity and diversity of the country's heritage. In 1998 the government, as a contribution towards a Northern Irish political settlement, amended the country's constitution to replace a territorial claim that Northern Ireland was part of the Irish state with a looser statement on entitlement to citizenship. In doing so it took the opportunity to add a clause affirming the affinity between the Irish nation and 'people of Irish ancestry living abroad who share its cultural identity and heritage'. Later, and in particular after the financial catastrophe of 2008, engagement with the diaspora acquired a more pragmatic dimension, as a means of stimulating tourism and encouraging investment. In 2014 a government reshuffle produced the first Minister for the Diaspora.[9]

What of the diaspora for whom President Robinson plugged in her candle? For some the emergence of a new Ireland, and the transformation of its standing in the world, reinforced a sense of identity. In parts of the United States the 1970s and 1980s had already seen a revival of enthusiasm for Irish culture. Cheap air travel allowed immigrants to maintain closer contact with their homeland, and so pass on firsthand knowledge to their children. The revival of Irish immigration in the 1980s brought new blood to ageing cultural groups. Digital communications permitted face-to-face contact and remote participation in events. Now the rise of a global Irish brand brought further encouragement. In the wake of Riverdance there were reports from New York and elsewhere of thriving classes in Irish dance and music, attracting pupils from a range of ethnic groups. Australia experienced a similar ethnic revival. In the 1960s there had been Celtic Clubs in Melbourne and Perth, an Irish Association in Queensland, and an Irish National Association in Sydney. By 1992 the Embassy of Ireland had contacts with 90 centres of activity, and by 2000 with 198. Argentina too saw a revival of Irish awareness. The nineteenth-century immigrants had initially held themselves apart from Argentine society, instead joining with British expatriates in an English-speaking bubble. By the early twentieth century the rise of Argentine nationalism, hostile to the British stranglehold on large parts of the country's economic life, made this stance less comfortable. Instead Argentines of Irish descent had preferred to merge into the Spanish-speaking population, even to the point, in some cases, of abandoning British-style clothing for the traditional dress of the gaucho. More recently, however, responding to the new profile of Irishness worldwide, there were reports of a new cultural shift: 'They celebrate St Patrick's Day, conspicuously drink beer, decorate their homes with shamrocks, and prefer tea and scones to the traditional *mate* and *bizcochitos*'.[10]

Not all interactions between the new Ireland and its diaspora were so positive. In Australia there were tensions between the older population of Irish birth or descent, socially and religiously conservative, and the products of an increasingly secular, commercialised and cosmopolitan Ireland who arrived in the 1980s and again following the crash of 2008. A similar cultural gulf opened up in the United States. Interviewed in 2004, a former state president of the Ancient Order of Hibernians who had emigrated forty years earlier made his feelings clear: 'Ireland has gone to the dogs. Ireland is not the country I left, I don't know what they think they are up to.' The cultural clash between old and new versions of Irishness became evident in the prolonged dispute, commencing in 1990, over demands by gay and lesbian groups to participate in the annual St Patrick's Day parades in New York and elsewhere. In 2000 excluded New Yorkers, following repeated rebuffs, established their own 'St Pat's for All' parade in the borough of Queens, and gradually began to attract the support of elected politicians, including Hillary Clinton. But it was only after 2014 and 2015, when the mayor of New York, Bill de Blasio, refused to take part in the official St Patrick's Day event, that its organisers had to give way: in 2016 the Lavender and Green Alliance were allowed to take their place in the parade, and de Blasio walked part of the way alongside them. In 2015 in Boston, the organisers of the St Patrick's Day parade had accepted the participation of two gay groups, OutVets and Boston Pride. The Boston decision, however, was by a vote of five to four. And in New York the following year a member of the Catholic League denounced the event in terms that would have made little sense to most inhabitants of the increasingly secular and cosmopolitan Irish Republic: 'They are making this an Irish parade, not a Catholic parade. It's contemptible.'[11]

In 1983 a historian of the Boston Irish dedicated one of his books to the memory of his father, 'who, in never missing Mass, a union meeting or an opportunity to vote, showed me what it was and is to be Irish, Catholic and American.' It was a warm and well-turned tribute. Yet, already by the time it was written, the world that it summed up, with its neat overlap of social, political and religious identities, was beginning to disappear.[12]

One part of this Irish-American identity, Catholic religious practice, had from the start been a product of self-definition rather than objective fact. A pair of surveys in the 1970s and 1980s revealed that a clear majority (54 or 56 per cent) of those who identified themselves as primarily of Irish ancestry were in fact Protestants. (In a third, from 1989–90, the figure—excluding those who disclaimed any religious affiliation—rose to 59 per cent.) The findings are less surprising than they seem at first sight. Large-scale migration from Ireland to the United States built up in the years after 1815. But for a century before there had been a smaller but still significant movement drawn mainly, though not exclusively, from Ulster. The genealogical trees of these predominantly Protestant immigrants had thus had that much longer to extend and multiply their branches. The minority of Catholics among these early immigrants, meanwhile, arrived in a vast landscape served by a handful of unevenly distributed missionary priests. Even in the nineteenth century Catholics who strayed into less well-served areas in the West and South drifted into other denominations so that, in the words of one observer, 'families named O'Donnell, Connor and Delahunty are now discovered drowsing in Protestant pews of Texas and Kansas'. Protestant emigration to the United States, moreover, did not stop in the 1830s. The immigrants simply became less visible. This was partly because they were so heavily outnumbered by their Catholic fellow countrymen. But in addition, as the investigators in 1930s Newburyport, Massachusetts, observed, they did not show the same inclination to form a separate ethnic group; instead they passed quietly into the ranks of the broader white population. Instead it was the Catholic Irish who made their church the centre of a close-knit community, to the point where it came to seem that Irish and Catholic were indeed synonymous.[13]

By the late twentieth century, however, the building blocks of a composite religious and political identity were dissolving one by one. The move to the suburbs already meant that, for growing numbers, neighbourhood life no longer revolved around the parish church and the clubs and societies linked to it. The parochial school no longer provided a bonding experience for each new generation. Men of Irish ancestry were still disproportionately represented among the parish clergy, and even more among the bishops. But their dominance was fading as Germans, Poles and other European Catholic nationalities, and (much more gradually) Hispanics and African Americans, began to rise in prominence. In religious terms, too, the church was beginning to lose its hold. Traditionalists were alienated by the liturgical reforms introduced by the Second Vatican Council (1962–5), in which, according to critics, continuity and mystery gave way to flat ceremonials, uninspiring English-language texts, and incongruous guitar music. More liberal-minded Catholics found their commitment shaken by the uncompromising teaching on contraception, divorce, and abortion. The sectional politicians of an earlier era, like John Fitzgerald and James Curley, had mocked birth control as a symptom of Protestant decadence. But as Catholics became part of the mainstream of American life they found themselves torn, as one critic has put it, between their loyalties 'to Western civilization's most open political and most closed religious systems'. Next, from the 1990s, came the revelations of widespread clerical paedophilia. As in Ireland itself, scandal of a particularly revolting kind combined with longer term social change, with catastrophic consequences. The proportion of American Catholics attending mass at least once a week, the minimum required by the church's rules, fell from 55 per cent in 1970 to 31 per cent by 2000 and to 21 per cent by 2018.[14]

Active participation in the labour movement was another part of the traditional Irish American identity. Irish influence reached its peak in the mid-twentieth century. Philip Murray, born in Scotland to Irish parents, was president of the Congress of Industrial Organizations (CIO), the key organisation in the mobilisation of industrial workers in the New Deal years, from 1940 until his death in 1952. George Meany, grandson of Irish immigrants, became head of the larger American Federation of Labor (AFL) in 1952. Three years later he negotiated with Murray's successor a merger of the two with himself as president of the new AFL-CIO, making him head of the most powerful labour organisation in the country. By the time Meany retired in 1979, however, the labour movement was no longer the force it had once been. Nor were the Irish so prominent in its ranks. Large numbers of Americans of Irish birth or descent were still blue-collar workers and union members, and some continued to rise to leadership positions. When Meany's successor, a Scottish American, retired in 1995 two Irish Americans competed for the presidency, and it was John Sweeney, son of an Irish-born bus driver from the Bronx, who went on to lead the AFL-CIO until 2009. But there was now a substantial section of Irish America, college educated and in white-collar employment, for whom the union hall, with its rituals, its companionship and its commitment, was no longer part of their daily life.

The third component of the traditional Irish American identity was an enthusiasm for partisan politics. But here too much had changed. The last of the machines that had made politics a face-to-face business, as much a part of the life of a neighbourhood as the local Catholic Church or the parochial school, had disappeared by the 1980s. Political allegiances, too, had become more fluid and conditional, as the decades-long commitment of Irish Catholics to the Democratic Party came under increasing strain. To the growing proportion of Irish-American voters who were now affluent suburbanites, the Republican Party, business friendly and tax averse, began to appear more attractive. But more was involved than economic interest. White immigrant groups, including the Irish, had long looked to the Democrats to defend them against the hostility of nativists and Protestants. But when, from the 1960s, the party began to perform the same protective function for Black Americans, its traditional supporters reacted strongly. Racial quotas for public employment, and the busing of children between districts as a means of breaking down segregation in schools, put Democratic candidates at odds with a large section of their Irish electoral base. So too did a growing cultural divide. On issues such as same-sex marriage and abortion, as well as on law and order and the war on drugs, it was the Republicans who were the party of traditional values. In 1968 almost two-thirds of voters of Irish Catholic background supported the Democratic candidate, Hubert Humphrey. In 1980, however, one exit poll suggested that just over half of Irish Americans had voted for the Republican presidential candidate, Ronald Reagan; in 1984 Reagan's share of their vote rose to 59 per cent. The same collapse of long-standing party allegiances was evident in Congressional elections. In the elections of 1994, for the first time, the majority of Irish Americans voted Republican. Ten years later, twenty-one Republicans of Irish Catholic background sat in the House of Representatives, compared to just nineteen Democrats. In the 2008 presidential election, 57 per cent of users of a major Irish-American website voted for the Democrat Barack Obama; in 2012, however, the figure was only 51 per cent. In the presidential race of 2016, the Democratic candidate Hillary Clinton performed strongly in traditional Irish strongholds such as South Boston. But across the United States as a whole some observers believed that just under half of the Irish-American vote had gone to the Republican candidate, Donald Trump.[15]

In ethnic terms too, the American Irish were no longer the cohesive body they had once been. A survey in 1969 found that only just under a third of heads of household of Irish descent were married to a person of the same ancestry. This figure, however, made no distinction between Catholic and Protestant. A survey carried out six years earlier suggested a sharp difference between the two, with roughly one in five Protestants of Irish ancestry choosing a bride of the same background compared to two out of five Catholics. That is further confirmation of the extent to which the descendants of Protestant immigrants, slightly more than half of the Irish-American population, had blended into the white American mainstream rather than constituting a distinct ethnic group. But it also means that more than half of Irish Catholic men also looked elsewhere. Before 1945 Irish-American Catholics who married outside their own ethnic group had favoured old immigrants like themselves, marrying English, Scottish or German partners who were either Catholic or willing to convert. After the Second World War, however, Germans became less acceptable, while Italians and eastern Europeans, formerly shunned as both low in status and just off the boat, had now become acceptable. Over time the preponderance of ethnically mixed marriages had a powerful cumulative effect. In the nationwide sample collected in 1963, three out of every five Catholics of Irish descent had some non-Irish ancestry. Among the minority of purely Irish descent, meanwhile, fewer than a third married partners of the same unmixed ancestry. In 1969 just over thirteen million Americans, 7 per cent of the population, reported their ancestry as Irish. But the number in whose veins there flowed only Irish blood was small, and declining.[16]

Identity, of course, is never a matter of statistical averages. It is a subjective state. Between 1991 and 1997 Reginald Byron, an American anthropologist based in Belfast and later in Swansea, Wales, investigated the world of people of Irish descent living in Albany, New York, a place regarded as 'uniquely "Irish" for a city of its size'. What he and his team discovered was a wide but shallow sense of Irishness. Just over two-thirds described themselves as 'very' interested in their ancestry, the rest as having 'some' interest. Three out of five had given concrete evidence of this interest by visiting Ireland, almost half in the hope of finding out something about their family history; about a quarter had visited more than once. A little under half reported themselves as sometimes eating what they considered distinctively Irish food, most commonly corned beef and cabbage or soda bread. A remarkable 70 per cent marked 17 March by wearing something green. Yet fewer than one in five regularly attended the annual St Patrick's Day parade (although seven in ten had seen it at some time in their lives), and only about the same proportion marked the day by a special meal at home or in a restaurant. Other acknowledgements of Irishness were unashamedly commercial. Albany shops offered books about Ireland and compilations of Irish jokes, proverbs or recipes, as well as plaques, ornaments or tableware with shamrocks or similar motifs, pieces of linen, pottery or glass, recordings of Irish folk music and Irish-related films. Here, Byron suggests, Irishness had become 'a commodity to be bought and sold', confirming the impression of an awareness of ethnic background expressed primarily through consumption.

Where politics is concerned, the number of Albany residents whose Irishness prompted them to concrete action was negligible. In Albany County, with around 90,000 adults of Irish descent, just 550 were members of the Ancient Order of Hibernians. The number joining the Irish Northern Aid Committee (Noraid), by this time the main organisation supporting the republican campaign in Northern Ireland, was smaller still. Roughly half of Byron's interviewees made comments that indicated a Catholic, nationalist version of Irish history, emphasising conquest, religious oppression, and a struggle for freedom from British rule. But for many the details remained vague. 'They ran out of potatoes in Ireland', one offered, 'and all came over to America.' Another 'used to know [about] St Patrick chasing the snakes out of Ireland and all that, years ago as a little kid'. This respondent, however, also mentioned that he had read *Trinity*, the first of two novels in which Leon Uris described the Irish independence struggle in the same rousing terms with which he had earlier chronicled the birth of Israel in his best-selling book *Exodus*. The respondent was not alone. A full half of the Albany Irish interviewed for Byron's project, in fact, answered questions about Irish history by citing the same novel, suggesting that it was the work of this American novelist, published in 1976, at the high point of the Northern Ireland conflict, that gave them an impression of the Irish past that their upbringing no longer supplied.[17]

'We've married Italian girls and moved to the suburbs.' With this pithy phrase, a disgruntled activist summed up the social changes that by the end of the twentieth century had undermined the distinctive cultural identity of the American Irish. Yet such complaints raise a question. If what had been key institutions of Irish-American life—the Catholic Church, the labour movement, grassroots political organisation—had been so comprehensively weakened, and if the sense of Irish identity itself had become so diluted and commercialised, then why, at just this time, did the affairs of Ireland become a significant issue in American political life? How were Irish Americans able to mount such an effective agitation, from the late 1960s onwards, in response to the crisis in Northern Ireland? And why—as was to happen in the mid-1990s—was an American president prepared to invest time and political capital in resolving a conflict in an obscure corner of Europe where the United States had no direct strategic interest?[18]

Numbers are one part of the answer. Since 1980 the ten-yearly census of the United States has asked respondents to describe their ancestry. As evidence of national origins, the results are of dubious value, reflecting differences in the time of arrival of particular nationalities, differences in the level of historical awareness encouraged by particular ethnic subcultures, and differences in the prestige attached to particular ancestries. From the point of view of politics, however, the findings, precisely because they include an element of self-definition, remain significant. In 2000 nineteen million Americans gave Irish as their only or main ancestry; another eleven million gave it as their second choice. A further 4.3 million described their ancestry as including 'Scotch-Irish', possibly indicating a desire to set themselves apart from Irish Americans as normally understood. But even without these, the thirty million Americans claiming an Irish ancestry made up just under 11 per cent of the population. That made them the second-largest ethnic group in the country, outnumbered only by those claiming a German ancestry (15.2 per cent), and almost twice as numerous as those who identified themselves as being of Italian descent (5.6 per cent). By now affluence, broadening opportunity and the passage of time had dispersed the Irish to every corner of the United States. But they remained particularly numerous in their old stronghold of the Northeast regions, where they accounted for 16 per cent of the population. In Massachusetts, the home state of two key figures in America's interventions in Irish affairs, Senator Edward 'Ted' Kennedy and House of Representatives Speaker Thomas 'Tip' O'Neill, the Irish population was more than twice the national average, 22.5 per cent. In Delaware, where Senator Joseph Biden was to emerge as the main opponent of the extradition to the United Kingdom of IRA fugitives, it was over 16 per cent.[19]

Even if the average Irish American's ethnic identity went no further than wearing a green tie on 17 March, this was a constituency worth cultivating. In New York, for example, where an estimated one in eight voters considered themselves Irish, the two leading candidates for the Democratic nomination in the mayoral contest of 1989 were Ed Koch, of Polish and Jewish background, and the African American David Dinkins. Both men committed themselves to campaigning against the extradition of Joe Doherty, a Belfast man wanted for the killing nine years earlier of an army officer in Belfast. Koch went so far as to publish an apology for his earlier suggestion that it was wrong to see British soldiers in Northern Ireland as an occupying force. In the event neither man seems to have benefitted significantly. Koch, the incumbent, failed to win renomination. In the mayoral election that followed Dinkins had the backing of the main IRA support organisation, Noraid, but received few Irish votes. He attended the 1991 St Patrick's Day parade but was booed and pelted with beer cans when he walked with the Irish Lesbian and Gay Organisation, which had been smuggled into the parade under the banner of another group. Two years later Dinkins lost the mayoral election to the social conservative, and Catholic, Rudi Giuliani. But the point was that both he and Koch thought the Irish vote important enough to be worth chasing—as, presumably, did members of the Massachusetts House of Representatives when in 1981 they passed a resolution calling for a British withdrawal from Northern Ireland.[20]

To numbers of potential voters must be added the significant number of men (for at this stage it was almost wholly men) of Irish background in positions of political power. The great Irish-dominated machines were now a thing of the past; local politicians had to share control of the cities they had once ruled with other, increasingly demanding ethnic groups. But in Washington, Irish power had grown since the 1930s, when the decline of long-standing religious and ethnic prejudices had permitted the first appointments at national level. In 1969, as the first British troops took control of the streets of Belfast, Derry and elsewhere, the key figures in Congress, Senate Majority Leader Mike Mansfield and Speaker of the House of Representatives John McCormack, were both of Irish background. These were men, now in the second half of their careers, who had spent their formative years in the type of traditional Irish-American environment that was being eroded by affluence and suburbanisation. Mansfield was born in New York to an Irish immigrant father, although brought up mainly in Montana. McCormack was the son of a Boston construction worker. A later Speaker, Tip O'Neill, was born in Boston in 1912, and the early chapters of his autobiography are enlivened with tales of the colourful doings of James Curley. It is worth considering how different the American response might have been if the Northern Irish conflict had begun two decades later than it did, when this transitional generation was no longer present.

Another part of the picture is the distinctive position that the Irish enjoyed within America's mosaic of ethnic identities. They— or at least those among them who were not what would later be called Scotch Irish—were not among the founders of white American society, like the English, Germans and Dutch. But they began to arrive in large numbers half a century before the Poles, Italians and other eastern and southern Europeans. As newcomers they had endured their share of nativist hostility and distrust. But already before the Second World War this was largely behind them. The mid-twentieth century image of the Irishman, on the stage, the screen and the printed page, was almost wholly positive. He was warm-hearted, sociable, and above all entirely American. When the time came, in the 1970s and after, to solicit attention to Irish issues, this accumulated cultural capital became a major asset. 'Brand Ireland', a Democratic Party activist explained in 2019, is 'incredibly strong, stronger than ever it seems. I see it all the time when I invite people to Irish American events, even if they're not Irish—it conjures up something that's going to be a good time; people will be lively. It conjures up an image that people want to be part of.' Anne Anderson, Ireland's ambassador in Washington between 2013 and 2017, agreed. Being Irish did not guarantee that you would get what you want. 'It gets the doors open for you', but then 'you have to walk through those doors and make the pitch'. But access was nevertheless crucial. 'My colleagues, ambassadors from similar sized states, and even larger states, they genuinely sometimes marvelled at the level of access that I had'.[21]

The ultimate demonstration of this Irish soft power, as it has been called, is the unique place in the political calendar of the United States that is occupied by St Patrick's Day. Irish Americans had asserted their right to commandeer the streets of New York and other cities from the mid-nineteenth century onwards. But formal observance by the White House began only in the 1950s, when the custom began of a representative of the Irish government presenting the president with a Waterford Crystal bowl containing shamrock. By the 1990s the event had expanded to include an early breakfast hosted by the vice president at his residence, the Naval Observatory; a lunch on Capitol Hill, hosted by the speaker of the House of Representatives; then the presentation of the shamrock, followed by a reception and supper hosted by the Irish embassy. Other ethnic groups have their officially sponsored day. In 1892 President Benjamin Harrison initiated Columbus Day, specifically to placate the Italian government, and American Italians, following the killing in New Orleans of eleven immigrants accused of complicity in the murder of a popular law officer. Since 1987 there has been a White House reception on or near Greek Independence Day, 25 March. But no other nationality is allowed to divert the entire Washington elite from its business for the whole of a fourteen-hour day.[22]

A further indication of the exceptional licence that the Irish expected from America, and to a large extent received, was the response to the arrival in the United States during the 1980s of tens of thousands of illegal immigrants. An Irish Immigration Reform Movement, founded in 1987, began a campaign to legalise what it claimed to be anything from 100,000 to 200,000 of these 'undocumented' Irish residents. (The United States Immigration and Naturalization Service put the number at under 40,000.) Their campaign was largely successful. Already in 1986 Brian Donnelly, a congressman from Boston, had forced the addition to an immigration reform act of 10,000 visas for each of thirty-six European countries, including Ireland, held to have been disadvantaged by the primacy that the 1965 act had given to family reunification. (The reform act of 1986 also included an amnesty for illegal immigrants who had entered the country before 1 January 1982, but that was too early for most of the Irish refugees from their country's early 1980s crash.) A further 45,000 of these 'Donnelly visas' were added in 1989–90. Of these a full 35 per cent were allocated to Irish applicants, one-third of whom were already living in the United States. In 1990 Representative Bruce Morrison of Connecticut secured the creation of a second package of 120,000 visas, of which 40 per cent were guaranteed to Ireland. By 1997, taking into account smaller packages and an extension of the Donnelly scheme, Irish applicants, either already in the United States or wishing to emigrate, had received around 72,000 visas. The United States embassy in Dublin suggested that by this means the problem of the undocumented Irish had been largely resolved by 1994.[23]

Representative John Bryant, a Texas Democrat of Ulster Scot ancestry, was one of the very few who spoke out against Morrison's scheme. He poured particular scorn on the tactic of attaching it to an immigration reform bill whose declared purpose was to promote greater 'diversity' in the immigrant population. 'Do we need more Irish people that look just like me, look just like Morrison . . . ?' The reality, he insisted, was that the Irish had come to the United States illegally. But 'because they have some friends in Congress they are going to get to stay here'. Outside Congress, too, what was striking was the level of sympathy for the undocumented Irish. Agents of the Immigration and Naturalization Service conducted occasional arrests and deportations. But urban mayors openly proclaimed their defiance of federal policy. In New York, Ed Koch insisted that Irish immigrants should not be deterred from making use of the city's schools and hospitals. 'They're not illegal to me, they're undocumented.' In Boston, Ray Flynn announced that 'the welcome mat is out' and created an office to provide Irish immigrants with legal aid. Newspapers too carried sympathetic depictions of the hardship of young people debarred by their lack of papers from moving on to secure careers, marriage and home ownership. The *Wall Street Journal* in 1987 quoted the words of one man who protested to his father that he was not doing anything wrong. 'I'm trying to make a future for myself.' The same claim could have been made by many hundreds of thousands of others, from Latin America and elsewhere, who likewise found themselves 'undocumented'. But it is hard to see their words being quoted with anything like the same understanding.[24]

15

A LAST HURRAH?

The United States and the Northern Ireland Conflict

Northern Ireland became a topic in world news in 1969. The region's problems went back to the settlement of 1920–1, which gave Ulster Protestants control of a devolved government in six Ulster counties. Confronted by a substantial and unreconciled Catholic minority comprising one-third of the population, successive Unionist governments resorted to electoral manipulation, and at times to heavy-handed repression, while reserving public employment and other benefits for their Protestant supporters. In the late 1960s a Northern Ireland civil rights movement demanded an end to discrimination in housing and other areas, and reform of the electoral system. Militant Protestants, reacting to what they saw as another Catholic, nationalist attack on the state that protected their liberties, staged violent counter demonstrations. In August 1969 the authorities in Derry and Belfast lost control, as Protestant and Catholic crowds fought one another with stones, petrol bombs and guns. The arrival of units of the British army was initially welcomed as offering protection to the outnumbered Catholics. Over the next eighteen months, however, the civil rights movement was shouldered aside by a new organisation, the Provisional IRA, created by young militants, based mainly in Northern Ireland, who had revolted against what they saw as the existing IRA's ineffective response to Protestant violence. The demand for reform within Northern Ireland gave way to a revived Irish republicanism, committed to a campaign of armed resistance that would force the British government to withdraw from Northern Ireland. Protestants meanwhile formed their own paramilitary organisation, the Ulster Defence Association, joining a smaller but vicious Ulster Volunteer Force already active since 1966. By the end of 1971 there had been 213 violent deaths—65 members of the police and army, 30 members of paramilitary groups and 118 civilians. During 1972 there were a further 479 killings. Once again the largest group—249—were non-combatants, caught in crossfire or killed by bombs placed in shops, offices, restaurants and bars, or in cars parked on busy streets.[1]

Northern Ireland's descent into murderous violence produced an immediate reaction on the other side of the Atlantic. Already in February 1967 James Heaney, a lawyer based in Buffalo, New York, had established the American Congress for Irish Freedom. His initiative grew out of contacts with the leaders of the early civil rights movement. But the Congress's aim, in another example of the recurring mismatch between Irish and Irish-American aspirations, was the traditional one of a British withdrawal from Northern Ireland. Over the next two years the American Congress for Irish Freedom became the most influential Irish-American body, lobbying politicians, pursuing a case against the British government before the European Commission on Human Rights, and calling for American companies not to invest in Northern Ireland. In the spring of 1970 two emissaries from the Provisional IRA arrived in New York. Both were veterans of earlier conflicts. Daithi O'Conaill from County Cork had been wounded in a gun battle with the Royal Ulster Constabulary during a short-lived IRA offensive against Northern Ireland in 1958. His companion, Joe Cahill, was a legendary figure within militant Northern Irish nationalism. In 1942, he had been sentenced to death, though later reprieved, for his part in the killing of a Belfast policeman. More recently he had been a prime mover in the split that had set the Provisional IRA on its blood-soaked course. The two men's mission was to establish a support organisation in the United States. At their instigation Michael Flannery, a former IRA fighter who had made a career in New York as an executive with an insurance company, founded the Irish Northern Aid Committee, commonly known as Noraid. Within a few months there were Noraid branches across New York and in other major cities such as Boston, Chicago and San Francisco. Recruits included large numbers of defectors from the American Congress for Irish Freedom, which by the end of the year had ceased to function. Noraid activists picketed British consulates and organised protests against visiting British royalty and politicians. But the main purpose was fund-raising. Organisers insisted that the money raised was for the families of activists imprisoned in Northern Ireland. The British and Irish authorities contended that it also funded the purchase of weapons for the IRA. The distinction was largely academic: even if Noraid did nothing except support the dependants of jailed activists, this meant that it covered what became a major expense for the IRA, freeing up funds for other, more directly murderous purposes. For the business of actually buying guns the Provisionals turned to a veteran republican, George Harrison, who for the next ten years became the movement's main supplier. Many of the weapons he delivered had come from Camp Lejeune in North Carolina, a Marine Corps base where soldiers regularly smuggled out firearms and ammunition for sale to local dealers.[2]

Support from the United States was of central importance in sustaining the Provisional IRA's twenty-five year campaign to force through political change by bloodshed. Yet the numbers involved were small. The American Congress for Irish Freedom claimed a core of 3,000 members, with several thousand sympathisers. Noraid had a membership of around 2,000 in 1976, rising to 5,000 by 1984. The print run of its newspaper, the *Irish People*, was just 13,000 in 1976. Even taking into account the much larger number of people who dropped money into a barroom collection box, or took part in a fund-raising dinner or card game, this was a tiny fraction of the thirty million self-declared Americans of Irish descent. Many of the leading activists in the United States were in fact Irish-born. Some had brought their allegiance to physical force republicanism with them across the Atlantic. Michael Flannery, founder of Noraid, had fought in the Irish War of Independence and the Irish Civil War, before emigrating in 1927. George Harrison, born in 1915, had been too young for these conflicts, but had been part of the IRA in his native Mayo before coming to the United States in 1938. Also involved were more recent immigrants, less likely than longer-established Irish Americans to have settled into assimilated middle-class comfort, and more attracted to organizations that put them in contact with their fellow countrymen. Another group, increasing in size over time, were Catholic immigrants from Northern Ireland, bringing with them the antipathies and resentments of the society from which they came. Among the great majority of the American-born of Irish descent, by contrast, a vague awareness of ancestry, all that survived of a once powerful ethnic identity, was no longer enough to inspire an active political response. In Albany, New York, more than two decades after the formation of the Provisional IRA, one resident memorably summed up her knowledge of what was happening 3,000 miles away: 'I know that somebody is fighting somebody else, [but] I am not quite sure what they are fighting about. They are killing each other, and it has something to do with religion [and] it has something to do with the English.'[3]

The minority of American-born of Irish descent who did nevertheless react to events in Northern Ireland, whether as supporters of Noraid or in other, less destructive ways, fell into two main groups. On the one hand there were those from families in which an older political tradition had been kept alive, often through individuals with direct personal experience of earlier struggles. Ray Flynn, mayor of Boston from 1984 to 1993 and for a time a Noraid supporter, recalled childhood visits with his grandfather to an Irish record shop in Roxbury, a meeting place for former members of the celebrated West Cork Brigade of the IRA. Pat Sullivan, the man behind the creation of a memorial park in Springfield, Massachusetts, for the centenary of the Irish rising of 1916, was inspired by memories of a County Kerry–born grandmother who had lived through the rising and its aftermath, and had told him stories of how 'the British soldiers would come through, and they would take pot-shots at her brothers when they were working in the fields and stuff'. Joseph Biden recalled his Aunt Gertie, who had terrified the young Joe with tales of the Black and Tans, the much-dreaded paramilitary force created by the British government in 1920 as part of its increasingly desperate attempts to regain control of Ireland. 'After she'd finished . . . I'd sit there or lie in bed and think at the slightest noise, "They're coming up the steps".' (Aunt Gertie, however, had been born in America, so her bloodcurdling atrocity stories, Biden surmised, came from more recent immigrants.)[4]

In other cases, by contrast, a commitment to the Irish nationalist cause had the opposite origin: in a reaction against the loss, within the family or in the wider community, of ethnic identity and historical memory. Tom Hayden, president of Students for a Democratic Society and a leading activist in the American New Left of the 1960s, recalled the complete lack of interest of his lower-middle-class, third-generation American parents in their Irish background. It was televised images from Northern Ireland, in 1968 and after, that made him realise 'what had been denied, that these marchers were somehow kin to me, that under the void of my identity I was Irish'. The discovery gave him not just an identity but a way of understanding his political commitment. Even when unaware of his heritage, he now felt, he had been 'Irish on the inside', inheriting from rebel ancestors the impulse to challenge oppression and injustice. Within a few years he was a regular visitor to Northern Ireland, and in time a close associate of leading figures in the republican movement.[5]

Tom Hayden's vision of an ancestry that made him, even when unaware of it, the heir to the United Irishmen, the Molly Maguires and the men of 1916 was an idiosyncratic one. But his whole-hearted embrace of his Irishness was part of a broader trend. The renewal of violent conflict in Northern Ireland coincided with the emergence in the United States of a white ethnic revival, as Jews, Italians, Poles and others rejected the goal of assimilation that had meant so much to earlier generations in favour of a restatement of their hyphenated identities. Ellis Island, closed in 1954 and reopened as a museum and heritage centre in 1990, replaced Plymouth Rock as the starting point in a new version of America's heroic story. In part, as in the case of Hayden, the revival was a reaction against what those involved came to see as the empty, conformist culture created by assimilation. But there was also what has been dubbed the Roots Too movement. The surge in Black consciousness, typified by Alex Haley's best-selling book and its television dramatisation, inspired a drive by other Americans to discover their ethnic heritages. It also provoked defensiveness: an insistence that the European immigrants of the nineteenth and twentieth centuries had never been part of the system of white privilege, but on the contrary had their own tale of hardship and discrimination.

The interaction of a revived American-Irish nationalism and a wider culture of ethnic self-assertion became evident in the controversy that developed in the 1990s over genocide studies. By the 1980s, in response to lobbying by Jewish organizations, sixteen states had recommended or ordered the inclusion in the school curriculum of the Nazi Holocaust. There followed campaigns from interested groups to include other examples of attempted genocide—against Armenians in the Ottoman Empire and Native Americans in the United States, in the Ukraine under Stalin, in Cambodia, Rwanda and Bosnia. In 1995, the 150th anniversary of the first failure of the potato in Ireland, Irish-American activists entered the field, arguing that the mass starvation that followed had been the result of deliberate government policy aimed at exterminating the Irish poor. So the Irish too were victims of genocide. The results were less impressive than in other campaigns at state level, such as the promotion of fair employment in Northern Ireland. Opponents, including respected historians, came forward to insist that the leap from the British government's undoubted mismanagement of the crisis to an allegation of deliberate mass murder was a step too far. There was also perhaps a feeling that such a blatant attempt to exploit by association the incomparable horrors visited on the Jews of Nazi-occupied Europe was in bad taste. But the Famine nevertheless won inclusion in what was by this time a rather overcrowded genocide studies curriculum in both New York and New Jersey.[6]

For Irish Americans of any vintage, support for a reborn militant nationalism brought them into contact with a culture different to their own. The activists who took to the streets of Belfast and elsewhere in 1968 and 1969 were part of a great wave of revolt against established institutions that took place across the Western world in the late 1960s, and their spokesmen framed their critique of Unionist abuses of power in the vocabulary of the radical counter-culture. That was a vocabulary with which most Irish Americans, as their growing disenchantment with the Democrats revealed, had little sympathy. When the civil rights campaigner Bernadette Devlin, fresh from the street fighting in Derry's Bogside, visited the United States in August 1969, she caused outrage by her support of the Black civil rights movement and by snubbing Chicago's mayor, Richard Daley, whose police had just launched a brutal attack on left-wing demonstrators gathered outside the Democratic National Convention. Even Irish Americans with more liberal views on race and political protest saw Devlin's emphasis on social and economic grievances as a dangerous departure from strictly nationalist goals. 'The ultimate objective' a columnist in the influential *Irish Echo* warned, 'is not to make our oppressed brethren in northeast Ireland more comfortable British subjects.' The difference in priorities narrowed somewhat after 1970, when activists like Devlin were eclipsed by the more traditionally minded Provisional IRA. Noraid, for its part, proved to be less uniformly reactionary than is sometimes recognised, particularly after a split in 1986 that saw the departure of some of its older Irish-born members. Noraid activists gave active support to Dinkins's mayoral campaigns in New York in 1989 and 1993; in 1984 the movement would even have backed the Rev. Jesse Jackson if he had run for president. But other supporters of militant Irish nationalism thought in very different terms: in Massachusetts in the 1980s protestors against integrated schooling were reported as chanting the slogan 'Niggers out of Boston, Brits out of Belfast'. And when Noraid's *Irish People* reprinted material from the Provisional IRA's newspaper *An Phoblacht* it did so selectively, highlighting the campaign against British rule while toning down or omitting references to anti-colonial struggles in Asia or the Americas, as well as to the socialist character of the imagined future Ireland.[7]

Apart from fund-raising and public demonstrations, different Irish-American organisations sought sympathetic hearers in Congress. Already in June 1969, before the first serious episode of communal violence in Northern Ireland, Tip O'Neill of Boston and Phillip Burton of California, encouraged by the American Congress for Irish Freedom, had organised a public letter in which one hundred congressmen had expressed their concern at the 'intolerance and discrimination' rooted in the laws of Northern Ireland. Simultaneously Senator Edward Kennedy telegraphed the Northern Irish Civil Rights Association to assure them that their cause was just. Two years later Kennedy took a stronger line. He joined with Abraham Ribicoff, a senator from Connecticut of Jewish Polish background but a long-term Kennedy family ally, to introduce a motion calling for the withdrawal of British troops from Northern Ireland, which in Kennedy's words was becoming 'Britain's Vietnam'. In 1974 a Redemptorist priest, Seán McManus, launched a new organisation, the Irish National Caucus. McManus, transferred by his church from Scotland to the United States on account of his political activities, was a Noraid organiser and an open supporter of the Provisional IRA. But the main role of the new body was to concentrate on lobbying in Washington. The Caucus effectively exploited the continued prominence of Irish Americans in the labour movement: Teddy Gleason, president of the International Longshoremen's Association, and George Meany of the AFL-CIO, were both directors. The following year the Caucus found an eager supporter within Congress. Mario Biaggi was the Democratic representative for a New York district straddling the Bronx and Queens. His constituents were mainly, like him, Italian Americans. But he had run, in 1973, for mayor of New York, and now had ambitions to try for one of the state's senate seats, both contests where the Irish vote might still carry weight. In 1977 he established an Ad Hoc Congressional Committee for Irish Affairs, which by 1979 claimed 130 members. In 1979 it scored a major success when an amendment by Biaggi to an important appropriations bill forced the State Department to suspend the licence that allowed American companies to supply firearms to the Royal Ulster Constabulary (RUC).[8]

In this early mobilisation of Irish-American opinion the Dublin government played no significant part. Its foreign policy had been dominated, throughout the 1960s, by the quest for membership of the European Economic Community. Sean Donlon, a diplomat who was to become a key figure in the Irish mission to the United States, later recalled his dismay at being transferred, in 1969, from Bonn to the Irish consulate in Boston. 'I was being moved from a whirlpool of Irish diplomatic activity to a quiet backwater where nothing happened.' Links with the Irish-American community were also weak, reflecting the continuing official view of emigrants as footloose deserters rather than victims of economic necessity. The Irish government's own position on the re-emergence of militant republicanism was in any case far from clear. In 1970 two ministers were sacked, and later put on trial, for their role in an attempt to import guns for the defence of Catholic areas in Northern Ireland.[9]

By the mid-1970s Dublin's policy had become clearer. The leaders of all the main parties were now agreed in seeing the Provisional IRA as a threat to stability in both north and south. Donlon and his colleague Michael Lillis, political counsellor at the Washington embassy, were thus free to begin the task of redirecting Irish-American political energies. In this they found a valuable ally in the Derry nationalist politician John Hume. Hume was a founder, and from 1979 the leader, of the Social Democratic and Labour Party (SDLP), which was by now the constitutional rival within Northern Ireland to the IRA and its political wing, Sinn Féin. He had made a special journey to West Germany in 1972 to lobby Edward Kennedy. A fellowship at Harvard in 1976 allowed him to renew that acquaintance, and through Kennedy to make contacts with other heavyweight figures. Thanks to Hume's efforts, along with those of Donlon and Lillie, Kennedy and O'Neill joined with two other senior Irish-American politicians, Hugh Carey, the governor of New York, and Daniel Patrick Moynihan, the newly elected senator for New York, in a public change of stance. All four had previously expressed some degree of support for the militant nationalist position. But on St Patrick's Day 1977 they issued a statement insisting that violence could never bring peace to Northern Ireland and calling on Americans to stop financing 'campaigns of death and destruction'.[10]

As a result of Hume, Donlon and Lillie's efforts, Irish America now spoke with two voices on Northern Ireland. Over the next two years O'Neill and his colleagues, having put themselves at odds with a large part of their Irish-American supporters, became aggrieved at the lack of response from Great Britain, where a precarious majority left the Labour government unable to contemplate any significant initiatives in Northern Ireland. During 1978 the group renewed its public attacks on British policy in Northern Ireland, focussing in particular on growing evidence of the use of torture in police interrogations. In May 1979 O'Neill threw his weight behind Biaggi's attack on arms sales to the RUC, which he said would be viewed as 'support for a particular faction in Northern Ireland'. But their opposition to the fellow travellers of a murderous IRA campaign remained firm. In 1980 news broke that the new Irish prime minister, Charles Haughey—one of those earlier put on trial for an apparent attempt to arm northern Catholics—intended to replace Donlon, by now Irish ambassador, in order to clear the way for his government to work more closely with Biaggi's Ad Hoc group, the Irish National Caucus, and even Noraid. Kennedy and O'Neill quickly let him know, in forceful telephone calls, that this was not acceptable, and Donlon remained in his post.

None of this manoeuvring, inside and outside Congress, made any impression on the federal government. The State Department's consistent position, continuing Woodrow Wilson's stance on the wider Irish question during and after the First World War, was that anything to do with Northern Ireland was a purely internal British concern. As a congressman and senator, John F. Kennedy had supported resolutions calling for Irish unity, the most recent being in 1956. Visiting Ireland as president in 1963 he was still willing to flatter his audience with references to Ireland's freedom after 'years of oppression', and pointedly declined to include Northern Ireland in his itinerary. But he also made clear that he would not say anything in public about the partition of the island. When the Irish ambassador tried, in preliminary talks, to suggest points Kennedy might use in private conversation, he 'looked as if another headache had struck him'. After 1969 the Nixon and Ford administrations adhered publicly to the doctrine that Northern Ireland was a matter for the British government alone. In practice, both gave substantial assistance to Great Britain, a key Cold War ally. The Justice Department, in a long legal battle, sought to force Noraid to register as the agent of a foreign power and to name the Provisional IRA as its principal. FBI agents meanwhile harassed and subpoenaed Noraid activists, with the explicit aim of frightening off potential recruits. In one notable case, in 1972, five New York men were required to travel 1,400 miles to appear before a grand jury in Fort Worth, Texas, then were jailed when they refused to answer questions. There were also prosecutions for gun running, unsuccessful in the case of the Harrison ring, but elsewhere leading to convictions and prison sentences. In 1971 the State Department detained and deported Joe Cahill as he attempted to make a return visit to the United States, and thereafter systematically refused visas to republican activists.[11]

The first small shift in the policy of strict non-intervention came in 1977. In the presidential election of the previous year, the Democratic candidate Jimmy Carter, a southern Protestant in need of northern ethnic votes, took part in an Irish National Caucus event in Pittsburgh. Earlier he had appeared at New York's St Patrick's Day parade wearing a badge inscribed 'England Get Out of Ireland'. (Later claims from his camp that the button had been pinned on his lapel by an activist and hastily removed were contradicted by two photographs taken at different times.) The furious reaction of the British and (perhaps more importantly) the Irish government led Carter to backtrack hastily, declaring his opposition to violence of any kind. But once in office he came under pressure from O'Neill and his allies to support their campaign for reform by peaceful means. The statement Carter produced in response was bland, denouncing violence and expressing his hope for 'a just solution that involves both sides of the community'. But pushed through over the objections of the State Department it provided a precedent for later steps towards a more activist policy.[12]

Carter's successor, in 1980, was Ronald Reagan. The composition of the new White House was a striking illustration of the changes that had taken place in the politics and culture of Irish America. Within the Cabinet were key men of Irish descent: William Clark, successively national security advisor and secretary of the interior; Donald Regan, secretary of the treasury; Raymond Donovan, secretary of labor; and William Casey, director of the CIA. Of these, however, only Clark, a wealthy Californian rancher, showed any particular interest in Ireland. He bought a house and kept horses there, and in 1981 caused a brief storm by suggesting that it was the hope of all Americans that political reconciliation would eventually lead to reunification. Reagan himself, in contrast, had no long-term record of interest in Ireland. Interviewed in 1979 by a journalist from the *Irish Times* he opened the proceedings by enquiring: 'Your paper is Dublin. That's south of the border, right?' The new president had initially believed that his own ancestry was English. When, during the 1980 presidential campaign, Irish diplomats revealed to him that they had traced his family back to Ballyporeen in County Tipperary, he asked them to keep the information to themselves until after the election. His election strategy, Clark told Donlon, was 'going for the WASP vote. There's no way he's going for the Irish Catholic vote except on abortion.' Once elected Reagan was happy to attend functions at the Irish embassy, and to be photographed, during a visit in 1984, being served a pint in Ballyporeen. Nancy Reagan, on the other hand, was reportedly never entirely reconciled to her husband's transformation from White Anglo-Saxon Protestant to son of the Irish diaspora.[13]

Reagan's affable acceptance of his Irish descent, however, did not inspire any dramatic change in the stance of the United States on the Northern Irish conflict. He publicly endorsed a new Congressional grouping, the Friends of Ireland, launched in 1981 by Kennedy, O'Neill and others, but resisted pressure to give active support to its work. On one memorable occasion Reagan terminated what was becoming an awkward conversation with Garret Fitzgerald, then Irish prime minister, by claiming that their telephone connection was breaking up. His only significant intervention was in May 1984, when he pressed the head of the British government, Margaret Thatcher, to moderate her initial contemptuous rejection of the latest Irish proposals for constitutional reform in Northern Ireland. Reagan may have been influenced by Casey. But the main reason for his intervention was the need, for the sake of his legislative programme, to maintain a relationship with O'Neill, the House Speaker. Awareness of American unease at the lack of progress in Northern Ireland probably did something to make Thatcher soften her stance. But confidential records of their meeting indicate that Reagan's exchange with Thatcher, his most important Cold War ally, was rather milder in tone than he later reported back to O'Neill. And any limited pressure he did exert was more than balanced by the assistance that his administration provided in the continuing war against militant republicanism. In June 1985 the British and American governments signed a new treaty, severely restricting the ability of fugitive IRA activists to resist extradition by claiming that their offences were political. The agreement met with strong opposition in the Senate's Committee on Foreign Relations, in particular from Delaware's Joseph Biden. But Reagan's allies in Congress deftly linked its approval to the passage of financial aid to support the workings of the new programme of joint action recently agreed by the British and Irish governments. In April 1986 Thatcher reinforced her claim on the support of both Reagan and Congress when she allowed British bases to be used for air strikes against Libya. The extradition treaty was passed in July, with the aid package following soon after.[14]

Even as Ronald Reagan manoeuvred to balance Congressional pressures and the needs of his Cold War alliance, the character of the Northern Ireland conflict was changing radically. Between March and October 1981 ten IRA prisoners in the region's main jail had died during a prolonged hunger strike in support of their demand to be treated as political prisoners. Their determined self-martyrdom undermined long-standing British attempts to present IRA violence as mere criminality, while the government's ostentatious indifference to their long-drawn-out deaths antagonised many, in both Ireland and the United States, not otherwise disposed to support political violence. It also inspired a change in republican tactics. As the hunger strike continued supporters had nominated one of the leading participants, Bobby Sands, for the vacant parliamentary seat of Fermanagh and South Tyrone. With other nationalist parties standing aside, Sands was elected. When he died, his election agent Owen Carron stood for and won the vacant seat. These victories, along with the election of two other hunger strikers to seats in the Dáil, the parliament of the Irish Republic, encouraged the Sinn Féin leadership to invest in electoral politics on a large scale. In elections in 1982 for a new Northern Irish Assembly, Sinn Féin candidates won 35 per cent of the nationalist vote, rising to 43 per cent in elections to the British parliament the following year, although in both cases those elected refused to take their seats. None of this implied the abandonment of traditional methods of pursuing the republican agenda. IRA operations in Northern Ireland included a bomb that killed eleven Protestants attending a First World War commemoration in November 1987, another explosion, in June 1988, that killed six soldiers participating in a 'fun run' for charity, a mortar attack on 10 Downing Street in February 1991, timed to coincide with a meeting of the British cabinet, and a landmine in January 1992 that killed eight men doing construction work on an army base. Instead, the first step had been taken towards a twin-track policy, in which a continuing campaign of murder and intimidation would run side by side with the pursuit of an appearance of democratic legitimacy through elections. It was the strategy memorably summed up by Sinn Féin's Danny Morrison when he asked a party convention in October 1991 whether anyone would object 'if with a ballot paper in this hand and an Armalite [rifle] in this hand, we take power in Ireland'.[15]

In the United States the emotive image of men starving themselves to death revived support for the republican cause. Contributions to Noraid, which had fallen off in the second half of the 1970s, rose dramatically. In 1983 the Ancient Order of Hibernians, headed since the previous year by an overt IRA sympathiser, chose Noraid founder Michael Flannery to be the grand marshal of the St Patrick's Day parade in New York, followed in 1984 and 1985 by Teddy Gleason and then Nassau County comptroller and Noraid supporter Peter King. But the movement was by this time facing a generational split. American-born members, led by Martin Galvin, the movement's director of publicity, had begun to argue that the organisation should develop its role as a pressure group within the United States. Irish-born traditionalists like Flannery wanted to keep the emphasis on fund-raising for the IRA's activities in Northern Ireland. Sinn Féin's decision to invest in electoral politics in both parts of Ireland drove the two sides further apart. In 1986 Sinn Féin agreed to modify its traditional refusal to participate in partitionist institutions by taking any seats it won in the Dáil. When a majority within Noraid backed the decision, Flannery, George Harrison and a few others withdrew in protest. This left Galvin free to move ahead with his more political strategy. Meanwhile the Irish National Caucus took up the continued problem of economic discrimination in Northern Ireland, reflected in high rates of unemployment among Catholics and their underrepresentation in skilled work. In 1984 activists drew up a code of conduct for American companies investing in the region. They adroitly labelled their objectives the MacBride Principles, after Seán MacBride, a one-time IRA chief of staff but latterly an internationally respected jurist and a founding member of Amnesty International. The Irish government, John Hume and his colleagues, and the Friends of Ireland were all concerned that excessive regulation would discourage American investment. But the campaign for the Principles, attractive for their appeal to common-sense fairness and free of the taint of violence, won widespread support. By 1994, fifteen states and more than thirty cities in the United States had passed legislation requiring companies operating in Northern Ireland to address employment practices.[16]

It was against this background of a freshly blurred line between violence and political action that a new American politician chose to plunge into Northern Irish issues. In April 1992 William Jefferson Clinton, governor of Arkansas and a candidate in the Democratic presidential primary, attended an Irish American Presidential Forum in New York. This was the third in a series of meetings, commencing in 1984, in which candidates in Democratic presidential primaries had been invited to lay out their policies on Irish issues. Clinton's motives for attending were, as he later admitted, opportunistic. He was, like Carter before him, a southern

Protestant in search of northern Catholic votes. He had just lost the Connecticut primary to Jerry Brown, the partly Irish (and Catholic) former governor of California. And the New York primary was just two days away. At the forum he offered a series of commitments: as president, he would send a peace envoy to Northern Ireland, he would support the MacBride Principles, and he would leave extradition cases to be decided by the courts, free of political interference. He also promised that Gerry Adams would receive an entry visa to the United States. Adams was president of Sinn Féin, and, in line with the party's twin-track strategy, had been elected to the British parliament, as member for West Belfast, in 1992. But he was also regarded by both the British and Irish governments as actively engaged in directing the IRA's campaign of bombings and killings. In October, now confirmed as the Democratic candidate, Clinton was to visit the Eire Pub in Dorchester, Massachusetts (pronounced 'eerie' by the locals), where in 1983 Ronald Reagan had famously dropped in for a drink. Around the same time Clinton was quoted as promising that with his election 'the Irish will have a friend in the White House'. Two weeks before polling day he wrote a public letter of thanks to the organisers of Irish Americans for Clinton/Gore. He repeated his promise to appoint a special envoy, declared his support for the MacBride Principles, and condemned collusion between the security forces in Northern Ireland and Protestant paramilitaries.[17]

In all of this Clinton was addressing a new type of Irish-American opinion. The question that forced him to commit himself on the Adams visa had come from Martin Galvin of Noraid. (When an Irish journalist asked immediately afterwards if he had known who he was talking to, Clinton replied, 'Come on, give me a break, I'm doing my best.') But the group that then formed behind Clinton's campaign was of a different character. The leading figures were Ray Flynn, Bruce Morrison and Niall O'Dowd. All three had been prominent in the 1980s campaign for concessions to undocumented Irish immigrants. Flynn, as mayor of Boston, had offered them a welcome mat; Morrison, as a congressman from Connecticut, had delivered the single largest batch of Irish visas; while O'Dowd's newspaper, *Irish Voice*, established in 1987, was a combative weekly aimed specifically at the new Irish immigrant population. The three were now united by a shared dissatisfaction with the pace of change in Northern Ireland. Flynn had renounced his early involvement with Noraid, but he remained active on Northern Irish issues such as the MacBride Principles. Morrison had left the Friends of Ireland for the Ad Hoc group, because of its stronger stand on human rights abuses by the security forces in Northern Ireland. O'Dowd was critical of the emphasis placed by diplomats like Donlon on containing Irish American support for terrorism, to the exclusion of more positive initiatives: 'What they effectively did was muzzle Ted Kennedy for 30 years, which was completely unproductive, in my opinion. . . . It was very easy to say "We're against violence", but on a practical level, I always knew you had to engage the people who were creating the violence.' In 1992 he gave Adams, still excluded from the United States, a monthly column in the *Irish Voice*. In the 1970s and for much of the 1980s Irish Americans had faced a binary choice, between the pro-IRA activists of Noraid and the Irish National Caucus and the moderate, strictly constitutional nationalism backed by the Friends of Ireland. Flynn, Morrison and O'Dowd offered a third way forward, one not tainted by direct support for terrorism but that pushed for a more proactive American policy towards Northern Ireland and was flexible on the question of how the IRA's political partner, Sinn Féin, should be treated.[18]

Following Clinton's election Irish Americans for Clinton/Gore reconstituted themselves as Americans for a New Irish Agenda. But translating campaign promises into action turned out, predictably, to be less than straightforward. Ray Flynn hoped to be rewarded for his efforts by becoming ambassador to Ireland. However

Edward Kennedy, whose support in the Senate would be vital to Clinton's plans for healthcare and other initiatives, had claimed that position for his sister, Jean Kennedy Smith, and Flynn had to be satisfied with a sunnier posting as ambassador to the Vatican. Clinton did propose appointing an envoy, though in the role of fact finder rather than negotiator, but dropped the idea when the Irish prime minister, Albert Reynolds, warned that this might compromise what he believed were promising private negotiations with his British counterpart, John Major. Clinton's public letter to his Irish-American supporters, moreover, had not repeated his promise to grant a visa to Adams, and the State Department, in April 1993, once again rejected an application. In response to the lack of action, Americans for a New Irish Agenda launched their own diplomatic initiative. In September, Bruce Morrison led a party to Ireland to meet nationalist and unionist leaders, including Sinn Féin and representatives of the Ulster Defence Assocation and the Ulster Volunteer Force. With him were Niall O'Dowd and two prominent Irish-American success stories from the corporate world. Bill Flynn, head of a major insurance company, had sponsored conferences on tolerance and conflict resolution, including one in Derry; Charles Feeney, the billionaire co-founder of the world's largest chain of duty-free shops, had donated generously to Irish causes north and south. The IRA facilitated the visit by calling a temporary ceasefire. On their return a non-profit organisation chaired by Flynn announced a conference on Northern Ireland, to be held in New York on 1 February 1994, with invitations to all the party leaders, including Adams. The visa issue was now firmly back on the table.

The White House had no official contact with Morrison's mission. However O'Dowd had reported regularly to a member of Edward Kennedy's staff, Trina Vargo, who passed on his reports to Nancy Soderberg, her predecessor in Kennedy's office and now a member of Clinton's National Security Council. Soderberg herself, as she later recalled, remained sceptical of the IRA's intentions. 'I said, "It's a week-long ceasefire! Give me a break. Come back when you're serious."' But others in the administration were impressed. Encouragement also came from other quarters. Albert Reynolds and John Hume, who had earlier supported the exclusion of Adams from the United States, now argued forcefully that a visa would advance the progress towards peace. They also secured the support of Jean Kennedy Smith, who in turn sought to persuade her brother. The decisive moment came at the funeral of Tip O'Neill on 10 January 1994, when John Hume assured a still hesitant Ted Kennedy that the time had come to give the Sinn Féin leader a hearing on American soil. Clinton himself was by this time open to persuasion. The collapse of the Soviet Union in 1989 and the end of the Cold War created a general sense that the United States had now to formulate a new vision of its foreign policy. It also reduced the importance of Britain as an ally. After embarrassing missteps over military operations in Bosnia, Somalia and Haiti, facilitating peace talks in Northern Ireland was a cheap and risk-free way for the administration to claim a diplomatic success. There was also the Irish vote in future elections to think about. On 29 January 1994, three days before the conference in New York, Clinton approved the Adams visa.[19]

Gerry Adams's forty-eight hour visit to New York, from 31 January to 2 February 1994, was an important step in his party's progress from terrorism to political action. But American policy was not made in a vacuum. By this time senior figures in the Sinn Féin leadership had clearly decided that armed action had served its purpose: the time had come to cash in the dividends of violence. Adams and others were already in talks with representatives of the British and Irish governments. But all this was taking place in secret, through a variety of what were described as backchannels. The contribution of the United States was to provide some immediate, tangible demonstrations of the benefits that might follow a change of course. Adams's first visa, in January 1994, was for forty-eight hours. A second, in September, after the IRA had announced a ceasefire, allowed him to undertake a two-week, ten-city tour. He also received a phone call from Vice President Al Gore, and had a meeting with State Department officials. On a third visit, in December, he was allowed into the White House to meet National Security Adviser Anthony Lake. In March 1995, in a further step towards legitimacy, Adams received an invitation to attend the St Patrick's Day lunch on Capitol Hill, hosted by the speaker of the House of Representatives, and the evening reception in the White House, and on both occasions shook hands with Clinton.[20]

In the short term none of this was quite enough. In February 1996 the IRA army council, under pressure from the rank and file, abandoned its ceasefire. The American response, however, was notably pragmatic. The new round of bombings and killings was a bump in the road, not a deal breaker. Niall O'Dowd continued to carry messages back and forth between Lake and Soderberg in the White House and Adams in Belfast. Adams received a visa allowing him to attend St Patrick's Day events in New York, Washington and Scranton, Pennsylvania. But there was no invitation to the White House, and no formal meetings with officials. Most important of all, he was forbidden to engage in fund-raising. The presence in Bruce Morrison's delegation of Chuck Feeney and Bill Flynn had been a reminder that there was by this time a substantial Irish presence in corporate America. In place of the crumpled five and ten dollar bills dropped into Noraid collection boxes in South Boston bars, there was now the possibility of tapping a vast reservoir of corporate and personal wealth. A first fund-raising tour in May 1995 had brought in almost $900,000; at one dinner at the Plaza Hotel in New York, 400 guests paid $1,000 a plate. But this was money available only to a party operating within the law, and with the permission of the United States government. Sinn Féin remained the political face of a formidable and still well-armed network of bombers and assassins. But the decision to order these forces back into action, as the terms of Adams's new visa made clear, now came at a high price.

By 1997 the coming to power of a Labour government under Tony Blair, and the announcement of a new IRA ceasefire in July, opened the way for multiparty talks on a peace settlement. The outline of that settlement, however, had already been determined. Joint declarations by the British and Irish government had acknowledged the sole right of the people of Ireland to decide their political future. But they also specified that the exercise of that right must involve the consent of separate majorities in both north and south. That stipulation ruled out, for the foreseeable future, any prospect of a unitary Irish state. So the purpose of the talks was to establish the terms on which Catholics could be reconciled to life within a Northern Ireland that remained part of the United Kingdom. The concessions—on police reform, power sharing political institutions, the symbolic acknowledgement of an Irish cultural identity—had to be sufficient to justify the Irish Republic in withdrawing its claim to the territory of Northern Ireland, and to induce the IRA to end its thirty-year insurgency. But they also had to stop short of frightening off the unionist participants. Here the United States was an important facilitator. The key figure was George Mitchell, the recently retired senator for Maine, who joined with a retired Canadian general, John de Chastelain, and a former Finnish president, Harri Holkeri, in chairing the multiparty talks. Mitchell was a skilful and resourceful chairman. He also took the bold decision that the talks would end, with or without an outcome, at midnight on 9 April 1998. This deadline was essential if any settlement was to be ratified by public vote before the 'marching season', when Orange bands made their raucous and provocative appearance on the summer streets and the possibilities for rational dialogue dwindled. But it also risked bringing the whole process to a disastrous halt. During a final fifty-eight-hour marathon session, phone calls from

Clinton, not just to the nationalist participants but also to the Ulster Unionist leader David Trimble, provided a vital push towards compromise. But even in this last stage it was Blair and the Irish prime minister, Bertie Ahern, who took the creative role, tweaking their respective positions on issues like cross-border institutions to create a middle ground which nationalists and unionists could, just about, accept. The result of their efforts was a wide-ranging agreement, signed by all the participants, on 10 April 1998. Even then, those involved were unable to agree on what to call the settlement. To unionists it was the Belfast Agreement, named from the city in which it was negotiated. To Catholics it was the Good Friday Agreement, named for the religious festival on which it was signed.

Throughout this process Sinn Féin faced the novel problem of dealing with two very different versions of Irish America. On one side stood the deep pockets and political influence of men like Chuck Feeney and Bill Flynn, whose support was never unconditional. The IRA ceasefire in 1994 followed tense meetings at which Feeney and others combined promises of further concessions from the Clinton administration with dire warnings of the consequences that would follow further deaths. But Adams and other Sinn Féin leaders had also to think of the other Irish America, which had sustained their movement through the grim years of the 1970s and 1980s. In August 1994, as negotiations for the first IRA ceasefire neared their end, progress was interrupted by a last-minute request: a visa for Joe Cahill. There was a moment of shock. 'Did you read this man's CV?' Clinton asked Albert Reynolds, when they spoke by phone. But the CV was the whole point: Cahill's standing as a warrior, and a killer, was what made him the ideal emissary to convince the militant wing of Irish-American nationalism, in Noraid and elsewhere, to support the abandonment of the military struggle for a united Ireland. Cahill got his visa and the movement's blue-collar American backers were for the moment reassured. Even so, there were signs that the deference being shown to the new type of wealthy backer, and the spectacle of fund-raising banquets with ticket prices far beyond the means of the average Noraid member, had begun to alienate traditional supporters.[21]

In these difficult circumstances Sinn Féin had now to sell a settlement it had initially rejected as 'an internal Northern Ireland solution' to its traditional American backers. It fell back on tried and trusted methods. Joe Cahill once again crossed the Atlantic to support this latest twist in strategy, delivering what one commentator unkindly described as his standard 'I stood at the foot of the gallows for Ireland' speech. He was accompanied by another figure of unimpeachable standing in republican circles. Martin Ferris was now a member of the Irish parliament. But he had earlier spent ten years in prison after having been captured off the coast of County Kerry on a ship laden with guns and explosives. Gerry Adams himself completed the charm offensive by appearing at Noraid's 1998 conference to pay tribute in person to its contribution to the cause. Not all were won over. Martin Galvin had earlier clashed with republican fundamentalists like Michael Flannery and the veteran arms procurer George Harrison when they opposed Sinn Féin's decision to take any seats it won in the Irish parliament. But now it was Galvin's turn to denounce the 1998 Agreement as a 'trap to ensnare republicans into administering British rule'. He and some others broke with Noraid, to align themselves with a range of dissident republican movements. But the greater part of the movement remained loyal. Sinn Féin's American base was secure.[22]

The Clinton presidency marked the high point of American involvement in the affairs of Northern Ireland. Clinton's successor, George W. Bush, continued the practice of appointing a special envoy. But where George Mitchell had reported to the White House, his successors, Richard Haass and Mitchell Reiss, were based in the State Department. In the event the president's lack of direct interest allowed both men to become forceful actors in their own right.

Haass, a hard-nosed career administrator with extensive experience of the Middle East, continued the policy of incentives and penalties begun under Clinton. The discovery in 2001 that members of the IRA had sold their services to the Revolutionary Armed Forces of Colombia (FARC), offering training in bomb-making and other military techniques, brought the threat of severe sanctions. But Sinn Féin were allowed to rehabilitate themselves by agreeing to the destruction of one of the stores of guns and explosives whose continued existence had become the main obstacle to a full political settlement. Reiss, in the changed atmosphere following Al Qaeda's attack on Washington and New York on 11 September 2001, took a harder line. On 20 December 2004 what were clearly members of the IRA stole £26.5 million in banknotes from the Belfast headquarters of the Northern Bank, after taking the families of two employees hostage. Six weeks later members of the IRA beat to death a forklift driver, Robert McCartney, following a personal quarrel in a Belfast bar. Adams once again found himself frozen out of official circles in Washington, and Reiss began rejecting applications for fund-raising visas. In response the IRA at last gave up its whole stock of armaments.

The other contribution of Haass and Reiss to the Northern Ireland settlement was less benign. The power-sharing executive set up following the 1998 Agreement was headed by members of the Ulster Unionist Party and the SDLP, representing the moderate wings of their respective tribal groupings. Haass, however, became increasingly critical of both. Instead, in common with elements in the Dublin government, he came to believe that the best hope for stability lay in a coming together of the extremes: on the nationalist side Sinn Féin, and on the other Ian Paisley's Democratic Unionist Party, which had boycotted George Mitchell's talks and had initially denounced the resulting settlement as a betrayal of Protestant Ulster. Haass and Reiss were not solely responsible for the outcome: thirty years of vicious conflict had created a society in which loud voices had a built-in advantage. But the American loss of faith in the moderate centre became a self-fulfilling prophecy: Northern Irish Assembly elections in 2003 showed the Democratic Unionists and Sinn Féin displacing the Ulster Unionists and the SDLP as the largest Protestant and Catholic parties. When a new executive took power, after a five year hiatus, in 2007, it was with Ian Paisley as first minister and Martin McGuinness of Sinn Féin as deputy first minister.[23]

The analogy is imperfect. But a settlement that left Northern Ireland in the hands of the political wing of the IRA, in pragmatic alliance with a unionist party that had its own history of questionable dealings with extremists, had a distinct whiff of the behaviour characteristic of a departing colonial power: the priority was not democracy or civility, but rather to find forceful local actors who would deliver a stable future. And indeed, with the departure of Mitchell Reiss, Northern Ireland became a peripheral concern in American foreign policy. Reiss's replacement, in 2007, was Paula Dobriansky, who held the post while continuing with her main job as Under Secretary of State for Global Affairs. During the presidential election of 2008, the campaign of Democratic candidate Barack Obama began by questioning whether an envoy was needed. When Obama's Republican rival John McCain took up the issue, encouraged by indignant Irish-American activists, the Obama camp took the line of least resistance and promised a 'senior envoy' who would build on the achievements of the Clinton administration. Hillary Clinton, Obama's secretary of state, duly appointed Declan Kelly, a businessman who had been a major contributor to her campaign for the Democratic nomination. However he was designated an 'economic' envoy. There was nevertheless a brief flurry of political activity in 2010 when the Ulster Unionist Party, in a feeble effort to out-Orange the Democratic Unionists, opposed a bill to complete the transfer to the devolved government of full control of justice and policing. Hillary Clinton spoke to the Ulster Unionist leader, while Kelly enlisted former American president George W. Bush to ask the British prime minister, David Cameron, to use his influence with the Ulster Unionists, who had recently formed an alliance with Cameron's Conservative Party. Neither appeal was successful (although the devolution of policing went ahead with the votes of the Democratic Unionists). Kelly resigned the following year, and it was not until 2014 that Obama nominated a successor, the former senator and one-time candidate for the Democratic presidential nomination Gary Hart. After the 2016 presidential elections, Donald Trump again left the position vacant, until May 2020, when he nominated his former chief of staff Mick Mulvaney.[24]

The fading out of the post of special envoy was a matter of common sense. With the IRA's weapons now disposed of, and Sinn Féin and the Democratic Unionist Party working together—pragmatically if not harmoniously—to divide between them the lion's share of power and patronage within a largely peaceful Northern Ireland, it was difficult to argue that any part of Ireland required America's day-by-day attention. The Irish ambassador, even as he lobbied the Obama campaign to commit to appointing an envoy, admitted as much to Trina Vargo: 'He said that Ireland wanted one because it made them feel special, but there was no substantial reason. . . . It was really more about the optics than the substance'. But the decline in interest in Irish matters also reflected the waning of Irish-American political influence. As a presidential candidate Obama did not bother to attend the Irish American Presidential Forum that had proved so important in the rise of Bill Clinton. Obama also resisted pressure to reopen the issue of Irish immigration. In December 2005 Niall O'Dowd and his brother-in-law Ciaran Staunton, a former Noraid activist, set up the Irish Lobby for Immigration Reform to demand an amnesty for what they claimed was the still substantial number of undocumented Irish living in fear of deportation. A similar campaign in the 1980s had secured the blatantly discriminatory Donnelly and Morrison visas. In 2008 both Hillary Clinton and Obama made clear that any renewed special treatment for the Irish was out of the question. Clinton tried to fudge the issue by talking of a comprehensive reform of immigration legislation. But when pressed in a televised debate she refused to support even the less substantial proposal that undocumented immigrants should be facilitated in getting the driving licences so many needed for work.[25]

The problem for activists like O'Dowd and Staunton was that, with Northern Ireland at peace, there was no great issue, other than the problems of a much-reduced community of illegal immigrants, around which Irish America could unite. Today, Noraid still describes itself as committed to the establishment of a democratic thirty-two county Ireland. In the same way marchers in New York's St Patrick's Day parade carry banners demanding 'England, Get Out of Ireland'—dating from the anti-partition campaign of 1948, and the only political slogan permitted in the parade. But with Sinn Féin serving as a senior partner in the government of a Northern Ireland that remains firmly part of the United Kingdom, the language in both cases seems to represent fidelity to the past rather than a call to action. There is also a newer organisation, the Friends of Sinn Féin, set up in 1994 as soon as the Clinton administration's fund-raising visas created the opportunity to tap the wealth of corporate Irish America. Between 1995 and 2014 the Friends raised $12 million, making Sinn Féin the best-funded political party in either part of Ireland. A more recent filing shows that in just the six months to April 2020 they collected $295,000. Their work has been from the start a very different operation to the crowdfunding of Noraid. Some large donations come from trade unions with a substantial Irish-American membership. But the list of donors is dominated by a single group, Irish-owned construction firms in New York and New Jersey. Of the $12 million reported up to 2014, in fact, $6.3 million came from New York State alone, with another million from New Jersey. An *Irish Times* analysis of the figures suggests that some of those paying $500 a head to attend the most important fund-raising event of the year, the annual dinner at the Sheraton hotel in Manhattan, have no interest in Ireland. Instead they are smaller contractors and suppliers of building materials anxious to ingratiate themselves with some of the most important players in the New York construction industry. Financial support from the United States remains central to the success of Sinn Féin. But what they rely on is now the support of a specific network, not of a cross-section of Irish America.[26]

Does this mean that the era of close American involvement in the affairs of Northern Ireland is over? Only a fool claims to predict the future, much less to declare an end of even a particular history. Brexit, the withdrawal of the United Kingdom from the European Union, has disrupted the delicate compromises and ambiguities of the Belfast or Good Friday Agreement. Instead it imposes a stark binary choice: either the creation of new legal and economic barriers between Northern Ireland and the Republic, now on opposite sides of the European Union's most westerly border, or the partial separation of Northern Ireland from the rest of the United Kingdom. Either has the potential to provoke renewed violence, from a resurgent republicanism or from a loyalist population that has already experienced the last quarter century as a progressive loss of status. The break with the European Union has also reinvigorated Scottish nationalism, calling into question the future of the United Kingdom as a federation of nations. Against this background it is easy to see how Ireland could once again become a matter of concern to politicians in the United States. There have already been warning shots. In 2019, as the implications of Brexit for the Northern Irish peace settlement started to become clear, House Speaker Nancy Pelosi led a congressional delegation to Ireland. And Joseph Biden, while on his way to becoming America's second president of Irish Catholic background, gave a public warning that any settlement that was to the detriment of Northern Ireland would mean that Britain could forget about a post-Brexit trade deal with the United States.

On the other side of the equation is the passage of time. Observers are agreed that there is no longer a significant Irish vote in the United States. Some electors might respond positively to an Irish name, or to a well-staged appearance on St Patrick's Day. But, as the Obama campaign clearly recognised in 2008, there is little to be gained or lost by a stand on specifically Irish issues. Instead the senators and congressmen who are active in this area choose to be so mainly because of their own ancestry and sense of identity. And it is here that change is likely to be seen. Pelosi's delegation in 2019 included 42-year-old Congressman Brendan Boyle from Philadelphia, whose father was an emigrant from County Donegal. By this time, however, Boyle was the only member of Congress to have an Irish-born parent. (There had been another, Joe Crowley of New York, whose mother was born in County Armagh, and who for twenty years chaired the Ad Hoc Congressional Committee for Irish Affairs. But in January 2019, in a sign of changing times, Crowley lost the Democratic nomination to the rising star of the party's left, Alexandria Ocasio-Cortez.) And even with Boyle's presence, as the *Irish Times* noted in its report on the visit, the average age of Pelosi's delegation was 60. Another Irish journalist, Caitríona Perry, likewise emphasises age and generational change. She points, for example, to two candidates for the Democratic nomination in the 2020 presidential contest. Joseph Biden, born in 1942, is emphatic in asserting his Irish ancestry. (He is in fact wholly Irish on his mother's side. His father's ancestors were mainly English, making him, by most reckonings, five-eighths Irish.) Beto O'Rourke, thirty years younger, bears a distinctively Irish surname, but he prefers to be known by the Mexican diminutive of his first name, Robert. The contrast in age and self-image suggests that it may well be chronology, more than anything else, that determines the nature of any further American intervention in Irish affairs. Today, as the prompt response to the Brexit negotiations shows, there are influential voices willing to make the problems of Ireland an issue of American policy. But how long that will continue, as one type of Irish American gives way to another, remains to be seen.[27]

16

GLOBAL IRELAND
REIMAGINED

During a period of nearly a century and a half, from the 1830s to the 1950s, around eight million inhabitants of a small island on the western edge of Europe spread out to different parts of the globe. Their dispersal was driven by two sets of forces: on the one hand, a skewed and underdeveloped economy at home, and on the other a wider world being transformed by technological advances, by ever more complex patterns of international trade, and by the seizure and exploitation of vast new lands. Irish settlement was limited largely to the English-speaking world: North America, Australia and New Zealand, with an outlier in Argentina. But in all but the last case they became a significant presence. In nineteenth-century Canada and New Zealand almost one in five of the white population was of

Irish descent; in Australia it was one in four. In the United States, during the first period of mass immigration, between 1820 and 1860, the Irish made up well over a third of new arrivals. In all of these destinations, moreover, immigrants of Irish birth and descent had an influence well above their numbers. Their early arrival, their command of English, and their familiarity with political institutions and processes combined to give them a prominent place in politics, in labour movements and in the Catholic Church. In the late nineteenth- and early twentieth-century United States, even as their share of population shrank, they retained a distinctive role as intermediaries between the great mass of recent immigrants and the host society.

In the wider history of world migration the Irish likewise represent an important chapter. As the institution of slavery slowly lost legitimacy it was they who emerged as the first example of what was to be the long-lasting alternative, the international trade in free but cheap labour. As early as 1834 George Cornewall Lewis, observing with horrified fascination the Irish migrants congregated in the industrial cities and towns of England and Scotland, was able to recognise the vital contribution that this despised underclass had made to the economic revolution that was transforming his society. The path that these Irish pioneered, marked by exploitation, discrimination and nativist hostility, was to be followed over the next two centuries by many others: Chinese and Indian workers around the Pacific Rim and beyond, eastern and southern Europeans in the United States, emigrants from former European colonies in Africa and Asia following the Second World War. The same pattern continues to the present day: all that is new is its extension from the affluent societies of the West to new centres of wealth, such as the oil-producing states of the Middle East, with their North African and Asian labourers, or, on a lesser scale, the tiger economies of South Asia itself. In contemporary Qatar investigations into the giant construction projects undertaken to prepare for the FIFA World Cup in 2022 have uncovered evidence of immigrant workers trapped in the country by debt, or by the confiscation of travel documents, housed in squalid, overcrowded barracks, and paid only a part of their agreed wages. There are also alarming reports of deaths, many attributed to being forced to labour out of doors in impossible temperatures. No one should be surprised. The pattern of migration, exploitation and discrimination that Lewis observed in the cellars and alleyways of the Irish districts of Manchester and Glasgow, and which he saw as a development without historical precedent, has become, in an ever more interconnected world, the norm.[1]

It is tempting to proceed to a solemn discussion of the lessons that the history of the Irish diaspora holds for the present, when both the United States and Europe struggle to cope with what seem to be overwhelming numbers seeking to penetrate their borders. But there is no point in presenting simplistic parallels. The story of the Irish diaspora differs in three important ways from anything that is happening today. First, it is true that the Irish stand out as an initially reviled immigrant group that achieved not just acceptance but influence beyond their numbers. But in doing so they had advantages not enjoyed, either at that time or later, by many other actual or would-be immigrants. They were white, Christian (although Catholic) and English speaking. Their migration, secondly, was to countries still in the process of settling lands only thinly populated by Indigenous peoples, whose claims to ownership were easily, often brutally, swept aside. So living space, whatever other issues mass immigration might throw up, was not a problem. Finally the admitting societies, especially the United States, took at most minimal responsibility for the welfare of the immigrants they admitted. They needed these newcomers to populate their frontiers and labour in their streets and factories. But they felt no obligation, apart from the limited efforts of private philanthropy, to address the problems associated with the presence of an impoverished and culturally disadvantaged underclass. Modern Western countries, despite the rightward shift of the last four decades, are more squeamish. Admitting large numbers of immigrants has implications for the provision of housing, education and health services, all areas that easily become contentious issues of domestic politics.

History, then, offers few easy answers to today's questions. What it can offer is a critical perspective on highly emotive issues. To examine past waves of anti-immigrant sentiment, such as the American nativism of the 1840s and 1850s (or, indeed, the reaction of well-established Irish Americans in mid-twentieth-century Washington Heights to new arrivals from the Dominican Republic), is to recognise the crude nature of the prejudices involved: the same charges recur, over and over again, in different time periods and against different groups of newcomers. To look more closely at the experience of emigrants themselves, meanwhile, even, at times, to hear their voices, is to be alerted to the dangers of a dehumanizing rhetoric. Contemporary policy makes much use of the distinction between involuntary migrants who are fleeing unendurable conditions, and 'economic' migrants who are simply seeking a higher standard of living. But the example of post-Famine Ireland, where living standards were rising even as large numbers had no prospect of achieving a life as independent adults except by emigrating, should make us wary of simplistic distinctions. Finally, and most important, there is the contrast between the economic priorities that led a range of overseas destinations to import Irish people in such numbers, and the cold reception those immigrants encountered on arrival. Here we are forced to recognise the collective hypocrisy, as alive today as at any time in the past, that allows affluent societies to stereotype and marginalise their migrant populations, while at the same time relying on them to do the work no one else is willing to undertake.

By the late nineteenth century several decades of massive emigration had created a strong transnational community. It was a community built around a Catholic faith, a popular history dominated by themes of resistance, defeat and oppression, and a loose body of folklore, music and dance. As such it did not include the entire Irish-born population, two-thirds as large as the population of Ireland itself, that now lived outside the island. Instead it was a sectional identity, effectively excluding the substantial number of Protestant emigrants, and not necessarily attractive to all expatriate Catholics. But for millions of the Irish-born and their descendants there was a powerful sense of common identity. In the development of this imagined community the nineteenth-century explosion of print culture had played a central part. Newspapers like Argentina's *Southern Cross* or Patrick Ford's *Irish World* provided regular information on events in a distant Ireland, drew on a common stock of poems, essays and fiction by Irish writers, and pillaged each other's pages to keep readers informed on developments in other parts of the diaspora. Successive Irish nationalist movements looked to this greater Ireland to underwrite their projects, creating support organisations and mounting regular fund-raising tours. In some parts of the diaspora, particularly in the United States, the bonds of a shared ethnic identity were reinforced by a powerful sense of collective grievance: emigrants and their descendants saw themselves as exiles, banished from their homeland through the negligence or malice of an alien government. But many others, whatever regrets and traumas they experienced in the process of migration, came to see the worldwide prominence of the Irish, and their role as founding members of thriving new societies, as a matter of pride. Cardinal Patrick Francis Moran of Sydney, in 1897, celebrated the 'marvellous expansion' of an 'Anglo-Celtic empire' that had come to comprise twenty million Irish Catholics.[2]

Moran wrote at the point when the empire he celebrated had just reached its peak. There were clear signs, by the end of the century, of cultural and political differences between the component parts of the diaspora. Irish Catholics in Australia and New Zealand were notably less strict in their religious observance, and less disposed to support the more militant varieties of Irish nationalism, than their counterparts in the United States. The events of 1916–23, inspiring a shared sense of solidarity with a homeland ravaged by revolution, guerrilla war and military repression, seemed in the short term to bring the different parts of the diaspora closer together. But the call to take part in the First World War also brought to the surface major differences in political outlook, as seen for example in the clash that came close to severing the link between the Canadian and American branches of the Ancient Order of Hibernians. Already by the time Moran spoke, meanwhile, what had been several streams of Irish emigration had narrowed to just two, to Great Britain and the United States. From the end of the 1920s it narrowed further still. Emigration remained a central part of Irish life, but the great majority now went no further than Great Britain. The diaspora, in other words, was no longer reinforced—except to a limited extent in the United States—by a continuing stream of new arrivals.

Against this background it might have been expected that, outside Great Britain, the sense of a distinctive Irish identity would gradually fade away. That this did not happen was testimony to the depth of the cultural footprint that Irish immigrants, through their early arrival, their numerical strength and their mastery of English, had already created. By the time the number of Irish-born in each country had begun to dwindle an idea of a distinctive Irish character had taken shape, symbolised in the prominence in popular culture of figures such as Gerald O'Hara, Patrick Durack and, once time had softened the outlines of the actual man, Ned Kelly. All this meant a diasporic Irish identity that was less susceptible than others to what has been called ethnic fade. And on these foundations, in the second half of the twentieth century, a new image of Irishness was constructed. As the inhabitants of the affluent West sought an alternative to the bland uniformity of a society of mass consumption in supposedly more authentic ethnic cultures, Ireland was well-placed to benefit. It stood out as having a marketable heritage, reassuringly rooted in a well-advertised and attractive, if tragic, history. In addition, and crucially, it was a heritage largely accessible through the English language. Already in the 1960s Irish performers like the Clancy Brothers prospered as part of a broader revival of folk and ethnic music. Later the Irish were prominent in what has been called the Roots Too movement, in which white ethnic groups responded to the example, or the challenge, of the campaign for Black civil rights by asserting their own historical and cultural identity. There was also, from the 1990s, the spectacular growth of the Celtic Tiger, adding a new air of glamour to the international image of Irishness.

All this helps to explain why, a century after mass long-distance migration came to an end, 'brand Ireland' remains a strong performer in cultural markets around the world. Its success has done more than allow Irish writers and performers to achieve reputations and audiences out of all proportion to the country's size. It has also, as the British government discovered to its discomfort in the long and painful negotiations over Brexit, given Irish diplomats, in both Washington and the European Union, an exceptional degree of soft power. Behind this success, however, lies a radical reinvention. The designers of the Irish pub, and the advertising agencies employed by the Irish Tourist Board, continue to rely heavily on the notion of authenticity, of an Irish people still in touch with its cultural roots. Yet the image with which they seek to woo global consumers is of a secular, fun-loving society that is far removed from the reality of Irish life before the middle of the twentieth century, and equally distant from the world of the emigrants who made up the spiritual empire celebrated by Cardinal Moran.[3]

What, then, is the future of the Irish diaspora? In 2020 the government of the Irish Republic issued a policy document titled *Global Ireland: Ireland's Diaspora Strategy 2020–2025*. The cover bears a striking and evocative image: the light, an electronic candle set inside a lamp, that Mary Robinson placed in a window of her official residence, following her election as president in 1990, as a beacon to 'our exiles and emigrants'. Yet the vision of the Irish diaspora set out in the strategy document itself is strikingly different to the connotations of loss and longing embodied in that phrase from three decades earlier. The Irish diaspora is now 'a diverse and dynamic global community'. Its members no longer huddle in ghettos, clinging to memories of a lost homeland. Instead they form a population that is 'increasingly multicultural, in which Irish identity can be one element of an individual's broader cultural background'. And in an Ireland that is now a society of net inward migration the definition of its diaspora has expanded to include not just Irish emigrants and their immediate or more distant descendants, but also a 'reverse diaspora' made up of those who have lived, worked or studied in Ireland before returning to their own country. There is also an 'affinity diaspora' of those whose links to Ireland are through participation in sport or cultural activities, or through academic study.[4]

These ambitious proposals for a new approach to the Irish diaspora have a broader context. An earlier policy document, *Global Ireland: Ireland's Global Footprint to 2025*, published in 2018, sets out a wide-ranging programme designed to 'increase the impact and effectiveness of our international presence', with the aim of making Ireland 'an island at the centre of the world'. The plan includes the opening of new embassies and consulates, with an increase in the overall number of diplomatic staff, additional investment in agencies charged with promoting tourism and investment, a drive to increase the number of international students studying in Ireland, and a greater emphasis on language teaching in Irish schools. In pursuing this goal of 'a stronger international presence', the diaspora are to be treated as an important resource. The extended network of embassies and consulates will provide improved services to the Irish abroad. Investment around the world in Irish Studies programmes, and in Irish cultural and sporting organisations, will maintain and strengthen the ties of Irish emigrants and their descendants to the homeland. There is also to be, in the inescapable managerial vocabulary of the early twenty-first century, 'a technologically enabled diaspora engagement project'.[5]

What is to be gained by 'doubling the scope and impact of Ireland's global footprint'? *Global Ireland* emphasises the opportunity for the country to play a greater part in matters of worldwide concern, such as climate change, peacekeeping and support for human rights. But the main emphasis is economic. Increasing the visibility and reputation of the 'Irish brand' will contribute to the goal of doubling exports to markets beyond the United Kingdom, doubling tourism earnings from traditional sources such as Germany and the United States, and tripling those from developing markets such as China. The election of Ireland to a two-year term on the United Nations Security Council during 2021–2 will likewise assist in 'raising Ireland's profile and boosting our reputation as an ideal partner for trade, investment and tourism'. The cultivation of the Irish diaspora is a further economic investment. Its members will provide 'strategic mentoring and guidance to Irish companies in pursuing trade and investment opportunities in overseas markets'. This firm emphasis on the economic future, however, also means that the outside world to which *Global Ireland* and the *Diaspora Strategy* look is one that has very little to do with the geography of the historical diaspora. The United States is unavoidably prominent. It is already the source of 70 per cent of foreign direct investment, with 700 companies employing around 150,000 workers. But this is a relationship with corporate America rather than Irish America. *Global Ireland* speaks explicitly of expanding Ireland's network beyond its traditional base, and the locations of new consulates and other agencies include Seattle, Miami, Raleigh-Durham and 'the economic hubs of Austin and Atlanta'. Elsewhere the emphasis is on a changing international order. 'As global economic and political power shifts east and south', the then Irish prime minister Leo Varadkar writes in his introduction, 'Ireland will respond by making new friends and improving long-standing relationships across Asia and the Global South.' The sites of investment in new or expanded embassies and consulates include Mexico City, Colombia and Chile, the Philippines, China, Mumbai, Tokyo, Bangkok, Morocco, Jordan and the United Arab Emirates. The only foreign language specifically mentioned in the strategy for schools (apart from provision for 'heritage speakers' of Portuguese, Lithuanian and Polish) is Mandarin Chinese.

The aspirations set out in *Global Ireland* are perfectly legitimate. A small open economy has no choice but to seek opportunities where it can find them, and to respond to changes in the wider world. But in terms of the history of the Irish diaspora, the document confirms the end of an era. The Ireland for which it speaks is no longer the impoverished, peripheral country that had no choice but to send away a substantial proportion of each new generation in order to secure a bare living for those who remained. It is an affluent, technologically sophisticated society that aspires to play a part on the world stage, a receiver as well as an exporter of migrants. The diaspora that forms part of its development plans, equally, is no longer concentrated in a handful of traditional emigrant destinations. It is a much looser, and more widely dispersed, collection of individuals and groups, no longer seen as exiles but as potential ambassadors for the Irish brand.

One further element in the *Diaspora Strategy* is worth noting. This is the commitment to hold a referendum to allow non-resident Irish citizens to vote in presidential elections. Legislation for that purpose, first introduced in 2019, is still before the Dáil, after being sidelined due to a general election. The proposal is at first sight an innocuous one. The Irish presidency is a largely ceremonial position, and the vote would still be confined to those members of the diaspora who hold Irish citizenship. But in 2017, when the idea was first floated, the response within Ireland was not wholeheartedly positive. Most European countries allow citizens living abroad to vote. But in Ireland, partition and a history of heavy emigration combine to magnify the potential consequences. The 1.9 million residents of Northern Ireland, and the 1.8 million Irish citizens living abroad, could between them yield enough votes to override the preferences of a domestic electorate that in 2020 stood at just 3.5 million. 'The sum of all fears', a columnist in the *Irish Times* observed, 'seems to be Gerry Adams in the Áras [Áras an Uachtaráin, the president's official residence] in 2025, propelled by a coalition of American barstool republicans and the Sinn Féin electoral machine in Northern Ireland.' Alongside this possibly dated stereotype, looking back to the heyday of Noraid and the Irish National Caucus, there was also a new consideration, the potentially malign influence of the large number of Irish-American voters who the year before had given their support to Donald Trump. How far reservations of this kind will influence any future referendum remains unclear. But the debate is a further indication of how far Ireland and its largest diasporic population have travelled in recent decades, and in what different directions.[6]

ACKNOWLEDGEMENTS

This book has its origins in a conversation with Bill Hamilton, now my agent, about the possibility of writing a book that might be read by someone other than my fellow historians. He suggested the Irish diaspora as a topic, and subsequently advised me on ways of adapting my writing to this new intended audience. I am grateful to Professor Mary Daly and Dr Michael Kennedy for their assistance with some tricky questions concerning the impact on Ireland of changes in American immigration policy in the 1960s. The Institute of Irish Studies at Queen's University, Belfast, has provided me with a much-appreciated base since my retirement from the School of History. Its director, Professor Peter Gray, has given helpful advice on several issues, particularly relating to the Famine. Professor Gray is also entitled to the thanks of historians everywhere for his work as director of the Irish Emigration Database, which has proved an invaluable resource. At Basic Books I wish to thank Lara Heimert for her very detailed comments on the penultimate version of the text. I am also grateful to Mike van Mantgem for his careful copy-editing, and to Kaitlin Carruthers-Busser for steering me through the different stages of the production process.

Mavis Bracegirdle, at a less than ideal time in her own life, read the entire manuscript and subjected it to the same frank and perceptive criticism she has given to every book I have written, across what is now well over half a lifetime. The book is dedicated to my granddaughters. At the ages of five and three they have remained magnificently indifferent to the whole process of its completion. But they will, I hope, enjoy seeing their names in print.

APPENDIX

A (Short) Note on Statistics

Statistics rarely make for gripping reading. But no discussion of emigration can avoid them. In the Irish case there is no one entirely reliable set of figures. Official returns are often imperfect. Up to 1847, for example, the American State Department's annual total of immigrants arriving from Ireland seems to have been calculated simply by taking 70 per cent of those sailing from Liverpool.[1] Other major problems are the large number of Irish immigrants who travelled overseas but departed from a British port, sometimes after an extended stay in Great Britain, and, in the first half of the nineteenth century, the substantial number of Irish immigrants who took the cheaper sea route to Canada, even though their intended destination was the United States. There are also variations in the way children were counted.

The statistics given within the chapters should all thus be taken as approximations. Five sets of figures are particularly relevant.

1. Estimates of emigration to North America 1825–1851

Records for people leaving Irish ports are available from 1825, collected by customs officials up to 1834 and then by government emigration agents. They are recognised to be seriously incomplete. In 1932, however, the pioneering American scholar of Irish emigration, William Forbes Adams, devised a formula for revising the official figures, and for adding an estimate of the number of Irish among passengers sailing from Liverpool to American ports. D. H. Akenson has since used Adams's formula to produce comparable figures for the period 1846–51.

EMIGRATION TO NORTH AMERICA 1825–51

	British North America	United States	Total
1825	8,893	4,286	13,179
1826–30	70,249	45,214	115,463
1831–5	171,037	73,102	244,139
1836–40*	85,886	96,231	182,117
1841–5	132,908	198,092	331,000
1846–50	229,830	710,200	940,030
1851	31,709	219,453	251,162

Source: W. F. Adams, Ireland and Irish Emigration to the New World: From 1815 to the Famine *(New Haven, 1932), 413–4; D. H. Akenson,* The Irish in Ontario: A Study in Rural History *(2nd ed. Montreal and Kingston, 1984), 30.*

* Adams was unable to supply data for 1836. The figure for 1836–40 is the total for the other four years increased by 25 per cent.

2. Recorded emigration from Ireland 1852–1914

From 1852 the Irish Registrar General published figures based on information collected by the police at each of the main Irish ports. Cormac Ó Gráda has argued that these returns under-record emigration to Great Britain, probably because movement back and forth within the United Kingdom was more difficult to categorise. He estimates that the total of 4 million emigrants between

1852 and 1910 should be increased to between 4.5 and 5 million, of whom around 1 million went to Great Britain.[2] But comparison with the alternative figures derived from changes in the population recorded at each census that cannot be accounted for by births and deaths (see section 4) suggests that the Registrar General's figures are in fact more accurate than Ó Gráda suggests. From 1876 the Registrar General's figures include the destination of emigrants. This makes it possible to compare the totals said to be leaving for the United States with the number of arrivals recorded, by this time more reliably, on the other side of the Atlantic.

EMIGRATION FROM IRELAND 1852–1914

(THOUSANDS)

	TOTAL EMIGRATION (REGISTRAR GENERAL)	EMIGRATION TO THE UNITED STATES (US STATISTICS)	EMIGRATION TO THE UNITED STATES (REGISTRAR GENERAL)
1852–60*	1,011	693	
1861–70	850	436	
1871–80	624	437	
1881–90	771	655	614
1891–1900	434	388	387
1901–10	346	339	274
1911–14	111	80	108

Source: Registrar General reprinted in Reports of the Commission on Emigration and Other Population Problems 1948–54 *(Dublin, 1954), 125, 318–9;* Bicentennial Edition: Historical Statistics of the United States, Colonial Times to 1970 *(Washington, 1975), 105–6.*

* Note that this figure is for only nine years. Akenson's estimate of 251,162 emigrants to North America in 1851 (see section 1) would suggest a total for the period 1851–60 of 1,262,520. The American statistics put the number of Irish immigrants entering the United States during 1851–60 at 914,114.

3. Emigration to Australia and New Zealand 1841–1910

In 1954 Irish government statisticians produced a set of estimates for emigration to Australia and New Zealand, using returns from the Colonial Land and Emigration Commissioners and the British Board of Trade, but containing 'elements of estimation, the basis of which varied from time to time'.[3] After 1876 these can be compared with the Registrar General's count of emigrants to different destinations (see section 2).

EMIGRATION TO AUSTRALIA AND NEW ZEALAND 1841–1910

	EMIGRATION COMMISSION (AUSTRALIA & NEW ZEALAND)	REGISTRAR GENERAL (AUSTRALIA)	REGISTRAR GENERAL (NEW ZEALAND)
1841–50	22,825		
1851–60	101,541		
1861–70	82,917		
1871–80	61,946		
1881–90	55,476	38,940	4,589
1891–1900	11,448	8,531	841
1901–10	11,885	4,802	1,214

Source: Commission on Emigration, *124–5, 314–5;* W. E. Vaughan and A. J. Fitzpatrick, Irish Historical Statistics: Population 1821–1971 *(Dublin, 1978), 264–5.*

4. Net emigration 1871–2011

From 1864 births, marriages and deaths had to be registered. This makes it possible, beginning with the censuses of 1871 and 1881, to establish what proportion of the change in total population recorded in each ten-year period is a result of the balance between births and deaths, and what must be attributed instead to persons entering and leaving the country. This provides an alternative set of estimates (though of net rather than gross emigration) for the period 1871–1914, and the most reliable figures available for the period after 1922.

By their nature these estimates can be calculated only for the ten-year intervals between censuses. In the period after 1921 figures for the numbers emigrating and entering the country in individual years are estimates derived from a range of administrative sources, including passenger manifests, returns from the British Board of Trade and, in more recent years, the Quarterly National Household Survey and its successor, the Quarterly Labour Force Survey.

NET EMIGRATION FROM IRELAND 1871–2011
(Thousands)

	Ireland	Irish Republic	Northern Ireland
1871–81	688	523	165
1881–91	733	593	139
1891–1901	452	386	66
1901–11	329	259	70
1911–26	498	398	100
1926–36	225	169	56
1936–46	225	186	39
1946–51	160	129	31

(continues)

(continued)

	IRELAND	IRISH REPUBLIC	NORTHERN IRELAND
1951–61	494	405	89
1961–71	186	129	57
1971–81	0	-108	108
1981–91	259	210	49
1991–2001	-115	-122	7
2001–11	-386	-349	-37

Source: John Fitzgerald, 'Irish Demography since 1740' in Eugenio F. Biagini and Mary E. Daly (eds.), The Cambridge Social History of Modern Ireland *(Cambridge, 2017), 23.*

Note: Since all figures are rounded to the nearest thousand, the total for the whole island is not always the exact sum of the figure for the two jurisdictions.

5. *The Diaspora*

Statistics on the number of Irish-born living in the United States, the main emigrant destination, are available in the ten-yearly American census.

IRISH-BORN POPULATION OF THE UNITED STATES 1850–1970

(THOUSANDS)

1850	962
1860	1,612
1870	1,856
1880	1,855
1890	1,872
1900	1,615
1910	1,352
1920	1,037
1930	924
1940	678
1950	520
1960	406
1970	291

Source: United States Census Bureau, Bicentennial Edition: Historical Statistics of the United States, Colonial Times to 1970 *(Washington, 1975), 117–8.*

Another useful way of seeing the diaspora in numerical terms is to look at the distribution of Irish-born people round the main emigrant destinations in 1891, the high point, in numerical terms, of the Irish diaspora.

NUMBER OF IRISH-BORN IN IRELAND AND IN THE MAIN EMIGRANT DESTINATIONS IN 1891, WITH THE PERCENTAGE OF IRISH-BORN IN THE POPULATION OF EACH REGION

(THOUSANDS)

IRELAND	GREAT BRITAIN	USA	CANADA	AUSTRALIA
NUMBER				
4,581	653	1,872	149	229
IRISH-BORN AS A PERCENTAGE OF THE LOCAL POPULATION				
97	2.0	3.0	3.1	7.2
% OF EX-PATRIATE IRISH-BORN IN EACH REGION				
	23	64	5	8

Source: NHI, VI, *640.*

Note: The original table includes among the 'migratory Irish' those living in Ireland but outside their native county. Hence the percentages in the final line differ from those in NHI, VI.

FURTHER READING

On Every Tide is a hybrid work. Where necessary, it draws on contemporary newspapers, reports, letters and diaries to flesh out the narrative with concrete detail and examples of individual experience. But the overall picture it presents rests firmly on the detailed research of several generations of historians. Since it is not a book aimed at an academic audience it does not give detailed references for well-known facts and generally accepted interpretations. However the Notes give the source of quotations, statistics, views attributable to a particular writer, and unusual or less well-known facts. The purpose of this short bibliographical note is to provide a starting point for readers who wish to explore some or all of the topics dealt with in more detail.

The Irish diaspora, as was emphasised in the introduction, was part of a much broader redistribution of population. This context is well covered in Walter Nugent, *Crossings: The Great Transatlantic Migrations, 1870–1914* (Bloomington, 1992) and R. L. Cohn, *Mass Migration, Under Sail: European Immigration to the Antebellum United States* (Cambridge, 2009). Kevin Kenny, *Diaspora: A Very Short Introduction* (Oxford, 2013) is a valuable review of a central concept.

For an analysis of the Irish background to the beginnings of mass migration, William Forbes Adams, *Ireland and Irish Emigration to the New World* (New Haven, 1932, reprinted Baltimore,

1993) remains invaluable. For later periods see T. W. Guinnane, *The Vanishing Irish: Households, Migration and the Rural Economy in Ireland, 1850–1914* (Princeton, 1997) and Mary Daly, *The Slow Failure: Population Decline and Independent Ireland, 1920–1973* (Madison, 2006), and for recent decades Bryan Fanning, *Migration and the Making of Ireland* (Dublin, 2018). For Northern Ireland see Johanne Devlin Trew, *Leaving the North: Migration and Memory, Northern Ireland* (Liverpool, 2014).

D. H. Akenson, *The Irish Diaspora: A Primer* (Belfast and Toronto, 1993) is a short, deliberately provocative comparative survey of the major Irish emigrant destinations. The only other attempt at a comprehensive overview is Tim Pat Coogan, *Wherever Green Is Worn: The Story of the Irish Diaspora* (London, 2000), a highly personal blend of travelogue, journalism and historical narrative. Malcolm Campbell, *Ireland's New Worlds: Immigrants, Politics and Society in the United States and Australia, 1815–1922* (Madison, 2008) and Cian T. McMahon, *The Global Dimensions of Irish Identity: Race, Nation and the Popular Press, 1840-1880* (Chapel Hill, 2015) are more focussed exercises in comparison between Australia and the United States. William Jenkins, *Between Raid and Rebellion: The Irish in Buffalo and Toronto, 1867–1916* (Montreal and Kingston, 2013) offers a comparative study of a different kind.

For the Irish in the United States, Kevin Kenny's *The American Irish: A History* (Harlow, 2000) has deservedly established itself as the standard introductory survey. In comparison, Jay Dolan's *The Irish Americans: A History* (New York, 2008), more selective and lighter in tone but informed throughout by sound historical scholarship, has perhaps been unfairly overlooked. Timothy J. Meagher, *The Columbia Guide to Irish American History* (New York, 2005) is another valuable resource. J. J. Lee and Marion R. Casey (eds.), *Making the Irish American: History and Heritage of the Irish in the United States* (New York, 2006) is a wide-ranging collection of essays that also includes a long review of the way in which writing on the subject has developed over time. James R. Barrett, *The Irish Way: Becoming Irish in the Multiethnic City* (New York, 2013) is a superb study of the relationship between the Irish and other immigrant groups in the late nineteenth and early twentieth-century city. An older work, K. A. Miller's *Emigrants and Exiles: Ireland and the Irish Exodus to North America* (Oxford, 1985) remains valuable for the wealth of detail it contains, although there is now much scepticism about its thesis that the lives of the Irish in America were shaped and constrained by a distinctive premodern mentality that they carried with them across the Atlantic.

Some of the most important work on the American Irish has been in studies of particular cities. Outstanding examples from more recent years are Tyler Anbinder's vivid account of a celebrated New York district in *Five Points: The 19th Century New York City Neighborhood That Invented Tap Dance, Stole Elections, and Became the World's Most Notorious Slum* (New York, 2001), and T. J. Meagher's *Inventing Irish America: Generation, Class and Ethnic Identity in a New England City, 1880–1928* (Notre Dame, 2001) on Worcester, Massachusetts. David Emmons, *Beyond the American Pale: The Irish in the West, 1845–1910* (Norman, OK, 2010) explores a region often neglected in studies of Irish America. For the largest Irish-American community the best starting point is R. H. Bayor and T. J. Meagher (eds.), *The New York Irish* (Baltimore, 1996). Michael Glazier (ed.), *The Encyclopedia of the Irish in America* (Notre Dame, 1999) is uneven but includes much valuable information.

For the political history of Irish America, David Brundage, *Irish Nationalists in America: The Politics of Exile, 1798–1998* (Oxford, 2016) is a comprehensive overview. Kevin Kenny, *Making Sense of the Molly Maguires* (Oxford, 1998) and Gillian O'Brien's *Blood Runs Green: The Murder That Transfixed Gilded Age Chicago* (Chicago, 2015) are revealing reconstructions of two dramatic episodes.

For Canada the best starting point remains C. J. Houston and W. J. Smyth, *Irish Emigration and Canadian Settlement: Patterns,*

Links and Letters (Toronto, 1990). Protestant politics are explored in W. J. Smyth, *Toronto: The Belfast of Canada: The Orange Order and the Shaping of Municipal Culture* (Toronto, 2015). David Wilson's two-volume biography *Thomas D'Arcy McGee* (Montreal and Kingston, 2008–11) examines a key figure in Irish Catholic public life. Mark G. McGowan, *The Waning of the Green: Catholics, the Irish and Identity in Toronto* (Montreal and Kingston, 1999) and *The Imperial Irish: Canada's Irish Catholics Fight the Great War, 1914–1918* (Montreal and Kingston, 2017) take the story forward into the early twentieth century.

The standard history of the Irish in Australia remains Patrick O'Farrell, *The Irish in Australia, 1788 to the Present* (3rd ed. Sydney, 2000). Elizabeth Malcolm and Diane Hall, *A New History of the Irish in Australia* (Sydney, 2018) sets out to supplement rather than replace O'Farrell's narrative by looking more closely at issues of race, ethnic stereotyping and gender. By far the best introduction to the many faces of Irish Australia, however, is David Fitzpatrick's magnificent *Oceans of Consolation: Personal Accounts of Irish Migration to Australia* (Cork, 1994), where meticulous background research transforms some quite ordinary sequences of family letters into vivid case studies.

For New Zealand, D. H. Akenson, *Half the World from Home: Perspectives on the Irish in New Zealand* (Wellington, 1990) is a pioneering survey. Angela McCarthy, *Irish Migrants in New Zealand, 1840–1937* (Woodbridge, 2005) focusses more narrowly on the attitudes and responses revealed in emigrant letters. For politics there is a detailed study by Richard Davis, *Irish Issues in New Zealand Politics, 1868–1922* (Dunedin, 1974).

For lesser emigrant destinations see Donal P. McCracken (ed.), *The Irish in Southern Africa, 1795–1910* (Durban, 1992) and Patrick Speight, *Irish-Argentine Identity in an Age of Political Challenge and Change, 1875–1983* (Oxford and New York, 2019). For the Irish in Great Britain the best introduction is Don MacRaild, *The*

Irish Diaspora in Britain, 1750-1939 (Basingstoke, 2010) and Enda Delaney, *The Irish in Post-War Britain* (Oxford, 2013).

Accounts of the recent past are inevitably provisional, liable to revision as new information emerges and long-term trends become clearer. Andrew Sanders, *The Long Peace Process: The United States of America and Northern Ireland, 1960–2008* (Liverpool, 2019) is the fullest narrative so far available. Mary-Alice C. Clancy, *Peace Without Consensus: Power Sharing Politics in Northern Ireland* (Farnham, Surrey, 2010) is a more focussed study, notable for the wide range of interviews with mostly anonymous British, American and Irish officials. Feargal Cochrane, *The End of Irish America? Globalisation and the Irish Diaspora* (Dublin, 2010) is a first attempt to assess the impact of Ireland's economic and cultural transformation on the country's place in the world.

NOTES

Abbreviations

IED: Irish Emigration Database, an extensive collection of emigrant letters and other documents, available at www.dippam.ac.uk/ied.

Miller Center: The Presidential Oral History Program archives oral history interviews of US presidents from Jimmy Carter to George W. Bush, as well as of Senator Edward Kennedy, Miller Center, University of Virginia. Available at Miller Center.org.

NHI: *A New History of Ireland, Vol. V: Ireland Under the Union I 1801–70* (Oxford, 1989), ed. W. E. Vaughan; *A New History of Ireland, Vol. VI: Ireland Under the Union II 1870–1921* (Oxford, 1996), ed. W. E. Vaughan.

PP: British Parliamentary Papers, a collection of reports by committees and other printed documents laid before the Houses of Parliament. Papers are identified by the year, the paper number, and the volume in which they appear, e.g., 1825 (509) 16. Sets are available in academic libraries and, to subscribers, in digitized form at https://parlipapers.proquest.com/parlipapers.

PRONI: Public Record Office of Northern Ireland, Belfast.

1. Diaspora

1. Mary Durack, *Kings in Grass Castles* (London, 1985), 19; Frances Devlin-Glass, 'The Irish in Grass Castles: Re-reading Victim Tropes in an Iconic Pioneering Text', in L. M. Geary and A. J. McCarthy (eds.), *Ireland, Australia and New Zealand: History, Politics and Culture* (Dublin, 2008), 104–18; Margaret Mitchell, *Gone with the Wind* (New York, 1973), 38–9, 44, 46, 51.

2. D. H. Akenson, *The Irish Diaspora: A Primer* (Belfast and Toronto, 1993), 69, 113, 263. All statistics on emigration are to some extent approximations, if not guesses. For the main sources, and the figures they seem to indicate, see Appendix.

3. *Report on the State of the Irish Poor in Great Britain* (PP 1836 (40) 34), iv, xxxvii.

4. Adam McKeown, 'Global Migration, 1846–1940', *Journal of World History*, 15/2 (2004), 155–89; Walter Nugent, *Crossings: The Great Transatlantic Migrations, 1870–1914* (Bloomington, 1995), chap. 12–3; John Berger and Jean Mohr, *A Seventh Man: Migrant Workers in Europe* (London, 1975), 16; Peter Gatrell, *The Unsettling of Europe: The Great Migration, 1945 to the Present* (London, 2019).

5. David Brion Davis, *Inhuman Bondage: The Rise and Fall of Slavery in the New World* (Oxford, 2006), 80, 124–31; Emma Christopher, Cassandra Pybus and Marcus Rediker (eds.), *Many Middle Passages: Forced Migration and the Making of the Modern World* (Berkeley and Los Angeles, 2007).

6. Karl Marx, *Capital: A Critical Analysis of Capitalist Production*, chap. 25, section 5,C; Patrick Speight, *Irish-Argentine Identity in an Age of Political Challenge and Change, 1875–1983* (Oxford/New York, 2019), 80.

7. Judy Collingwood, 'Irish Workhouse Children in Australia' in John O'Brien and Pauric Travers (eds.), *The Irish Emigrant Experience in Australia* (Swords, Co. Dublin, 1991), 49; K. P. T. Tankard, 'Drama and Disappointment: The *Lady Kennaway* Girls', in D. P. McCracken (ed.), *The Irish in Southern Africa, 1795–1910* (Durban, 1992), 278–86.

8. Kevin Kenny, 'Diaspora and Comparison: The Global Irish as a Case Study', *Journal of American History*, 90/1 (2003), 134–62; Enda Delaney, Kevin Kenny and Donald MacRaild, 'Symposium: Perspectives on the Irish Diaspora', *Irish Economic & Social History*, 33 (2006), 35–58; Liam Kennedy, *Unhappy the Land: The Most Oppressed People Ever, the Irish* (Sallins, Co. Kildare, 2013).

2. The Beginning of Mass Migration

1. All estimates of Irish emigration in the eighteenth century rely heavily on guesswork. For a recent summary see Patrick Griffin, '"Irish" Migration to America in the Eighteenth Century? Or the Strange Case of the "Scots/Irish"', in James Kelly (ed.), *The Cambridge History of Ireland, Vol. 3: 1730–1880* (Cambridge, 2018), 596. For the period after 1783 see M. A. Jones, 'Ulster Emigration, 1783–1815', in E. R. R. Green (ed.), *Essays in Scotch-Irish History* (London, 1969), 46–68. For problems with the much-quoted analysis of the 1790 census see D. H. Akenson, *Being Had: Historians, Evidence and the Irish in North America* (Ontario, 1985), chap. 2.

2. J. D. Post, *The Last Great Subsistence Crisis in the Western World* (Baltimore, 1977), 98–107; *Belfast Newsletter*, 12 September 1817. For statistics on emigration after 1825 see Appendix. For the earlier figures, estimates based on less complete data, W. F. Adams, *Ireland and Irish Emigration to the New World: From 1815 to the Famine* (New Haven, 1932), 421–2, 426.

3. Cormac Ó Gráda, 'Across the Briny Ocean: Some Thoughts on Irish Emigration to America, 1800–1850' in T. M. Devine and David Dickson (eds.), *Ireland and Scotland, 1600–1850* (Edinburgh, 1983); Adams, *Ireland and Irish Emigration*, 119–20, 187–96.

4. Joel Mokyr and Cormac Ó Gráda, 'Poor and Getting Poorer? Living Standards in Ireland Before the Famine', *Economic History Review*, 61/2 (1988); Cormac Ó Gráda, *Ireland: A New Economic History 1780–1939* (Oxford, 1994), 80–5; *First Report of His Majesty's Commissioners for Inquiring into the Condition of the Poorer Classes of Ireland* [hereafter *Poor Enquiry*], Supplement to Appendix F (PP 1836 (39) 34), 269; Anderson family correspondence (PRONI D1859, reproduced in IED).

5. *Census of Ireland, 1841* (PP 1843 (504) 24), xxxvi; Garret Fitzgerald, 'The Decline of the Irish Language 1771–1871', in Mary Daly and David Dickson (eds.), *The*

Origins of Popular Literacy in Ireland: Language Change and Educational Develop-ment 1700–1920 (Dublin, 1990), 72.

6. Fergus O'Ferrall, *Catholic Emancipation: Daniel O'Connell and the Birth of Irish Democracy, 1820–30* (Dublin, 1987); S. J. Connolly, *Priests and People in Pre-Famine Ireland, 1780–1845* (Dublin, 1981).

7. *Evidence Taken Before Her Majesty's Commission on the Occupation of Land in Ireland,* Part 2 (PP 1845 (616) 20), 959; *Report on the State of the Irish Poor in Great Britain* (PP 1836 (40) 34), 32.

8. B. S. Elliott, *Irish Migrants in the Canadas: A New Approach* (2nd ed. Montreal and Kingston, 2010); Helen Cowan, *British Emigration to British North America: The First Hundred Years* (revised ed. Toronto, 1961), 65–84. For the survival of Robin-son's settlements see D. H. Akenson, *The Irish in Ontario: A Study in Rural History* (2nd ed. Montreal and Kingston, 1999), 40–1.

9. For the Caulfield estate, Cowan, *British Emigration*, 214–5. For the other fig-ures on landlord assistance see David Fitzpatrick in *NHI, V,* 615. For arrears of rent, *Poor Enquiry,* Supplement to Appendix F, 177.

10. Adams, *Ireland and Irish Emigration*, 161–2; *Poor Enquiry*, Appendix F (PP 1836 (38) 33), 133.

11. Based on lists of passengers arriving at New York during 1820–48 and Boston during 1822–39, analysed in Ó Gráda, 'Across the Briny Ocean', 119–20, 123–4.

12. Charlotte J. Erickson, 'Emigration from the British Isles to the U.S.A. in 1841: Part 1. Emigration from the British Isles', *Population Studies*, 43 (1989), 360–1; *Commission on the Occupation of Land*, 91, 315.

13. Adams, *Ireland and Irish Emigration*, 222; *Poor Enquiry*, Appendix F, 134; *Report of the Select Committee on the Operation of the Passenger Acts* (PP 1851 (632) 19), 619–20.

14. Oliver MacDonagh, *A Pattern of Government Growth, 1800–1860: The Pas-senger Acts and their Enforcement* (London, 1961), 49, 148. For the Irish sea crossing see *Captain Denham's Report on Passenger Accommodation in Steamers Between Ire-land and Liverpool* (PP 1849 (339) 51), and for general accounts of sailing conditions M. A. Jones, 'Transatlantic Steerage Conditions from Sail to Steam, 1819–1920', in Brigid Flemming Larsen et al. (eds.), *On Distant Shores* (Aalborg, Denmark, 1993); Philip Taylor, *The Distant Magnet: European Emigration to the USA* (London, 1971), chap. 7. Steerage was so called because the cables connecting the helm to the rudder ran through this part of the ship.

15. *Second Report of the Select Committee on Emigration from the United King-dom* (PP 1826–7 (237) 5), 74, evidence of A. C. Buchanan; Raymond Cohn, *Mass Migration Under Sail: European Immigration to the Antebellum United States* (Cam-bridge, 2009), 149. For the supposed 'coffin ships' of the Famine era see above pp 59-60.

16. C. P. Lucas (ed.), *Lord Durham's Report on the Affairs of British North America* (3 vols, Oxford, 1912), ii, 212–7; C. J. Houston and W. J. Smyth, *Irish Emigration and Canadian Settlement: Patterns, Links and Letters* (Toronto, 1990), 25–6.

17. *Report on the Affairs of British North America, Appendix B* (PP 1839 (3–III) 17), 114. For the census of 1871 see above pp 264-5.

18. *Emigration: Report of Commissioners* (PP 1831–2 (724) 32), 22. For Irish settlement in urban Canada in this period see Robert Grace, 'Irish Immigration and Settlement in a Catholic City: Quebec, 1842–61', *Canadian Historical Review*, 84/2 (2003), 217–51; Lucille Campey, *Ontario and Quebec's Irish Pioneers: Farmers, Labourers and Lumberjacks* (Toronto, 2018), 53–4, 89–91; Andrew Holman, '"Different Feelings": Corktown and the Catholic Irish in Early Hamilton, 1832–47', *Canadian Journal of Irish Studies*, 23/1 (1997), 41–66.

19. *Report on the Affairs of British North America, Appendix B*, 67. For sectarian clashes see Michael S. Cross, '"The Shiners" War: Social Violence in the Ottawa Valley in the 1830s', *Canadian Historical Review*, 54/1 (1973), 1–26; Jane G. V. McGaughey, *Violent Loyalties: Manliness, Migration and the Irish in the Canadas, 1798–1841* (Liverpool, 2020), 135–66; above p. 269.

20. Anderson Letters (PRONI D1859, reproduced in IED). For the background to this family's emigration see above p. 21.

21. Joseph Schafer (ed.), *Memoirs of Jeremiah Curtin*, (Madison, 1940), 31–40.

22. Raymond Cohn, *Mass Migration Under Sail: European Immigration to the Antebellum United States* (Cambridge, 2009), 170. The case for not underestimating Irish rural settlement in the period before 1845 is effectively made by David Doyle, in *NHI, V*, 709–11.

23. Graham Hodges, '"Desirable Companions and Lovers": Irish and African Americans in the Sixth Ward, 1830–70', in Ronald H. Bayor and Timothy J. Meagher (eds.), *The New York Irish* (Baltimore and London, 1996), 110; Peter Way, *Common Labour: Workers and the Digging of North American Canals 1780–1860* (Cambridge, 1993); William Jenkins, *Between Raid and Rebellion: The Irish in Buffalo and Toronto, 1867–1916* (Montreal and Kingston, 2013), 86, 88. It is not possible to quantify this shifting balance between rural and urban Irish settlement. Studies suggesting that already by 1845 most immigrants were joining the urban working class generally draw on statistics from the 1850s, which of course include the great mass of economic refugees arriving during the Famine.

24. Robert Ernst, *Immigrant Life in New York City* (Port Washington, NY, 1949), 66; Brian C. Mitchell, *The Paddy Camps: The Irish of Lowell, 1821–61* (Urbana and Chicago, 1988).

25. G. B. Dickason, *Irish Settlers to the Cape: History of the Clanwilliam 1820 Settlers from Cork Harbour* (Cape Town, 1973), 67. See also W. J. Forgrave, 'The 1820 Irish Settlement at Clanwilliam, Northwestern Cape' in D. P. McCracken (ed.), *The Irish in Southern Africa, 1795–1910* (Durban, 1992).

26. Stephen Nicholas (ed.), *Convict Workers: Reinterpreting Australia's Past* (Cambridge, 1988), 45–7. The older idea that most convicts had been transported for acts of social or political rebellion had already been rejected by A. G. L. Shaw, *Convicts and the Colonies: A Study of Penal Transportation from Great Britain and Ireland to Australia and Other Parts of the British Empire* (New York, 1966, Melbourne, 1977); George Rudé, *Protest and Punishment: The Story of the Social and Political Prisoners Transported to Australia, 1788–1868* (Oxford, 1978). For statistics on convict numbers see Patrick O'Farrell, *The Irish in Australia: 1798 to the Present* (3rd ed. Sydney, 2000), 23, 36.

27. Bob Reece (ed.), *Exiles from Erin: Convict Lives in Ireland and Australia* (Dublin, 1991), 151–70, 139–40; Rudé, *Protest and Punishment*, 5. For convict women see Elizabeth Rushen and Perry McIntyre, *Fair Game: Australia's First Immigrant Women* (Spit Junction, NSW, 2010); Deborah Oxley, *Convict Maids: The Forced Migration of Women to Australia* (Cambridge, 1996).

28. Rushen and McIntyre, *Fair Game*, 14, 80, 83; R. B. Madgwick, *Emigration into Eastern Australia* (Sydney, 1969), 234; John McDonald and Eric Richards, 'The Great Emigration of 1841: Recruitment for New South Wales in British Emigration Fields', *Population Studies*, 51/3 (1997), 337–55; Ralph Mansfield, *Analytical View of the Census of New South Wales for the Year 1846* (Sydney, 1847), 104.

29. Graham Davis, *Land! Irish Pioneers in Mexican and Revolutionary Texas* (College Station, TX, 2002).

30. Patrick McKenna, 'Irish Migration to Argentina' in Patrick O'Sullivan (ed.), *The Irish World Wide, Vol. 1: Patterns of Migration* (Leicester, 1992), 63–83; Tim Fanning, *Don Juan O'Brien: An Irish Adventurer in Nineteenth-Century South America* (Cork, 2020), 46–57. Some of the details in McKenna's account are corrected in Patrick Speight, *Irish-Argentine Identity in an Age of Political Challenge and Change, 1875–1983* (Oxford/New York, 2019), 43–53.

31. Edmundo Murray, 'The Irish Road to Argentina', *History Ireland*, 12/3 (2004), 29; Helen Kelly, *Irish 'Ingleses': The Irish Immigrant Experience in Argentina, 1840–1920* (Dublin, 2009), 53–5. There is no reliable figure for the Irish population, because Argentine records list all immigrants from the British Isles as *Inglés*. The figure of 30,000 is quoted in McKenna, 'Irish Migration to Argentina', 80. It is broadly compatible with a report by the archbishop of Buenos Aires fifteen years later that there were 28,000 Irish in Argentina. An alternative estimate suggests a much lower figure of 5,246 Irish-born and 3,377 Argentinian-born in 1869. But this is derived from incomplete listings, using a combination of surnames and religious denomination to identify the Irish. See Kelly, *Irish 'Ingleses'*, 43–52.

3. Flight from Famine

1. The literature on the Famine is very large. For an excellent recent overview see Ciarán Ó Murchadha, *The Great Famine: Ireland's Agony 1845–52* (London, 2011). For the last recorded death from starvation see Ó Murchadha, *The Great Famine*, 177–8.

2. *Daily News*, reprinted in *Irish Examiner*, 11 September 1848. The complex chronology of emigration in these first Famine years is picked apart in Oliver Mac-Donagh's 'Irish Emigration to the United States of America and the British Colonies During the Famine' in R. D. Edwards and T. D. Williams (eds.), *The Great Famine: Studies in Irish History, 1845–52* (New York, 1956), 319–27.

3. For shifts in government thinking see Peter Gray, *Famine, Land and Politics: British Government and Irish Society, 1843–50* (Dublin, 1999), 232, 238–9, 279, 299.

4. Gerard Moran, *Sending out Ireland's Poor: Assisted Emigration to North America in the Nineteenth Century* (Dublin, 2004), chap. 3.

5. J. S. Donnelly in *NHI, V*, 337; MacDonagh, 'Irish Emigration', 332–40; Moran, *Sending out Ireland's Poor*, chap. 2. For landlords see also Tyler Anbinder,

'Lord Palmerston and the Irish Famine Emigration', *Historical Journal*, 44/2 (2001), 441–69; Desmond Norton, 'Lord Palmerston and the Irish Famine Emigration: A Rejoinder', *Historical Journal*, 46/1 (2003), 155–65; Emily Slinger, 'From Sligo to St John's: The Gore-Booth Assisted Emigration Scheme 1847', in Graham Davis (ed.), *In Search of a Better Life: British and Irish Migration* (Stroud, 2011).

6. K. A. Miller, *Emigrants and Exiles: Ireland and the Irish Exodus to North America* (New York, 1985), 295. For the geography of Famine emigration two main sources are available. S. H. Cousens's pioneering study, 'The Regional Pattern of Emigration During the Great Irish Famine, 1846–51', in *Transactions of the Institute of British Geographers*, 28 (1960) mapped population loss between 1841 and 1851 minus recorded mortality. Tyler Anbinder and Hope McCaffrey, 'Which Irish Men and Women Immigrated to the United States During the Great Famine Migration of 1846–54?', *Irish Historical Studies*, 39/156 (2015), offers an analysis based on 18,000 immigrants arriving in New York.

7. *Papers Relative to Emigration to the British Provinces of North America* (PP 1847 (777) 39), 26–7; Francis Costello, 'The Deer Island Graves, Boston: The Irish Famine and Irish-American Tradition' in Patrick O'Sullivan (ed.), *The Irish World Wide: History, Heritage, Identity, Vol. 5, The Meaning of the Famine* (London, 2000), 121; *Papers Relative to Emigration to the British Provinces of North America* (PP 1847–8 (964) 47), 13–15; Cowan, *British Emigration to British North America*, 163–4.

8. *Captain Denham's Report on Passenger Accommodation in Steamers Between Ireland and Liverpool* (PP 1849 (339) 51). For the *Londonderry*, Frank Neal, *Black '47: Britain and the Famine Irish* (Basingstoke, 1998), 73–4.

9. Terry Coleman, *Passage to America* (London, 1972), 205–17; MacDonagh, *Pattern of Government Growth*, 225; *Report of the Select Committee on the Operation of the Passenger Acts* (PP 1851 (632) 19), 484.

10. *A Letter to the Colonial Land and Emigration Committees Detailing Treatment of Passengers on Board Emigrant Ship* 'Washington' (PP 1851 (198) 40), 5; *Select Committee on the Operation of the Passenger Acts*, 428, 491.

11. *Select Committee on the Operation of the Passenger Acts*, 409; *A Letter to the Colonial Land and Emigration Committees*, 5.

12. *Papers Relative to Emigration to the British Provinces of North America* (PP 1847–8 (932) 47), 14; (PP 1847–8 (964) 47), 16–17.

13. Reports of Chief Medical Officer George Douglas, 17, 29, 31 May 1847, in *Journal of the Legislative Assembly of the Province of Canada, Vol. 6: Session 1847* (Montreal, 1847), Appendix L, unpaginated; Marianna O'Gallagher and Rose Masson Dompierre, *Eyewitness Grosse Isle 1847* (Quebec, 1995), 325. See also Marianna O'Gallagher, *Grosse Ile: Gateway to Canada 1832–1937* (Quebec, 1984); Donald McKay, *Flight from Famine: The Coming of the Irish to Canada* (Toronto, 1990), chaps. 14–15.

14. *Papers Relative to Emigration to the British Provinces of North America* (PP 1847–8 (971) 47), 50; McKay, *Flight from Famine*, 291.

15. Maude Charest-Auger, 'Les Réactions Montréalaises á l'Epidémie de Typhus de 1847' (MA Thesis, University du Quebec á Montréal, 2012), www.archipel .uqam.ca/4645/1/M12336.pdf (accessed 8 December 2016), 112 and Appendix D;

Papers Relative to Emigration to the British Provinces of North America (PP 1847–8 (971) 47), 50.

16. A. L. Geston and T. C. Jones, 'Typhus Fever: Report of an Epidemic in New York City in 1847', *Journal of Infectious Diseases*, 136/6 (1977), 816, 820; Costello, 'The Deer Island Graves', 119.

17. For 'coffin ships' see David A. Wilson, *Thomas D'Arcy McGee, Vol. 1: Passion, Reason and Politics, 1825–1857* (Montreal and Kingston, 2008), 192; Cian T. McMahon, 'Tracking the Great Famine's "Coffin Ships" Across the Digital Deep', *Éire-Ireland*, 56/1–2 (2021), 81–109. For mortality statistics Cian T. McMahon, *The Coffin Ship: Life and Death at Sea During the Great Irish Famine* (New York, 2021), 151–8; *Papers Relative to Emigration to the British Provinces of North America* (PP 1847–8 (971) 47), 50; *Papers Relative to Emigration to the British Provinces of North America* (PP 1847–8 (932) 47), 4–5; Raymond Cohn, *Mass Migration Under Sail: European Immigration to the Antebellum United States* (Cambridge, 2009), 137–52; Cormac Ó Gráda, *Black '47 and Beyond: The Great Irish Famine* (Princeton, 1999), 106–7; MacDonagh, *Pattern of Government Growth*, 213.

18. The widely quoted figure of 200,000–300,000 emigrants to Great Britain seems to originate with Miller, *Emigrants and Exiles*, 291.

19. Neal, *Black '47*, 62, 160, 177–9, 280; Lewis Darwen et al., '"Irish Fever" in Britain During the Great Famine: Disease and the Legacy of 'Black '47', *Irish Historical Studies*, 44/166 (2020), 270–94.

20. Margaret Slocomb, *Among Australia's Pioneers: Chinese Indentured Pastoral Workers on the Northern Frontier 1848–c. 1880* (Bloomington, IN, 2014), 74.

21. MacDonagh, 'Irish Emigration', 358–9.

22. Trevor McClaughlin, 'Lost Children? Irish Famine Orphans in Australia', *History Ireland*, 8/4 (2000), 31, 33.

23. Trevor McClaughlin, *Barefoot and Pregnant: Irish Famine Orphans in Australia* (Melbourne, 1991); Moran, *Sending out Ireland's Poor*, 129–32.

24. Miller, *Emigrants and Exiles*, 506–20; Patrick O'Farrell, 'Lost in Transit: Australian Reaction to the Irish and Scots Famines, 1845–50', in O'Sullivan (ed.), *The Meaning of the Famine*; Perry McIntyre, 'The Irish in Australia: Remembering and Commemorating the Great Famine', in Ciarán Reilly (ed.), *The Famine Irish: Emigration and the Great Hunger* (Dublin, 2016), 181–92. For the campaign to push Ireland into the genocide curriculum see above p. 417.

25. Michael Quigley, 'Languages of Memory: Jeremiah Gallagher and the Grosse Île Famine Monument' in Reilly (ed.), *The Famine Irish*, 209–22.

26. The Registrar General, whose figures on overall emigration are cited elsewhere, did not begin to record emigrant destinations until 1876. These are the figures compiled around 1950 for an Irish government report, using returns from the Colonial Land and Emigration Department and the Board of Trade: *Reports of the Commission on Emigration and Other Population Problems 1948–54* (Dublin, 1954), 314. For the influence of nativism see Raymond L. Cohn, 'Nativism and the End of the Mass Migration of the 1840s and 1850s', *Journal of Economic History*, 60/2 (2000), 361–83.

27. For a recent overview of the post-Famine economy see Andy Bielenberg, 'The Irish Economy, 1815–1880: Agricultural Transition, the Communications Revolution and the Limits of Industrialisation', in James Kelly (ed.), *The Cambridge History of Ireland, Vol. 3: 1730–1880* (Cambridge, 2018), 179–203. For the long-term impact of blight see Peter Solar, 'The Great Famine Was No Ordinary Subsistence Crisis', in E. M. Crawford (ed.), *Famine: The Irish Experience 900–1900* (Edinburgh, 1989), 112–33. For farm size see J. S. Donnelly, *The Great Irish Potato Famine* (Stroud, 2001), 161; L. P. Curtis in *NHI, VI*, 148.

28. The classic account of the Irish matchmaking system is K. H. Connell, 'Catholicism and Marriage in the Century After the Famine' in *Irish Peasant Society* (Oxford, 1968). See also Liam Kennedy, 'Farm Succession in Modern Ireland: Elements of a Theory of Inheritance', *Economic History Review*, 44/3 (1991), 477–99; Timothy W. Guinnane, *The Vanishing Irish: Households, Migration and the Rural Economy in Ireland 1850–1914* (Princeton, NJ, 1997), 133–65.

29. This is the argument of Guinnane, *The Vanishing Irish*.

30. Miller, *Emigrants and Exiles*, 453–69.

31. Sarah Roddy, *Population, Providence and Empire: The Churches and Emigration from Nineteenth-Century Ireland* (Manchester, 2014), 44.

32. Guinnane, *The Vanishing Irish*, 133–65; Margaret Lynch-Brennan, *The Irish Bridget: Irish Immigrant Women in Domestic Service in America, 1840–1930* (Syracuse, NY, 2009), 27.

33. *Irish Examiner*, 20 April 1866; *Reports with Regard to the Accommodation and Treatment of Emigrants on Board Atlantic Steam Ships* (PP 1881 (c. 2995) 82), 32, 34; Regina Donlon, *German and Irish Immigrants in the Midwestern United States, 1850–1900* (London, 2018), 42–3. For the American wake see also Arnold Schrier, *Ireland and the American Emigration, 1850–1900* (Chester Springs, PA, 1997); Miller, *Emigrants and Exiles*, 557–60.

34. E. E. Griggs to John Orr, 8 November 1850; John Orr to E. E. Griggs, 22 January 1851 (IED). For John Orr's American career see above p. 105.

4. Castle Garden and Beyond

1. Angus Maddison, *Contours of the World Economy, 1–2030 AD* (Oxford, 2007), 379, Table A4. If we add the territories that later became Italy and Germany, the United States slips to ninth place.

2. John Killick, 'Transatlantic Steerage Fares, British and Irish Migration and Return Migration, 1815–60', *Economic History Review*, 67/1 (2014), 170–91; K. Theodore Hoppen, *Elections, Politics and Society in Ireland 1832–85* (Oxford, 1984), 100, 113; *Irish Examiner*, 20 April 1866. For remittances see Arnold Schrier, *Ireland and the American Emigration, 1850–1900* (Chester Springs, PA, 1997), 103–12.

3. *Cork Examiner*, 19 October 1857, reprinted from the *Morning Herald*; *Eighteenth Report of the Emigration Commissioners*, 1858 (PP 1857–8 (c. 2395) 24), 15–17; John Anderson to Jane Anderson, 10 July 1857 (IED).

4. Raymond L. Cohn, 'The Transition from Sail to Steam in Immigration to the United States', *Journal of Economic History*, 65/2 (2005), 469–95.

5. *Reports with Regard to the Accommodation and Treatment of Emigrants on Board Atlantic Steam Ships* (PP 1881 (c. 2995) 82); Friedrich Kapp, *Immigration and the Commissioners of Emigration of the State of New York* (New York, 1870), 38.

6. *Reports with Regard to Accommodation and Treatment*, 13.

7. *Cork Constitution* in *Kerry Evening Post*, 18 April 1860; *Irish Examiner*, 20 April 1866; *Reports with Regard to the Accommodation and Treatment*, 6; Robert Gavin, W. P. Kelly and Dolores O'Reilly, *Atlantic Gateway: The Port and City of Londonderry Since 1700* (Dublin, 2009), 99–104.

8. *Report of the Select Committee Appointed by the Legislature of New York, to Examine into Frauds upon Emigrants: 1847* (Albany, 1847), 85–122; Kapp, *Immigration and the Commissioners of Emigration*, 111–15.

9. 'An Hour in Castle Garden', *New York Tribune*, 25 July 1867.

10. Hidetaka Hirota, *Expelling the Poor: Atlantic Seaboard States and the Nineteenth-Century Origins of American Immigration Policy* (New York, 2017), 56, 77, 127, 144, 216.

11. Kapp, *Immigration*, 58; Hirota, *Expelling the Poor*, 115–8, 163.

12. For strong farmers 'running away with the crops' see Earl of Clarendon, Lord Lieutenant, quoted in Oliver MacDonagh, 'Irish Emigration to the United States of America and the British Colonies During the Famine' in R. D. Edwards and T. D. Williams (eds.), *The Great Famine: Studies in Irish History, 1845–52* (New York, 1956), 326; 'Emigration', *Leinster Express*, 6 October 1849; *Irish American*, quoted in Robert Ernst, *Immigrant Life in New York City, 1825–63* (Port Washington, 1965), 62; Joseph P. Ferrie, *Yankeys Now: Immigrants in the Antebellum United States, 1840–1860* (New York, 1999), 69. Greenlees's and Hanlon's letters are reprinted in Ronald Wells, *Ulster Migration to America: Letters from Three Irish Families* (New York, 1991).

13. David Noel Doyle, 'The Irish as Urban Pioneers in the United States, 1850–1870', *Journal of American Ethnic History*, 10/1–2 (1991), 36–59; *Ninth Census of the United States: Statistics of Population, Tables I to VIII* (Washington, DC,1872), 389.

14. J. F. Maguire, *The Irish in America* (New York, 1868), 220. For sponsored colonization see J. P. Shannon, *Catholic Colonization on the Western Frontier* (New Haven, 1957), and for Hughes, John Loughery, *Dagger John; Archbishop John Hughes and the Making of Irish America* (London, 2018), 267–71.

15. Shannon, *Catholic Colonization*, 59, 67–70, 107–14, 136, 167–71, 261–2.

16. Joseph Shafer, *Four Wisconsin Counties: Prairie and Forest* (Madison, 1927), 85–9; Grace McDonald, *History of the Irish in Wisconsin in the Nineteenth Century*, (New York, 1976), 11; Ann Regan, *Irish in Minnesota* (St Paul, MN, 2002), 7; Malcolm Campbell, *Ireland's New Worlds: Immigrants, Politics and Society in the United States and Australia, 1815–1922* (Madison, WI, 2008), 70–1. For the Connemara immigrants see Shannon, *Catholic Colonization*, 154–66.

17. Shannon, *Catholic Colonization*, 103–7; average wages for Massachusetts, 1874, in Stephan Thernstrom, *Poverty and Progress: Social Mobility in a Nineteenth-Century City* (New York, 1969), 94.

18. Robert Ernst, *Immigrant Life in New York City, 1825–63* (Port Washington, NY, 1963), 213, 219; Richard Stott, *Workers in the Metropolis: Class, Ethnicity and*

Youth in Antebellum New York City (Ithaca, 1990), 94; Dennis Clark, *The Irish in Philadelphia* (Philadelphia, 1973), 74–5; Oscar Handlin, *Boston's Immigrants* (Cambridge, MA, 1959), 250–1. The idea that the majority of Irish were manual labourers was comprehensively refuted by David N. Doyle in *NHI, VI*, 750–3. For comparative proportions of unskilled see Ferrie, *Yankeys Now*, 17.

19. For the phrase 'mediocre skills' see Stott, *Workers in the Metropolis*, 89. For the subdivision of shoemaking Bruce Laurie, *Artisans into Workers: Labor in Nineteenth-Century America* (Urbana and Chicago, 1989), 41. Employment statistics in Ernst, *Immigrant Life*, 216–7; Handlin, *Boston's Immigrants*, 250–1.

20. Ernst, *Immigrant Life*, 83.

21. Stott, *Workers in the Metropolis*, 128–38.

22. Internal Health Department, *Report on the Cholera in Boston in 1849* (Boston, 1850), 15; Tyler Anbinder, *Five Points: The 19th-Century New York City Neighborhood That Invented Tap Dance, Stole Elections, and Became the World's Most Notorious Slum* (New York, 2001); 'The Five Points Site', www.gsa.gov/about-us/regions /welcome-to-the-northeast-caribbean-region-2/about-region-2/five-points-site-new -york (accessed 12 March 2021).

23. Anbinder, *Five Points*, 72–91; Stott, *Workers in the Metropolis*, 169–72, 202–3, 214–22; Tyler Anbinder, *City of Dreams: The 400-Year Epic History of Immigrant New York* (Boston and New York, 2016), 149–58; Maguire, *The Irish in America*, 231–3.

24. Clark, *Irish in Philadelphia*, 40–4; Thernstrom, *Poverty and Progress*, 117–22; William Jenkins, *Between Raid and Rebellion: The Irish in Buffalo and Toronto, 1867–1916* (Montreal and Kingston, 2013), 83–4; Timothy J. Meagher, *Inventing Irish America: Generation, Class and Ethnic Identity in a New England City, 1880–1928* (Notre Dame, 2001), 60–1.

25. John Ferguson to family, 10 January 1873; Mary Anne Ferguson to Maggy Ferguson, n.d. (IED); Stott, *Workers in the Metropolis*, 173–81.

26. *Report on Population of the United States at the Eleventh Census, 1890*, Vol. 1, Part 2 (Washington, DC, 1897), cxlvii, cliv; Margaret Lynch-Brennan, *The Irish Bridget: Irish Immigrant Women in Domestic Service in America, 1840–1930* (New York, 2009), 84; Hasia R. Diner, *Erin's Daughters in America: Irish Immigrant Women in the Nineteenth Century* (Baltimore, 1983), 89.

27. Virginia F. Townsend, 'Our Irish Girls', *Arthur's Illustrated Home Magazine*, xliii (Philadelphia, 1875), 667–71; 'The Morals and Manners of the Kitchen', *The Nation*, xvi (1873), 6.

28. Lynch-Brennan, *The Irish Bridget*, 91, 130–8. For male wages in Philadelphia see John Ferguson's letters, 1 January 1872, 10 January 1873 (IED).

29. Lynch-Brennan, *The Irish Bridget*, 109–11.

30. S.C.H. 'A Cabinet Question', *Lippincott's Magazine*, 9 (March 1872), 357–9; 'The Hired Girl', *Daily Inter Ocean*, 4 October 1890.

31. Lynch-Brennan, *Irish Bridget*, 151–3.

32. Dennis Clark, 'Irish Women Workers and American Labor Patterns: The Philadelphia Story', in Patrick O'Sullivan (ed.), *The Irish World Wide, Vol. 4: Irish Women and Irish Migration* (London, 1995), 121; Ernst, *Immigrant Life in New York*,

68; Diner, *Erin's Daughters in America*, 77. For the sewing machine ('one week does to learn') see John Ferguson to Joseph and Eliza Jane, 10 May 1875 (IED).

33. 'An Hour in Castle Garden', *New York Tribune*, 25 July 1867.

34. Diner, *Erin's Daughters in America*, 106–19; Mark C. Foley and Timothy W. Guinnane, 'Did Irish Marriage Patterns Survive the Emigrant Voyage? Irish-American Nuptiality, 1880–1920', *Irish Economic and Social History*, 26 (1999), 15–34.

35. Ferrie, *Yankeys Now*, 142–5; Grace McDonald, *History of the Irish in Wisconsin in the Nineteenth Century* (New York, 1976), 106–7; Regan, *Irish in Minnesota*, 28. David M. Emmons, *Beyond the American Pale: The Irish in the West, 1845–1910* (Norman, OK, 2010) is a general survey.

36. Some of John Orr's letters are in PRONI T3103, while others, in private possession, are reproduced in IED; Letters of William Williamson and his brothers are in PRONI T2680, reproduced in IED.

37. James Walsh, 'The Irish in the New America: "Way out West"', in David Doyle and Owen Dudley Edwards (eds.), *America and Ireland, 1776–1976: The American Identity and the Irish Connection* (Westport, CT, 1980), 165–6.

38. R. A. Burchell, *The San Francisco Irish, 1848–1880* (Manchester, 1979), 8, 54–60.

39. JoEllen Vinyard, *The Irish on the Urban Frontier: Nineteenth-Century Detroit* (New York, 1976), 60–3, 314–8; Regan, *Irish in Minnesota*, 33–4; Regina Donlon, *German and Irish Immigrants in the Midwestern United States, 1850–1900* (London, 2018), 70–77; Edward Hanlon to Father, 8 January 1860 (Wells, *Ulster igration*, 80–1). Vinyard uses an 'index of dissimilarity', where 100 would mean that the Irish were represented in the poorer occupations in proportion to their share of the overall population. On this scale San Francisco scores 112, Detroit 118 and St Louis 120, as compared to 123 for New York, 129 for Brooklyn and 130 for Boston.

40. Timothy M. O'Neill, 'Miners in Migration: The Case of Nineteenth-Century Irish and Irish-American Copper Miners', in Kevin Kenny (ed.), *New Directions in Irish-American History* (Madison, 2003), 61–74; Graham Davis and Matthew Goulding, 'Irish Hard-Rock Miners in Ireland, Britain and the United States', in Graham Davis (ed.), *In Search of a Better Life: British and Irish Migration* (Stroud, 2011), 179–95; David M. Emmons, *The Butte Irish: Class and Ethnicity in an American Mining Town, 1875–1925* (Urbana and Chicago, 1989).

41. David T. Gleeson, *The Irish in the South, 1815–1877* (Chapel Hill, 2001); Joe Regan, 'The Large Irish Enslavers of Antebellum Louisiana', *American Nineteenth Century History*, 21/3 (2020), 211–35.

42. James Anderson to William Anderson, 4 May 1857 (IED); Richard Nicholl to Lucy Nicholl, 7 November 1868 (IED); Emmons, *Beyond the American Pale*, 152–7, 215.

43. John Orr to Rev. John Orr, 13 June 1850 (IED); Burchell, *The San Francisco Irish*, 153; Richard White, *The Republic for Which It Stands: The United States During Reconstruction and the Gilded Age, 1865–1896* (Oxford, 2017), 157, 520–2.

44. Journal of J. B. Hamilton, 1859 (IED); Robert McElderry to Thomas McElderry, 11 March 1852 (IED); William McElderry to Thomas McElderry, 17

December 1853, 1 December 1854 (IED); William Hill to David Hill, 24 January 1855, 2 September 1865, 8 March 1872 (IED). For Hill's anti-Orange and anti-British views see above p. 203.

45. Emmons, *Beyond the American Pale*, 16.

46. John Doherty to Father, 24 November 1850 (PRONI T2606/4); Mary Doherty to her sister Isabella, 1 July 1860 (PRONI T2606/9).

47. Ferrie, *Yankeys Now*, 87–8.

48. Rebecca A. Fried, 'No Irish Need Deny: Evidence for the Historicity of NINA Restrictions in Advertisements and Signs', *Journal of Social History*, 49/4 (2016), 829–54; Meagher, *Inventing Irish America*, 47, 102; Thernstrom, *Poverty and Progress*, 101.

49. Ernst, *Immigrant Life*, 200–1; Clark, *Irish in Philadelphia*, 46, 49; Internal Health Department, *Report on the Cholera in Boston*, 15. For mortality in general see Doyle in *NHI, VI*, 747–8.

50. Ferrie, *Yankeys Now*, 127, 189.

51. Tyler Anbinder, 'Moving Beyond "Rags to Riches": New York's Irish Famine Immigrants and Their Surprising Savings Accounts', *Journal of American History*, 99/3 (2012), 752. For wages see Stott, *Workers in the Metropolis*, 60.

5. Soldiers and Citizens

1. Matthew Brooks to Rebecca Clark, 3 March 1863 and undated (IED); Maris A. Vinovskis, 'Have Social Historians Lost the Civil War? Some Preliminary Demographic Speculations', *Journal of American History*, 76/1 (1989), 37. For the conventional account see Robert L. O'Connell, *Of Arms and Men: A History of War, Weapons and Aggression* (Oxford, 1989), 196–202. Brent Nosworthy, *The Bloody Crucible of Courage: Fighting Methods and Combat Experience of the American Civil War* (London, 2005), chaps. 2 and 30, corrects a number of myths and oversimplifications.

2. Samuel Morse, *Foreign Conspiracy Against the Liberties of the United States* (New York, 1835), 5; Nancy Lusignan Schultz, *Fire and Roses: The Burning of the Charlestown Convent, 1834* (New York, 2000); Michael Feldberg, *The Philadelphia Riots of 1844: A Study of Ethnic Conflict* (Westport, CT, 1975).

3. Tyler Anbinder, *Nativism and Slavery: The Northern Know Nothings and the Politics of the 1850s* (New York, 1992).

4. Regina Donlon, *German and Irish Immigrants in the Midwestern United States, 1850–1900* (London, 2018), 181–4; Wallace S. Hutcheon, 'The Louisville Riots of August 1855', *Register of the Kentucky Historical Society*, 69/2 (1971), 150–72; R. A. Burchell, *The San Francisco Irish, 1848–1880* (Manchester, 1979), 127–31.

5. Graham Hodges, '"Desirable Companions and Lovers": Irish and African Americans in the Sixth Ward 1830–70', in Ronald H. Bayor and Timothy J. Meagher (eds.), *The New York Irish* (Baltimore and London, 1996); *Pilot*, quoted in Dennis P. Ryan, *Beyond the Ballot Box: A Social History of the Boston Irish, 1845–1917* (London and Toronto, 1983), 131; Susannah Ural Bruce, *The Harp and the Eagle: Irish-American Volunteers and the Union Army, 1861–1865* (New York, 2006), 24–31, 540.

6. L. F. Kohl and M. C. Richard (eds.), *Irish Green and Union Blue: The Civil War Letters of Peter Welsh* (New York, 1986), 65–6 (3 February 1863).

7. MacMahon quoted in D. T. Gleeson, *The Green and the Gray: The Irish in the Confederate States of America* (Chapel Hill, NC, 2013), 115 (I have corrected the somewhat garbled quote from the original text); Mitchel quoted in Cian McMahon, *The Global Dimensions of Irish Identity: Race, Nation and the Popular Press, 1840–1880* (Chapel Hill, NC, 2015), 101–2.

8. Peter F. Stevens, *The Rogue's March: John Riley and the St Patrick's Battalion, 1846–48* (Washington, DC, 1999); Bruce, *The Harp and the Eagle*, 1–6; Gleeson, *The Green and the Gray*, 54–60; James McPherson, *Battle Cry of Freedom: The Civil War Era* (Oxford, 1988), 606–8.

9. 'Tuam Plaque in Memory of Dick Dowling', *Tuam Herald*, 30 May 1998; 'US Tension Spreads to Tuam with Bid to Move Dick Dowling', *Tuam Herald*, 23 August 2017.

10. Kohl and Richard, *Irish Green and Union Blue*, 66; Rory T. Cornish, 'An Irish Republican Abroad: Thomas Francis Meagher in the United States, 1852–65' in John Hearne and R. T. Cornish (eds.), *Thomas Francis Meagher: The Making of an Irish American* (Dublin, 2005), 139–62.

11. Mitchel quoted in Bruce, *The Harp and the Eagle*, 84; Craig A. Warren, '"Oh, God, What a Pity!" The Irish Brigade at Fredericksburg and the Creation of Myth', *Civil War History*, 47/3 (2001), 193–221; Gleeson, *The Green and the Gray*, 104–5.

12. John Loughery, *Dagger John: Archbishop John Hughes and the Making of Irish America* (Ithaca and London, 2018), 1–21, 295–304; Gleeson, *The Green and the Gray*, chap. 5; text of *In Supremo Apostolatus* in www.papalencyclicals.net/greg16/g16sup.htm (accessed 21 July 2019).

13. Kerby A. Miller, *Emigrants and Exiles: Ireland and the Irish Exodus to North America* (New York, 1985), 359; Joseph Hernon, *Celts, Catholics and Copperheads: Ireland Views the American Civil War* (Columbus, OH, 1968), 11–38.

14. Bernadette Whelan, *American Government in Ireland, 1790–1913: A History of the US Consular Service* (Manchester, 2010), 124–48; Charles P. Cullop, 'An Unequal Duel: Union Recruiting in Ireland, 1863–1864', *Civil War History*, 13/2 (1967), 101–13.

15. *Correspondence Respecting the Enlistment of British Subjects* (PP 1864 (Cd 3385, 3395) 62).

16. Bruce, *The Harp and the Eagle*, 70–2, 167.

17. Casualty figures from Bruce, *The Harp and the Eagle*, 119, 132, 156, 166; Meagher quotation, 118. For Meagher as military commander see also Hearne and Cornish (eds.), *Thomas Francis Meagher*, 149–55.

18. Edward K. Spann, 'Union Green: The Irish Community and the Civil War', in Bayor and Meagher (eds.), *The New York Irish*, 203. For McClellan as an Irishman see Bruce, *The Harp and the Eagle*, 85.

19. Iver Bernstein, *The New York City Draft Riots: Their Significance for American Society and Politics in the Age of the Civil War* (New York, 1990), 25–35. For the numbers killed see page 288, n. 8. The actual death toll is generally assumed to have

been much higher than 105, though contemporary claims for figures in excess of 1,000 are hard to credit.

20. Kevin Kenny, 'Abraham Lincoln and the American Irish', *American Journal of Irish Studies*, 10 (2013), 51–2; Allan Nevins and M. H. Thomas (eds.), *The Diary of George Templeton Strong, Vol. 3: The Civil War, 1860–1865* (New York, 1952), 335, 339, 343.

21. Dale T. Knobel, *Paddy and the Republic: Ethnicity and Nationality in Antebellum America* (Middleton, CT, 1986), 104–28.

22. Above p. 417. The classic statement of the view that the Irish had to struggle to escape being classified as non-white is Noel Ignatiev, *How the Irish Became White* (New York, 1995). For an excellent, balanced review of the whole issue see Kevin Kenny, *The American Irish: A History* (London, 2000), 69–71.

23. 'How to Keep a Girl', *Puck*, 5 December 1883. I am grateful for this reference to my former student Ms Nicole Holmes.

6. Beneath the Southern Cross

1. Hamish Maxwell-Stuart, '"And All My Great Hardships Endured": Irish Convicts in Van Diemen's Land', in Niall Whelehan (ed.), *Transnational Perspectives on Modern Irish History* (New York, 2015), 69–87.

2. Katherine Foxhall, *Health, Medicine and the Sea: Australian Voyages c. 1815–1860* (Manchester, 2012); Don Charlwood, *The Long Farewell* (Ringwood, VIC, 1981).

3. John McDonald and Ralph Shlomowitz, 'Mortality on Immigrant Voyages to Australia in the 19th Century', *Explorations in Economic History*, 27 (1990), 84–113; Robin Haines and Ralph Shlomowitz, 'Deaths of Babies Born on Government Assisted Voyages to South Australia in the Nineteenth Century', *Health and History*, 6/1 (2004), 113–124.

4. Stawell quoted in Geoffrey Serle, *The Golden Age: A History of the Colony of Victoria 1851–1861* (Melbourne, 1963), 49n; L. M. Geary, 'Australia Felix: Irish Doctors in Nineteenth-Century Victoria', in Patrick O'Sullivan (ed.), *The Irish World Wide, Vol. 2: The Irish in the New Communities* (London, 1992), 162–79; Michael Gladwyn, 'Ireland, Empire and Australian Anglicanism, 1788–1850', in Colin Barr and Hilary M. Carey (eds.), *Religion and Greater Ireland: Christianity and Irish Global Networks, 1750–1950* (Montreal and Kingston, 2015), 297–318. Lecale and Down Historical Society, transcripts of The James Cumine Parkinson Letters, available at www.lecalehistory.co.uk/parkinson/index.html (accessed 3 February 2018).

5. The characteristics of the Irish immigrant population are surveyed in David Fitzpatrick, *Oceans of Consolation: Personal Accounts of Irish Migration to Australia* (Cork, 1994), 6–16.

6. For employers' complaints see *Papers Relative to Emigration to the Australian Colonies* (PP 1857 (144) 10), 221, 133, 144–5. Michael Normile of County Clare, printed in Fitzpatrick, *Oceans of Consolation*, 71–2; Elizabeth Malcolm and Dianne Hall, *A New History of the Irish in Australia* (Sydney, 2018), chap. 5, 6.

7. D. H. Akenson, *Small Differences: Irish Catholics and Irish Protestants, 1815–1922* (Kingston and Montreal, 1988), 185.

8. Lindsay J. Proudfoot and Dianne P. Hall, *Imperial Spaces: Placing the Irish and Scots in Colonial Australia* (Manchester, 2013), 186, 172–3; Dianne Hall, 'Irishness, Protestantism, and Colonial Identity in New South Wales', in Barr and Carey (eds.), *Religion and Greater Ireland*, 319–39. For a general discussion see Fitzpatrick, *Oceans of Consolation*, 16.

9. Fitzpatrick, *Oceans of Consolation*, 78, 182–3; Patrick O'Farrell, *Letters from Irish Australia 1825–1929* (Belfast, 1984), 104.

10. R. V. Jackson, *Australian Economic Development in the Nineteenth Century* (Canberra, 1977), 100–4, 119–24; Beverley Kingston, *The Oxford History of Australia, Vol. 3, 1860–1900: Glad, Confident Morning* (Melbourne, 1993), 51–6.

11. Fitzpatrick, *Oceans of Consolation*, 171, 265; O'Farrell, *Letters from Irish Australia*, 140.

12. Fitzpatrick, *Oceans of Consolation*, 213, 216, 218–9.

13. Proudfoot and Hall, *Imperial Spaces*, 117; Eric Richards, 'Irish Life and Progress in Colonial South Australia', *Irish Historical Studies*, 27/107 (1991), 230; M. E. R. McGinley, 'The Irish in Queensland: An Overview' in O'Brien and Travers (eds.), *The Irish Emigrant Experience*, 109–12. For agricultural opportunities in general see Kingston, *Glad, Confident Morning*, chap. 1.

14. Proudfoot and Hall, *Imperial Spaces*, 112; Durack, *Kings in Grass Castles* (London, 1985), 60–1; O'Farrell, *Letters from Irish Australia*, 189.

15. O'Farrell, *Letters from Irish Australia*, 138, 194–6, 216.

16. John Mitchel, *Jail Journal, or Five Years in British Prisons* (New York, 1854), 281.

17. Ann McGrath, 'Shamrock Aborigines: The Irish, the Aboriginal Australians and Their Children' in Graeme Morton and David A. Wilson (eds.), *Irish and Scottish Encounters with Indigenous Peoples: Canada, the United States, New Zealand and Australia* (Montreal and Kingston, 2013).

18. Fitzpatrick, *Oceans of Consolation*, 78; O'Farrell, *Letters from Irish Australia*, 67–8, 76; Durack, *Kings in Grass Castles*, 62–3, 112; Frances Devlin-Glass, 'The Irish in Grass Castles: Re-reading Victim Tropes in an Iconic Pioneering Text' in L. M. Geary and A. J. McCarthy (eds.), *Ireland, Australia and New Zealand: History, Politics and Culture* (Dublin, 2008). For the revealing comment of another settler, Patrick Coady Buckley, illegitimate son of an Irish female convict, see Proudfoot and Hall, *Imperial Spaces*, 143.

19. Serle, *The Golden Age*, 161–9. The fullest contemporary account is Raffaello Carboni, *The Eureka Stockade: The Consequence of Some Pirates Wanting on Quarterdeck a Rebellion* (Melbourne, 1855). Peter Lalor's account, published in the *Ballarat Times*, 14 July 1855, was reprinted in the Irish newspaper *Nation*, 14 July 1855, and, in part, in the *Irish Examiner*, 23 July 1855. See also John Bastin (ed.), 'Eureka—an Eye-Witness Account', *Australian Quarterly*, 28/4 (1956), 76–83.

20. Jan Kociumbas, *The Oxford History of Australia, Volume 2: 1770–1860* (Melbourne, 1992), 300–11; Geoffrey Blainey, *The Rush That Never Ended: A History of Australian Mining* (Melbourne, 1963).

21. Carboni, *Eureka Stockade*, 58, 60, 66. Lalor's political background is discussed in C. Kiernan, 'Peter Lalor, the Enigma of Eureka', in *Labour and the Gold Fields* (Canberra, 1968), 11–16.

22. Charles Gavan Duffy, *My Life in Two Hemispheres* (2 vols., London, 1903), ii.133–4.

23. Serle, *The Golden Age*, 255, 312; Patrick O'Farrell, *The Catholic Church and Community, in Australia: A History* (Melbourne, 1977) 99; Malcolm and Hall, *New History*, chap. 9.

24. For most of what follows see Patrick O'Farrell, *Catholic Church*. For the church act of 1836 see also Hazel King, *Richard Bourke* (Melbourne, 1971), chap. 17.

25. G. A. Bremner, *Imperial Gothic: Religious Architecture and High Anglican Culture in the British Empire, c. 1840–1870* (New Haven/London, 2013), 234.

26. O'Farrell, *Catholic Church*, 40–9, 78–82; Colin Barr, *Ireland's Empire: The Roman Catholic Church in the English-Speaking World* (Cambridge, 2020), chap. 6. Cullen was not directly involved in James Quinn's appointment. Barr speculates that it was promoted by the politically astute bishop of Melbourne, James Goold, as a way of gaining Cullen's favour.

27. Malcolm and Hall, *New History*, 282, 287–8.

28. O'Farrell, *Letters from Irish Australia*, 57. For Orangeism see Patrick O'Farrell, *The Irish in Australia: 1788 to the Present* (3rd ed. Sydney, 2000), 100–105; Proudfoot and Hall, *Imperial Spaces*, chap. 7; David Fitzpatrick, 'Exporting Brotherhood: Orangeism in South Australia', *Immigrants & Minorities*, 23/2–3 (2005), 277–310.

29. O'Farrell, *Catholic Church*, 59, 74, 184, 203–5, 280; Fitzpatrick, *Oceans of Consolation*, 17–18. For Ireland's devotional revolution see Emmet Larkin, *The Historical Dimensions of Irish Catholicism* (Washington, DC, 1984); S. J. Connolly, *Priests and People in Pre-Famine Ireland, 1780–1845* (Dublin, 2001). It is important to note that this view of a mid-nineteenth-century transformation of religious practice has been challenged. For an up-to-date review of the question see Colin Barr, 'The Re-energising of Catholicism, 1790–1880' in James Kelly (ed.), *The Cambridge History of Ireland, Vol. 3: 1730–1880* (Cambridge, 2018), 281–5.

30. Proudfoot and Hall, *Imperial Spaces*, 189.

31. A digitised version of the letter, with transcript, is available from the State Library of Victoria at http://handle.slv.vic.gov.au/10381/211066 (accessed 27 March 2020). For the Irish associates of the Kelly gang, Bob Reece, 'Ned Kelly's Father' in Bob Reece (ed.), *Exiles from Erin: Convict Lives in Ireland and Australia* (Dublin, 1991), 239.

32. O'Farrell, *Irish in Australia*, 141–2; Malcolm and Hall, *New History*, chap. 7.

33. Reece, 'Ned Kelly's Father', 227. The school Ned Kelly briefly attended was a state school run by a Scotsman, but there may have been provision for some form of separate religious instruction.

34. Reece (ed.), *Exiles from Erin*, 304. Jack Donahoe, born in Dublin in 1806 and transported in 1825, was shot dead by the police near Sydney in 1830. The protagonists in different versions of the folk ballad 'The Wild Colonial Boy' invariably have the initials 'JD', suggesting that Donahoe may have provided the model (*Australian Dictionary of Biography*, https://adb.anu.edu.au/biography/donohoe -john-jack-1985/text2413, accessed 10 July 2021).

35. Ciara Breathnach, 'Recruiting Irish Migrants for Life in New Zealand 1870–75', in Geary and McCarthy (eds.), *Ireland, Australia and New Zealand*, 14– 31; James Belich, *Making Peoples: A History of the New Zealanders from Polynesian Settlement to the End of the Nineteenth Century* (Honolulu, 1996), 316. For overall population and the number of Irish-born see D. H. Akenson, *Half the World from Home: Perspectives on the Irish in New Zealand, 1860–1950* (Wellington, 1990), 40, 63.

36. Figures collected in Ireland on emigrants heading for New Zealand between 1876 and 1890 show 36 per cent as coming from Ulster and 46 per cent from Munster (Akenson, *Half the World from Home*, 70–1). An analysis of death certificates of those arriving between 1871 and 1890 reverses the proportions, at 43 per cent from Ulster and 35 per cent from Munster (Angela McCarthy, *Irish Migrants in New Zealand: 'The Desired Haven'* (Woodbridge, 2005), 56). Where religion is concerned, the picture is unclear. Akenson (*Half the World from Home*, 65–74) uses a comparison between the number of New Zealanders estimated to have been of Irish descent and the size of the Catholic population, at a time when few Catholics came to New Zealand from anywhere other than Ireland, to suggest that only around a quarter of Irish immigrants can have been Protestant. The higher figure of 45 per cent or more is based on studies of death certificates (McCarthy, *Irish Migrants in New Zealand*, 61). One possible explanation for the discrepancy might be that Catholics were more numerous in the large floating population moving back and forth between Australia and New Zealand, while Protestants were better represented among those who settled permanently in New Zealand and (eventually) died there.

37. A. Bradley, Auckland, to Samuel Carse, 1 September 1864 (PRONI D4405/1/1/1/56); William Graham to James Graham, 20 July 1884 (PRONI T3886/A/2); Akenson, *Half the World from Home*, 54–9, 65–84; D. H. Akenson, *The Irish Diaspora, A Primer* (Toronto, 1993), 87–90.

38. Edmund Bohan, 'The Irish in New Zealand Politics, 1860–1880', in Brad Patterson (ed.), *The Irish in New Zealand* (Wellington, 2002), 54–6.

39. Richard P. Davis, *Irish Issues in New Zealand Politics, 1868–1922* (Dunedin, 1974), 11–22; Lyndon Fraser, *Castles of Gold: A History of New Zealand's West Coast Irish* (Dunedin, 2007), 133–45; Sean Brosnahan, 'The "Battle of the Borough" and the "Saige O'Timaru": Sectarian Riot in Colonial Canterbury', *New Zealand Journal of History*, 28/1 (1994), 41–59.

40. Akenson, *Half the World from Home*, 123–58; Brad Patterson, 'New Zealand's Ulster Plantation Revisited', in Geary and McCarthy (eds.), *Ireland, Australia and New Zealand*, 46–58; McCarthy, *Irish Migrants*, 240–1.

41. Barr, *Ireland's Empire*, 464–5.

42. Hugh Jackson, 'The Late Victorian Decline in Churchgoing: Some New Zealand Evidence', *Archives de Sciences Sociales des Religions*, 56/1 (1983), 100–1; Davis, *Irish Issues in New Zealand Politics*, chap. 8; Akenson, *Half the World from Home*, 167–73; Lyndon Fraser, *To Tara via Holyhead: Irish Catholic Immigrants in Nineteenth-Century Christchurch* (Auckland, 1997), 57–8.

43. Belich, *Making Peoples*, 243; William Graham to James Graham, 9 November 1884 (PRONI T3886/A/4); McCarthy, *Irish Migrants*, 225.

7. The Making of Irish America

1. David T. Gleeson, *The Green and the Gray: The Irish in the Confederate States of America* (Chapel Hill, NC, 2013), chap. 6; Susannah Ural Bruce, *The Harp and the Eagle: Irish-American Volunteers and the Union Army, 1861–1865* (New York, 2006), chap. 6.

2. Michael A. Gordon, *The Orange Riots: Irish Political Violence in New York City, 1870 and 1871* (Ithaca, 1993). For the parallels drawn by newspapers with 1863 see pp. 78–9, 167.

3. Kevin Kenny, *Making Sense of the Molly Maguires* (New York, 1998).

4. Kenny, *Making Sense of the Molly Maguires*, 117–29.

5. Bruce, *The Harp and the Eagle*, 257–62.

6. John Loughery, *Dagger John: Archbishop John Hughes and the Making of Irish America* (Ithaca and London, 2018), 60. For ratios of priests to people see Kerby A. Miller, *Emigrants and Exiles: Ireland and the Irish Exodus to North America* (New York, 1985), 331–2. For American church attendance rates see Jay P. Dolan, *The American Catholic Experience: A History from Colonial Times to the Present* (Notre Dame, 1992), 207, and Hugh McLeod, 'Catholicism and the New York Irish 1880–1910' in Jim Obelkevich et al. (eds.), *Disciplines of Faith: Studies in Religion, Politics and Patriarchy* (London, 1987), 338. The rates of 90 per cent or more in Ireland are those recorded in the 1970s. See S. J. Connolly, *Priests and People in Pre-Famine Ireland, 1780–1845* (2nd ed. Dublin, 2001), 102.

7. David Doyle, in *NHI, V*, 713–4; M. R. O'Connell, *John Ireland and the American Catholic Church* (St Paul, MN, 1988), 305–7; Colin Barr, *Ireland's Empire: The Roman Catholic Church in the English-Speaking World 1829–1914* (Cambridge, 2020), chap. 1; Dolan, *American Catholic Experience*, 143–4.

8. Ellen Skerret, 'The Catholic Dimension' in L. J. McCaffrey et al., *The Irish in Chicago* (Urbana and Chicago, 1987), 24–5, 56n.4.

9. Barr, *Ireland's Empire*, 65, 75; David T. Gleeson, *The Irish in the South, 1815–1877* (Chapel Hill, 2001), 82.

10. Hasia Diner, *Erin's Daughters in America* (Baltimore, 1983), 130.

11. Dolan, *American Catholic Experience*, 205–6.

12. Dolan, *American Catholic Experience*, 262–78; Skerrett, 'The Catholic Dimension', 43; R. A. Burchell, *The San Francisco Irish, 1848–1880* (Manchester, 1979), 166. For inferior standards in parochial schools, Timothy J. Meagher, *Inventing Irish America: Generation, Class and Ethnic Identity in a New England City, 1880–1928* (Notre Dame, 2001), 156–62; Dennis P. Ryan, *Beyond the Ballot Box: A*

Social History of the Boston Irish (East Brunswick, NJ, 1983), 65–72. For teachers of Irish background, see above p. 230.

13. Dolan, *American Catholic Experience*, 308–20; O'Connell, *John Ireland*, chap. 18. The regional dimension is suggested in L. J. McCaffrey, *Textures of Irish America* (New York, 1992), 64–5.

14. J. E. Roohan, *American Catholics and the Social Question, 1865–1900* (New York, 1976), 280–331.

15. Kevin E. O'Brien (ed.) *My Life in the Irish Brigade: The Civil War Memoirs of Private William McCarter, 116th Pennsylvania Infantry* (Campbell, CA, 1996), 49.

16. Andrew Greenless to John Greenless, 30 May 1859 (IED); William Hill to David Hill, 7 July 1859 (IED). See also W. McSparron to his niece Margaret Ann, 30 July 1863 (IED). For Hill's anti-Orange and anti-British views see William Hill to David Hill, 24 January 1855, 8 March 1872.

17. For Orange numbers see Michael Feldberg, *The Philadelphia Riots of 1844: A Study of Ethnic Conflict* (Westport, CT, 1975), 118–9, n. 29; Gordon, *The Orange Riots*; Mary C. Kelly, *The Shamrock and the Lily: The New York Irish and the Creation of a Transatlantic Identity, 1845–1921* (New York, 2005), 86, 100; Michael Glazier (ed.), *The Encyclopedia of the Irish in America* (Notre Dame, 1999), 748.

18. K. A. Miller et al., *Irish Migrants in the Land of Canaan* (Oxford, 2003), 446–51; John Francis Maguire, *The Irish in America* (New York, 1868), 308–12.

19. JoEllen Vinyard, *The Irish on the Urban Frontier: Nineteenth-Century Detroit* (New York, 1976), 103–4; Tyler Anbinder, *City of Dreams: The 400-Year Epic History of Immigrant New York* (Boston and New York, 2016), 149–50.

20. Burchell, *The San Francisco Irish*, 46–9; Vinyard, *The Irish on the Urban Frontier*, 94–104; McCaffrey et al., *The Irish in Chicago*, 7; Meagher, *Inventing Irish America*, 60; Robert Ernst, *Immigrant Life in New York City* (Port Washington, NY, 1949), 39–40; Tyler Anbinder, *Five Points: The 19th-Century New York City Neighborhood That Invented Tap Dance, Stole Elections, and Became the World's Most Notorious Slum* (New York, 2001), 43.

21. Stephan Thernstrom, *The Other Bostonians: Poverty and Progress in the American Metropolis, 1880–1970* (Boston, 1973), 209. The exact figures, representing the percentage of each group that would have to be moved to another area to achieve the same distribution as the native-born white population, are English 13, Irish 15, German 31 and Italian 74. For geographical mobility see Vinyard, *The Irish on the Urban Frontier*, 70; Joseph P. Ferrie, *Yankeys Now: Immigrants in the Antebellum United States, 1840–1860* (New York, 1999), chap. 7.

22. The role of spatial segregation in the development of a multi-ethnic America has been much debated. For a useful overview see Kathleen Neils Conzen, 'Immigrants, Immigrant Neighborhoods, and Ethnic Identity: Historical Issues', *Journal of American History*, 66/3 (1979), 603–15.

23. Burchell, *San Francisco Irish*, 78–81; Meagher, *Inventing Irish America*, 58, 123; Vinyard, *The Irish on the Urban Frontier*, 111, 192.

24. David Doyle, 'The Remaking of Irish America, 1845–80', in *NHI, VI*, 736–7.

25. Ralph Wilcox, 'Irish Americans in Sport: The Nineteenth Century', in Joseph Lee and Marion Casey (eds.), *Making the Irish American: History and Heritage of the*

Irish in the United States (New York, 2006), 444–7; William V. Shannon, *The American Irish* (New York, 1966), 95–102.

26. Quotations in Anbinder, *Five Points*, 188; Mick Moloney, 'Irish American Popular Music', in Lee and Casey (eds.), *Making the Irish American*, 388. More generally W. H. A. Williams, *'Twas Only an Irishman's Dream: The Image of Ireland and the Irish in American Popular Song Lyrics, 1800–1920* (Urbana and Chicago, 1996).

27. Burchell, *San Francisco Irish*, 96–9.

28. Sallie A. Marston, 'Neighbourhood and Politics: Irish Ethnicity in Nineteenth-Century Lowell', *Annals of the Association of American Geographers*, 78/3 (1988), 414–32; John T. Ridge, 'Irish County Societies in New York, 1880–1914', in Bayor and Meagher (eds.), *The New York Irish*, 275–300.

29. Mike Cronin and Daryl Adair, *The Wearing of the Green: A History of St Patrick's Day* (London, 2002), 34–8, 64–76; *Cincinnati Daily Gazette*, 18 March 1869; *New York Tribune*, 18 March 1868. For refrigerated shamrock see Cronin and Adair, *The Wearing of the Green*, 72.

30. *New York Tribune*, 18 March 1857; *Boston Journal*, 18 March 1868; Dennis Clark, *The Irish in Philadelphia* (Philadelphia, 1973), 127; 'St Patrick's Day, the Procession and Parade', *Daily Critic* (Washington, DC), 17 March 1874; Russell quoted in Dennis Clark, *Hibernia America: The Irish and Regional Cultures* (New York, 1986), 56.

31. William Leonard Joyce, *Editors and Ethnicity: A History of the Irish-America Press, 1848–1883* (New York, 1976); Matthew Frye Jacobson, *Special Sorrows: The Diasporic Imagination of Irish, Polish and Jewish Immigrants in the United States* (Cambridge, MA, 1995), 57–64; Burchell, *The San Francisco Irish*, 175–7. For the politics of the Irish-American press see above pp 239-40.

32. Patrick Ford's explanation for why there was no Irish-American daily, cited in Joyce, *Editors and Ethnicity*, 176, n. 18.

33. Meagher, *Inventing Irish America*, 68–9, 72.

8. The Politics of Irish America

1. William L. Riordan, *Plunkitt of Tammany Hall*, ed. Terence J. McDonald (Boston, 1994).

2. Terry Golway, *Machine Made: Tammany Hall and the Creation of Modern American Politics* (New York, 2014), 112, 153–6, 194–200. For Tweed's cultivation of the Irish see R. H. Bayor and T. J. Meagher, *The New York Irish* (Baltimore, 1996), 102.

3. Amy Bridges, *A City in the Republic: Antebellum New York and the Origins of Machine Politics* (Cambridge, 1984).

4. Steven Erie, *Rainbow's End: Irish-Americans and the Dilemmas of Urban Machine Politics, 1840–1985* (Berkeley, 1988), 33–5.

5. Erie, *Rainbow's End*, 45–57.

6. Jane Addams, 'Why the Ward Boss Rules' (1898), printed in Riordan, *Plunkitt of Tammany Hall*, 117–22; Thomas H. O'Connor, *The Boston Irish: A Political History* (Boston, 1995), 122.

7. R. A. Burchell, *The San Francisco Irish, 1848–1880* (Manchester, 1979), chap. 7; Alexander Callow, 'San Francisco's Blind Boss', *Pacific Historical Review*, 25/3 (1956), 261–79.

8. Craig Brown and Charles N. Halaby, 'Machine Politics in America, 1870–1945', *Journal of Interdisciplinary History*, 17/3 (1987), 587–612; Michael F. Funchion, 'The Political and Nationalist Dimensions' in L. J. McCaffrey et al., *The Irish in Chicago* (Urbana and Chicago, 1987); R. A. Morton, '"A Man of Belial": Roger C. Sullivan, the Progressive Democracy and the Senatorial Elections of 1914', *Journal of the Illinois State Historical Society*, 91/3 (1998), 133–59; H. L. Platt, 'Jane Addams and the Ward Boss Revisited', *Environmental History*, 5/2 (2000), 194–222.

9. Collins quoted in Jack Beatty, *The Rascal King: The Life and Times of James Michael Curley (1874–1958)* (Reading, MA, 1992), 7; Doris Kearns Goodwin, *The Fitzgeralds and the Kennedys: An American Saga* (London, 1988), 119, 193. See also O'Connor, *Boston Irish*, 164–5.

10. David Montgomery, *Beyond Equality: Labor and the Radical Republicans 1862–1872* (New York, 1967), 373–6; Erie, *Rainbow's End*, 27–8.

11. Erie, *Rainbow's End*, 5; Bayor and Meagher, *The New York Irish*, 97; McCaffrey et al., *The Irish in Chicago*, 62; Dennis Clark, *The Irish in Philadelphia* (Philadelphia, 1973), 130; Timothy J. Meagher, *Inventing Irish America: Generation, Class and Ethnic Identity in a New England City, 1880–1928* (Notre Dame, 2001), 43; James R. Barrett, *The Irish Way: Becoming American in the Multiethnic City* (New York, 2012), 129, 221.

12. For senators see www.senate.gov/senators/Foreign_born.htm (accessed 19 October 2019); Burchell, *San Francisco Irish*, 186–7. *Irish World*, quoted in Golway, *Machine Made*, 83; list of Congressmen in 1890–2 in David Noel Doyle, *Irish Americans, Native Rights and National Empires* (New York, 1976), 125, n. 6.

13. Montgomery, *Beyond Equality*, 126–7, 198–9.

14. Robert E. Weir, *Beyond Labor's Veil: The Culture of the Knights of Labor* (University Park, PA, 1996), 93; Bruce Laurie, *Artisans into Workers: Labor in Nineteenth-Century America* (Urbana and Chicago, 1997), 161; Richard White, *The Republic for Which It Stands: The United States During Reconstruction and the Gilded Age 1865–1896* (Oxford, 2017), 157, 520–2.

15. Susan Levine, 'Labor's True Woman: Domesticity and Equal Rights in the Knights of Labor', *Journal of American History*, 70/2 (1983), 334.

16. William Porter to Robert Porter, 26 October 1869 (IED); Eric Foner, 'Class, Ethnicity and Radicalism in the Gilded Age: The Land League and Irish America', in *Politics and Ideology in the Age of the Civil War* (Oxford, 1980), 189; *Irish World*, quoted in David Brundage, *Irish Nationalism in America: The Politics of Exile 1798–1998* (Oxford, 2016), 115.

17. Quoted in Matthew Frye Jacobson, *Special Sorrows: The Diasporic Imagination of Irish, Polish and Jewish Immigrants in the United States* (Cambridge, MA, 1995), 177, 205. More generally see Doyle, *Irish Americans, Native Rights and National Empires*, chap. 7.

18. Laurie, *Artisans into Workers*, 176–209.

19. L. F. Kohl and M. C. Richard (eds.), *Irish Green and Union Blue: The Civil War Letters of Peter Welsh* (New York, 1986), 100–4; Elizabeth Gurley Flynn, *The Rebel Girl: An Autobiography* (New York, 1955), 23–6.

20. Jacobson, *Special Sorrows*, 57–64; William Leonard Joyce, *Editors and Ethnicity: A History of the Irish-America Press, 1848–1883* (New York, 1976); James Paul Rodeechko, *Patrick Ford and His Search for America: A Case Study of Irish-American Journalism 1870–1913* (New York, 1976).

21. Kyle Hughes and Donald MacRaild, *Ribbon Societies in Nineteenth-Century Ireland and Its Diaspora: The Persistence of Tradition* (Liverpool, 2018), 290–1; John Ridge, 'Ancient Order of Hibernians', in Michael Glazier (ed.), *The Encyclopedia of the Irish in America* (Notre Dame, 1999), 26–8.

22. For the Order's progress towards acceptance by the Catholic Church see Kevin Kenny, *Making Sense of the Molly Maguires* (New York, 1998), 278–80. For its role as a cultural pressure group, Meagher, *Inventing Irish America*, 247–53; W. H. A. Williams, *'Twas Only an Irishman's Dream: The Image of Ireland and the Irish in American Popular Song Lyrics* (Urbana and Chicago, 1996), 200–10.

23. The idea that Irish-American nationalism was primarily a quest for respectability and advancement within the United States was first put forward in Thomas N. Brown, *Irish-American Nationalism* (Philadelphia and New York, 1966). (For Davitt's words see page 24.) Kerby A. Miller, *Emigrants and Exiles: Ireland and the Irish Exodus to North America* (New York, 1985), 335–44, stresses instead the Anglophobia that immigrants brought with them from Ireland. But this leaves unexplained the different development of Irish politics in Canada and Australia.

24. Angela Murphy, *American Slavery, Irish Freedom: Abolition, Immigrant Citizenship and the Transatlantic Movement for Irish Repeal* (Baton Rouge, 2010).

25. Joseph Denieffe, *A Personal Narrative of the Irish Revolutionary Brotherhood* (New York, 1906), 3.

26. Brian Griffin, '"Scallions, Pikes and Bog Oak Ornaments": The Irish Republican Brotherhood and the Chicago Fenian Fair, 1864', *Studia Hibernica*, 29 (1995–7), 85–97.

27. For the limited revolutionary enthusiasm of rank-and-file Fenians see R. V. Comerford, *The Fenians in Context: Irish Politics and Society 1848–82* (Dublin, 1985). Comerford's thesis of 'patriotism as pastime', at first received with scepticism, and even indignation, now seems to be widely accepted.

28. Patrick Steward and Bryan McGovern, *The Fenians: Irish Rebellion in the North Atlantic World* (Knoxville, 2013); Hereward Senior, *The Last Invasion of Canada: The Fenian Raids, 1866–1870* (Toronto and Oxford, 1991).

29. Many historians write of 'the Clan na Gael'. In this they may be following the practice of John Devoy, *Recollections of an Irish Rebel* (New York, 1929). Devoy, however, had never succeeded in mastering Irish (Patrick Maume, 'Devoy, John', in James McGuire and James Quinn [eds.], *Dictionary of Irish Biography* [Cambridge, 2009], http://dib.cambridge.org /viewReadPage.do?articleId=a2562). In that language, no definite article is needed where the phrase specifies which *Clan* (family or grouping) is being talked about.

So the correct form is 'Clan na Gael' but 'the Clan'. On the same principle see later references to the Irish parliament as Dáil Éireann but 'the Dáil'.

30. The international context is the central theme of the most recent study: Niall Whelehan, *The Dynamiters: Irish Nationalism and Political Violence in the Wider World, 1867–1900* (Cambridge, 2012).

31. Gillian O'Brien, *Blood Runs Green: The Murder That Transfixed Gilded Age Chicago* (Chicago and London, 2015).

32. Victor A. Walsh, '"A Fanatic Heart": The Cause of Irish-American Nationalism in Pittsburgh During the Gilded Age', *Journal of Social History*, 15/2 (1981), 187–204; Whelehan, *The Dynamiters*, chap. 4 and 241–2.

33. Finlay Peter Dunne, *Mr Dooley and the Chicago Irish: The Autobiography of a Nineteenth-Century Ethnic Group ed.*, Charles Fanning (Washington, DC, 1976), 286. For 'had his rollers on' in a context that seems to point to being drunk see page 85.

9. The Other America

1. David A. Wilson, *Thomas D'Arcy McGee, Vol. 1, Passion, Reason and Politics, 1825–57* (Montreal and Kingston, 2008); *Thomas D'Arcy McGee, Vol. 2, The Extreme Moderate, 1857–68* (Montreal and Kingston, 2011); 'Was Patrick James Whelan a Fenian and Did He Assassinate Thomas D'Arcy McGee?', in David A. Wilson (ed.), *Irish Nationalism in Canada* (Montreal and Kingston, 2009), 52–83.

2. The Registrar General's returns (see Appendix) do not cover the whole period. So these are the statistics compiled around 1950 for an Irish government report, using returns to the Colonial Land and Emigration Commissioners and the Board of Trade: *Reports of the Commission on Emigration and Other Population Problems 1948–54* (Dublin, 1954), 314–5. For population in the early 1840s see C. J. Houston and W. J. Smyth, *Irish Emigration and Canadian Settlement: Patterns, Links and Letters* (Belfast and Toronto, 1990), 25.

3. Marjory Harper, 'Enticing the Emigrant: Canadian Agents in Ireland and Scotland, c. 1870–1920', *Scottish Historical Review*, 83/215 (2004), 41–58.

4. John Gorman to Philip Gorman, 6 January 1866 (IED).

5. D. H. Akenson, *The Irish Diaspora: A Primer* (Toronto and Belfast, 1993), 261–3. Enumerators were instructed to record origin 'as given by the person questioned': *Manual Containing the Census Act and the Instructions to Officers Employed in the Taking of the First Census of Canada* (Ottawa, 1871), 23.

6. Houston and Smyth, *Irish Emigration and Canadian Settlement*, 226–9, using data from Darroch and Ornstein's study of a sample of census returns (see note 8).

7. Nathaniel Carrothers to William Carrothers, 5 December 1853, in Houston and Smyth, *Irish Emigration and Canadian Settlement*, 257–9.

8. A. G. Darroch and M. D. Ornstein, 'Ethnicity and Occupational Structure in Canada in 1871: The Vertical Mosaic in Historical Perspective', *Canadian Historical Review*, 61/3 (1980); Gordon Darroch and Lee Soltow, *Poverty and Inequality in Victorian Ontario: Structural Patterns and Cultural Communities in the 1871 Census* (Toronto, 1994), 41, 53–8, 85–9, 90–3. The work of Darroch and his collaborators confirms the picture of a flourishing farming population of Irish origin put forward,

on the basis of much more limited evidence, by D. H. Akenson, *The Irish in Ontario: A Study in Rural History* (Montreal and Kingston, 1984).

9. Darroch and Ornstein, 'Ethnicity and Occupational Structure', 325–8; Livio di Matteo, 'The Wealth of the Irish in Nineteenth-Century Ontario', *Social Science History*, 20/2 (1996), 209–34.

10. Darroch and Ornstein, 'Ethnicity and Occupational Structure', table 6. Michael B. Katz, *The People of Hamilton, Canada West: Family and Class in a Mid-Nineteenth-Century City* (Cambridge, MA, 1975), 26, 60–8, 143–60, 165–73; Robert Grace, 'Irish Immigration and Settlement in a Catholic City: Quebec, 1842–61', *Canadian Historical Review*, 84/2 (2003), 245–50; Donald Mackay, *Flight from Famine: The Coming of the Irish to Canada* (Toronto and London, 1990), 323. For the possibility that Hamilton was particularly likely to attract poor Famine immigrants see Cecil Houston and W. J. Smyth, 'The Irish Abroad: Better Questions Through a Better Source: The Canadian Census', *Irish Geography*, 13 (1980), 1–19.

11. *Canada: A Handy Guide for the Farmer and Labourer* (Edinburgh, 1870), 60–2; Marilyn Barber, *Irish Domestic Servants in Canada* (Ottawa, 1991), 1–6; L. R. McClean and Marilyn Barber, 'In Search of Comfort and Independence: Irish Immigrant Domestic Servants Encounter the Courts, Jails and Asylums in Nineteenth-Century Ontario', in Marlene Epp et al. (eds.), *Sisters or Strangers: Immigrant, Ethnic and Racialized Women in Canadian History* (Toronto, 2004), 133–60; Katz, *The People of Hamilton*, 27, 66; William Jenkins, *Between Raid and Rebellion: The Irish in Buffalo and Toronto, 1867–1916* (Montreal and Kingston, 2013), 67–71.

12. For life cycle see Katz, *The People of Hamilton*, 270–2. For married women's work, Andrew C. Holman, '"Different Feelings": Corktown and the Catholic Irish in Early Hamilton, 1832–1847', *Canadian Journal of Irish Studies*, 23/1 (1997), 41–66.

13. Peter Ludlow and Terence Murphy, 'The Irish in Imperial Halifax, Nova Scotia', in Daniel Roberts and Jonathan Wright (eds.), *Ireland's Imperial Connections, 1775–1947* (Basingstoke, 2019). For the Halifax toasts see Mark McGowan, *Michael Power: The Struggle to Build the Catholic Church on the Canadian Frontier* (Montreal and Kingston, 2005), 21, and for the coronation Bonnie Huskins, 'Public Feasting and the Negotiation of Class in Mid-19th-Century Saint John and Halifax', *Labour/ Le Travail*, 37 (1996), 21, 26.

14. Kevin James, 'Dynamics of Ethnic-Associational Culture in a Nineteenth-Century City: Saint Patrick's Society of Montreal, 1834–56', *Canadian Journal of Irish Studies*, 26/1 (2000).

15. C. J. Houston and W. J. Smyth, *The Sash Canada Wore: A Historical Geography of the Orange Order in Canada* (Toronto, 1980), 24; Scott See, '"Mickeys and Demons" vs. "Bigots and Boobies"', *Acadiensis*, 21/1 (1991), 110–31.

16. For membership see Houston and Smyth, *The Sash Canada Wore*, 84–91, 190, n. 42 and for the social dimension chap. 6. See also David Wilson (ed.), *The Orange Order in Canada* (Dublin, 2007), especially the chapter by Eric Kaufmann.

17. William Smyth, *Toronto, the Belfast of Canada: The Orange Order and the Shaping of Municipal Culture* (Toronto, 2015), 137–46.

18. Brian Clarke, 'Religious Riot as Pastime: Orange Young Britons, Parades and Public Life in Victorian Toronto', in Wilson (ed.), *The Orange Order in Canada*, 109–27.

19. For Belfast see A. C. Hepburn, *A Past Apart: Studies in the History of Catholic Belfast 1850–1950* (Belfast, 1996), 50.

20. G. F. G. Stanley, 'The Caraquet Riots of 1875', *Acadiensis*, 2/1 (1972), 2. The letters of Macdonald and the mayor are reproduced in *The Archivist's Pencil*, http://archives-archtoronto.blogspot.com/2016/05/the-corpus-christi-riot-of-1864.html (accessed 4 March 2020).

21. Fay Trombley, 'Thomas Louis Connolly, an Archbishop's Role in Politics', in Terence Murphy and C. J. Byrne (eds.), *Religion and Identity: The Experience of Irish and Scottish Catholics in Atlantic Canada* (Saint John's, NL, 1987), 125.

22. Stanley, 'The Caraquet Riots of 1875'; Stephen T. Rusak, 'The Canadian "Concordat" of 1897', *Catholic Historical Review*, 77/2 (1991), 209–34.

23. Shane Lynn, 'Friends of Ireland: Early O'Connellism in Lower Canada', *Irish Historical Studies*, 40/157 (2016), 43–65; Michael Cottrell, 'Green and Orange in Mid-Nineteenth-Century Toronto: The Guy Fawkes' Day Episode of 1864', *Canadian Journal of Irish Studies*, 19/1 (1993), 12–21.

24. D. C. Lyne and P. M. Toner, 'Fenianism in Canada 1874–84', *Studia Hibernica*, 12 (1972), 27–76; P. M. Toner, 'The Fanatic Heart of the North' in David Wilson (ed.), *Irish Nationalism in Canada* (Montreal and Kingston, 2009), 34–51. For the Grosse Île memorial, above pp 67–8.

25. Quoted in Mark McGowan, *The Waning of the Green: Catholics, the Irish, and Identity in Toronto 1887–1922* (Montreal and Kingston, 1999), 196.

26. Lynn, 'Friends of Ireland', 52; Maureen Slattery, 'Irish Radicalism and the Roman Catholic Church in Quebec and Ireland 1833–1834: O'Callaghan and O'Connell Compared', *CCHA, Canadian Studies*, 63 (1997), 29–58.

27. Quoted in David Wilson, 'The Narcissism of Nationalism: Irish Images of Quebec, 1847–66', *Canadian Journal of Irish Studies*, 33/1 (2007), 19.

28. Mark McGowan, 'The Tale and Trials of a "Double Minority": The Irish and French Catholic Engagement for the Soul of the Canadian Church, 1815–1947', in Colin Barr and Hilary M. Carey (eds.), *Religion and Greater Ireland: Christianity and Irish Global Networks, 1750–1950* (Montreal and Kingston, 2015), 97–123.

10. An Irish World

1. *Report of the Immigration Commission: Steerage Conditions—1911* (Washington, DC, 1911), 5–12.

2. *Hearings Before the Committee on Immigration and Naturalization . . . December 13 to 20, 1921 . . . February 9 and 13, 1922* (Washington, DC, 1922), 257–77. For Anna Herkner's account of the sexual harassment she witnessed while travelling disguised as a Bohemian peasant in 1911 see *Report of the Immigration Commission: Steerage Conditions—1911*, 21–3; M. A. Jones, 'Transatlantic Steerage Conditions from Sail to Steam 1819–1920', in Brigid Flemming Larsen et al. (eds.), *On Distant Shores* (Aalborg, Denmark, 1993), 77–8.

3. Tyler Anbinder, *City of Dreams: The 400-Year Epic History of Immigrant New York* (Boston and New York, 2017), 331–46.

4. David Fitzpatrick, *The Americanization of Ireland: Migration and Settlement 1841–1925* (Cambridge, 2020), 7, 9–14, 136, 141; Thomas Archdeacon, *Becoming American: An Ethnic History* (New York, 1983), 139; Description of a recent visit to Philadelphia, listed as 29 July 1868 but clearly dating from c. 1901 (IED).

5. For the Irish-born overseas see Appendix. For estimates of the multi-generational Irish population D. H. Akenson, *The Irish Diaspora: A Primer (Toronto and Belfast, 1993)*, 69, 113, 263; Donald MacRaild, *The Irish in Britain 1800–1914* (Dundalk, 2006), 1; David Brundage, *Irish Nationalism in America: The Politics of Exile 1798–1998* (Oxford, 2016), 113.

6. 1900 data in E. P. Hutchinson, *Immigrants and Their Children, 1850–1950* (New York, 1976), 178, 188, tables 35a, 35b. For parity with the native-born see Kevin Kenny, *The American Irish: A History* (Harlow, 2000), 185; David Noel Doyle, *Irish Americans, Native Rights and National Empires* (New York, 1976), 42–5.

7. Kerry Soper, 'From Swarthy Ape to Sympathetic Everyman and Subversive Trickster: The Development of Irish Caricature in American Comic Strips Between 1890 and 1920', *Journal of American Studies*, 39/2 (2005), 257–96.

8. James T. Farrell, *Young Lonigan* (New York, 2001); Frederick L. Hoffman, 'The General Death-Rate of Large American Cities 1871–1904', *Publications of the American Statistical Association*, 10/73 (1906), 20; Niles Carpenter, *Immigrants and Their Children 1920* (Washington, DC, 1927), 197–206; D. N. Doyle, 'The Remaking of Irish America 1845–80' in *NHI, VI*, 748; Nancy Sheper Hughes, *Saints, Scholars and Schizophrenics: Mental Illness in Rural Ireland* (Berkeley, 1979), 72.

9. Archdeacon, *Becoming American*, 118.

10. James Barrett, *The Irish Way: Becoming American in the Multiethnic City* (New York, 2012), 116–22.

11. Barrett, *The Irish Way*, 150–4, 208; Steven P. Erie, *Rainbow's End: Irish-Americans and the Dilemmas of Urban Machine Politics, 1840–1985* (Berkeley, 1988), 63–4.

12. Barrett, *The Irish Way*, 66–74.

13. Quoted in Barrett, *The Irish Way*, 2.

14. C. G. Pooley, 'Segregation or Integration? The Residential Experience of the Irish in Mid-Victorian Britain', in R. Swift and S. Gilley (eds.), *The Irish in Britain 1815–1839* (Savage, MD, 1989), 70–1. David Fitzpatrick, 'The Irish in Britain, 1871–1921', in *NHI, VI*, 662–4, documents the lack of upward social mobility. D. M. MacRaild, *Irish Migrants in Modern Britain, 1750–1922* (Basingstoke, 1999), chap. 2, offers a more optimistic account, but this relies rather heavily on the special case of the north of England iron industry.

15. Gearóid Ó Tuathaigh, 'The Irish in Nineteenth-Century Britain: Problems of Integration', *Transactions of the Royal Historical Society*, 31 (1981), 156.

16. Fitzpatrick, 'The Irish in Britain', 668–9.

17. Brian Jenkins, *The Fenian Problem: Insurgency and Terrorism in a Liberal State* (Liverpool, 2008), 337–40.

18. D. M. MacRaild, *Faith, Fraternity and Fighting: The Orange Order and Irish Migrants in Northern England, c. 1850–1920* (Liverpool, 2005).

19. The contrast between the Irish experience in the United States and in other destinations is a central theme of Akenson, *The Irish Diaspora,* and Malcolm Campbell, *Ireland's New Worlds: Immigrants, Politics and Society in the United States and Australia, 1815–1922* (Madison, WI, 2008). For the Irish in the western United States see above pp 106–8.

20. Helen Kelly, *Irish 'Ingleses', The Irish Immigrant Experience in Argentina 1840–1920* (Dublin, 2009), 55; Patrick Speight, *Irish-Argentine Identity in an Age of Political Challenge and Change, 1875–1983* (Oxford/New York, 2019), 17–20.

21. Patrick McKenna, 'Irish Migration to Argentina', in Patrick O'Sullivan (ed.), *The Irish World Wide, Vol. 1: Patterns of Migration* (Leicester, 1992), 63–83; John Murray, 'The Irish and Others in Argentina', *Studies,* 38/152 (1949), 380–2; Stephen Collins, 'Murder, Sainthood and Irishness in Argentina', *Irish Times,* 5 November 2013; Speight, *Irish-Argentine Identity,* 203.

22. Claire Healy, 'The Irish "Ingleses" in Nineteenth-Century Buenos Aires', *History Ireland,* 16/4 (2006), 37–40.

11. War and Revolution

1. Michael Keyes, *Funding the Nation: Money and Nationalist Politics in Nineteenth-Century Ireland* (Dublin, 2011).

2. For numbers in 1903, David Fitzpatrick, 'Exporting Brotherhood: Orangeism in South Australia', *Immigrants and Minorities,* 23/2–3 (2005), 277–310. For the Council of the World, see D. M. MacRaild, *Faith, Fraternity and Fighting: The Orange Order and Irish Migrants in Northern England, c. 1850–1920* (Liverpool, 2005), 302–3, and for the more exotic aspects of Canadian Orangeism, C. J. Houston and W. J. Smyth, *The Sash Canada Wore: A Historical Geography of the Orange Order in Canada* (Toronto, 1980), 95, 162.

3. Elizabeth Malcolm and Dianne Hall, *A New History of the Irish in Australia* (Sydney, 2018), 46. For the connection with Imperial Federation, Richard Davis, *Irish Issues in New Zealand Politics, 1868–1922* (Dunedin, 1974), chap. 7; Thomas Mohr, 'Irish Home Rule and Constitutional Reform in the British Empire, 1885–1914', *French Journal of British Studies,* 24/2 (2019), 1–17.

4. Michael Doorley, *Justice Daniel Cohalan, 1865–1946: American Patriot and Irish-American Nationalist* (Cork, 2019).

5. *National German-American Alliance: Hearings Before the Subcommittee of the Committee on the Judiciary, United States Senate* (Washington, DC, 1918), 646.

6. Úna Ní Bhroiméil, *Building Irish Identity in America, 1870–1915: The Gaelic Revival* (Dublin, 2003); Paul Darby, *Gaelic Games, Nationalism and the Irish Diaspora in the United States* (Dublin, 2009).

7. Dennis Ryan and Kevin Wamsley, 'A Grand Game of Hurling and Football: Sport and Irish Nationalism in Toronto', *Canadian Journal of Irish Studies,* 30/1 (2004), 21–31; Patrick O'Farrell, *The Irish in Australia: 1788 to the Present* (3rd ed. Sydney, 2000), 186–7.

8. Redmond quoted in Alan Ward, *Ireland and Anglo-American Relations 1899–1921* (London, 1969), 15.

9. Malcolm Campbell, 'Emigrant Responses to War and Revolution, 1914–21: Irish Opinion in the United States and Australia', *Irish Historical* Studies, 32/125 (2000), 78–83; Mark McGowan, *The Imperial Irish: Canada's Irish Catholics Fight the Great War, 1914–1918* (Montreal and Kingston, 2017), 62–7, 76–80, 217–8.

10. McGowan, *The Imperial Irish*, 28; Mike Cronin and Daryl Adair, *The Wearing of the Green: A History of St Patrick's Day* (London, 2002), 114.

11. Jedd Kildea, 'Australian Catholics and Conscription in the Great War', *Journal of Religious History*, 26/3 (2002), 298–313; Hall and Malcolm, *Irish in Australia*, 312–22. For different reports of Mannix's words, Val Noone, 'Class Factors in the Radicalisation of Archbishop Daniel Mannix, 1913–17', *Labour History*, 106 (2014), 199–200.

12. O'Farrell, *Irish in Australia*, 284; T. E. Hachey, 'The Quarantine of Archbishop Mannix: A British Preventive Policy During the Anglo-Irish Troubles', *Irish University Review*, 1/1 (1970), 111–30.

13. Cronin and Adair, *The Wearing of the Green*, 113–32. Different figures have been given for the number of Catholics among the Victoria Cross holders. Tim Sullivan identifies all fourteen, and bases his figure of eight on their enlistment papers. See 'An Illusion of Unity: Irish Australia, the Great War and the 1920 St Patrick's Day Parade', *Agora*, 55/1 (2020), 24–31 (online journal www.htav.asn.au /documents/item/3390, accessed 24 July 2020).

14. Catalogue entry in the New Zealand National Library, https://natlib.govt .nz/records/22400921 (accessed 23 July 2020); James Watson, *W. F. Massey: New Zealand* (London, 2010), 145–7. The encyclical, *Ne Temere*, was mainly concerned to impose strict conditions on Catholics wishing to marry a person of another faith, and to make the church's acknowledgement of the marriage as grudging and mean-spirited as possible. But it was also taken as denying the validity of marriages involving a Catholic but not celebrated by a priest. The 1920 act made it a crime to challenge the legitimacy of a legally valid marriage. There were no prosecutions under the act.

15. Malcolm Campbell, *Ireland's New Worlds: Immigrants, Politics and Society in the United States and Australia, 1815–1922* (Madison, 2008), 175; Jimmy Yan, 'Labour Radicalism and Irish Revolution in Australia' in Fearghal McGarry (ed.), *Century Ireland: Global Irish Revolution*, www.rte.ie/centuryireland/index.php/articles /labour-radicalism-irish-revolution-in-australia (accessed 24 June 2021).

16. Lar Joyce, 'The 69th "Fighting Irish" Regiment in the First World War', *History Ireland*, 26/6 (2018), 35.

17. Ward, *Ireland and Anglo-American Relations*; Michael Doorley, *Irish American Diaspora Nationalism: The Friends of Irish Freedom, 1916–35* (Dublin, 2005).

18. Michael Hopkinson, 'President Woodrow Wilson and the Irish Question', *Studia Hibernica* 27 (1993), 89–111. For Wilson's supposed Orange prejudices see the comments of Devoy, quoted in Robert Schmuhl, *Ireland's Exiled Children: America and the Easter Rising* (Oxford, 2016), 37. For his comments on Barry see Ward, *Ireland and Anglo-American Relations*, 81–2, and for Roosevelt *New York Tribune*, 11

September 1895. See also Roosevelt's use of the phrase, in a slightly different context, in *Boston Journal*, 19 April 1892.

19. De Valera quoted in Ward, *Ireland and Anglo-American Relations*, 219; Gallagher quoted in Doorley, *Cohalan*, 157–8.

20. For 1916 see Doorley, *Cohalan*, 93–4, and for 1920 Ward, *Ireland and Anglo-American Relations*, 221–4; R. A. Burchell, 'Did the Irish and German Voters Desert the Democrats in 1920? A Tentative Statistical Answer', *Journal of American Studies*, 6/1 (1972), 153–64.

21. Timothy J. Meagher, *Inventing Irish America: Generation, Class and Ethnic Identity in a New England City, 1880–1928* (Notre Dame, 2001), 349–58.

12. In the Melting Pot

1. Mike Cronin and Daryl Adair, *The Wearing of the Green: A History of St Patrick's Day* (London, 2002), 109–10. The twenty-six-county state created by the Anglo-Irish Treaty of 1921 was initially called the Irish Free State. After 1937, with the introduction of a new constitution, the government insisted that the English name of the state was 'Ireland', a tendentious formulation liable to cause confusion. The state became a republic in 1949, but the official name remained 'Ireland'. In the interests of clarity, the southern state is referred to here, according to context, as the Irish Free State, independent Ireland, or the Irish Republic.

2. Dáil quoted in Enda Delaney, *Demography, State and Society: Irish Migration to Britain, 1921–71* (Liverpool, 2000), 57. For statistics see Delaney, *Demography, State and Society*, 48–9; Mary Daly, 'Migration Since 1914', in Thomas Bartlett (ed.), *The Cambridge History of Ireland, Vol. 4: 1880 to the Present* (Cambridge, 2018), 539, 551.

3. Andy Bielenberg, 'Exodus: The Emigration of Southern Irish Protestants During the Irish War of Independence and the Civil War', *Past & Present*, 218 (2013), 199–233; Delaney, *Demography, State and Society*, 69–83.

4. Mary E. Daly, *The Slow Failure: Population Decline and Independent Ireland, 1920–1973* (Madison, WI, 2006).

5. Damian Hannan quoted in Delaney, *Demography, State and Society*, 247; Robert Kennedy, *The Irish: Emigration, Marriage and Fertility* (Berkeley, 1973), 168–9. For the sense of malaise see Clair Wills, *The Best Are Leaving: Emigration and Post-War Irish Culture* (Cambridge, 2015).

6. Johanne Devlin Trew, *Leaving the North: Migration and Memory, Northern Ireland 1921–2011* (Liverpool, 2013).

7. Matthew O'Brien, 'Transatlantic Connections and the Sharp Edge of the Great Depression', *Éire-Ireland*, 37/1–2 (2002), 38–57.

8. *Reports of the Commission on Emigration and Other Population Problems 1948–54* (Dublin 1954), 316; Delaney, *Demography, State and Society*, 45, 130, 234.

9. Rory O'Dwyer, 'A "Roof-Raising Affair": Éamon de Valera's Tour of Australia and New Zealand', in L. M. Geary and A. J. McCarthy (eds.), *Ireland, Australia and New Zealand* (Dublin, 2008), 211–23.

10. Oliver MacDonagh, 'The Irish in Australia: A General View', in Oliver MacDonagh and W. F. Mandle (eds.), *Ireland and Irish-Australia* (London, 1986), 168–9;

D. H. Akenson, *Half the World from Home: Perspectives on the Irish in New Zealand, 1860–1950* (Wellington, 1990), 74–82.

11. Christopher van der Krogt, 'Catholic Religious Identity and Social Integration in Interwar New Zealand', *Catholic Historical Review*, 86/1 (2000), 47–65. For statistics on church attendance, schools and mixed marriage see Patrick O'Farrell, *The Catholic Church and Community in Australia: A History* (Melbourne, 1977), 280, 352, 369; Akenson, *Half the World from Home*, 161–73. For the boorish products of All Hallows Patrick O'Farrell, *Vanished Kingdoms: Irish in Australia and New Zealand: A Personal Excursion* (Kensington, NSW, 1990), 103.

12. O'Regan quoted in Sean Brosnahan, 'Parties or Politics: Wellington's IRA 1922–8', in Brad Patterson (ed.), *The Irish in New Zealand: Historical Contexts and Perspectives* (Wellington, 2002), 76; O'Farrell, *Vanished Kingdoms*, xvii. For attendance at De Valera's Australian meetings see Patrick O'Farrell, *The Irish in Australia: 1798 to the Present* (3rd ed. Sydney, 2000), 304–5, a more critical account than O'Dwyer's 'A "Roof Raising Affair"'.

13. Declan O'Connell and John Warhurst, 'Church and Class: Irish-Australian Labour Loyalties and the 1955 Split', *Saothar*, 8 (1982), 54–7.

14. O'Farrell, *Catholic Church and Community*, 399–401; Akenson, *Half the World from Home*, 184–9.

15. Keith Jeffery, 'Distance and Proximity in Service to the Empire: Ulster and New Zealand Between the Wars', in Robert Holland and Sarah Stockwell (eds.), *Ambiguities of Empire* (New York, 2009), 113; Philip Ollerenshaw, 'Northern Ireland and the British Empire-Commonwealth, 1923–61', *Irish Historical Studies*, 36/142 (2008), 231, 240.

16. *Irish Press*, 19 May 1950; Seamus Smyth, 'In Defence of Ulster: The Visit of Sir Basil Brooke to North America, Spring 1950', *Canadian Journal of Irish Studies*, 33/2 (2007), 10–18.

17. 'Too much insistence upon "British"': quoted in W. J. Smyth, *Toronto: The Belfast of Canada: The Orange Order and the Shaping of Municipal Culture* (Toronto, 2015), 32. For the decline of Orangeism David Wilson (ed.), *The Orange Order in Canada* (Dublin, 2007), 177; C. J. Houston and W. J. Smyth, *The Sash Canada Wore: The Historical Geography of the Orange Order in Canada* (Toronto, 1980), 162, 167. For the Irish component in the population Sheila T. McGree and Victoria M. Esses, 'The Irish in Canada: A Demographic Study Based on the 1986 Census', *Canadian Journal of Irish Studies*, 16/1 (1990), 4–5. The figure is based on self-identification, with respondents allowed to name multiple national origins.

18. Ollerenshaw, 'Northern Ireland and the British Empire-Commonwealth', 238.

19. E. P. Hutchinson, *Emigrants and Their Children, 1850–1950* (New York, 1956), 224–41. For the figure of three-quarters, Kevin Kenny, *The American Irish: A History* (Harlow, 2000), 227.

20. Stephan Thernstrom, *The Other Bostonians: Poverty and Progress in the American Metropolis, 1880–1970* (Cambridge, MA, 1973), 139, 141; W. W. Lloyd Warner and Leo Srole, *The Social Systems of American Ethnic Groups* (New Haven and

London, 1945), 93–4; Jack Beatty, *The Rascal King: The Life and Times of James Michael Curley (1874–1958)* (Reading, MA, 1992), 234. Warner and Srole's volume, one of a six-part series, reflects research done during 1930-5.

21. Marion R. Casey, 'Irish Americans on the Move in New York City' in R. H. Bayor and T. J. Meagher (eds.), *The New York Irish* (Baltimore, 1996), 395–415; Warner and Srole, *Social Systems*, 35–40.

22. Ruby Jo Reeves Kennedy, 'Single or Triple Melting-Pot? Intermarriage in New Haven, 1870–1940', *American Journal of Sociology*, 49/4 (1944), 331–9. More than 90 per cent of the marriages in Kennedy's tables where both parties were Irish were celebrated in Catholic churches (page 58). This would indicate that her 'Irish' are in fact Irish Catholics—probably because she used a combination of surname and religion to identify nationality when working through the marriage registers. For the Ne Temere decree see above p. 498, note 14.

23. Mary Burke, 'Grace Kelly, Philadelphia and the Politics of Irish Lace', *American Journal of Irish Studies*, 15 (2019), 31–23.

24. Thernstrom, *Other Bostonians*, 138–42; Steven Erie, *Rainbow's End: Irish Americans and the Dilemmas of Urban Machine Politics, 1840–1985* (Berkeley, 1988), 238–46.

25. Lawrence J. McCaffrey, *Textures of Irish America* (New York, 1992), xiii–xiv.

26. Thernstrom, *Other Bostonians*, 61–70. For Jewish and Irish entrepreneurship and incomes see Thernstrom, *Other Bostonians*, 136–7.

27. Nathan Glazer and Daniel Patrick Moynihan, *Beyond the Melting Pot: The Negroes, Puerto Ricans, Jews, Italians, and Irish of New York City* (2nd ed. Cambridge, MA, 1970), xcvii.

28. Warner and Srole, *Social Systems of American Ethnic Groups*, 241. For the decline of the GAA in the interwar years see Paul Darby, *Gaelic Games, Nationalism and the Irish Diaspora in the United States* (Dublin, 2009), 85–101, and for the Hibernians Matthew O'Brien, '"Hibernians on the March": Irish America and Ethnic Patriotism in the Mid-Twentieth Century', *Éire-Ireland*, 40/1–2 (2005), 170–82.

29. For Newburyport Protestants see Warner and Srole, *Social Systems*, 293. For the Catholic Church, Jay P. Dolan, *The Irish Americans: A History* (New York, 2008), 231.

30. Timothy J. Meagher, *The Columbia Guide to Irish American History* (New York, 2005), 143–4, 274–5; John T. McGreevy, 'Thinking on One's Own: Catholicism in the American Intellectual Imagination, 1928–60', *Journal of American History*, 84/1 (1997), 100–4.

31. Brian Hanley, 'Irish Republicans in Interwar New York', *Irish Journal of American Studies Online*, 1 (2009), 48–61; Gavin Wilk, *Transatlantic Defiance: The Militant Irish Republican Movement in America, 1923–45* (Manchester, 2014). For the emigration of anti-Treaty veterans, Gavin Foster, 'No "Wild Geese" this Time? IRA Emigration After the Irish Civil War', *Éire-Ireland*, 47 (2012), 94–122.

32. Richard English, '"Paying No Heed to Public Clamour": Irish Republican Solipsism in the 1930s', *Irish Historical Studies*, 28/112 (1993).

33. Elizabeth Keane, 'All Politics Is Local: The USA and the Anti-Partition Movement During the First Inter-Party Government', *Irish Studies Review*, 15/3 (2007), 299–300; Edwin O'Connor, *The Last Hurrah* (Boston, n.d.), 255.

13. From Tammany to Camelot

1. For a statistical analysis of the prevalence in different decades of urban machines see M. C. Brown and C. N. Halaby, 'Machine Politics in America, 1870–1945', *Journal of Interdisciplinary History*, 17/3 (1987), 587–612.

2. Steven Erie, *Rainbow's End: Irish-Americans and the Dilemmas of Urban Machine Politics, 1840–1985* (Berkeley, 1988), 85, 124, 214; Reginald Byron, *Irish America* (Oxford, 1999), 176–7; L. W. Dorsett, *Franklin D. Roosevelt and the Big City Bosses* (Port Washington, NY, 1977), 104, 105.

3. Matthew O'Brien, 'Transatlantic Connections and the Sharp Edge of the Great Depression', *Éire-Ireland*, 37/1–2 (2002), 43–7; Allan J. Lichtman, *Prejudice and the Old Politics: The Presidential Election of 1928* (Lanham, MD, 2000), 60; Robert A. Slayton, *Empire Statesman: The Rise and Redemption of Al Smith* (New York, 2001), ix.

4. For Jewish competition see James Barrett, *The Irish Way: Becoming American in the Multiethnic City* (New York, 2012), 229.

5. Jack Beatty, *The Rascal King: The Life and Times of James Michael Curley (1874–1958)* (Reading, MA, 1992), 170, 393; William Shannon, *The American Irish: A Political and Social Portrait* (rev. ed., New York, 1966), 216.

6. David M. Kennedy, *Freedom from Fear: The American People in Depression and War, 1929–45* (Oxford, 1999), 227–34; Beatty, *Rascal King*, 454.

7. Dorsett, *Franklin D. Roosevelt and the City Bosses*, 92. For Curley and Poland see Beatty, *The Rascal King*, 330.

8. Erie, *Rainbow's End*, 88, 298 n. 8; Beatty, *The Rascal King*, 294, 410, 417.

9. Kennedy, *Freedom from Fear*, 285, 320. For the wider social background, see Lizabeth Cohen, *Making a New Deal: Industrial Workers in Chicago, 1919–39* (2nd ed. Cambridge, 2008).

10. R. H. Bayor and T. J. Meagher (eds.), *The New York Irish* (Baltimore, 1996), 339; Terry Golway, *Machine Made: Tammany Hall and the Creation of Modern American Politics* (New York, 2014), 290–300; Dorsett, *Franklin D. Roosevelt and the City Bosses*, chap. 4.

11. Erie, *Rainbow's End*, 118–28; Thomas H. O'Connor, *The Boston Irish: A Political History* (Boston, 1995), 285–303.

12. U.S. Bureau of the Census, *Current Population Report*, Series P-20, No. 221, 'Characteristics of the Population by Ethnic Origin: November 1969' (U.S. Government Printing Office, Washington, D.C., 1971). For example, 30 per cent of Irish men and 21 per cent of Irish women were in professional and managerial jobs, compared to 28 per cent and 19 per cent of the overall population. Twenty-one per cent of men were skilled workers or foremen, compared to 20 per cent of the overall population.

13. Andrew Greeley, *The Irish Americans: The Rise to Money and Power* (New York, 1981), 1–8, 106–14.

14. Bayor and Meagher, *New York Irish*, 421; Timothy J. Meagher, *The Columbia Guide to Irish American History* (New York, 2005), 133; Robert W. Snyder, 'The Neighbourhood Changed: The Irish of Washington Heights and Inwood Since 1945', in Bayor and Meagher (eds.), *The New York Irish*, 439–60.

15. Greeley, *The Irish Americans*, 148; Byron, *Irish America*, 75.

16. Byron, *Irish America*, 177, 182. For Irish mayors in 1965, Shannon, *The American Irish*, 432.

17. The range of opportunities that the New Deal opened up for Irishmen is outlined in Shannon, *The American Irish*, 327–48. See also Kennedy, *Freedom from Fear*, 285. For Joseph Kennedy see Fredrik Logevall, *JFK, Vol. 1: 1917–1956* (London, 2020), 152–3, 301.

18. Shannon, *American Irish*, 412–13.

19. Joseph L. Rosenberg, 'The 1941 Mission of Frank Aiken to the United States: An American Perspective', *Irish Historical Studies*, 22/86 (1980), 162–77.

20. Matthew J. O'Brien, 'Wartime Revisions of Irish American Catholicism: Stars, Stripes and Shamrocks', *US Catholic Historian*, 22/3 (2004), 75–96; Brian Hanley, '"No English Enemy . . . Ever Stooped so Low": Mike Quill, de Valera's Visit to the German Legation, and Irish-American Attitudes During World War II', *Radharc*, 5/7 (2004–6), 245–64.

21. Robert Dallek, *An Unfinished Life: John F. Kennedy, 1917–63* (New York, 2003), chaps. 7–8. For Humphrey's campaign song see page 253.

22. Dallek, *An Unfinished Life*, 625, 126; Doris Kearns Goodwin, *The Fitzgeralds and the Kennedys: An American Saga* (London, 1988), 538; Logevall, *JFK*, 56; Sylvia Ellis, 'The Historical Significance of President Kennedy's Visit to Ireland in June 1963', *Irish Studies Review*, 16/2 (2008), 115.

23. 'Kenneth P. O'Donnell Dies at 53', *New York Times*, 10 September 1977 (Salinger's background was French and New York Jewish, Sorensen's Danish and Russian Jewish); Steven Gould Axelrod, 'Frost and the Cold War', in Mark Richardson (ed.), *Robert Frost in Context* (Cambridge, 2014), 210; Goodwin, *The Fitzgeralds and the Kennedys*, 708; Logevall, *JFK*, 524.

14. 'We've married Italian girls and moved to the suburbs'

1. O'Neill quoted in Tim Pat Coogan, *Wherever Green is Worn: The Story of the Irish Diaspora* (London, 2000), 265–6, and in Ray O'Hanlon, *Unintended Consequences: The Story of Irish Immigration to the U.S. and How America's Door Was Closed to the Irish* (Newbridge, Co. Kildare, 2021), 213. Irish official quoted in Mary Daly, *The Slow Failure: Population Decline and Independent Ireland, 1920–1973* (Madison, WI, 2006), 327. The former Irish diplomat is Sean Donlon, in Garret Fitzgerald Interview, 28 September 2005, Edward M. Kennedy Oral History Project, Miller Centre, University of Virginia, 24.

2. See Appendix.

3. Central Statistics Office, 'Population Change and Historical Perspective', in Census 2016 Summary Results (Dublin, 2017), 10, www.cso.ie/en/media/csoie /releasespublications/documents/population/2017/Chapter_1_Population _change_and_historical_perspective.pdf (accessed 11 December 2020); M. E. Daly,

'Migration Since 1914', in Thomas Bartlett (ed.), *The Cambridge History of Ireland, Vol. 4: 1880 to the Present* (Cambridge, 2018), 533; Irial Glynn, with Tomás Kelly and Piaras MacÉinrí, *The Re-Emergence of Emigration from Ireland: New Trends in an Old Story* (Washington, DC, 2015), 6.

4. Daly, 'Migration Since 1914', 534; Glynn et al., *Re-Emergence of Emigration*, 7–8, 11; Bryan Fanning, *Migration and the Making of Ireland* (Dublin, 2018), 152–6; A. P. Lobo and J. J. Salvo, 'Resurgent Irish Immigration to the US in the 1980s and Early 1990s: A Socio-Demographic Profile', *International Migration*, 36/2 (1998), 257–80.

5. Central Statistics Office, *Census 2011, Profile 6—Migration and Diversity* (Dublin, 2012), 7, 11; Fanning, *Migration and the Making of Ireland*, 211–20; Irial Glynn, 'Migration and Integration Since 1991', in M. E. Daly and Eugenio Biagini (eds.), *The Cambridge Social History of Ireland* (Cambridge, 2017), 571–3. For returning Irish emigrants in 1998–9 see Enda Delaney, *Irish Emigration Since 1921* (Dundalk, 2002), 7.

6. Fanning, *Migration and the Making of Ireland*, 159–67, 181–91.

7. Faith Survey, Irish Census 2016, https://faithsurvey.co.uk/irish-census.html (accessed 16 December 2020); Louise Fuller, *Irish Catholicism Since 1950: The Undoing of a Culture* (Dublin, 2004).

8. Feargal Cochrane, *The End of Irish America: Globalisation and the Irish Diaspora* (Dublin, 2010), chap. 6. For the basing of the Irish pub on the post-1960s lounge bar, Vincent Comerford, *Inventing the Nation: Ireland* (London, 2003), 199.

9. 'Cherishing the Irish Diaspora: President Mary Robinson on a Matter of Public Importance 2 February 1995', President of Ireland, Media Library, https://president .ie/en/media-library/speeches/cherishing-the-irish-diaspora (accessed 19 November 2021).

10. Rebecca S. Miller, 'Irish Traditional Music in the United States', in J. J. Lee and Marion Casey (eds.), *Making the Irish American: History and Heritage of the Irish in the United States* (New York, 2006), 414–5; Marion Casey, 'Before Riverdance', in Lee and Casey (eds.), *Making the Irish American*, 422–3; Patrick O'Farrell, *The Irish in Australia: 1788 to the Present* (3rd ed. Sydney, 2000), 321, 330–3; Edmundo Murray, *Becoming Irlandés: Private Narratives of the Irish Emigration to Argentina* (Buenos Aires, 2005), 6.

11. O'Farrell, *Irish in Australia*, 311–21; Cochrane, *The End of Irish America*, 41. For the parade controversy *New York Times*, 1 March 2013, 15 March 2015, 10 January 2016, 17 March 2016; 'New York City Mayor Ends Boycott of St Patrick's Day Parade as Gay Ban Dropped', *Guardian*, 3 March 2016. See also Cochrane, *The End of Irish America*, chap. 5; Mike Cronin and Daryl Adair, *The Wearing of the Green: A History of St Patrick's Day* (London 2002), 222–6.

12. Dennis P. Ryan, *Beyond the Ballot Box: A Social History of the Boston Irish, 1845–1917* (London and Toronto, 1983).

13. D. H. Akenson, 'The Historiography of the Irish in the United States of America', in Patrick O'Sullivan (ed.), *The Irish World Wide, Vol. 2: The Irish in the New Communities* (Leicester, 1992), 100–1; Thomas Beer, in 1941, quoted in

W. V. Shannon, *The American Irish: A Political and Social Portrait* (2nd ed. New York, 1966), viii. Beer's comments are close to those of John Lynch, Catholic bishop of Toronto, who had earlier been a missionary priest in the United States. In a polemic against emigration from Ireland, published in 1864, Lynch wrote of visiting a town in Texas where the shops bore names like O'Doherty, McCarthy and O'Brien, yet there was only one Catholic to be found: *Wexford People*, 21 May 1864. For Newburyport see above p. 352.

14. For liturgical change and contraception see Lawrence J. McCaffrey, *Textures of Irish America* (Syracuse, 1992), 87, 84, 87. For religious practice Faith Survey, American Catholic Statistics (1985–2018), https://faithsurvey.co.uk/american -catholic-statistics.html (accessed 22 December 2020).

15. These are the statistics brought together in McCaffrey, *Textures of Irish America*, 120–1; Jay P. Dolan, *The Irish Americans: A History* (New York, 2008), 292–4. They slip disconcertingly back and forth between 'Irish', 'Catholic' and 'Irish Catholic', and it is not always clear how carefully the three are distinguished. For 2008–16 see IrishCentral.com, www.irishcentral.com/news/president-barack -obama-has-narrow-lead-over-mitt-romney-among-irish-american-voters-in -irishcentral-poll-176994391-237755741 (accessed 1 February 2021); 'St Patrick's Day Events Highlight an Irish Divide over Trump', *New York Times*, 16 March 2017.

16. US Bureau of the Census, *Current Population Report*, 'Characteristics of the Population by Ethnic Origin, November 1969' (Washington, DC, 1971); Reginald Byron, *Irish America* (Oxford, 1999), 153; Marjorie R. Fallows, *Irish Americans: Identity and Assimilation* (Englewood Cliffs, NJ, 1979), 65, 105; Richard D. Alba, 'Social Assimilation Among American Catholic National-Origin Groups', *American Sociological Review*, 41/6 (1976), 1035–6.

17. Byron, *Irish America*, 127–33, 249–58, 115, 259–60. See in particular the vivid account, by one of Byron's researchers, of an Irish festival held in nearby New Durham on 26 May 1991 (262–3).

18. Unnamed board member of the Irish Arts Centre in the Bronx quoted in Ronald Bayor and Timothy Meagher (eds.), *The New York Irish* (Baltimore and London, 1996), 437.

19. US Bureau of the Census, *Census 2000 Brief: Ancestry 2000* (June 2004), available at www.census.gov.

20. Andrew Sanders, *The Long Peace Process: The United States of America and Northern Ireland, 1960–2008* (Liverpool, 2019), 186–9; Brian Hanley, 'The Politics of NORAID', *Irish Political Studies*, 19/1 (2004), 14–15.

21. Caitríona Perry, *The Tribe: The Inside Story of Irish Power and Influence in US Politics* (Dublin, 2019), 75, 130.

22. Perry, *The Tribe*, 157–73.

23. Lobo and Salvo, 'Resurgent Irish Immigration', 259, 261–3; Ray O'Hanlon, *The New Irish Americans* (Niwot, CO, 1998), 61–87, 108.

24. O'Hanlon, *The New Irish Americans*, 102, 42, 70, 85, 53. See also Matthew Frye Jacobson, *Roots Too: White Ethnic Revival in Post–Civil Rights America* (Cambridge, MA, 2006), 389–96.

15. A Last Hurrah?

1. There is a large literature on the Northern Irish conflict, much of it partisan. Two books offering balanced accounts, and focussing on opposite sides of the divide, are Richard English, *Armed Struggle: A History of the IRA* (London, 2003) and Susan McKay, *Northern Protestants: An Unsettled People* (2nd ed. Belfast, 2005). Note that, although most Northern Irish nationalists would say that their hope is for an all-island Irish Republic, 'republican' is generally used to distinguish supporters of the IRA and its political wing, Sinn Féin, from more moderate, non-violent, nationalist groups. Statistics on deaths are bedevilled by problems of definition. The figures given here are from a database published in the *Guardian* in 2010: https://theguardian.com/news/datablog/2010/jun/10/deaths-in-northern-ireland-conflict-data (accessed 3 January 2022).

2. Andrew Wilson, *Irish America and the Ulster Conflict 1968–1995* (Washington, DC, 1995); Jack Holland, *The American Connection: U.S. Guns, Money and Influence in Northern Ireland* (New York, 1987).

3. Brian Hanley, 'The Politics of Noraid', *Irish Political Studies*, 19/1 (2004), 1–4; Reginald Byron, *Irish America* (Oxford, 1999), 121.

4. Caitríone Perry, *The Tribe: The Inside Story of Irish Power and Influence in US Politics* (Dublin, 2019), 25, 46–7; *Irish America*, April 1987, https://irishamerica.com/2020/08/senator-joe-biden (accessed 25 January 2021).

5. Tom Hayden, *Irish on the Inside: In Search of the Soul of Irish America* (London, 2001), 66, 100–1.

6. Matthew Frye Jacobson, *Roots Too: White Ethnic Revival in Post–Civil Rights America* (Cambridge, MA, 2006); Thomas Archdeacon, 'The Irish Famine in American School Curricula', *Éire-Ireland*, 37/1–2 (2002), 130–52; Liam Kennedy, *Unhappy the Land: The Most Oppressed People Ever, the Irish?* (Dublin, 2016), chap. 5.

7. Matthew O'Brien, 'Irish America, Race and Bernadette Devlin's 1969 American Tour', *New Hibernia Review*, 14/2 (2010), 84–101; Hanley, 'The Politics of Noraid'; Holland, *The American Connection*, 48–57. For the busing protests see Wilson, *Irish America and the Ulster Conflict*, 33, and for the 1986 split, see above p. 427.

8. Wilson, *Irish America and the Ulster Conflict*, 99–105. For Kennedy's telegram, *Irish Times*, 26 June 1969.

9. Sean Donlon, 'Bringing Irish Diplomatic and Political Influence to Bear on Washington', *Irish Times*, 25 January 1993.

10. Maurice Fitzpatrick, *John Hume in America: From Derry to DC* (Dublin, 2017). Donlon and Lillis offer detailed accounts in what is labelled an interview with Garret Fitzgerald, 28 September 2005, Edward M. Kennedy Oral History Project, Miller Center. See also the interview with John Hume in the same collection.

11. Sylvia Ellis, 'The Historical Significance of President Kennedy's Visit to Ireland in June 1963', *Irish Studies Review*, 16/2 (2008), 122; Andrew Sanders, *The Long Peace Process: The United States of America and Northern Ireland, 1960–2008* (Liverpool, 2019), chap. 1–2; Holland, *The American Connection*, 27–47.

12. For Carter's badge see Sanders, *The Long Peace Process*, 87–8.

13. Sean Donlon, 'Reagan's Irish Connection', *Irish Times*, 14 January 1989, and a fuller account by Donlon printed in Sanders, *The Long Peace Process*, 140–1. For the WASP vote see Fitzgerald Interview, 27. For the location of Dublin, Conor O'Clery in *Irish Times*, 6 November 2015. For Clark's role as Reagan's most committed adviser on Irish issues see Sean Donlon's reminiscences in *Irish Times*, 25 January 1993, and Wilson, *Irish America and the Ulster Conflict*, 243–4, and for his remarks on reunification *Irish Times*, 8 December 1981.

14. James Cooper, '"The Situation Over There Really Bothers Me": Ronald Reagan and the Northern Ireland Conflict', *Irish Historical Studies*, 14/159 (2017).

15. English, *Armed Struggle*, 225.

16. Wilson, *Irish America and the Ulster Conflict*, 268–77.

17. Conor O'Clery, *The Greening of the White House* (Dublin, 1996), 18–25; *Irish Times*, 1, 5 October 1992. For Clinton's own account see Bill Clinton, *My Life* (London, 2005), 401.

18. Niall O'Dowd interview, 18 November 2010, Edward M. Kennedy Oral History Project, Miller Center 8.

19. Nancy Soderberg interview, 10–11 May 2007, William J. Clinton Presidential History Project, Miller Center, 64–5; Garret Fitzgerald interview [with Michael Lillis and Sean Donlon], 28 September 2005, Edward M. Kennedy Oral History Project, Miller Center, 31; O'Clery, *Greening of the White House*, 78. Clinton's motives are analysed in Mary-Alice Clancy, *Peace Without Consensus: Power Sharing Politics in Northern Ireland* (Farnham, Surrey, 2010), 62–7; Timothy J. Lynch, *Turf War: The Clinton Administration and Northern Ireland* (London and New York, 2004), 35–56.

20. For an incisive account of Sinn Féin's disengagement from violence, deftly unpicking fact and myth, see Henry McDonald, *Gunsmoke and Mirrors: How Sinn Féin Dressed Up Defeat as Victory* (Dublin, 2008).

21. O'Clery, *Greening of the White House*, 139–49, 153; Ed Moloney, *A Secret History of the IRA* (2nd ed. London, 2007), 460–1.

22. 'Noraid Seems Free of Cordite Whiffs as it Backs Adams on NI Agreement', *Irish Times*, 6 June 1998; 'Republican Rebels Gain Strength', *Observer*, 25 June 2000. For Cahill's standard speech, Moloney, *Secret History*, 382, and for 'an internal Northern Ireland solution' George Mitchell, *Making Peace* (New York, 1999), 133.

23. Clancy, *Peace Without Consensus*, 120–8, 171–5; Sanders, *The Long Peace Process*, 259–69. For the FARC episode see Henry McDonald, Kamal Ahmed and Ed Vulliamy, 'How America Held the IRA over a Barrel', *Guardian*, 28 October 2001, and for Reiss's own retrospective account Mitchell Reiss, 'The Troubles We've Seen', *The American Interest*, 3/6 (2008) www.the-american-interest .com/2008/07/01/the-troubles-weve-seen (accessed 19 February 2021).

24. Sanders, *The Long Peace Process*, 269–76; 'UUP to Defy Pressure and Vote No on Policing', *Irish Times*, 9 March 2010; 'Northern Ireland Executive Now in a Position to Move Forward', *Irish Times*, 10 March 2010. For dealings between the Democratic Unionists and loyalist paramilitaries see Ian Cobain, 'Troubled Past: The Paramilitary Connection That Still Haunts the DUP', *Guardian*, 27 June 2017.

25. Trina Vargo, *Shenanigans: The US-Ireland Relationship in Uncertain Times* (New York, 2019), 46–7; Niall Stanage, *Redemption Song: Barack Obama: From Hope to Reality* (2nd ed. Dublin, 2009), 170–80.

26. For 'Britain Get Out of Ireland', *New York Times*, 16 March 2018; for Friends of Sinn Féin, *Irish Times*, 5 March 2015, 8 September 2020.

27. 'Pelosi's Visit Part of an Enduring Friendship', *Irish Times*, 25 April 2019; Perry, *The Tribe*, 236–7.

16. Global Ireland Reimagined

1. Amnesty International, *The Ugly Side of the Beautiful Game: Exploitation of Migrant Workers on a Qatar 2022 World Cup Site* (London, 2016); 'Revealed: 6,500 Migrant Workers Have Died in Qatar Since World Cup Awarded', *Guardian*, 23 February 2021.

2. Colin Barr, *Ireland's Empire: The Roman Catholic Church in the English-Speaking World, 1829–1914* (Cambridge, 2020), 2.

3. For Irish soft power, see the resentful, and slightly baffled, comments of the right-wing British periodical the *Economist*: 'The Irish Conquest of America', *Economist*, 16 March 2019, and 'How Ireland Gets Its Way: An Unlikely Diplomatic Superpower', *Economist*, 18 July 2020. See also the comments of a senior Irish diplomat, above p. 406.

4. Government of Ireland, *Global Ireland: Ireland's Diaspora Strategy 2020–2025*, www.dfa.ie/media/globalirish/Diaspora-Strategy-2020-English.pdf (accessed 3 March 2021).

5. Government of Ireland, *Global Ireland: Ireland's Global Footprint to 2025*, www.ireland.ie/media/ireland/stories/globaldiaspora/Global-Ireland-in-English.pdf (accessed 3 March 2021).

6. John McManus, 'Taoiseach Blows Out Mary Robinson's Light', *Irish Times*, 18 March 2017.

17. Appendix: A (Short) Note on Statistics

1. Raymond L. Cohn, *Mass Migration Under Sail: European Immigration to the Antebellum United States* (Cambridge, 2009), 26–7.

2. Cormac Ó Gráda, 'A Note on Nineteenth-Century Irish Emigration Statistics', *Population Studies*, 29/1 (1975), 143–9.

3. *Reports of the Commission on Emigration and Other Population Problems 1948–1954* (Dublin, 1954), 316.

INDEX

abolitionism (US), 125–126, 138
Aboriginal people (Australia), 157–159
Act of Union, 195, 202, 243, 258
Ad Hoc Congressional Committee for Irish Affairs, 419–420, 421, 429, 441
Adams, Gerry, 428, 429, 430, 431–433, 434–435, 436
Addams, Jane, 225
AFL-CIO, 399, 419
African Americans
  affirmative action and, 374
  domestic service, 98, 101
  Labor movement and, 233, 238
  Great Migration by, 98, 364
  Irish attitudes to, 111–112, 138–139, 364–365, 373, 399–400
  suburbanisation and, 373
  See also slavery
agriculture. *See* farming/agriculture
Ahern, Bertie, 434
Aiken, Frank, 335, 336, 377–378
Albany, New York, 401–403
Alfred, Duke of Edinburgh, 170, 172, 183
All Hallows College, 167–168, 169, 185, 197, 302, 338
Alternative für Deutschland, 390
American Association for the Recognition of the Irish Republic, 355
American Congress for Irish Freedom, 412–414, 419
American Federation of Labor (AFL), 237–238, 399

American Land League, 234–235, 238, 255
American Party (Know-Nothings), 68, 123–125, 140, 142, 258
American Protective Association, 291–292
American Red Cross, 378
American Republican Party, 122
American Society of Hibernians, 213
American wake, 74
American War of Independence, 18
Americanism, 200–201
Americans for a New Irish Agenda, 429–430
Amnesty International, 427
An Phoblacht, 418
Ancient Order of Foresters, 214
Ancient Order of Hibernians
  Catholic Church and, 202
  Clan na Gael movement and, 309
  decreasing membership in, 351–352, 402
  ethnic revival and, 326
  First World War and, 313–314, 448
  Gaelic League of America and, 310
  Grosse Île monument and, 67
  middle class and, 213
  multiple branches of, 214
  overview of, 240–241
  parishes and, 199
  patriotism and, 255
  Redmond and, 311
  St Patrick's Day parade and, 426
Anderson, Anne, 406
Anderson, David, 21, 33–34

Anderson, John, 21, 33–34
Anderson, Joseph, 21, 34
Anderson, Robert, 21, 34
Anderson, William, 21
Angels with Dirty Faces, 347
Anglo-Irish Treaty, 328, 354–355
Anglophobia, 238–239, 255, 320
anti-Catholic sentiment/violence, 122,
  123, 126, 291, 362–363, 378
anti-immigrant sentiment, 5–6, 7,
  121–124, 136–138, 140–142, 150,
  291–292, 390
anti-Orange riot
  Australia, 170
  Canada, 269, 272, 277–278
  New Zealand, 183–184
  New York, 190–191, 193, 241
anti-partition movement, 335, 342,
  356
antisemitism, 365–366, 378, 379
Aquinas, St Thomas, 353
Argentina, 5, 7, 10, 41–42, 43,
  301–303, 395
Armstrong, Thomas, 42, 302
assembly lines. *See* factory system
assimilation, 171–173, 186, 208,
  227–228, 350–353, 416
Association for the Recognition of the
  Irish Republic, 323, 325
Australia
  de Valera's visit to, 335–336
  emigration to, 2–5, 11, 38–40,
    63–66, 113, 143–145, 289–290,
    388–389, 460
  Eureka Stockade, 159–163
  Gold Rush, 144
  Irish in
    aboriginal people, relations with,
      157–159
    antagonism towards, 65–66, 150,
      166, 169–171, 315, 316
    Catholic Church and, 166–169,
      337–338, 340, 447–448
    crime and policing, involvement
      in, 175–176

dispersed settlement of, 151–152
employment and economic status,
  148–151, 155–157, 336
experience contrasted to United
  States, 89, 154–155, 301
generational conflict among,
  395–396
Gold Rush and, 159–163
land ownership among, 9–10,
  155–157
middle class immigrants,
  148–149
nationalism and, 66–67,
  172–177, 305–307, 311–318,
  319–320, 338–339, 395
number of, 40, 43, 290, 329, 444,
  464
politics and, 159–166, 172, 313,
  339–341
Protestants, 169–171, 306–307
sports among, 311
journey to, 146–147
living standards in, 153
transportation to, 8–9, 38–39,
  145–146, 250
Australian League for an Undivided
  Ireland, 339

Baez, Joan, 392
Bakery Hill. *See* Eureka Stockade
Balch, Emily, 297
Ball, Alice, 65
Balance, John, 182
Ballarat, Victoria, 159–162, 165, 336
Baltic, 317
Barry, John, 321
Barry, Leonora, 234
baseball, 210
Beecher, Lyman, 126
Belfast Agreement, 434, 440
Belfast Weekly News, 13
Bell, David, 202
Benevolent Irish Society, 268
Beyond the Melting Pot (Moynihan and
  Glazer), 350–351

Biaggi, Mario, 419–420, 421
Biden, Joseph, 404, 415, 425,
    440–441
Big Jim McLain, 380
birth control, 228, 353, 364, 391, 398
Black and Tans, 415
Blair, Tony, 433, 434
Board of Alien Commissioners, 84
Board of State Charities, 84
Boer War, 309
Boston, 82, 92, 93, 122, 227–228,
    364–365, 370–371
Boston Pride, 396
Boucicault, Dion, 211
Bourke, Richard, 318
Bowers, Harry F., 291
Bowery Theatre, 211
boxing, 210
Boyle, Brendan, 441
Boyne, Battle of the, 204
Brazil, 7, 8, 389
Brennan, Matthew, 222
Brexit, 440, 442, 449
'Bridget', 99, 101, 218, 267, 292
Bringing Up Father, 292
British North America. *See* Canada
    (formerly British North America)
British North America Act, 276
Brooke, Basil, 341–342, 343–344
Brooks, Matthew, 119–120
Broughton, William, 167
Brown, Jerry, 428
Browne, Patrick, 42
Bryant, John, 408
Buchanan, Alexander Carlisle, 54–55
Buchanan, James, 243
Buckley, Christopher Augustine,
    226–227
Buckley, Patrick, 182
Buffalo, New York, 35–36, 96
Burns, Anthony, 125
Burton, Phillip, 419
Bush, George W., 435, 438
Butt, Isaac, 279
Butte, Montana, 109, 113

Byrnes, Thomas Joseph, 165
Byron, Reginald, 401–403

Cagney, James, 347
Cahill, Joe, 413, 422, 434–435
California, 105–107
Cameron, David, 438
Canada (formerly British North
    America)
    as emigrant destination, 28–29,
        31–33, 60, 262
    Brooke, Sir Basil, visit to, 341–343
    Catholic Church in, 275–277,
        281–282
    Craig, Sir James, visit to, 341
    emigration to, 7,24, 55–58, 82, 113,
        261, 331, 332, 389
    French Canadians, Irish and,
        280–282
    Fenian movement and, 244,
        247–249, 259–260, 278–279
    Irish in
        employment and economic status,
            32–33, 264–267
        First World War, 313, 315
        nationalism and, 67–68, 277–
            280, 307, 313–315, 319
        numbers, 5, 43, 263, 289–290,
            329, 443–444
        politics, 258–261, 274–275
        religious balance among,
            263–264
        rural settlement by, 32, 264–265
    Orange Order in, 204, 269–274,
        306, 343
    religious divisions in, 269–270,
        272–273, 275–277
Canadian Confederation, 248, 259
Canadian Pacific Railway, 263
Canadian Shield, 31, 262
canal building, 35, 110
Cape Colony, 11
Cape of Good Hope, 37
capitalism, predatory, 235–236
Carboni, Raffaello, 162

caricatures, 141–142, 150, 292
Carnegie, Andrew, 235, 237
Carr, Edward, 170
Carr, Hugh, 85
Carron, Owen, 425
Carson, Edward, 314
Carter, Jimmy, 422–423
Casement, Roger, 312, 314
Casey, William, 423, 424
Castle Garden, 82–84, 103, 287
Catalpa, 250
Catholic Church
    Ancient Order of Hibernians and,
      240–241
    in Argentina, 42, 302–303
    in Ireland, 194–195, 391
    Irish domination of, 167–169,
      184–185, 196–198, 281–282
    and emigration from Ireland, 72–73
    education and, 169, 170, 186,
      199–200, 275–277
    ethnic parishes and, 197, 296
    Fenian Brotherhood and, 245
    marriage and, 330, 338, 347
    newer immigrants and, 296–297
    paedophilia, clerical, 391, 398
    See also individual destinations
Catholic Church Extension Society,
    282
Catholic Colonization Bureau, 88
Catholic Emancipation, 166, 195, 202,
    277
Catholic Intelligencer, 216
Catholic League, 396
Catholic Social Studies Movement,
    340
Caulfield estate, 25
Celtic, 286
Celtic Clubs, 395
Celtic Park, 310
'Celtic Tiger', 387–388, 389, 449
census, ancestry and,
    Canada, 263
    United States, 403–404
Central Park, 190

Cermak, Anton, 370
chain migration, 42, 43, 155, 205, 301
Chancellorsville, battle of, 137
Charitable Irish Society, 268
Chartist movement, 162, 193
Chicago Evening Post, 256
Chicago Triangle, 252, 308
Chiffley, Ben, 339
Chinese, 7, 8, 111, 141, 233, 389, 444
cholera, 56, 59, 75, 94, 105, 280
Christian Brothers, 316, 318
Christian Front, 366
Church Act (Australia), 166
Church of Ireland, 148
civil rights movement
    Northern Ireland, 411–412, 418
    United States 381, 418, 449
Civil War, Irish, 328, 330, 335,
    354–355, 414
Civil War, U.S.
    British reparations following, 245,
      249
    casualties, 119–121, 137
    Catholic church and, 132–133
    commemoration of, 189–190,
      193–194
    conscription and, 138–140
    draft riots and, 138–140
    emigration, and 133–136
    ethnic units in, 129–130
    Fenian Brotherhood and, 245
    impact of, 119–120, 133–135
    Irish response to, 126–134
    recruitment in Ireland for, 134–136
    weaponry of, 120–121
Clan na Gael movement, 67, 250–254,
    278, 308–309, 310, 311–312, 323,
    354–355
Clancy Brothers, 392, 449
Clark, William, 423–424
Clarke, Tom, 312
clearances, 49, 59, 117–118
Cleary, William, 313
Cleburne, Patrick, 129
Clerkenwell explosion, 300

Clinton, Hillary, 396, 400, 437–438, 439
Clinton, William Jefferson, 427–430, 431, 432, 434, 435
clothing trade/garment industry, 10, 36, 102–103
'coffin ships', 59
Cohalan, Daniel, 308–309, 310, 312–313, 320, 321, 323–325, 326, 328, 354
Cohan, George M., 347–348
Cold War, 379
Colleen Bawn, The (Boucicault), 211
Collins, Patrick, 228, 231, 364
Colonial Land and Emigration Commissioners, 147, 149
Colored Orphan Asylum, 139
Columbian Artillery, 125
Columbian Order. *See* Tammany Hall
Columbus, Christopher, 326
Columbus Day, 407
Committee of Vigilance, 124, 226
Common Council (Boston), 228
Common Schools Act (1871), 276
Communism, 340, 366, 379–380, 381
Confederacy, 127, 128, 129, 131–133, 245
Congress of Industrial Organizations (CIO), 399
Connell family, 157
Connolly, Richard 'Slippery Dick', 221
Connolly, Thomas, 275, 276
conscription, 134, 135, 138–140, 315–316, 318, 378
construction industry, 92, 104, 151, 334, 348, 439–440
Convention of Irish Societies, 214–215
Conyngham, David Power, 194
Cook, James, 38
Cooke, Henry, 342
copper mines, 108–109
Corbett, Jim ('Gentleman Jim'), 210
Corcoran, Michael, 129–130, 131, 136
Corcoran, Thomas, 375
Corning, Erastus, 2nd, 374

Corrigan, Michael, 201
Cosgrave, W. T., 354
Costigan, John, 279
Coughlin, Charles, 365–366, 379
Council of the American Irish Historical Society, 308
Craig, James, 341–342
Crawford, Alexander, 159
Crimean War, 11, 203, 244
Croke, Thomas, 185
Croker, Richard, 222
Cronin, Patrick, 254, 308
Crosby, Bing, 348
Crowley, Joe, 441
Crump, Edward, 367–368
Cullen, Paul, 168, 184–185, 196, 245
Cunard Line, 80
Curley, James, 345, 356, 364–365, 367, 368, 376–377, 398, 405
Curtin, David, 34
Curtin, Jeremiah, 34

Dáil Éireann, 314, 319, 322, 329, 425, 427, 452
Daley, Richard, 374, 382, 383, 418
Daly, Marcus, 109
Davis, Jefferson, 129
Davitt, Michael, 242–243, 251
de Blasio, Bill, 396
de Chastelain, John, 433
de Sapio, Carmine, 370
de Valera, Éamon, 322–324, 325–326, 328, 335–337, 338, 340, 351, 354–356, 377, 379, 390
de Vere, Stephen, 54
Deer Island, 58
Democratic County Committee, 370
Democratic Labour Party, 340–341
Democratic National Convention, 418
Democratic Party, 219, 226, 228–229, 399–400
Democratic Unionist Party, 436–437
Democratic-Republican Party, 121
Denieffe, Joseph, 244

deportations, 62, 84–85, 408, 422, 438
Devlin, Bernadette, 418
devotional revolution, 172, 194, 198, 296
Devoy, John, 250, 251–252, 278, 308, 311, 312, 354
diaspora
  Irish government and, 394, 449–453
  statistics of, 4–5, 289–290, 328–329
  unity and diversity in, 305–308, 327–328, 446–448
  use of term, 12–13
diet
  in Australia, 153
  on ships, 52, 54
  in United States, 97
Dignan, Patrick, 182
Dillon, John, 307
Dinkins, David, 404–405, 418
discrimination, 99, 115–116, 141, 150
Dobriansky, Paula, 437
Dogtown, 108
Doheny, Michael, 244
Doherty, Joe, 404
Doherty, John, 113–114
domestic labour, 10–11, 12, 103, 267–268
domestic service, 36, 63, 64, 73, 84, 98–102, 115, 150, 233, 267, 290, 299, 334, 344
Dominicans, 373
Dominion of Canada, 259, 263
Donahoe, Jack, 177, 487n34
Donahoe, Patrick, 216
Donlon, Sean, 420, 421, 424, 429
Donnelly, Brian, 407–408, 439
Donovan, Raymond, 423
Dooley, Mr, 256
Doran, Lillian, 73–74
Dowling, Richard, 129
Downey, John, 106
draft riots, 139, 142, 191

Dryer, Albert, 316, 339
Dublin Lying-in Hospital, 148
Dubliners, The, 392
Duffy, Charles Gavan, 163–164, 166, 170, 177, 260
Duffy, Francis Patrick, 347
Dunne, Finley Peter, 256
Durack, Mary, 2–4
Durack, Patrick, 2–4, 156, 159, 448
Durkin, Martin, 377
dysentery, 56, 105

Easter Rising, 314, 318, 319, 322
economic crisis of 2008, 388
Ed Sullivan Show, The, 392
Edgeworth, Henry (Abbé de Firmont), 17–18
Edison, Thomas, 109
education
  Catholic Church and, 169, 170, 186, 199–200, 275–277
  funding for, 341
  increasing demand for, 22
  Irish history and, 351–352
  middle class and, 148
  suburbanisation and, 373
Eisenhower, Dwight, 377
Elizabeth and Sarah, 51
Ellis Island, 287–288, 416
Ely, Joseph, 367
Emancipation Proclamation, 138
Emerald Guards, 130, 132
Emigrant Savings Bank, 100, 117–118
emigrants
  age, 26
  family groups, 26–27
  gender balance, 11–12, 27–28, 149–150, 180
  Protestant, 18–19, 42, 148, 180, 300, 306–307, 329–331, 487n36
  regional origins, 18–19, 50, 71,149, 179
  socioeconomic background, 50, 149, 388–389

emigrant vessels
  'coffin ships', 59
  conditions on board, 28–31, 51–55,
    79–81, 146–148, 286–287
  fares, 25–26, 29, 60, 78–79
  mortality on board, 31, 51, 59–60,
    81, 147–148
  steamships, 80, 146
  steerage, 30, 54, 78, 80–81,
    146–147, 286, 473n14
  violence towards passengers, 53–55,
    79
emigration, from Ireland
  assisted, 24–25, 39–40, 48–49,
    144–145, 149–150, 178–180
  destinations and routes, 18–19,
    25–26, 29, 50–51, 55, 60, 81–82,
    332–334, 386, 388–389
  numbers, 4–5, 18–19, 43, 46–47,
    68–69, 145, 178–179, 285, 329,
    332–334, 386–389
  returnees, 288–289, 389
emigration, global, 7–8, 285–286,
  444–445
Emmet, Robert, 203, 244
Emmet Monument Association, 244
England, John, 216
English (language), 22, 209
entrepreneurs, Irish America fails to
  produce, 348–349
Erie Canal, 35
Erin Prairie, Wisconsin, 104–105
Erina Coronet Band, 213
Erin's Hope, 250
ethnic fade, 448
ethnic parishes/units, 129–130, 296
Eureka Stockade, revolt at, 160–163,
  165, 336
European Commission on Human
  Rights, 413
European Economic Community, 420
European Union, 390, 440
Evatt, H. V., 340
evictions, 49
explosives, 252

factory system, 92–93, 102, 361. *See
  also* manufacturing sector
Fahy, Anthony, 42, 302–303
Farley, James, 375, 376
farm succession, 70–71, 73
farming/agriculture, 20, 26, 47–48,
  72, 86, 89–90, 106–107, 109–110,
  155–156, 264–265, 332. *See also*
  Great Famine
Farrell, J. T., 292–293, 346
Federalists, 121, 204
Feehan, Patrick, 252
Feeney, Charles, 430, 432, 434
Fenian Brotherhood/movement
  in Australia, 145, 172
  Hibernians and, 240, 277
  invasion of Canada by, 239,
    247–249
  in Ireland, 171
  Irish Legion and, 131
  Manchester Martyrs and,
    259–260
  in New Zealand, 187
  Parnell and, 234
  religious divisions and, 183,
    269–270
  rise of in Great Britain, 299–300
  in United States, 202, 244–251
Fenian Sisterhood, 245
Ferris, Martin, 435
Fianna Fáil, 331, 335, 355
FIFA World Cup, 445
Fighting 69th, The, 347
film, Irish in, 347–348
First Battle of Bull Run, 130, 131
First World War, 312, 314, 320–321,
  332, 335, 337, 448
Fitzgerald, Garret, 424
Fitzgerald, James Edward, 181
Fitzgerald, John 'Honey Fitz', 228,
  364, 376, 380, 383, 398
Fitzhugh and Grimshaw, 23
Fitzpatrick, John, 132
Fitzwilliam estate, 49
Five Points, 95, 118, 125, 206–207

Flannery, Michael, 413, 414, 426–427, 435

Flynn, Bill, 430, 432, 434

Flynn, Edward, 369

Flynn, Elizabeth Gurley, 239, 255

Flynn, Ray, 408, 415, 428–430

Fogarty, John, 356

Forbes, Genevieve, 286–288

Ford, Austin, 354

Ford, Gerald, 422

Ford, Patrick, 217, 229, 235, 236, 239, 252, 311, 447

Foresters, 271

Foster, Vere, 54, 60, 79

Fraser, Peter, 335, 336

Fredericksburg, battle of, 137

Freeman's Journal, 163

Freemasons, 204

Friendly Sons of Erin, 240

Friendly Sons of St Patrick, 202, 213

Friends of Ireland societies, 277, 280, 322, 424, 427, 429

Friends of Irish Freedom, 312, 320, 323, 324, 325

Friends of Sinn Féin, 439–440

frontier, in United States, 33–35, 78, 85–86

Frost, Robert, 383

Fugitive Slave Act, 125

Gaelic American, 309, 354, 378

Gaelic Athletic Association, 310, 326

Gaelic League of America, 308, 310, 326

Gallagher, Jeremiah, 67, 278–279

Gallagher, Michael, 325

Galvin, Martin, 426, 427, 428, 435

Gangs of New York, 95

Garibaldi, Giuseppe, 307

genocide studies, 417

George, Henry, 236

George, Lloyd, 317

German immigrants, comparison to, 209–210

German Triangle, 296

Gettysburg, battle of, 137, 194

Gibbons, James, 201

Giuliani, Rudy, 405

Glazer, Nathan, 350–351, 368

Gleason, Teddy, 419, 426

Global Ireland: Ireland's Diaspora Strategy 2020–2025, 449–450, 451, 452

Global Ireland: Ireland's Global Footprint to 2025, 450–452

global trade, 28–29

Going My Way, 348

gold/gold mining, 105–106, 144, 159–163, 178, 263

Gompers, Samuel, 237–238

Gone with the Wind (Mitchell), 2–4

Good Friday Agreement. *See* Belfast Agreement

Gore, Al, 432

Goulburn, Henry, 24

Gould, Jay, 235, 237

Goyder, George, 155

Grace, William, 231

Grand Army of the Republic, 189–190

Grand Central Station, 295

Grant, Ulysses S., 121, 216, 229, 249

Great Britain

  bombing campaigns in, 252–254, 355, 426

  emigration to, 60–63, 297–300, 333–334, 388

  Irish in

    employment 5–6, 9, 298–299, 334

    number, 43, 289–290

    politics, 299–300

    Orange Order in, 300–301

Great Depression, 332, 333, 350, 353, 369

Great Famine

  background, 45–46

  commemoration and popular memory, 66–68

  and concept of diaspora, 12

  demographic impact, 46

emigration due to, 46–47, 50–51, 60–61, 63–66, 68, 71
genocide studies and, 417
government response to, 47–48
impact on Irish society, 5, 43, 46, 69–72
Great Migration. *See* African Americans
Great National Irish Fair, 246
Great Western Railway, 264
Greek Independence Day, 407
Greenlees, Andrew, 86, 89, 203
Grosse Île, 55–57, 59, 67–68, 279
Guinness, 393
Guy Fawkes Day demonstration, 278, 282

Haass, Richard, 435–436
Hague, Frank, 367, 370
Haley, Alex, 416
Hall, A. Oakey, 190
Hamilton, J. B., 111–112
Hanlon, Edward, 86, 89, 108
Hannegan, Robert Emmet, 377
Harding, Warren, 325
Harrigan, Edward, 211
Harrison, Benjamin, 407
Harrison, Carter H., 227
Harrison, Carter H., II, 227
Harrison, George, 413–414, 422, 427, 435
Hart, Gary, 438
Hart, Tony, 211
Harvard University, 132
Haughey, Charles, 421
Hayden, Tom, 416
Hayes, Sean, 354
Heaney, James, 412
Hell's Kitchen, 222
Heron, Denis, 72
Herzog, Isaac, 390
Hewetson, James, 40
Hibernian Benevolent Society, 277–278, 310
Hibernians (Civil War unit), 130

Hill, William, 112, 203–204
Hitler, Adolf, 379
Hobson, William, 177–178
Hoffman, John T., 190–191
Holkeri, Harri, 433
Holland, John Philip, 251, 252
Holocaust studies, 141, 417
Holy Family parish, 199
Holy Name Society, 380
Home Rule Party/movement, 13, 173, 202, 234, 251, 253, 279, 300, 305–306, 307, 311–312, 319
homeownership, 96, 109, 117, 180–181, 372
Homestead Act, 86
Hoover, Herbert, 362
Hopkins, John Patrick, 231
Horrors of Transportation, The, 39
Horton, Robert Wilmot, 24
House Un-American Activities Committee, 380
housing, 94–97, 117, 153, 156–157, 346, 372
Hudson's Bay Company, 248
Hughes, Archbishop John, 87, 132–133, 140, 194, 199, 245
Hume, John, 420–421, 427, 431
Humphrey, Hubert, 381, 400
hunger strikes, 425, 426
'hyphenated Americans', 321, 324

Illinois and Michigan Canal, 35
immigration reform (United States), 385–387, 388, 407–408, 438–439
Impellitteri, Vincent, 370
Imperial Grand Orange Council of the World, 306
In Supremo Apostolatus, 132
indentured service, 8
India, revolt against British rule in, 244
Indigenous populations, 110–111, 157–159, 177–178, 186–187
Industrial Workers of the World, 234
infrastructure, political machines and, 224–225

inheritance, impact of on emigration patterns, 70–71, 73
International Longshoremen's Association, 419
Inwood, 373
Ireland
cultural change in, 21–23, 391–392
diplomacy and 'soft power', 406–407, 420–421, 449
economic development of, 5, 20–22, 45–46, 69–70, 78–79, 331–333, 386–388
immigration, 389–391
Irish Free State and Republic, 499n1
Revolution and Civil War, 314–315, 328, 330, 335, 354–355, 414
Ireland, Archbishop John, 88, 89, 90, 196, 200
Irish American Athletic Club, 310
Irish American Benevolent Society, 213
Irish American Presidential Forum, 427, 438
Irish Americans for Clinton/Gore, 428, 429
Irish Association, 395
Irish Athletic Club of Boston, 310
Irish Brigade, 130–131, 136, 137, 194, 203
Irish Catholic Colonization Association, 87–88
Irish Echo, 418
Irish Emigration Society, 85, 202
Irish Historical Society, 205
Irish Immigration Reform Movement, 407
Irish Land League, 242–243
Irish language, 22, 209, 278, 310, 330, 492n29
Irish Lesbian and Gay Organisation, 405
Irish Lobby for Immigration Reform, 438

Irish National Association, 316, 339, 395
Irish National Caucus, 419, 421, 422–423, 427, 429
Irish National Federation of America, 202
Irish News, 239
Irish Northern Aid Committee (Noraid), 402, 405, 413–415, 418, 421, 422, 426, 428, 434–435
Irish Parliamentary Party. *See* Home Rule movement/party
Irish People, 414, 418
Irish Protestant Benevolent Society, 269
Irish pubs, 393, 449
Irish Race Convention, 312, 320–321
Irish Rebellions
Irish Republic Brotherhood (1867), 250
Irish Volunteers (1916), 314
United Irishmen (1798) 112, 121, 161, 203, 313, 336
Young Ireland (1848), 145 243–244, 258,
Irish Republican Army (IRA), 314, 319, 330, 354–355, 404–405, 413, 425–426, 430–431, 432–433, 434, 436
Irish Republican Brotherhood, 312, 316, 323. *See also* Fenian Brotherhood
Irish Republican Union, 243–244
Irish republicanism, 506n1. *See also* Fenian Brotherhood, Irish Republican Army, Irish Republican Brotherhood, Provisional IRA
Irish Times, 453
Irish tourism, 392–393, 394, 449
Irish Victory Fund, 320, 324
Irish Voice, 429
Irish Volunteers, 130, 132
Irish War of Independence, 414
Irish World, 217, 235, 237, 239, 311, 354, 378, 447

Irish-American, 216–217
Irishmen's Civil and Military
    Republican Union, 244
Italians, 294–295, 296, 348–349, 369,
    407

Jackson, Jesse, 418
Jacksonians, 204
Jefferson, Thomas, 121
Jeffersonians, 204
Jennings, Patrick, 165
Jerilderie letter (Kelly), 174–175,
    176–177, 242
Jesuit, 216
Jewish immigrants, 348, 350, 364,
    365–366, 390
Jiggs. *See Bringing Up Father*
Johnson, Andrew, 249
Johnson, Lyndon, 381
Johnson-Reed Immigration Act (1924),
    333
Jones, Mary 'Mother Jones', 234

Katzer, Frederick, 196
Kearney, Denis, 111
Kearsarge, USS, 135
Kelly, Declan, 437–438
Kelly, Dickie, 303
Kelly, Edward, 368, 370, 374
Kelly, Edward 'Ned', 173–177, 242,
    448
Kelly, Grace, 348
Kelly, 'Honest John', 222
Kelly, Thomas, 250
Kelso, James, 190–191
Kennedy, Edward 'Ted', 380, 404, 419,
    420–421, 424, 429, 430, 431
Kennedy, John Fitzgerald, 380–384,
    422
Kennedy, Joseph, 376, 379, 380–381,
    382
Kennedy, Joseph, Jr., 380
Kennedy, Kathleen, 383
Kennedy, Patrick Joseph, 380, 383
Kennedy, Robert, 379

Kerry Men's Association, 214
Kerry Patch, 107–108, 207
Kidder, Jerome, 135–136
Killian, Bernard Doan, 247, 278
kindness, political machines and,
    225–226
King, George, 274
King, Peter, 426
Kings in Grass Castles (Durack), 2–4
kinship ties, 208
Knights of Columbus, 326, 352–353
Knights of Labor, 111, 201, 233–234,
    235, 237, 291
Knights of St Patrick, 213
Know-Nothings, 68, 123–125, 140,
    142, 229, 258
Koch, Ed, 404–405, 408
Ku Klux Klan, 326, 362, 363

La Guardia, Fiorello, 369–370, 378
labour movement/unions, 193, 201–
    202, 231–238, 295–296, 319–320,
    369, 374, 398–399, 419
Labour Party (Australia), 339–341
'lace curtain' Irish, 292, 345, 363
Lake, Anthony, 432
Lalor, James Fintan, 161
Lalor, Peter, 160, 161, 162, 165–166,
    176
land ownership, 9–10, 155–157, 266.
    See also homeownership
landlords, 25, 49, 234–235, 251
Landsdowne, Lord, 279
Lang, John Dunmore, 65, 169–170
Lansdowne estate, 117–118
Last Conquest of Ireland (Perhaps), The
    (Mitchel), 66
Last Hurrah, The (O'Connor), 356–357
Laurier, Wilfrid, 277
Lavender and Green Alliance, 396
Lawrence, David, 370
League of Nations, 322, 324, 335
Lee, Robert E., 121
Lewis, George Cornewall, 5–7, 9, 10,
    61, 298, 344, 443–444

LGBT community, 396, 405
Liberal Party, 186, 277, 300, 307, 341
Liberal-Conservative Party, 258–259, 281
life expectancy, 116, 293–294
Lillis, Michael, 420
Limerick Guards, 214
Lincoln, Abraham, 126, 138, 140, 228–229, 245
linen, 20, 332
Liston, James, 318–319
literacy, 22, 149, 288
Loafing Leprechaun, 393
Lodge, Henry Cabot, 237
Lodge, Henry Cabot, Jr., 364–365, 380
Lomasney, Martin, 226, 228
Londonderry, 52
Lonigan, Bill 'Studs', 293
Lorne, Marquis of, 278
Louis XVI, 17–18
Louise, Princess, 278
Louisiana, purchase of from France, 40
Louisiana Zouaves, 130
Louisville, Kentucky, 124
Lowell, Massachusetts, 35, 36, 92, 102, 213
Lowell Irish Benevolent Society, 213
Lughnasa, 23
Lynch, Patrick, 132–133, 216

MacBride, Séan, 427, 428
MacBride Principles, 427, 429
Macdonald, John A., 259, 260, 274, 279
Macrossan, John Murtagh, 165
Maguire, George, 230
Maguire, John Francis, 87, 95–96, 97, 118, 205, 349
Maguire, Patrick, 228
Mahon, Denis, 49
Mahon, Hugh, 316–317
Major, John, 430
Makem, Tommy, 392
Malthus, Robert, 24, 43

Manchester Coronet Band, 213
Manchester Martyrs, 183, 259
Mannix, Daniel, 315–316, 317–318, 336, 339
Mansfield, Mike, 356, 405
manual labor, new world economy and, 7–9
manufacturing sector, 20, 331, 333, 388, 391. *See also* factory system
Maori, 177–178, 186–187
Marine Hospital, New York, 58
Marist Brothers, 184–185, 318
Maritime Commission, 376
marriage
    intermarriage
        with African Americans, 125
        interfaith, 169, 172, 186, 319, 329–330, 338, 347
        interethnic, 186, 208–209, 303, 346–347, 351, 401
    Ireland, 70–71, 73, 332
    United States, 103–104
Marriage Amendment Bill, 319
Marshall Plan, 356
Marx, Karl, 9
Marye's Heights, 130
Massachusetts, pauper immigrants expelled from, 84
Massey, William, 180, 182, 319
Maxwell, John, 153–154, 157
McAdoo, William Gibbs, 362
McCaffrey, Lawrence, 349, 350
McCain, John, 437
McCance, John, 154
McCarter, William, 203
McCarthy, Joseph, 379–380, 384
McCartney, Robert, 436
McClellan, George, 137, 138
McColl, Ewan, 392
McCool, Finn, 246
McCoppin, Frank, 230
McCormack, John, 405
McCrystal, Edward, 67–68
McGarrity, Joseph, 308, 312, 354, 355

McGee, Thomas D'Arcy, 59, 118, 257–260, 272, 274
McGloin, James, 40–41
McGuinness, Martin, 437
McLaughlin, Hugh, 233
McLaughlin, William, 232
McLoughlin, C. J., 313–314
McMahon, T. W., 127
McManus, George, 292
McManus, Séan, 419
McManus, Terence Bellew, 245
McMullen, John, 40–41
McNamara, Francis, 38–39
McParland, James, 192
McQuaid, Bernard, 201
Meagher, Thomas Francis, 130, 131, 132, 137, 194, 203, 228–229, 239
Meany, George, 399, 419
Meath Football Club, 214
medical examinations, 287, 288
'mediocre skills', 92
'melting pot', 350–351
Menzies, Robert, 341
Mexican-American War, 243
Mexico, 40
military technology, 120–121
militia companies, 127, 136, 211, 212, 213–214, 215
Minié, Claude-Étienne, 120
mining, 108–109, 113, 144, 159–163, 191–193
Minnesota Colonization Company, 88
Mitchel, John, 66, 127, 131, 157, 244
Mitchell, George, 433, 435, 436
Mitchell, James, 377
Mitchell, Margaret, 2–4
'mixed marriage'. *See* marriage
Molly Maguires, 191–193, 241
Molly Malone's, 393
Monroe Doctrine, 324
Montgomery Guards, 212
Moran, Patrick Francis, 168–169, 179, 184, 447, 448
Morrison, Bruce, 408, 428–429, 430, 432, 439

Morrison, Danny, 426
Morse, Samuel, 122
Most Holy Trinity Parish, 197, 206
Moville, Ireland, 82
Moynihan, Daniel Patrick, 350–351, 368
Mulligan Guard, 211
Mulvaney, Mick, 438
Mulvihill, William, 42
Murphy, Frank, 375
Murphy, Michael, 277–278
Murphy, 'Silent Charley', 222, 308, 321
Murphy, Tom, 229
Murray, James, 168
Murray, Philip, 398–399
Myall Creek massacre, 158–159, 166

Napoleon III, Emperor, 133
Napper Tandy Light Artillery Company, 212
Nash, Patrick, 370
National German-American Alliance, 309
National Guard, 139, 190–191
National Health Service (United Kingdom), 334
national parishes, 197
nationalism, Irish
  in Australia, 66, 172–177, 305–307, 311, 319–320, 338
  in Canada, 67–68, 259, 277–280, 282, 305–307, 310
  diasporic identity and, 305–307
  genocide studies and, 417–418
  in Great Britain, 299–300
  in United States, 219, 234–235, 238, 243–256, 308–314, 320–326, 353–354
Native Americans, conflicts with, 110–111
nativism, 122–125, 137–138, 142, 205
Ne Temere, 347
needle trades, 102–103

neighbourhoods, in United States, 205–209
New Deal, 359, 366–368, 370, 375
New Departure, 251
New Jersey Medical Center, 360
New Left, 416
New Orleans, 82, 110
New South Wales, 11, 38–39, 40, 43, 144, 145, 169–170
New York, 29, 35, 78, 82–84, 91–92, 93. *See also individual politicians*
New York Commissioners of Emigration, 81, 82–83, 84–85
New York Gaelic Athletic Association, 351
New Zealand
    colonization of, 177–178
    emigration to, 144–145, 178–180, 290, 460
    Irish in
        Catholic church and, 184–186, 337–338
        economic status, 180–181, 336
        numbers, 5, 178, 180, 290, 329, 460
        nationalism among, 305–307, 319, 338–339
        Orange Order, 183–184, 306
        politics, and, 181–183, 341
        Protestants, 180–184, 487n36
    Maori, Irish relations with, 186–187
    religious conflict in, 183–184, 318–319
New Zealand Tablet, 179
Newburyport, Massachusetts, 96, 115, 117, 345–346, 350, 351–352, 397
newspapers, 216–218, 239–240, 447
Nixon, Richard, 377, 381, 382, 422
nomination system (New Zealand), 179
Normile, Michael, 150, 152, 159
Northern Ireland
    conscription in, 378
    conflict in, 411–412
    creation of, 328
    economic development, 332–333
    emigration from, 332, 341–343
    emigration to, 330
    and US politics, 15, 355–357, 403–406, 412–442
Northern Irish Civil Rights Association, 419
Northern Pacific Railway, 248
Nuestra Señora del Refugio, 41
Nugent, Robert, 139

Obama, Barack, 400, 437, 438–439, 441
O'Brien, Charlotte, 81
O'Brien, Henry, 139
O'Brien, Hugh, 231
O'Brien, John Thomond, 41–42
O'Brien, Lawrence, 383
O'Brien, Pat, 347
O'Brien, William, 113, 279, 336
O'Callaghan, Edmund Bailey, 280
Ocasio-Cortez, Alexandria, 441
O'Conaill, Daithi, 413
O'Connell, Daniel, 22, 64, 161, 166, 173, 195, 216, 243, 258, 299, 374–375
O'Connor (poor immigrant), 85
O'Connor, Edwin, 356–357
O'Connor, Thomas, 41
Oddfellows, 271
O'Donnell, Kenny, 383
O'Dowd, Niall, 428–429, 430, 432, 438–439
O'Dwyer, Michael, 336
O'Dwyer, William, 370
O'Farrell, Henry James, 170–171, 172, 183
O'Farrell, Patrick, 338–339
O'Hara, Gerald, 1–4, 110, 448
O'Hara, Maureen, 348
O'Higgins, Ambrose, 18
Oliver, Dennis J., 106
O'Loghlen, Bryan, 165, 170
O'Mahoney, Ellen, 245

O'Mahony, John, 244, 246, 247, 250
O'Malley, Chuck, 348
O'Mulcahy, William, 88
165th Regiment, 320
O'Neill, John, 247–249
O'Neill, Thomas 'Tip', 386, 404, 405, 419, 421, 423, 424, 431
Ontario, 31–32
Orange Order/Orangeism, 13–14, 170–171, 183–184, 190–191, 203, 204, 241, 258, 259, 269–274, 300, 306–307, 343
Order of the Star-Spangled Banner, 122–123
O'Regan, Patrick, 339
Oregon Territory, 243
O'Reilly, John Boyle, 132, 239
O'Rourke, Beto, 441
Orr, John, 75, 105, 111
O'Shanassy, John, 164–165, 170
O'Sullivan, Edward, 152
O'Sullivan, Maureen, 348
OutVets, 396
Overland Campaign, 121

paedophilia. *See* Catholic church
Paisley, Ian, 436–437
Palmerston estate, 49
Panama Canal, 309
Papineau, Louis-Joseph, 280
Paris Peace Conference, 321, 322
Parkinson, James, 148–149
Parnell, Charles Stewart, 234–235, 251, 253, 305–306
Partridge Island, New Brunswick, 57, 58, 59
Passenger Acts (British), 30, 47, 53, 79, 147
Passenger Acts (United States), 55, 79
passenger brokers, 23
patriotes, 280–281
'peacocking', 156
Pearl Harbor, 378
Pearse, Patrick, 312

pedestrianism, 210
Pelosi, Nancy, 440, 441
Pendergast, Thomas, 367, 376–377
People's Charter, 162
Perry, Caitríona, 441
Philippines, 236–237, 389
Phytophthora infestans, 43, 45–46, 69
Pilot, 216–217, 239
Pinkerton National Detective Agency, 192
Pius IX, Pope, 133
plebiscites, 315–316, 339
Pledge of Allegiance, 353
Plimsoll, Samuel, 59
ploughs, steel, 90
Plumbers and Pipefitters Union, 377
Plunkett, John Hubert, 159, 166
Plunkitt, George Washington, 219–221, 222–223
Plunkitt of Tammany Hall (Riordan), 220–221
Polding, John, 167–168, 169
police, Irish in 122, 139, 175, 230, 271, 297, 349, 380
political asylum, 390
political machines, 223–226, 229–230, 295, 359–361, 366–368, 374–375. *See also* Tammany Hall
Poor Law Guardians, 48
Poor Law Unions, 62, 64
Poor Laws, 61, 62, 84
Porter, William, 235
potato, as staple food, 45. *See also* Great Famine
Powderly, Terence, 233, 237
Power, Harry, 173
Power, James, 40–41
Power, Michael, 275
Powers, David, 383–384
Progress and Poverty (George), 236
progressive reform movement, 228
Prohibition, 362
Protestant Political Association, 318, 319

Provisional IRA, 412, 413–414, 418, 419, 420, 422
Public Works Administration, 366, 368

quarantine stations, 56–58, 62
Quebec, 273–274, 275, 280, 281
Quebec City, 32–33
Queen, 38
Queensland, 155–156
Queenstown, Ireland, 81–82
Question of Questions, The (Lang), 169–170
Quinlan, John, 132–133
Quinn, James, 168
Quinn, Matthew, 168

Rassemblement National, 390
Reagan, Nancy, 424
Reagan, Ronald, 400, 423–425, 428
Reconstruction Finance Corporation, 375
Red Rover, 39
Redmond, John, 279, 306, 311–312
Reform League, 162
Reform Party, 182, 258–259, 319
Regan, Donald, 423
Reiss, Mitchell, 435–436, 437
remittances, 23–24, 79, 91, 100, 144
Repeal Association (US), 243
Repeal of the Act of Union, 277
Repeal Party, 161, 166, 299
Representation of the People Act, 253
Republican Party, 125, 228–229, 399–400
Rerum Novarum, 340
residential segregation, 205–209, 272
returnees, 289, 387
Revolutionary Armed Forces of Colombia (FARC), 436
Reynolds, Albert, 430, 431, 434
Ribbon Society, 240
Ribbonmen, 299
Ribicoff, Abraham, 419
Ridgeway, Battle of, 247–248

rifled musket, 120
Riordan, William, 220–221
River Plate Steamship Company, 42
Riverdance, 392, 395
Roberts, William Randall, 246
Robillard, Ellen, 2
Robinson, Mary, 12, 66, 391–392, 394–395, 450
Robinson, Peter, 24
Rodgers, Elizabeth, 234
Roman Republic, 162
Roney, Frank, 94
Roosevelt, Franklin D., 366–368, 369, 375, 378
Roosevelt, Theodore, 236, 321
Roots Too movement, 416, 449
Rossa, Jeremiah O'Donovan, 229, 250, 252, 278
row houses, 96
rowing, 210
Royal Ulster Constabulary (RUC), 420, 421
'runners', 82, 287
Russell, John, 48
Russell, William, 216
Russo-Japanese War, 309
Ryan, James, 376
Ryan, Paddy, 210

Saint Vincent de Paul Society, 199
Salinger, Pierre, 384
San Patricio de Hibernia, 41
San Patricios, 128
Sands, Bobby, 425
sanitation
    at Castle Garden, 82
    on ships, 30, 53
Santamaria, Bartholomew Augustine ('Bob'), 340
Sargeant Light Guards, 213–214
Scorsese, Martin, 95
'Scotch Irish', 205, 404
Scotch-Irish Society of the United States of America, 205
Scottish nationalism, 440

scurvy, 105
Second Vatican Council, 398
Second World War, 331, 333, 334, 335, 377, 378–379, 380
secret societies, 191–193, 240–241
Securities and Exchange Commission, 376
Seddon, Richard, 182
Seeger, Pete, 392
segregation, 205–209, 374, 418, 489n21
selectors, 155–157, 175
Self-Determination for Ireland Leagues, 319, 336, 339
self-improvement, associations/societies and, 212–214
Senate Wing, 246–247, 250
September 11 attacks, 388, 436
Seward, William, 133, 134, 249
Shamrock Aboriginal Warriors, 158
Shamrock Friendly Association, 213
Shamrock Guards, 130
'shanty Irish', 345
Sheridan Guards, 214
Shields, James, 129, 231
Shiners' War, 33, 280
shipbuilding, 332
Siney, John, 193, 233
Sinn Féin, 314, 317, 319, 322, 325, 328, 335, 420, 425–437, 439–440
Sisters of Mercy, 198, 302
Sisters of the Good Shepherd, 198
Sisters of the Holy Cross, 198
69th New York Infantry Regiment, 129–130, 132, 136, 139, 236, 320
Skeffington, Frank, 356–357
'Skirmishing Fund', 252, 255
slavery, 8–9, 109–110, 111–112, 123, 124–126, 127, 132, 243, 443
Smith, Al, 361–363, 367, 369, 381
Smith, Frank, 279–280
Smith, Joan Kennedy, 430, 431
Social Democratic and Labour Party (SDLP), 420, 436–437
Soderberg, Nancy, 430–431, 432

Soldiers' National Cemetery, 126
Sons and Daughters of Ireland Protestant Association, 342
Sons of the Emerald Isle, 213
Sorensen, Ted, 381, 383
South Africa, 5, 37
Southern Celts, 130
Southern Cross, 303, 447
Spalding, John, 200, 245
Spalding, Martin, 133
Spellman, Francis, 353, 380
spinning industry, 27
sports, 210, 214, 255, 310–311
St Andrew's Society, 269
St George's Society, 269
St John, 51
St John's Eve, 22–23
St Joseph's Benevolent Society, 213
St Patrick's Catholic Union, 213
St Patrick's Day, 214–216, 241, 259, 317–318, 328, 351, 396, 406–407, 423, 432
St Patrick's Society, 260, 268–269
St Patrick's Temperance Association, 213
Stafford, Edward, 181
Staten Island, 58
Staunton, Ciaran, 438–439
Stawell, William Foster, 148
'steam heat' Irish, 292–293
steamships, 80–81, 146
steerage, 30, 54, 78, 80–81, 146–147, 286, 473n14
Stephens, James, 244, 246, 250
Stevenson, Adlai, 381
Stewart, George Vesey, 184
Storrow, James Jackson, 228
Stowe, Harriet Beecher, 126
Strong, George Templeton, 140
Students for a Democratic Society, 416
suburbanisation (US), 372–374, 398
Suez Canal, 146
Sullivan, Alexander, 252
Sullivan, John, 106

Sullivan, John L., 210
Sullivan, Pat, 415
Sullivan, Roger, 227, 231, 253–254
Superior and Bayfield railroad, 104
Sweeney, John, 399
Sweeny, Peter 'Brains', 221
Sweeny, Thomas William, 129
Sweetman, John, 88

Tambora volcano, 18–19
Tammany Hall, 139, 140, 193, 215,
    221–223, 225–226, 230–231, 236,
    308, 361, 369–370
Tasmania (Van Diemen's Land), 38,
    113, 145, 149, 151, 157, 174
teaching, Irish women employed in,
    230, 291, 297, 344
temperance movement, 199, 212, 213,
    271
tenant right, 26
tenements, 94, 95–96, 97
Texas, Irish settlement in, 40–41
textile industry, 92, 102
Thatcher, Margaret, 424–425
theatre (US), 211–212
Therry, Roger, 166
third class passage, 286–287
Thoreau, Henry David, 51
Thynne, Andrew, 165
timber trade, 28, 37
Tobin, Maurice, 376–377
Tole, John, 182
transatlantic traffic, 28–31
transcontinental railroad, 78
Triangle, 252
Triangle Shirtwaist Factory, 361
Trinity (Uris), 402–403
Truman, Harry S., 344, 356,
    376–377
Trump, Donald, 400, 438, 453
tuberculosis, 292
Tumulty, Joseph, 321
Tweed, William 'Boss', 221–222, 224,
    229, 250
28th Massachusetts Infantry, 136

Twigg, James Hamilton, 152
Tyler, Robert, 243
typhus, 56, 57–58, 61, 62–63

Ullathorne, William, 167
Ulster Defence Association, 412, 430
Ulster Unionist Party, 436–438
Ulster Volunteer Force, 412, 430
undocumented immigrants, 407–409,
    428–429, 438–439
Union Party, 366
unions. *See* labour movement/unions
United Brotherhood, 278
United Irish League, 306, 311, 312
United Irish Societies, 255
United Irishmen, 121, 161, 205, 240,
    252, 278, 299
United Labor Party, 236
United Nations Security Council, 451
United Protestant Immigrants' Home,
    269
United States
    emigration to, 18–19, 33–36,
        58, 68–69, 77–85, 133–134,
        285–289, 333, 354, 386, 388
    immigration policy, 82–85,
        287–288, 385–386, 407–409,
        439
    Ireland as a foreign policy issue,
        320–322, 355–357, 421–425,
        427–438
    Irish in
        American patriotism and,
            352–353
        antagonism towards, 84–85,
            99, 101, 121–125, 136–142,
            190–194, 291–292, 347–348,
            361–363
        culture and community of,
            205–218, 351–352, 373,
            400–403
        Catholic church and, 194–202,
            352–353, 373, 397–398
        employment of, 35–36, 91–94,
            229–230, 290–291

economic status of, 91, 94–98,
114–118, 107–108, 344–346,
348–350, 371–372
frontier, presence on, 18, 33–35,
85–86
generational conflict among, 396
geographical dispersal of,
104–110
labour movement, in, 231–238,
398–399
military service, 111, 126–137,
236–237, 243, 313, 315, 320
nationalism among, 66, 131,
238–256, 308–313, 320–326,
343–344, 353–357, 402–402,
412–420, 439–440
'new immigrants, relations with,
293–297, 346–347, 363,
368–371
numbers, 18, 43, 60, 329,
403–404, 463
politics, 219–231, 359–371,
374–377, 399–400, 440–442
Protestants among, 190–191,
202–205, 397
racist depictions of, 141–142
rural and urban settlement,
33–36, 85–91
'Scotch Irish',204–205, 404
suburbanisation of, 372–373, 398
nativism, 68, 121–125, 137–138,
140–142, 291
United States Catholic Miscellany, 216
upward mobility
in Great Britain, 298
in Canada, 266
in United States, 114–115, 292–293,
344–346
Uris, Leon, 402–403
Ursuline convent, destruction of, 122,
124, 126

Van Buren, Martin, 243
Van Diemen's Land. *See* Tasmania
Vanishing Irish, The, 332

Varadkar, Leo, 452
Vargo, Tina, 430, 438
Vaughan, Roger, 168
Versailles, Treaty of, 322
Victoria, Queen, 268, 278, 300
Victoria Cross, 318
Vindicator, 280
Vogel, Julius, 178–179
volunteer fire companies, 212, 223
von Igel, Wolf, 312–313, 320
voting rates (US), 223–224
voting rights, 163, 165, 234, 452–453

Waitangi, Treaty of, 178
Walker, Jimmy, 369
Walsh, David, 367
Ward, Joseph, 182–183, 318
ward bosses, 227–228
Washington, George, 30
Washington Heights, 346, 373
Washington Park, 346
Waverley Cemetery, 336
Wayne, John, 380
Welsh, Peter, 126, 130, 238–239, 242,
255
Whelan, Patrick James, 260
Whig Party, 122
White, David, 120
Williamson, Bill, 105
Williamson, James, 106
Wilson, Woodrow, 320–322, 324, 325,
422
women
AFL and, 238
emigration of, 10–12, 27–28,
39–40, 64–66, 71, 73–74,
149–150, 180
employment
Australia, 149–150
Canada, 267–268
Great Britain, 298–299, 334
United States, 36, 98–104, 230,
290–291, 344
experience on board ship, 53, 81,
147–148, 286–287

women (*continued*)
    exported as a commodity, 10–11, 39,
      64–66
    Fenian movement and, 245
    Ireland, status and prospects in, 22,
      27, 73–74, 331–332
    Knights of Labor and, 233–234
    as returnees, 289
    social clubs for (US), 214
    transported to Australia, 39
Worcester, Massachusetts, 96–97
workhouse-orphans scheme, 64–67,
  144, 170
Workingmen's Benevolent
  Association, 193
Workingmen's Party, 111, 226
Works Progress Administration, 366

World's Fair, St Louis, 310
Wren, John, 317
Wyndham estate, 25

Xhosa people, 37

Yellow Ford, battle commemorated,
  255
Young Britons, 272–273
Young Ireland movement, 59, 64,
  130, 145, 161, 163, 243–244,
  258
Young Men's Catholic Literary
  Association, 213
Young Men's Catholic Lyceum, 213

Zangwill, Israel. *See* 'melting pot'

Sean Connolly is professor of Irish history (emeritus) and visiting research fellow at the Institute of Irish Studies at Queen's University, Belfast. He is the author of five books, including *Contested Island* and *Divided Kingdom*, and was general editor of *The Oxford Companion to Irish History*. Born in Dublin, he lives in Belfast.